Sacred Storytelling

Sacred Storytelling

The Autobiography of Johannes Strieter (1829–1920)
and Related Sources

Johannes Strieter

TRANSLATED BY
Nathaniel J. Biebert

RESOURCE *Publications* · Eugene, Oregon

SACRED STORYTELLING
The Autobiography of Johannes Strieter (1829–1920) and Related Sources

Copyright © 2020 Nathaniel J. Biebert. All rights reserved. Except for brief quotations in critical publications or reviews, no part of this book may be reproduced in any manner without prior written permission from the publisher. Write: Permissions, Wipf and Stock Publishers, 199 W. 8th Ave., Suite 3, Eugene, OR 97401.

Resource Publications
An Imprint of Wipf and Stock Publishers
199 W. 8th Ave., Suite 3
Eugene, OR 97401

www.wipfandstock.com

PAPERBACK ISBN: 978-1-7252-7743-4
HARDCOVER ISBN: 978-1-7252-7742-7
EBOOK ISBN: 978-1-7252-7744-1

As a reconteur [*sic*] of past reminiscences
[the Rev. Strieter] has but few rivals.

—*Wausau Daily Record-Herald*, August 15, 1910,
front page, first column

Fig. 1: Johannes Strieter at Age Eighty-Five, printed in St. John's Anniversary Committee,
History of St. John's Evangelical Lutheran Church, Garfield Heights, Ohio (1929)

Contents

List of Illustrations | ix
Translator's Preface | xi
Acknowledgements | xvii
Original Preface | xxiii
Preliminary Remarks | xxv

Chapter 1: Youth | 1
Chapter 2: Seminary | 21
Chapter 3: Into the Ministry | 44
Chapter 4: Newburgh | 62
Chapter 5: Wisconsin | 69
    Hardships and Happenings | 89
    Battle with the Fanatics | 119
    My Departure from Injunland | 128
Chapter 6: Aurora | 130
Chapter 7: Peru | 139
Chapter 8: Proviso | 143
    Saloon and Ball | 146
    Lodge | 153
Chapter 9: Pleasant Experiences | 158

Appendix I: Strieter Ancestry | 181
Appendix II: Strieter Children | 187
Appendix III: Indian Missions in Huron and Saginaw Counties, Michigan | 191
Appendix IV: Announcements Pertaining to Strieter's Ministry | 222
Appendix V: Sketch of the Parents of the Ernst Girls by Henry F. Rahe | 228

CONTENTS

*Appendix VI: Beginnings of Organized Lutheranism in
         Marquette County, Wisconsin* | 234
Appendix VII: Early Relationship between the Missouri and Wisconsin Synods | 260
Appendix VIII: Johann Jacob Hoffmann | 269
Appendix IX: J. J. Kern Letters | 281
Appendix X: Death and Burial of C. F. W. Walther | 344
Appendix XI: Jubilee Report | 351
Appendix XII: Johannes Strieter's Obituary | 356

About the Translator | 359

Subject Index | 361
Name Index | 367
Place Index | 377
Scripture Index | 389

Illustrations

1. Johannes Strieter at Age Eighty-Five | v
2. Johannes and Elizabeth Strieter | xxv
3. Johannes Strieter's Baptismal Font in Affalterbach (2013) | 1
4. Partially Restored Fresco in Affalterbach (2013) | 3
5. Evangelical Church in Affalterbach (2013) | 5
6. Strieter Homestead in Freedom Township (2020) | 10
7. Bethel United Church of Christ Cemetery (2013) | 14
8. Rev. Johann Jacob Friedrich Auch, Johannes Strieter's Brother-in-Law | 14
9. Rev. Johann Konrad Wilhelm Löhe | 22
10. Map of the Franconian Colonies in Michigan (1849) | 23
11. Rev. Ferdinand Sievers | 26
12. Friedrich August Crämer (between 1830 and 1844) | 27
13. The Church and Parsonage in Frankenmuth (c. 1859) | 28
14. The Mill in Frankenmuth (1865) | 29
15. Rev. Johann Heinrich Philip Gräbner | 30
16. Church Bells in the Forest in Frankenmuth (2020) | 31
17. Rev. Sievers's Frame Parsonage Built in 1849 | 34
18. Dorothea Crämer | 36
19. Concordia Seminary Buildings in Ft. Wayne—Then and Now | 41
20. Site of Strieter's Accident in Ohio (2020) | 47
21. Daniel Haag's Gravestone (2020) | 53
22. Page 82 in Strieter's Manuscript | 57
23. Johannes and Elizabeth Strieter's Wedding Picture | 58
24. First Church and School of St. John's Lutheran, Garfield Heights, Ohio (after 1859) | 63
25. Partial Map of Cuyahoga County, Ohio (1858) | 63
26. Interior of the First Church of St. John's Lutheran, Garfield Heights, Ohio (after 1859) | 67
27. Arnold Cemetery, Mt. Hope, Ohio (2020) | 68
28. Map of Marquette County, Wis., circa 1860 | 71

29. Rev. Peter Heinrich Dicke | 76
30. Wilhelm and Marie Stelter's Gravestones (2016) | 77
31. Friedrich and Wilhelmine Krenz's and Dorothea S. Anklam's Gravestones (2012) | 86
32. Partial Map of Wisconsin (1860) | 87
33. Site of Strieter's Accident in Marquette County, Wis. (2016) | 90
34. Foundation of the Old Parsonage Stable (2016) | 91
35. Fierke Family Burial Plot (2019) | 92
36. J. J. Hoffmann | 100
37. Johannes Strieter (mid- to late 1860s) | 114
38. August Crämer, Friedrich Wyneken, and Wilhelm Sihler with Full Beards | 115
39. First Church of St. John's Lutheran, Peru, Ind. | 140
40. Immanuel Lutheran Church in the Town of Proviso, Ill. (before 1905) | 144
41. J. C. W. Lindemann | 147
42. Heinrich List | 153
43. C. F. W. Walther | 161
44. Immanuel Lutheran Church's Parsonage in the Town of Proviso, Ill. (before 1905) | 164
45. Johannes and Elizabeth Strieter | 167
46. Strieter Family Portrait (c. 1892) | 168
47. Johannes Strieter Relaxing Outdoors | 170
48. Karoline Sievers | 172
49. Rev. Peter P. Andres | 173
50. Second Church of St. John's Lutheran, Garfield Heights, Ohio (before 1905) | 175
51. August J. C. Schefft | 177
52. Family of Friedrich Strieter (c. 1910) | 187
53. Crucifix with Skull and Serpent at St. Lorenz Lutheran Church, Frankenmuth (2020) | 197
54. Missionary Johann Friedrich Maier's Gravestone (2020) | 220
55. Ernst Adolph Schultz | 238
56. Rev. Martin Stephan, Jr. | 239
57. Postcard of Naugart, Wis. (1909) | 270
58. Rev. Eduard Moldehnke | 270
59. Rev. J. J. Hoffmann | 278
60. Taegesville, Wis. (1911) | 280
61. August and Mathilda Kickbusch | 352
62. Postcard of Naugart, Wis. (1912) | 355
63. Johannes Strieter Reading, with Elizabeth Standing Nearby | 357
64. Johannes and Elizabeth Strieter's Gravestone (2013) | 358

Translator's Preface

The task of writing a fitting preface for a work such as this is so overwhelming that I hardly know where to begin—especially when it is followed by an original preface written by a man who actually knew the autobiographer personally. I suppose I should start by acknowledging the tremendous debt I owe the autobiographer, the late Pastor Johannes Strieter. When, in 2011, I first discovered a copy of Orlan Warnke's translation of Strieter's Wisconsin chapters (what constitutes Chapter 5 in the present book) in the files of St. Paul-Naugart,[1] I was no scholar of American Lutheran history and, apart from several key church history figures, was not a huge fan of history in general. History was little more than a series of dates I couldn't remember. But once I started reading Pastor Strieter's reminiscences, I couldn't stop turning the pages and devouring the content. I had to know more about the people, places, and circumstances of which he spoke. Pastor Strieter, by his own admission, was no particularly gifted, learned, or noteworthy man, but he most certainly had a good memory and a head full of horse sense, and was a highly gifted raconteur or story-teller. Through Pastor Strieter's autobiography, I came to realize what the study of history actually is at its core—people, in all of their beauty and ugliness, simplicity and complexity, feats and failings, humor, hardships, relationships, religious convictions, and whatever else defines humanity and whatever else humanity does under the ruling, protecting, blessing, and limiting hand of God. And in realizing this, history suddenly became instructive and applicable far beyond any classroom instruction (though history teaches one not to downplay that either). After all, humans—for all the considerable differences that may exist between cultures and generations—are still and always humans. And it is precisely humans that we humans are primarily here to interact with.

One of my purposes, then, in providing this translation is to help others to love and appreciate history as I have been led to love and appreciate it myself.

---

1. Naugart is the local name for the intersection of Naugart Drive and Berlin Lane, near which the church is located; the Naugart post office was located on the northeast corner of the intersection from 1889–1939. Today the post office from which the church gets its mail is located in Athens, Wisconsin.

But Strieter's autobiography will also help people learn and retain history. Though Johannes Strieter is not a name that students of church history or American history are required to remember, the path of his life intersects with that of numerous distinguished persons—August Crämer, Friedrich Wyneken, J. C. W. Lindemann, C. F. W. Walther, and John Pritzlaff, just to name a handful. Here we can view the Ojibwe, the Civil War, the establishment and founding of roads, cities, churches, and schools, and travel by sea, lake, river, canal, railroad, horseback, buggy, stagecoach, and on foot through the lens of Strieter's firsthand experience. Encountered this way, the names and landmarks of history take on life and linger in our memory. Friedrich Wyneken the promoter of American mission work and president of the Lutheran Church-Missouri Synod is much easier to remember when we also know him as the willing participant in a rousing game of duck-duck-goose.

This volume should also prove an especially helpful tool for those charged with the tasks of preaching and teaching in the Christian church, and especially in the Evangelical Lutheran Church.[2] One can make anything to be taught a little more memorable with a fitting, memorable story, and there are plenty of fitting, memorable stories to illustrate the truths of Holy Scripture here. My own congregation has gotten used to me sharing "Strieter stories" in sermons and Bible classes to illustrate what the Bible says about baptism, the Lord's Supper, the power of God's word and forgiveness, the protection afforded by God's angels, and so much more.

But one certainly does not have to be a pastor or teacher in the church to appreciate this book. For the Christian layperson looking for good, readable, interesting, Christian literature of a non-technical nature, this book will not disappoint. And even for a non-Christian reader, it can provide many hours of enjoyable diversion and amusement. As the writer of the original preface says, the book is "a string of instructive, gripping, delightful, encouraging experiences, events, and anecdotes." Who doesn't like a collection of good stories told well?

A chief benefit that the book provides in abundance is perspective. I highly doubt that the time spent recollecting and mulling over this book will be time in which much complaining takes place. If any of the characters on the following pages were to overhear us lamenting how we have no air conditioning, or how the dishwasher is on the fritz, or how the delivery date for our online order got delayed, or how our car broke down in an area without cell service, forcing us to walk several miles to the nearest gas station, or about the restrictions on what we can have in our dorm room, or how the congregation can't agree on the particulars of its proposed church expansion project, they would rightly laugh themselves sick.

---

2. For those unacquainted with Lutheranism, this is not the name of a particular denomination, but a label that applies to all those Christians who treasure the gospel of Jesus, and who also take the Lutheran Confessions seriously (as contained in the Book of Concord of 1580) as accurate and reliable witnesses to the truths of Holy Scripture.

Another chief benefit is the shot of courage it gives to us who serve in positions of high responsibility to say what needs to be said and to do what needs to be done, out of love for God and the souls he has redeemed with his blood. Sometimes tender love needs to wear a tough exterior, but in this book we can take counsel with Pastor Strieter and hear him saying, "If I could do it, and live to tell the tale, then you can too."

Perhaps the strongest takeaway, at least for me, is to note the abundant fruit produced by an endeavor rightly undertaken. As Strieter himself details in his Preliminary Remarks, this book almost didn't happen, because even though his relatives were encouraging him to write his memoirs, he couldn't view it as anything but a self-serving, self-trumpeting endeavor. And he refused to engage in such. It wasn't until his relatives started playing the right notes, by telling him that his autobiography would give glory to God and be of benefit to them, that he conceded and wrote down the story of his life—and even then, "only . . . for the two reasons specified,"[3] namely to glorify God and serve his fellowman. I am convinced that, if he had not begun his task in the Lord's name as he did, this book would not be in front of you today. Bach composed his music "to the glory of God alone" and "in Jesus's name," and his music is still being heard all around the world more than two and half centuries after his death, treasured by countless thousands far more than the latest hits and trending YouTube music videos. So too with Strieter's autobiography. God was not going to let this interesting and instructive work so intentionally undertaken to his glory die out so quickly. Instead, here it is, presented afresh in a new language, for at least a few more generations to benefit from and enjoy, unless Jesus should make his return first.

Johannes Strieter wrote his autobiography on 241 sheets of lined paper, not including a couple different insertions to supplement some of the material. His original manuscript is in the possession of the Concordia Historical Institute in St. Louis. As he himself indicated in his original Preliminary Remarks, once he finished the manuscript, he handed it over to his brother-in-law, Friedrich Leutner (1848–1916) of Cleveland, for editing and publishing. Unfortunately for the original German readers, Leutner went a little heavy on the editing, trying to make Strieter and those in his camp a little more polished and refined than they actually were. The liberties in his editing increased as he progressed through Strieter's manuscript. Sometimes it was innocent enough—for example, when he would unify the verb tenses in a given story. But in a few cases, his liberal editing ended up falsifying elements of the story Strieter was telling. And more broadly, the printed book of 1905, *Lebenslauf des Johannes Strieter, Pastor Emeritus, von ihm selbst erzählt und geschrieben*, lacked something of the character, charm, and authenticity of Strieter's original. I document the most glaring examples of Leutner's editing in the footnotes. There is also one place where the printer (whether Leutner or a professional he paid) completely skipped a line in Strieter's original, making the original German sentence unintelligible in

---

3. See p. xxvi.

the context. And it was the printed German book that those undertaking English translations used as the basis for their work.

Johannes's son Carl (1865–1952; Johannes consistently calls him Karl) was the first to translate the autobiography into English. Carl's work was reproduced through the efforts of Johannes's grandsons E. J. Strieter and Col. Edwin O. List (retired at the time). I obtained my copy of Carl's translation from Trinity Lutheran Church in Burr Ridge, Illinois. I hereby wish to thank this congregation for generously mailing me a copy at my request, gratis, in 2012. Among the main weaknesses of this translation, in addition to its lack of wide availability, are its antiquated expressions and occasional mistranslations arising from the fact that English was not Carl's first language. In addition, Carl inexplicably omitted some parts, making his translation an abridgment. His translation's strength, however, lies in the fact that he himself experienced much of the content firsthand. There are consequently places where Carl's version is less translation and more paraphrase and/or explanation, which can be helpful for understanding. I have done my best to note these places in the footnotes.

As already noted, the Wisconsin chapters were separately translated by Orlan Warnke (1914–2013), who was apparently unaware of Carl's translation. Mr. Warnke grew up and lived much of his life in the area Strieter inhabited in Wisconsin. He appears to have translated Strieter's Wisconsin chapters sometime prior to 1986 in conjunction with genealogy work he was doing, since he was descended from people whom Pastor Strieter served. Mr. Warnke's preface is interesting and worthwhile reading in its own right, and his translation is far superior in quality to Carl's. Still, it does leave something to be desired in places (even Warnke himself says that the end product was "the result of persistence rather than skill") and it, too, contains a few minor omissions.

I have no shame in admitting that I used the previous two translations as consultants. I also came into the possession of another translation by a certain Milton Bauer, about whom I otherwise know nothing. (I don't even remember how his translation came into my hands.) His work only comprises most of Chapter 1. Since it came into my possession comparatively late and also has omissions and mistranslations, I consulted it relatively little. Frankenmuth historian Herman Zehnder (*Teach My People the Truth* [1970], 47) also refers to at least a partial translation by Louis Hölter, the writer of the Original Preface, but I know nothing further about that.

Even though I came down rather hard on the printed *Lebenslauf des Johannes Strieter* earlier, I cannot overstate its value in one important regard: It was my Rosetta Stone for learning to read and understand the *Kurrentschrift* (German cursive) of Strieter's original manuscript, and in fact for learning to read and understand *Kurrentschrift* in general. As a result, I am able to make a claim about the present book that is somewhat unique in the world of published translations: By translating directly from Strieter's original manuscript, this English book in many ways more accurately and faithfully represents what Strieter wished to communicate to his audience than the original printed book did in Strieter's mother tongue. I did not refrain from editing his content entirely; I did, for instance, correct incorrectly spelled names of persons and places and then noted his original spellings in footnotes. But on the whole, I did my best to let Strieter speak as Strieter. If he switched verb tenses mid-paragraph or mid-sentence, I did the same. If he shared something rough or crude that someone else said, or he himself, I translated it in all its roughness or crudeness. The writer of the Original Preface, Rev. Louis Hölter, said that the autobiography manuscript represented the author as he lived and breathed, and that's what I did my best to replicate. I didn't want a manuscript that could be handed in to a university English professor for an A. I wanted a manuscript through which you could just imagine this seventy-five-year-old, straightforward, dedicated, immigrant, veteran warhorse of a pastor telling you these stories in person, from the chair adjacent to yours in the evening light of your living room.

All the footnotes in the autobiography are my own, as are any extended information and commentary in the captions of the pictures. I have also included twelve appendices—almost equal in length collectively to the autobiography itself—that present information and primary source content meant to supplement Strieter's autobiography. My own interests and experience—especially as a pastor having formerly served two congregations that can trace their origins back to Strieter's ministry in Wisconsin—admittedly influenced what I chose to include in this section. I am sure, for example, that dozens of additional appendices could have been included to supplement what Strieter says about his time in Aurora and Proviso, Illinois. I simply did not have the time to pursue these additional rabbit holes. Permit me to assure those who live in areas Strieter lived and served that are untouched-on in the appendices that I did not intend to slight you in any way.

Of course, I cannot and dare not conclude this preface without imitating the subject of this book. If this translation were to serve no other purpose than furthering my own name or reputation, then this book, together with everything in my possession related to it, should be burned and forgotten. "[Jesus] must become greater; I must become less" (John 3:30). I ask the Lord to forgive and remove any self-centered and self-promoting thoughts in my heart as I present this book, and to use it solely to glorify his saving name, to further the work of his kingdom, and to serve to the benefit of my fellow Christians and fellow human beings.

Nathaniel J. Biebert
August 2, 2020
Trinity 8
Austin, Texas

Acknowledgements

I must begin by acknowledging the members of St. Paul Lutheran-Naugart in the town of Berlin and Grace Lutheran in the village of Maine, Wisconsin (both in the countryside northwest of Wausau), for their generous support of my ministry during the beginning and development of my research and translation. They also directly supported this project with the donations from a midweek Lenten supper. As already mentioned in my preface, these congregations are some of the modern fruit of Pastor Strieter's labor in Wisconsin. I doubt I would have ever discovered the man and his autobiography if I had not been called as their pastor. It was also a daughter of St. Paul Lutheran, Judith (Zamzow) Tepe, who asked me after my slide presentation at the congregation's one hundred and fiftieth anniversary celebration if I would be publishing my work in a book. That was the first verbal encouragement I received to undertake what resulted in the present volume. Since countrysides change much more gradually than cities through the years, it was easy to imagine and be captivated by the stories Strieter told from his time in that area as I drove around visiting members and otherwise carrying out my ministry. I promised these congregations when I accepted the call to my current congregation in Austin, Texas, that I would continue to set aside time to work at completing the Strieter autobiography and publishing it. I thank God that he has enabled me to keep that promise.

DuWayne Zamzow, a member of St. Paul-Naugart and of the Pommerscher Verein-Central Wisconsin, gifted me copies of *Berlin's Memories in 1976* (the centennial history of the town of Berlin in Marathon County), *"Declaring God's Glory: Yesterday, Today and Tomorrow"* (the one hundred and fiftieth anniversary book of St. John Lutheran, Fall Creek, Wis.), and his *Zamzow Family Memoirs*, all of which I have benefitted from in my research. He also generously supported this project financially.

Laurel Hoffmann of the Pommerscher Verein-Central Wisconsin Library in the town (not city) of Berlin, Wis., pointed me to literary and pictorial resources related to the early history of the town of Berlin and the surrounding area. My copy of *Prussian Netzelanders and Other German Immigrants* by Brian Podoll has been checked out from her library for a *long* time.

ACKNOWLEDGEMENTS

Kevin Anklam was always willing to talk about Pastor Strieter's travels with me during my visits with his father-in-law. Kevin especially helped me to understand the workings of Strieter's (buckboard) buggy and accordingly to accurately translate the sections where Strieter talks about it in detail.

I must also express my gratitude to my current congregation in South Austin, who have been equally as supportive of my ministry and continuing research and education as my previous congregations, and who always perk up when I say, "It's time for another Strieter story." I could not have finished this project without that support.

The Concordia Historical Institute has been of tremendous assistance along the way, especially Laura Marrs (who provided me with my first biographical sketch of Pastor Strieter), Shawn Barnett (who facilitated my reception of digital scans of Strieter's original manuscript), Ben Nickodemus, and Mark Bliese. They have readily, kindly, and capably fielded my numerous inquiries.

Archivist Susan Willems of the Wisconsin Evangelical Lutheran Synod spent countless hours willingly, tirelessly, and graciously assisting me by locating and scanning the letters in Appendices VI and IX (and whatever preliminary transcriptions and translations were available), so that I could transcribe and translate them. She is the first full-time archivist my synod has hired, and I pray that, if God wills, she retains the position for many years to come.

The kind staff of the Marathon County Historical Society in Wausau, Wis., helped me to conceptualize Wausau (or Big Bull, as Strieter calls it) in its early days, when Strieter passed through.

Mary Nuechterlein of the Frankenmuth Historical Association and Dave Maves of the St. Lorenz Heritage Committee in Frankenmuth, Mich., provided me with valuable assistance and recommendations through their email correspondence. I also thank Daniel Haubenstricker of the Heritage Committee for his guided tour of the St. Lorenz Log Cabin, Museum, and Church on July 15, 2020, and the printed resources he freely shared.

Lana Gits and Patricia Reaves of the Franzosenbusch Heritage Project (http://www.fhproject.org) furnished me with names and information pertaining to Strieter's service in the town of Proviso, Illinois.

Winfried "Joe" Strieter, Susan Hawkins, and Frederick Strieter—all descendants of Pastor Strieter—supplied me with many encouragements, artifacts, and pieces of information, including a number of the photographs in the present book. They have also given me a firsthand taste of the Strieter personality, conviction, warmth, and *Gemütlichkeit*. I cannot overstate their importance to this project or sufficiently thank them for all of their contributions to it. Nelson Wesenberg, whose mother was a great-granddaughter of Pastor Strieter, also contacted me out of the blue at a late stage in this project and provided me with some valuable photos.

I must acknowledge the many congregations, not mentioned elsewhere, that freely shared anniversary books, artifacts, and other resources with me, and also lent

ACKNOWLEDGEMENTS

me aid in other ways: Immanuel Lutheran, Hillside, Ill., especially Rev. Ted Vratny; Salem Lutheran-Scio, Ann Arbor, Mich., especially Mildred Crawford (who gave me, among other things, "The Schmid Letters" and "The Life and Labors of Friedrich Schmid," both translated by Emerson E. Hutzel); St. Lorenz Lutheran, Frankenmuth, Mich. (I've already mentioned a few members separately); St. Paul Lutheran-Frankenlust, Bay City, Mich., especially Rev. Dennis Matyas; Immanuel Lutheran-Frankentrost, Saginaw, Mich., especially Rev. Mark Loest; St. John Lutheran, Garfield Heights, Ohio, especially Karen Dutton, director of Christian education; St. John's Lutheran, Peru, especially Rev. Kenneth Greenwald; St. John Lutheran-Wien, Edgar, Wis., especially Rev. Jeffrey Lambrecht; St. John's Lutheran, Portage, Wis.; St. Paul's Lutheran, Sheboygan Falls, Wis.; St. John Lutheran, Plymouth, Wis., especially Rev. Thomas Burton; Immanuel Lutheran, Mayville, Wis., especially Secretary Kim Kamrath; Trinity Lutheran, Oshkosh, Wis., especially Rev. Kelly Leary; and St. John's Lutheran, Princeton, Wis., especially Rev. John Stelter.

On the memorable evening of October 2, 2013, Gerhard Gall and Doris Schelling, residents of Affalterbach, Germany, kindly helped me look up information on the Strieter family in the parish records and gave my wife and me a tour of the church in which Johannes Strieter was baptized. They also provided me with the information in Appendix I. Mr. Gall acquainted me with Paul Sauer's history of Affalterbach[1] and Ms. Schelling, who shares some of Johannes Strieter's ancestry, freely shared the results of her research into the ancestry of Johannes's parents, Jacob Strieter and Maria Wiesenauer.

Jim Bunke, the curator of the Luckhard Museum in Sebewaing, Mich., specially opened up the museum for me on a weekday and gave me a complimentary copy of *Faith in the Forest* by Charles F. Luckhard.

Cathy Zell of the Wisconsin Lutheran Seminary Library kept patiently and generously extending the due date on my copy of Strieter's *Lebenslauf* and was also very accommodating in opening up the archives room for me when the archives were still housed on the seminary campus.

Joan Ingraham and Kathleen McGwin of the Marquette County Historical Society of Westfield, Wis., have provided me with much information and encouragement. Kathleen also mailed me two complimentary copies of *Lebensbrot*, the collection of vacancy sermons that Strieter preached in 1904.[2]

Rev. em. John Dolan of Montello, whose wife Carol is a descendant of Farmer Johann Schultz of Appendix VI, has been especially encouraging, hospitable, and helpful to me in researching the history of Lutheranism in Marquette County, Wis., before, during, and after Strieter's service there. He has been my indispensable collaborator for several installments of my serial, "Johannes Strieter: Raconteur of Past Reminiscences" in the *WELS Historical Institute Journal*, which is cited in several places in the

---

1. See p. 181, n. 1.
2. See p. 176 and nn. 50–52.

present volume. I also thank Prof. John Brenner for his willingness to edit and publish this serial in the *Journal*.

Dennis and Nora Beskow welcomed my wife and me into their home during the afternoon of June 18, 2013, to discuss the history of Budsin, the later name given to Strieter's home base in Wisconsin. They were my first in-person contacts in the area. The complimentary copy of *A Historical Stroll through the Churches of Marquette County* they later mailed me has been especially valuable.

Rev. Thomas Mickelson spent hours with my wife and me on March 29, 2016, as I rummaged through his church (St. John Lutheran, Budsin) and the attic and front porch of his parsonage, searching for the congregational records Strieter kept in Wisconsin. Pastor Mickelson finally found a slip of paper with the combination to the safe in the parish hall of St. Paul Lutheran in the town of Newton, which led us to the discovery. It felt like we had successfully completed an Indiana Jones-like treasure hunt. In this connection, I also owe a debt of gratitude to Rev. Bryan Lundquist who gave me a helpful tip about the location of those records.

On my Strieter study- and photo trips in 2013 and 2020, Rev. Douglas and Kathy Hartley of Ann Arbor, Mich., Rev. Jeffrey and Jenny Schmidt of Flushing, Mich., Rev. Stephen and Charis Kuehl of Powell, Ohio, and Rev. Joshua and Julie Krieger of Livonia, Mich., all graciously put me up in their homes and provided ample hospitality.

Rev. Kirk Lahmann, Rev. Caleb Bassett, Rev. Steven Kruschel, and Rev. Abram Degner proofread, and provided feedback on, the autobiography portion of the manuscript; Rev. em. John Dolan and Rev. Bassett did the same with the front matter; and and my wife Katie proofread everything. (Any mistakes in spelling, grammar, and/or content should, however, be placed squarely at my feet, not theirs.)

And what more can I say about my wife? Who not only puts up with, but continues to cherish, a husband who dives into a project headlong like this over the course of nine years? (My lack of planning the evening we met with Gerhard Gall and Doris Schelling in Affalterbach, Germany, meant that we had to spend a mostly sleepless night in our compact rental car.) She is truly a "wife of noble character" (Prov. 31:10). For your love, companionship, support, listening ears, careful eyes, and so much more, Katie, thank you.

Finally, I must thank the triune God himself. He is the one ultimately responsible for the facts that I was raised in the same confessional Lutheran faith as Pastor Strieter, called to the same high and holy profession as he, and called to serve in an area where he once served. God is the one ultimately responsible for my interest in German, the excellent education I received in that language at Luther Preparatory School and Martin Luther College, and my ability to read, understand, and translate it. He has richly blessed my efforts, caused much help to spring up from places where I was not seeking it, and kept my wife and me safe on many travels by land and by air. Last but most important, God is the one ultimately responsible for the sure hope of eternal life that I have in the blood of Jesus his Son. I speak from the heart with King

David and Father Strieter: "Bless the Lord, O my soul, and all that is within me, bless the name of his holiness. Bless the Lord, O my soul, and forget not all the good things he has dealt you" (Psalm 103:1,2).

To God alone the glory!

Original Preface

The venerable author of this autobiography relates within it that the idea of becoming a pastor had been awakened in his heart in his youth. Feeling his unworthiness, he chose an ash tree in the vicinity of his homestead as an altar and at that ash repeatedly implored God on his knees to please take this idea away from him, since he was unfit for the ministry. But the One who governs the heart leads him into the preaching ministry. After he has been active in God's vineyard for half a century, and the same God has put him into retirement, he is asked to compose an account of his life's story. In humility he earnestly resists this request. But the reasons cited—namely, that in this way he could promote the glory of God and the building up of his kingdom even now, since his Lord had deprived him of the work he was accustomed to, and that he should not bury his talent in the handkerchief like that [cf. Matt. 25:14–30], and so on—have pressed the quill into his hand. "Thus the Lord governs hearts" [cf. Psalm 33:15] will be the judgment of the Christian readers of this book.

The undersigned, who was once confirmed and won over to work in God's vineyard by this venerable spiritual father, has let himself be persuaded to write a preface only after much resisting, and for this purpose he has read through the manuscript repeatedly. The cliff which threatens to ruin a work like this has thankfully been avoided. This self-authored biography is not a self-trumpeting. It is rather a work praising the One who entered the author's name in the Book of Life with the precious blood of Christ at his baptism, just as the author's father wrote in the family Bible. Consequently, the entire work is not a narrative laboriously pieced together and forced into a desired format. If you had the pleasure of hearing the author, especially on the occasion of the various conferences and synod conventions, or of simply interacting with him otherwise, and if you now got the chance to read this book, you will immediately acknowledge: This is Pastor Strieter as he lives and breathes, in his seriousness and humor, as he talks, jokes, thinks, reports, and admonishes. And what a string of instructive, gripping, delightful, encouraging experiences, events, and anecdotes! You have to laugh; right after that you would like to cry! A preface should be short, but this one would get very long if we were only to pick out pieces here and there from the full work.

ORIGINAL PREFACE

Biographies like this are wells for church historians. From this mine many a building stone can be taken for a history of our precious synod.[1] Here an eyewitness tells the story of the Franconian colonies in Michigan, established in the backwoods, and the story of the Indian mission there, and the story of our institution in Fort Wayne from the years when the initial passion was still burning. Here we see the young laborer, pressed into the ministry prematurely by the church's need, in hopeless and in productive mission stations, also ministering to a wide and broad field where he never preached less than four or more than nine times a week and covered some 6,000 miles during the year with his horse. Here we find the spiritual shepherd relaxing at home, even though seldom ministering to just one congregation. As we watch, he leads many well-known figures past our eyes, e.g. Walther, Crämer, Wyneken, Fuerbringer, Schwan, Lindemann, Sihler, Sievers, Hattstädt, Ruhland, Jox, Brauer, Wunder, Wagner. Some he leads past quickly, others leisurely. He tells the story of conflicts with sects, lodges, and false brothers, of cross and distress within and without, but also of pleasant experiences in an extremely happy marriage, in the genuine love of penitent Christians, and in the fruit harvested already on earth from seed that had been scattered years earlier. And all of this is done in the original, unique style of the straightforward and steady evangelical Missourian warhorse, who has cleared, dug, plowed, planted, and watered for more than fifty years exactly where God placed him, and who now presents here both old and new from the treasure of his rich experience [cf. Matt. 13:52].

Many a preacher, teacher, or listener still living among us like a pillar from ancient times will read the memories from the author's youth shared here and will live in them for hours at a time, and they will also evoke his own such memories. Many a person will be refreshed by these recollections in the quiet hours after exhausting work. Many a person will take away helpful tips and ready weapons from the author's pastoral activity and will utilize and apply them according to his own gifts. For every reader there is some benefit inside.

Dear, beloved fellow believer, take and read. You will not regret it.

God has taken the pastoral ministry in a congregation away from the beloved Father Strieter through the deafness imposed on him. May God help him to see in these years that he has taken his hands out of his lap at God's own direction, in order to strengthen his fellow pilgrims on their way to the city of eternal rest through this autobiography. Finally, up to the present Father Strieter has in fact fact belonged, along with the apostle Paul, to those who are poor, but who make many rich, to those who have nothing, yet possess everything [cf. 2 Cor. 6:10]. So for him and his life's companion, may God also partially use the proceeds from the sale of this little book to answer the petition, "Give us this day our daily bread"!

L[ouis] Hölter
Chicago, December 4, 1904

1. Namely, the Lutheran Church-Missouri Synod.

Preliminary Remarks

I had not given any thought to writing down the story of my life. But on January 17, 1904, against my will, our golden wedding was celebrated in Frankenlust, Michigan.

Fig. 2: Johannes and Elizabeth Strieter, unknown year, photo printed in St. John's Anniversary Committee, *History of St. John's Evangelical Lutheran Church, Garfield Heights, Ohio* (1929)

We had to go into the church, and Pastor Andres, our dear spiritual shepherd, gave a speech, though I did not understand a single word of it on account of my deafness. The house of my son-in-law, H[einrich] List, teacher in Frankenlust, was filled with people. There was a meal, speeches were given, presents were not wanting either, and congratulatory letters turned up. In one of them—written by my brother-in-law Leutner, teacher in Cleveland, Pastor Zorn's congregation—I was asked to write my life's story, and to do so to the honor of God and as a favor to my family. I simply wrote it off. I confess, however, that the two reasons bounced around in my head, for God does not want his works to be kept secret, and a person should serve his family and other people who are dear to him if he can. Yet another letter came from my dear nephew, H[enry] Rahe, with a similar request. And soon everybody was blowing the same horn: "Write!" So then, I will write. But it is only being done for the two reasons specified. I also wanted to note that everything I write is going into the hands of my brother-in-law Leutner for revision and then from his hands to the press.[1]

J. Strieter

---

1. This sentence was crossed out, presumably by Leutner himself, and not included in the print edition, since Leutner wanted the readers to think of it only as Strieter's work and not his own. Since this translation remains as faithful as possible to Strieter's original manuscript, and not to Leutner's edition, this sentence does not apply to the present work.

Chapter 1

Youth

I was born in Affalterbach, Marbach Jurisdiction [*Oberamt*], Kingdom of Württemberg. Regarding my birth and baptism, here are my sainted father's own words:

> On the 9th of September, 1829, I, Jacob Strieter, became the father of a baby boy. He was born into the world between one and two in the morning. On the 11th of September he was brought to Holy Baptism and received the name Johannes, and his name was entered in the Book of Life with the precious blood of Christ.

Fig. 3. The font at which Johannes was baptized, built in 1778, 2013, photo.

Affalterbach—a small market town with a population of 500 back then, on the country road between Marbach and Winnenden, two hours from either city. In the middle of the town was a crossroads. On the left-hand corner, as you stand facing Winnenden, was an inn, the Lamb Inn [*Lammwirt*], and on the right-hand was an inn, the Oxen Inn [*Ochsenwirt*]. Everything above there was called the Upper Village [*Oberdorf*]. From the Oxen Inn it went somewhat downhill, and down there was called the Lower Village [*Unterdorf*]. In the Lower Village, off to the side, was the well. It was a good well, from which everybody fetched their water for men and livestock.

In the Lower Village my father had a house of his own. We lived upstairs, and the livestock were stalled beneath us. Facing the street, which ran past below, were two windows. One evening fireworks were set off in the distance. We had the window open, were leaning out, and were eagerly watching them. My sister shoved me to the side, I shoved her back and shoved my sister right out the window. She fell headfirst, one story down onto a stone slab. Father brought her up seemingly dead. But she soon came to again.

My parents were Jacob Strieter and Maria Katharina Wiesenauer. They had eight children:

1. Rosina,
2. Dorothea,
3. Katharina,
4. Christiana,
5. Jacob Friedrich,
6. Margaretha, the one I threw out the window,
7. Johannes, and
8. a girl who died young,[1] so I ended up being the youngest.

My father was born on July 17, 1789, my mother on November 28, 1791.

My father was a shepherd at first. He sent his shepherd-servant with his flock to graze in the Bavarian countryside, while he guarded other people's flocks at home. The servant came home and the flock was mangy, 500 sheep, and Father had to have them cheaply slaughtered. With the proceeds he bought himself some more acreage, in addition to the acres he already had, and now took up farming.

---

1. Barbara was born on Dec. 28, 1831, and died on Jan. 8, 1832.

Fig. 4. Partially restored fresco in the Evangelical Church of Affalterbach, 2013, photo. This fresco on the north wall of the sanctuary appears to have once once encircled the sanctuary, depicting important stories from the Bible. On the far left, Adam and Eve are expelled from the Garden of Eden. The next panel appears to depict Cain's murder of his brother Abel. Whether this fresco was visible when Johannes attended church there as a little boy is unknown.

My parents were pious; especially my father was a devout Christian. He held family devotions three times each day. In the morning he read a chapter from the New Testament; those of us children who could read also had to have the book in front of us and each one also had to read several verses. At midday he read from the Old Testament and in the evening from a devotional book, mostly from Arndt's *Wahrem Christentum* [*True Christianity*].² My father was kind to his children, but still stern in his discipline. He did not permit his children to keep any frivolous, worldly company and did not let any of them on the dance floor. My father had an old hymnal, the Württemberg hymnal [*das Württemberger Gesangbuch*] of 1740, which was bound together with the New Testament. In the Testament were brief annotations on the verses, by Brenz,³ I believe. This little book was a wedding present from his father-in-law, Johann Martin Wiesenauer, who was also a pious man. My niece, Lizzie Liken in Sebewaing, Michigan, still has this little book. From this hymnal, whose hymns still had doctrinally sound lyrics, my parents would sing. My parents liked to sing in general. When my mother sat at the spinning wheel, she would sing spiritual songs almost continuously. My father, too, would sing almost constantly, when his work permitted it. How often I would hear "Christ, the Life of All the Living." My father also had many fine sayings, such as:

---

2. The fuller title is *Vier Bücher vom Wahren* [or *von Wahrem*] *Christentum* (Four Books on True Christianity). Johann Arndt (1555–1621) is best known for this work and for being the pastor of the young Johann Gerhard, who would become one of Lutheranism's greatest theologians.

3. Johannes Brenz (1499–1570), a fellow reformer and correspondent of Martin Luther, who participated with him in the Sacramentarian Controversy and the Marburg Colloquy of 1529.

"No fire, axe, or knifepoint | shall sever me from you."[4]

"I still have a Savior surely | from my sins, who's mine securely, | all my lifetime never forsakes me, | till before his throne he takes me."[5]

He also had the custom that, when the prayer bell tolled, he would remove his cap, fold his hands, and pray with his family loud and in chorus: "Lord Jesus Christ, with us abide, | for round us falls the eventide."

Another custom he had, when he would set out to go somewhere or would begin a task, was to say, "In God's name."

One time my father was in his vineyard and I took his pruning knife, went off to the side a ways, and cut something off, then went to Father and said, "Father, look what a nice twig I have!"

He said, "Yeah, you have cut off my young little tree." But he did not punish me any further.

One time there was gunfire in the direction of Wolfsölden,[6] a tiny little village on the Murr River where the mill was located.[7] I followed the sound of the shooting, but I did not stay on the path; instead I went in at an angle. I came to the clay pit, where there was a bed of clay. It was nice and smooth and had a yellow tint to it. I tried to get across there, but I sank in up to my waist and got stuck. I was scared and cried out. Then someone came over from the road and got me out. But now I didn't look for the shooting any more, but made my way home. The whole way I was gazing down at my yellow legs. My sister Margaretha, who was three years older, took off my little britches and washed them in the ditch opposite our house.

We had a pastor named Götz.[8] He was a very strict, moral man, but a rationalist. When he visited a sick person, he would tell him that he should overcome all pain with manly strength. When he began his instruction, which my brother attended, he began with this: "The earth turns on its axis." My brother said that at home, and Father told him, "Child, you must not believe that. Our dear God says, 'The sun rises at the end of the sky and goes around until it's back at the same end' [Eccles. 1:5], and he knows better."

---

4. From st. 13 of Paul's Gerhardt's hymn, "If God Himself Be for Me." The *you* refers to Jesus.

5. The final lines of st. 13 of "Komm, mein Herz, in Jesu Leiden," a German Communion hymn by Ernst Gottlieb Woltersdorf sung to the tune of "Soul, Adorn Yourself with Gladness." Based on the context of these hymn verse excerpts, Jacob Strieter appears to have employed these sayings during hard times.

6. Strieter spelled it Wolfselten, which is basically a phonetic spelling. See also n. 7.

7. Wolfsölden, just east of Affalterbach, is actually located on the Buchenbach (Beech Tree Creek), a tributary of the Murr River. Still today on Google Maps you can see a *Mühlkanal* (mill canal) off of the Buchenbach. Both the creek and the canal run along *Mühlenweg* (Mill Lane).

8. According to Evangelische Kirchengemeinde Affalterbach's website, M. Carl Gottlieb Goez (or Götz, as Strieter spells it) was pastor from 1818–1837 (http://www.kirche-affalterbach.de; accessed July 26, 2015).

Fig. 5. Evangelical Church in Affalterbach, 2013, photo.

The pastor's wife was pious though. If anyone was seriously ill, then she would come after the pastor, even to the poorest people, and she would bring something good along and read to the sick person from the New Testament.

My father was a shepherd at first, as already mentioned, and during that time people would often send for him now and then when something was on their livestock, especially on their sheep. He had a beautiful sharp knife, with a white handle made of bone, maybe eight inches long. When he was called out somewhere, he would stick the knife in the inner side pocket of his coat. One time he had been out, came home, and forgot to take out his knife. He went to chop some wood. The knife was situated in the pocket with the point facing Father's waist, and when he swung down he stabbed himself in the side with the knife. Father swelled up badly and was in a lot of pain and almost suffocated to death. Then came the pastor's wife and brought some olive oil and told Mother to give some of it to Father and to apply it to the swelling in a hot press using a rag. Mother did this, and Father got better again.

I also attended the school in Affalterbach for one year. This school was a little ways off the country road, toward Marbach. That's where the church was too. There were two classrooms. In the lower level the schoolmaster held class with the smaller children, and in the upper level his son, who was called Provisor, taught the bigger children. Both were enormous wardens. In the lower classroom I was in the first row. He sat behind his desk, on which he had a long blackthorn the width of a finger. If someone in the back misbehaved, he would laugh, "Ha ha!", take his stick, then usually come striding out, up over our heads, until he reached the culprit. And then down it came in all its force. Oh, what dread I had for that old teacher, but I never received any beatings.

One time I was heading home from school; it was already late. There was music coming from the Oxen. Before the Oxen we had to veer right to go home. I was trotting along slowly behind my siblings. But when I heard the music, I followed the music. They were dancing in there. On one side there was an elevation, on which the musicians were sitting. An old codger was playing the bass viol; my Injunlanders called it the *Brumm*.[9] I clambered up and sat down next to the *Brumm* player and kept peering in at the gaps in order to find out where the sound was coming from. How long I was sitting I do not know, but suddenly my sister grabbed me by the arm, pulled me down and marched on home with me. My father was across the field in Winnenden and had just come home. He was sitting in the middle of the living room and had his small leather cap on. He pulled me between his knees. "Where have you been?"

"In the Oxen."

He laid me over his knees, took his small leather cap off and counted on my backside with it. "There, next time you'll stay with your brother and sisters."

In 1837 my father formed his emigration ideas. The choice was between Russia and North America, the United States. It was said that the Russian tsar was very kind to German Lutherans and helped them to find a home. But my father still decided in favor of America, and he had in fact selected Ann Arbor, Michigan, as his destination. Pastor Götz sent for my father and urged him to stay. He showed him on the map a body of water that was called Lake Erie. He told him that we would have to cross it, and that it was a very turbulent body of water where a very large number of ships sank. My father related this to us, but cheered us up by saying, "Our dear Lord God is also on the water."

We got ready for our departure. Another family and a few young men from Affalterbach and several families from the surrounding villages also got ready to go. My father hired a coachman with two big old horses and a large wagon covered with white fabric; that's where everything was packed up. Mother and we small children were allowed to sit up top; the others had to walk. Now we were off to America. When we came to the Oxen, the innkeeper ran to the wagon with a flask of wine, managed to grab hold of my father, wept and cried out, "Now our prayer-man is leaving us."

We traveled to Bremen. It was a long, deplorable trip. The cover over us got cracks in it here and there, and the water would drip through them when it rained. The coachman was a drunken wretch [*Strick*]. He drank in every single inn, especially the ones where we spent the night, and no one could get him away from it. If the young men had not looked after his horses, the poor animals would have died.

Finally we arrived in Bremen. My father soon became acquainted with Christian brothers, especially a certain Kalbfleisch family. At a synod convention—I believe the

---

9. Strieter will talk more about "his Injunlanders" in Chapter 5 (pp. 83, 84) *Brummen* means to growl or rumble, and in telecommunications a *Brumm* is a hum.

location was called Collinsville[10]—an old lady invited me over and told me that she had gotten acquainted with my father in Bremen. In Bremen they loaded us on a small vessel on a river,[11] and now we were headed to Bremerhaven. That's also where we thought we were going to die; at one point our small vessel was sitting on the ground. After a while the water was coming toward us like a mountain, and we thought it was going to cover us.[12] In the harbor two ships were ready—a beautiful new vessel with three masts, a speedy sailer called *Louise*, and an old vessel with two masts which was called *Leondine*. We really wanted to take the *Louise*, but there was no more room on it, and so we had to board the *Leondine* in disappointment.[13]

We were off, and so too began the seasickness. My poor mother almost never left her bed. We ate sailors' fare—black, tough hardtack. Up on deck was a walled-in firestove on which a large kettle was stored. The cook handed it over for cooking every day. If the girls did not feel well, then the young men did the cooking. They had beans which were put in the water in the kettle, along with a nasty piece of salt pork. Then they were cooked. The beans on the bottom were burnt, and those above them were hard. And then there was the grease on top, as thick as a finger. When midday came, then the people came with bowls and took their portion. But we Swabians had never eaten such food. In Affalterbach, in the morning we would have a bread soup with fried potatoes, at midday millet gruel [*Hirsbrei*], creamed corn [*Welschkornbrei*], potato wedges and spaetzle [*Kartoffelschnitz und Knöpfle*], fried spaetzle and salad, pancakes and salad, steam dumplings [*Dampfnudeln*], yapper slappers [*Maulschellen*] (filled dumplings), meatballs or sausage balls, and so on. There wasn't a lot of meat, but some. But salt pork—never.

My sisters took our portion of pork raw, then they roasted it well and filled an entire metal tub [*Blechstipich*] with it and brought it over to us. They broke the hardtack into pieces with the hammer, put the fragments in a bowl and poured hot water over them and melted them, and thus made a good soup that we could eat.

We had a good trip. No one died, and a little girl was born, who was baptized Leondine.[14] Only once were the hatches closed on account of a storm. There was one time during the night that something slid past against us and our ship tipped way over to one side. In the morning the captain—he was still rather young, a short and most delightful fellow—told us: "Another ship was sailing toward us and would have just about drilled us into the ground." From then on the young men had to blow a

---

10. In Illinois. Strieter is once again fast forwarding briefly.

11. The Weser River

12. Strieter is describing what it looked like to him when he approached the sea for the first time.

13. Something is amiss in this recollection, since the passenger manifest that includes the Strieter family identifies their ship as "Barque Leontine." A barque is typically a three-masted ship, as opposed to a brig, which has two masts.

14. See n. 13. The manifest lists a Leontine Math as the twenty-day-old daughter of the forty-three-year-old Cathariena (*sic*) Math, a maidservant by occupation. This would date Leontine's birth to July 4, 1837.

signal. They had a long brass reed available and they positioned themselves at the front and one of them blew until he was out of breath, then the second one blew, then the third and so forth, the whole night through, in order to warn the other ships to stay away from us.

On Sunday it was always quiet. My father would go onto the deck; everybody gathered around him. Even the sailors had to be quiet. The captain would lean against a mast. There a hymn would be sung, and my father would read a sermon from Ludwig Hofacker[15] and would pray.

We were about halfway there when the captain showed us a ship over yonder and said, "That is the *Louise*." We arrived happily in New York, and two days later the *Louise* did too—the beautiful, new, speedy sailer.

Now we boarded a small ship, and that brought us to the canal.[16] On the canal we were now headed for Buffalo. The canal men were really nasty: If anyone went on shore, they would not let them back on. My father even fetched us some bread once, and when he was about to jump on, the helmsman veered away, and my father fell into the water up to his neck and his two loaves of bread were floating on the water.

We arrived in Buffalo and knew that we now had to go on the turbulent Lake Erie. We were quite uneasy and had a look at the water. We thought that it would rage and bluster out there, like it did on the Sea of Gennesaret when the Savior sailed across it with his disciples, but the water was completely tame. We boarded a steamboat, and that quickly brought us safe and sound to Detroit. There people had been arranged to meet us with transportation. The elder Auch was also there, the father of my eventual brother-in-law. They loaded us up and drove us to Ann Arbor. From Ann Arbor we headed several more miles further—to the west, I believe—to Scio. There was a large settlement of Württembergers there, together with their pastor Friedrich Schmid, an alumnus of Basel.[17] In the middle the frame church stood on the one corner, the parsonage on the other corner, and behind the church lay the cemetery.[18] A mile or so to the west there were forty acres of land on which a log house was located a ways off the path. That was the property of a bachelor, Karl Müller, a tailor. He did not live in his house though, but went around sewing in people's homes. For back then it was different from today. If you needed clothes back then, you fetched the tailor. We moved

---

15. Ludwig Hofacker (1798–1828) was a pietistic Lutheran pastor in Stuttgart and Rielingshausen. He was renowned for his passionate Christ-centered preaching; his church would often already be crowded an hour before the service began.

16. The Erie Canal

17. Friedrich Schmid (Strieter consistently spelled it Schmidt in his manuscript) was born on Sept. 6, 1807, in Walldorf near Nagold, Württemberg, Germany. In March 1828 he entered the Basel Mission Institute. He was ordained a Lutheran minister on April 7, 1833. German immigrants in Washtenaw County had previously requested a pastor from Basel and so Schmid was sent to America, arriving in Ann Arbor in August 1833. What became Salem Lutheran Church in Scio was organized on Sept. 20, 1833.

18. The frame church, thirty by forty feet, was erected in 1836. Pastor Schmid built a house across from the church in the summer of 1836 and moved his family into it in September.

into his house. The owner ended up marrying my oldest sister Rosina. Their youngest son is the Pastor Müller in Deerfield, Michigan. We stayed in Scio through the winter. In the spring of 1838 we moved seven to eight miles further south to the town of Freedom, Washtenaw County, Michigan.

There Father bought himself forty acres of uncultivated land for a hundred dollars. Before that he had already bought himself a cow for twenty dollars, and so his supply of money was used up now. The forty acres lay perhaps a quarter mile off of the road from Manchester to Ann Arbor, somewhat more towards Manchester. There were many Germans there too, Württembergers, and in the township of Bridgewater bordering on the south, Hessians; my brother-in-law Müller was also a Hessian. There was no church there. Service was held in a log public schoolhouse, a mile or so east of us.[19] My father erected a log house and cleared land for farming. My brother Jacob, five years older than I, helped him bravely, and so did I, as much as I could. My sisters worked as servants and gave their earnings to Father. Back then girls did not get three or four dollars a week, but seventy-five cents or at best one dollar. Pastor Schmid preached for us in the schoolhouse; he had many preaching stations. One time after the sermon he stationed my father in front of himself and delivered an address. Then my father knelt down, and the pastor solemnly blessed him. From then on my father preached five Sundays and Pastor Schmid on the sixth. Later, up at the intersection, from which we lived a quarter mile to the north, a log church was built and a cemetery was laid out, which is also where my parents are sleeping.[20] My father preached in the church and also taught school during the winter for three months at a time—both, however, without any actual pay. I attended school under my father for three winters.

---

19. This was eventually known as the Kuebler District schoolhouse.

20. The German Evangelical Bethel Congregation was officially organized by Pastor Schmid in the fall of 1840. At the same time an acre was deeded to the congregation for a cemetery and a log church was erected on that acre. Today this church is Bethel United Church of Christ, located on the southeast corner of Bethel Church Road and Schneider Road. Johannes and his family lived a quarter mile north of there on what is today Schneider Road (see Figs. 6 & 7).

Fig. 6. The land purchased and cleared by the Strieter family
in Freedom Township, 2020, photo.

I also attended some classes in the public school in the aforementioned schoolhouse. There we had a certain Jerry Cramer for several terms. He was an absolutely outstanding teacher, though very strict, but also kind and fair. One time a small Catholic girl was crying; her name was Eva Crämer. "Eve, why are you crying?" he asked. She pointed at a big girl who had stolen her picture; it was his[21] cousin. He inquired about it, and sure enough, she had it, a little Catholic picture of Mary. He sent a boy out to fetch a stick. He brought a hazel stick, about as thick as a finger and three feet long. The teacher grabbed the thieving girl by the hand, brought her on the floor, and gave her a real proper lashing over her back.

In my class there was a big, lazy brat, who never knew his spelling lesson. A lot was "spelled [*gespellt*]" back then. One morning the teacher told him, "If you do not know your 'spelling lesson' this evening, if you miss just one word, then you will receive your punishment." The guy studied now, but still missed one word. Then the schoolmaster took his ruler and lashed him three times on each hand so hard that the young man told me the next morning that his hands were so swollen that he couldn't chop any wood.

One time the teacher showed us a thing made of lead that looked like a half dollar, with a hole and a string in it. He told us, "Whoever does not miss a single word in spelling this evening, gets this thing around his neck and may take it home until

---

21. Leutner corrected this to "her," but perhaps Strieter is referring to the teacher, in order to show just how fair he was.

tomorrow." Now we went at it. I was the top speller. Lillie Allen was standing next to me. Whenever a word was given to me, she would look at me, expecting me to miss it, but I didn't miss, and now I received the thing around my neck. How proud I was, and with what pleasure I showed my lead thing to my parents and siblings.

In 1843 I was confirmed in the spring by Pastor Schmid in Scio. We were positioned according to age. I was the second last. In the back of the Württemberg catechism [*Württemberger Kinderlehre*] are questions and answers for confirmation. There were enough for everyone to answer two. Whoever was good at learning learned them all; whoever was bad at learning learned the two questions and answers that would come up at his or her turn. The pastor held his classes in the church. They did not last very long. When it was time to start, we children sat in our place, Mr. Pastor would come in, say an *ex corde* prayer with his eyes half-closed and turned toward heaven, and then begin. With his hands behind his back he would walk up and down the aisle and talk. What did he say? This is the only thing I still remember: Once while he was walking, the stovepipe above him wobbled. I looked up and thought, "If that falls down, it's going to hit the pastor on the head." He noticed this, stood still, and asked what I was looking at. He never did ask anything from the catechism, never posed one question. In general he did nothing but talk, and towards the end I learned a couple psalm verses and some hymn verses from Hiller.[22] Hiller was also our hymnal in church. The questions, mentioned before, were assigned, as was the confirmation hymn that was supposed to be sung at the confirmation.

On Confirmation Day we had to go to his house. There he gave us a serious speech: We should not fall away. He would be able to see it in our eyes if we had fallen away. We cried emotional tears as we solemnly resolved that we would not fall away. He went away, soon came back, and his knees were dusty; he had apparently been praying on his knees. We headed to the church, the pastor in the lead; we followed along behind him. The altar was encircled by a railing. We had to take our seats inside it. He delivered an address, but I have no idea what that was about either. He stepped in front of the altar; we had to sing our hymn, and now he quizzed us on our questions. We knew the answers. Individually we went up to him, knelt down, and he solemnly blessed us with his hand laid upon us, and he read our commemorative passage from a small slip of paper. Mine was not a complete passage from the Bible, but his own words that were based on a Bible passage. For the Lord's Supper we had to go to the altar two at a time. On the plate lay cut-up, ordinary bread, maybe about the length and width of a finger, and two drinking glasses stood there, filled with wine. He took one of those little pieces of bread, broke it in two and put a half-piece in everyone's hand. He also put the glass in everyone's hand. I don't remember anything else about any confession and absolution. No one announced for the Supper. Later I saw a Catholic woman go to the Supper with everyone else.

---

22. Strieter is referring to Philipp Friedrich Hiller's *Geistliches Liederkästlein* (Small Treasure of Spiritual Songs).

It was around that time, I believe, that Schmid founded the so-called Michigan Synod. He wanted to start a mission among the Chippewas in Huron County, on the eastern shore of Huron or Saginaw Bay.[23] He had selected my brother-in-law,[24] who married my second sister Dorothea, to be his missionary. My brother-in-law left his farm and went to attend the university in Ann Arbor. Later he ran to Schmid every day to learn theology from him. Candidate Auch was ordained. The head of the Michigan Synod was Metzger from Liverpool, Medina County, Ohio.[25] He came from Liverpool and delivered the sermon.[26] Candidate Auch told me afterwards that he had seen Metzger drinking a bowl of punch before he went to church. The sermon certainly fit the description—a crude rant against the Catholics. As he preached, the spit flew out of his mouth.

23. In a letter dated April 1, 1843, Pastor Schmid wrote:

You know from my last letter to you [dated February 5, 1842] that we are willing to do something among the aborigines of this land, to bring them the gospel. The Lord has since that time guided us so that we hope to carry out this enduring desire within the coming year. We organized a mission society and took in a number of young men who will prepare themselves to carry the flag of the cross of Christ to the poor Indians. . . . For nine years I have been here and labored in the part of the vineyard of the Lord assigned to me without my joining a Lutheran synod, partly because Michigan is so far from the other states where the synods exist, and partly because the synods include too many who are unbelievers. But to become more solidly founded and to be able to work unhindered in the Kingdom of God, we—Brother Metzger, Brother Cronnenwett [in the previous letter spelled Kronewett and in a subsequent letter Kronenwett], whom we ordained last year and who served with blessing in several congregations in the state of Ohio, and I—formed a synod, in order to be able to ordain our pupils in the future.

See Acknowledgements for source information. This synod is now called the First Michigan Synod in retrospect, because when Schmid didn't strictly insist on subscription to the Book of Concord, four pastors, who had joined the synod soon after its founding, left and became founding members of the Missouri Synod. The first Michigan Synod, also called the Missionary Synod of the West, disbanded shortly thereafter. Strieter will talk more about this later (pp. 23–24).

24. Johann Jacob Friedrich Auch

25. Rev. Georg Wilhelm Emmanuel Metzger, a native of Württemberg, Germany, was pastor of what is today Zion Evangelical Lutheran Church in Valley City, Liverpool Township, Ohio. When he arrived in 1834, the congregation had a log church more than a mile south of Valley City, also called Liverpool Center. In May 1838, a frame church was dedicated about a mile further to the southeast. This caused dissatisfaction with some of the members, who left that congregation and started their own, Emmanuel in Valley City, today Emmanuel United Church of Christ. Metzger appears to have served the mother congregation until his death in 1855. Rev. Karl August Wilhelm Röbbelen, sent by Wilhelm Löhe (whom Strieter will mention later), was also installed in Valley City in 1846; his relationship to Metzger and his congregation is unclear. (Röbbelen joined the Missouri Synod in 1849 and accepted a call to Frankenmuth in 1851.) Around 1850, there was another division in the mother church, which resulted in the founding of St. Paul in Valley City (LC-MS). The mother church Zion eventually joined the American Lutheran Church and is today a member of the ELCA.

26. In a letter dated December 21, 1844, Pastor Schmid wrote:

We celebrated our first annual festival here in Michigan this past summer in the month of June. Friends of the mission from near and far gathered. . . . Brothers Metzger, Kronenwett, and Richter served as pastors. Our first pupil, J. F. Auch was festively ordained by us to bring the Word of Life to the Indians.

Auch moved to Sebewaing, Huron County.[27] Schmid trained another man, Sinke, a ladies' tailor from Germany by profession. He was a very short little man, physically and intellectually lacking. Schmid also trained another man, Maier. All three also preached by us in Freedom. Auch made it through and so did Maier, but Sinke got pathetically stuck right away in the beginning and got down from the pulpit after several fruitless attempts. Schmid sent Sinke and Maier to Auch in Sebewaing. Sinke tailored there and mended clothes for the Indian boys, since Auch was running an Indian school.[28] Maier, however, mostly served the station in Shebeyang.[29] Schmid and my father wanted me to become a missionary too, and to be trained by Schmid as well. I had no desire for that. Schmid was repulsive to me, especially since people commonly spoke about his greed. I worked the field with my father.

My third sister Katharina married Friedrich Luckhardt who, even though he had no experience as a farmer, bought forty acres of land and took up farming. My fourth sister Christiana married Christian Bach, a farmer, whose father bought him sixty acres of land over in Bridgewater, where my brother-in-law Müller also moved. My youngest sister Margaretha married a blacksmith, Johann Killinger, who had twenty acres of land near his smithy. My brother Jacob married a girl who had recently come from Germany, Christiana Trinkler. We called her Nana. My brother-in-law Killinger asked my father to let me help him. So I worked with him in his smithy and in his field. I even had it in mind to learn that fine trade, but it was not the will of our dear God. I got very sick with typhoid [*Nervenfieber*] and had to go home. My sainted mother was sick for a year; she suffered from gout. She died on October 4, 1847, at age fifty-six. Ten months later, on July 27, 1848, my father died at age sixty.[30] He was

---

27. In a letter dated November 21, 1845—which Pastor Schmid appears to have written in stages—he wrote:

> After our mission festival, which took place during the first days of the month of June, and our emissaries had been consecrated for this holy work, preparations were made for their journey which took place in the name of the Lord on June 17. Brothers Auch, Dumser, and Sinke, and the wife of the first mentioned [Dorothea née Strieter] left together and arrived safely in Saginaw, a small village, where they will remain for a few weeks, and then go about 25 to 28 miles farther to the Indians who are living near Lake Huron, to which place Brothers Dumser and Sinke were assigned.... In Sebewaing on Lake Huron our brothers, Auch, Dumser, and Sinke, have already erected a mission house on a part of the eighty acres which the mission purchased. The school for Indian children is now to begin, to which the Indians are not only willing, but are asking permission, to send their children in order to partake of Christ and his eternal grace.

28. In a letter dated January 31, 1848, Pastor Schmid wrote:

> Our school for Indians is quite large; poor, helpless children who wandered about like wild creatures, naked and deeply sunk in the forests, are now neatly dressed, are required to learn to read, write, etc. in the school here and to listen to the word of Jesus, their Savior, with reverence.

29. Johann Friedrich Maier (Strieter spelled it Meyer) worked at the Shebeyang (or Shebahyonk) mission, near the present-day unincorporated community of Weale, on Saginaw Bay near the mouth of Shebahyonk (now Shebeon) Creek, about seven miles northeast of Sebewaing.

30. Actually fifty-nine years, ten days, according to the birth information Strieter gives earlier. Schmid's death entry for Jacob Strieter says he died on July 28 and that he was fifty-nine years, eleven

only in bed for two days. Just after New Year's of 1850 I set my bundle on my back to go and visit my brother-in-law and my sister in Sebewaing.

Fig. 7. Bethel United Church of Christ Cemetery (formerly German Evangelical Bethel Church), where Johannes Strieter's parents are buried, 2013, photo.

Fig. 8. Rev. Johann Jacob Friedrich Auch, Johannes Strieter's brother-in-law, in his later years. Image courtesy of the Luckhard Museum, Sebewaing, Mich.

---

days old.

I marched from Ann Arbor to Saginaw. There my brother-in-law picked me up with the sled. Saginaw at that time had one street along the river, one inn, one store, several liquor dens, and a row of small houses. Lower Saginaw, now Bay City, also had one small street along the river, one liquor den where people could also buy all sorts of small and sundry items, and a small number of small houses. But there was a large sawmill nearby, and on the road to Upper Saginaw another very large one, and on the east side of the river, now East Saginaw, yet another large sawmill. My sister had no children. She had a mishap with her first delivery. They were now very happy to see me. I was always the favorite with my siblings. I now made myself as useful as I could; I even taught a little school with the dear Indian children.

I really loved the Indians. I also frequently went with Missionary Maier to Shebeyang. One time I came down with the fever, dumb ague; it makes you shiver a little and then you have to sleep and it gives you the most terrible thirst and frightening dreams and hallucinations. A squaw stayed with me. She laid a bulrush mat on the ground for me, on which I lay down in front of the fire. I was craving water. She bends her head forward, forces her mouth open, and makes the sound, "Ohch." But I wanted water. She gave me some and right away her prophecy was fulfilled.[31]

I continued to go with dear Maier anyway and had fun with him at his expense. He was no horseman. There I would ride next to him and would knock his stirrup off his foot. Then I would put my horse into a brisk trot and his horse would want to do the same, and he had to hang on tight to the mane. If we came to a wet spot, I would go right through with his horse behind me so that the water would splatter all over him. Once in a while he would scold, but most of the time he laughed.

One time I went with him to a sick woman. Back in the sugar maple woods, a little old woman who was almost a hundred years old had taken ill. They brought her home to her wigwam. There she lay on a bulrush mat with an old squaw attending to her. Next to her lay a dead bird, green, with long legs; I believe we called it a waterhen. She kept setting the bird here and there and stroking it. The missionary told me later that it was her guardian spirit that would supposedly bring her to the Indian heaven. The missionary spoke with her about heaven, but she would not listen to any of it. She said she was too old. Especially the other woman was very surly.

The religion of the Indians was described to me this way: They believe that there is a great good spirit, Gishaemanido, and an evil spirit, Machimanido.[32] Each one has many spirits in its service, which are in the animals and all around us. For example, a rattlesnake is an evil spirit. When it storms really badly, that is caused by the evil spirit, and you have to appease it with offerings. My brother-in-law once had an Indian with him in a ship when the waves were high; the Indian threw tobacco in the water. In

---

31. In other words, Johannes threw up.

32. These names are variously spelled. According to "The Ojibwe People's Dictionary" online, *gichi-manidoo* means *great spirit* or *god* and *maji-manidoo* means *evil spirit* or *demon* (https://ojibwe.lib.umn.edu; accessed April 21, 2020).

the far west, they say, is a beautiful land with magnificent sugar maple forests and beautiful lakes and rivers. There is a lot of game and a lot of fish, but no pale-face comes there. That's where eternal peace is found. Along the border of that land runs a deep, narrow, dark stream, with a narrow footbridge going across. A bad Indian falls off and perishes in the stream, but a good Indian gets across.[33] Everyone chooses his own guardian spirit, like that woman chose the bird. When she was buried, I went to find her grave. There a split piece of wood was embedded in the ground at the head, and her bird was painted in green on top of it.

The Indians liked me: "Bushu, bushu John," they would say.[34] I even witnessed one of their festivals. They had assembled near the creek[35] in an open area. With short, thin sticks, perhaps one and a half feet high, they had staked off a longish space. In the middle stood a man with the drum, which was a hollow log covered with deerhide on both ends. He had a mallet in his hand, and now he began beating on the deerhide with gusto. Another man stood next to him with a gourd, a vegetable like a pumpkin, a thick, round mass with a handle. When it is dry, it is very hard, and the seed rattles when you pound it against your hand. He now took his one hand with the thing and began pounding it forcefully against the other, so that it rattled. That was the music. When they had played for a while, a man and a woman stepped into the circle, their hands crossed against their chest and an animal pelt hanging over their arms with the scalp still on it, a weasel, a muskrat, a mink, etc. They skipped along one after the other. Pretty soon the man thrusts his pelt into a woman's face and shouts, "Hui!" and she then jumps in too. The woman does the same to a man, and pretty soon the space is filled. Those in the middle play the music and the others go skipping along to it, one after the other. And then pretty soon two of them leave the ring and go over into the nearby thicket. The chief, Nage-jikamik,[36] Great Chief, lies on the ground nearby and

33. Cf. Herman F. Zehnder, *Teach My People the Truth: The Story of Frankenmuth, Michigan* (Herman F. Zehnder, 1970), 43–47.

34. According to "The Ojibwe People's Dictionary" online (see n. 32), *boozhoo* means *hello!* or *greetings!*

35. The two streams that immediately present themselves for consideration are the Sebewaing River and the Shebeon (Shebahyonk) Creek. But Strieter could also be referring to one of the tributaries of the Sebewaing River, such as Volz Creek. See also the next n.

36. Original spelling: Nage-dschikamik. Strieter spelled this name two slightly different ways in his manuscript—Nage-dschikamik here, and Nagedschickamik later. Contributing to the confusion about the identity of this chief and the location of this powwow are the following: a) Local historian Charles F. Luckhard identified the chief of the Sebewaing Ojibwe band as Nock-tschi-ko-me and the chief of the Shebahyonk band as Me-gan-ig-isch-ik (*Faith in the Forest* [Charles F. Luckhard, 1952], 20,33)—neither of which matches well with the name Strieter gives. b) Zehnder quotes a July 25, 1845 letter by August Crämer in which Crämer supposedly called Nocktschikome the chief at Shebahyonk (*op. cit.*, 70), but later Zehnder refers to "Chief Meganigischik of Shebahyonk" (*ibid.*, 83). c) When Strieter mentions Nagedschickamik later (p. 33), he seems to be associated with Shebahyonk (a careful reading, however, reveals that Strieter only puts translator Jacob Graverad in that area). d) In Appendix III, no. 6, Crämer refers to the entire Shebahyonk village as a small, committed congregation (p. 207). In no. 9, he refers to Shebahyonk's chief as "the committed chief" (p. 216) while referring to "the great faithlessness" of Sebewaing's chief and "the miserable condition of his heart," calling him

has a large liquor jug in his arm. A Frenchman who knew the language was with me. The chief spoke with me through him. He told me, "They are celebrating a festival of thanks to the great spirit." I had the interpreter tell him that that was not how a person thanks the great spirit. He replied, "He is a very great spirit, not as particular as people are. It doesn't matter to him whether you people kneel down and pray, or whether we dance." The next morning I went back to the festival area. There lay the chief dead-drunk, with his squaw sitting next to him, watching over him.

In the spring a mission house was to be built in Shebeyang, for which we needed boards.[37] My brother-in-law and I took our seats in the mission boat, which was twenty feet long[38] with a mast and sail. We had no wind and had to "pole" the boat, that is, propel it with poles. Toward evening we came to a small little stream, navigated into it, made a tent, brought our blankets and our trunk inside, made ourselves a fire, and cooked ourselves tea and eggs. We had bread too. We ate and went to sleep.

During the night the wind came from the other side and drove the water from the little stream out into the bay, and our boat sat there on the sand. We packed everything back in and now worked at getting our boat into the water. We had to go into the water. Boots and stockings came off and now, with our poles stuck in under the boat, we lifted up and shoved back and forth, until the thing was floating. We got in and put our stockings and boots on—people wore boots back then—and off we went. We had wind, but the wind was too "close"; we could not reach the lighthouse at the mouth of the Saginaw River.[39] We navigated to shore and I say, "I am getting the fever." That doesn't help any; I start yawning and getting the chills. We stood for a while, but night is approaching; we have to get going. We propel our boat again, until we reached the river. Then Auch took a rope, went up on shore and pulled the thing, and I was supposed to keep it away from shore with a pole. But I wanted to sleep now that I had the chills, for it was the dumb ague. Bump, my boat hits the shore, and I wake up and shove it back off. The wind was making little ripples, and I think, "That is a turned down bed; you should just go crawl in." Bump, my boat hits the shore again, and I shove it back off.

---

a "gray-haired sorcerer and scoundrel" (p. 217). (In no. 10, it is not completely clear which "Indian congregation" and chief Missionary Auch is referring to.) Taken all together, and preferring primary sources to secondary ones, it appears that this powwow took place near the Sebewaing River or one of its tributaries, and that the chief Strieter refers to was the chief of the Sebewaing band. As for the name Strieter gives him, according to "The Ojibwe People's Dictionary" online (see n. 32), *great* is *gichi-* and *chief* is *ogimaa* or *ogimaakaan*. (The *Na-* or *No-* at the beginning may have been a first person indicator, so that his name meant, "I am a great chief.") It is also remotely possible that Strieter (and his companions?) mistranslated the name; *nagaji'* means "to be familiar with, accustomed to, used to making; to know how to handle."

37. See Appendix III, no. 9, p. 215, esp. n. 25.
38. "and ten wide" was originally added, but then crossed out in pencil.
39. That is, the wind was blowing from the direction they wanted to go.

Finally there is a little house on the prairie in the distance. My brother-in-law says, "Those are Frenchmen. Let's go and find out if they'll put us up for the night." We go over; the house is locked. A little ways away is another house; we see light there. Off we go over there. There we find two women, the mother from the first house and her daughter in the second house. Their husbands were out fishing. There were two beautiful children in the cradle, one with the head at one end, the other with the head at the other. One belonged to the mother and the other to the daughter. Auch asked if we could stay overnight. They said sure. Pretty soon the mother takes off with her baby, and the daughter plunders her bed to make one for us on the floor. I slept gloriously. In the morning the woman bakes buckwheat cakes and roasts salt pork and fish. Oh, how great it tasted—better than on the ocean. Auch asks her what we owe, but she doesn't want anything. I say, "Give her a half-dollar." He took out his money-bag and gives her a brand new half-dollar. Then she laughed anyhow, and was very pleased as she examined the half-dollar in her hand.

We returned to the boat and were off. We traveled to the sawmill and my brother-in-law bought wood. But we have to go to Upper Saginaw, because everything else could only be bought there. There I came down with my fever again. My brother-in-law brings me to the inn. A fat woman brings me upstairs to a bed. Every moment she comes and wakes me up in English: "You mustn't sleep." We headed back up to Lower Saginaw and stayed overnight with a Frenchman. There we had boiled potatoes [*Pellkartoffeln*], salt pork, and fish.

We now loaded our boat full of lumber, so that it was only a hand-length above the water, and we made our way to the bay. We had strong wind, but when we got near the mouth of the river, the wind was too "close" to us and we had to drop the sail and grab for the poles. We work tremendously hard; the waves keep throwing us back against the right shore. Finally we're around the corner.[40] In front of us a sailing ship lay at anchor. It had a large float of boards hanging at the side, which were to be loaded in once the water had quieted. We tied our boat to the float and had our first good look at the bay. The water was very turbulent, the waves were running high, and there were whitecaps everywhere. The captain appeared on his ship and shouted to us that we should go back into the river. He said the water was much too high for our boat and he could not hold us; his anchor had enough weight to hold already.

My brother-in-law says, "John, what should we do?"

I say, "Not go back; we don't want to go through all that work again."

He says, "If you're up for it, let's keep going." He tied the sail in until it was a piece as large as a tablecloth. I untie the rope, and he hoists the sail. Whoosh, we whizzed on past the ship out into the open, stormy bay.

At first I definitely felt very strange. When the boat was at the top of a high wave, I would think, "Now it's going to rush down into the trough and right down to the ground." But look, just like that it was back at the top of another wave. My

---

40. At the mouth of the Saginaw River, the eastern bank projected into the bay somewhat.

brother-in-law began to sing. Then I relaxed and thought, "If he is singing, there must not be anything to worry about." But the boat traveled so horribly that it tilted way to the front, as if it were going to stand up on its head, and the water was constantly washing in at the front, so that I had to bail water almost continuously. In two hours we were at the mouth of the Sebewaing River.[41]

I would like to relate a few more snippets from my youth.

When I was just a boy, my sister Christiana worked in Manchester for a merchant, [Mr.] Keith. There were two brothers; the oldest was an old bachelor, and the younger one was married but had no children. The younger, a short and very friendly man, brought my sister home in the buggy for a visit and went to my father, asking him to relinquish me to him. He wanted to take me in as his son. He would give me a good training, and if I turned out well, I would go into his business. He had a large general store. He really pressed my father, and toward me he was uncommonly friendly. I took a terrible liking to the idea too, but my father shook his head: "Nothing good will come of it. Deceit sticks between buyer and seller like a nail in the wall. There you will turn into a worldling on me and will too easily get eternally lost on me." Our dear God would not have it that I become a rich storekeeper.

Another small occurrence: There were two eighty-acre plots next to each other, running south to north lengthwise. The eastern eighty were divided. On the southern forty a Hessian family, the Gosenheimers, lived on the southern end. He was a master tailor. Mrs. Gosenheimer's sister was there, and they had a boy, somewhat smaller and younger than I. They took us into their home until my father had built his log house. Our house was erected on the northern half of the eighty, along the eastern end. On the western eighty a man, [Mr.] Hoberger, lived on the west side. One time my father sent me to him on an errand very early in the morning. I headed through the woods. When I was halfway or so, a large marsh lay in front of me to the right. Over there, beyond the marsh, was a field. An animal, black, is coming towards me across the field. I stopped and asked myself, "What could it be? It's not a sheep; it's hanging its head to the ground. It's also not a pig; it's much too big. It's not a dog either." It came to the fence; then I could tell what it was. It climbed up on the rails and then tumbled down. Ah, it's a bear. The brute came lumbering right at me. "What should you do? Run away? Then he'll run after you. Climb up a tree? He'll certainly climb too." I positioned myself behind a tree. I had a dog with me. He soon saw the fellow too and started growling softly. I told him to stop. When the bear, a frightfully large fellow, was still fifteen rods [eighty-two and a half yards] or so in front of me, I thought, "This is it!" I stepped forward, and Mr. Bear looked up and sees me, hesitates a little while and . . . then turns aside somewhat to the left and

---

41. Someone, probably Leutner, inserted in pencil after this: "so we had done about thirty miles in two hours."

starts running. Now I felt relieved, took care of my errand, and returned home and and told my story. Soon after that the poor fellow was shot.

Another occurrence: We had a lake to the north, a mile or so away, Lake Pleasant. We, my brother and I, often bathed in it. One time we swam far out and then turned around for shore. We were maybe a few rods [twenty yards] or so from shore when I thought, "You can certainly wade now," and let myself down. But the water went over my head. Now because I was so certain, I started swallowing water right away and immediately I was out. My brother, five years older, was much bigger. He noticed it immediately and grabbed me—he was able to stand—and held me up until I came to my senses.

Another little story: One day we rode the horses to the waterhole, twenty rods [110 yards] or so from the stable, but didn't have any bridles, nothing in our hand but the halter strap. After the waterhole we rode a bit farther, a short pleasure ride. We turned, and I put my horse into a gallop, with my brother and his horse following, and now race the horses back as fast as they'll go. On the way it occurs to me: "The stable door is still open. If your horse rushes on in, you're dead." I get scared, but can't do anything but jump off, and I'm going much too fast for that. In front of the stable door there was a tall manure pile. Before I came to it, I forcefully shouted, "Hoh!" Suddenly my horse stopped and next thing I knew, I was lying on my back on the manure, with my head toward the horse.

One more: It was winter and my mother was visiting my sister Rosina in Scio—Karl Müller's place—and got sick. She suffered a lot from rheumatism, and that's what she had now. She was referred to an old English doctor, who was not actually practicing any more and lived on his farm; it was maybe ten miles or so west of us. We received word at home that we should go to the doctor and get medicine for her. I get on the horse and ride to the doctor. From the doctor though I ride off straight for Müller's. It was bitterly cold, and evening was setting in. I was riding over there on a newly installed road[42] toward the path on which Müller's lay. Suddenly I have to go down a very steep hill. My horse's hind feet slipped and he sat down on his backside and did not get back up until we reached the bottom. Now I was headed to Müller's. My horse was tired, and I was too. I was riding slowly. All at once I became very sleepy. I had already heard that you should not fall asleep, otherwise you were dead.[43] I forced my eyes wide open, but I was already pretty much out. It seemed to me like I was seeing a rider on a large, black horse hurrying toward me in a dream. While I was dreaming this, next thing I knew that horse was running right past me. My dream was actually happening. That collision woke me up, and now I put my horse in a drive, and pretty soon I was there.

---

42. Perhaps what is today M-52.
43. Leutner changed this to: "otherwise you would freeze to death."

Chapter 2

Seminary

In the first half of the [18]40s the men sent by Löhe[1] came with their colonies. First came Ernst and Burger.[2] Burger soon died, leaving behind a widow and two little boys. The oldest eventually married the daughter of my youngest sister, Margaretha, and currently still resides in Adrian, Michigan. Then came Hattstädt to Monroe, Michigan.[3] He and Sievers are, to my knowledge, the only ones in our synod who never took a call elsewhere. Crämer and his Franconians came and established a colony on the Cass River, fourteen miles east of Saginaw.[4] Gräbner and his Franconians came and settled eight or so miles north of Frankenmuth[5]—the name they gave to the spot just mentioned—and they named their spot Frankentrost.[6] Sievers and his Franconians came and settled on the western shore of the Saginaw River, opposite

---

1. Johann Konrad Wilhelm Löhe (1808–1872) was a confessional Lutheran pastor in the village of Neuendettelsau in Franconia, Bavaria, Germany, from 1837 until the end of his life. In 1841 Friedrich Conrad Dietrich Wyneken traveled around Germany pleading the cause of the spiritually needy Lutherans in America. From his small village Löhe answered the plea impressively. (See the following notes.)

2. Adam Ernst (1815–1895), formerly a journeyman shoemaker, and Johann Georg Burger (1816–1847), one of Ernst's friends, were two volunteer helpers whom Löhe sent to America in 1842. Ernst eventually became a member of the Ohio Synod, and Burger eventually ministered in Hancock and Van Wert Counties in Ohio.

3. Georg Wilhelm Christoph Hattstädt (1811–1884) was sent to America by Löhe in 1844.

4. Friedrich August Crämer (1812–1891) met Löhe in 1844 and was sent to America in 1845. He was pastor in Frankenmuth until 1850, when he accepted a call to be a professor at the practical seminary in Fort Wayne, Indiana. See also next n.

5. All the names the Franconians gave their settlements were personalized paraphrases for God. *Frankenmuth* means *(Source of the) Franconians' Courage*. A Historic Site sign outside of St. Lorenz Evangelical Lutheran Church on West Tuscola Street tells the story of Crämer and the city's founding.

6. Johann Heinrich Philip Gräbner (1819–1898) was sent to America by Löhe in 1847. *Frankentrost* means *(Source of the) Franconians' Comfort*. Today Frankentrost is a small unincorporated community about eight miles east of Saginaw, identified by Immanuel Evangelical Lutheran Church (LC-MS) on the southwest corner of M-46 and Mueller Road.

Lower Saginaw, and called their spot Frankenlust.[7] Clöter was in Upper Saginaw.[8] Kühn came with Franconians, but they mostly stayed in Detroit; only one family and a number of bachelors came along to Frankenmuth. Kühn was to establish the colony of Frankenhilf.[9] Friedrich Lochner also came with Sievers.[10]

Fig. 9. Rev. Johann Konrad Wilhelm Löhe, pastor in Neuendettelsau, Bavaria, from 1837–1872. He was responsible for sending many confessional Lutheran pastors and laypeople to the United States to serve the spiritual needs of German immigrants and to evangelize the Native Americans.

7. Georg Ernst Christian Ferdinand Sievers (1816–1893) was sent to America by Löhe in 1847 and became pastor in Frankenlust, Michigan. *Frankenlust* means *(Source of the) Franconians' Joy* or *(God the) Franconians' Delight*. Today the location of the original colony is marked by St. Paul Lutheran Church on the southwest side of Bay City on the southern corner of Westside Saginaw Road (M-84) and Ziegler Road.

8. Ernst Ottomar Clöter (1825–1897) was sent to America by Löhe in 1849. He was installed as pastor of Holy Cross Lutheran Church in Saginaw by Pastor Sievers on November 30, 1849.

9. *Frankenhilf* means *(God the) Helper of the Franconians*. Eventually this colony was founded in 1851. Today it is the village of Richville.

10. Strieter is in error here. Friedrich Johann Carl Lochner (1822–1902) came with Crämer in 1845, not with Sievers in 1847. Lochner was first the pastor of a United (combination of Lutheran and Reformed) congregation in Toledo, Ohio, but left when he failed to have it constituted as a Lutheran congregation. He then served Lutheran churches in Madison and Macoupin Counties, Ill.; Milwaukee, Wis.; and Springfield, Ill., where he was also an instructor at Concordia Seminary.

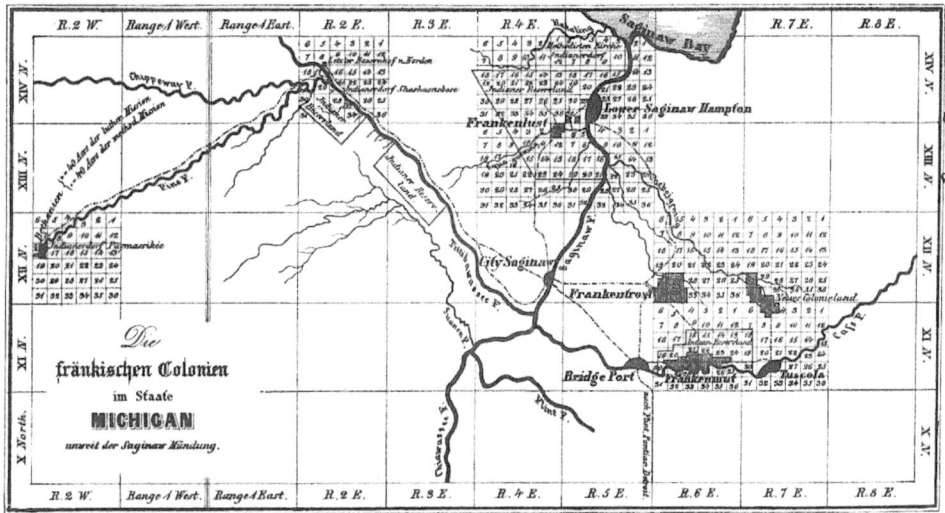

Fig. 10. *Die fränkischen Colonien im Staate Michigan unweit der Saginaw Mündung,* map printed in Wilhelm Löhe, *Etwas über die deutsch-lutherischen Niederlassungen in der Grafschaft Saginaw, Staat Michigan* (1849). Ferdinand Sievers included the original version of this map with his April 18, 1849 letter to Löhe. The "Neues Colonieland" east of Franketrost marks the site for Frankenhilf.

Hattstädt, Crämer, and Lochner traveled to Ann Arbor to Parson Schmid and held a conference with him. Schmid made a very Lutheran impression and professed his loyalty to the symbolical books of the Lutheran Church[11] without qualification. They now established fellowship, and the mission was to be run jointly, for Crämer was also doing mission work among the Chippewas.[12] Missionaries Auch and Maier now

11. This refers to the Lutheran Confessions contained in the Book of Concord of 1580.

12. In a letter dated November 21, 1845—which Pastor Schmid appears to have written in stages— he wrote:

> In a very surprising but very pleasant manner, brotherly participation and help was offered us from Bavaria, without any request on our part or knowledge thereof. The Lord arranged to have real help from the old fatherland in our Indian mission, which in this part of the world has received very little support up to this time. A small colony of believing souls, with their own preacher, arrived here last summer in order to work as a mission colony among the Indians, and to be as a light to them. They occupied a fitting location on the Cass River in Saginaw County, buying a piece of land which I had selected before their arrival. There is also a piece of land for the mission.... Reverend Mr. Löhe, who wrote us concerning the whole matter, expressed his wish and the wishes of many other participating friends, namely to spread the kingdom of Christ also among the poor Indians. In doing this, he asked nothing of us up to this point which would be contrary to our conscience and conviction; pure teaching and adherence to the Lord and the Holy Sacrament, according to the creed of our Evangelical Lutheran Church, is his condition, with which we, who for many [sic] years have founded a Lutheran synod, are in agreement, convinced that up to this point our Evangelical Lutheran Church has remained pure and true in her teaching and the administration of the sacraments, adhering to God's holy word, and in doing so we here have never been led into controversy with either the Reformed or the Lutherans. As far as forms and customs are concerned, we shall continue to love them and will put incidentals in their relation to the great prime things, and I would never like to render

established close brotherly fellowship with the Franconian pastors and held conferences with them. But it wasn't too long before Schmid separated from the Franconians and went his own way again. Indeed, the Franconians were decried as half-Catholic: They burned candles at the Lord's Supper; the pastor chanted at the altar; he turned his back to the people; he made the sign of the cross. Especially the sign of the cross was regarded as the living Satan. Missionaries Auch and Maier, however, remained with the Franconians. In 1847 our synod, the Missouri Synod, was called into being in Chicago, and now the Franconians joined this synod, including Missionaries Auch and Maier. Thus the mission in Sebewaing and Shebeyang came into our synod.[13]

> judgment of any sort about our brothers who call themselves Evangelical.... If the brothers of Bavaria do not ask anything which is contrary to our conscience, then we can very well carry on our work of the Lord with them.... A colony has settled on the Cass River about twenty-five miles from the above-mentioned [mission] station [in Sebewaing]. Pastor Crämer, who suffers from fever a great deal, hopes in a short time to begin a school for Indian children. At the present time they are very busy erecting a building for a mission house.
>
> See Acknowledgements for source information.
>
> 13. See Appendix III, nos. 1 & 6. In his letter dated January 31, 1848, Pastor Schmid gives no hint of any strife. But in his next letter to the Basel Mission Institute, written three years later, on April 29, 1851, he records the breakup from his perspective:
>
> For nearly eighteen years I have served numerous congregations here with the Holy Word and Sacrament, in which there are Lutheran and Reformed from the homeland. Yet I have never had to experience the slightest criticism on the part of the Reformed because of teachings and creed. As far as church practice is concerned, I maintain everything according to our Württemberger church, except that we from early times did not have Communion wafers. If the divine truth is proclaimed in a godly and powerful manner and the pastor lives in the strength of the gospel, then the truth-loving and the truth-seeking people of both confessions can get together through the strength of the Word; and this will also occur without any attempt to force a union. For that reason there are, I think, many in the congregation here whose parents were Reformed, but I am not certain of it. I do not inquire about it, for they are united and happy with and through the proclaimed Word of the cross and the holy sacraments. Firmness in the teachings and in the creed is required here, and if this exists, then the Spirit of the Lord will be with his Word.... As far as the rigid Old Lutherans are concerned, with whom I have come into contact without learning to know them, I respect their sound teachings, but these people are mostly lacking in living faith, and for that reason there is so little love and so much harshness toward others. Their rigid ceremony and their strong condemnation of others are terrible things to me.... I could not join this synod [the Missouri Synod], out of conviction. We too had a synod among us here, but it lacked firm foundation and therefore collapsed; some wanted an organization strictly Lutheran, others not so strict, and as a result a lengthy paper was drawn up but when one wanted to follow its path, the wind blew it away.... That we have erected a mission here and that we have already worked a year among the Indians with blessing in this state is already known, and that our missionaries joined the Old Lutherans and that they demanded from us what we couldn't do, you probably also know. Thus we had no choice but to turn over the mission with its missionaries to the Old Lutherans, and thus our mission endeavor is restricted.
>
> In a letter dated February 9, 1857, Schmid reports that he had joined the Ohio Synod the previous fall, but in a letter dated November 14, 1859, he says that the Ohio Synod did not suit him because of "their stiff and strict forms and ceremonies," and on March 19, 1861, he reported that he and several brothers had resurrected the Michigan Synod (the so-called Second Michigan Synod) in December 1860. Pinpointing Schmid's theological position is difficult. He certainly seems to have breathed an evangelical spirit, and it seems that the early Missourians could have learned something

The mission house in Shebeyang was built; I helped as much as I could. A long log house, made of squared fir trunks, divided in the middle, one half the missionary's residence and the other the church and school. It was dedicated. Baierlein from Bethany preached; Jacob Graverad translated.[14] His father, an Englishman, a former liquor dealer among the Indians, was formerly Auch's translator. But the Indians who already understood some English told Auch, "Graverad does not say what you say at all. He often says the opposite." So Auch dismissed the elder and employed the younger. The tall Jacob definitely knew how to speak good Indian, but was bad at English. He called everything "she." (Maier married Auch's sister Dorothea. She was confirmed with me, and now lived in Shebeyang.)[15]

The idea now occurred to me of becoming a minister [*Diener*] of the Church myself, even if only as a teacher. I carried the idea around with me and couldn't get rid of it. So I sought refuge in prayer. Over at the edge of the woods stood a white ash, behind which I knelt down and prayed, but mostly that God would please remove the idea from my heart, because I was unfit. Daily, often several times, I went to find my prayer altar, but the idea only grew more and more intense.

Finally I opened up about it to my brother-in-law Auch. He advised me against it at first, citing, actually, the fact that I was not especially gifted for becoming a missionary and being a missionary's assistant was too unstable, the fact that I did not have the educational background for such studies, and the fact that I did not have the means either. In all these points he was absolutely correct. Instead he now made me a proposal: "Stay with us. We have no children. You'll be like our very own." He offered me a horse as a gift, a young and beautiful animal, and—get this—he told me he had 700 dollars available, if I'm not mistaken, and that he wanted to lend it to me without interest as long as I wanted. I should use the money to acquire some land. The land they were sitting on and the surrounding land was school property and would soon be for sale, fifty cents an acre. In five years there would be a village here, he said, and I could resell the acres for a hundred dollars apiece. He had purchased forty acres at the mouth of the river in order to cut off the speculators. The Indians were prophesying an abundant whitefish harvest in the fall. He said I should buy myself a bag net, hire a man, buy barrels and salt, stretch the net across the creek in the evening and pull it out full in the morning. Out in the distance, a mile or so, were two small little islands; a ship could moor along one of them. I could take my fish there with our boat and get

---

from him in this regard. But the Missourians' charge against Schmid of doctrinal duplicity is also hard to refute. In the final analysis, Schmid made too big a deal out of the Missourians' ceremonies (something Schmid himself said in his Nov. 21, 1845 letter that he did not want to do) and his accusation against these early Missourians for lacking a living faith is unfounded, as evidenced, among other things, by this autobiography.

14. See Appendix III, no. 9, p. 216. Eduard Raimund Baierlein arrived in Frankenmuth to serve as a missionary to the Ojibwe in 1847. He labored at the Bethany mission station in St. Louis, Michigan, about thirty-four miles west of Saginaw, from 1848–1853.

15. Leutner eliminated this parenthetical remark from the print edition.

three and a half to four dollars a barrel. And the promised catch of fish did turn out to be so abundant that a Frenchman and his assistant caught 1,200 barrels full off of Fish Point, which is what they called a promontory sticking out into the water not too far from the river's mouth. The village also came true.

"Thousands!" I thought. "This way you can become a fairly rich man without a lot of work. You should do it." But I didn't accept right away.

Auch said, "Think it over."

I now often ran back to my white ash, but the more I prayed, mostly to be rid of the idea of studying,[16] the more fervent the idea became.

"So," my brother-in-law asked one day, "what do you want to do?"

I said, "I want to stay true to my idea."

"Fine," he said. "The next conference is at my place. I will present it to Crämer then."

Fig. 11. Rev. Ferdinand Sievers, pastor of St. Paul Lutheran, Frankenlust, Mich., from 1848–1893

Auch traveled to Saginaw with his boat and brought Crämer, Gräbner, Clöter, Sievers, Baierlein, Kühn and a guy named Sommer, who was still supposed to be at the seminary, and Mr. Bergrat Koch, Sievers's father-in-law, who had just recently brought his daughter from Germany to be dear Pastor Sievers's wife. The conference

---

16. Strieter is not saying that the studying aspect of entering the ministry was particularly unpleasant or intimidating to him. The emphasis is on *rid*, not on *studying*. His prayers mostly consisted of requests to be rid of the idea of studying for the ministry, rather than more neutral requests such as: "Please help me to reach a decision and to be at peace with my decision, and bless whatever decision I make to your glory."

was held in the schoolroom.¹⁷ After the conference the gentlemen, especially Crämer, had another serious debate, with Mr. Koch. Mr. Koch thought that the secular arm was needed for the spread of the Church, and we were lacking that here. Crämer and the others didn't want to have anything to do with any secular arm.

Fig. 12. Friedrich August Crämer, between 1830 and 1844 in Bavaria.
Image courtesy of the Frankenmuth Historical Association.

Crämer took me aside and said, "You, sir, are going with me to Frankenmuth, and I will see if you've got what it takes. If you are fit, then you will go to the seminary in Fort Wayne, and if not, you will go back to Sebewaing."

I packed my bundle. Maier's wife was also there. When it was time to go, the two Doras [*Dorles*]¹⁸ cried, and I did too. Auch brought the group to Saginaw by boat. Then I headed to Frankenmuth on foot.

There was a young man my age there, Kundinger, Crämer's sister's son, who was supposed to be trained yet and then become Kühn's schoolmaster in Frankenhilf. Old man Moll of Frankentrost said, "Help the Franconians [*Hilf den Franken*] is what we should call it."¹⁹ Crämer gave the two of us daily instruction in the Augsburg Confession, and Teacher Pinkepank, who lived with his wife, Moll's daughter, across

17. For more on this conference, see Appendix III, no. 9, p. 215.

18. That is, the two Dorotheas—Auch's wife (Strieter's sister) and Maier's wife (Auch's sister, who had been confirmed with Strieter).

19. In other words, they had named the settlement Frankenhilf—*(God the) Helper of the Franconians*—but the way things were going, Moll thought a better name would be Hilf den Franken—*(God) Help the Franconians*.

the street on the north side—also a long log house that was half residence and half schoolhouse—taught us in reading, writing, singing, etc. after he was done teaching school. We also did some scraping on the violin. Kühn gave me a Book of Concord and a small little book called *Luthers Leben* [Luther's Life].[20]

Fig. 13. Friedrich Lochner, *Die Kirche und das Pfarrhaus zu Frankenmuth* (oriented westward), c. 1859, watercolor. Image courtesy of Concordia Historical Institute, St. Louis, Missouri. The 1846 log church and 1852 frame church (the latter was not yet built when Strieter was there) are on the left (south) and the combination school-teacherage is on the right (north). Note also the cemetery and the framework with the two bells on the north side of the church near the road.

Since I was not happy with how I was doing, I was expecting my dismissal from Crämer every day. But look here: One morning after the class hour he clapped me on the shoulder: "Cheer up, my dear Strieter. You are doing quite well, sir. You are going to go to the seminary." Now I got excited.

Crämer's house stood on the south side of the path, north of the Cass River, and was a log house. A kitchen took up the entire space on the west side. The eastern side was divided—a small section towards the road was a combination bedroom and study. There he would sit, the diligent Crämer, at his small, simple desk in front of the window. The other section was a living room. There the stairs went up. The upstairs, under the roof, was also bisected. In the back room toward the west slept the maid and the children, and we slept in the front room—Kühn, Kundinger, and I. There were bedbugs aplenty.

---

20. This was possibly *Luthers Leben für christliche Leser insgemein* (Luther's Life for Christian Readers in General) by Moritz Meurer (Dresden: Justus Naumann, 1850). This was an abridgment of Meurer's more scholarly multi-volume work.

Every day there was service in the morning and in the evening. There would be singing, then Crämer would mount the low, small pulpit and preach. Later on we took turns singing; the men would sing one line and the women would sing the next. It was incredibly lovely. Every Friday there was private confession and every Sunday there was Lord's Supper. The log church stood somewhat uphill to the west of the parsonage. Next to the church was a framework in which two bells hung, one larger and one smaller, which the dear Franconians had brought along with them from Germany. Every day the prayer bells were rung. Then everybody would stop what they were doing on the path, in the field, in the house, the men would remove their caps, hands were folded and they prayed, "Lord Jesus Christ, with us abide," and so on. It was just too lovely!

But the dear Franconians had their fun too. One time I was sitting by a dear man who was telling me how it was in Germany. He told me how the light afternoon meal [*Vesperbrot*] had been brought out to the field and there had been beer with it. When he came to the part about the beer, he paused, turned his face upward and called out, "Oh, a brewsky—I sure could go for one! [*O a Bierla wenn i hätt!*]"

Fig. 14. Anonymous itinerant artist, *Mühle zu Frankenmuth im Jahr 1865*, watercolor, commissioned by Mrs. Anna Hubinger, wife of Johann Matthias Hubinger. Image courtesy of the Frankenmuth Historical Association.

There were two large, handsome men there, the Hubinger brothers. The older one ran the farm, the younger one the mill that they had constructed on the Cass River. Everything was built very solidly and laboriously. Because of that the water could do nothing but drive either the saw or the milling gear. A fine, strong dam was there, which had a swing-gate and an exit chute in the middle. To the east of Frankenmuth lay Tuscola, several miles away. The people there sued the Hubingers because of their dam, since the Tuscolans were floating timber downstream. One day Crämer said to me, "You, sir, are going with the Hubingers to Tuscola today for their hearing. Take what is spoken in English and make it German." The two men and I went up there. We had to wait a long time, but finally headed out of the village to a schoolhouse. Hubingers had arranged for an attorney from Saginaw, who arrived on horseback. His pants were torn up at the bottom. Now the affair was underway. The attorney gave a lengthy speech and read from a book that he had brought along under his arm. The judge rendered his decision: Not guilty. We went home in cheerful spirits, and the Tuscolans left the Hubingers in peace.

Fig. 15. Rev. Johann Heinrich Philip Gräbner, pastor of Immanuel Lutheran, Frankentrost, Mich., from 1847–1853

One time Crämer sent me to Frankentrost to fetch Pastor Gräbner. I don't remember what the deal was. It was Sunday afternoon. I walked through the beautiful woods. Come to an opening where a path stretches out and small log houses are standing on both sides. In the middle was a long log house, partitioned: The western half was pastor's residence, and the eastern was church and school. I went inside. Pastor Gräbner was right in the middle of Catechism instruction. I whispered in his ear, but he calmly went on teaching until class was over. Then he went to the other side with me. It was one room. In the one corner stood an oven, in the other a bed with a curtain around it, and next to it a desk in front of the window. It was a living room, a bedroom, and a study. Gräbner put on his long boots, slipped into a coat, lit up a

German pipe with a porcelain bowl, hung his tobacco pouch on his coat button, took his large walking-stick in hand, and now we headed to Frankenmuth.

Fig. 16. The original St. Lorenz bells in their present-day framework, 2020, photo.

Also in Frankenmuth both bells were rung every Friday at 3 o'clock, to signal the suffering of Christ. I frequently rang the large bell, even one time with Crämer.

It was time to tackle Frankenhilf. A carpenter was there from Huntington, Indiana, who was, I believe, acquainted with the Franconians. Out there in the virgin forest, seven miles or so northeast of Frankenmuth, tree trunks were felled and rolled on each other in square, about the height of a man, and now it was time for dedication. Kühn went out there and took me along to sing. They still did not have any Missouri hymnals there. They had brought along just a thin little book from Löhe, as big as a Fibel,[21] which had beautiful songs in it. I had to sing "The Lord Hath Helped Me Hitherto."[22] Kühn delivered an address on those words [1 Sam. 7:12] to the carpenter, a handful of young fellows, and Father Amman, the only head of household with a family. Kühn cried a lot as he gave it, and I felt deeply sorry for him. His Frankenhilf must have weighed very heavily on his heart. Now we headed back home through the thick virgin forest on the Indian path.

21. A German primer

22. This three-stanza hymn was penned by Ämilie Juliane (1637–1706), countess of Schwarzburg-Rudolstadt. It was sung to the tune, "All Glory Be to God on High." Juliane's hymn was translated into English by August Crull and is, for example, no. 71 in the *Evangelical Lutheran Hymnary*.

It was time to go to the synod convention, I believe in St. Louis.[23] My sister in Sebewaing had a maid from Frankenmuth, a very well-behaved child. She had to go home to get married. My brother-in-law took his seat on one horse, the maid on the other, and they rode to Frankenmuth through the woods, forty miles. I was supposed to go down with him to keep my sister company until the pastors came back. We rode off to Frankentrost.[24] On the other side of Frankentrost we met up with an old path and continued on that. We came across a pole bridge that looked suspicious at the end. The wood was rotted, you could see some water there, and it looked very marshy. "We'll get stuck there," says my brother-in-law.

I had the young horse. "I'll get over," I said. Turned my horse around and got a running start. Just like that, I was across. Like a fox my horse easily cleared the spot, which was perhaps three paces wide. He does the exact same, but his horse didn't quite jump far enough and his back legs sank all the way down into the muck. He got out right away though. When we were close to the bay we came to a river, which was deep, not very wide. Fortunately a canoe was available in front of us. We take the saddles off, each of us takes his horse to the side and off we go. The horses pulled that little boat across splendidly. On the other side, saddles back on, and we continue.

My brother-in-law now traveled to the convention. Back then you went up around the lake and then down on the Mississippi; it took a long time.

We had an Indian (and that's what we called him; he was hard of hearing) who would go up to the prairie very early in the morning and shoot a young buck, and every time his daughter of twelve years would bring us a nice piece, a leg or a loin. We were not able to stow it. I tell my sister, "Just tell the child that she shouldn't bring us any more."

"Yeah," she says, "I don't dare do that, otherwise the old woman will be insulted." We ate what we could; the rest we secretly gave to the pigs.

While I was there I had another ride too. I'm taking a young horse out of the stall, on which no one has ever sat, but like a dummy I leave the door open behind me. I swing myself up on it, but just like that it wheels around and goes inside to its stall. I tried to keep myself steady with my heel in the back and with my hand holding tight to its neck, but I fell on my back against the threshold and the horse goes right over me. It stepped down at my waist between my legs and scraped me badly, and came down with the other foot at my neck and also took the skin with it there. My back was in considerable pain and the scraped skin stung, but I went and got my horse out again, but close the door this time, and get on again. But now it went like mad. I let it run as long as it pleased, then I rode home slowly, and from then on the horse went fine.

23. This convention, which went from October 2–12, 1850, was the one at which Pastor Crämer was called to be a professor at the seminary in Fort Wayne.

24. The maid stayed in Frankenmuth to get married, and Strieter took her horse back to Sebewaing with his brother-in-law.

One evening my sister looks out the window and cries, "Oh boy, here comes the crazy doctor." An old bachelor lived in Scio, a cultured and learned man, widely traveled. They said that he had gone out of his mind due to a failed love affair. When he was alone, he would chatter away to himself; otherwise you couldn't notice anything strange about him when he was with someone. He had already been there[25] earlier and traded for rarities from the Indians and sent them to Germany. He came and brought a box with all kinds of small and sundry items for exchanging. He now took off every morning and returned in the evening. One time it was cold and wet, and my doctor comes home and has a wound on his hand; he said he had scraped himself. The hand was swelling up. My sister says, "Mr. Doctor, let me bandage your hand, sir."

He replies, "Oh no, Mrs. Missionary, it has to heal that way."

He comes home again; his hand is even more swollen and the wound looks bad. Then he takes a sharp knife and pricks around in the wound over and over. My sister says, "Mr. Doctor, you are really aggravating your hand. Please let me tie something on it."

He replies, "Oh no, Mrs. Missionary, there is already rotten flesh in it, and it has to be cut out," and he keeps working around on his hand with the knife. Then he takes off again, and when he comes home he goes upstairs and doesn't eat any supper. In the morning he doesn't come down. I go up there and call him, but he doesn't want to come down. We eat, and then my sister goes and brings him down and makes him a bed in an adjacent room, but by now she has to undo his coat and shirt with the knife, because his hand and arm were so swollen and were more black than white. "Mrs. Missionary," he cried out, "I have the black gangrene. The hand or the whole arm must come off. Please fetch a doctor."

I took my seat on the horse, took another one next to me, and went down to Shebeyang to fetch Jacob Graverad. When I arrived, a squaw told me that they were over yonder on the island. I jumped into a canoe and went over. There I found him. He went with me, borrowed Nagejickamik's[26] pony from him and rode to Frankenmuth to fetch Dr. Koch. Scarcely was our Jacob gone when my brother-in-law comes home and sniffs around in the air. "What smells in here so noticeably?"

My sister opens the door to the doctor's room and says, "See for yourself." My brother-in-law, for being a missionary, was a decent doctor. He puts some olive oil in a receptacle, makes it hot, soaks a rag in it and covers the doctor's entire arm with it and stays up with him through the night. In the morning the arm is fine again, and nothing bad can be seen on the hand but the wound.

In the morning[27] my half-Indian [Jacob Graverad] comes on horseback, along with the doctor. When he came in, my doctor calls out from his bed, "Mr. Doctor, you

---

25. Namely, in the Sebewaing area
26. See p. 16, n. 36.
27. Leutner corrects this to "Here comes," implying that Jacob Graverad and the Frankenmuth doctor arrived that same morning, but by repeating "In the morning" Strieter is probably saying that

come too late. You see, sir, I am an old, widely traveled physician. I have even doctored the wives of the sultan in Turkey, and I am unable to help myself. Mr. Missionary here knows more than I; he has cured my hand for me."

Koch ate, we foddered his horse, the doctor gave him ten dollars, and he rode back home.

My brother-in-law transported me back with the boat. By Lower Saginaw we took a little detour. By an island in the river we turned right and went into a tributary[28] to go to Frankenlust. The river was quite full of logs and one could scarcely get through; there were also a lot of reeds and grass in it. We came to a clearing. There in the distance stood a little log church, and not far from that a frame house that was still not quite finished. That was the parsonage, and it was actually owned by the pastor. His wife got 13,000 dollars, I believe, from her father to bring along,[29] and dear Sievers used it to build himself a house back in the woods and to help many people out of poverty. When we entered the house, a handsome, very friendly man stood before us, Pastor Sievers. From the side door stepped in a beautiful[30] young lady in the prime of her youth, a half-year older than I, and introduced herself to us as Mrs. Pastor Sievers.[31]

Fig. 17. Rev. Sievers's frame parsonage built in 1849. Image courtesy of St. Paul Lutheran-Frankenlust, Bay City, Mich. The house cost between $800 and $900 and was commonly called *das weiße Schloß*, "the white castle," in local conversation.

Jacob and Dr. Koch didn't arrive until two mornings after Auch first applied the hot press.

28. Squaquaning Creek, as spelled in a posthumous biography of Pastor Ferdinand Sievers (the modern spelling is Squaconning), is described thus: "about 150 feet wide and about six feet deep at its greatest depth, amply covered with reeds" (*Der Lutheraner* 51, no. 10 [May 7, 1895] 79).

29. Leutner crossed this out and replaced it with: "His wife received a fortune from her father, as she told me."

30. Strieter had *schöne*, but Leutner replaced it with *schmucke*, "well dressed, fashionable." Strieter's effusive words probably made Leutner uncomfortable.

31. Karoline Wilhelmine Auguste née Koch, born on Feb. 6, 1829.

From there we headed back to the Saginaw River and up to Upper Saginaw. There my brother-in-law bought me some black cloth for a suit. I marched to Frankenmuth feeling very happy about my fine, handsome cloth. In Frankenmuth lived a Bernthal family on the lower street (two streets led to Saginaw, the upper and the lower)[32] next to the river, where the church was also located. The family lived west of the church.[33] The old father was a wagonmaker and worked diligently in his workshop. They had several sons and, I think, a few daughters too. The second son, if I'm not mistaken, was a tailor, and he made me my suit, the handsomest one I had in my life, and also the best; I had the suit for a very long time. I worked off the tailor's fee with the cradle in the wheatfield.[34] Things were definitely still tight for the people. As soon as possible the wheat was threshed. The sound of it would carry up to us in bed very early in the morning: one-two-three-four, one-two-three-four.[35] It was a splendid thing to hear. Women came from Frankentrost, each one with a small sack of grain on her head, three or four in a row, to go to the mill and then back home. It was so nice in Frankenmuth, and our dear God let me experience a tremendous number of blessings there. May he reward it all!

Crämer never stopped concerning himself with the Indians either. In an old shanty not far from the church lived an old chief with his old wife—who was pushed to the side though—with a few of her youngest boys, and with his young wife and a few of her small children.[36] All of them would come to the parsonage after church on Sunday and Crämer would give them a speech. His son Heinrich had to translate; they called

32. The upper street would be Genesee Street, which turns into Junction Road, and the lower street would be Tuscola Street, which turns into Tuscola Road, and eventually joins with Junction Road several miles west of town.

33. Lit.: "from the church in the direction of Saginaw." Leutner crossed this phrase out.

34. The cradle is also called the grain cradle or cradle scythe. It consists of an arrangement of fingers attached to the handle of a scythe, such that the cut grain falls on the fingers and can be cleanly laid down in a swath for collection. A grain cradle is on display in one of the rooms of the upper floor of the Luckhard Museum in Sebewaing, Mich.

35. Representing either one person threshing in sets of four strokes with a flail, or four people threshing together, each taking a stroke in turn.

36. "In Frankenmuth itself an Indian family lived on the mission land, whose head, an Indian witch doctor or medicine man, was called Oldshim. He himself did not become a Christian, since his witch doctor practices gave him great enjoyment and he didn't want to give them up. He also wanted to go where his fathers had gone before him after this life was over. Yet for all that, he formally gave his two children and his two little grandchildren over to the mission for rearing and eventual instruction. This ultimately led to these four children being promptly baptized, once Oldshim had given his permission" (Friedrich Lochner, "Ehrengedächtniß des seligen Herrn Friedrich August Crämer, Professors der Theologie und Directors des praktisch-theologischen Seminars zu Springfield, Ill." in *Der Lutheraner* 47, no. 23 [Nov. 10, 1891] 182). "[The medicine man's] name was Oglajo but . . . the Yankees in the area had nicknamed [him] 'Old Jim.' When the Germans pronounced this as 'Old Chim,' many people, including some unwary historians, assumed that the Indian's name was 'Oldshim'" (Zehnder, *Teach My People the Truth*, 82).

him Wabshkentip, White Head, because he had very light-colored hair.[37] The old chief would justify himself though, wherever he could. After the service they would get a bowl full of corn soup with bacon, which they were mighty glad to eat.

Fig. 18. Dorothea Crämer, wife of Rev. August Crämer. The Ojibwe children referred to her as "Mother" on account of the care they received from her, including washing, grooming, and delousing.

Crämer told me he had a call to be a professor in Fort Wayne, and that I should now go home to Freedom, bid my siblings farewell and adieu, and then meet up with him in Detroit for the continued journey to Fort Wayne. My brother-in-law had made me a trunk. I shut my things inside it and it was supposed to make the trip together with Crämer's luggage. I took just a few things with me and marched back to Ann Arbor. In the evening I arrived there and rode with a man to my old home. It was late when I arrived at the farmyard. My brother had a large, handsome dog, white with large yellow spots; it originally belonged to a nigger[38] in the South. Everything was

37. According to "The Ojibwe People's Dictionary" online (https://ojibwe.lib.umn.edu; accessed April 21, 2020), *waabishkindibe* means *he has white hair*. Heinrich was about ten years old at this time and was not Crämer's natural son, but the son of his wife Dorothea, whom Crämer had met on the ship during the voyage to America and had married shortly after landing.

38. This was a common way of referring to black people at the time, both by those who wished to refer to them disparagingly and by naïve immigrants who simply heard others using the label and didn't know any better. The word itself originates from the Latin word *niger*, meaning *black (man)*. Leutner put quotation marks around the word, indicating his own uncertainty about the appropriateness of the term.

already dark in the house. The dog began to bark. I said, "Penter, come." He stopped barking and came to me. I knock.

"Who's outside?" I heard my brother say.

"Your brother."

He got up, his wife too, and opened the door. The dog went inside with me, posted himself in front of me, begins to sniff me up until he had reached my face. Then he let out a loud yap and started licking me all over; I couldn't escape.

I visited my siblings in Freedom and Bridgewater. They provided me with a number of other items and I said my farewell. My brother brought me to Ann Arbor, and there I boarded the railroad car, for the first time in my life. A railroad ran from Detroit to Jacksonburg.[39] I arrived in Detroit at nighttime. There some guys were standing in front of a chain and hollering dreadfully; they wanted people for their hotel. I waited till everybody was gone. Then a man comes to me and asks if I wanted to spend the night. "Sure." He took me along. When I was with my siblings I had also bought myself a hunting bag [*Büchsenranzen*][40] and put my effects in it. He took my hunting bag for me, hung the strap over his shoulder, and off we went. We walked a good piece, then he turned to the side, opened a door, and there we were.

I heard Irish voices coming from the kitchen. The man asked if I wanted to eat. I said sure. He went to the kitchen and soon came a piece of beefsteak with potatoes and bread. The steak was tough and bloody, but I was hungry and relished the meal. Pretty soon he asked if I wanted to go to bed. I said sure. Then he took a tallow candle—that's what people had back then—opened a door, and we went up the stairs. There stood a bed right in front and some more behind it. By the first bed he said I should undress. I lay my pants on the chair, hang my waistcoat with my pocket watch on a nail, and crawl in. He grabbed my pocket book out of my pocket, grabbed my watch, and laid both of them under my pillow for me and left. In the morning I ate again and paid twenty-five cents.

I now went to find Pastor Schaller.[41] On the slope not too far from there, toward the river, stood a large, simple, old frame house, where a brother-in-law of Pastor Schmid from Scio lived,[42] and upstairs, Pastor Schaller. He was just coming down the stairs, and

---

39. Jacksonburg(h), Michigan, was founded in 1830. Its name was changed to Jacksonapolis and then shortened to Jackson in 1838, but apparently it continued to be called Jacksonburg informally.

40. Also called a game bag, somewhat akin to a messenger bag today.

41. Johann Gottlieb Michael Schaller (1819–1887) came to America in 1848, largely at the encouragement of Löhe (see n. 1). After accepting a call to Philadelphia in 1848 and Baltimore in 1850, he accepted a call to Trinity in Detroit in the fall of 1850; he had not even been installed yet when Strieter met him. He had joined the Missouri Synod in 1849 and was won over to Walther's position on the doctrine of church and ministry at the synod convention in St. Louis in 1850. He was the father of John Schaller (b. Dec. 10, 1859), who eventually became a professor at and the president of both Dr. Martin Luther College in New Ulm, Minn., and Wisconsin Lutheran Seminary in Mequon, Wis.

42. From Pastor Schmid's letter dated March 19, 1861, we know that Pastor Hattstädt (see n. 3) married a sister of his. But Strieter is likely talking about a different brother-in-law here, since Hattstädt, as Strieter notes on p. 21, remained in Monroe for the duration of his ministry.

I introduced myself to him. He had a journeyman cobbler in his congregation—married, had no children. He directed me to him. Eight days I stayed with those folks. They lived quite a ways out, in the upstairs of a Catholic tailor's house. I frequently conversed with the tailor. He was a strict Catholic. One time I'm chopping some kindling for my hostess with a small hatchet. Over yonder across the fence, in the next lot, stood an old, single-story frame house, from which quite a few women would come out. One woman, fairly young, stationed herself in front of me, laid her hands on the fence and her chin on top, and stared at me without saying a word. I keep pecking away at it, and the wench won't leave. I toss my hatchet to the side and run inside to the tailor: "I say, what kind of people are actually over in that place?"

He says, "Those are whores, who want to entice you over there." And he also gave me a speech, warning me never to get mixed up with bad women folk.

In my host's shop I bought myself a new pair of boots. They were definitely a little too big, but he said, "You are still growing, sir," and that he had made them himself; I was getting a good deal. And he was right.

After eight days Schaller told me I should head out on my own. I went down to the river and boarded the ship. Took deck passage though, since I didn't have a lot of money. The ship set sail for Toledo, where I wanted to go. Soon I noticed a young fellow who was my size and age, who was dressed like a sailor with a little sailor cap on his head. He made my acquaintance right away and told me that his home was between Tecumseh and Clinton.[43] He said his father was a farmer, but he could not stand it on the farm; he was a sailor. He was now going home for a visit. When it was midday and the meal was taken below for the sailors, he slipped down into an opening and motioned for me to follow. Down there we ate a marvelous meal together, but he told me afterwards that now it was our turn to treat the guys, and that's what we did. He asked me where I was from and what my name was and where I was headed and what I wanted to be. I told him.

"Oh, you fool!" He called me that in English. "Come with me to my parents, and when I go away again, I am going to the ocean and I can make a fine sailor out of you. You don't need to be afraid of me; I'm no bad guy."

I found the fellow extraordinarily pleasant and I was always happy when I was on a ship. My favorite picture as a child was a ship with three masts in full sail. We arrived in Toledo, grabbed the fellow's trunk at both ends, and went to the hotel. We ate together and slept in the same bed. In the morning he paid the bill. "Now John, what do you say?"

I said, "I'm still going to go to Fort Wayne."

"Then good bye," he said.

---

43. More than fifty miles northwest of Toledo in Michigan

I got on the canal boat and rode to Fort Wayne.[44] There I went to find the seminary right away. Steinbach[45] later told me that when they saw me approaching with my hunting bag, they said, "What kind of hobo do we have here?"

The student gentlemen directed me over here to Dr. Sihler.[46] He was sitting in the kitchen and was in the middle of fixing a pony for his son Christian; he was tying his colorful silk handkerchief on one of its wooden legs. I said who I was, where I came from, and why I was there. He asked about Crämer; I had no information to give him. I arrived in Fort Wayne on October 10, 1850, and the dear Crämer ended up arriving on the twenty-fourth.[47] Dr. Sihler called upstairs, "Rauschert!" Above his small study the Dr. had a room that was also our lecture hall. Two students who boarded with Sihler lived in it, Rauschert and Werfelmann.[48] Rauschert came down. Sihler said, "Please bring Strieter to Mrs. Bornemann." She was a widow who foddered me for a while. "Do you have money, sir?" the doctor asked me.

"No."

"Do you have anyone who can provide for you?"

"No."

"That's fine. Payment is due every quarter-year. When it's due, go to Mr. Griebel and he will give you money." That's what happened. Every quarter cost three dollars, which I would go and get from my patron. The people in the country brought us a bunch of stuff—whole or half hogs and so much fine sausage. I soon filled out at the seminary.

---

44. Via the Wabash and Erie Canal, running parallel to the Maumee River

45. Ferdinand Steinbach from Saxe-Weimar

46. Wilhelm Sihler (1801–1885) was won over to confessional Lutheranism from rationalism. After serving as a private tutor for a number of years, he came to America in 1843 in answer to Pastor Friedrich Wyneken's pleas for help. He initially joined the Ohio Synod, but left it in 1845 due to its lax confessionalism and unionistic practices at the time. With the support of Löhe he started a *Nothelferseminar* ("emergency helper seminary") in Fort Wayne, Ind., in 1846. Its purpose was to train pastors as thoroughly but also as expeditiously as possible so that they could provide the pastoral care urgently needed by the many German immigrants and fledgling congregations. Its students were given instruction in confessional Lutheran doctrine and pastoral practice, especially preaching and teaching, but they received no mandatory instruction in the Hebrew and Greek of the Scriptures. This seminary was deeded to the newly formed Missouri Synod in 1847. Dr. Sihler was president of the seminary from 1846–1861. He was also vice president of the Missouri Synod and overseer of the synod's congregations in Ohio, Indiana, and Michigan from 1847–1854.

47. Strieter's arrival on Oct. 10 is unlikely. The 1850 synod convention was held from October 2–12. Even if some pastors, like Strieter's brother-in-law Auch, came home early, Strieter says that he was in Sebewaing keeping his sister company during the convention and that he didn't return to Frankenmuth until Auch returned home. So Strieter would have needed time to return to Frankenmuth, pack his belongings, hike to the town of Freedom, say goodbye to his siblings in the area, ride the train to Detroit, spend a week with the cobbler there, take the ship to Toledo, and then take the canal boat to Fort Wayne—all between the time Auch returned from the convention and October 10. We do know for sure that Crämer arrived a) after Strieter and b) on October 24 (*Der Lutheraner* 7, no. 7 [Nov. 26, 1850] 56). Perhaps Strieter arrived around Oct. 20.

48. Jakob Rauschert from Franconia and Heinrich Werfelmann from Hanover

But now the studying really began. It was almost enough to drive a man insane. Crämer gave the twenty of us guys a dreadful amount of homework. Many a night I only slept for two hours. We soon contracted a lot of headaches. Classes started at eight; at ten there was a piece of bread, but dry. At midday we got our beans; at one, back at it until four. Then we would head down to the St. Joe, behind the milldam, for a bath.[49] Occasionally the doctor would come and take one with us.

Ottmann[50] and I were the best swimmers. One time when the water was very high, Ottmann said to me, "Let's try to swim across." Off we go. On the other side, he says we should try to see how close to the dam we can swim past. Off we go, but that took some work. When we came to the middle, the water wanted to take us away. We breasted the water and at the same time worked our way sideways. We finally arrived, but completely exhausted. We looked at each other and said nothing. That night the water brought a tree trunk with roots and branches, but left it lying on top of the dam. Sommer,[51] the same one I had already gotten to know in Sebewaing, a very friendly and very active person, tried to replicate our work of art the next day. But when he came to the middle of the current, it dragged him downstream and he was left hanging in the branches of the tree trunk. He sat down on the trunk and began to sing. But we hollered at him, "Okay, just get over here; we already know what it's like."

He worked his way over to us along his tree, and once he was on dry land he started in: "O you dear brothers, do not do that again. That is putting God to the test. If the tree had not been there, the water would have taken me away, and death would have claimed me by now." There were large boulders down below. Later Pastor Kalb, who was supposed to become a professor at the teacher seminary, drowned at that spot, and Fleischmann,[52] who tried to save him, almost did too.[53]

---

49. In the print edition, Leutner changed "the St. Joe" to "the river." This change was justified, since the river to which Strieter refers is the Maumee, not the St. Joseph. Still today there is a dam on the Maumee due north of the seminary's original location, just west of the Anthony Boulevard bridge.

50. Friedrich Ottmann from Franconia

51. Wilhelm Sommer from Saxon Lusatia

52. Philipp Fleischmann (1815–1878) was a professor and director of the teacher seminary in Fort Wayne from 1857 until his resignation due to eye trouble in 1864.

53. The opening article of the July 27, 1858 issue of *Der Lutheraner* (14, no. 25), penned by Dr. Sihler, details the tragic death of Pastor J. Paul Kalb (1828–1858) on June 8. He was bathing in the spot Strieter mentions here, between four and five p.m., with Professor Fleischmann. Fleischmann, "some distance away from [Kalb], all at once saw him disappearing and hurried over to his rescue, since he is skilled at swimming." But "after he had already succeeded in expending all his energy in bringing his dear friend close to the shore, by God's ordaining his arm suddenly became paralyzed on him and he was robbed of his senses in such a way that he could no longer hold on to, no longer see his friend, no longer tear him away from the deep into which he had now sunk, and only with the utmost effort, more dead than alive, did he himself reach the not too distant shore, where he lay powerless for some time and could only still manage one loud, prolonged, agonizing cry from his constricted chest." Kalb's body was not found until ten days later, five miles downstream.

I had been in Fort Wayne for six weeks when I had to teach a Catechism lesson on the Seventh Commandment.[54] We had to go over to Dr. Sihler's residence several times each week. There the lectures and Catechism lessons were held up in Rauschert's and Werfelmann's room. The catechist in question had to go and get six to seven youngsters from Teacher Wolf. They would go upstairs and sit down on a bench. The seminary students would stand around them against the wall, the doctor would sit on a chair, Mr. Catechist in front of his boys, and now we were ready to go. That gave us some angst.

Fig. 19. *Above*: W. Mackwitz, *Das alte Anstaltsgebäude zu Fort Wayne*, date unknown, engraving printed in M. Lücke, *Zum 50-jährigen Jubiläum des praktischen evang.-lutherischen Concordia-Seminars zu Springfield, Ill.* (1896). This engraving depicts Concordia-Ft. Wayne's first campus, a fifteen-acre site on the Maumee River, purchased from the widow of Col. Marshall S. Wines. The seminary occupied this site from 1849–1861. At first the site only consisted of the land, the building on the left (called the Wines Cottage), and a nice fruit and vegetable garden. Dr. Sihler occupied the ground floor of the cottage's residence,

---

54. "You shall not steal," according to the Roman Catholic and Lutheran numbering of the commandments.

and the two upstairs rooms were converted into dorm rooms, one of which doubled as a classroom. The middle building (just the shorter part with the larger chimney) is the Wolter House, built in 1850 and named after Professor August Wolter, who died from cholera in 1849. The Wolter House consisted of four rooms and a large dormitory. The final buildings on the right—the larger, house-like seminary addition to the Wolter House and the English Academy (the largest building)—were not built until 1857 (after Strieter's time). *Below:* The Wilfred Uytengsu, Sr. Center, 2020, photo. This administration building of the Indiana Institute of Technology, which bought the campus in 1953 and moved to it in 1957, constitutes all that remains of the original Concordia-Ft. Wayne buildings.

I had already gotten to know the Seventh Commandment pretty well from experience. I explored everyday life with the students and showed how all people in every station are thieves. At the conclusion the doctor would ask every row for their assessment. He himself went last. To my knowledge no one criticized me, not even Mr. Doctor; in fact he praised me highly for being so practical. I was pleased and encouraged by that. Soon I also had to give a lecture on the false teachings about the Lord's Supper. For that, however, I borrowed from a lecture by Ottmann, which I utilized well. Dr. Sihler praised me again, but he didn't know that I had plowed with someone else's heifer, and I didn't say anything either.[55]

One time I had to do a funeral for a child out in the bush, in the house. When we were singing, two people behind me were looking over my shoulders and singing robustly, but in the middle of the verse they sang differently and knocked me off the saddle. I had the music book and was following along too casually. During the next verse it happened to me again, but during the third verse I watched what I was doing and went at it fearsomely, also turned my face towards them a little; now I stayed on track.

I also catechized in the surrounding area. One time I even had to mount Sihler's pulpit to give a funeral sermon. One time I had to go to Huntington to preach for Pastor Stecher around the holidays.[56] For that Dr. Sihler advised me to borrow a horse from a farmer. The man gave me a big, black brute that was still young. I get on, put my umbrella under my arm, and start out. I was riding on the tow-path for the canal. It starts to rain and I open my umbrella, but now my Black takes off. Fortunately I soon came to a quagmire; my brute got all fours stuck up to his belly. By the time he worked his way out, I had my umbrella closed. The man told me later that he had forgotten to say that I should not open an umbrella, because the horse could not stand that.

Crämer accepted a call to a congregation on the side and made me his vicar; it was called Nothstein. A man lived there who had that name, and others lived in the

---

55. The ironic placement of this story about the "borrowed" lecture after the story of his Catechism lesson on the Seventh Commandment was doubtless intentional.

56. German: *zur Festzeit*. This usually refers to the time around Christmas, when pastors were even busier than they are today, since oftentimes services were not only held on Christmas Eve and Christmas Day, but also on Second Christmas Day (St. Stephen's Day), New Year's Eve (St. Sylvester's Day), and New Year's Day, besides Sundays.

surrounding bush. It was twelve miles away.[57] Every fourteen days I had to go out there. In the morning I would head out on foot, preach and hold Catechism instruction with the little children, and head back in the afternoon. I was relieved by others twice; otherwise I kept my arrangement. One time the St. Joe River[58] was very swollen. Behind Rudisill's was a small bridge over a brook that came from the marsh,[59] but now the Joe had taken the little bridge away, and the water was flowing in reverse from the river into the marsh, and with considerable strength. What now? I looked for a staff, found a branch, took it in hand, and started off into the water. In the middle it just about knocked me over, but I got across anyway; the water went up to my waist. I still had two miles to go, but now I ran.

57. There is a Notestine Cemetery, established in 1834, on a small hill on the river side of St Joe Road, just north of the intersection with Notestine Road in Cedar Creek Township. Even though it is only eight and three-fifths miles from the site of the seminary campus today, there were doubtless fewer bridges over the Maumee and fewer roads in general, and the existing roads were much more primitive.

58. See n. 49. Again, Leutner has just "the river." However, this time Strieter's memory is correct. See also the next sentence.

59. This was likely in the same location as the bridge on St Joe Road just north of the intersection with Maplecrest Road, one-and-a-half miles southwest of Notestine Cemetery.

Chapter 3

Into the Ministry

In 1852, synod convention was in Fort Wayne at the end of June and beginning of July. A pastor came from Holmes County, Ohio, B[esel],[1] a Basel student who colloquized and was accepted into fellowship. He came to Crämer and requested a preacher for a congregation by Coshocton which he had taken from a United preacher.[2] Crämer sent for me and told me that I had to take my examination and had to go with B[esel]. Röder[3] and I were actually slated to be missionaries to the Indians. Crämer even gave us private instruction. What a delight that was.[4] He had the book of Matthew in Chippewa, and there Röder would now take his seat on one side and I on the other, each with his Testament open. Crämer would read to us in Indian and we would repeat it. Then we would copy down the dreadful words, and now we were supposed to memorize them. Chippewa had long, gnarly [*welsche*] words. But the reason for that was because the language had so few words and everything had to be paraphrased. Miessler, subsequently a doctor in Chicago, who became Baierlein's successor in Bethany, told me when he left us (much to our chagrin) that Chippewa had its roots in Hebrew.[5] I asked Crämer not to send me away yet, but all pleading was in vain.

At eight o'clock I had to take my seat in front of my Crämer and Dr. Sihler. Several other men were also there, and my schoolmates were behind me. Crämer examined me until ten o'clock; then, after a short break, the doctor tackled me. His first question was, "Strieter, what's in Matthew 13?" Fortunately I knew. But now I

---

1. The 1852 convention proceedings for the Missouri Synod list among the voting preachers a Friedrich Besel in Holmes County, Ohio. He was headquartered outside of Mount Hope (called Middle Town in an 1861 map of Holmes County) to the southwest, where there is still an Arnold Cemetery (see Fig. 27). Besel left the Missouri Synod and joined the Iowa Synod in 1881.

2. "United" refers to the Prussion Union, which merged the Lutheran and Reformed Churches in Prussia.

3. Edmund Röder from Prussian Lusatia

4. German: *Das war charmant.* Judging from how he continues, Strieter is apparently being somewhat sarcastic.

5. Ernst Gustav Hermann Miessler (1826–1916) worked with Baierlein at the Bethany mission station from 1851–1853, when he succeeded him. He left the preaching ministry in 1871 to study and practice medicine in Chicago, which he did from 1874–1899.

was also supposed to say what was taught in those parables. How that went I don't remember anymore, but I received a certificate saying I was sufficiently qualified for the preaching ministry [*Predigtamt*].[6]

On July 4 we headed out from Fort Wayne on the canal amid fanfare [*mit Musik*]. In Toledo we got on the steamer that went to Sandusky; from there to Monroe; from there to Detroit; from there to Cleveland. At midday there was bloody beefsteak, etc. Schaller and others would not eat the steak, but Schwan[7] and I dug in. In the evening Schaller thought that if the steak was served again, he would eat it, but it did not return. In Cleveland B[esel] and I went with Schwan, who lived not too far away in a small little frame house; his son Paul was a small boy.[8]

We went a stretch on the railroad,[9] then continued on the canal. We disembarked in Massillon, I think the place was called. On the shore stood an old, respectable Pennsylvany Dutch[10] farmer by the name of Arnold.[11] He received us joyfully and went with us up the street to a small inn. A young man from the east, a baker, was with us, who was going to visit his mother up there.[12] Arnold had a fourteen-year-old lad with him who worked for him. Now the horses were retrieved—four splendid animals, the oldest eight years old—and harnessed to a wagon. The old father had brought a load of wheat to market. His wagon did not have a box, but planks on the side, with a small board across them on which B[esel] took his seat with Arnold. The baker set his trunk behind them, and he and I sat on that. Behind us there was a plow and a barrel of salt.[13] The back left horse had a saddle on his

---

6. Strieter received a "satis" diploma. This is a standout sentence in the autobiography, and many pastors can doubtless relate to it when recalling their seminary education.

7. Heinrich Christian Schwan (1819–1905) had been taken up as a member of the Missouri Synod in 1850. He served as pastor of Zion in Cleveland, today the second oldest church in the synod, from 1851–1899. He helped to popularize the use of the Christmas tree in American churches by placing one in Zion in 1851. He was known as a staunch, tactful, sharp, wise, modest, and refined Lutheran pastor.

8. Paul was born on Jan. 1, 1851. To get the full effect of this clause, by the time Strieter wrote these words, Paul was fifty-three years old, had been the pastor of St. Paul's Ev. Lutheran Church in Cleveland, a daughter of his father's congregation, for twenty-four years, and had been in the pastoral ministry for thirty-one years.

9. Perhaps to Akron

10. The Pennsylvania Dutch were early German immigrants to America in the seventeenth and eighteenth centuries from what is today western and southwestern Germany. Many were refugees of war. Usually *Dutch* refers to the people of the Netherlands and their language, but in the label *Pennsylvania Dutch* it is an Americanization of *Deutsch*, meaning *German*. The label Pennsylvania Dutch was also used to refer to their particular dialect and their descendants.

11. Strieter is doubtless referring to Jacob Arnold, born Sept. 24, 1787, and not to his son Johann (b. June 1, 1817), since Strieter later calls him "the old father"; Jacob was sixty-four years old and had seven sons ranging from thirty-seven to twenty-three years old at the time. See also nn. 22 & 23.

12. Namely, where they were headed.

13. Leutner changed this to a sack of salt.

back, the front left horse had the reins, and the young lad took his seat in the saddle. I inquire, "Can the boy even drive?"

"Oh sure, he drove the whole way here."

We started out; the horses went at a walk. When we went slightly downhill, they trotted a little and then continued at a walk again. Arnold had a lot of questions about the synod convention and B[esel] told him about it. Now we went uphill, for quite a long time—the hill must have been a mile long, or high, I should say. The path wound up the hill like a snake. At the top we went straight again, then downhill. It wasn't long before the back left horse whinnied and bolted, and now we were off and running, all four as fast as they could.

B[esel] shouted, "Hoh!"

Arnold shouted, "Hoh!"

But the horses didn't want to hoh.

Arnold shouted to the boy, "Hang on tight!" Arnold grabbed the pieces of wood in front of him and hung on and let the horses run as they wished.

At first I thought, "You should go to the end and drop yourself down; it's not that high." But then another thought came to me right away: "You are the only one who can maybe still provide some help. When the horse stops kicking out, then you can make your way out on the tongue and get on the horse behind the boy[14] and draw the front horses to the side." But the animal wouldn't stop kicking out. You could constantly see the shiny horseshoes on the bottom of his feet sparkling in the air. On the right the water had torn a deep ditch, in places at least six feet deep or so. The wagon often ran so close to this ditch that I thought, "Now it's going to tip over," but it always kept going past.

Finally we came to the climax. There's just one man who is trying to come up the hill with his load. "Now," I thought, "something's going to happen." I was right. He quickly swerves out of the way once he saw us coming, but his back wheel was still stuck on the rut. Our back axle meets with his, and just like that I was lying over yonder, not far from the fence. A small sandbank was there, runoff from the hill; I shoot like an arrow headfirst into the sand there, making a hole in the sand as big as a hen's nest. Right next to the hole I made, a handbreadth or so away, a stone is lying in the ground and protruding from the ground, as large as a plate. I sit up and rub the sand out of my ears and think, "Well, the good Lord definitely protected you from a sudden death." For if I had landed on that stone, I would have knocked my brains out. My baker slid down fairly close to me without injury, ran to me right away—"Are you hurt?"—and marveled with me at my good fortune that I didn't hit the stone.

On the path stood the baker's trunk, planks were lying around, and behind me, over there along the fence, were the back wheels, the plow, and the salt barrel, with half of it spilled out from the bottom. The others are gone. We looked, and here comes my B[esel]. He had hung on tight to the wooden crosspiece where the shaft sits that holds

---

14. Namely behind the boy on the same horse he was occupying, the back left horse.

the front and back parts of the wagon together, thinking that the back wheels were still on and would run him over and kill him, and he let himself be dragged over the stones of the washed-out path. Finally he couldn't take it any more and let go. There he lay, untouched. He scrapes himself up and limps toward us: "O my head! O my shoulders! O my hips! O my legs!" The blood was already running into his shoes.

Over yonder stood a house, from where they had witnessed everything. The man came over and took B[esel] with him, hitched up his buggy, loaded B[esel] up, and went home with him.

My baker and I bring the trunk and planks to the side and get started after our cart. Below ran a small brook and a little bridge.[15] On the other side it immediately went up the bank at a steep angle. At the top, it's dug out and the path bends off to the left a bit. There the wheel ran up and flings the old father over the side,[16] so hard that his shoulder turned yellow and black, and he had to carry his arm in a sling. But he still went after his horses.

Fig. 20. The approximate site of Strieter's accident in Ohio, 2020, photo. The ditches on both sides of the road are still deep, and the road is still traveled by many horse-drawn carriages.

---

15. The best candidate for this brook seems to be what is called Camp Run in an 1856 map of Wayne County, Ohio (https://www.loc.gov/item/2012592397/), about three-fifths of a mile southwest of West Lebanon. (See the bridge in the distance in Fig. 20.)

16. If I'm imagining this correctly, the horses turned left with the path at the top of the hill on the other side of the bridge, but were going so fast that the wagon ran up partially onto the bank, thus tipping to the left, with the right front wheel higher than the left front wheel, and knocking Jacob Arnold out onto the path over the left side of the wagon.

They went through the valley and back up the hill on the other side. There the saddlehorse tumbled and the boy fell, right between the horses, who dragged him by the saddle strap up the hill over the stones. When they reached the top, the strap ripped, and my boy lies there. There was a house there too, close to the path. The people come out and carry the boy inside. The man hitches a horse to a stone drag; they lay the boy on it and bring him to the inn, several miles or so further.

In front of the inn, where the horses usually stopped for a midday rest,[17] stood a post and a water trough. The horses ran through between the post and the corner of the building. They still had the axle and one wheel on the tongue and they ran against the corner of the building so hard that they tore out a large stone at the bottom. The inn shook so much that the ladies inside thought there was an earthquake and ran outside, but they quickly saw what had happened. The one ran to the field to get the men; it was harvest time. The other one ran around the stall and grabbed the front horses by the head so that they would not race any further. They had run from the watering hole across the street along the stall towards the fence.

When my baker and I also arrived, the boy was lying on the floor. His mother was with him, a widow who didn't live far from there. The doctor was also with him, and the others were standing around him, including old man Arnold, and he was holding his arm.[18] The poor boy! His back looked like a piece of fresh meat, his arm was broken,[19] his shoulder was separated,[20] his leg was broken, and several ribs were broken.[21]

When the doctor was finished, he said he did not know what he looked like on the inside, but everything seemed to be alright, and these external injuries would heal quickly. I comforted the wailing mother as well as I could. (After six to eight weeks the lad was fine again.)

B[esel] brought the bad news home and now all the sons of the old father—I believe there were four of them[22]—came on horseback to see what had happened to "Dad." They gathered up the wagon and loaded everything back up. The old father said to me, "Jack (Jacob) will stay here"—his youngest, a handsome young man, eighteen years old[23]—"and I will too, and you take Jack's horse and ride home with the others."

---

17. Probably what the 1856 map (see n. 15) identifies as the Eagle Tavern in Mount Eaton, along the town square.

18. The antecedents of "he" and "his" are unclear. Based on what he said earlier, Strieter could be referring to Jacob Arnold holding his own arm. But based on what he will say shortly, he could be saying that Arnold was holding the boy's broken arm for the doctor.

19. Leutner changed this to "crushed" (*zerquetscht*).

20. Leutner changed this to "dislocated" (*ausgerenkt*).

21. Leutner changed this to "cracked" (*geknickt*).

22. He had seven total—Daniel, Johann, Georg, Jacob, Jonas, Heinrich, and Ludwig.

23. Something is amiss here. Jacob Arnold's youngest son was Ludwig, and he was twenty-three years old at the time. He also had a son named Jacob, but he was his fourth oldest son and was twenty-nine years old.

INTO THE MINISTRY

I say, "No, Father Arnold, you take the horse and ride home, and I will stay with the wagon."

Arnold got on and left. My Jack gets his four horses out of the stall and hitches them up, takes his seat in the saddle, but brought along his blacksnake. My baker and I sit on the trunk again. Jack heads out. Right away the path goes somewhat downhill and my horse on the right whinnies again and starts to cut loose. But my Jack lashes him around the belly, so that it whistles. The horse jumps forward. Then he turns his whip around and whacks the animal on the forehead with the thick, yellow[24] knob so hard that I expected the animal to collapse. If the horse jumped forward, it gets one on the forehead; if it jumped backwards, it gets one around the belly. "Just wait, I'll run off on *you!* [*Wart, ich will dir weglofen!*]" Jack said. He put them into a strong trot, shouted, "Hoh!" and bump, they stopped, and he repeated that a number of times. It didn't take long and the horses were like lambs.

When I arrived at B[esel]'s, he was lying in bed and he informed me that I had to preach the next day. I went to his books with a heavy heart and tried to put something decent together. Across the street stood an old house where church was to be held.[25] The folks came and I led the singing and preached. Preached again a week later, and later in several more places. When B[esel] was healed up, he took me in the buggy and now it was time to go to my Roscoe[26] congregation. Roscoe lay across the river along the hills, and there was a village on this side too, Coshocton. There[27] we turned in at a Prussian Lutheran's house, whom B[esel] had praised highly, and ate at midday. We went into an adjoining room, but now I had an experience. All at once the man started in and began scolding terribly: B[esel] had promised them an older preacher and now he was bringing a candidate. B[esel] became very uneasy, but there was nothing he could do.

---

24. Carl Strieter translates *gelben* as *brass*.

25. An 1861 map of Holmes County shows the parsonage for the Lutheran church on the east side of what is today Township Road 362, one-tenth of a mile north of its intersection with Township Road 618 (modern address: 7482 Township Road 362, Millersburg). The old house Strieter mentions here was therefore directly across the road to the west from that site. Though the site of the old house is simply a field today, there is coincidentally a cemetery in the middle of that field, west of where the old house would have stood. That cemetery, however, was not begun until early in the twentieth century. The first cemetery was Arnold Cemetery, just a tenth of a mile further south.

26. Strieter first wrote "Coshocton" and then appears to have crossed it out himself and written "Rosco." The reason for the confusion is obvious when looking at any map (including one of Coshocton County from the 1850s). Coshocton lies at the confluence of three rivers; the Tuscarawas and Walhonding Rivers join and become the Muskingum. Coshocton lay on the eastern side of the Tuscarawas and Muskingum. Roscoe Village lay west of the Walhonding and Muskingum. (Politically, it belongs to Coshocton today.) Strieter and Besel came from the north and would have had two river crossing options—across the Tuscarawas to Coshocton or across the Walhonding to Roscoe Village. Since Strieter says in the next sentence that his destination lay "along the hills," he was right to make the correction to Roscoe.

27. This appears to refer to Roscoe Village.

We left and headed out into the very hilly country, turned in at an administrator's house and discovered that while B[esel] was at the convention, the old preacher had returned and the people had taken him back in. His people had deposed him on account of an offense against the Sixth Commandment. What happened was that he was spending the night with the administrator—Memmel was his name. During the night the mom hears her daughter scream. In the morning the mom asks, "Jane, why'd you scream [*was hast g'schria*]?"

"O Mom, do you have to ask me?"

"Jane, why'd you scream?"

"The parson came to my bed, and I got really scared. Then he says to me, 'Child, I didn't really do anything to you. Just don't tell anyone, so that I don't get a bad reputation.' And I did promise him, Mom, so just don't say anything."

But her brothers had also heard her scream and noticed what was up, and they spread it around. Because of that, the pastor stayed away. But after his shame had subsided, he returned and confessed, and his people thought that that could happen to anyone, and they kept him.

The next day there was church in the schoolhouse over yonder behind the hill. Memmel went with his family, a widow and a few men came, and a young man came whose mother had died. B[esel] gave a funeral sermon first, and then I am supposed to preach. After church the men said that they had taken the old parson back in, so they did not need me. B[esel] went home; I was supposed to stay for a week and preach in Roscoe.[28] I did, but the Prussian Lutheran still wanted an older preacher, and so I was also unneeded there.

I rode back to B[esel] again by stagecoach and wrote to my Professor Crämer. He wrote that I should go to Steinbach in Liverpool;[29] he had an ancillary congregation that I could perhaps take over. I take my seat on the stagecoach and ride to Medina. From there I go on foot to Steinbach, who lived with the dear Haseroth. I taught school for Steinbach for a few days while he went to Schwan in Cleveland to get some advice. He brought me to Elyria and then held an outdoor meeting on the South Ridge.[30] In Elyria there were two families. There was a dear Theisen family; he worked in the mill and her brother, Philipp Theiss, a tailor, was also in that family.[31]

---

28. Strieter originally had Coshocton here too (see n. 26).

29. See p. 12, n. 25. Today this is St. Paul Evangelical Lutheran Church in Valley City, Ohio, at the corner of Lester Road and Center Road.

30. What today is Lowell Street and Telegraph Road used to be known as South Ridge Road. (Even a glance at a modern map of Ohio will reveal a North Ridge Road about three miles north of Lowell Street.) Strieter later makes it clear that church was held in the schoolhouse on the South Ridge and that this school was "two miles away" from Elyria. The *Map of Lorain County Ohio* published in 1857 by Matthews and Taintor from surveys by John F. Geil shows the location of this schoolhouse—just south of the corner of Lowell Street and Murray Ridge Road, across from what is today the North Murray Ridge Cemetery.

31. Peter Theisen (b. May 30, 1805) and his wife Maria Elizabeth (née Theiss) Theisen (b. Dec. 27, 1810) came to Elyria with their four children and two of Maria's brothers, Friedrich Gottfried Theiss

There was also a Böse family. Between Elyria and South Ridge lived a Württemberger, S[chaible],[32] and then there were a few Bavarians and Hessians living in the area, ten families or so. Steinbach drew up a short document, and on Sunday it is to be accepted and signed, and with that I would be called. But he told me, "There is a man here named Z.[33] Do not let him sign; he is an arch-drunkard."

Sunday came. I preach and now it's time for the signing. Z. was first. I told him my orders; he left the schoolhouse. Then a man started in: "I demand bread at the Supper though, otherwise I will not sign."

I read: "The Holy Supper shall be administered according to the manner and custom of the Lutheran Church." I say, "In the manner and custom of the Lutheran Church, wafers are used." He stands up and leaves, and his wife follows.[34]

I am to have a salary of sixty dollars for the year and am to be fed on rotation; I am to go to someone different every quarter-year. On October 10, 1852, I was called and gave my first sermon.[35]

I went to live with T[heisen] in the village and was treated like a lord there. In front was a large room. My table and my bed were there, and there I taught school to six children or so. One Sunday I would preach in Elyria and those from the South Ridge,

---

and Jacob Theiss, in 1842. In 1843 Maria's brothers Philipp Theiss (b. Nov. 14, 1816) and Heinrich Theiss (b. Jan. 30, 1819) and Heinrich's wife Barbara (Hoffman) arrived in Elyria in 1843. The Theisens eventually ended up in Wisconsin, Friedrich Theiss in Cleveland, and Philipp and Heinrich Theiss in South Dakota.

32. The *Commemorative Biographical Record of the Counties of Huron and Lorain, Ohio* (Chicago: J. H. Beers & Co., 1894) provides a biographical sketch of Jacob Schaible and his family on pages 1102–3. After suffering an extended illness, Jacob Schaible emigrated from Württemberg with his wife Catharine Barbara née Ramsayer and five children—Agnes Barbara, Margaretha Maria, Johann Friedrich, Catharine Henrietta, and Jacob E.—in May 1848. They arrived in Elyria on August 1. Jacob soon "purchased land one mile west of Elyria, built a small house, and settled on his farm, which was nearly all covered with underbrush and forest. He immediately began to clear and improve his property." By the time he finished doing so, he would have "one of the best farms in the county." But until then, the Schaibles lived an extremely frugal life, as Strieter will show. By the time Strieter arrived, the Schaibles had two additional children, Caroline and Carl Heinrich (Charles Henry).

33. Leutner inexplicably corrected this to B.

34. The use of leavened bread at the time was an outward indication that a pastor or congregation was unionistic or doctrinally lax, since leavened bread was used in the church of the Prussian Union. This was, however, a somewhat unfortunate development. We do know for a fact that Jesus used matzah or unleavened bread when he instituted the Lord's Supper, but *description* is not necessarily *prescription*. What Jesus through his Holy Spirit had his inspired Evangelists record was not a "Continue to do this" with unleavened bread (ἄζυμος), but a "Continue to do this" simply with bread (ἄρτος) (Matt. 26:26; Mark 14:22; Luke 22:19; 1 Cor. 11:23–24). All else being equal, unleavened or leavened bread may be used. In fact, leavened bread was regularly used in the early days of the Christian Church, and the great Lutheran theologian Johann Gerhard wrote, "The usage of leavened or unleavened bread in the holy Lord's Supper is to be left to the discretion of Christian freedom and . . . no unnecessary conflict in the Church of God should be initiated on account of this" (*A Comprehensive Explanation of Holy Baptism and the Lord's Supper*, Chapter 7). Pastor Strieter would have done well to explain the matter further.

35. I.e., as a regularly called pastor.

two miles away, would come over here; the next Sunday church was there and those in Elyria went out there. After the sermon I also gave Christian instruction.

I lived for my quarter-year at T[heisen]'s place in town. One time I was not feeling well. My host said he had a small, white powder that I should take. I take the powder and feel completely miserable. I have to go through the garden to the throne,[36] but get such pains there that I can't even move. My hostess comes and calls, "Mr. Pastor, you've been in there so long. Why don't you get dressed and we'll get you out of there." I pull myself together and the mother and the maid bring me into the house and lay me on my bed.

No sooner do I lie down than I get the cramp in both calves, so that my flesh pulls together into a clump. I yell, and they rub. I yell, "Get me a pail full of cold water!" The maid gets some water, and I put both feet into the cold water and the cramp goes away. But I thought, "You are never taking that powder again."

Later I lived at S.'s house over in the woods. They had a frame house. In the front they had a small, low addition, where they lived. Then the actual house. That had a large room and a bedroom, a fireplace, but no stove. The inside of the house was not plastered [*geplästert*]. It was winter. When I would put wood on, she would come and douse it with water on me and say the chimney was starting to burn. My dear neighborlady, F., brought a bed. Not far from there was an old log schoolhouse where I taught school. When I arrived in the morning, I first had to shovel out the snow. There was a stove there, but bad wood. They brought up the logs that had already sat in the water for ten years and sawed them into blocks. I would split them and make a fire. But it wouldn't burn. My kids would come; I would position them around the stove and I would stand behind them. The whole winter I never got one foot warm and I contracted a terrible head cold, which I didn't get rid of until I was in Wisconsin. In the evening a group would come and I would teach them hymns for an hour [*hielt Singstunde*].

My Mrs. S. was one short, angry little woman. She had two boys. The small one was terribly dumb and couldn't grasp anything at all. The whole winter we taught the three letters *a*, *b*, *c*. She would help: "Johnny, what's this? Say *a*. What's this? Say *b*. Now, what's this?"—pointing back to *a*. He doesn't know. "You Satan, won't you just say it?" and she lays into him. The boy starts crying. Then she says, "No, no, my Johnny, stop that and I won't smack you any more." The boy rubs his eyes. "Johnny, what's this?" She tells him. "What's this?" She tells him. Back to the first letter. He doesn't know what it is. She lays into him again: "You Satan, won't you just say it?" The boy starts crying loudly.

I go in there: "Ach, just leave the child in peace." That's how it went every day.

---

36. German: *zum Pabst*. *Pabst* or *Papst* is the word for *pope*. In many Protestant regions *zum Papst gehen* ("go to the pope") was slang for using the lavatory or, in this case, the outhouse, alluding to the papal throne.

One time the husband was by the fire in the country[37] and didn't come right away when she called him for dinner. Then she tried to bash his brains in with the fire poker. He just barely got out of the way so that he didn't catch anything.

A family came from Germany. The poor wife became frightfully homesick and lost her mind. I visited her regularly. With God's help I get her straightened out again. I went to live with F.[38] I stayed there longer than usual. There I had it nice.

Fig. 21. The final resting place of Daniel Haag (1825–1872) in North Murray Ridge Cemetery, outside of Elyria, Ohio, 2020, photo. Haag was the sermon sleeper who appreciated Strieter's rebuke and was responsible for the congregation's restart in 1858, four years after Strieter left.

I had a man who always went to sleep on me during church. As soon as the sermon started, his head would start to hang. He came to announce for the Supper. I said, "But my dear man, you are always sleeping during the sermon." Yeah, he couldn't help it, he said. I said, "Let me give you a good piece of advice, sir. Come to church with the

37. I.e., clearing land
38. Presumably the initial of the last name of the family that had recently immigrated

thought, 'Today I am going to hear for once what the pastor knows.' Then, when you are there, pray really earnestly that our dear God would please drive the sleep away. If it comes anyway, then bite yourself on the tongue, and make it a good one." And sure enough, from then on my dear man was a very attentive listener.

Later everything closed down there for a while. Jüngel was now Steinbach's successor in Liverpool.[39] He told me, "H[aag] came to me and asked me to start there again, because some people had moved into the area. He said he would have me picked up with the buggy and brought back home and would give me five dollars every time."

"Wow, that is a lot! How did that happen?"

"Yeah, he said, 'Pastor Strieter sowed seed in my heart, and now it's coming up.'"

I also began preaching in Vermilion. Several families lived there. When I had preached on the South Ridge, I would eat at H[aag]'s at midday, then march eighteen miles to Vermilion, preach in the evening and teach hymns for an hour, and on Monday and Tuesday I would teach school to eight kids or so. On Tuesday after school I would walk my eighteen miles back down and teach school the rest of the week back on the South Ridge. My miller T[heisen][40] had no more work in Elyria and had to go looking for work. He moved with his family to Liverpool.

In the spring of 1853 I was ordained by Schwan. He preached on the Good Shepherd. It fit well, and I earnestly made up my mind to become a good undershepherd. Steinbach assisted.[41]

I now came to S[chaible]'s for meals.[42] There, next to the main room, was a small room that was to be mine. I cobbled a table together and bought myself a water pitcher and a glass. The room smelled terribly bad; it had been the cat's den for years. When I went to bed, I felt things crawling all over my body. I got out of bed; everything was covered in red.[43] I got dressed and sat down at my table and laid my head on the table. That's how I carried on.

One day the wife asks, "Don't you go to bed, sir?"

I say, "There are bedbugs." She and her daughter[44] go at it and start washing, but it didn't help a thing; I had to stay at the table. The family simply did not live well. I could not eat their bread. It was three fingers high and so hard that you could have used it as

---

39. Heinrich Jüngel, originally from Hesse-Darmstadt, was installed as Steinbach's successor at St. Paul Lutheran Church in Liverpool (see n. 29) on Dec. 14, 1854. Strieter is telling a story here that happened later, after he moved to Newburgh, Ohio, to illustrate how this conversation, and the sermons now attended to as a result of this conversation, bore fruit for this sleeping man, whom he identifies as Mr. H. in the next sentence.

40. The print edition mistakenly reads F. for T.

41. See Appendix IV, no. 1.

42. It appears to be Leutner who crossed out "for meals" and added, "on the rotation." This was the final home where Strieter lodged on rotation, from October–December 1853.

43. Bedbugs

44. Margaretha Maria, now sixteen years old. Their oldest daughter, Agnes Barbara, had already married Friedrich Gottfried Theiss by this time, as will be made clear.

a projectile and smashed in a person's brains. Each morning he ran into town to fetch some meat, but every time he brought the udder, which he got for free or for a few cents. That went into the water and was brought to the table together with the gravy when it was just tolerably well boiled. Fortunately they always brought baked potatoes to the table. Then I could at least peel off the skin and eat my potatoes with salt, and I also would drink some water. The potatoes and the water did not fill me up, however, and it started to take a terrible toll on me. When I walked to my schoolhouse on the South Ridge, I would have to stop and rest several times.[45] How often I stood behind my table and thought, "It's time for you to go and tell your people, 'I can't go on like this any more,'" but I never actually did so; I just kept on toughing it out.

One time my dear Ph[ilipp] T[heiss] loaded me on his buggy and drove me to Steinbach. Along the way he started in, "Sir, I would like to have a word with you on a matter of special importance."

I said, "Okay, what is it?"

He said, "You must marry, so that you can get away from the S[chaible] family; death will claim you there."

I said, "What are you saying? Sixty dollars a year—and that's not coming in—and moving around every quarter year?"

He said, "You are always preaching to us about trusting in God; you should also take your own preaching to heart and have trust in God. God is clearly showing you that you need to marry, otherwise you may as well resign. And now let me also tell you whom you should take; take Lisbeth." In Vermilion lived a Widow Ernst[46] with six little daughters.[47] The oldest she had sent to Steinbach to the German school, since there was nothing happening in Vermilion, and to be confirmed by him.[48] After confirmation the mother sent her daughter to Elyria, so that she would have church and Christian instruction, and she made her home away from home at T's.[49]

Before this I got a letter from my brother, who wrote that L. had told him that he should write to me and ask me whether I wanted his daughter M. for my wife. One tramp after another was coming to inquire after her, but he had promised my father that I would have his M. I wrote that I could not entertain any thought of marriage at this time; if God wanted to have it, he would surely work it out. In the meantime M. should not be bound to me. After a year my brother wrote to me that M. had married and had died while giving birth to her first child. I would have received a rich wife, but I would not have kept her; thus God cares for us without us even knowing it.

45. In spite of the fact that it was only about seven-tenths of a mile to the west.
46. Leutner wrote out her full name: "a widow, Anna Kunigunda Ernst."
47. See Appendix V, pars. 7, 9, 11–15.
48. Leutner rearranged and partially recomposed the sentence: "The oldest, Lisbeth, she had sent to Steinbach to the parochial school and for confirmation, since nothing was happening in Vermilion."
49. This was probably the Theisen home originally, but depending on when Peter Theisen lost his job and when his family moved to the town of Liverpool, it may have belonged to the Theiss brothers by this point.

We came to Steinbach. When he looked at me, he clapped his hands together: "Man, what do you look like? Whose house are you at?"

"At S[chaible]'s."

"That's enough of that; death will claim you there. You need to marry, so that you can get away from there."

"Marry with sixty dollars a year? How am I supposed to provide for a wife like that?"

He said, "The God who provides just for you now will then provide for both." He continued, "You should take Lisbeth."

I said I would have taken her gladly, but she was too young for me.

We drove home, but from Elyria we went straight to Vermilion in order to hold service there in the evening. T[heiss]'s brother, H[einrich] T[heiss], was in the forest cutting wood for ship-building. When he came home: "Are you still at S[chaible]'s, sir? One can tell just by looking at you. Death will claim you in that sh—house.[50] Get yourself away from there."

"Whereto?"

"Marry someone. Take Lisbeth." She was right above us.[51]

I said, "And where do I go with her?"

He said, "To Mother Ernst." She had a house in Vermilion. "You'll be taken care of there."

I said, "All good things come in three; this is from God."[52]

Mother Ernst and her little daughters came to church. I preached and taught hymns for an hour. Afterward Lisbeth went into the adjoining room to practice the melodion. I now say to Mother Ernst, in the presence of H[einrich] T[heiss] and Ph[ilipp] T[heiss], what was said to me three times in succession. She says, "If you want my Lisbeth, sir, I give her to you with a happy heart." We call Lisbeth out of the room[53] and the betrothal took place.

---

50. German: *dem S—haus*, with the original letters between *S* and *haus* erased. Carl rendered the word *pigsty*, but the usual words for *pigsty* are *Schweinestall* or *Schweinekoben*, and there really isn't room for the letters *chwein* anyway. It is possible that Heinrich simply said, "in the Schaible house," but usually Strieter uses English cursive letters for family names and initials, and the *S* here is in German cursive.

51. This episode seems to have happened during the brief stop in Elyria before continuing to Vermilion for the service. Elizabeth was in the upstairs of the Theiss home, getting ready to accompany Strieter and the two Theiss brothers on the twenty-mile buggy ride to Vermilion, as this conversation was taking place.

52. Strieter is referring to the fact that he was told to marry Elizabeth Ernst three times that day, by three different men. There was doubtless some behind-the-scenes orchestration on the part of one or more parties.

53. Whatever Strieter originally wrote after this, either he or his wife, upon review, really did not want to go to press. It is struck through in pencil and the entire bottom third of the page is torn away (see Fig. 22), along with the top sixth of the next page. Though crossed out very thickly, the words in the next one-and-a-third lines (before the page is torn away) can be made out: "*& ich will nun meine Sache wichtig & feierlich machen &*": "and I now try to be momentous and solemn as I make

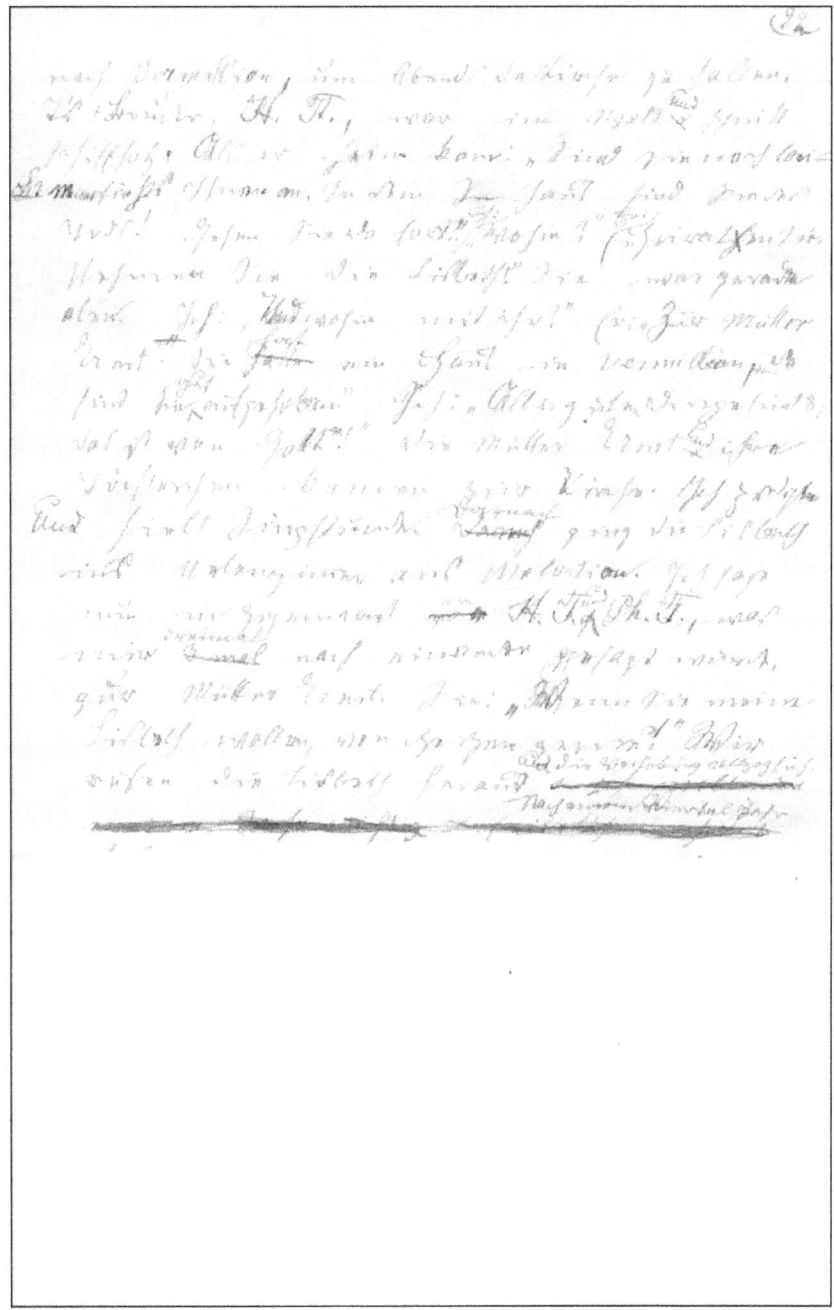

Fig. 22. Page 82 in Strieter's manuscript, where his betrothal to Elizabeth was originally described in detail. The outline represents how large the sheet would have been if the bottom third had not been torn away. See n. 53.

---

my case, and . . ." All of that, and whatever else was below it, was replaced with: "and the betrothal took place. After a quarter year."

After a quarter-year I rode with my Lisbeth to Elyria via railroad. There I borrowed a horse from the livery stable and we drove to Steinbach. He married us. On the way home I wanted to hurry and I cracked one on the horse with the whip. Then it lashes out in back and its leg goes over the shaft. I have to unharness in order to get my horse free. After a while I lash again and my horse also lashes again and, sure enough, over the shaft again. I note that the beast knows his stuff, and I am now forced to drive at a steady pace.

I forgot to mention something, that the judge in Elyria wouldn't give me a license. He asked whether the girl was eighteen. I said, "No."

He said, "Since you are honest enough to tell me that, I must also be honest with you and tell you that I can only give you a license with the consent of her parents." So I had to get her mother, who told the gentleman that I could have her daughter. Lisbeth was born in Brownhelm, not far from Vermilion, on Aug. 24, 1838, and we were married on Jan. 17, 1854. There was certainly no eighteen years between those two dates.[54]

Fig. 23. Johannes and Elizabeth Strieter's Wedding Picture, photo printed in Armin Schroeder, ed., *A Picture Book of the Past: The St. John's Visitor for 1942 and 1943*. Image courtesy of Winfried Strieter. Even though this is labeled as their "wedding picture," what Strieter says about his beard later suggests that the picture might not have been taken until the early 1860s.

54. Elizabeth was fifteen years old at the time of her marriage to Johannes, who was twenty-four. According to court documents shared with me by Susan Hawkins (see Acknowledgements), Johannes first appeared before the judge on Jan. 3, and then returned with his prospective mother-in-law on Jan. 16. She signed a sheet of paper which stated: "I Cornelia Ernst mother of Elizabeth Ernst do hereby affirm in the Probate Court und give my free consent to the marriage of my said daughter with John Strieter." Someone must have asked Widow Ernst for her name, and "Cornelia" was the best the person could make of "Cunigunde," which is how she signed the statement.

We took the railroad cars from Elyria to Vermilion. When we arrived, Lisbeth's cousin, H. Ernst, peeked in through the door and sees us sitting. Then he disappeared. We went to Mother. As already said, she had her own house in Vermilion. The T[heiss]es[55] were already there. We sit down at the table and eat our good noodle soup, which Mother had cooked for us. There goes a racket outside. There was a large open space in front of the house. There stood a whole crowd, big and small, making a shivaree that was tremendous. Among other things they had planed the edges of a large merchandise box and smeared it with resin, and had done likewise with a scantling, and now two people were sawing on the box. Boom, boom, it rumbled dreadfully. My H[einrich] T[heiss] says, "You're going to have to give those guys some money to get them out of here." But I didn't have any. The last cent was spent on the trip. He reached into his money bag and took out a handful of small stuff—apparently he had caught wind of what was going to happen—and gives it to me.

I went out and asked who the captain was. They pointed me to a large fellow. I give my handful of money to him and thank them for their kindness. They say in English, "Hurrah for Mr. Strieter! Hurrah for Libby Ernst!" and they bounce off to the saloon. After that, those guys were uncommonly friendly. Actually, they had a small bone to pick with me, since Libby Ernst was pretty much the Bride of Vermilion.[56] She was a beautiful, sensible, and virtuous girl and a good student. During winter the sailors would lodge in Vermilion. Lisbeth's cousins were also sailors. One of them, Caspar Ernst, went to the college [*Hochschule*] in Oberlin every winter. He would pester Mother to let Lisbeth go along with him to the school. He said he would take care of everything; it wouldn't cost her a cent.[57] Mother would say, "Lisbeth knows enough to get along in the world. She is not going to Oberlin." Others would come and want to take her to a party or a ball, but Mother says, "Lisbeth is staying at home."

But throughout the winter they frequently had "spelling school." That was always a big deal. Everybody would flock there, so that the large schoolhouse was crammed full. It was conducted like this: Two Choosers were elected, who posted themselves up at the desk opposite each other and now chose their Spellers. Soon the aisle was filled up in two rows back to the door. The Choosers elected were always the two best spellers, and that was Gust Pelton and Libby Ernst. The spelling started. The schoolmaster gave the words. During her final months there they had a fine schoolmaster, Mr. Salos. Pretty soon the rows were spelled down, since whoever missed a word had to sit down. Eventually only Gust Pelton and Libby Ernst would be standing there. It might occasionally happen that one of these two would spell down the other, but most of the time they would say in English, "We will give up." Even Mr. Salos one time posted himself opposite Libby when she was the only one

---

55. The print edition mistakenly reads F. for T. (cf. n. 40).
56. Leutner crossed out this sentence.
57. See Appendix V, par. 4. Elizabeth did have a cousin Caspar (or Casper) Ernst, but it appears that her cousin Louis was the one who offered to take care of her schooling.

still standing, and someone else gave the words. But Libby spelled down Mr. Salos too. In this way Libby was generally popular, and the boys were understandably not too happy that the minister had caught Libby.

I now lived at Mother's house and was treated fine and dandy. I held church, two days of school, and went down to the South Ridge and taught school the remaining days and still preached on the South Ridge, since everything was finished in Elyria. T[heisen]s[58] had moved to Liverpool and B[öse] moved back to Germany. Apart from that there was only a German joiner still there, who never came to church though, and a Catholic store-clerk.

Even on the South Ridge I only had seven to eight listeners left; the others moved back to Germany, especially the Hessians. Here's how that came about: S[chaible]'s daughter—the lovely house I mentioned earlier—married a brother-in-law of T[heisen] the miller who, as already mentioned, ran out of work.[59] He now sat around and often sat with his small little daughter on the front steps.[60] Then his sister-in-law[61] started talking badly about him, saying that he just sat there to look at the women to see if they were . . .[62] She said that to a woman and her mother, and they immediately repeated it to the T[heisen]s. T[heisen] went to her and confronted her about it and was probably a bit harsh. The young woman ran home right away and complained about the experience to her parents.

I came home, for I was still living in the S[chaible] house at the time, and was met with dark faces. The daughter had already left again. I asked what was the matter. Then she starts in and relates how T[heisen] had treated her daughter. I went over and spoke with T[heisen] and then with the young sister-in-law, but she denies everything. T[heisen] says, "I have my witnesses." They were brought and both the young woman and her old mother verified that she had said it.

I dismissed the witnesses and said, "Now there's no more denying it." She now confessed that she had said it and apologized.

I stayed overnight. When I came home, I was immediately asked how it went. I say, "Very well; they have reconciled."

"What!" S[chaible] pounded on the table. "My daughter has reconciled with that milljack?" And right away he went over to see her. Then she started making an angry face again, and my hosts were now like people possessed by the devil. Before that the old man would eat with me, while the others ate outside. But now the small

---

58. The print edition mistakenly reads F. for T. (cf. nn. 40 & 55).
59. Agnes Barbara Schaible married Friedrich Gottfried Theiss, one of Elizabeth Theisen's brothers.
60. Sarah M. Theisen was born on July 14, 1852, and was thus about a year old at this time.
61. Namely "S[chaible]'s daughter," Agnes Barbara.
62. I am unsure why Strieter only put a dash here. Perhaps Agnes accused him of simply judging every passing woman's appearance (pretty, ugly, etc.), or perhaps she used a more provocative word that Strieter wasn't comfortable using, such as *reizend*, "attractive, fetching." Leutner supplied the word *schön*, "pretty."

boy[63] would call into my little room, "Dinner!" When I came out, no one was there and the door was closed. I ate by myself. I also used to prepare a family devotion. When the man and I had eaten, I would call the others inside and I would read and pray. But now he read outside and would yell loudly, so that I couldn't help but hear it. None of them gave me a kind look any more. I let things go on like this for a while and then I spoke with the old folks. They looked at the floor and said nothing. I spoke with the old man in private, but to no avail.

I thought, "Okay, it's time to have a serious talk with this man." We were walking to church; he was carrying my robe [*Chorrock*]. I start in and confront the man with his sin. I especially confronted him with the Fifth Petition[64] and sincerely admonished him that he needed to break his stubbornness.

We now stood still and I stopped talking. Then he goes across under his chin with his hand and announces, "Mr. Pastor, this head will have to come off before I will reconcile with that milljack."

I say, "If that's how you are going to talk, then you, sir, are no Christian."

"So!" he says and marches off ahead of me into the schoolhouse, laid his bundle on the table, and went home.

The following Sunday only seven to eight people came to church on the South Ridge. The others, mostly Hessians, stayed away. I go to them and speak with them. Then one gave this excuse, the other that excuse. I found out that S[chaible] had gone around and had told the people that they should not go to listen to me in church any more; I was half-Catholic. He had seen in one of my books that it said "you should bless yourself with the holy cross," and signs of the cross were printed in it.[65] That was why they stayed away. But I continued to preach to the few people on the South Ridge. I always went the eighteen miles from Vermilion on foot, there and back. It was a very difficult walk for me, for the poor, misled people weighed really heavily on my heart. My few remained faithful. One widow Z. even moved up to Vermilion and later moved with us to Newburgh.

63. Jacob E., eight years old at the time

64. That is, he referred especially to the man's ignoring of the Fifth Petition of the Lord's Prayer: "Forgive us our trespasses, as we forgive those who trespass against us."

65. Jacob Schaible probably saw a page from Strieter's copy of Luther's Small Catechism, whether printed separately or as part of the Book of Concord. In the section on "How the Father, as the Head of the Family, Should Teach His Household to Bless Themselves in the Morning and Evening," Luther says that in the morning and in the evening, before praying, "you should bless yourself with the holy cross."

Chapter 4

Newburgh

In 1854 a small portion of Zion's Congregation in Cleveland, Mr. Pastor Schwan's congregation, branched off and formed an independent congregation in Independence, Cuyahoga Co., Ohio—near Newburgh, two miles south[1]—and named it St. John Congregation.[2] Twenty or so families combined to form it. They built a little frame church and a small parsonage behind it.[3] They called me to be their pastor. In October 1854 I moved there with my young wife, the mother-in-law, and her five younger little daughters.[4] On the Eighteenth Sunday after Trinity I was installed by Pastor Schwan, with Pastor Kühn from Euclid and Pastor Steinbach from Liverpool assisting. The church was dedicated at the same time. Pastor Kühn delivered the sermon. Pastor Steinbach read the dedication prayer.[5] On the Nineteenth Sunday after Trinity I delivered my inaugural sermon.

---

1. Strieter originally had "east"; it is unclear who made the correction. The 1858 *Map of Cuyahoga County Ohio* (Philadelphia: S. H. Matthews) shows a Newburgh Village at what is today the intersection of Miles and Broadway Avenues in Cleveland. From there it is 2.3 miles southeast to the former site of the church at what is today the southeast corner of the intersection of Turney and Granger Roads.

2. Today this is St. John's Lutheran Church of Garfield Heights.

3. Fig. 25 shows the parsonage to the immediate east of the church, so the frame church must have faced west. It also shows the house to the immediate east of the parsonage as belonging to H. H. Boening (*sic*), whom Strieter mentions in the next paragraph. About the first parsonage, one historical account of the congregation says, "It was an unassuming little house, which did not distinguish itself in the least from the cottages of the first settlers" (St. John's Anniversary Committee, *History of St. John's Evangelical Lutheran Church, Garfield Heights, Ohio* [1929], 14).

4. See Appendix V, pars. 15,16.

5. See Appendix IV, no. 2.

Fig. 24. The First Church and School, after 1859, photo printed in St. John's Anniversary Committee, *History of St. John's Evangelical Lutheran Church, Garfield Heights, Ohio* (1929).

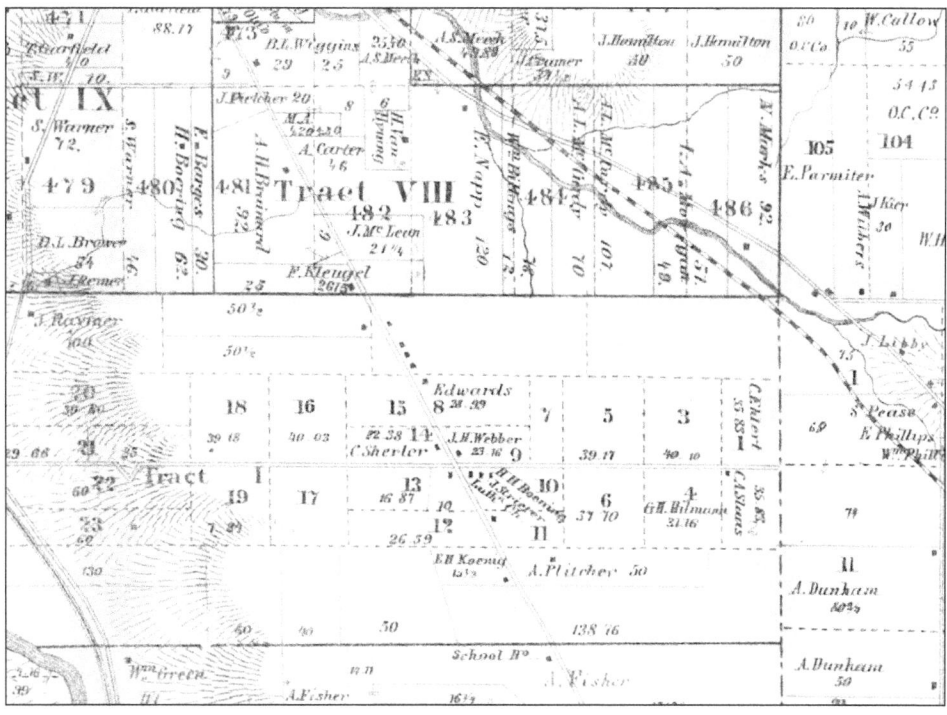

Fig. 25. *Map of Cuyahoga County Ohio* (Philadelphia: S. H. Matthews, 1858), partial. Note the crossroads and "Luthn. Ch.," "J. Strieter," and "H. H. Boening" on the SE corner of the intersection. The congregation was founded in the home of Casper Heinrich Scherler, shown on the NW corner of the intersection. The intersection was first called German Corners, then South Newburgh Centre. Today it is the center of Garfield Heights.

I would preach and then teach school to twenty or so children during the week. With the exception of one family and a widow Z., they were Hanoverians. Father H[ermann] H[einrich] Böhning was the senior member.[6] When we met to elect our board of administrators and to determine the salary (I was to have two hundred dollars per year), Father Böhning said, "I will give this much." Then he went through the ranks that way, and asked at the end if they were happy with that. "Yes," they said, cheerfully and unanimously. Besides the two hundred dollars they also gave wood for fuel and a lot of other stuff. They took very good care of us. There I had it quite nice for a change. The people loved me and bore with my weakness very patiently.[7] They also loved my wife very much. The girls M[ary] B[öhning] and M[ary] B[orges] gave her a new dress every year. They also liked the mother-in-law and the girls. The dear people came very regularly to church, to Christian instruction, and the men to congregational meetings. There was a very brotherly spirit among us.

My church attendees [*Kirchkinder*] enjoyed listening to God's word. It also had its fruit. One time Widow Z. came to me and said that her neighborlady had brought her an entire basketful of goodies, and when she asked why she was doing this, she had answered, "On Sunday the pastor preached about love, and it went to my heart."

One time H[einrich] B[icker] spoke his mind to me rather quite freely and definitely said more than he should have. The next day he came: "Mr. Pastor, I have as many regrets about what I said as I have hairs on my head."

One time I noticed that a certain man had peered into the glass a little too deeply. The next morning there was a knock at the door. I said, "In here [*Herein*]," which is what we said back then. In comes my man So-and-so. I say, "Please have a seat." He takes a seat. I say, "Now, my dear man, what brings you to me this early?"

He says, "Oh, sir, you already know what," and he started to cry and pleaded with me to please forgive him.

One time I stayed overnight at Father Böhning's. Before going to bed he read from the Bible, prayed, and sang with his family the entire hymn, "Now Rest Beneath Night's Shadow,"[8] and my, how lovely. My Newburgers, as people called us, were good singers in general. We would also sing in four parts. My Ernst Böhning sang a splendid bass, and my Friedrich Tönsing[9] a fine tenor. Mary Böhning and Mary Borges sang the first part along with several others, and W[ilhel]m and John Böhning sang alto.

---

6. Böhning was born on April 3, 1798.

7. Strieter more than once mentions "his weakness," and he seems to be referring to something in particular. Later in this chapter he specifies this weakness by referring to the delivery of his sermons.

8. The original hymn has nine stanzas.

9. Apparently a good friend of the Strieter family, since he sponsored Johannes and Elisabeth's second-born, Emma.

Almost every Sunday we were taken to someone's home after the service. Often we were at Father Böhning's. The good old mother[10] cooked us pea beans [*Vicebauna*] with a long, speckled sausage in there and meat. Beforehand there would be a milk soup with these tiny little dumplings. My, how delicious that was! The Borges family also invited us often and took us along, and others did too.

I received a call from the vicinity of Baltimore, but the congregation would not release me. Another one from the vicinity of Columbus, Ohio, but again I was not released; and another one from old Frankentrost, but I was not released then either.

Now my Jüngel[11] came to me one day. I say, "What brings you to me so unexpectedly?"

He says, "Tomorrow morning I will tell you." In the morning he took a letter from Dr. Sihler out of his pocket with an enclosed call and accompanying note from W[ilhel]m Stelter, from Crystal Lake, Marquette Co., Wisconsin. In these was stated that there were over 300 families there, who had been deserted by their preacher and left for the fanatics, Albright's people.[12] Help had to be provided immediately. He[13] had thought of us both.

Jüngel said, "I cannot and dare not leave. I have recently received a United congregation in Amherst, which I dare not abandon. You must go."

I presented it to my congregation. Fritz Tönsing was chairman.[14] It was discussed back and forth, all of it in favor of my staying. Finally the chairman says, "I will call the question now, so that we know where we stand. All in favor of letting our pastor move, say, 'Yes.'"

Everybody was silent.

"All opposed, 'No.'"

"No," everybody called out.

Tönsing smiled and said, "I am going to ask again, but a bit differently: All who are convinced in their conscience that we need to let our pastor move, say, 'Yes.'"

"Yes," they said, though very meekly. That was in Nov. 1859.

With my neighboring ministers [*Amtsnachbarn*] I was on good terms. I visited them, and they me. Held conferences with each other regularly. In Cleveland was Schwan. He was our senior. In Ohio City, now West Cleveland, my dear Lindemann; already at the seminary we had gotten along very well.[15] In Euclid was Kühn. In

---

10. H. H. Böhning's wife, Maria Eleonora (Stoffer-Blase) Böhning

11. See p. 54, n. 39.

12. For more on these families, see *WELS Historical Institute Journal* 37, no. 2 (Fall 2019) 1–56, and 38 no. 1 (Spring 2020) 1–41.

13. That is, Dr. Sihler

14. Fritz is a nickname for Friedrich, mentioned earlier.

15. Johann Christoph *Wilhelm* Lindemann, originally from Hanover, had enrolled at Fort Wayne during the 1851–1852 school year.

Liverpool, first Steinbach, then Jüngel, who was also at the seminary with me and we were always close friends.

I know that one time Schwan and Lindemann marched the five miles out to me. I walked to Schwan after school almost every Monday. We also went with each other to take baths in the lake[16] and went on walks. Then we would set to work on our sermon for next Sunday. He had the Latin Harmony[17] and I had Luther. He would read, then I would read. Now he would ask, "Strieter, what should we use?" I then had to start outlining, and he would laugh sometimes, but sometimes he commended me too. One time he said, "Your outline is absolutely excellent. If Walther had it, he would make a sensational sermon, but you, sir, are too stiff."

I said, "Yeah, how does one go about becoming more smooth?"

He said, "Copy someone else's sermons, so that you get into a different channel. Take Fresenius.[18]" I buy myself Fresenius right away[19] and start copying—word for word, in fact—and I learn it. Sunday I mount the pulpit and repeat everything beautifully up through half of the first part; at this point I lose my line of thought. My Tönsing was sitting close to the front and looking me right in the eye. As I was losing my spot, he looked down at his feet. I do not get back on track; everything gets jumbled together. Finally in my anxiety I say, "Amen." Before everyone leaves, I signal my Tönsing: "Did you notice something today, sir?"

---

16. Leutner specifies Lake Erie.

17. This refers to the *Harmonia Quatuor Evangelistarum* (Harmony of the Four Evangelists), a harmonizing of and commentary on the four Gospels begun by Martin Chemnitz, continued by Polycarp Leyser, and completed by Johann Gerhard in 1627.

18. Johann Philipp Fresenius (1705–1761) was a pietistic Lutheran pastor at Nieder-Wiesen, Giessen, Darmstadt, and Frankfurt am Main, who remained loyal to the Lutheran Confessions and opposed the Moravians.

19. Since it appears that Schwan and Strieter studied and preached on the Gospels together, the book Strieter bought was probably *Heilsame Betrachtungen über die Sonn- und Festtags-Evangelia* (Beneficial Reflections on the Sunday and Festival Gospels), first published in 1750. Fresenius also had a book of sermons on Epistle texts published in 1754.

Fig. 26. The Church Interior, after 1859, photo printed in St. John's Anniversary Committee, *History of St. John's Evangelical Lutheran Church, Garfield Heights, Ohio* (1929).

"Yes sir, I did. You lost your spot."

I put my Fresenius in the corner though, and went back to making my own sermon, after I had made a proper study of my Luther, especially his House Postil.[20] This was my method: When I was finished with Luther, I started thinking and prepared the whole thing in my mind right up to the Amen, and then I wrote it and delivered it that way.

One time conference was held by me. Jüngel brought his neighboring United minister along. He already had all sorts of United ideas during the conference. Theology was also discussed during the meal. In response to some remarks Lindemann made, the United gentleman said, "That all depends on how you look at it."

Lindemann lifted his plate into the air: "How you look at it? This is a plate, no matter how I might look at it."

The gentleman was silent, but after the meal he took his hat and left.

---

20. There were two editions of Luther's House Postil (a postil is a book of sermons). The first was published in 1544 by Veit Dietrich, formerly Luther's personal secretary. The second was published in 1559 by Andreas Poach, a former student of Luther, on the basis of the notebooks of Georg Rörer, a deacon at the Wittenberg parish church and tireless transcriber and copier of Luther's sermons. (Thus Poach's edition is sometimes also called Rörer's edition.) From the next chapter we know that Strieter possessed the German volumes of the first Erlangen edition of Luther's works (1826–1857). Volumes 1–6 of that edition (1826) contained Luther's House Postil, interspersing the sermons found in both Dietrich's and Poach's original editions.

Fig. 27. Site of the first St. John's Lutheran Church, Mt. Hope, Ohio, 2020, photo. Note that this cemetery is also where Jacob Arnold is buried (see p. 45, n. 11, and p. 49, n. 25).

One time Lindemann and I had to go to Holmes Co., Ohio, where I had been together with B[esel], to dedicate a church. Engelbert was there now.[21] Lindemann preached in the morning, and I in the afternoon. Because of the sermon I gave, I continued to get quite a bit of razzing. That's because I was betrayed.[22] I had my dear old Pennsylvany Dutchmen in front of me and was going right along in my sermon and said that on the Last Day the good Lord would call out, "Jack, John, George, come out!" and just like that they would be standing there with glorified bodies. To my Pennsylvany Dutchmen it wasn't funny at all; they all had completely serious faces. The dear old Arnold had already told me earlier, "I think you are a pretty smart fellow [*Ich denk, du bist a ziemlich smarter Kerl*]."

---

21. Wilhelm Engelbert, originally from Nassau, had enrolled at Fort Wayne during the 1852–1853 school year and had graduated in 1855.

22. Namely, Pastor Lindemann told the other pastors about Strieter's sermon when they got back. See Appendix IV, no. 3.

Chapter 5

Wisconsin

In Nov. 1859 I set out for Wisconsin with my wife and three children.[1] We couldn't take Mother along, because we ourselves still didn't know where we were staying, and because the cold winter was just around the corner and she had trouble with coughing, especially in winter. She moved with the girls to the city of Cleveland.[2]

We traveled to Milwaukee. My wife had a girlfriend from school there, K. T., who was married to F. E. They took us in. I now wrote to W[ilhel]m Stelter. But in his letter to Dr. Sihler the good man had written his township, Crystal Lake, at the top, but nowhere did he indicate his P.O., which was called Stone Hill. I addressed Crystal Lake, but get no reply because he didn't receive my letter. I wrote again—no reply. A week later I tell my wife, "We're setting out."

We rode by railroad as far as Ripon. There I inquire and learn that we had to drive to Princeton. I ordered a wagon; the luggage went up into it. The wife takes a seat next to the driver with the two young ones and I take a seat with my Friedrich in the back on a crate. At first it went pretty well. Then came . . . Injunland paths.

Injunland: They told me that it had belonged to the Indians and had been purchased from them for one cent per acre.[3] To the eye a very beautiful area, hilly, richly furnished with marshes, rivers, and lakes, but meager sand-soil.

    1. See Appendix II, nos. 1–4.
    2. See Appendix V, pars. 17,18.
    3. "[On] Oct. 18, 1848, the Government obtained the Indian title to all of the lands claimed by the Menomonees [sic] within the State of Wisconsin. This treaty was made at Lake Poygan, and the purchase included the tract lying north and west of the Fox River between the Wolf and Wisconsin Rivers, including nearly all of Waushara County, much of Marquette County, and some of Green Lake County, long known as 'the Indian Land.' In return the Indians accepted a grant of land previously ceded by the Chippewas of the Mississippi and Lake Superior and by the Pillogu [sic; should be Pillager] band of Chippewas [guaranteed to contain not less than 600,000 acres]. It was stipulated in the treaty that the Indians might remain on 'the Indian lands' for two years, or until notified by the Government that the lands were wanted. In the fall of 1852 they were so notified, and removed to Wolf River" (*Portrait and Biographical Album of Green Lake, Marquette and Waushara Counties, Wisconsin* [Chicago: Acme Publishing Co., 1890], 203.2). Not mentioned is the stipulated government payment of $350,000. See Charles J. Kappler, ed., *Indian Affairs: Laws and Treaties*, vol. 2 (Washington: Government Printing Office, 1904), 572–74, for the full text of the treaty. Settler E. J. Dartt wrote in a letter to *The Oxford Times* (of Oxford, Wis., west of Montello) in 1915: "I came to Montello March 13, 1847,

When we arrived in Princeton, people were there who were going to be my members. Immediately the word got out: The preacher is here. They were Poseners, who addressed me as Preacher, and my wife as Mrs. Priestette [*Frau Priestergen*]. A man came to me, C[hristoph] T[agatz]; I was supposed to turn in at his place. Another man also took a seat on the wagon, and off we go.

Now came the real Injunland paths with their pole bridges across the marshes. "That damn . . . wooden country," the driver cursed in English, as my wife later told me.[4] We arrived at C[hristoph] T[agatz]'s place in the evening. Over there across the path lived Father T[agatz], who came to see us right away.[5] Everything looked and sounded very injunlandish. In the evening we had a meal, also injunlandish. Didn't quite taste right. At night the dear Mrs. T[agatz], a beautiful young wife—they had no children yet[6]—threw some rye straw on the floor which Grandmother T[agatz] had brought,[7] and we spread our bedding on it.[8] Sleep didn't want to come either, but my fatigue got the better of me. I soon wake up again though, and hear my wife sobbing so softly. It was hard on me too. I heard and saw her do this for several days and nights. Then I said, "Lisbeth dear, you must not cry any more. Our dear God has brought us here and he will surely be with us." Now she got a hold of herself.

A house had been built on W[ilhel]m Stelter's land, and two acres fenced in, for my predecessor, D[iehlmann].[9] The house was built in German fashion—timber framing

---

and lived with the Indians one and a half years before any other white settler came to this section of the country" (http://www.wiroots.org/wimarquette/oldsettdartt.html; accessed Aug. 14, 2019).

4. Leutner crossed out "dam [*sic*] . . ." and replaced it with a dash in the printed edition. The word *fluchte*, "cursed," was also misprinted as *flüsterte*, "whispered."

5. "Father Tagatz" was Martin, who was fifty-seven years old at the time. He passed away on Jan. 5, 1867, and was buried on Jan. 7. Here Strieter originally wrote: "When I spoke about the marshes, he says in front of my wife, 'Yeah, there you'll sink up to [here a blank perhaps representing something inappropriate].' Her eyes grew wide." It appears that Johannes himself crossed this out, perhaps at Elizabeth's urging.

6. Christoph Tagatz's wife was Louise née Schätzke, and though she had no children at the time, she appears to have been pregnant, as their daughter Emilie Pauline was born on June 9, 1860, and baptized by Strieter on July 1.

7. Though it is possible that "Grandmother T." refers to Martin Tagatz's mother (see n. 5), there is no burial record for such a woman. Strieter may be referring to Martin's wife, Anna Justine née Mesall or Missal, who was forty-nine at the time. She passed away on Sept. 30, 1874, and was buried on Oct. 2.

8. The original sentence read: "The dear Mrs. T[agatz] . . . threw some beds on the floor which Grandmother T[agatz] had brought, and we lay down on them." The correction to "rye straw" seems too detailed to have been made up by Leutner.

9. Today this property has the address W3276 County Road E in the town of Crystal Lake (mailing address Neshkoro). The parsonage Strieter is describing appears to have been built in the summer of 1858. Strieter later also mentions a log stable that was built on the property. Eventually the property was expanded to four acres, and in 1876 a new parsonage was built. A new barn appears to have been built at some point too, the foundation of which still serves as a flower garden today. The property ceased to be used for the parsonage after 1898.

See Appendix VI, pp. 247ff, and the *WELS Historical Institute Journal* 38 no. 1 (Spring 2020) 13–32, for more on Konrad Diehlmann. In the summer of 1859, Diehlmann insisted that his Marquette Co.

[*Fachwerk*] and filled out with clay. It had two rooms and a small bedroom. I bought myself a six-year-old horse, Charley, for sixty dollars, hitched him to a sled and drive to Wautoma and get myself two stoves, bedsteads, etc., and we moved in.

On the second day of Christmas 1859, I preached for the first time—in the morning in the town schoolhouse and in the afternoon at Welke's, nearly twelve miles away or so. I now preached at Tagatz's;[10] at Schmidt's; at Kiesow's, later Donning's; at Buchholz's; at Warnke's; near Neshkoro, at Rörke's; in the vicinity of Westfield; in Berlin; in Fairwater.[11] To Buchholz's it was twelve miles, to Fairwater twenty-five miles, to Berlin twenty-five; to the other places it was not especially far. I never preached less than four and never more than nine times a week and almost always traveled 6,000 or so miles a year with my horse. When I preached at Buchholz's, I would take off at seven o'clock, preach, drive another ten or so miles to Warnke's[12] (in the winter it was closer[13]), preach again, and then nine or so miles home. At first I took along something to eat, but it didn't work; in the winter it was frozen and in the summer it was dry as bark. Then I gave it up and ate just like my horse, at seven in the morning and seven in the evening.

> Fig. 28 (following two pages). Map of Strieter's area of service in Wisconsin c. 1860. The date in parentheses next to each village denotes when it was platted. Dotted lines represent Indian paths as documented by surveyors George B. Sargent and William P. Huntington in 1851 and 1852. I filled in the other roads—those I felt were important to the immigrants in this story—using my best judgment on the basis of later plat maps (1860, 1876, 1878, 1900) and current roads. The house-like symbol, when accompanied by "S.H.," denotes a schoolhouse, otherwise a residence. The S.H. or community center on the western #14 plot, where the so-called Tagatz's congregation met, was built between 1857 and 1859, probably in the summer of 1858 around the same time as the parsonage. A cross denotes a church building, with the year it was built in parentheses. The small envelope symbol denotes a post office.

---

congregations give him a release in order to salvage his reputation. He also requested and was granted a release from the Wisconsin Synod. He then moved to the town of Randolph, Columbia Co., Wis., where he served two congregations—one near his new home and one in the town of Dayton in Green Lake Co.

10. This refers to the already-mentioned schoolhouse by Tagatz's, built between 1857 and 1859, probably in the summer of 1858 around the same time as the parsonage; see Fig. 28. It was located near the present address of W2983 Eagle Road. There is still a Matz-Tagatz Cemetery on Eagle Road, three and a half miles west of Germania and three-tenths of a mile east of State Road 22.

11. Some of the congregations that still exist today as a result of Strieter's ministry, in addition to those mentioned in nn. 12, 19, & 20 below, are as follows: St. John's Lutheran, Budsin / rural Neshkoro; Trinity Lutheran, Little Mecan / rural Montello; Zion Lutheran, Neshkoro; Immanuel Lutheran, Westfield; St. John's Lutheran, Berlin; St. Paul's Lutheran, Fairburn / rural Berlin (an 1899 daughter of St. John's); and Zion Lutheran, Fairwater.

12. See Fig. 28. A log church on Peter Warnke's property (unknown year of construction) was in use until 1876, when a new church was built in Germania. This congregation became known as St. Peter's Lutheran. It closed in March 1962. The original log church has long since been torn down, but its foundations were still visible in 1970. Also, the unused church building in Germania remains standing, and there is a Germania Lutheran Cemetery on Eagle Road east of Germania.

13. It was closer in the winter because he could take the sled across the frozen marshes.

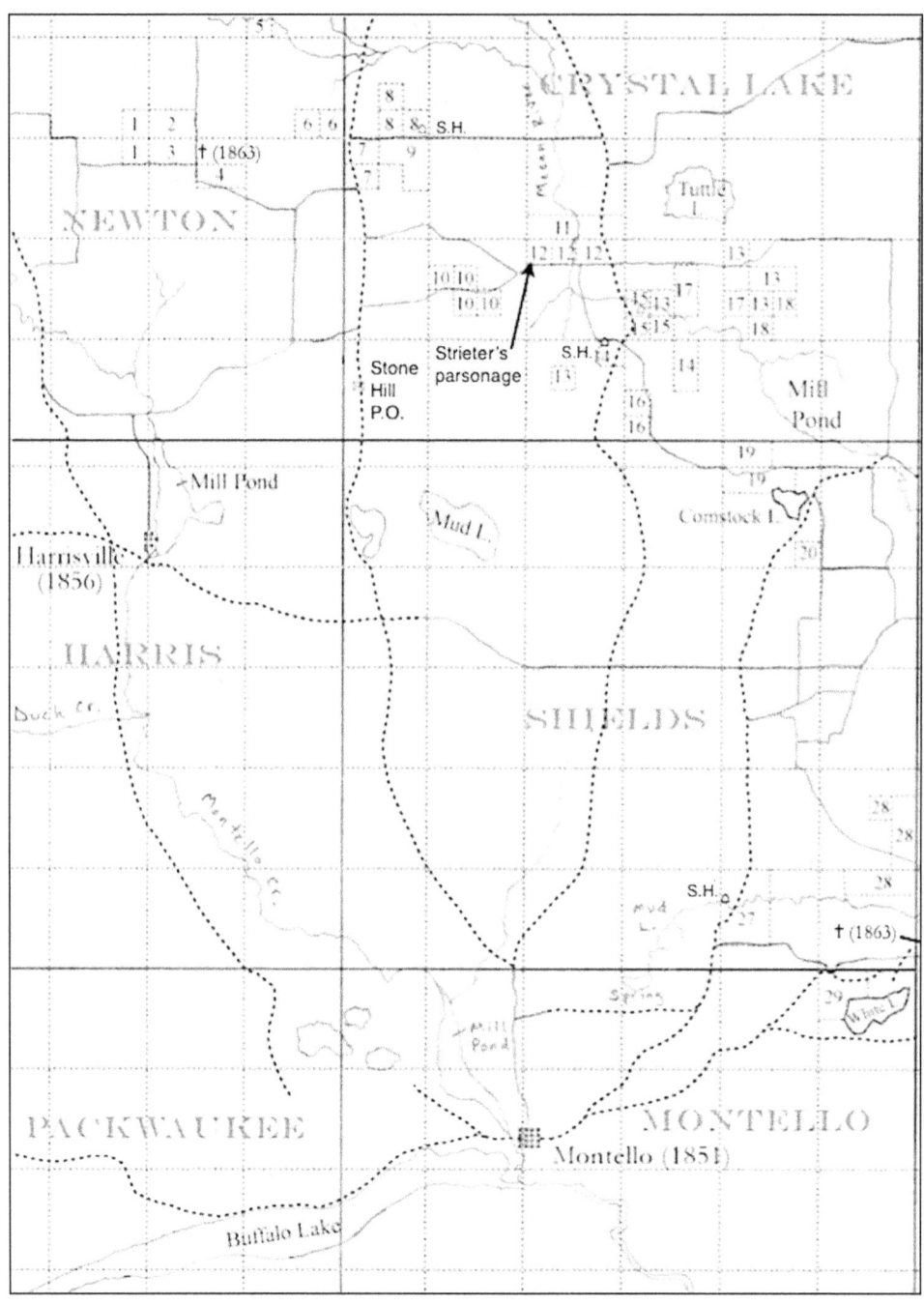

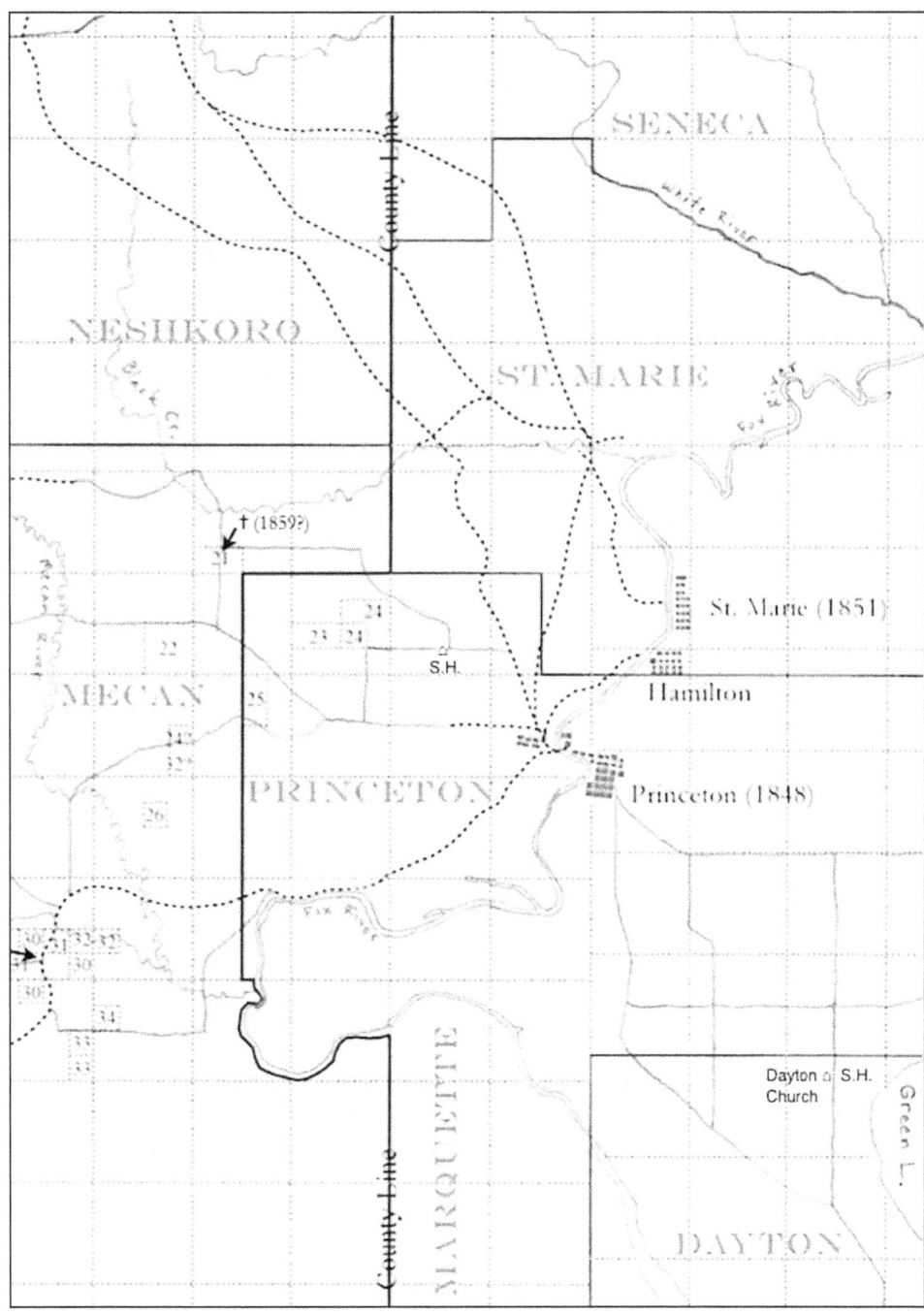

The owners of the numbered properties, along with their date of purchase, are as follows (properties are listed W to E, N to S when stacked vertically):

1. Johann Kopplin: 1855? (patent 12/15/56); July 13, 1854

2. Johann Kopplin: July 13, 1854; then Friedrich Kiesow and Gottlieb Klempe: Aug. 12, 1856

3. Carl Stubbe: Nov. 9, 1853 (moved to Fall Creek in 1856); then Gottlieb Donning: Aug. 17, 1856. An August Donning (Gottlieb's middle name?) must have purchased the land across the road, since courthouse records indicate that he and his wife Auguste donated the land on which the first church was built, where the cemetery now lies.

4. August Kopplin: 1858? (patent 8/10/59)

5. Ferdinand Holz: 1856? (patent 4/1/57)

6. Wilhelm Fierke/Virke: 1857? (patent 10/1/58); 1853/54?. Fierke helped the congregations get organized so that they could call their first full-time pastor in 1857.

7. Andrew Fenske: Nov. 21, 1854; Aug. 15, 1856

8. Michael Schmidt/Smith: Jan. 15, 1856; Feb. 5, 1856; Dec. 30, 1853. At some point (probably during the ministry of Strieter's predecessor, Konrad Diehlmann) a schoolhouse was built on his property and services began to be held there. Although services were also held at Friedrich Kiesow's (#2) at some point, a case could be made that Lutheran immigrants living in or around plots 1–9 first met here, which may have contributed to some of the later division that occurred during Strieter's ministry (see Appendix IX).

9. Daniel Barz: Sept. 3, 1856

10. August Kohnke/Kuhnke: Nov. 15, 1855; Aug. 11, 1856; Dec. 7, 1856; Nov. 15, 1855. His wife Johanne Henriette née Krenz is the woman whose mother, Dorothea Sophie Anklam, encouraged Strieter to visit the Pomeranian immigrants northwest of Wausau in Marathon Co.

11. Samuel Fischer: Nov. 13, 1852. See Appendix VI, No. 73.

12. William/Wilhelm Stelter: Jan. 15, 1856; Nov. 7, 1853; Nov. 12, 1852 (moved to Fall Creek in 1860 and sold his land to Julius Breitenfeld, also a member and administrator of the so-called Tagatz congregation). Stelter also helped the congregations get organized in 1857 and became one of the first administrators. He eventually donated two acres (probably in the summer of 1858) for parsonage property.

13. August Tagatz (parents: Martin Tagatz—one of the first administrators—and Justine née Mesall): Oct. 6, 1853; April 2, 1856; Nov. 21, 1854; Nov. 14, 1856 (eighty acres); April 2, 1856

14. (Christoph?) Julius Tagatz: Oct. 16, 1856; Nov. 14, 1856

15. Andrew Hol(t)z: Nov. 12, 1852; Aug. 11, 1856; Nov. 27, 1856

16. Gottfried Stelter: Oct 24, 1854; Jan. 15, 1856 (moved to Fall Creek in 1860)

17. Ludwig Krueger: Nov. 25, 1853; Nov. 26, 1857

18. Ludwig Kohnke: Oct. 28, 1856; June 2, 1858

19. Johann Friedrich Warnke: Aug. 1857; July 3, 1856

20. August Gruhlke: Nov. 24, 1853. He conducted separate services at his house, and eventually also in Princeton, during Diehlmann's and Strieter's ministries, due to his group being put under discipline by Pastor Martin Stephan, Jr. in 1855 or 1856. He left with others for Minnesota in 1862.

21. Peter Warnke: Sept. 26, 1853. The services held at the "log church" on his property (until 1876) were originally held at the schoolhouse east of John Teske's (#24).

22. Wilhelm Krenz: Jan. 1, 1853 (eventually moved to Fall Creek). One of the first administrators.

23. Gottlieb Glenz: July 25, 1853

24. John Teske (different from #31 & 32): Dec. 24, 1852 (120 acres); Oct. 23, 1858. Gottlieb Reim, a Wisconsin Synod pastor, held at least two services either in his house or in the schoolhouse east of his property prior to the arrival of Strieter's predecessor, Konrad Diehlmann. (The plots marked "24? 32?" were purchased by a John Teske on July 20, 1857, but I am unsure which one.)

25. Gottlieb Teske: May 21, 1853

26. Ferdinand Bahr: May 13, 1856. One of the first administrators.

27. Johann Gottlieb Welke: June 1, 1853 (minus one-half acre identified by the schoolhouse). Strieter's predecessor, Diehlmann, boarded with Welke until the parsonage was built around the summer of 1858. Services were also held at the schoolhouse surrounded by his property before being moved to Emil Ludke's property.

28. Michael Buchholz: Aug. 13, 1854. Strieter mentions him as an administrator. He also refers the services held for his congregation as taking place "at Buchholz's," even though they took place on Emil Ludke's property, not his.

29. Ernst Schultz: Sept. 4, 1855. A son of Johann Schultz (#34). Like his father, he also conducted some of the earliest reading services among the immigrants.

30. August Schwanke: Jan. 16, 1858; March 22, 1856; Sept. 19, 1857. One of the first administrators.

31. Emil Ludke and John Ludwig Teske: Aug. 9, 1856 (W plot seems not to have included the one acre and 134 rods east of the state road). Ludke eventually donated land for the 1863 church, which is now known locally as Emmanuel Big Mecan.

32. John Ludwig Teske: Sept. 24, 1857; unknown date

33. Si(e)gesmund Luetke: Sept. 23, 1853; Dec. 5, 1854. One of the first administrators.

34. Johann Schultz: July 12, 1853. He conducted some of the first reading services among the immigrants and played a key role in getting them to request their first full-time pastor from the Wisconsin Synod, Konrad Diehlmann. Friend of August Gruhlke. Though his influence seems to have waned after Diehlmann left and Strieter arrived, he continued to carry some respect in the area. (See Appendix VI for more.)

On January 15, 1860, Pastor P[eter] H[einrich] Dicke from Mayville installed me.[14] I picked him up from Ripon and also brought him back there. In Ripon he bought me an old buggy for thirty dollars with his own money and lent it to me without interest until I could pay it off.

---

14. See Appendix IV, no. 4. Peter Heinrich Dicke had enrolled at Fort Wayne during the 1851–1852 school year and had graduated in 1853, first serving as an adjunct pastor in Frankenlust, Mich., before accepting a call to Frankentrost in 1854. The June 30, 1857 issue of *Der Lutheraner* reports that he was installed as pastor of "the three Lutheran congregations by Mayville, Dodge County, Wisconsin," on Ascension Day, May 21, 1857, "on the occasion of the celebration of a church dedication" (p. 183).

Fig. 29. Rev. Peter Heinrich Dicke (1822–1911), unknown year, photo. Image courtesy of St. Paul Lutheran-Frankenlust, Bay City, Mich.

I held instruction in the summer, and did so at Tagatz's, at Buchholz's, at Warnke's, also in Fairwater at Röske's. We took children from Berlin into our home. I confirmed in Fairwater at Röske's; the others I assembled at Tagatz's or at Stelter's and confirmed under the green trees in groups of fifty or so, and held the Supper there too. Children came to me from twelve miles away. I also taught some school.

The people were in the habit of not standing around in front of the schoolhouse or residence, but of going inside and singing until I arrived. They had Bollhagen's hymnal,[15] which in the main part had our hymns more or less unaltered. Then it had several appendices, and those had rationalistic hymns. One man told me, "Our pastor in Germany always had us sing from the second appendix." That one had the worst hymns.[16] I looked up all the hymns that were in our St. Louis hymnal[17] and wrote the

15. Laurentius David Bollhagen (1683–1738) first issued his *Heilige Lippen- und Herzensopfer einer gläubigen Seele oder Vollständiges Gesangbuch* (Holy Offerings from the Lips and Heart of a Believing Soul or Complete Hymnal) in 1724 for use in public worship in Pomerania. It was reprinted several times after his death. In nineteenth century editions the first word was changed from *Heilige* to *Heiliges* (A Holy Offering).

16. The second appendix contained such hymns as "Rejoice, Rejoice, Believers" (*Christian Worship* 7), "The Bridegroom Soon Will Call Us" (*CW* 10), "Come, Oh, Come, Life-Giving Spirit" (*CW* 181), "Alleluia! Let Praises Ring" (*CW* 241), and "Renew Me, O Eternal Light" (*CW* 471). While these particular hymns may not have borne the brunt of his displeasure, the section did have a strong representation of Pietistic hymns and hymnwriters, who put the focus on mankind's devotion to and acceptance of God rather than God's gracious work in human hearts and faithfulness to mankind for Jesus's sake. Hymn no. 1203 by J. P. v. Schult is one example that would have probably been distasteful to Strieter.

17. The *Kirchen-Gesangbuch für Evangelisch-Lutherische Gemeinden ungeänderter Augsburgischer*

page number in Bollhagen's hymnal on the side, purchased hymnals from Barthel[18] and sold them, and brought our hymnal into use among the people. At first I would say, "In my hymnal, no. *x*, in Bollhagen's, page *x*."

The people sang well and knew all the melodies. It never happened to me once that we were unable to sing a hymn. Almost everywhere I had some men who would act as the precentor. I would begin, and some good singer would take it up. Then I would save my voice as much as possible.

Fig. 30. The final resting place of Wilhelm Stelter (1817–1907) and his wife Marie (1823–1922) in St. John Lutheran Cemetery, Fall Creek, Wis., 2016, photo. Stelter helped found what is today St. John Lutheran Church in Budsin and St. John Lutheran in Fall Creek, Wis.

One time I noticed over at Buchholz's that every last person was standing in front of the church. (There they soon built a log church thatched with straw,[19] and soon another one just like it at Donning's.[20]) When I got there, someone said, "Father died the day before yesterday. Please give a funeral sermon before you go into the church." I announce the hymn, "Who Knows When Death May Overtake Me," and while they are singing, I think of a text for myself and what I am going to say.

Confession, first published in 1847, also colloquially known as "Walther's hymnal."

18. Martin C. Barthel (1838–1899) was the first "general agent" of publishing interests of the Missouri Synod (1860) and the first manager of Concordia Publishing House in St. Louis (1869–1891).

19. Today this is Emmanuel Lutheran, Big Mecan / rural Montello, located at the corner of Evergreen Lane and Town Hall Road, just south of State Road 23. The church Strieter describes here was built in 1863 at what is today the east end of Emmanuel Lutheran Cemetery.

20. Today this is St. Paul's Lutheran, town of Newton / rural Westfield, located at the corner of 10th Road and 11th Road.

With the Supper I now had some anxiety. My Stelter—he was an administrator [*Vorsteher*] and a very dear Christian—said, "When we were abroad, people announced for the Supper with the schoolteacher or with the custodian. No one went to the preacher."

Where do you even start? I give a speech and show what the Lutheran custom was, namely to announce for the Supper beforehand with the pastor, and how necessary this was for me and them.

But the reply was, "We're not used to that," meaning that it wasn't necessary either.

A former schoolmaster from Germany[21] wanted to know where it stood in the Bible that you had to announce for the Supper. I had already cited the passages, "We are stewards" [cf. 1 Cor. 4:1], and, "Do not throw your pearls to the sows" [Matt. 7:6], and now I pointed to the passage, "Confess your sins to each other" [James 5:16]; they confessed their sins to John.[22] He was quiet. But they still could not and would not see the necessity of the practice.[23]

I say, "But what then if it is absolutely necessary for me to say something to someone for the sake of my conscience?"

They reply, "Then just say it."

I say, "In front of everyone?"

"But of course."

"Fine, that's what I'll do."

I now let everyone give me his or her name, and I always write it down. When I held Supper at Buchholz's for the first time, I had seventy-five male and seventy-five female names in my book. After that I addressed the following questions to them: Do you believe from the heart in Jesus Christ as your Savior? Do you believe that in the

---

21. Immigrants Johann Schultz, Ernst Adolph Schultz, August Gruhlke, and Wilhelm Fierke were all former schoolmasters from Germany. Since Gruhlke basically ran his own private church and was not served by Strieter, this probably refers to one of the other three.

22. Either Strieter was mistakenly thinking, either at the time or when recalling the incident later, that the passage was found in one of John's epistles, instead of in James, or he was combining James 5:16 with 1 John 1:9 in his mind.

23. The practice of announcing with the pastor before partaking of the Lord's Supper can trace its ancestry back to private confession, which in turn dates all the way back to around 250 AD in the Eastern Church. The Eastern Church historians Socrates Scholasticus and Sozomen both relate that the office of penitentiary, a minister appointed for hearing private confessions, also thereby helped people to prepare to receive the Lord's Supper (Socrates, 5.19; Sozomen, 7.16). The Bible nowhere explicitly necessitates private confession or announcing, but it does command us to examine ourselves before receiving the Supper and warns us of the consequences of treating the Supper lightly (1 Cor. 11:27–32). Strieter was also correct to cite 1 Corinthians 4:1 and Matthew 7:6, which emphasize the pastor's role in relation to the Lord's Supper, namely to be a faithful administrator of it and not to knowingly or willingly distribute it to those who are continuing in some sin. Many Lutheran churches in America today no longer practice announcing, probably due to the difficulty of putting it into practice in our fast-paced, busy society and in larger churches. However, there is usually still some form of registration required so that the pastor is able a) to take note of those planning to partake of the Supper and to speak to them beforehand or afterward if needed, and b) to keep track of whether or not any of his congregation's members are failing to make use of the Supper.

Supper the true body and blood of Christ is eaten and drunk under bread and wine? Are you reconciled, and do you intend to partake of the Holy Supper as repentant sinners? These questions were answered yes in chorus.

But it didn't take long before it happened as I thought it would. One time I'm driving home from Princeton and see how someone is unhitching his oxen from the cart and letting them drink and hitching them back up again, and he's so drunk that he can hardly get it done. On Sunday there's Supper at W[arnke]'s. My man is sitting way in the back, but gives his name too.

I say, "But my dear sir, I have something to say to you. I saw you there completely drunk, did I not?"

He says, "Yeah."

I say, "Does this happen with you at other times, sir?"

He says, "Yeah."

I say, "You, sir, are a drunkard then. A drunkard cannot inherit the kingdom of God; God's word condemns him [1 Cor. 6:10]. He can only bring a curse on himself if he takes the Holy Supper."

He says yeah, he was sorry and would amend his ways.

I say, "You must repent, sir, sincerely, acknowledge your sin and hasten in faith with your sins to your Savior. Repentant, as a Christian, you must go to the Supper."

He says, "Yes, I will do that."

I say, "I will give you the Supper then, but I will be watching you to see whether you are serious about amending your ways."

Later, on the way home, a man is standing at the bottom of the little hill where I have to turn: "Mr. Preacher, one moment." I halt. "I wanted to go to the Supper too. Will you accept me, sir?"

"You know my questions. What is your position on them?"

He says, "I am not reconciled. My brother-in-law N. and I are mortal enemies, and I would sooner go to hell than forgive him."

"My dear man, how then are you going to go to the Supper? Doesn't the Lord say that if you do not forgive people their failings, then the heavenly Father will not forgive you either [Matt. 6:15]?"

"I know well that according to the teaching of Jesus I cannot go to the Supper."

The Supper is at B[uchholz]'s. After the names are recorded, a father stands up: "Mr. Preacher, So-and-so and Such-and-such, my daughter and my son-in-law, have also announced. They are at enmity with us."

I ask the accused; they admit it. "Then reconcile with each other immediately. All four of you step into the aisle and extend your hands in reconciliation." They do so.

A mother stands up: "Mr. Preacher, So-and-so, my son, has also announced. He drinks. Please admonish him."

I admonish him.

The Lord's Supper is at T[agatz]'s. There I learn that H. doesn't believe in any devil. He announces.

"Mr. H., is it true what I hear about you, sir, that you deny the existence of the devil?"

He says, "How am I supposed to believe that there is a devil? No one has ever seen him yet."

"Sure someone has seen him—there in the wilderness [Matt. 4:1–11]. Haven't you heard that account yet, sir?"

"Oh sure, but I can't believe it."

"Then you do not believe God's word, sir. Then you also cannot believe the doctrine of the Supper. So you cannot go to the Supper."

In the course of time here comes one administrator, there comes another: "Mr. Preacher, the people don't like having you tell them their shame right to their face in front of everyone."

I say, "That's exactly what I suspected."

I now present again how necessary it is to announce. This time they want to announce. I now say that I will set a day on which they should announce; for those far away I will hold it so that they should announce by my buggy before church. And that's how it went. That's how I got announcing going.

One time I'm driving to B[uchholz's] to hear announcements for the Supper in the church. On the way someone calls to me, "Mr. Preacher, we wanted to go to the Supper too. Will you write us down here?"

"Gladly."

"But the question is whether I am allowed to go?"

"Why wouldn't you be?"

"Yeah, I am in conflict with my neighbor P., who let his cattle into my pasture. I tell him about it, but to no avail. Then I sue him and he is found guilty. But in front of the court he comes up to me and socks me one in the face and goes to the judge and lays five dollars down. I go to him later and confront him with his wrong, but he says, 'I paid for that.'"

I say, "If you have offered him reconciliation and he doesn't want it, then you, sir, can go to the Supper, but he cannot."

I reach my destination. Sure enough, my P. comes and announces. I confront him with what M. said. He admits it, but also refers to his five dollars. I say, "Listen here, sir, you know better than that. You know that you cannot make up for your sins with five dollars. You must ask M. for forgiveness."

He won't do that.

"Then you cannot go to the Supper either."

He makes a sour face and leaves.

After the service the administrators have some other business, and I come out of the sacristy with my basket. (I always had to bring everything with me.) My P. is still there too and starts in: "Listen, you administrators, I have something to tell you. I am in conflict with M. To him he gives the Supper, but not to me."

I now present the affair to them. Then my administrators said, "The preacher has handled the matter exactly right."

Later a woman came: "Mr. P. has threatened to give you a sound thrashing, sir. I would definitely watch out; he is a wild man."

"Did he say that to you, ma'am?"

"Yes."

"Good, please give him my regards and tell him that here under the hay is a small little gun, loaded and ready. If he should attack me in the woods like a murderous robber, I will shoot him stone dead." He didn't come though.

One time a woman asked me to stop by her place sometime; she had something to tell me about. I stop by. There she relates this: Over in Germany she had been a rich farmer's daughter, and her husband had been her father's servant, and because he was such a good person, she had fallen in love with him and suggested that they get married. But he had said, "Get that idea out of your head. Your father will not agree to it, and if he did agree to it, our wealth would come from you, since I have nothing, and it is not good when the wife makes her husband rich. You have a temper; if you fly off the handle at some point, you'll rub it in my face."

"I promise him that I will say nothing about it all my life.

"I approach my mother and she approaches my father. 'Fine,' says my father, 'I will give you this much money and then you can both go to America.'

"We got married. My father gives me money and we came to America and bought ourselves the land here. Now imagine, sir, I just recently get annoyed over something and say to my husband, 'You didn't have *anything* but your jacket.'

"He doesn't say a word, but shoots me a look. Oh, that look went right through my heart. If only he weren't so good. But I have such a good man. He can go anywhere he likes and while this man or that one comes home and has had too much, mine never does. And he is so good to me and the children. And now I had promised him I would never rub it in his face, and now I did it anyway. So do you think that God can forgive me my sin?"

I say, "First of all, ma'am, you must apologize to your husband, and he must forgive you first."

"Ah, I have already asked him for forgiveness many times, and he has said to me, 'Just forget about it; everything is fine.'"

"Good, now ask our dear God for forgiveness too."

"Oh, how often I have done that!"

"Okay, what more do you want then? Everything is all good now. Now your husband has forgiven and God has forgiven, and you don't need any forgiveness beyond that."

"God has really forgiven me too?"

"Why, in the Fifth Petition he says he has."[24]

Now she was happy.

One time a man came to me with his wife and told me that his wife was going out of her mind. He had heard that such women should be given a good, sound beating. Should he give it a try?

I say, "Of course not. How is that going to help? You must be kind, sir."

I speak with the woman. She said that one child after another died on her when it was born, and that was God's punishment for her sins. I point her to her Savior and recite passages to her. She listens to it, but that's it. I arrange to meet the man again and again. Finally have no idea what else to say. One time I had her in front of me again and I ask her whether she really wanted to be saved.

"Oh sure!" she exclaims.

"Good, and God wants it too and affirms it with an oath [see Heb. 6:13–20]. Now who's going to prevent it?"

Suddenly she lifts up her head and, with joy beaming from her face, cries, "That is true!" From then on she stayed happy.

Yes, when God's hour has struck, he helps through a simple little word.

One time a man came and told me that his woman was a Jewess. They were not married yet and his girl, twelve years old, was also not baptized yet.

I say, "Come over and bring the woman along."

He came. I start with Moses and the Prophets and prove to the woman that Jesus of Nazareth is the Messiah promised by the prophets and ask her what her position is on that. But she gave me no answer. He says, "Come on, talk to the preacher." She remains stock-still.

I arrange to meet her again. She comes and I take her alone and start again and ask what she thinks, but she remains stock-still. If I talk about something else, she is quite talkative. If I start talking about Jesus, her head turns to the ground and not a word. I cannot make any progress with the woman.

I tell the man, "So I cannot marry you, sir. Since the woman does not believe in Jesus, I also cannot marry her in the name of Jesus. Go to the justice of the peace. Your child, though, I will instruct and baptize." The child is sent to me, and I instruct and baptize it in the presence of witnesses. But the mother did not show her face.[25]

---

24. If Jesus taught us to pray, "Forgive us our trespasses," in the Lord's Prayer, then the implication is that God is truly able and willing to do so.

25. The man in this story was Gottlieb Busse and "his woman" was Charlotte Jacobson. Their twelve-year-old daughter was Julie Busse, born on Feb. 15, 1851. (Thus most of the events in this story took place in 1863.) Strieter baptized her on March 27, 1864, in the presence of Julius and Rose Breitenfeld and his own wife Elizabeth.

While I'm on the subject of the Jewess, I will add this: One woman asked me, "Mr. Preacher, is your wife not a Jewess? She has such large, black eyes and such heavy, black hair."

I also had to deal with the musicians. Especially at weddings they knew how to have a good time. If it was going to be a proper one, it lasted three days and three nights, and there would be music-playing, dancing, and boozing. The performers were my churchgoers. One of them, a teacher from abroad, knew better than to go to the Supper, but always went to church. The others—there were four of them usually—also went to the Supper. I speak with the musicians, but accomplish nothing except that they become defiant towards me. I thought, "You must put up with this for the time being." But it didn't take long before I just couldn't give the performers the Supper any more in good conscience, though they still went to church and their wives also went to the Supper. Not just at weddings, but also at get-togethers things often got out of hand, and I had to rebuke and instruct and had much opposition from the flesh and often unpleasant confrontations. Ah, many sighs were sent to heaven, many tears were shed. My short impromptu prayer was always: "Comfort me once again with your help and let your joyful Spirit uphold me!" [Ps. 51:12].[26]

I did most of my studying when I was riding, driving, or sitting. I had Luther, the Erlangen edition, the German volumes, which I picked up cheaply in Euclid from one of Kühn's members through Kühn's negotiation. Luther's House Postil was my constant companion, as well as another extra volume.[27] I read my Luther, and my manner and method of preparing my sermon in my mind, as already noted,[28] now came in very handy. First I would go through my Gospel, then I would run through my Luther, then I would outline, then I would think and organize, then I would preach in front of the

---

26. One of the evil characteristics of Pietism enumerated by Valentin Ernst Loescher (1673–1749) in *The Complete Timotheus Verinus* (Milwaukee: Northwestern, 1998) is precisionism in matters of adiaphora, that is, unyielding strictness in matters neither explicitly commanded nor forbidden in Holy Scripture (pp. 150-60). Pietists like Joachim Lange (1670-1744), Gottfried Vockerodt (1665-1727), August Hermann Francke (1663-1727), and Paul Anton (1661-1730) taught that producing or attending comedies, joking, and dancing were sinful. Pietists took activities that often lead to sin—e.g. dancing often leads to lust and self-abandon (cf. Matt. 5:28; Rom. 13:14; Gal. 5:19-23), and joking often leads to obscenity or coarseness (cf. Eph. 5:4)—and wrongly labeled them sinful in themselves. The effects of the Pietistic movement can still be felt in the Lutheran Church today, and Strieter was not exempt from them in his day either, even though he certainly knew about Pietism and opposed it in principle. One can appreciate his concern: Lust, drunkenness, and self-abandonment are all sins, and certainly those sins abound in the kind of raucous scenes he is describing. However, while acknowledging that we do not know all the details and live in a much different time and therefore must be cautious in judgment, it could be that Strieter went too far in refusing the Lord's Supper to the musicians. (But perhaps he would say we admit too many today.)

27. See p. 67 and n. 20.

28. See p. 67.

group in question in my mind all the way from the first word to the last, and would then step confidently in front of my people. I never preached long.

For confessional services I used the Catechism exclusively, simply covering part by part in order, but I didn't just preach outright, but asked a lot of questions, doing more catechesis and often asking questions and taking answers, so that I would also know whether they understood it. Especially a former teacher F.[29] answered me very often.

I did not labor in vain. Quite often it was expressed: "We never heard such sermons abroad." Quite a few tears were cried; quite often there was grieving over the fleshly condition.

The people were not to blame, for they must have had miserable preachers—rationalists, hirelings, belly-servers [cf. Rom. 16:18], and babblers. You could tell from the things that were occasionally said. One man, Administrator B., was asked to tell me one time that I should preach more humbly. I say, "I am constantly striving to be humble and am not aware of anything particularly arrogant in my sermons."

"Oh, that's not what I meant. What I mean is this: Our preachers would often have the whole church in tears when they preached."

"Oh, I see. You mean that I should preach more emotionally?" They had had it as their goal to elicit the emotions, so that they would be praised for how wonderfully they had preached.

Especially for funerals they must have had this practice, for one man even gave me two dollars before his mother's funeral. That was unheard of. He said, "Please give a nice address; my mother was a good woman."

But I read as my text, "Death is the wages of sin" [Rom. 6:23], and preached law and gospel.

One man told me, "What my pastor [*Seelsorger*] in Germany liked best was when he sat down with the musicians at weddings and played the *Brumm*"—the bass viol.

They could also be bribed, which I noticed too. One time a man came from twelve miles away and brought us two beautiful, nicely dressed ducks, and soon he started in, telling me that he was in conflict with his neighbor, and I should settle it, and he gave me to understand that I should take his side.

Another man asked if he could ride with me to the next congregation. I invited him up. Soon he pulled a small, folded-up paper parcel from his pocket and handed it to me saying, "Mr. Preacher, I would very much like to give you some pay."

"You certainly don't owe me any pay, sir. You're just a servant on the prairie."

"Even so, I want to give it to you this one time. Please take it; I am happy to give it."

I took it, stick it in my waistcoat pocket and say, "Thank you very much."

Pretty soon he started in: "Mr. Preacher, you have a girl as your maid, whom I would very much like to have as my wife. You will put in a good word for me, won't you?"

29. Probably Fierke (see n. 21; also p. 308, n. 83).

I say, "Listen here, sir, I did not study for the matchmaking trade, but let me give you a good piece of advice: Ask L.'s parents"—he had none himself—"and if they say yes, ask L., and if she also says yes, come to me and I will marry you."

He was quiet. In front of my house he got down and went on his way. My L. saw us coming and I hardly get into the house: "Papa, what did he want from you, sir?"

"He wanted you."

"Just what I thought. How often have I already told that guy that I do not want him."

"Yeah, but he gave me money too," and I pull out my small parcel. There are five dollars. "You poor guy, spending so much money for nothing."

My L. laughs and claps her hands: "If only it were ten!"

Whenever anyone came with a gift, I was suspicious. But they soon learned to think differently.

I was not able to spend a lot of time teaching school, since I was in the saddle or on the buggy or sled pretty much day and night, but I adapted my instruction to cover school subjects as much as possible. I obtained a young teacher from Addison, L.,[30] and when he went to C., a D.[31] I fixed one up myself, my dear F[erdinand] R[öske],[32] whom I instructed and confirmed privately with his older brother. He lived with me at home.

One day my neighborlady K[ohnke] came to see me with an old woman. She said it was her mother from Big Bull. Up there behind Wausau flows the Wisconsin River. Above Wausau it has a falls, which the log drivers called Bull; near Wausau another, which they called Big Bull; farther down yet another, which they called Grandfather Bull. Thus the location of Wausau acquired the name Big Bull. No one called it anything else. When I would write, I put the address Big Bull and it would get there fine.[33]

30. Leutner changed this to: "from Ft. Wayne, Lossner." A Heinrich Lossner appears as a baptismal witness in Strieter's records (including for one of his sons) up through January 1864.

31. Leutner replaced "a D." with: "Dress came." An Ernst Dress appears in Strieter's records in Oct. 1864. There is also a Heinrich Dress that appears in Feb. 1865; Strieter may have been confusing his name with that of his former teacher (see previous n.), or the teacher's full name was Ernst Heinrich Dress.

32. The printed book has H. R., and Strieter's original manuscript appears to read H. K., but a comparison of Strieter's description here to the records he kept and to what he says later in the chapter (see pp. 89 & 117) reveal that the young man in question is Wilhelm Ferdinand Röske, born on May 7, 1844, and confirmed with his older brother Carl Friedrich Jr. (b. May 27, 1841) on Oct. 31, 1863. Their parents, Carl Friedrich Sr. and Louise (Goethe) Röske, were from the town of Harris in Marquette County.

33. Strieter has these waterfalls backwards, though he has Wausau correct. According to historian Louis Marchetti, quoting a July 1906 speech given by the Hon. John C. Clarke, who had come to Wausau in 1845: "The name of 'Bull Falls' which is attached to nearly all the rapids in the Wisconsin river, of which there are many, was given by the voyageurs of the American Fur Company, who in going north from Indian station, known as Dubay, heard a terrible roaring sound, which upon

The old mother told me that up there behind the village, in the woods, in a ten- to twenty-mile circle, there lived many people, Pomeranians, who had no pastor. The Pomeranians said Pastor.[34] Three years ago already their pastor had abandoned them and had gone to run a sawmill. I should please come up to them too. I promise her I will and now go to Big Bull too.[35]

Fig. 31. The final resting place of Friedrich (1830–1905) and Wilhelmine (1841–1908) Krenz (*center*) and Dorothea Sophie Anklam (1811–1890; *left*) in Big Hill Cemetery in the town of Berlin, Marathon Co., Wis., 2012, photo. Dorothea was the mother of both Friedrich and Johanne Henriette (Krenz) Kohnke, the latter of which was one of Pastor's Strieter's members and neighbors in Marquette County, Wis. (see Fig. 28). Dorothea was

investigation proved to come from the falls at Mosinee, and they named them 'Toro' [*Taureau*, 'Bull']; moving north they found a larger rapids, and to them they gave the name of 'Gros Toro' [*Gros Taureau*, 'Big Bull']. Still further along they encountered the great falls, and these they named 'Grand Pere Toro' [*Grand-père Taureau*, 'Grandfather Bull']. From these names all the other falls have received the names they are known by" (*History of Marathon County Wisconsin and Representative Citizens* [Chicago: Richmond-Arnold, 1913], 65). However, the name "Bull" might actually be derived from the French words *beau lieu*, meaning "beautiful place." (Cf. Beaulieu Rapids on Fig. 32.) Wausau's original name is reflected today in businesses like Bull Falls Brewery and Big Bull Falls Landscaping and in the annual Big Bull Falls Blues Fest.

34. That is, as opposed to Preacher [*Prediger*] or Parson [*Pfarrer*].

35. A careful examination of Strieter's records and the records of his eventual assistant, J. J. Hoffmann, reveal Strieter's neighborlady to be Johanne Henriette Kohnke (née Krenz), and her mother to be Dorothea Sophie Anklam (née Lau; 1811–1890). Dorothea had been previously married to Johann Daniel Krenz, who had died around the early 1840s in Germany. She was forty-eight at the time she visited Strieter. Her husband August Anklam and her son Friedrich Krenz ended up being founding members of the first Lutheran congregation northwest of Wausau, founded on March 11, 1861, and Friedrich was also elected the first president and donated the land for the first parsonage.

visiting her daughter when she encouraged Pastor Strieter to visit and minister to the Pomeranian immigrants living in the rural Wausau area. That one conversation ultimately resulted in the founding of more than twenty congregations in Marathon, Portage, and Clark Counties. Dorothea's son Friedrich was elected president of the first Lutheran congregation in the town of Berlin, Marathon Co. (and perhaps the first Lutheran congregation in all of Marathon Co.), at its organizational meeting on March 11, 1861. He also donated the land for the first parsonage along what is now County Road A, about a quarter-mile west of the intersection with County Road O. He served in the Union Army from 1864–1865, surviving both the Battle of Nashville and Sherman's March to the Sea. He has since gained some local historical attention for the beautiful, faith-filled letters he wrote home to his wife during his service.

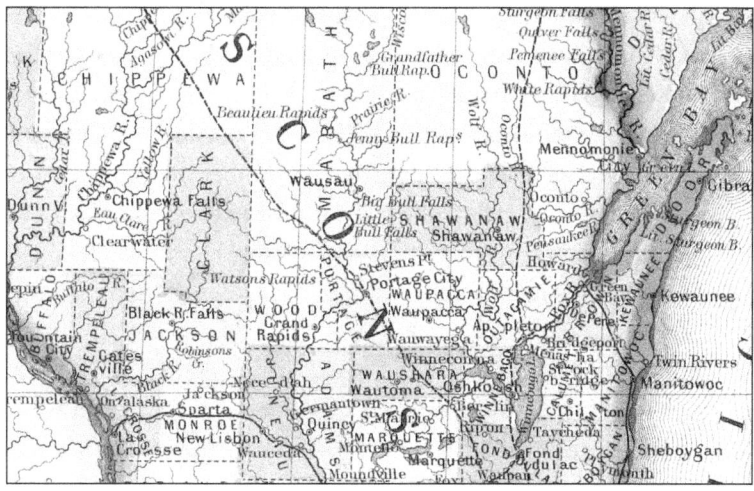

Fig. 32. S. A. Mitchell, Jr., *County Map of Michigan, and Wisconsin*, 1860, partial. Note the early names for Mosinee (Little Bull Falls), Wausau (Big Bull Falls), and Merrill (Jenny Bull Rapids), and how Marathon County extended north all the way to the state line at the time. Strieter required a full two days to travel from his home in Marquette Co. to the town of Berlin, northwest of Wausau, in Marathon Co. Today the trip takes two hours.

I made the trip there in two days every time, and back in two, 120 miles to the first preaching station. I would make it to Stevens Point the first day, the second, all the way there. If I couldn't reach it, then to Wausau and to the first preaching station bright and early the next morning. Preached there at many stations, in schoolhouses and residences, usually nine times during the week, distributed the Supper and baptized. Preached also in Stevens Point.[36]

36. Some of the churches that still exist today as a result of Strieter's ministry in rural Wausau and Stevens Point include: St. Paul Lutheran, Naugart (mailing address Athens); Grace Lutheran, village of Maine (mailing address Wausau; branch-off congregation from Immanuel mentioned below); Trinity Lutheran, town of Berlin (mailing address Merrill); Faith Lutheran, village of Maine (mailing address Merrill; the result of a combination of St. John's Lutheran, town of Scott, and Zion Lutheran, town of Maine, the cemeteries of which still remain); St. John's Lutheran, town of Hamburg (mailing address Merrill); St. Peter Lutheran, Little Chicago (mailing address Marathon); and St. Paul Lutheran, Stevens

One time I received a very fine letter in which I was asked if I would also preach to them sometime. I said I would and set a time. On the appointed day a person comes on foot and gives the impression that he is the writer—a man, single, in his thirties or so. He absolutely refused to eat with us. I hitch up and bid him have a seat, but he won't. He goes along in front of me for fifteen miles or so. How often I halted and urged him to have a seat, but no sir.

We headed towards Portage, to the right. Finally we go past a lake on an elevation. Down there in the valley stands the residence.[37] His brother, older, a widower, approaches me and calls out, "Welcome, sir, you who are blessed by the Lord" [cf. Gen. 24:31]. I get down and go into the house. The runner makes a good meal, and now we head into a neighboring house for church. After church I ask if I should come back, but the runner says that he will write again. They must not have been pleased with me.

When they returned home my escort has to check on his fires on his land that had to be cleared. In the meantime the older brother opens up a large trunk and shows me his brother's books and pamphlets and periodicals—Latin, Greek, etc., periodicals from Germany by Rudelbach,[38] etc.—and tells me that his brother is very learned and that he learns everything on his own. But he forbade me from saying anything to his brother. He said about himself that he had to marry again, but an inner voice was telling him it had to be a young woman. They turned to the Iowans,[39] as I learned later.

Many of my Injunlanders moved to Fall Creek, in the vicinity of Eau Claire. They wrote to me to come to them too. Went there frequently.[40] Had to go twenty-five to thirty miles or so to Pardeeville,[41] then on the railroad to Tomah, then another ninety miles by stagecoach.

Now something about:

Point. There used to be an Immanuel Lutheran, town of Maine, in the unincorporated community of Taegesville; see Fig. 60. There also used to be a Dreieinigkeit (Trinity) Lutheran, town of Berlin, about two miles east of Little Chicago, whose cemetery, now called Friedenshain, remains. A red granite monument across from St. Paul, Naugart, just over one mile south of County Road F on Berlin Lane, commemorates the Pomeranian immigrants who settled the area.

37. The printer misprinted "schoolhouse."

38. Andreas Gottlob Rudelbach (1792–1862) was a Dano-German theologian who edited, among other things, the *Zeitschrift für die gesammte lutherische Theologie und Kirche* (Periodical for the Collective Lutheran Church and Its Theology) (1839ff).

39. That is, the Iowa Synod, which had been founded in 1854. In 1930 it merged with the Ohio Synod and the Buffalo Synod to form what is now called the "Old" American Lutheran Church. In 1960 another merger produced the "New" American Lutheran Church, which in 1988 merged with two other church bodies to become the present-day Evangelical Lutheran Church in America (ELCA).

40. Today this is St. John's Lutheran on County Road JJ south of Fall Creek. Strieter will say more about this group later.

41. Strieter spelled it Parteville.

WISCONSIN

Hardships and Happenings[42]

Whenever it worked out, I would also take my wife along. Yes, we even did some fishing. We would make three seats on the buggy and the wife, the five children,[43] the schoolmaster, and L. would climb in and we'd head for the milldam, towards Harrisville. There we'd mostly catch a nice mess of black bass.[44] What a thrill that was!

One winter we also had a bad cold spell. It was Christmas and the Supper was supposed to be held at Tagatz's. My administrator B.[45] comes with his face all wrapped up: "Are we still going?"

"Yes."

"There won't be any church though."

He and my schoolmaster R[öske] head out.[46] I hitch up, Mama and L. climb in the sled and take my effects in their lap. They sat in the box and I throw the buffalo blanket over them, get in, and away we go. The horse is running at a terrific clip. Before the schoolhouse I have to make a turn and I knock the sled over.[47] My wife gets back in the sled, and I get the buffalo over her. L. runs ahead fifty steps or so to the schoolhouse and already has white blotches on both cheeks as big as a dollar. B. tells her that; she gets some snow to draw the frost back out. They had a fire going in the stove and had moved the table over by it. The wife sets my effects on the table; I drive to T[agatz's] to nail my sled box back down. Even when I get back, my wine in the bottle still looks like chopped ice. We have to return home without having church.

---

42. Leutner made "Hardships and Happenings" a separate chapter in the original book, but Strieter appears to have intended it as a subsection within the Wisconsin chapter.

43. See Appendix II, nos. 1–6.

44. If the fishing back then was the same as today, these were largemouth bass.

45. This could be Julius Breitenfeld.

46. Based on the information Strieter provides here and on nn. 30–32, it appears that this cold spell happened in late 1863 or early 1864.

47. This accident seems to have taken place at what is today the corner of 15th Drive and Eagle Road (today State Road 22 basically runs right through that intersection), as Strieter was attempting to turn left (east) onto Eagle Road. This confirms that there was once a schoolhouse about fifty steps east of this intersection. (See n. 10.)

Fig. 33. Site of Pastor Strieter's accident in the town of Crystal Lake, Marquette Co., Wis., 2016, photo. Note the sharp left turn in the road, now called 15th Drive. The road it intersects with in the picture, State Road 22, did not exist back then.

For a full week we led a camp life. In the living room stood a box stove with one hole on top. On the floor above us stood the meat barrel. I go up to the schoolmaster and say, "We have to bring the meat downstairs, otherwise all of it will freeze into one clump, and we won't have any meat to eat then." I grab the top of the barrel and he grabs the bottom, but it starts to get too heavy for him. He jumps off to the side and lets the barrel crash. It rolls into the wall so hard that the house shakes. But that was our good fortune, for it had already frozen all the way through, and the collision broke everything up into pieces.

I go out with my face bundled up and fill my arm with wood, then my schoolmaster goes out with his face bundled up and makes another armful, and we stack a pile in the corner.

The well in front of the house, twelve feet deep, was frozen in. We take the pump out and lower a ladder down, chop the ice apart, and draw water with a small bowl. The water came out of the sand and was not deep, but the well never gave out. Soon we had another small hole, from which we would remove the ice chunks and draw water with a small little cup.

Fig. 34. Foundation of the old parsonage stable, 2016, photo. See p. 70, n. 9.

My stable was a log stable surrounded with straw and thatched with hay. But whenever I came into the stable, my horse, a dark chestnut, and my brown cow were snow-white, and I would wipe the frost off again. My hens also roosted in the corner of that stable. They would not get down, and I had to hold their feed in front of them, their water too. I held water in front of the livestock in the stable, but they didn't want any. For several days they drank nothing. Then I went down to the Mecan and chopped the ice up. I chopped a hole as deep as the axe-handle was long. Finally the axe broke through and the water shot up as high as our house. My schoolmaster and my boy[48] brought the livestock, but they didn't get them there. The horse yanked himself free from the schoolmaster's hand and went home, and the cow followed after.

Since the stove had only one hole, L. boiled potatoes on it. We had a hole under the floor where the stove stood. That's where the potatoes were, and they didn't get any frost. They were boiled, meat was roasted, then coffee was made. We would eat and L. would start all over again.

At night we brought the beds out and threw them around the stove. There we would lie down for bed, the whole herd of us. Before falling asleep I would give the command: "Whoever wakes up, stick wood in the stove." When the stove was full of coals, we scooped them into an iron kettle and dumped them outside so that there would be room for more wood.

---

48. Doubtless Friedrich, the oldest

Fig. 35. The Fierke family burial plot in the town of Newton, Marquette Co., Wis., 2019, photo. This plot, located along what is today County Road Y, is a visible reminder of the ministerial acts Strieter had to conduct as the result of tragedies. Wilhelm Fierke's thirty-eight-year-old wife Caroline and his son Gustav, just shy of twelve, were victims of a farmhouse fire on Jan. 3, 1860. Caroline died that same day, while Gustav died four days later. They were buried on the property where the fire had taken place on Jan. 6 and 9, respectively. Wilhelm remarried on June 17 that same year.

Several people froze to death.[49] A week later I drove to Buchholz's for church. A man had died, and I was supposed to give a funeral address in the house before church, and since I had to drive fourteen miles or so, I headed out early. Several times I had to stop and rub the ice off around my horse's mouth so that it could breathe. I drove through the woods. When I came into the open, the wind blasted me in the face and I suddenly get a stinging pain in my head, as though someone had stabbed an awl into me. I quickly get my head under the buffalo and start rubbing my forehead. Someone later told me, "One more sting, sir, and death would have claimed you." I felt the effects for a long time.

One time I was driving over a creek that ran very swiftly and was never frozen over otherwise, but now it was. I go in. Halfway across the ice breaks, and my horse sinks in the water up to its belly. The wheels plant themselves in the ice and the singletree breaks off. I grab the reins at the very end and let my horse through, call to it, and it stops. I get down—the ice held me—and tie my horse up and cover it up, tie the reins to the shaft, pound the ice down, and try to pull the buggy out after me, but not a chance. I go and get my horse and tie the traces to the reins and have the horse pull the buggy out. I take

---

49. See n. 46. According to Strieter's records, three people died between March 5–8, 1864, but then Strieter would be incorrect about it being Christmastime.

the halter strap, tie the singletree together, hitch the horse and off we go. But the horse ran so fast that I had my hands full controlling it.

One time I'm driving home at night and have to cross a marsh. They had cut a path through there in the fall, stuck a ditch on both sides,[50] thrown twigs in, and piled the dirt from the ditches on top. All of it was an icy plane. My horse is trotting along, unfortunately directly above the ditch, so that it was hollow beneath the horse. Suddenly it breaks through and is now situated in a hole just as large as the length and width of the horse, and its legs sink into the mire so that the ice is exactly level with the horse's back. I get down and think, "You should go over to that house and get somebody." It was forty rods or so [about 220 yards] away. I start walking and make it as far as the fence. "Wait," I thought, "you'd better not. You can't just leave the horse by itself." I go back again, grab my horse under the mouth and say, "Fanny, come." Then the horse pulls its front leg up, sets its foot on the ice, and just like that it was out of there.

One time a young man told me he would like to ride with me to the next church. He gets on. I was already using the buggy. When we came to the marsh, two miles wide or so, I asked, "How good does it look? Will it still hold?"

"Oh sure, just fine."

I say, "It'd still be best for me to drive around."

"Oh no, yesterday they were still driving hay over it. Just keep going."

I go in. It works. Every so often the horse puts its foot through, but nothing serious. We come to the far edge. There everything is a pool of water. We go in. Bump, my horse is situated in it so that the water is level with its back. I say, "Now you're going to have to get down, sir." I had shoes on. He climbs down into the water. "Undo the horse, sir. Grab it by the head and say, 'Come.'" The horse heaves itself up and works itself out. "Tie it up, sir, and come grab the buffalo and cover the horse up. Alright, now pull the buggy onto the land." He pulls, but it won't budge. "Go get the reins, sir, and tie them tightly to the buggy and take the reins over your shoulder." He does it and now starts pulling like an ox. Bump, there he lies, prostrate in the water. I didn't dare laugh, but very secretly thought, "Serves you right. Why did you lure me in here?" He gets up and pulls again and thankfully[51] gets the buggy onto the land. We hitch the horse and off we go, but now it ran. My young man got down by the church. Where he went to, I don't know.

One time my wife and I were driving home from Berlin and also had to cross a marsh. We come to water; my horse goes in up to its waist. Two young men, one bigger and one smaller, came along with fishing poles and I ask them to help. They

---

50. In typesetting, the printer inadvertently skipped almost a whole line in Strieter's manuscript, so that in the book this sentence began: "In the fall they had stuck a ditch there."

51. Strieter originally had: "actually."

did. We unhitched the horse and all three of us pulled Mama across and continued on our way.

I also want to say something about my horse:

As soon as I arrived in Injunland, I bought my Charley from a Catholic for sixty dollars. Since I had no money though, the dear Buchholz put up security until I could pay. The brute was very nasty though. The moment he was hitched up he would want to take off, and Mama and the maid would have to hold him, one on each side, until I was in the buggy. As soon as they let go, away he went. If I restrained him, then he would immediately rear up. If I let him run, then he would run for all he was worth for two miles or so. He also proved his nastiness by darting to the side at every stone or stump, and right after that he would take off blindly—it could be in any direction—and would do so as quick as lighting.

He soon had to pay for his nastiness, or rather I did, for he got the heaves on me and began to limp with his front leg. Now he behaved; I could let him stand wherever I wanted without tying him up. But a lame horse would not suit me.

I drove to Big Bull. There I turned in at an innkeeper's place,[52] later too. The gentleman was uncommonly friendly towards me, never would take any pay from me, and I always had to eat with him at the family table. I drove to Wausau and from there out into the bush. I stopped at the first farmer's place and held church.[53] That night it rained heavily, and now my buggy was finished. The man took it apart, loaded it onto his wagon, drove it back to Wausau, put it back together, and I left.

When I come back to my innkeeper in Stevens Point, whose name was Avery,[54] I complain to him about my trouble with my lame horse. He says, "I think I can help you," and leads me into his stable and shows me a black mare, supposedly eight years old, strongly built. He says, "Let's try harnessing her to your buggy." We get on and drive

---

52. Strieter left on Monday, Oct. 1, 1860, stayed in Stevens Point that night, and stayed in Wausau the night of Oct. 2. See next n.

53. Strieter held church for the first time in the Wausau area on Wednesday, Oct. 3. He also baptized eight children that day. The farmer appears to have been Carl Kufahl, who lived on the east side of what is today North 72nd Avenue, almost half a mile north of the intersection with County Road A, though he may have had a temporary log house or shanty closer to the intersection at the time. He later donated some of his property for the site of Immanuel Lutheran Church (see Fig. 60). See Appendix XI for some of the reminiscences Strieter shared six years after penning this autobiography, when he returned to the Wausau area in 1910 for a fiftieth anniversary celebration.

54. In his manuscript, Strieter spelled it Evreÿ here, then Evrÿ and Evry later. Leutner corrected it to Everey here and Everay later. The printer consistently printed Everay. However, Strieter appears to be referring to the Avery House. "During the Civil war the great hotel was the Avery House, upon the site of which the Mansion House was afterward erected. It changed hands in May, 1863, Mr. Avery retiring and George A. Spurr assuming control" (*A Standard History of Portage County Wisconsin*, vol. 1 [Chicago and New York: The Lewis Publishing Company, 1919], 156). An 1876 plat map of Portage County also shows a W. Avery and a J. N. Avery owning land just west of Stevens Point, which fits Strieter's later description of him as having a farm outside of town. The Avery House was located just north of the town square, on the southeast corner of N. Second and Brown Streets.

around in the city. "She supposedly balks," he says. But the animal travels as nicely as can be. "Alright," says my innkeeper, "continue on your way now. If she goes, then you're taken care of; if she doesn't, then bring her back and I'll make everything right."

I take off. My horse travels fine. Midday arrives. I drive over to the shade of a nearby leafy tree and give my Kate oats in the pail that I had with me. In a few minutes she has the half pailful gone. I put the bridle on and take my seat, but my horse won't take one step. I get down and grab it at the head and pull it along after me. Not far ahead of me lies a village—I believe it was called Plainfield. I think, "You should leave the buggy there, ride back and get your lame Charley back."

I arrive at the lodging yard, take the harness off, put the buffalo on the horse's back and start to ride back. "Wait," I thought, "this simply won't work. You made arrangements with M. T.[55] to bring you to Ripon tonight. You're going to the synod convention in St. Louis."[56] I turn around, put the harness back on, hitch up, and start pulling my Kate along after me again. I come to a small grove, take my seat in the buggy again, hang my head, and consider the miserable predicament I'm in. Kate hangs her head too and goes to sleep. I quietly grab my whip, lash her a good one under the belly and yell, "Gid up!"[57] She lurches forward, runs like mad, and I head home on the run.

My T. is already there. I tell my wife about my trade and tell her that she should now drive with the horse every day; perhaps we'd get it in shape. I eat, take my traveling bag, and take off for Ripon, thirty miles. There I get on the train cars for St. Louis. My wife writes, "I drive every day. Your horse travels fine." I come home. Then she tells me, "M. T. came and wanted to go somewhere with Kate. I let him have her, then she balked. He goes in front of her and tries to hit her. Then she goes off on him, tears his coat up and tries to attack him with her front feet so that he has to crawl underneath a bush[58] for protection, and now she won't go for me any more either."

I hitch her back up, but nope, she won't budge. I put the saddle on and ride to Stevens Point. There I hear that Avery is outside of town on his farm. I go and find him and tell him what the deal is. He shows me a pony, white, somewhat yellowish, with black mane and black tail, a fat fellow. Rocky is his name. He says, "He goes, and is a fine riding horse. Give me twenty dollars for him." He writes a bill with a pencil; I sign and get up on Rocky and take off.

Oh, how fine he gallops, how thrilled I am, how I thank God for my little horse. Now I was taken care of. Now I can drive and ride, and my wife and children are delighted with the handsome and nice Rocky. I now do a lot of riding and read my Luther on my Rocky. When he gallops, it's like I'm sitting in a rocking chair.

---

55. This could be Martin Tagatz.
56. The 1860 synod convention in St. Louis was held from Wed., Oct. 10, to Sat., Oct. 20.
57. Strieter spelled this *Girab* (pronounced like "gear up").
58. The book mistakenly printed *Tisch* (table) for *Busch*.

It was winter, I'm riding to Big Bull, it starts to snow and keeps on snowing and snowing. The snow gets deeper and deeper. I can't ride fast any more, stay overnight halfway to Stevens Point.[59] Gets terribly cold. I'm lying in the bed and freezing, finally get up, go out, open a door and, on a hope and a prayer, call out in English, "Landlord!"

"Hey" is the answer I get. I ask him to get up. He comes.

"I have to go."

He accompanies me out to the stable, puts the saddle on. I pay and take off; it was two o'clock. But now how cold it is under the bright sky and in the air. At seven I arrive at my Avery, who tries to take off my shawl, but shawl and beard are one icy clump there. I first have to hold my head by the stove for a while until it thaws. I eat and get back on my pony to go to Big Bull. Again cannot ride hard; the snow is too deep and too loose. At eight in the evening I finally arrive in Wausau. I head for the inn and have my little horse brought into the stable. "Let me take care of the pony," says the hostler.

I say, "No, let me take care of the pony," have him make a straw-bed for him, stick some hay in, give him water—he wasn't warm—and four quarts of oats. That done, we now go into the house. I let them give me something to eat, then go to bed.

Bright and early I get on my horse and head out into the bush and still make it on time for church, according to the arrangements I had made.[60]

Another time I take the sled.[61] The K[ohnke] neighborlady also sends a sackful of buckwheat groats with me to give her mother, and I had my box with books that I always brought along—hymnals, Bibles, postils, catechisms, prayer books, Bible histories—and a basket with my Communion equipment and a traveling bag with my robe [*Chorrock*]. I preach and hold the Supper here and there. Have to drive a long stretch through the beautiful virgin forest. There lies a tree stem across the path. Four feet off the ground it had broken off and is lying on the stump and, on the opposite side, on its branches, three feet high or so off the ground. I cannot go around; there is thick underbrush both left and right. I undo my Rocky from the sled and draw him around to the other side and cover him up and now work at getting my sled onto the stem. It was heavy, and I have to exert myself tremendously. Finally I have it on top, but what now? I have no other choice but to let it go. Down it slides, but somewhat crooked. I crawl through underneath and try to lift the shaft up, but oh boy, it must have gotten stuck under something there. I cannot get it up and have to push my sled backwards onto the tree again so that I can get the shaft loose. Finally. I hitch my pony, but now I had shoes on—my feet were wrapped

---

59. I.e., in Plainfield. He appears to have stayed there on Monday night, Nov. 26, 1860.

60. Namely, on Wed., Nov. 28. He baptized one baby on Thurs., three on Fri., three on Sun., and three on Tues..

61. He departed on this third and final mission trip to Wausau on Mon., Jan. 14, 1861. He baptized three children that evening in Stevens Point. He stayed overnight in Wausau on Tues., and arrived at his destination on Wed. morning, Jan. 16. He baptized two children that day, two on Thurs., four on Sat., and one on Tues.

in a wool cloth and I had fur shoes over that. The snow gets into my shoes, melts, and it's getting cold now, since night was falling.

I hitch my horse and continue on to my destination. I arrive, my horse is taken off my hands, and I go inside. Sit down in front of the stove and try to take off my shoes and also my stockings, to rub my cold feet and warm them up. But the stockings are frozen tight to the skin, and I first have to stick my feet in the stove to thaw the ice.

Soon I went to bed. I was lying for a while when I get a bed partner. He was lying for a while, then he called out, "Yes, yes, Father Luther said so." After a short pause: "Yes, yes, Father Luther said so." Again after a while: "Yes, yes, Father Luther said so."

I say, "What exactly did Father Luther say?"

He doesn't say a word.

When I woke up in the morning, my bed partner was gone. I ask my hostess what sort of man that was. Then she told me that he was a follower of Grabau.[62] He had come here with a bundle of money, had bought himself a bunch of land and had used his money to help others get land. He said that we were not the true Lutheran Church; he and his adherents were. Those he had tied to his purse strings stuck with him and he would read to them from Luther and act as their pastor.

We now drove through the bush over to the gardener, which is what he had been in Germany, and held church in his house. After church I say to the people, "Keep an eye on your pigs; there is a bear in the area. Back there in the woods I saw his tracks."

When I came back,[63] they told me that scarcely had I left when one day the sun had shone nice and bright and after that it had frozen again. Then the snow had frozen hard, and way up there stood a beech tree that had still had nuts that now fell down. Then they had lured the mother pig over there to glean the beechnuts. Pretty soon the pig had started squealing terribly, and the bear was sitting by it and wolfing down its flesh from its living body. The father had loaded the old shotgun, and since he didn't have any shot, put stones in. The boy grabbed the axe and the father the gun and off they went to the bear.

When they got close to him, he growled, and the father had aimed and lowered the gun again. The son yelled, "Father, shoot already!"

But the father said, "Yeah, if I don't hit him right, then he'll go off on us."

The son said, "I've got the axe here; I'll chop his head."

The father aimed again and lowered the weapon again.

---

62. Johannes Andreas August Grabau (1804–1879) was imprisoned in Erfurt in 1837 for opposing the Prussian Union (union of Lutheran and Reformed Churches in Prussia). With the help of friends he escaped and went to Berlin, where he continued his ministry secretly. He was arrested and imprisoned again in 1838. He was permitted to emigrate in 1839 and did so with about one thousand other Prussians. A small group stayed in Albany, while Grabau and the majority settled in Buffalo, where he served as a pastor for nearly forty years. In 1845, he helped organize what came to be called the Buffalo Synod, a distant ancestor of today's ELCA. Grabau butted heads with the Missouri Synod over his extreme views on ordination and the authority of the ministry, among other things.

63. Most likely for J. J. Hoffmann's installation on Sun., Aug. 25, 1861.

Then the boy said, "Father, give me the weapon. I'll shoot," and the bear lay down on his side. Shot him in the ear. They brought their pig home on the hand-sled and laid it in front of the stove and tended to it. Its whole side had already been eaten away down to the ribs. But after recuperating, it made it back on its feet. They sold the bear's hide, oil, and meat and made, if I'm not mistaken, sixteen dollars.

When the story came to an end, the father exclaimed, "If only another bear would come!"

I drove home.[64] It was cold. Between Stevens Point and Wautoma I come to a place where I had previously turned left. I can see just fine how high the snow is, but think that the pathway still must be firm, for we would often go on trips six feet high above ground. The freshly fallen snow would always get trampled down firm again. But look, my pony sinks so deep into the snow that I can only still see his head and tail. I undo the horse, pull the sled back, and now trample around in the snow so that my horse can get some air, and I bring it out of there and hitch it back up. At this point a man comes who tells me that I had to turn left further down.

I make it through the woods back onto the open prairie. Then I come to two sleds loaded down with sacks. On the front sled were three yoke of oxen, on the back sled two yoke. The back sled driver lets his sled stand, comes to the front sled, and now one man beats on the oxen on this side, the other on the other side, until they have dragged the sled forward several rods or so [about twenty to thirty yards]. Then they go and get the back sled that far in the same manner. I'm finally able to pass the sleds and I come to my inn[65] and think, "You should stay overnight."

I have my little horse unharnessed and go inside. After a while two Jews come, one younger and one older, with a sled full of pelts which they had obtained from the Indians by trade. When they had warmed up and were about to leave, I ask where they were still planning on getting to tonight. "To Berlin," was the answer.

To Berlin—that was at least another thirty to forty miles. Why, if they can do that, you can still make it home too.

I have my little horse hitched back up and I follow the Jews. The snow was dug out on the right and thus we could sled through along the fence and snowbank. All at once my Jews disappeared. Then I reach the corner. The snow was dug out across the path to the other side and was so high that I couldn't see the Jews any more when they turned the bend. Further along it bends back to the right, with the fence on the left and the snowbank on the right.

Then, all at once: Stop. There stood my Jews and I behind them, with a sled loaded with sacks in front of us that wants to come this way. Right away a troop of oxen comes, driven by two men, who also want to go up the way we were going. After a brief discussion, it was decided: "The big ox there in front must create a pathway." The ox now gets some beatings and he burrows through the snow. When

---

64. Strieter is resuming his previous story, before the incident with the bear and the pig.
65. The inn in Plainfield he has already mentioned twice

he makes it forward a few feet or so, then he is given a rest again, then they lay into him again, until he is finally around the sled in front of us. The others now had it easier. Once the oxen were gone, the driver in front of us also now tries to get out of the way for us, since we couldn't; we had a snowbank six to eight feet high on the right. But his grays won't draw one trace tight. He had to unload all of his sacks and they then drew the empty sled around. Now there is a clear pathway and my Jews now try to get going, but now one of their horses won't budge. They had a big old yellow horse on the right, and a young little animal on the left, four years old or so, who won't budge. They now lash at the tired little animal mercilessly. The younger man goes and stands in front and beats him between the ears with the thick end of the whip handle. But the animal takes the beating and doesn't move a muscle. I ask them to please not beat the animal like that. They should grab the big horse by the bridle and talk to him nicely to get him to draw the sled tight first. They did that and it worked. Away they go now, with me following along.

In Wautoma they turn left to go to Berlin, and I turn right to go to my homestead. I still had twelve miles. For a stretch it was going well, for I had a pathway, but now I had to leave the pathway and turn left. The snow is deep there. My Rocky is almost knee-deep in the snow. It's not long before I have no idea where I am any more. I'm freezing terribly, throw the reins over my head and wrap myself in the buffalo. It is getting colder and colder. I think, "This night you will freeze to death." I start praying that our dear God would please take my poor soul to himself if my final hour had arrived. Then the thought of the wife with her four little children occurs to me. "No," I said to our dear God, "you cannot let me freeze to death. Bring me home alive to my family once more." Sleep wants to overpower me. But I keep moving my arms and legs over and over and keep praying unceasingly to my God to please have mercy on me.

All at once I come upon a track and also see a house on the left. I look at it and recognize it; it's the Borsack schoolhouse.[66] I say, "Gid up, Rocky!" and in fifteen minutes I am in my yard. I go inside. My wife gets out of her warm nest and lies down with the children, and I get in. She throws everything we have on me, also gives me something warm to drink, but I am freezing so badly that my teeth are chattering. It was three o'clock in the morning. I had been sitting on the sled and had eaten nothing from seven o'clock in the morning to three o'clock in the morning.

I finally fall asleep and don't wake up until around ten and now I want to go and get my mail, which we would get three times a week. I had three miles to travel and think, "The poor Rocky is so tired; just go on foot." But that won't work. The snow is so deep and so loose that I can't make any headway. Then I think, "Go and get Rocky and put the saddle on and ride slowly."

---

66. The Borsack schoolhouse stood on what is today the northern side of the intersection of County Road E with State Road 22, three quarters of a mile north of the present-day St. John's Lutheran Church in Budsin and one and a half miles from Strieter's house. Later in the chapter he identifies "W[ilhel]m Borsack," a Methodist, as his neighbor (p. 120).

I go and get my Rocky and retrieve my mail items, let my little horse in through the small gate and have the wooden nail in my hand that gets pegged in front. My Rocky doesn't quite go through far enough. I give him just a few taps in the rear and say, "Rocky, a little farther." He whinnies and turns right—two acres were fenced in—down along the fence, then up along it over there, and three times or so around the yard going along the fence, so that the snow and the halter strap were flying in the air. Oh, was I glad to see that.

I wrote to Professor Crämer for an assistant. He replied that he was sending me J. J. Hoffmann. He said that he was still young and unsteady [*leicht angelegt*]; he was not yet able to be independent. He needed to work under me for at least another year yet, and I was supposed to keep a good eye on him.

Fig. 36. J. J. Hoffmann, unknown year, photo. Image courtesy of St. Paul Lutheran-Naugart, Athens, Wis.

Hoffmann came. An impressive, youthful person, very gifted. I really liked him. But soon noticed that he was a weak character. His favorite was idling away the time in the kitchen with the wife and the maid. I had him preach at Tagatz's and told the congregation that this was my assistant.[67] We would do the work together. He would work especially in Big Bull, but would also preach here, and I would go

---

67. See Appendix IV, no. 5.

back up to Big Bull from time to time. Were they quite alright with that? They gave a unanimous "Yes."

I now bought Fanny, a five-year-old dark chestnut, a beautiful animal, for 120 dollars, a high price at the time and I had to pay in gold[68] coin. But I obtained it on a one-year loan, and with zero interest. I now gave Hoffmann my good Rocky for eighty dollars, the price he cost me,[69] also on a loan without interest, and for as long as it took him to get the money.[70] I did that because Fanny was no riding horse, but was a fine runner in the buggy, easily trotting twelve miles an hour.

I now say to Hoffmann that he should go up to Big Bull and should stay fourteen days and come back home. He went and came back after fourteen days. I had him preach again at Schmidt's. After the sermon he asked me on the way home how I had liked his sermon. On the previous Friday I had already given him Luther to study. But he soon set the book aside and went to find my wife and conversed with her, and not until Saturday evening did he jot a little bit down. I told him in answer to his question: "To be blunt, I have no idea what you said. Hoffmann, you're going to turn into a miserable babbler this way. Why don't you leave your studies of Greek and French"—since he had told me he was pursuing those—"and read Luther, so that you can preach something decent?"

He hung his head.

He went back to Big Bull, soon comes back, and said that he had had them call him as an independent pastor.[71] I ask him how he could dare do that behind my

---

68. "or silver" was crossed out in lead and then in ink.

69. Strieter had traded a sixty-dollar horse for Rocky, plus paid another twenty dollars.

70. It appears that it took Hoffmann well over two years to pay off his eighty-dollar loan from Strieter. From the "Receipts and Thanks [*Quittung und Dank*]" section of the Sept. 15, 1863 issue of *Der Lutheraner*: "I hereby certify that I have, through Mr. Dr. Sihler's intervention, received $25.00 from his congregation in Fort Wayne for the full covering of the debts incurred for my previous and current horse. At the same time I most sincerely thank that dear congregation and wish her rich blessings from our profoundly benevolent God, who has also attested his benevolence to me precisely through this unexpected gift. Wausau, Aug. 26, 1863. J. Jacob Hoffmann."

71. A document has been preserved, titled "Formation of the Congregation in the Town of Berlin, Marathon County, Wisconsin," apparently authored by the August Schmidt mentioned later in this footnote. It reads in part:

After the Lutherans in the vicinity of Wausau had asked Mr. Pastor J. Strieter from the towns of Newton, Christal [*sic*] Lake, and Shields, Marquette County, Wisconsin, to visit them and he had refreshed them with the word of God three times, Pastor Hoffmann, formerly a student at the seminary in Fort Wayne, Indiana, and assistant pastor of the aforementioned congregations, came to these people, and after he traveled through the area, a meeting for the purpose of founding a congregation was held on March 11, 1861, the proceedings of which are inserted here:

Proceedings of the congregational meeting for the towns of Berlin and Stettin, Marathon County, Wisconsin, assembled in the district schoolhouse near Mr. Heinrich Beilke on March 11, 1861.

The meeting was opened by Mr. Pastor Hoffmann with prayer. Mr. Friedrich Krentz was elected president, and Mr. August Schmidt was elected secretary. — After Mr. Pastor

back. Didn't he know that the congregation belonged to me? I also now told him what Crämer had written me. He apologized to me. I now had to put a good face on the bad affair and install him.[72] The man also came to a sad end. My dear old Strasen,[73] long time president of the Wisconsin District of the Synod of Missouri, Ohio, and Other States, can sing a sad song about Hoffmann. So can the dear Dr. Schwan, president of the synod at large at the time.[74]

And now some more about the hardships.

One time I was driving across a marsh, alongside the road, because the road was completely impassable. Came to the end where there was standing water, and I note, "There you will get stuck." There was a pile of fence rails lying there which I went and brought over, then lay one next to the other and build a bridge, pull the horse onto it, keep taking out the ones in back and putting them down in front again, kept on doing that until I reached firm ground. But now I arrived too late. The people were gone.

One time I was driving to Berlin for preaching and I wanted to take a box of books home with me from the depot. The railroad went from Ripon to Berlin. Got up very early, for I was in a hurry to get home, for I was almost always in a hurry. It's not yet day. The valley below, where the depot was located, was filled with fog, but I saw light through the window in the depot. I was heading for that; I could not see the path. All at once I jerked forward and then just as quickly backward again, so that I thought the evil foe was taking me on. I have to wait once I'm there. The man wasn't there yet. Day breaks and I think, "You should at least go see what the deal was there." Look here, there was a hole dug—someone was presumably looking for sand—six to eight feet or so long, three feet or so wide and just as deep. I had driven over that. I looked at it and wondered just how the horse got across that. It did not see the pit and plunged right in. But my Fanny was nimble.

One time Pastor Brandt, a Norwegian, came to me and wanted to get across to his ancillary congregation by Puckaway Lake—a farmer had brought him from another ancillary congregation—and he asked me for Communion wine and if I could take him there. We were driving there. On the shore of the lake stood a little

---

Hoffmann was given an explanation of his compensation . . . he was unanimously called by the following persons, who hereby organized themselves as an evangelical Lutheran congregation, to conduct the ministry among them according to the confessional writings of the Lutheran Church.

This is followed by the names of fifty-eight adult males, not including the secretary himself, for a total of fifty-nine. The location of the district schoolhouse mentioned here (a log building at the time) is today occupied by an empty, unused brick schoolhouse on the southeast corner of Naugart Drive and Berlin Lane. See also Fig. 57.

72. See Appendix IV, no. 6.

73. Strieter spelled it Strassen. Karl (or Carl) Johannes August Strasen (1827–1909) was a pastor in Watertown, Wisconsin. He also served as president of the Northwestern District from 1875–1880 and of the Wisconsin District from 1880–1885.

74. See Appendix VIII. H. C. Schwan was president of the Missouri Synod from 1878–1899.

house. Out came a friendly man and greeted me by name. I asked him if he knew me. He said, "I am in your church as often as you preach at Buchholz's, sir." It must have been six miles away or so.

I say, "So you can understand me, sir?"

He says, "Not much at first, but soon more, and now, sir, I understand every word you say."

The two of us pastors, the man, his wife, and several little children take our seats in a skiff, for I wanted to hear the sermon, and we go across the lake. In the distance at the bottom of the hill was a house where church was to be held. My dear Brandt now had announcement first, then confession, then began to preach. But pretty soon my watch told me, "You have to go," for I had seventeen to eighteen miles or so. I stand up and leave. My dear Brandt follows me out and bids me adieu, but sends a young man with me who's supposed to show me to a rowboat. He showed me to a dinky little rowboat with two oars. I get in and go at it, towards the house in the distance. Soon I notice that the thing is definitely leaking. There's the water coming in, and at a pretty good rate too. I started rowing away for all I was worth. The water is rising. I already have to set my feet up against a crossboard, so that I don't fill my shoes. I can't bail the water; I don't know if there's a container available. Even if there is, I still don't dare let the oars rest, for the wind was strong and blowing sideways; it would have driven me up to the upper end and the lake was fairly long. So I had to work. My little boat is already over half-full of water. I started getting anxious. I'm sweating; my hands ache. Finally I am on the shore, but completely wiped out with my hands full of calluses.

During the winter I was driving across that lake one time with Fanny, over the ice. The lake is not deep and is very springy; the Fox River flows through it lengthwise.[75] I'm moving right along. I want to get to Fairwater, and it's much closer going from Buchholz's than going around by Princeton. There, not far from me, the ice bows up and the water spurts into the air. A little farther, the same thing on the other side. It's getting worse and worse. I have to keep dodging the spurting places left and right. My Fanny also notices the fun and sweeps away across the ice like a fox. I am getting anxious and ask the good Lord to please not let me break through. I make it across.

Something about hardships pertaining to Fall Creek. I go up there one time, drive to Montello, twelve miles. (I also had twelve miles to Princeton, and twelve to Wautoma. Four hundred steps or so off of the Mecan, to the west, was my house.) I take the wife along so that she can take the horse back home. From Montello I take the stagecoach to Pardeeville, from there to Tomah on the railroad. Then it was ninety or so miles to Eau Claire on the stagecoach. Before it gets to Eau Claire, I get off and head off to the right on foot to Fall Creek to my people, who with few exceptions had been my church attendees [*Kirchkinder*] in Injunland.

75. Puckaway Lake is only five feet deep at its deepest point.

How happy they were when I stepped into their midst in front of the schoolhouse. Man and woman embraced my neck and kissed me. Oh, with what pleasure I preached to them![76]

On the way home, while riding on the stagecoach day and night, the driver, who had apparently fallen asleep, lost his way and drove into the bushes. He halts and shouts that we men should get out and should look for the road because he didn't know where he was. There were two other men besides me in the box, and several ladies. We get out. The one man looks around and shouts, "Here is the path!" But the coach was situated on a slope. He has to turn around, so we three position ourselves on a ledge, grab on top, and lean backwards to keep the coach balanced so that it doesn't tip over, and we make it back on the road.

I had written my wife to pick me up in Montello, but she doesn't get the letter; when I arrive in Montello, there's not a woman there. What now? I have no other choice but to walk twelve miles. I was not at all accustomed to walking; I was always on the horse or on the buggy. I don't get very far before my feet are aching and the soles of my feet are burning like the blazes. I sit down, take shoes and stockings off, and try walking barefoot, but that wouldn't work at all. The sand was so hot, and every little stone was irritating. I put my stockings back on and now walk home in stockings, ten miles or so.

---

76. Strieter appears to have departed for his first trip to Fall Creek on or around Mon., Nov. 12, 1860, since he recorded two baptisms he performed in "Eau Clair" on Nov. 14, 1860. According to *Declaring God's Glory: Yesterday, Today and Tomorrow* (Aug. 17, 2014), the commemorative book celebrating the one hundred and fiftieth anniversary of St. John Lutheran Church in Fall Creek, "it was Wilhelm Stelter who convinced Strieter to make the trip to the Fall Creek Valley." This is consistent with Strieter's records, since Strieter calls him "my Stelter" and "a very dear Christian" in the previous chapter, and since he includes Wilhelm Stelter as a witness to the first of the just-mentioned baptisms, that of Florendine Caroline Stubbe. *Declaring God's Glory* also claims that since "there was no local pastor" in 1863, Strieter "was called and twice made the 200-mile trip to conduct church services, baptize children and perform marriages" there. But this is highly unlikely, since a) Strieter's records do not include any 1863 visits to Fall Creek, and b) Candidate Theodor Gustav Adolph Krumsieg was ordained and installed as the congregation's first regular pastor on Sept. 28, 1862, and was installed at his next parish in Fond du Lac County on Dec. 13, 1863. Even allowing for time to move from Eau Claire County to Fond du Lac County and for a delay in making arrangements to have a pastor install him in his new parish, it does not seem likely that Strieter would have had time to arrange and make two 200-mile trips to Fall Creek in the time available between Krumsieg's departure and the end of the year in 1863. c) Fall Creek must have obtained a pastor not long after Krumsieg's departure, since Strieter goes on to talk about another trip there in early April 1864 to conduct an investigation into the accusations against their pastor, a trip for which there *is* evidence in his records. That means that there had to be time for the new pastor to get settled in Fall Creek and for the relationship between him and his new congregation to deteriorate. Finally, d) *Declaring God's Glory* speaks of two trips Strieter made, and there is evidence of two trips in his records—one in 1860 and one in 1864, but none in 1863. The only discrepancy between what he shares here and his records is that he goes on to mention how "the sand was so hot" against his bare feet on the final leg of his return trip, so that he finished the trip in stocking feet, which hardly seems possible in a Wisconsin November. Perhaps the conclusion of this trip got jumbled with another one in his memory, or perhaps it was an abnormally warm November day.

Another time I was up there we rode to Black River Falls on the stagecoach.[77] There we were told that the stage could not go any farther because of the bad roads. The four horses were hitched to a lumber wagon, three thin boards laid across the box. On the front board the driver took his seat. On the second board a man and a woman, each with a child in his or her lap; the boy was bigger and the girl was smaller. On the back board, I and a short young lady. Others wanted to come too, but we were told, "The horses can't pull that much." It was just starting to get dark when we took off.[78]

We come to a frightful hill. The two of us men have to get down. The horses cannot pull us all. The driver, the two ladies, and the little children stay up. The ground was loose, yellow sand. The horses run in a gallop as best they can, ten steps or so, catch their breath again, and then another burst like that, until they are on top. We get back on and away we go.

Wasn't all that long before the little lady next to me gets sleepy, lays her little hands on my knee and her little head on top and drifts off. The people in front of me also fall asleep and were so careless that each one has his or her child's little head facing out. Then all at once the man's child hangs his head down over the box. I reach out between the two of them, grab it by its little robe and pull it back in. Then the wife's baby hangs its head out and I pull it back in. So it went the whole night. Having arrived at a station in the morning, we drink some coffee. Then the wife expressed her thanks that I had "watched [*gewatscht*]" their children so well.

I had been commissioned by my President Fürbringer[79] to conduct an investigation. There was a preacher there by this point.[80] I preached to a schoolhouse full of people, then the investigation got going. A number of complaints were brought forward; unfortunately they turned out to be true. The pastor asked for forgiveness, and since there were no criminal offenses, I asked the congregation to pardon him and retain him. But they didn't want to; they still thought it would be better if he left, because things were ruined for good by that point. He was relocated out west after that, and became a very good pastor there, even a visitor.[81] He has long since gone to heaven.

---

77. For this final trip, Strieter records five baptisms he performed in Fall Creek on Sunday, April 3, 1864, after baptizing the son of his neighborlady on Tues., March 29. Thus he departed on or around Wed., March 30.

78. Most likely the evening of Fri., April 1

79. Ottomar Fürbringer (1810–1892) was president of the Northern District of the Missouri Synod from 1854–1872 and from 1874–1882.

80. The preacher under investigation remains a mystery, though someone with more time and ambition could doubtless discover his identify. Even the one hundred and fiftieth anniversary book for St. John, Fall Creek, does not mention any preacher between Theodore Krumsieg and Wilhelm Julius Friedrich. The latter preached his first sermon in Fall Creek on Aug. 7, 1864, and was ordained and installed on Oct. 2.

81. A visitor is sometimes called a circuit pastor today. He was answerable to the district president and responsible for visiting the pastors in his area.

I received a slip of paper on which a bunch of places were recorded for me that I was supposed to visit and do mission work. A man promised me a riding horse. Bright and early[82] one man hitches his horses to his wagon, another brings me a horse, a big gelding, and says, "He has the heaves [*die Heafs*], but he won't keel over. Just keep riding him at a good clip, sir."

I get on my gelding. The other man takes off; I follow after. He puts them into a trot, and I put my gelding into a gallop. But right away I think, "Oh boy, oh boy, how is this going to turn out?" For he galloped so high and was throwing me into the saddle with full force. The consequences came soon enough. I get colic, and have to call to the man to stop, then take a seat in his wagon and tie the old boy to the back. The pains get worse and worse; the man finally has to drive at a crawl. I tell him to take me to an apothecary. He did so. The gentleman was in the middle of sweeping out. I tell him that I'm sick. He says, "Yeah, I can see that." He disappears into his hideout and mixes me up something proper, a half-glass full of yellow stuff. How it tasted, I don't remember anymore, but I scarcely had it down before my belly gets red-hot and my pain is gone.

I get on my gelding and head for Chippewa Falls, leave my horse on this side, and I take the ferry across the river. Over there the path goes along between the river and the hill, toward the village. There stands a little house right next to the path, and behind it, at the bottom of the hill, a new brewery with "Gerhard" on it. "He has to be German; you should stop in there."

The man was a young, friendly man; no beer belly on him. He directed me into the village. There, situated in the valley, stands a saloon in the center. I make my way there, address the bartender in German, and he answers me in German. I say who I am and why I was there. He says that he doesn't care much for church. Over there in that little house by the hill lives a cobbler, he says; I should stop in by him.

I head over. The cobbler is beating his leather. He stutters and says that yeah, a pastor had been there earlier, and the people from the country had come in to hear him preach. The preacher was supposed to eat at his place at noon, and they were going to give him twenty-five cents each time. They still owed him fifty cents, and he wanted nothing more to do with it.

During the conversation, a door opens up and a woman walks in the door and soon picks up on the discussion. She speaks fine German. "Whoa," I thought, "this is a sophisticated woman." She gives me several zingers, but gentle ones, the gist of them being how people were expected to fodder the vagabonding[83] preachers for free. I get red, stand up, and say, "Listen here, ma'am, I am an honest pastor and no lowlife." I pat my money-bag and say, "I have money. If you give me a meal, ma'am, I will pay you" [cf. 2 Thess. 3:6–12]. She turns friendly and apologizes.

---

82. On Mon., April 4
83. The printer misread *herumlaufenden* for Strieter's *herumstreichenden*.

Now they told me that there were not many in the village and there were people scattered in the country, but they could not be called together now on such short notice. "Okay, I will ride up to Yellow River and come back the day after tomorrow. Could the people be called together by then?"

Yeah, he didn't have any time at all, he said, and besides that, he didn't know anybody either. I myself could not go and do it, for I was always scheduled in advance from place to place. So I was unable to preach in Chippewa Falls.

I go back to the brewer, stay overnight at his place and ask, "What kind of a cobbler's wife is that? She did not grow up here."

"Yeah, a military officer brought her along from Germany and jilted her, and in her need she took the cobbler as a husband."

I cross the river[84] and get on my gelding and head up to Yellow River. I arrive at a settlement of Swabians, my own countrymen, turn into a house where two brothers live, who had two sisters as their wives. Each had a baby. They were in the middle of cooking sugar.[85] So in the morning the one woman would go into the bush and the other would stay with the children. In the afternoon they would switch. In the evening many people came. In the morning a nice large group assembles in the schoolhouse.[86] I announce my hymn and start singing; they sing along, very well, but somewhat slowly. I start to preach. Then a man calls out, "Mr. Parson [*Pfarrer*], a little louder; there are people here who can't hear well." So now I belt it out.

After church I warn the people not to get involved with every single wandering preacher, but to come together on Sunday, sing a hymn, and a man should read a sermon out loud. A preacher would probably be coming to Fall Creek soon and he would serve them too.

They respond, "Yeah, we thought that you were just going to stay with us, sir."

"Yeah, dear friends, that simply will not work. Just take heart and stick tightly together and hold reading service. The good Lord will not abandon you, and he will give you a preacher." They bade me a fond farewell and expressed their many thanks.

I head back to Chippewa Falls and continue on to Menomonie, but have to gallop; the fellow will only walk or gallop. Soon the inside of my legs are in a lot of pain, but what can I do? I have to keep going.

Before Menomonie I arrive at a settlement and turn in at the house of the man to whom I was directed. He asked if I was Pastor Moldehnke.[87]

"No, I am Pastor Strieter." "Great," I thought, "now you have ended up in Moldehnke's ward, the traveling preacher of the Wisconsin Synod."

---

84. On Tues., April 5
85. That is, boiling maple sap down to syrup
86. On Wed., April 6
87. Strieter spelled it Mohldehnke. See n. 90.

In the morning I go to the schoolhouse.[88] Was completely full. Before I know what's happening they start to sing, but I don't know the words and don't recognize the melody either. When they stopped, I stood up and asked if this congregation belonged to Pastor Moldehnke.

"Yes, Pastor Moldehnke has preached here before."

I say, "Then I am not permitted to preach."[89]

They say, "You are Lutheran too, sir, from what we've heard. Go ahead and give us a sermon. You are already here anyway, and we so seldom get an actual sermon."

"Alright, then I will preach, but tell Pastor Moldehnke when he comes not to look at this as if I were trying to interfere in his ministry [*Amt*]. I was directed here and did not know that he had already preached here. He should regard it as a guest sermon." They said they would deliver the message.[90]

I state my hymn, start singing, then preach. Also warn them to watch out for the fanatics, the Methodists. The wife of the Methodist preacher was even in church, as I was later informed. They took a hat collection and gave it to me.

In general I received money almost everywhere.[91] I have already wondered to myself why our traveling preachers today often have to be supported almost entirely from the fund. I never needed to apply to the fund for assistance. When I went to Big Bull, I would bring home a whole bag full of money. Indeed—ten-cent pieces, five-cent pieces, very small three-cent pieces, very large two-cent pieces, a sixpence, a shilling, rarely two shillings. I would empty my bag onto the table for my wife and she would sort it all and put each sort into a little purse and revel in her treasure.

---

88. On Thurs., April 7

89. This is the closest Strieter comes to alluding to the poor relationship between the Missouri and Wisconsin Synods at the time. (By the time he wrote his autobiography, the two were in fellowship with each other, so he doubtless omitted much more that he might have said otherwise.) The Wisconsin Synod at the time was notorious among the pastors of the Missouri Synod for interfering in their territory. See Appendix VII.

90. Pastor Eduard Moldehnke of the Wisconsin Synod made three well-documented mission trips between 1861 and 1862, but in none of these does he mention stopping or preaching near Menomonie. However, at the 1863 Wisconsin Synod convention, President Johannes Bading reported that "during the course of spring [1863], journeys were also made in Minnesota and four stations were visited. Furthermore 14 new stations were established in western Wisconsin, so that altogether 22 stations in Wisconsin and Minnesota are being served by the traveling preacher" (*WELS Historical Institute Journal* 16, no. 2 [Oct. 1998] 47). At that same convention, it was resolved to release Pastor Moldehnke from his position so that he could serve as instructor of the seminary-college to be started in Watertown. Pastor Moldehnke agreed to the new position, provided he be given three more months to wind up his traveling preacher activities, which was granted. He did not make any more preaching trips on behalf of the synod after that (though he did make one on behalf of the Minnesota Synod). President Streissguth did report at the 1866 convention that "the congregations in and near Menomonee [*sic*]" were still awaiting a pastor in vain, and that Pastor H. Kittel of La Crosse had paid them a visit at Streissguth's request "to bolster [their] declining spirit" (*ibid.* 18, no. 2 [Oct. 2000] 13).

91. Strieter digresses before returning to his mission trip in western Wisconsin and Minnesota.

One time I had to ride way out of the way and baptize three children for a man. When I was finished, he counted thirty-seven cents into my hand. I say, "Certainly this is all the money you have, sir?"

"Yes."

"Okay, then I will give it back to you and add that much more."

He started to cry: "Ach, it is meant to be a thank offering that my children are now baptized, and you won't accept it, sir?"

"Okay, if it is meant to be a thank offering, I will take it."

One time a woman came. "Mr. Pastor, I am a widow and don't have any money, but would really like to give you something. Here is a small sack of nuts; please take them along for your children."

My people in the Injunland gave me two hundred dollars and rye for bread and some for the horse, some wheat too.

I now hurried from Menomonie to Durand, across the river on the ferry, up the hill, into a saloon. "Are you German, sir?"

"Yes indeed."

I say who I am and why I was there.

He says, "Yeah, there would no doubt be people here, but where can we assemble?"

I say, "There's room enough right here."

He says, "You want to preach in the saloon, sir?"

"Certainly!"

"Okay." He goes and gets my horse into the stable and shows me in through the door to his family. I stay overnight.

In the morning a nice large group assembles.[92] I announce the stanzas of my hymn and start singing. They sing along. I position myself with my back against the counter, the liquor bottles behind me, and start preaching. Soon the door opens up and a man pokes his head in, but quickly bangs the door shut again. Another man does the same, and another. It's comical, and I have to control myself so that I don't lose my focus. After the sermon I baptize two more children.[93]

From Durand I make my way toward Eau Claire. In the distance by the hill I see an old little house and think, "You should just stop in there once." The door is open, opposite another door. In the middle of the living room sits the father with his head hung down. I call out, "Good day, father."

He says, "A German voice! Do come in, sir."

Soon an old little mother comes in through the other door. He told me that they had had three children, two sons and a daughter. The one son had drowned while floating logs, the other had been shot and killed in battle—the Civil War

---

92. On Fri., April 8

93. Strieter records baptizing four children in Durand on this day—Christian Lorenz Kuhn, August Wilhelm Zeising, Wilhelm Heinrich Wetterroth, and Anna Elisabeth Catenhusen.

[*Rebellionskrieg*] was going on at the time—and the daughter had recently married and now they were all alone.

I comforted them with their Savior and asked if they had a Bible.

"Yes, other good books too."

I told them just to keep reading them and to pray persistently and remain firm in faith in their Savior. He would not abandon them.

He says, "Oh, dear Pastor, couldn't you please give us the Holy Supper?"

I say, "Dear father, I have absolutely nothing with me. Hold on to the spiritual use of the Supper, sir. Apply to yourself the merit of Jesus, which he has won for you by giving over his body and shedding his blood. Then you will have the blessing of the Supper even without actually taking it." But I make up my mind: "That is not going to happen to you again." From then on I always took some wine and wafers along, even when I rode.

I commended the dear folks to our dear God and took my leave.

I rode towards Eau Claire. On the other side of a bridge across a river I was supposed to turn right. Back there were also people to whom I was supposed to preach. I lose the barely visible track, ride up a high hill; the other side slopes down like a roof. Both of my gelding's hind feet slip out and he sits down on his backside and doesn't get back up until the bottom. At the bottom I bend a bit left and find the track again. Come into the open, turn in at the first house and tell the woman who I am and why I was there. She leaves me her child and runs to call her husband. He is a friendly man and, as I soon notice, Christian. I stay overnight and preach in the house to a number of listeners.[94]

I ride back over onto the Eau Claire Road. There I am supposed to go over across the prairie to a house and visit a family where especially the wife is really committed, but find the house locked. I go back over and continue on the road. I come to a new house where a staghorn is fixed on a post, so it was a tavern. On the porch [*Poartch*] stands a man. "Are you by chance the Lutheran preacher, sir?"

"Yes."

"Please come on in." He took my horse from me and leads me into the saloon. "Do you want something to drink, sir?"

"No, thank you."

"Then go into this room," and he opens the door for me.

There sit a number of women and also a man, and against the wall sit four nice girls, dressed in white, with a blue[95] ribbon around their waists, and one woman has a child in her arm. The little children are seated according to size. I am supposed to baptize the children. I take down their names and give a short address, telling the adults and the little children what baptism is, that they were making a covenant with the triune

---

94. On Sat., April 9. Strieter's two baptisms "by Mondovi" were of Johann Ludwig Heinrich Machmeyer and Heinrich Schreiner.

95. The printer misread *buntes* for Strieter's *blaues*.

God, the Father, the Son, and the Holy Spirit, that they would put on Christ. They should believe that from the heart and hold on to this covenant of grace.[96]

I now read the rite and ask the biggest one, "Do you desire to be baptized?"

"Yes," says the child, leans its little head over the water and lets itself be baptized. Same with the second, the third, and the tiny little Trude too, the baby the woman was holding. Oh, it was too beautiful. I got to experience the same thing one time in Berlin.[97]

After the baptism they give me coffee and cake, then I continue riding to Eau Claire, turn in at my young carpenter's place, who brings me to a widow.[98] I cannot preach there.

Ride back to Fall Creek and turn my gelding back in, get driven back to Eau Claire, take my seat on a small steamer, and head down the river to Reads Landing.[99] Arrive there towards evening, go up the rise. A saloon is there and I go in: "Are you German, sir?"

"Yes indeed."

"Do you have something to eat?"

He pours me a glass of beer, gives me a piece of sausage and a piece of bread. I take that to a corner, sit down and set it on a barrel and try to consume it. The beer doesn't

---

96. In confessional Lutheran circles today, this would be considered an improper way of speaking about baptism. Baptism is a one-sided covenant in which God does all the acting, not a two-sided covenant. In baptism God saves us (Mark 16:16; Titus 3:4–5; 1 Pet. 3:20–21), forgives our sins (Acts 2:38; 22:16), clothes us with Christ (Gal. 3:26–27), makes us heirs of eternal life (Titus 3:4–7), and makes a pledge to us that we will have a good conscience before him (1 Pet. 3:21). This of course does not benefit us apart from faith in Christ (Mark 16:16), but baptism is precisely one of the means through which God gives us faith (Gal. 3:26–27; Col. 2:11–12). Strieter does allude to this proper view of baptism when he calls baptism a "covenant of grace," which it cannot be unless it is one-sided. The language of two-sidedness crept into Lutheranism over time, especially in trying to describe the purpose of the confirmation rite which, though not sinful, is not instituted or commanded in Scripture. One faulty explanation of confirmation is that it is a renewing of our baptismal covenant, which we cannot in fact renew, since we had no part in making that covenant in the first place.

97. Strieter appears to be faltering a bit in his memory here. He did baptize four children in the town of Brunswick in Eau Claire County on April 9, but they were not all girls, and the baby's name was not Gertrude. He baptized Anna Louise Wüst (b. Sept. 6, 1856), Amalie Caroline Wüst (b. Nov. 13, 1857), and Carl Friedrich W. Wüst (no birthdate given)—all children of Johann and Maria (Damas) Wüst—and also Marva Peisch (b. Nov. 22, 1863), the daughter of Johann and Amalie (Würtenberger) Peisch. The similar experience he had in Berlin actually occurred less than a month later, on May 1, when he baptized four daughters of August and Barbara (Ander) Schipinsky—Pauline Wilhelmine (b. Dec. 14, 1852), Emilie Clara (b. May 17, 1854), Louise Wilhelmine (b. Oct. 14, 1855), and Anna Friederike (b. May 29, 1860).

98. I have followed Leutner's abridgment here. Strieter's manuscript reads: "*der führt mich zu einer Wittwe* [sic], *die einzigen Lutheraner im,*" followed by a large space, followed by a word that appears to start with *St*, but is indiscernible because of the lines stricken through it and the attempted corrections written over the top of it. Whatever the case, Strieter's records indicate he did baptize two children in Eau Claire on Sun., April 10.

99. Strieter spelled it Reeds Landing. Reads Landing lies on the western shore of the Mississippi River where the Chippewa River empties into it.

taste good; I let it stand. The sausage is dry and doesn't taste good either. I chew on the bread. Then all at once a bunch of guys come in and take their places at the counter and get some drinks. In the middle stands a short man, a blacksmith, who right away starts mocking and says that the Bible is a book of lies. This is too much for me. I stand up and go up to the person: "Listen here, sir, you say the Bible is a book of lies. Let me ask you: If you were to get completely drunk right now, and you went home and abused your wife and children like a tyrant, would that be right?"

The keeper interjects, "Yeah, that's what he often does."

"No," the man answers.

"Okay, the same thing is also found in the Bible, for there it is: 'You husbands, show common sense as you live with your wives' [1 Pet. 3:7]. Now how can the same thing that is the truth in your mouth be a lie in the Bible?"

He was quiet, and one-two-three, the room was empty.

In the corner a door is open and a woman stands in the doorway and calls out that supper is ready. The saloonkeeper says, "Mister, are you a parson?"

"Yes."

"Please come and eat with us."

I go in. There a large, roasted fish is sitting on the table; I couldn't take my eyes off of it. We sit down.

"Mr. Parson, please say a prayer."

I say a prayer and dig in.

He asks, "Do you know Professor Walther,[100] sir?"

"Oh sure, quite well."

"I was in St. Louis at the confectioner X.'s"—I can't remember the name, but he was a well-known individual. "Walther often tried to convert me, but he did not succeed."

"Too bad. You need to be converted if you want to go to heaven."

"Mr. Parson, time will tell. A mocker I am not."

"Couldn't a person preach here then?"

"Yeah, look here, sir. Earlier a man came and passed himself off as a preacher, held church, told the people that traveling cost money and that they should take a collection for him. They do that. He takes the money and goes to the nearest saloon and wastes it on drink. Several others did the same. A person loses all his desire after that."

My steamer comes and I get on board for La Crosse. The boat gets under way and I go inside. Soon I go back outside. There stands a large man with a raincoat [*Wachsrock*] on, at the front and looking out. I go inside and outside more than once, and in the morning the man is still standing in the same spot. He now goes inside and another man takes his place.[101] I learn that the night-watchman was the captain. A noble figure, getting old already, with a hooked nose.

100. C. F. W. Walther (1811–1887)

101. This sentence was omitted by the printer.

The thought now occurs to me: "This man stands in one spot the entire night in order to maneuver his boat safely down the river. What dedication! What, and you're going to get tired? It's going to be too much for you? You're going to get testy—you who work on immortal souls for your Savior?"

I come to La Crosse and take my seat on the train cars for Pardeeville. There stands my Fanny in the innkeeper's stable, whom I have left there for so long this time. I hitch up and take off. Haven't gone too far when I start to feel ill. I drive under an oak, let my horse munch on a bush, and I lie down on the ground and throw up. But nothing comes out except sour, bitter water, and some blood at the end. I'm so dizzy, the whole world is spinning, and my head aches badly. It's getting to be evening; I simply have to get going. I crawl to my buggy and claw my way up, hold on tight to the seat on both sides, and take off. Have to drive at a walk though; my head won't take it. Reach home toward morning,[102] lie down for a little rest and try to take my clothes off. But my underpants have crusted together with the grime, so that I first have to soak them with a wet, hot cloth. My legs from the top down to the knees are completely sore. That came from getting thrown around in the saddle.

I attended the conventions and conferences. One time I didn't go to the local conference because I was sick. I also was not at the 1854 convention in St. Louis because I was very poor and had no money for traveling. I also was not at one delegate convention and had my alternate go, because I was deaf and wouldn't have been able to hear anything anyways.[103] Otherwise, to my knowledge, I was at all the conventions and conferences from 1853 up to my retirement from the ministry. More than once I baptized my newborn baby and then departed, or it was born to me while I was gone. Never did I submit the excuse: "domestic circumstances."[104]

At the beginning of the sixties I came to the convention in St. Louis with a full beard and had to put up with a lot of teasing.[105] This is how it happened: I was shaving at a farmer's place in Big Bull. He didn't have a mirror; there was only a small triangular piece of a mirror in the house. It had been stuck into a crack in one of the beams in the log house. That was okay, but the razor was like a saw and the heavy, bitter tears ran down my cheeks.

---

102. Strieter appears to have concluded his investigation/mission trip on Tues., April 12—nearly two weeks away from home.

103. As Strieter will relate in Chapter 8, he grew deaf toward the end of his ministry.

104. Leutner changed Strieter's "*häusliche Umstände*" to "*Familienverhältnisse wegen*."

105. The Missouri Synod Convention was held in St. Louis from October 10–20, 1860.

Fig. 37. Johannes Strieter, perhaps mid- to late 1860s, photo.
Image courtesy of Susan Hawkins.

Then I asked myself, "Did our dear God really cause the beard to grow so that we could torture ourselves with it so shamefully?" and I answered, "No." And from then on I let everything grow as it pleased. To this day I never again had a razor put to my face.

In St. Louis Missionary Clöter took a liking to my beard. Later we had convention in Monroe, Mich., and Clöter came with the full beard too.[106] In the evening there

---

106. The Northern District Convention took place in Monroe, Michigan, from May 29 to June 4, 1861.

was supposed to be conference, but there wasn't a lot going on. My Jox[107] right away nominated Strieter to conduct the meeting; I had to take the chair and Clöter was made secretary. Jox wanted to have the two bearded men up in front. Soon many people were following my example with the full beard, even my dear Prof. Crämer.

Fig. 38. *Left to right:* Prof. August Crämer, Synod President Friedrich Wyneken, and Dr. Wilhelm Sihler with full beards, engravings printed in M. Lücke, *Zum 50-jährigen Jubiläum des praktischen evang.-lutherischen Concordia-Seminars zu Springfield, Ill.* (1896). Strieter (humorously?) suggests that he started the full beard trend in the Missouri Synod.

One time we had convention in Watertown and I drove there with Fanny, seventy-five miles.[108] One time conference was in Lebanon and I also drove the eighty miles there to Babylon.[109] One time conference was in Woodland, and I also drove there.[110] One time it was in Freistadt, and I also drove there.[111] There we camped in the late Fürbringer's study.[112] Beds were positioned on the floor on both sides. Our feet were touching in the middle. Outside[113] stood a bed for two. Ruhland lingered downstairs a bit long. Stecher and Steinbach slipped into the bed, to Ruhland's chagrin. Whether he liked it or not, he would have to join us in the camp. Strasen was lying up by the door and says, "You guys leave the last spot open for Ruhland and when he comes marching through, each of you give him a kick." He had to get undressed outside.[114] Once he's in by us, Strasen gives him one. He turns around and starts griping. In the meantime he gets one from the other side. Then he sees the game we're playing and strikes out for his bed, but he gets his kick from both sides all the way down. Having reached the end,

107. Pastor Johannes Heinrich Jox of Immanuel Lutheran Church in Kirchhayn, Wisconsin
108. The Northern District Convention took place in Watertown from June 18–24, 1862.
109. The Wisconsin Pastoral Conference met in Lebanon from May 5–7, 1863.
110. The Milwaukee Pastoral Conference met in Woodland from April 26–28, 1864.
111. The Wisconsin Pastoral Conference met in Freistadt from September 9–11, 1862.
112. This may have been an honorary name for the study due to Ottomar Fuerbringer's faithful service in Freistadt from 1851–1858. By the time this conference was held, Friedrich Boeling had been using this study since the beginning of 1861.
113. Leutner's correction is probably more correct: "In the room next door."
114. See previous n.

he starts in: "You despicable people." But we are laughing hysterically and he starts laughing too. Oh, Ruhland was just terrific.[115]

One time conference was in Mayville, where Dicke was.[116] I drove there. As I was unhitching, my horse was nibbling around at the dung. Everyone was standing outside when I came. Then the dear Synod President Wyneken exclaimed, "Look, Strieter's horse is so hungry, it's feeding on dung, and so shamefully lean. We should take up a collection so that Strieter can buy oats."

But my Dicke came to my aid: "That horse is not lean. It is thin and empty right now because it has run forty miles.[117] No horse looks round after doing that."

One time conference was at Jox's place in Kirchhayn.[118] Dr. Sihler was also there. In the evening someone called in through the window, "Is there still room in the camp?" It was our old, dear President Wyneken.[119] The joy was great. During the midday break we went under the green trees and played Plumpsack.[120] Link set it up.[121] The old gentlemen had to play too. Link especially had it in for Wyneken. He often had to get out of the ring and received some terrific whackings from Link. Wyneken would laugh his head off and run. Even the old Dr. had to take his turns.

We were very brotherly together and were attentive during the sessions. Back then it never occurred to anyone to read the newspaper during that time or to tell something to the guy next to him. Our headmen were Strasen and Link, and they supplied most of the papers. Wyneken called us the Brimstone Boys [*Schwefelbande*].[122]

---

115. Something is amiss in this story, since Friedrich Carl Theodor Ruhland (1836–1879; see Appendix VII), had moved from Oshkosh, Wisconsin, to Wolcottsville, Niagara County, New York, and had been installed as pastor of St. Michael's Church there on July 6, 1862, before the conference in Freistadt was held. (It also does not seem likely that the study in Freistadt would have been upstairs.) Since it does not seem likely that Strieter was mistaken about Ruhland, the main character in the story, perhaps he was mistaken about the location. Perhaps this occurred at the conference Ruhland himself hosted from May 11–14, 1860 (which would explain why he was irritated about not getting to sleep in the bigger bed), or at the one in Milwaukee on May 3–4, 1861. Ruhland eventually became the first president of the Evangelical Lutheran Free Church in Germany.

116. I was unable to locate any announcement for a conference in Mayville during Strieter's years of service in Wisconsin on the pages of *Der Lutheraner*. However, it may have been held in early May 1862, since the Wisconsin Pastoral Conference usually met around that time in other years.

117. The distance between Strieter's homestead and Mayville was more like seventy miles, but Strieter most likely divided the journey between two days.

118. The Wisconsin Pastoral Conference met in Kirchhayn from September 3–5, 1861.

119. Fifty-one years old at the time

120. A German version of Duck-duck-goose played with a knotted handkerchief

121. Pastor Georg Link of Immanuel, Lebanon

122. According to the Grimm Brothers' *Deutsches Wörterbuch*, *Schwefelbande*, lit. "sulfur gang," denotes "a sorry or slipshod gathering, a rabble, especially in more vulgar parlance and used colloquially." It supposedly originated as a "nickname for *Sulphuria*, a students' club in Jena that was notorious for not giving satisfaction," and the Grimm Brothers also suggest that the label alludes to the devil or hell.

I voted for the first time in my life, for Stephen A. Douglas,[123] and was thus registered in the roll of citizens. That resulted in me getting drafted [*gedräfted*].[124] I presented myself in Berlin. The captain told me that I probably wouldn't come up because a number of men had been drafted and only six[125] were needed. I had a high number; they would probably have their number six man before they got to me. But he told me when I should report back.

The time came. Nobody knew how it would turn out. My dear Ferdinand Röske, my teacher, got the horse ready and was going to come along. Now came the terrible moment of parting. My wife fell around my neck and cried, "O Papa! O Papa!" The children grabbed me around the body at my legs and arms and cried, "O Papa! O Papa!"

I had to leave. Having arrived in Berlin, I went to the office. There I was told, "You have to go; almost everyone before you was ineligible." He would give me two hours to find a substitute. He actually didn't have any right to do that, but since I was a minister, he would show me the courtesy.

I go out. There stands a man who is waiting for such an opportunity. I take him inside, but the gentleman said, "He is better than you, but he has a bald head and therefore I am not allowed to take him, since I am only allowed to enlist first class men as substitutes."

Outside I was told, "Down there are half-breed Indians who will go for cheap."

I said, "I am not taking an Indian. I want the kind of man who knows what he's doing."

Then a young, impressive guy comes and offers to go for me, but says right away that he demands 725 dollars. I lead him inside. He is good.

I run to my Fischer, in whose house I held church, and ask if he would act as surety for me at the bank so that I could have 725 greenbacks for twenty-four hours. "Oh sure!" he says.

We head to the bank. Fischer says, "Give the gentleman 725 greenbacks in my name." He counts them out for me.

I go over and give the person his greenbacks. He is delighted. "Seven hundred dollars I will send to my wife—I have a wife and a child—and twenty-five I will keep as spending money."

I send my Ferdinand home to bring the good news and arrange for him to come back in the morning, and with my companion I take the railroad to Milwaukee, go to my friend So-and-so[126] and share my need with him. He goes with me to Mr.

---

123. In the 1860 presidential election

124. See Appendix IV, no. 7, p. 224. It appears that Strieter was not drafted until 1864.

125. Both here and in the next line, Strieter originally had "four," but the correction appears to be his own and not Leutner's.

126. Leutner replaced this with F. E., so he must have known the identity of Strieter's friend.

Such-and-such, but he won't help.[127] He goes with me to Pritzlaff, whose name I can certainly share. The gentleman is in his hardware store bright and early and is in the middle of sweeping his office.[128] My escort remains standing outside by the door. I go inside and bid good morning and say my situation, that I would very much like 725 greenbacks to be able to pay my banker by tonight, and he would get his money back little by little.[129]

He said he had given Pastor N. Beyer money for a substitute, but he had been released from duty. I could go and get that money for myself.

I say, "Beyer is up on the Wolf River. That is impossible for me, to retrieve that money in time."

Pritzlaff continues sweeping in silence. After a pause I say, "Mr. P[ritzlaff], if you are unable or if you are unwilling to help, please say so."

He looks up at the ceiling. "Yeah? And what would you do then?"

I say, "Whatever God wills."

He throws his broom into the corner, goes to his desk and writes, and hands me the slip of paper. I express my thanks and go out to my So-and-so and hand him my paper. He says, "Now you've got help." Off he goes with me to the bank and presents his slip, and the gentleman counts up 725 greenbacks, which I tuck away and now board the train for Berlin, give the banker the money and ask how much I owe.

He says, "Nothing," and full of joy, I go home to my family, who laugh and rejoice with me a thousand times over.

But now we did even more saving—for we had to be frugal enough as it was in those terribly expensive times—so that the debts would be paid. All the money was supposed to be sent to Lochner.[130] Everybody helped. Money was coming in from all sides. Pastor Hügli of Detroit, Michigan, sent money to Pastor Fr[iedrich] Lochner along with a note that, in return, Strieter had to pluck a tuft of hair from his beard and send it to him.

After I moved to Aurora I sent one more payment. Lochner sent a portion of it back to me along with a note that it was all paid up. God has surely given and will give the dear Pritzlaff his reward of grace for what he did [Luke 6:38], so too to the others who helped.

---

127. Leutner struck this sentence and it was omitted from the book.

128. Pritzlaff's store was eventually incorporated as the John Pritzlaff Hardware Company, which has gained some fame in Milwaukee's history. At the time of this story, Pritzlaff was at his original store on the corner of what is today North Old World 3rd Street and West State Street. Eventually he would build a new store at what is today 311 North Plankinton Avenue, where his company would become, as it has been called, "somewhat like the Amazon.com of the late 19th and early 20th centuries." Pritzlaff died on March 18, 1900.

129. Leutner struck everything after "my situation" and it was omitted from the book.

130. See Appendix IV, no. 7.

WISCONSIN

Battle with the Fanatics[131]

Dr. Sihler and the dear W[ilhel]m Stelter had already told me in their accompanying letter back when I was in Newburgh that the Methodists, the Albright people—we called them Jumpers—were thick in that area and look, six or so of their so-called preachers[132] were running around from house to house. They already had a good number.

When I first got to Injunland I had to hold church in the schoolhouse and in residences. One time over in the bush in the schoolhouse behind Welke's. I am there somewhat early, since coming too late was not my practice. An old teacher from abroad, Sch.,[133] is there already and starts in: "Mr. Preacher, what's going to be done about the Methodists? They had invited your predecessor to a debate, and he didn't show. They really whooped it up when that happened. What are you going to do, sir?"

I say, "For starters, I am not going to concern myself with the fanatics[134] one bit. If they attack, however, then they'll get what they've got coming."

He says, "Yeah, but will you always have the right words to say right away, sir?"

"Don't worry about it, dear Father Sch., and I won't worry about it either."

I'm holding church by Neshkoro one time. During the sermon there I said, "Just believe in your Savior and everything will be fine."

Just then a woman calls out, "No, no!"

I say, "What is missing then?"

She says, "A person must also repent."

I say, "Can a believer be unrepentant?"

She was silent.

I say, "Keep quiet for now, ma'am; after church we can talk more."

I finish my sermon, but during the hymn after the sermon she disappears.

One evening there's a knock at my door and three men come in. The one says politely that they would very much like to speak with me, if I would permit it. I say sure.

He asks if I am converted.

"Sure!"

---

131. Leutner also made this a separate chapter in the original book (see n. 42), but Strieter appears to have intended it as another subsection within the Wisconsin chapter.

132. This word is in English in Strieter's original.

133. This might be the same Johann Schultz who authored many of the letters in Appendix VI.

134. German: *Schwärmer*. The Grimm Brothers' *Deutsches Wörterbuch* defines *schwärmen*, the correponding verb, this way: "to travel or conduct oneself as, with, or in a swarm." The term is primarily used in apiculture, but it then can connote, outwardly, any kind of mob activity or wild, impulsive, or dissolute behavior, and, inwardly, "human ideas that fall out of line with a particular course," including the inclination toward error and heresy in the realm of religion. In Lutheran usage, this family of words describes the seeking of God and his truth outside of the means of grace (e.g. in visions, dreams, nature, natural human reason, etc.). The means of grace—the gospel of Christ in word and in the two sacraments—is the "course"; departing from that course is *Schwärmerei*, fanaticism. *Schwärmer* could also be translated, besides *fanatic(s)*, as *mad/crazy raver(s)*. Traditionally it has been translated *enthusiast(s)*, but *enthusiasm* is now used in a predominantly positive sense as a synonym for *zeal*, and the German family of words does not typically have a positive sense.

Could I give the time and hour of my conversion?

"The first hour of my conversion was the hour of my holy baptism, and at this hour I am still in the faith, so I am converted."

"Sir, if you cannot give a time and hour after your baptism when you were converted, then you are not converted."

"Can you prove to me from my life that I am unconverted, sir?"

"No."

"Then, sir, you also had better not say to me that I am unconverted. You can only judge what you can see; it is God who looks at the heart [1 Sam. 16:7]. If you say that I am unconverted without being able to prove it, then you are judging my heart and you are declaring me to be a child of the devil and pronouncing the judgment of damnation on me. And if you do not repent of that, the saying will apply to you: 'With the measure with which you measure, it will be measured to you' [Matt. 7:2]. Do you wish to retract your terrible judgment, sir?"

"No, my spirit tells me it's true."

"I do not wish to hear anything about your spirit, sir. Here is the door."

They go.

It's not long before three others come. One is my neighbor, W[ilhel]m Borsack. He starts by asking if a person is still a sinner after his conversion.

"Yes."

"No, someone who is converted is not a sinner anymore."

I say, "Let's hear what God's word says." I look up Hebrews 12 and read, "'Let us put off the sin that keeps on clinging to us.' What do you say to that, sir?"

He says, "Let me reflect for a bit." After a pause: "Look, sir, here's what it's like: I am sitting here; my old Adam is lying there in the corner and is dead. But now I have to watch out that he does not wake up again and come at me."

I say, "If the fellow is dead, sir, then you do not need to watch out. If that's the case, you are safe from him."

He says, "Please don't laugh. This is an important matter."

I say, "I'm not laughing one bit. But listen, sir, here it is: 'keeps on clinging.' If something is lying there in the corner, it can't be clinging to you. What do you say now?"

He smacks his hand on his knee, stomps his foot on the floor, and shouts, "And if it's there ten times, it still can't be true!"

"What? You want to be a sinless saint, yet say in response to God's word, 'And if it's there ten times, it still can't be true'? You are a despicable blasphemer, sir. Please leave quickly; I fear the devil will snatch you before my very eyes."

They leave.

I have confirmation at Stelter's under the trees; also hold the Supper right away.[135] When I was finished, a man comes, approaches me and says, "You just told the children that Christ's body is under the bread in the Supper, sir. That you must prove."

I say, "That I can do very easily."

Now another man approaches me: "Mr. Preacher, you started speaking around ten o'clock and now it is after one. You take your seat on your buggy now and drive home, and if this bullheaded fellow wants something, he should come another time."

I call out, "Listen, everyone! Come to my yard fourteen days from now, after four; I will prove it then."[136]

At the appointed time, I come home from the preaching place. The yard is covered in people. We shoved a wagon in front of the house. I grab my Bible, get up on the wagon, and call out, "Alright, where is my opponent?" There comes Michael[137] Jahns out of the crowd with his Bible under his arm. I say, "Get up here, sir. You position yourself in front of the seat and I'll stand behind it, so that everyone can see and hear us without a problem."

He gets up and says, "Let us now pray."

I say, "You should have done that beforehand, sir. I have already prayed, and I do not pray with you. Go ahead and begin."

He says, "Look up St. Matthew, please, and read the words of institution." I do so. "Look up St. Mark." I do so. "Look up St. Luke." I do so. "Now look up St. John."

I say, "The words of institution are not found there."

He says, "Yes, I was well aware of that. I just wanted to test you."

I say, "That's fine. But let me tell you where else the words are found—1 Corinthians, in the eleventh chapter. I will read that too. Now, what next?"

"See, sir, there you find bread, bread, bread!" He is shouting dreadfully.

One of the men standing below says, "Yes, we hear that it was bread. It wouldn't have been just crust; they wouldn't have been able to eat it then."

"Shut up!" Jahns says.

I say, "Now I will also shout as loud as you, sir: Body, body, body! What do you say to that?"

He says, "But how can it be his body? It has ascended into heaven."

"Precisely for that reason. Now he enjoys the full use of his divine majesty, also according to his humanity. Now that's happened, his body can truly be in the bread."[138]

135. This appears to have been on Sun., July 15, 1860.

136. See previous n. Strieter confirmed another group of thirteen the following Sunday, July 22, so the debate was held July 29.

137. Strieter spelled it Michel, probably because he pronounced it MIGH-kel, as we do, and he wanted to distinguish it from the German name Michael, which would have been pronounced MIKH-uh-ail.

138. This is one valid argument for the real presence of Jesus's body and blood in the Lord's Supper, but it is not sufficient by itself, since by itself it logically dismisses the possibility of the real presence

He says, "But you cannot see and cannot taste his body. So it cannot be there either."

I say, "You cannot see and cannot taste your soul, sir. So I have to say that you have no soul."

He says, "Then what sort of blood supply does Christ have to possess, if he is going to give it to drink to so many thousands?"

I say, "Sir, if you were to say, 'Drink my blood,' then that would be a valid question, but not when Christ says it. He is omnipotent and can do as he pleases. What do you say in response to the words, 'This is my body,' which I read to you from God's word four times?"

"I say it is not his body."

"Who tells you that, sir?"

"The Spirit tells me that."

"Your spirit says the opposite of what the Spirit of God says in his Word. In paradise God said, 'Do not eat from the tree; you will die' [Gen. 2:17]. But the devil said, 'Eat; you will not die' [Gen. 3:4–5]. Thus the devil says the opposite. So too here: God says, 'This is my body,' and you, sir, say, 'It is not his body.' Thus it is the devil who is speaking from your mouth."

He gets down from the wagon. Below they try to stop him: "Stay up there and prove that there is no body."

He says, "Let me go."

One man holds an old tree-root in front of him and says, "Just put that book away, for our doctrine is found in there, while yours is found in this old piece of wood and in your burnt-up braincase."

B[orsack] comes up and says, "You people simply do not have the Spirit at all. It's impossible to talk with you."

Another man says, "B[orsack], when you tore up that girl's pinafore up there in the woods, was that also the Holy Spirit?"

They leave.

Word got around that there was going to be a camp meeting. It was supposed to get started on Wednesday and last until the next Wednesday. That Sunday arrives. I have to go over to B[uchholz's] and W[arnke's], but come home a little after four or so. I say to the wife, "Hop on. We are going to the camp meeting." It was a half mile or so away from the house on the other side of the Mecan on the knoll. We go over. We tie the horse up outside the camp village and the two of us walk into the village towards the preaching stand. Three or was it four men are up there. One is standing and giving a speech. He was just saying, "I'm gonna stop after goin' on a bit more [*Mer wolla halt no Bisele angeha*]."[139]

---

when Jesus first instituted the Supper, before he ascended into heaven.

139. Everything that the speakers will say at this camp meeting Strieter records in a low German dialect. In the realm of American English, this would be somewhat akin to the "hillbilly" English

Another is sitting very solemnly in the middle, an impressive fellow, with a plumpish face and dark beard, somewhat corpulent, average height, in his forties or so. A man stands up from the audience, apparently someone who knew me, and says something in the gentleman's ear. He stands up and tugs at the speaker's coat, who then says a few more words and sits down. Now the gentleman stands up, puffs himself up, raises his hand, points it at me (I am leaning against a tree three rods [sixteen and half yards] or so directly in front of him): "You mustn't think that yer da only one that knows summat; other people have learnt summat too."

"Amen! Hallelujah!" shout a number of throats.

He continues: "Confirmation is shameful humbug. Confirmation is gobbledygook, and gobbledygook is shameful humbug. 'Course, I'm still gonna cel'brate da Supper." He looks up 1 Corinthians 11 and reads the words of institution, puts the book down, and says, "Here it says it is his body. Well, it cert'nly is his body. But ya shouldn't think that it was his actu'l body. I'm well aware that Luther wrote on da table wit' da chalk, 'This is my body.'[140] Maybe it's still there."

"Amen! Amen! Hallelujah!" come the shouts from the masses.

He continues: "I say, it's not his body. Why? 'Cause I can't grasp wit' my sound reason how his body can be in da bread. And what I can't grasp wit' my sound reason, I'm cert'nly not gonna have anything to do wit' [*do will a mit Leib und Seel net he*]."

"Amen! Amen! Amen! Hallelujah! Hallelujah! Hallelujah!" The shouts ring out so loud that they echo in the woods.

I say to my wife, "Come on, I've had enough now." We go home. I sit down at the desk and write: "To Whom It May Concern [*Herr N. N.*]: A few moments ago I heard you say that in the Supper, Christ's body is not in the bread because you could not grasp it with your sound reason. Now you should know, sir, that a preacher of the gospel does not prove his doctrine with his sound reason, but with God's word. If you do not prove what you have said for me from God's word, then you are a fanatic and a false prophet. J. Strieter."

Scarcely had I finished when Michael Jahns comes around the corner on his way to the meeting. I call him and give him the letter, saying, "Please give this letter to the gentleman who spoke up there when I was there."

He says, "Yes of course. That is Brother Blank; I'll give him the letter."

Bright and early Monday morning, my Michael comes and says, "Brother Blank gives his regards and told me to tell you that he has read the letter, but he does not have any time at all right now. For something like this, he says you need to have Bible against Bible."

---

spoken in the backwoods of the South. Strieter had no inherent prejudice against low German dialects as such (for example, the Pomeranians he visited in the Wausau area spoke Plattdüütsch), but in this case he uses it to reinforce the inferiority of Methodist doctrine and preaching. Leutner, however, made the speakers sound even more unrefined in the printed edition.

140. The speaker was referring to the Marburg Colloquy of 1529.

Right after that a top buggy comes, and then another one with Brother Blank sitting in it. He drives slowly until he is within ten rods [fifty-five yards] or so of the house. I am standing in the doorway. Then he cracks the whip and—just like that—he's past. Now he drives slowly again. That was on the Monday after the Wednesday, and there was supposed to be camp meeting until the coming Wednesday.[141] After the buggies come the freight wagons with the whole kit and caboodle loaded up and heading home.[142]

In Injunland I had no more trouble from the Jumpers; they were even friendly.[143] Now I had definitely held the field against the fanatics, yet I would have liked to have confounded them even more thoroughly. I thought, "You should consult Luther once. He knows everything else; he will also know how to do this."

I consult him and find this: "You should not debate with the fanatics. They do not stick to the point, but bounce around this way and that. If you let them prove their case—whew, do their trousers stink then!"[144]

I thought, "Just wait until you guys come back to me."

I am up in Big Bull and am preaching in the schoolhouse by Beilke's, and after the sermon I warn against the Methodists, for I had heard that they had also broken in here.[145] I said that they were fanatics, who robbed them of baptism, absolution, and the Supper and put their bench of repentance[146] in their place. When the people were leaving, someone tapped me on the shoulder. I turn around. There in front of me stands a burly guy, twenty-five to thirty years old or so, average height, and he says, "I also belong to the brotherhood that you called fanatics. You will have to prove that, sir."

I say, "I would be very happy to." I call out, "Listen, you people, this gentleman demands proof that his organization are fanatics. Let us go into the schoolhouse once again; I will furnish the proof."

---

141. Leutner crossed out this sentence. See next n.

142. Leutner inserted here: "They had already concluded the camp meeting on Monday instead of Wednesday."

143. Sometime during this ordeal, or perhaps after it, there seems to have been another incident. In his Dec. 2, 1861 report to Johannes Bading, president of the Wisconsin Synod, traveling missionary Eduard Moldehnke reports of his chance meeting with J. J. Hoffmann in Wausau. He remarks: "[Hoffmann's] mentor, Strieter, once got involved in such a fierce argument on the street with the Methodist preacher in Princeton (where Strieter works) that the two novices lined up against each other with clubs for protection. It ended with the two worthy men spitting in each other's face."

144. I was unable to locate or verify this quote.

145. This sermon took place on Dec. 2, 1860. "The schoolhouse by Beilke's" was a log schoolhouse on the southeast corner of what is today Naugart Drive and Berlin Lane in the town of Berlin, Marathon County, Wisconsin. It was eventually replaced by a frame schoolhouse, and then by a brick schoolhouse, which is still standing today, though no longer in use. Heinrich Beilke and his wife, Auguste née Neumann, lived on the property cater-cornered from the schoolhouse; the 1881 plat map shows them with 160 acres there. According to *Berlin's Memories in 1976*, the bicentennial history of the township, Heinrich had been a builder of stone roads, arrived in 1857, and built a small log house.

146. The bench or stool of repentance was a piece of furniture in the worship space where people would publicly confess their sins and promise to amend their lives and dedicate them to Christ.

Then a man steps in front of me: "Mr. Pastor, you are supposed to baptize a child over at Beilke's. If he wishes to have proof, he may come over there."

I go over into the indicated house and baptize the baby.[147] Pretty soon the house starts filling up. Pieces of wood get set up like sawhorses, boards get laid on them, and the table gets covered. There was bacon, rye bread, and groats. I am supposed to say a prayer. The head of the house rises with a bottle—"Prost!"—and puts the bottle to his lips, takes a drink, and passes it around. It also comes to me. I hold it up to my mouth too; I don't remember anymore if I actually sampled some. I thought, "Oh great, they have brandy. How is this going to turn out?" But my fears were unfounded. The bottle did make the rounds several more times later, but my gathering stayed very nice.

After dinner my attacker comes and says, "Brother Schaefer"—that was his preacher[148]—"doesn't want to come. He says that today is the Sabbath, and one should not desecrate the day of the Lord with quarreling."

A large Pomeranian retorts, "Are we really intending to quarrel? The proof that you are fanatics is going to be furnished from God's word, and I think that's exactly what Sunday is there for."

He said yeah, he couldn't help it, and leaves.

My dear folks start singing songs from the hymnal, including Christmas songs. I am asked if they may also sing secular songs.

I say, "Oh sure, as long as they are appropriate." Now they start singing those songs too, and my! That was glorious. Oh, how it rang out into the beautiful woods. But the accompaniment was mostly sung by the older women. Finally the Bible was brought to me. We sang an evening hymn and I read and say a prayer and the people leave.

My host mother opens a bedroom door and says to me I should sleep there. I sleep and don't wake up until broad daylight, and I hear, "Now Brother Schaefer is coming." I get out of my bed and get dressed, shove my hair back, and go out. Right away the door opens and in comes a short little gentleman with a white necktie on, who bids a friendly good morning. Another elderly man is with him, my attacker's father, and a younger, lanky person, who was Pennsylvany Dutch and the public schoolmaster in the schoolhouse.

Mr. Schaefer starts in: "This brother told me that you had called us fanatics, sir.[149] So I merely wanted to tell you: You have the people in Injunland in mind. We call them fanatics too, but we are episcopal Methodists."

---

147. Johann Heinrich Carl Beilke, who was one month old. His sponsors were Carl Stege, J. Schöneberg, and Emilie Bratz.

148. In the same letter referred to in n. 143 above (written exactly one year later), traveling preacher Eduard Moldehnke spoke of a blacksmith named Schaefer who worked in the rural Wausau area among those with Methodist leanings. He made it sound as though Schaefer's followers were not too loyal and would desert him as soon as a Lutheran preacher established himself there. (Moldehnke did not consider J. J. Hoffmann, Strieter's successor in the area, to be a competent Lutheran preacher.)

149. Thus the attacker himself, the burly twenty-five- to thirty-year-old, was also present.

I say, "I already knew that those are Albright's people and that you and your people are episcopal, sir. But I call you fanatics too. The proof shall now be furnished. Tell me, please, what should a preacher of the gospel use to prove his doctrine?"

He says, "God's word."

I ask, "God's word, black and white?"

He says, "Yes."

A loaf of bread was still lying on the table, as was the Bible. I say, "Tell me, please, what is the essence of baptism?"

He says, "Essence? How am I supposed to understand that? God is an essence too."

I say, "I will make clear to you what essence is, sir. Here sits a loaf of bread. At first it was rye, which the father had milled. The mother mixed the flour with water, added sourdough, kneaded it, and baked it. If you ask me about the essence of the bread, I will answer, 'Flour and water.' Now tell me, please, what the essence of baptism is."

He still won't take a stab at it.

"Fine, I will let you off the hook for that, but tell me, please, what the benefit of baptism is."

He won't take a stab at that either. He says, "Baptism is a holy sacrament."

I say, "That merely tells me what people call baptism, sir, but please tell me, what does it give?"

Now the teacher speaks up: "Mr. Pastor, if you will permit it, I will tell you."

I say, "Please, speak."

He says, "According to our doctrine, baptism is not only the reception of a person into the visible fellowship of the church, but also a picture of his inner birth, also called his rebirth."

I turn to Schaefer: "See, sir, he said it." I continue: "Please read me those words from your book."

He pulls a small booklet out of his pocket, a little bigger than the Little Habermann,[150] and reads the same words.

I say, "I also have a booklet in my pocket with the same format. You read Article 10 in 'Articles of Faith and Rules for Living,' right?"

"Yes," he says.

"Okay, in my booklet Article 10 reads thus: 'Baptism is not only a sign of the reception of a person into the visible fellowship of the church, but also a sign of his inner birth, also called his rebirth.' In your book it says 'picture' and here it says 'sign.' What is the difference here between 'sign' and 'picture'?"

He says, "Yeah, there is no difference."[151]

---

150. The Little Habermann (*das Habermännlein*) was the nickname given to the popular Christian prayerbook by Johann Habermann, which first appeared in Wittenberg in 1567.

151. From "In your book" to here was stricken through in Strieter's manuscript in both pencil and ink, and "a sign of his inner birth" was changed to "a picture of his inner birth." It appears that Leutner

"Your booklet is the booklet of the episcopals; mine is that of the Albright people. You see, sir, you have the exact same doctrine about baptism. But now to the proof. Here is the Bible." I shoved it over to him. "Please read to me from God's word that baptism is a picture."

He pages this way and pages that way.

I say, "Give me the book, sir, and tell me what I should read."

He pulls another booklet from his pocket, looks up a spot and says, "Read John 3:5."

I read, "Unless someone is born of the water and Spirit, he cannot enter the kingdom of God." I say, "Does it say here that baptism is a picture?"

He says, "Yeah, you see, sir, if according to the Spirit you—"

I interrupt, "Please drop the explaining. I did not ask you for your explanation of this passage, but whether it says here that baptism is a picture. Does it say that here?"

"No," he says.

"Next passage," I say.

He names the next baptism passage. I look it up and read it and ask, "Does it say here that baptism is a picture?"

He says, "Yeah, you see, sir—"

I interrupt, "Please drop the explaining; I am asking you in the strongest terms. You promised me, sir, that you would prove your doctrine from God's word, black and white." I say, "Next passage."

He now names for me the baptism passages one by one. I read each one and ask each time, "Does it say here that baptism is a picture?" I force him to answer. He says no each time.

Mr. Schaefer is done with his passages and says then, "I do not have my concordance here. If I had that, I could find the passage."

The old man starts in: "May I speak?"

I say, "Sure."

He says, "Somewhere in the Bible it says something about signs, but I don't know where." Anyhow, he meant Romans 4:11, but I didn't give him a hand.

Now his son, my attacker, starts in: "Yeah, you are definitely not letting Brother Schaefer do any talking at all. If he were allowed to talk, he could prove it."

I say, "You, sir, are a snot-nosed brat. Be quiet until someone asks you."[152]

I turn to Schaefer: "Have you now proved to me from God's word, black and white, that baptism is a picture, sir?"

"No."

"Okay, sir, then you and your people are fanatics until you do so."

---

wanted to simplify Strieter's conversation.

152. This exchange between Strieter and the twenty-five- to thirty-year-old son was also stricken through in both pencil and ink. Leutner likely surmised that it would not paint Strieter in the best light.

He says, "Yeah, my bishop is coming up here soon to admit the converted souls into the church, and he can prove it to you."

I write my address on a page of my little pocket notebook, tear it out, and give it to him: "When your bishop comes, please write to me a week in advance. Write where and when he is going to meet me; I will be on the scene." He tucks his piece of paper away and they leave. I have yet to receive that letter regarding the bishop to this day.

Later I come up there and Beilke tells me (he had heard everything as it was happening, along with his wife and in-laws[153]): They had stopped in for a drink at Kickbusch's in the village. There that fellow, my attacker, had told the assembled crowd while standing at the counter that his Schaefer had utterly defeated me. He had just come in and had heard what he said. Then he had gone right up to the guy and had said, "What did you just say about our pastor? Say it one more time and I will smack your yapper so hard, the blood won't stop running.[154] Didn't our pastor ask ten times, 'Does it say here that baptism is a picture?', and your padre [*Pfaffe*] had to say no every time? Didn't our pastor finally ask whether he had proved his doctrine with the Bible, and Schaefer had to say no? I guess we can see what kind of converted people you guys are—lying so shamelessly."

To my people in Injunland and in Big Bull I said, "If a fanatic comes and requires this or that, and you are able to help, then do so. If he starts in and tries to convert you, or even begins to pray, then tell him to leave immediately. And if he will not leave, then grab the broom and chase him out like you would a dog,[155] even if he's a preacher. Then the people won't give you any trouble. Do not go to their assembly."

My Departure from Injunland[156]

One time Pastor Strasen and Pastor Link were visiting us with their wives and stayed a day and two nights. On the way home we accompanied them for a piece. My wife sat on Strasen's wagon and Link sat next to me. He started asking about my work, about my hardships, about my health. Thinking nothing of it, I talked about my health, that I had been having stomach pains for the last half-year, had bloating after every meal. He says, "It's time for you to get out of here. It's been long enough now; otherwise you'll be done for." We part ways.

---

153. Auguste Beilke's parents appear to have been David Neumann, who was one of the founding members of what is today St. Paul Lutheran Church-Naugart and who died on March 16, 1875, at age eighty-four, and Louisa (Schwan) Neumann, who died on Nov. 3, 1889, less than two months shy of her ninety-third birthday. (Her burial entry lists her survivors as "five adult children.")

154. Leutner cleaned this up a little in the book: "one more time and I will give you a sound thrashing."

155. Leutner also cleaned this up in the book: "then grab the broom and sweep him out."

156. Leutner also made this a separate chapter in the original book (see nn. 42 & 131), but Strieter appears to have intended it as another subsection within the Wisconsin chapter.

It isn't long before four calls arrive—the first from Aurora, Ill., and one from Yorkville, Ill., soon followed it. They are calling me jointly.[157] The one from Aurora was written by J. P. Beyer; the accompanying letter was written by Pastor Wunder—both pastors in Chicago. I wrote a few words to my President Fürbringer in Frankenmuth, asking for advice and enclosing Wunder's letter. Soon came the reply: "My dear Strieter, the call from Aurora is from God. Go in his name, sir. Just take care that a capable, practical man succeeds you. Yours, Ottomar Fürbringer."

I travel to the conference in Milwaukee and lay the matter before the conference.[158] Unanimously they say, "Go."

Now I announced it at the main stations and arranged for the administrators to meet at my place to act in the name of the congregations. They came. I lay the call from Aurora before them and read Fürbringer's letter and share the advice of the conference; they already knew how matters stood at their own congregations. One man was there who was holding a grudge against me; I had said something disagreeable to him earlier and he told me later that he felt offended, but there was nothing I could do to help him.[159] He said right away, "If it's from God, then we should go along with it." The others didn't want to hear anything about that.

The discussion goes back and forth. I say, "I will go out and leave all of you alone, so that you can really speak your minds freely. But I'll tell you this: If you agree that God's will is for me to stay, then the call will go back to the post office tomorrow." I leave.

After a quarter-hour or so I come back. "Now, what is the result?" Yeah, they thought that I should accept the call. The reason they cited was that the Schmidt folks would come back if a new pastor were there. There were ten or so who had left because they didn't get their way with the service time, namely from the other portion of the congregation, and had gotten themselves a man from Princeton.[160] But they were mistaken about that.[161] Two didn't want to vote yes, but said they would yield to the others.

Now I wrote that I was coming. We headed out in the spring of 1865.

---

157. Leutner struck this sentence.

158. I was unable to locate any announcement in *Der Lutheraner* for a conference in Milwaukee in late 1864 or early 1865. The 1865 Wisconsin Conference was held in Racine after Strieter left. There may be something amiss in Strieter's recollection.

159. Leutner struck everything after the semicolon in this sentence.

160. See Appendix IX, pp. 301ff. This was a much bigger affair than Strieter lets on here.

161. Namely, the members of the Schmidt congregation didn't come back after Strieter left.

Chapter 6

Aurora

In the spring of 1865 I came to Aurora, Illinois.[1] I was welcomed with great joy. I had Aurora and Yorkville, also called Long Grove. Soon I was also going to Squaw Grove[2] and Pierceville,[3] Plano too, and right away I had five preaching stations again. In Aurora they were mostly Bavarians, in Squaw Grove and Yorkville Hanoverians, in Pierceville Württembergers and Hessians. Plano I don't remember. There wasn't a lot going on there; they were probably mostly railroad workers.

In Aurora I soon came into great tribulation. When I held the first congregational meeting, twelve men presented themselves. "Is that all?"

"Yes."

Oh, the thought went straight to my heart, "What have you done? You leave hundreds of families there in the lurch to run after these few?" The tears of the dear Buchholz and others appeared before my soul and accused me.[4] I thought that the heavens were going to fall down on me and the earth was going to swallow me up.

If I had had nothing good to fall back on, I would have despaired, but I asked myself, "What did you do to end up here?" And I could find nothing. Especially my remark to the administrators was my sheet anchor, when I said that my call from Aurora would go back to the post office the next morning if that's what they decided.

In Aurora we lived with F. M. Downstairs was a room—the living room—and behind the entrance a small space for cooking. The upstairs had the exact same

---

1. See Appendix IV, no. 8. The Aurora church was located on the southeast corner of the intersection of Benton and Jackson Streets. Today this is Iglesía Luterana San Pablo, a daughter congregation of the now relocated St. Paul Church.

2. The village of Squaw Grove was one-half mile west of present-day Hinckley.

3. The historic location of the Pierceville Post Office is four and a half miles north of Hinckley on Somonauk Road. The present-day Pierce Town Hall is at the end of Somonauk Road, where it intersects with Perry Road.

4. See Appendix IX. God willing, a future installment in the *WELS Historical Institute Journal* (perhaps 39, no. 2, and 40, no. 1) will detail the confusion and rivalry that prevailed in Marquette County, Wis., after Strieter left, which eventually led to a split in the Mecan congregation (what Strieter called "Buchholz's") into Emmanuel, Big Mecan, which was served by Rev. August Zernecke and Wisconsin Synod pastors from then on, and Trinity, Little Mecan, which was officially organized in 1866 and served by Missouri Synod pastors from then on.

arrangement. The room in front was the sleeping room for everyone, and the small little nook in back was my study. There was no school held anywhere; there was no schoolhouse anywhere. Only in Aurora did they have a small frame church, which they managed to keep in the lawsuit with the former congregation, from whom they had separated. In Aurora we soon called a teacher, Teacher D. He held school in the church. But soon a schoolhouse was built. Even the women did drudgery work for the masons. Soon D. was teaching a large school.

Aurora and Yorkville were served on one Sunday, 9:30 in Aurora and 2:30 in Yorkville on rotation, for two Sundays in a row, and the third Sunday in Squaw Grove and Pierceville. It was twenty-five miles to get there. It was eighteen to Yorkville, which Fanny had to run between services; I had brought her along. I would go out to Plano from Yorkville, probably from Squaw Grove too, in the late afternoon. In Yorkville I had twenty families or so, likewise in Squaw Grove, ten or so in Pierceville. In Yorkville church was held in the schoolhouses, partly in the village, partly all around in the country. In Squaw Grove, likewise in Pierceville, we had a specific schoolhouse, in Plano too.

In Yorkville a church was supposed to be built, but where to put it? In Brown's schoolhouse a congregational meeting was held after church.[5] Administrator F. H. proposed the grove between the congregation and the village as the spot and cited as his reason that they had their thicket there, where they could get firewood with the sled in winter and the children could travel to school without a problem. But it was said that was almost completely out of the way and the entire congregation, with few exceptions, would have to go hunting for the church. H. stood up: "I resign from my position as administrator and member of the Building Committee." He stayed there and another man was elected in his place.

A congregation member who lived about right in the middle offered land for the church and cemetery, which was accepted, and soon the little church was standing there all paid for.[6] The way it would be paid for was also settled right away in that first meeting. They said, "W. K., how much?"

"Seventy-five dollars," and so forth. F. H. was saved for last. He also specified an amount, out of shame, for he didn't do his part for a long time.

Now the school was also on my mind. I started talking about it with W. K. and F. K.[7] and soon found a hearing, for their house was full of kids and they were committed Christians. I went to my friend in Addison, Prof. and Director Lindemann, and I place my cause before him. He said, "I will give you a fine person, B.," who

---

5. From an 1870 map of Kendall Township, it appears that Brown's schoolhouse was on the southeast corner of the intersection of what is today Walker Road and State Road 47.

6. The first church was built on the east side of what is today Immanuel Road, about two-fifths of a mile north of the intersection with Walker Road. Immanuel Lutheran Cemetery is not far from there. The present church, affiliated with the ELCA, is on the east side of Immanuel Road south of the intersection with Walker Road.

7. Perhaps F. Kollmann, who didn't live far from the church.

had taken part in the entire Civil War [*Rebellionskrieg*]. "He'll get a school up and running for you."

I present it to the congregation, but then F. H. resists it right away: We didn't have any money for a teacher and we also didn't have a schoolhouse.

I said that we shouldn't concern ourselves with the pay right now. That would turn up just fine, for if the congregation called a teacher, then they would also have it in mind to pay him. And as for the building, we had a fine building right here.

F. H. said that was a house of God and was not there for the children to rub their greasy fingers all over it and cut the benches to bits.

I said, "It can be used as a school precisely because it is a house of God, for a Christian school is a divine service [*Gottesdienst*]. And as for cutting the benches to bits, I can personally vouch that the teacher we get would not let any benches get cut to bits."

H. K. stepped up and said that we didn't need a German school; we needed English. He only spoke English with his children too, even though he couldn't pronounce a single word correctly. And he said that when the children were fourteen years old, they were sent to the pastor for instruction; that was religion enough. Later we unfortunately had to excommunicate that person.

My B. came. I present to him that he is going to have to lodge with a family, that he was going to have to start school with fifteen children, that the pay was far from settled.

He says, "None of that matters to me one bit. I came here to hold school."

School got going. F. H. and H. K. naturally did not send their children. Things went fine with the school and also with the Catechism instruction. If I had to preach in the morning, then Catechism instruction was taught by the teacher in the afternoon, and vice versa; that's how it was in Aurora and in Yorkville. In Squaw Grove and Pierceville I soon obtained a separate pastor. Now there were both, sermon and Catechism instruction, every Sunday in Aurora and Yorkville. How delighted I was.

The Americans were furious now, for they had only a few children. They wanted to shoot the Dutch minister and hang the Dutch schoolmaster.

Christmas came. The first evening Christmas service was in Aurora and the second in Yorkville. But my B. had prepared everything and pulled it off so nicely that a guy's heart could just sing for joy. The children sang so nicely, recited their parts so nicely, gave their answers so nicely, they had written such nice letters to their parents. Everybody was astounded. At the end, F. H. comes and asks the teacher about getting a Fibel, and pretty soon his children are coming too.

An American reproached our W. K. for doing wrong by his children by not having them learn English. W. K. told him, "My children do learn English and know more than yours."

The man replied that he would take his chances.

"Good," says W. K., "you'll see." He tells it to B., who takes W. K.'s daughter and goes over there. B. sets his A. next to the other man's children and has them read. A. reads better than the others. He has them spell. A. spells the others down. He poses questions pertaining to geography. The questions where the other children get stuck, A. answers. The neighbor says, "I will be quiet now," and was very friendly toward our teacher from then on.

Something on Squaw Grove and Pierceville:[8]

After church in S[quaw Grove], H. and his wife and So-and-so and his wife are still in the schoolhouse. H. presses So-and-so for clergy pay.[9] He says he has no money. Mrs. H. says, "You've got money for whiskey." But now the others let fly at her with a flood of words. All four go out. Everybody converges into a knot and in such a way I had never before heard or seen in my life. Everybody was screaming all over the place—these at them, those people at these people. All I could tell was that there were two factions. Any intervention on my part was completely impossible; the shouting and the fury were too intense. I got myself out of there; you can imagine the emotional state I was in on the road.

A few days go by, I get a telegram saying I should come to the funeral. Mrs. So-and-so had died, the woman who really went off at Mrs. H. in the schoolhouse. I'm supposed to take the railroad to N.[10] and from there a man will bring me out there with the buggy. I go down there, the man is at the depot and heads out with me.

"What are you going to preach? What are you going to do?" Sighing and thinking and anxiety were all jumbled together in my heart. In the house of the deceased it wasn't a big deal; I sang and read a psalm. But now I'm in the schoolhouse. I don't remember any more what text I selected; all I remember is that I gave them a stern repentance sermon and set before them God's often sudden judgment and earnestly admonished them to repentance. All of them were hanging their heads.

My man transported me back to the railroad and praises my sermon. I say nothing more than, "I told them the truth." The man whose wife had died comes to me right away because I had supposedly said to the man, "I sure told him the truth." I say, "Tomorrow I will be in N. and you will too, sir. Then the man will tell what I said."

"Fine."

I go there. So-and-so comes too. I say, "Listen, sir, this is what So-and-so says."

---

8. Leutner made this a separate chapter in the original book, but Strieter appears to have intended it as a subsection in the Aurora chapter. I, however, did not give it the usual subsection formatting here, due to its informal nature, the fact that there are no other subsections in this chapter, and the fact that he resumes talking about Aurora afterward.

9. Back then, no regular offering was gathered during worship. The pastor's salary was determined by how much each adult male member pledged annually on behalf of himself and his household. These pledges were usually recorded by the congregational secretary.

10. This abbreviation is unclear. Strieter may be using it to indicate he no longer remembers where it was, like we use "X" today.

He says, "No, sir, this is what you said," and says my words, "and that's what I said to So-and-so."

He replies, "No, this is what you said."

"No, this is what I said."

I go home. It comes time for church in Squaw Grove and Pierceville. I go there and preach about reconciliation, what it is and how necessary it is. After the service I say, "Now all of you stay here and be reconciled."

Mrs. H. stands up and confesses and apologizes. H. too, and so throughout. One man does not want to. His elderly father urges him with tears, but nope, he leaves without reconciling. God's judgment soon visited him. From then on things went well in Squaw Grove.

I had to hold instruction there with some adults. Two large young men come. The one told me right away I shouldn't take too long; he wanted to get married. Two very large girls come. The one has a golden watch, frequently pulls it out and checks it. The one young man shoots his tobacco spit way up into the aisle, one after the other. I start out by reciting a few sentences from the Catechism and then right away ask them to repeat what was said. Then I also relate Bible stories. When I related that Eve was created from Adam's rib, the girl with the watch smirks. I act as though I didn't notice anything, and when I tell them stories I try to be earnest and pleasant and as simple as if I had small children in front of me, and I do this every time.

Doesn't take long before the girl stops bringing her watch, stops smiling too, and the guy stops spitting his tobacco juice while I'm teaching; they became very serious and I confirm them.

At the same time I had a woman. She already had several children, small ones, and could not come to the schoolhouse. I went to her, also recite to her, but ugh, nothing sticks in her head. Have to stick with just the bare essentials.

Having my students repeat the Catechism after me—time was was very much lacking for that: In the morning in the schoolhouse by H.'s, then in the house of this woman, then to Z.'s schoolhouse, then another woman in her home, then twenty-five miles home.

I tell her husband that he should have his wife repeat the text of the Catechism after him for as long as it took until she knew it and named him a few passages too. He complained he didn't have any time; he had a lot of work and no servant. I told him that if that was the case, he should have his wife repeat it after him in bed at night. He promised and kept his word. I confirmed her in their home in the presence of a few administrators. Now there's supposed to be Lord's Supper. The woman's husband asked me if he could also go to the Supper with his wife.

I asked, "Why wouldn't you?"

He said he was Reformed. He had learned that in the Supper there was merely bread and wine as a remembrance.

I say, "Okay, what then, sir, did you have your wife repeat after you all this time?"

"This is my body; this is my blood."

"Okay, do you also know where that's found?"

"In Matthew, Mark, Luke, and St. Paul."

"Okay, whom are you going to believe then, sir, your teachers in E. or God's word?"

"Yeah, if I want to be a Christian and be saved, I have to believe God's word."

"Good, then believe that, sir, and go with your wife to the Supper."

He did.

As already indicated, I had another woman in P[ierceville]. The mother, a widow living in her daughter's house, had told me that her daughter was not yet confirmed either. I could come on over sometime. The daughter also had a child already. She speaks English and shows no inclination. I urge her and she finally gives in. The mother holds the child, the woman takes her seat on the bed, I sit on a chair in front of her, and now it's time to get started.

I ask if she understands German.

"Not well."

I say, "I will speak German and if there's a word you don't understand, then tell me and I will say it in English."

Already during my second visit I say, "Mary, just speak German."

She tells me yeah, she speaks Pennsylvany Dutch; I would laugh at her then.

I say, "You're being ridiculous. Out with it now."

Now she speaks German.

My, how committed dear Mary became. How well she understood everything and how joyfully she answers my questions. When the time for confirmation comes, I offer to confirm her in her home. "No, sir," she says, "I am going to the children in the schoolhouse and will confess my faith publicly."

Later she moved to a village. Pastor Norden, who was there by then, received a letter to come over and to give Mary the Lord's Supper; she was sick. She had a growth above the opening to her stomach. She asked Norden if he knew me; he was supposed to tell me to visit her so that she might see me one more time before she died. But she soon died.

As happy as I was in Aurora in the beginning, things turned just as sour later. Already on account of the liturgy, which I had introduced with their approval, one man stubbornly stayed away. I heard that his wife, who had withdrawn along with her husband, was practicing incantation. I inquire and learn that there was a little book that was going from house to house, in which you could find a remedy for anything. I have the book handed over. It is just about as thick as our Dietrich's Catechism. I read it and have no idea what to make of these absolutely horribly blasphemous spells. I show it to the woman to whom it belongs and ask her to please burn that book, which she did.[11]

---

11. In the manuscript, the examples that follow at this point are not included on the same page

I will only provide a few of them as proof:
For worm in the finger:

> Christ, Peter, and John
> > went out to the field.
> They plowed three furrows;
> > they plowed up three worms.
> The one was called Black,
> > the second one White,
> > > the third one Red.
> Worm in the finger,
> > be dead!

(Blow out over the finger three times and speak the three holy names.[12])
For stomachache and colic:

> Jerusalem, Jerusalem,
> > you city of kings,
> you who have crucified
> > our Lord Christ,
> you have turned
> > into water and blood
> and for stomachache and colic
> > are a remedy good.

(Hit stomach three times with open hand and say the three holy names.)
For burns:

> Christ was hanged,
> now I have been burned.
> > If his hanging harms him none,
> > so too my burning harms me none.

(Blow out over it three times and speak the three holy names.)

But now what to do with the congregation? I have no choice; they need to be instructed and rebuked. I gather up the courage and deliver a sermon on rituals or incantations and quote a few of the shameful spells. I hear that it has stirred up bad blood.

---

as what precedes them and what follows them at "But now what to do." Here Leutner inserted, "Put the two supplements here." The "two supplements," containing the examples and written on smaller sheets of paper, begin, "I will only provide a few as proof" (see the next sentence here), which suggests a certain reluctance on Strieter's part and that they were written only at Leutner's special request, perhaps to make the book more interesting. Carl Strieter does not include any of the examples in his translation.

12. Apparently the names of the three persons of the Trinity

Another thing: My Bavarians[13] liked to drink beer. For a while there were actually three beer gardens east of the city. I rebuked all the running over there that took place. One man actually had to do public penance in church.[14] I visited another man. After I said my piece, he said, "I am simply going to drink my beer and it's also going to be too much. I am well aware of that, but I won't give it up and you, sir, cannot tolerate it. I will leave the congregation. My old lady can stay there. But I will continue to pay my share as I have and we will remain good friends." That's what he does.

Now people start making insinuations to me about my "strictness." It is time to go to the convention in St. Louis.[15] The teacher is to be the delegate for it and is tasked with asking the president to see to it that I am relocated. The reason he is to give is that in the morning church is too early and in the afternoon it is too late, so the congregation cannot grow. They had to have a preacher of their own, that is, one just for them.

I had heard nothing of the sort before this. It was very troubling to me and I said, "The congregation is not able to grow. We already have everyone who can be had. We cannot accept those who belong to the lodge and the few freethinkers; they don't want to have anything whatsoever to do with us anyway. Sure, there are a number of people who have not joined yet, but they go to church, go to the Lord's Supper, and pay their dues. There is nothing else to draw on for growth. If the congregation is going to grow, there's first going to have to be an influx of people from the outside."

They stand by their decision. The teacher submitted his case to the dear President Bünger. But he responded, "What more does the congregation want? They already have everything—church every Sunday and Catechism instruction. They should just be content."

The year after that convention is in Fort Wayne.[16] My schoolmaster is to be the delegate again and is to present my relocation to the president again. Now I rebuked them earnestly: They should not bring about change unilaterally, but wait until God changed things.

They stand by it, however, and the teacher has to bring the matter before Bünger again, and actually in writing this time. Bünger hands me the letter to read for myself. I say, "I do not want to read the letter, but this time please give the people what they

---

13. See the first paragraph of the chapter; this is a shorthand way of referring to the members in Aurora.

14. Penance is usually associated with the Roman Catholic Church, but it is clear from early church fathers like Irenaeus, Tertullian, and Eusebius that publicly expressing remorse, especially for more grievous and public sins, was a common practice early on in the Christian church. Sometimes the penitents would even occupy a special "place of penance" in the church, separate from the main group. The practice of public penance was done away with in the main by the mid-third century in the Eastern Church and the mid-fifth century in the Western Church, but the practice has been resurrected from time to time as deemed necessary, including in the Lutheran Church.

15. The 1868 Western District Convention in St. Louis began on May 6.

16. The 1869 Missouri Synod Convention in Ft. Wayne began on Sept. 1.

want. So far we have gotten along like brothers; I fear if the people don't get their way now, things might turn sour."

He said, "Jox is looking for a pastor; I will tell him about this."

Jox comes to me: "When I get home, you will receive a call from Peru, Indiana."

After a few days the call arrives. I announce: "Next Sunday church will be at 2:30 and after church there will be a congregational meeting. I have a call and we have to deal with it."

I drive to Yorkville, but that afternoon they hold a meeting[17] and call Pastor Reinke. During the week I learn what happened. Sunday comes. I preach in Y[orkville] in the morning and in Aurora in the afternoon. After church I go home; someone comes and asks me to come to the meeting. I tell him, "Please tell the people I would have nothing to do in their meeting." He left. Now two men came and asked me to come. I go over there. Now one man after the other came to me and offered me his hand and apologized and said that Reinke had sent the call back; I should stay.

One man would not give me his hand, saying his conscience would not let him. When asked why, he said because he believed that I myself did not believe what I preached.

I asked how he knew that.

Because I got down from the pulpit so casually after the sermon. (The pulpit stairs were in the nave of the church.)

Now the others started putting pressure on him. So I said, "Just leave M. alone. I know my M.; he is a Christian. The devil is just tripping him up right now; he'll be set right again soon enough." And that's what happened. I was barely gone when a humble letter of apology arrived. I said,[18] "As soon as I learned that you had called Reinke, I wrote to Jox that I was coming. Next Sunday I am giving my farewell sermon."

They ask me to write to Jox; he should revoke my acceptance and I should send the call back.

"I will write to Jox," I say, "but I already know it is futile."

So it was. I also had to bring the sad news to my dear people in Yorkville that I had to leave. They were quite upset, but had to go along with it. Yes, those dear Yorkvillers—the things they did for us. When I came out of church, there were all sorts of parcels, bowls, and sacks in my buggy. When I came back, the empty containers were gone and others in their place, before I could figure out who had done it.[19] They also supplied me with oats and hay for my horse. God will repay it all.

17. Namely, in Aurora after he left.

18. Strieter is resuming his story about what happened at the meeting.

19. In other words, Strieter emptied the various containers at home during the week and brought them back on his final Sunday there, but when he came out after church, they had already been replaced with different containers filled up with more gifts.

Chapter 7

Peru

In the autumn of 1869 I came to Peru, Indiana.[1] There I had a dear teacher[2] with a good school. Besides Peru I was soon preaching in the vicinity of Moorefield at Father Springer's (everybody was Pennsylvany Dutch there),[3] at J. Betzner's in the bush,[4] in Rochester, in Whippoorwill, and at See's (that was the name of the man I first called on there). His place was located in the vicinity of the Eel River. In Peru the congregation numbered fifty voting members. At Springer's there were eighteen or so. At Betzner's just four families. In Rochester there were five families. In Whippoorwill there were eight families. I could get to Rochester by railroad; I had to ride to the other places. Those in Whippoorwill came and got me from Rochester.

1. See Appendix IV, no. 9. The church was located on the west corner of what is today West 2nd and South Hood Streets.
2. Leutner corrected this to: "There I had the dear Teacher K." He obtained the initial from when Strieter gives it later. The teacher's name was Heinrich Kors (1833–1911).
3. Moorefield was the original name of North Grove; Strieter spelled it Morefield. This preaching station appears to have been a schoolhouse about 1.7 miles southwest of North Grove.
4. J. Betzner appears to have lived about two miles west of Bunker Hill in Pipe Creek Township, on the south side of the road.

Fig. 39. Kingman Brothers, St. John's Evangelical Lutheran Church, Peru, Ind., from 1861–1875, publ. 1877, drawing. Image courtesy of St. John's, Peru. See n. 1.

They did have a parsonage in Peru, but it was terribly cold in the winter; it was jerry-built. Peru lies in the Wabash Valley; it soon turned into a real valley of tears for me. Mama came from Aurora later, bringing a sick child (that's why she couldn't come along right away), and it soon died on us.[5] The summers were very dry, and the lowlands would therefore dry out and the air would become full of fever stuff. Sickness would appear everywhere. Three or four would often be sick in bed at the same time in our house. Even dear Mama was overtaken by congested fever during the noon meal, and right away she was completely gone. But God blessed the efforts of the homeopathic doctor, who gave her so much quinine that it was suppressed right away after the first attack. The dear man did all his work for free.

A lady notified me that her husband didn't believe there was a devil. I spoke with him and suggested to him that he meet with the teacher and several other brothers at my place on an evening each week and go through the doctrine of the devil, to which he agreed. But we accomplished nothing. He said, "A snake is s'posed to have chatted, Mr.

---

5. See Appendix II, no. 8.

Pastor? You, sir, ever heard a snake chat? I'm s'posed to believe such nonsense? That guy who appeared to Christ in the wilderness was a chief of that band of robbers."

We finally had to give it up. Just between the two of us I asked him, "Do you honestly believe, sir, that Christ is God's Son?"

He said, "I too am God's son."

I asked, "What, sir, do you say to the words, 'conceived by the Holy Spirit'?"

He said, "That sounds to me exactly like if I went away on a trip to Germany and when I came back after a year, my old lady was fat and when I asked, 'Where'd you get that from?' and she said, 'From the Holy Spirit.'"[6]

I said, "So in your eyes, sir, Christ is the child of a whore?"

He said, "Yeah, what else could he be?"

I said, "Then we are done with you, sir. We must excommunicate you."

He said, "That's what you must do, if you want to act in accordance with the Bible." He promised that he would also come to the meeting. The excommunication went quickly, and on Sunday it was announced from the pulpit. Up till then he had been giving a hundred dollars of clergy pay.

One church discipline case I inherited from my predecessor, Jox. Jox had preached that whoever goes to the Supper twice a year purely out of custom is a hypocrite. Someone attacked him for that in a letter and called him a hypocrite and a liar. Jox already brought the matter to the congregation's attention, but it was interrupted by my arrival, so I had to continue. We could not get anywhere with the person. He would not give proof and also would not retract. We had to excommunicate him too.

One time we elected H. G. as an administrator, a man of very keen intelligence and excellent demeanor. I barely had a chance to rejoice over his election when my teacher comes and tells me that H. G. wants to open a saloon. I speak with him right away. "Yes." I summoned him before the board. All pleading and exhorting was useless. At the next meeting he and his brother show up and declare at the end that they are leaving the congregation and are refusing all admonition. They left.

Another man became an Oddfellow. One man withdrew because Jox had offended him. Several moved away. A number died, and we came down to thirty.

My Teacher K[ors] accepted another call, and I had to hold school. One afternoon I suddenly got a stinging pain in my eye, as if someone had stabbed a needle into my eye. I rub and rub, but the pain keeps getting worse and I had to dismiss the children. That night was a horrible one. Pretty soon the other eye starts stinging too. My eyes, especially the first, were completely bloodshot. They fetched our Dr. B., but he said, "I don't like to do anything with the eyes. Fetch someone else." Someone else is fetched. He says the same thing, but advises that we wrap a rotten apple on them. Our neighborlady comes and names a doctor who would take the case. He is fetched. He says, "I will be right back," and leaves. He does come back soon and brings along

---

6. Leutner crossed out the man's answer and replaced it with: "He gave a completely blasphemous answer. It shouldn't be repeated."

three leeches, attaches two to the worst eye and one to the other. As they start sucking, it was just like the burning was being brushed off with the hand.

One time I was called to an old man who wanted to see me. I went up a staircase. Upstairs in a large living room sat the old man. I say, "Good day, grandfather!"

He says, "Good day, Mr. Parson!"

I ask, "You want something from me, sir?" He never attended my church and was a heavy whiskey drinker.

"Yes, I would very much like to have the Supper before I die."

I say, "To benefit from the Supper a repentant heart is required."

He says, "I am completely prepared."

I say, "But I have to ask anyway, sir, how is it going with your old sins?"

Agitated, he asks, "What sins?"

"Your despising of God's word and your drinking."

He says, "Out the door!", and I leave. He soon died, and they got an English pastor to do the funeral.

At Father S[pringer]'s out there by Moorefield I often turned in and was there overnight most of the time. He says in an anglicized Pennsylvany Dutch, "Now, Mr. Parson, some take the wafers and some take the bread; some take it in the hand and some in the chops. What is the difference?" The Reformed had withdrawn, or they came to church but stayed away from the Supper.

I show him the difference, but the next time: "Now, what is the difference?" and so on. I simply could not make it clear for the old man; he would always keep coming back to his "difference." One of his children was a daughter G. who suffered from tuberculosis. She was a very pious child. I began Catechism instruction. She was already in her twenties, but she answered so alertly and joyfully.

I was directed to a Z., who was sick in bed. I speak with him and invited him to church.

He says in Pennsylvany Dutch, "It can't be done."

I ask, "But why not?"

He says, "In a past meeting the topic of bread and wafers for the Supper came up. When I desired bread, Mother J. then said to me, 'Whoever is not worthy with wafers is certainly not worthy with bread,' and someone spit at me."

One time I was riding up there. I had to go through a forest. Suddenly a storm broke out. Then a tree toppled down in front of me across the path. My horse jumped over it. On the right, right next to me, a treetop toppled down, on the left a large branch. My horse got all excited and swept on through. Fortunately I came into the open.

Chapter 8

Proviso

Without me expecting it, a call came to me from Proviso, Cook County, Illinois, thirteen miles west of Chicago.[1] I asked my dear Dr. Sihler for advice and he advised me to accept the call. I presented the call to the congregation. Someone asked if I could run the school. I said sure, but not five days a week on account of the preaching stations I went to each week. They said there should be five days of school, for the sake of the non-member children, so it would be better for me to accept the call. I accepted the call.

The wife again could not accompany me right away on account of a sick child, so I set out with the kids and arrived at K. P.'s in Proviso on March 12, 1873. The next morning he drove me up to the church, a large, beautiful frame church whose steeple had a view far across the prairie. It stands at an intersection,[2] next to the schoolhouse and the teacherage; a couple hundred steps to the south is the parsonage. In the northwest street corner, back a ways, in a grove, stands a building almost just as large. I ask my K. P. what that building is.

---

1. Today this is Immanuel Lutheran Church (LC-MS), 2317 South Wolf Road, Hillside, Illinois. Hillside still belongs to Proviso Township.
2. Today this is the intersection of West Cermak Road and South Wolf Road.

Fig. 40. Immanuel Ev. Luth. Church in Proviso, Ill., photo printed in *Lebenslauf des Johannes Strieter* (1905)

"That's a chapel of the devil, a dance hall."

I asked whether the owner belonged to the congregation, to which he said yes. He also had a saloon. I was also told that both were frequently visited by the congregation.

Soon Mama arrived too. The first visit we were paid was by the wife of the owner of the just-mentioned establishment with a basketful of goodies for the kitchen and two bottles of wine for me.

When I came to Proviso,[3] 125 families called me their pastor, but only thirty-seven names appeared beneath the constitution. They once had a constitution in which it said that the congregation consisted of two congregations, a church congregation and a school congregation, and there were a lot more names beneath that one. Now they wanted to combine the two into one and to draw up a new constitution and the majority were refusing to sign it. They invoked the fact that they had signed once and that was enough. This happened before my time and should have been avoided, and the combining should have been done in a different way. It made for a lot of unpleasantness.

3. See Appendix IV, no. 10.

The congregation had two schools—one, the larger, in the East District, the other in the West District. The eastern one, by the church, was vacant; the western one had a teacher, but he soon caused us a lot of grief. We finally had to dismiss him from his position and also excommunicate him.[4] In the western school we then had Teacher W[iegrefe]. But when those members moved and joined neighboring congregations, it closed down. In the East District we had Teacher L[eutheusser], Teacher M[ack], Teacher H[erter], Teacher K[aeppel],[5] Teacher V[oigt], and Teacher D[aenzer].

When I got there, I was told that the sermon was on Sunday morning and Catechism instruction in the afternoon, but in the afternoon almost none of the adults came. I presented this to the congregation, that the Catechism was not merely for the children, but also for the adults. But they did not think they could come twice. I then proposed having a brief catechesis right after the sermon, to which they agreed. But now some of them[6] headed out of the church after the sermon. That troubled me a lot. I instructed and exhorted, but it didn't help. Then I started rebuking in earnest; that helped. We arranged for the Supper on the first Sunday of every month and on Maundy Thursday. Running out early also ceased when the Supper was celebrated.

For depositing into the treasury, they had this arrangement: Each family member had to pay fifty cents to the church treasury.[7] The school treasury was extra, five dollars per child per year plus a dollar heating fee.[8] The building treasury was divided up according to land—forty acres this much, twice forty this much, etc. But see, every year on accounting day it was read off: fifty dollar deficit, a hundred dollar deficit, 150 dollar deficit. The pastor and teacher got paid, but the treasurer had to dig into his own pocket. I wanted to remedy this and proposed to the congregation that they do away with the compulsory system and introduce freewill contributions. They did not want to go along with that at all. One man thought that, if we did that, I would have to die of hunger. I told him that before it got to that point I would come to him for a piece of bread. Would he give me one?

"Oh sure!"

"Great, then there's no danger." I said they should try it for a year on a trial basis. They agreed to that. I gave a sermon on giving to the church treasury, and look, when the year was up, we had a surplus. Now a resolution was passed and freewill payments were introduced, and up until my departure we always closed with a surplus.

The election of officers went like this: Someone nominated a candidate, someone else supported it, and it was voted on, until we had three candidates, then the administrator was elected by oral vote from those three.[9] The congregation had five

---

4. This was F. Polsdorfer, the West District schoolteacher from 1871–1878.
5. In the chronological order, Teachers Herter and Kaeppel should be switched.
6. Leutner intensifies this, saying it was "many of them" (*zum großen Teil*).
7. Carl Strieter says that this was a weekly obligation.
8. German: *einen Thaler Feuergeld*. Carl translated: "$1.00 for coal and wood."
9. Here Leutner added: "And under patriarchal circumstances that worked really well."

administrators; four were collectors and the fifth was treasurer. These five were now all in all, and it worked wonderfully. But my, what kind of administrators I often got, some of them people who secretly worked against me.

I now proposed a different arrangement to the congregation, namely to elect by ballot and to do so twice. The first time every man should write a name, and from these the three highest should be candidates. The second time one of those three should be written down, and the one with the most votes should be administrator. They agreed to this. I now gave a speech before the election, in which I showed what kind of a man an administrator should be and with what conscientiousness he should be elected. And see, from now on I got the best men.

I also introduced installation of the administrators. At the resolution of the congregation, ten points were established as the duties of an administrator. They were not only put into the minutes, but were also read at every installation, affirmed by the administrator-elect with a handshake, and he would kneel and be consecrated with the laying on of hands,[10] and a written copy of his duties were then handed to him. I would give a speech; in it I would first address the administrator and then the congregation.

The effect was marvelous. While people seemed to be scrambling for administrator positions before, now no one wanted a turn anymore. When H. was elected, he begged to be set free. When this did not happen, he consented with tears. A. was elected; he also didn't want it. When he was not released, he asked, "Mr. Pastor, just don't be too hard on me, please." And from then on, the administrators discharged their office faithfully, including going to their school, usually four times a year. One time two of them also came to the confirmation class.[11] In my final years there I held this during the summer, on every schoolday from nine to ten, as long as school was in session. That worked the best.

Now to the:

Saloon and Ball[12]

K. P. had already told me what was going on with that. I was soon to experience it for myself. My church members' horses often stood in front of the saloon for hours at a time. I myself saw drunks come out. Games were played there, including games for money. The ball made its appearance. People streamed in from all four sides, arriving in the evening and returning home in the morning.

At that time I had a dear friend at the seminary in Addison,[13] Prof. Lindemann, Sr.

---

10. This clause was omitted in Leutner's print edition.
11. This sentence to the end of the paragraph is omitted in Carl Strieter's translation.
12. Leutner made this a separate chapter in the original book, but Strieter appears to have intended it as a subsection in the Proviso chapter.
13. The Lutheran Teacher Seminary, today Concordia University Chicago. The seminary was

Fig. 41. J. C. W. Lindemann, engraving printed in W. H. T. Dau, ed., *Ebenezer: Reviews of the Work of the Missouri Synod during Three Quarters of a Century* (1922).

I bemoaned my trouble to him and asked for advice. He said, "Strieter, you must break the spell. It is impossible for the gospel to penetrate such hearts that are so preoccupied with serving the flesh. Take it on, in God's name."[14]

---

founded in 1864, with the campus center and north wing built that year. The south wing was added in 1873. The campus is pictured in the January 30, 1906 issue of *Der Lutheraner* (p. 37). A monument marking the location of the seminary stands at the northeast corner of the Addison Village Hall along West Lake Street.

14. See p. 83, n. 26. The influence of Pietism can once again be felt here. That a strict attitude against dancing was not the traditional Lutheran position is evident from a sermon on John 2:1–11 that Martin Luther himself published in 1525. In it he said (Weimar Edition 17/2:64):

Is it then also a sin to play music [*pfeyffen*] and dance at a wedding, since people say that much sinning comes from dancing? Whether the Jews had dances I do not know. But since it is the custom of the country, just like inviting guests, decorating, eating and drinking and being merry, I see no reason to condemn it, except for its excess, when it is lewd or there is too much. But the fact that sins are committed in that case is not the fault of dancing by itself, since things like that happen just as much at meals and in church, just as it is not the fault of eating and drinking when some people turn into swine while engaged in them. But where things are conducted in a chaste manner, I will let weddings have their rites and customs and dances without objection. Faith and love are not lost by dancing or by sitting, when you do them in a chaste and moderate manner. Young children certainly dance without sinning; do as they do and become a child, then dancing will not harm you. Otherwise, if dancing were a sin in itself, then we must not

I went now to X.'s and encounter his wife in the saloon. I tell her that I would very much like to speak with them. She says I should just speak. I say that we could be overheard in the saloon; I would prefer that they go someplace private with me. She called her husband over, opened a door, and up the stairs we go, opened another door on the left; there was a bedroom there. She sat on the bed, I on a chair in front of her, and he stood somewhat behind me off to the side. I now began with holy baptism, presented the baptismal blessing, reminded them of the baptismal covenant, described the sinful activity, reminded them of death and judgment, and begged them to give it up. Told them also that H. wanted to buy the dance hall from them, put it on his land, and turn it into a cheese factory. They could expand their small store. I tried my best to make it so that they had all the information necessary to come out without any loss.

I asked them what they had to say to that.

He says, "What do you think?"

During my speech, she had lowered her head, grabbed the edge of her apron, and twisted it around and around with her fingers. Now she pulled herself together and said, "No, we're not going to give it up. We've put too much into it."

I said that I was very sorry, but that from that day on I too would be changing my tune, and left.

Now I went at it, instructed, exhorted, rebuked, and coaxed privately, and in the confessional assembly delivered a sermon on the ball, showing that it was not a fruit of the tree of the Church, but of the tree of the world.

It came up in the meeting and there were long and intense discussions. Every possible defense was presented. Their fathers had danced, their grandfathers and great-grandfathers—did I wish to condemn them all? There was dancing in the military. If the young men did not learn to dance, then they would be scorned. One man accused me of having eleven commandments; he had only learned ten and my eleventh said: "Don't go to the ball."

I said, "I only have ten too, but all ten are against the ball. My First Commandment says, 'We should fear, love, and trust in God above all things.' Do you do that at the ball, sir?"

He was silent.

"My Second says, 'We should pray, praise, and give thanks.' Do you do that at the ball, sir?"

He was silent.

"My Third says, 'We should gladly hear and learn God's word.' Do you do that at the ball, sir?"

He was silent.[15]

---

allow children to do it either.

Persistent encouragements along these lines may have been more appropriate than an encouragement to eliminate ballroom dancing entirely. But see next n.

15. Even though I am unsure whether Pastor Strieter received and implemented good advice in

"My Fourth says, 'We should honor our parents and those in authority.' Do you see it, sir, as an honorable thing in the sight of God and all people when your children are skilled at running around at the ball? I could go through all the Commandments in their entirety like that, sir, but this should suffice to show you that I do not need any eleventh commandment against the ball."

My passages were especially: "Do not conform yourselves to this world" [Rom. 12:2]. "You cannot be partakers of the Lord's table and the devil's table at the same time" [1 Cor. 10:21b]. "Do everything in the name of Jesus" [Col. 3:17].

One man exclaimed, "If a person can really do everything in the name of Jesus, should I then haul manure in the name of Jesus too?"

I said, "By all means, sir, and everything that you cannot do in the name of Jesus, you must discontinue."

The battle carried on.

Finally, after I had announced the Holy Supper again, I declared that from this day forward I was no longer letting anybody come to the Lord's Table that would not discontinue their godless, carnal activity for me, and I turned twenty-five people away.

At the next meeting a man stood up at the end: "Before we close, I have something else to bring up. I ask you, Mr. Pastor, how many did you refuse at the last announcing?"

"Twenty-five."

"There you see it. The pastor is destroying our entire congregation. And now I ask you, Mr. Pastor, are you going to continue this madness?"

"I will not yield one hair, do with me what you wish. The moment I would yield, I would be putting the devil in this pulpit."

I was expecting the motion to depose the pastor, but he sat down and everybody was quiet. After a pause, someone said, "I make a motion we adjourn." Supported, carried.

As I was leaving, Father D. claps me on the shoulder and whispers in my ear, "Stand firm, sir; you are getting it done."

I would frequently send three men to X. to exhort him, but to no avail. Before one meeting I again sent three men, who invited him to the meeting, but he was rude and sent us the message that he was not coming to our meeting and would not put up with the admonishers from now on. He was unanimously declared to be one who had excluded himself and put himself under the ban. Now the battle was won. My church members stayed away from any further balls, and those who had been turned away all came back. I was assured that Mr. X. repeatedly had to pay his musicians out of his own pocket. Even privately hosted dances died out; at least, I didn't hear of any in my final years there.

---

addressing this matter, the silence on the part of the members certainly speaks in his defense. If they could not say that they were dancing in Jesus's name and glorifying God with their dancing, or even that such godly dancing was possible, then perhaps Strieter was right to attack it so.

Now this X. opened a cheese factory and my people brought their milk there, and some would also once again tie up their horses in front of the saloon on the way home. Payday was every month and took place in the saloon. Some of them would stay there for a long time too. Toward evening I myself saw an otherwise dear old father going home in a very drunken state; he was staggering back and forth so badly he could scarcely walk.[16]

"So, this is the new trap the devil has set for you. What now?" I exhorted and rebuked again and delivered two sermons on how we should act toward those who are excommunicated. After that I was sued by X.; he said I had caused him 5,000 dollars in losses in his hotel—he didn't even have one, just a completely ordinary saloon—and in his cheese factory—I never said a word against it—and he was still going to get that 5,000. The case was supposed to come up in court. I hired a lawyer and went to the courthouse in Chicago. But X.'s lawyers gave his case and his deposit back to him beforehand. Now there was peace. It also wasn't too long before the gentleman gave up his factory too.[17]

After I arrived in Proviso, I took over Lyons right away, a village six miles to the east.[18] At first I went there every fourteen days, as they desired, then every Sunday afternoon. That was a desolate, drunken hole, and every Sunday wagonfulls of people came from the city[19] to drink and dance. Not far from the church, which the congregation had constructed cheaply, there was a beer garden, and it was completely open in between. People would be gambling and dancing there while I was preaching, and the high clarinet and its waltzes would echo in loudly through the windows. My M., a regular churchgoer and active member, but a feisty character, tolerated this several times. Then, when the clarinet had really let itself be heard again, he went after church to the owner and told him, "Today is the last time, or else on Monday you know exactly where I'm gonna be."

Now things were fine. They would play and dance merrily, but a lookout was posted to watch for the arrival of the Holy Joe, and as soon as I set foot in the church, poof, everything was quiet all the way up until I went back out, then boom, back at it again.

I then handed Lyons off to my neighboring minister Bohlen, who was much closer and, in my opinion, could better minister to the brothers' needs.[20] At the same

16. Leutner omitted everything after the semicolon.

17. Leutner changed these two sentences to read: "Now there was peace, though it didn't last very long. The man gave up his factory." The combination of Strieter's details, old property maps of Cook County, and an announcement of creamery machinery for sale in the June 29, 1903 edition of *The Elgin Dairy Report* reveal the man's identity—C. Thiele.

18. Today this is Zion Evangelical Lutheran Church, 7930 Ogden Avenue, Lyons, Illinois—exactly six miles from Immanuel, Hillside.

19. Presumably Chicago

20. Pastor Wessel Bohlen was serving Zion Evangelical Lutheran Church, today at 5865 South

time I started up in La Grange and Hinsdale, then also in Downer's Grove and Grossdale.[21] Twenty banded together in La Grange[22] and not quite as many in Hinsdale.[23] In Downer's Grove and Grossdale it was small. In Hinsdale they built a church on a purchased lot.[24] In La Grange S[ieling] donated a small piece of land and a schoolhouse was erected. Soon had a nice school going too. We called Pastor Molthan to Hindsdale[25] and Pastor Ullrich to La Grange.[26]

Back when I was still in Aurora, my right ear started humming. I went to the doctor and he asked about my earlier work, etc. I told him a bunch of stuff, and he thought

---

Archer Road, Summit, Illinois. Zion, Summit, is just under four miles south from Zion, Lyons.

21. Grossdale was the original name of Brookfield, Illinois. Today there are Missouri Synod congregations in both of these latter cities, but they were founded in 1909 and 1902, respectively.

22. Today this is St. John's Lutheran Church at the corner of 47th Street and Brainard Avenue, La Grange, Illinois.

23. Today this is Zion Lutheran Church at 204 South Grant Street, Hinsdale, Illinois—four and a half miles southwest of Immanuel, Hillside, and about seven and a half miles almost due west of St. John's, La Grange.

24. The history of Zion, Hinsdale, available online, opens as follows (http://www.zionlutheranhinsdale.org/about/history/; accessed May 8, 2017):

The history of Zion Lutheran Church began in Hinsdale, Illinois on November 14, 1886, when the first service was held in the old Fullersberg schoolhouse. Dr. E. A. Kraus, president of Concordia Teachers College, presided over the service. In January of 1887, Rev. John Strieter of Immanuel, Hillside, began conducting bi-monthly services for the Hinsdale community. . . . The community responded with much enthusiasm to these services and on April 15, 1888, a congregation was officially formed, with 21 members signing the charter. ZION was the name given to the new, and proud congregation. In April, 1888, a vacant lot at Vine and Second Streets [just one block west of the current location] was purchased for the purpose of building a house of worship. The church, complete with tower and bell, was completed for the cost of $2,515, $1,000 of which was raised by the small congregation. The building was dedicated on October 14, 1888. 1889 also [saw] the purchase of land, as five acres north of Hinsdale were purchased as a cemetery plot for the Hinsdale congregation.

See also Appendix IV, no. 12.

25. See Appendix IV, no. 13.

26. The history of St. John's, La Grange, available online, opens as follows (http://www.sjlagrange.com/church/History.html; accessed May 8, 2017):

On May 30, 1886, an historic meeting took place at the home of Louis Sieling of LaGrange. Twenty men prayerfully decided to organize a Lutheran Christian congregation at LaGrange and to begin at once to build a place of worship which could also serve as a school house for a Christian Day School. During the summer of 1886, a frame school house, 26 x 38 feet, was completed on land donated by Louis Sieling, and on September 19th of that year the building was dedicated to God's glory for use as a church and school. On September 26, St. John's congregation was formally organized. From 1886 until 1893, Rev. John Strieter of Immanuel, Proviso (Hillside), conducted worship services every Sunday afternoon. During these years, Mr. Fred Polsdoerfer, Mr. Louis Luecker, and Mr. Charles Strieter taught at the school. In 1893, St. John's called Rev. Alex Ullrich to be in charge of both church and school.

See also Appendix IV, no. 14.

that both ears would go deaf eventually; all the freezing was especially to blame.[27] The hearing in my right ear disappeared almost entirely. When I still had La Grange, it also started in my left ear, so that I couldn't hear nearly anything at all anymore. I was at the conference, the big one, and out of all that was said the entire time I heard exactly one word, from the mouth of the dear, old Brauer, now departed, who was sitting in my vicinity and had a loud voice. At the end I asked my brothers whether I shouldn't resign my position. They advised: No.

Pretty soon I got out of bed one morning and could hear; it came back during the night. My left ear could hear again for eight years or so.

In 1901 the deafness came back. I asked my visitor[28] to come and called the brothers to a meeting and and asked them if they didn't want to take my position from me. But they said: No.

In 1902, I asked the visitor to come again and now told my people how the instruction was weighing on my conscience. I could not hear any child's answer anymore and had to confirm haphazardly. After a lengthy speech by the dear Grosse from Addison, they agreed. They resolved to give me a hundred dollars and to take up a collection for me every quarter-year as long as I lived. On Cantate Sunday I delivered my farewell sermon on Acts 20:32, and on Rogate Sunday I held Lord's Supper in the morning and in the afternoon installed my successor, Pastor C[hristoph] Drögemüller.[29] Pastors Ullrich from La Grange and Gübert from Hinsdale assisted. I and my wife moved in with the son-in-law H[einrich] List in Frankenlust, where he is a teacher.

27. Carl Strieter, doubtless recalling actual conversations, translates quite freely: "The doctor whom I consulted thought that the freezing I had to endure in Wisconsin was the cause. Deafness or hard-of-hearing often are the result of such freezing."

28. One of a number of pastoral deputies of a district president, sometimes also called a circuit pastor today.

29. Carl includes the dates of each Sunday—April 27 and May 4, respectively. See Appendix IV, no. 15.

Fig. 42. Heinrich List, teacher of St. Paul Lutheran School-Frankenlust, Bay City, Mich., from 1899–1942. Image courtesy of St. Paul Lutheran-Frankenlust.

Lodge[30]

In Proviso I was sued by an Oddfellow, if I'm not mistaken. It happened like this: A child who was baptized died on him and he asked me to come and give the funeral address in his house. He never came to my church. When I was there, I told him he was a sinner and that he could only be saved through repentance. Told him also what repentance was and how necessary it was because of death and judgment. I got on his bad side for saying that. When he met me on the sidewalk one time, I bid him good day—I didn't have a clue about his spite—and he told me not to bid him good day anymore.

A girl, thirteen years old or so, threw a rolled up piece of paper to a boy during my devotion at the school. When he picked it up, I took it away from him and ask, "L., should I read out loud what you have written?"

She said, "No."

I asked, "What do you deserve now?"

She said, "Punishment."

"And that's what you will get, for sin needs to be punished."

I send a boy outside to get me a stick. He brought a small switch that had sprouted on a plum tree. I call her up to me and lash her, not especially hard, three times across her shoulders. She did not cry, but grabbed me by the hand then and said in a very sweet voice, "Mr. Pastor, please do not hit me anymore. I will not do it again."

"Good, then take your seat." She was the daughter of a widow, who was the sister of the man who did not want any more greetings from me.

---

30. See n. 12. Leutner also made this a separate chapter in the original book, but Strieter appears to have intended it as another subsection in the Proviso chapter.

It's not long before I'm at the school and a gentleman hands me a written invitation to appear before Judge N.[31] on such-and-such a day. When it was time for me to appear, my elders got a lawyer to accompany me and gave him five dollars afterwards. The plaintiff G. also had a redheaded lawyer and brought three witnesses, my students, the cousins of the girl. The opposing lawyer asked the boys if I had spoken with them beforehand.

"Yes."

What had I said?

That they should tell the truth.

What kind of man was I?

I was a very good man.

Could they tell when a man was angry?

"Oh, sure."

Had I been angry when I was hitting?

"No, he was just fine."

He now gave it up. Then one of them exclaimed in English, "Oh, she needed a whipping."

The judge now called my lawyer up to speak. He said his speech would be superfluous, since his[32] own witnesses had already beat him. Then the judge rendered his verdict: "Not guilty."

As the boys were going out the door, they shouted, "Hurrah for Mr. Strieter!" That lawyer was very nice to me afterwards though, even tipped his hat to me.

I soon received an anonymous letter, three pages long, in which I was called every name in the book. I was even called a Sabbath-breaker because I attended to my business on Sundays, and a bunch of other stuff.

One time I was asked to visit a sick man. The wife came to my church; he did not. I had a talk with him and at the end gave him the Holy Supper. He died. Then the wife came to tell me, but she said her husband had been an Oddfellow; was there anything I could do? I told her I would give a funeral address at the house, but the Oddfellows were not allowed to show up with their badges. When I was finished, they could have the body if they wanted. She was okay with that. The gentlemen came with fanfare until they got close to the house, then they were quiet and holed up in the wood shack until I was gone.

In Wisconsin I was also sued by the Oddfellows and convicted. I was staying there for several days and was holding some school and instruction with older and younger children. One day a boy of eleven years or so was really nasty; he shamelessly defied me. I take him just outside, pick up a switch, and lash him four times on his cushion. He behaved himself then. Right after that I have to appear before a nearby judge. A man, a

---

31. This abbreviation is unclear. Strieter may be using it to indicate he no longer remembers who it was, like we use "X" today.

32. Leutner prevents any confusion by changing "his" to "the opponent's."

farmer, steps forward as the lawyer and says that they are all Oddfellows here and they were going to show me that I could not mistreat the son of an Oddfellow. The father had died and was apparently an Oddfellow, which I did not know. Three men were sitting there as jury. Then he said they could fine me for twenty-five dollars. The gentlemen went into an adjacent room and came right back with their twenty-five dollar fine. The father with whom I was staying was there and said, "The twenty-five dollars will be paid, and you will continue holding your school, sir." That's what happened. I confirmed the older children in R.[33] I have no idea who paid the twenty-five dollars.

In R. I was told that R., who was going to my church, was also an Oddfellow. I went to see him and spoke with him, telling him among other things that in their pocket manual, on any number of seventy-some pages, it said that faith in Christ was no better and no more certain than the faith of the Jews, Turks, and heathens.

He says, "The book that you have is a counterfeit, sir."

I bring along my book for him. He says that he will show it to their chaplain, a Methodist minister. He gave me my book back, saying that the chaplain had explained it this way: As Christians we believe in Christ, but as Oddfellows we believe what the booklet says. The booklet I had was genuine.

I say, "But, my dear R., then our dear Lord God will one day have to split you into two parts, and let the Christ-half go to heaven and the Oddfellow-half go to hell."

He says, "Mr. Pastor, when I die, my wife will get 2,000 dollars from the lodge; she will not get anything from the church. I am through with your church, sir."

One time my wife and I were visiting his relatives along the canal.[34] While I am speaking with the husband, my wife was paging through a thick book that was lying on the table. On the way home she says "Hey, your P. in H[insdale] is a lodge member; I read his name in the book."

I speak with P. He says, "Oh, that is just an aid association."

I ask for the constitution. He gave it to me along with the songs that are sung during the meetings. I page through the thing and see that the order, which was called Ancient Order of the United Workmen, if I'm not mistaken, was a lodge, pure and simple. The songs praised their works of drying the tears of widows and orphans, and were directed to the Great Spirit and Great Father.

I speak with P., but he says that the order has already cost him over 600 dollars. If he leaves, his money will be wasted. Then it came back to the 2,000 dollars his wife would receive when he died. He would rather part ways with the congregation than with the order. And that's what he did.

Another man belonged to it and he quit.[35]

---

33. R. appears to be the first letter of the city in Wisconsin where Strieter was staying for a stint.

34. Most likely the Illinois and Michigan Canal. Johannes does not exactly specify that they were Mr. R.'s relatives, but his son Carl does so specify in his translation, and the context supports him.

35. Leutner adds for clarification that what this gentleman quit was the lodge, not the church.

We are holding a small conference at my place one time when my neighboring minister B[ohlen] said to me, "Your G. in L[a] G[range] belongs to the lodge. I saw him at a funeral wearing a badge."

I go to see G., but then he too said it was just an aid association. He belonged to the same lodge. Also can't get anywhere with him. He was an administrator in L[a] G[range]. I asked if any others from the congregation belonged to it.

Four to five others.

Who were they?

He wouldn't tell me.

I make it known that I am going to give three sermons against the lodge.

The first was on the passage, "You shall worship God, your Lord" [Matt. 4:10], and I read from the booklet that they believed in a higher being, saying that in the whole booklet it was never said who this higher being is. In fact, their headmen said that they phrased it that way precisely so that those who didn't believe in the God of the Bible could be accepted, thus a deliberate denial of the true God. Consequently, that confession was that of a heathen; the higher being was an idol. But now Paul said that what the heathens sacrificed to idols, they were sacrificing to demons. Whoever was therefore subscribing to this confession of faith was renouncing his covenant God, to whom he had sworn allegiance in his baptism,[36] and was signing himself over to the devil.

When I came back, someone handed me a piece of paper before I went in. It said that they didn't want to be a Lutheran congregation, but an evangelical one. I should resign from my position. Twenty names at the bottom, perhaps six to seven of them from my church members and the rest I mostly didn't know at all. I give the second sermon on the passage: "Do not tug at the foreign yoke together with the unbelievers, etc." [2 Cor. 6:14], and now I lash out at the brotherhood. Then I read the note, but omit the names, after I had said how many names were there, and I said that none of this would happen, and announce my third sermon.

When I come, a note is again handed to me, written in English, very stylishly and with fancy words; in it I was asked to resign my position for the sake of peace and the same twenty names are at the bottom. I give my third sermon on the passage: "Cursed is the one who trusts in man" [Jer. 17:5], read the note again, but in German, and repeat my declaration, but announce that there will be a congregational meeting after church next time.

Earlier they had asked me to write a constitution. I did that and brought it along. After the sermon I ask everyone to stay here. Everybody stayed. On the right side of the altar sat three rows of girls, some of them girls I had confirmed, some from neighboring congregations, but who with the permission of their pastor went to church and to the Supper by me. Scarcely had I begun to speak when a furious guy jumps up: "So, we have the devil for our God?" and out into the aisle he comes. My girls, as if by command, get up and position themselves in a circle around me, with their faces

36. See p. 111, n. 96.

toward me, and the person now keeps on swinging away at me with his fist over the girls' shoulders and heads. When he had vented, he ran off.

One man started in, saying I should prove that they did not mean the true God when they talked about the higher being.

I said that the true God was only in Christ, for John says that whoever does not have Christ does not have God [2 John 9]. He was the one who should show me just one occurrence of the name of Christ in his book.

He replies, "Christ has no business in the association; he doesn't belong in there."

"Okay, you dear people, now you have their own admission that the lodge as such has no Christ, and thus no God, but the devil."

Another man said he had given twenty-five dollars toward the building. We should return him his money.

I say, "I also gave twenty-five dollars, but do not demand it back."

Another man said that we had absolutely no right to lay claim to this property, since the congregation was not yet incorporated.

I pull out a note and hand it to my son,[37] who was the teacher at the time, and I say, "Read it."

He read that St. John Congregation was incorporated.

The man said, "Now who did that?"

"I did," I said.

One after the other left. Now I read my constitution, which contained a paragraph against the lodges. It was unanimously adopted. We had peace.

Pretty soon I learned that those who had left, along with some others, had sent for a United man from the city who was now preaching to them, and that they were trying to fish for my people. One of mine had even been in their church and said, "Oh, he preaches just beautifully!"

I said to my son, "Now it's time for you to leave. I must give the little group a shepherd who can keep them together." I went to my dear Succop, my president at the time; he thought the same thing. My son received a call, and we called the dear Ullrich, who was released to us in St. Louis. He came immediately after his examination. The United man was soon forced to give up, and the better ones of those who had left came back. Ullrich even got Grossdale back,[38] which had been lost to the United man.[39]

---

37. Leutner identifies Karl (Carl) as the son in question.

38. See n. 21.

39. Since Alexander Ullrich was called, ordained, and installed in 1893 as a result of the lodge situation, it appears that Strieter delivered his three sermons against the lodges in 1892 or early 1893.

Chapter 9

Pleasant Experiences

In L[a] G[range] the school had already folded on us twice and the people had lost all courage. I waited a while, then I began to talk about it again. But no one had the heart. I said, "We have many young people here, especially girls, so that, for example, if some who drew a large salary, three or four dollars a week, were to give one dollar per month, we could easily support a teacher, and I would also give my share to the cause." All who were in favor of it should raise their hand. Beforehand I had proposed my son Karl from Minnesota.[1] Everyone raised their hand, and now we got to calling, and we soon got a fine school, for my son came to everyone's delight, and he put his heart into the work.

In Big Bull I had a beautiful dream one time. Church was at Father Kufahl's;[2] it was all crammed full. After church many stayed and made me tell stories. Finally the room emptied out at a late hour. Mother Kufahl says, "You can sleep here, sir," and everbody went out and I lie down along the wall, very tired. Father Kufahl lay down in front of me. I dream I am hearing the angels singing and it is so beautiful. I am enjoying the song, when I wake up; there sat Father Kufahl with Mother, his oldest son and his wife, and his other son around the table, and he was holding his morning devotion. They were singing a morning hymn to the tune of "Jesus Christ, My Sure Defense."[3]

---

1. Strieter spelled it Minnasota. Leutner omits this sentence and simply inserts Karl's name into the last sentence of the paragraph.

2. Strieter spelled it: Kufall's. (It is variously spelled Kufahl, Kupfahl, Kuphal, and Kuphahl in the earliest church records.) See p. 94, n. 53.

3. The people sitting around the table, in the order Strieter lists them, appear to have been Carl Kufahl, Sr., his wife Anna née Schunkeler, Carl Kufahl, Jr., his wife Emilie née Nass, and Daniel Kufahl, who was fourteen years old. Strieter appears to have been at their house on Wed., Oct. 3 and Fri., Nov. 30, 1860, and Wed., Jan. 16, 1861. The *Hamburgisches Gesangbuch für den öffentlichen Gottesdienst und die häusliche Andacht* (Hamburg Hymnal for Public Worship and Family Devotions) of 1843 (and numerous subsequent editions) contained a five-stanza morning hymn titled "Kommst du, süßes Morgenlicht," to be sung to the tune of "Jesus lebt, mit ihm auch ich [Jesus Lives! The Victory's Won]," which has the same tune as "Jesus Christ, My Sure Defense."

One time synod convention was in F[ort] W[ayne].[4] I stayed with Mr. Orff, I'm pretty sure was his name. He told me about a musician, a phenomenal piano player, who had come this way and would frequently board with him, an utterly peculiar person. There were many people visiting me, and they would make me tell stories. The musician would sit in a corner and listen. One time I am telling stories again and mention the cold weather, especially my feet freezing; I was in Wisconsin. Then Strasen said, "There I can help you. Have your wife knit you two pair of stockings from heavy thread. Put those on and over them a pair of kipskin[5] boots a couple sizes too big, and a pair of buffalo hide shoes over those. Then you will keep your feet warm." My musician hears that, and when it's time for me to return home, he is standing on the porch [*Poarch*] with a travel bag in his hand: "Here, Mr. Pastor, please take this along, but do not say whom you got it from," and he left. In the satchel were two large balls of heavy, black, wool yarn, a large pair of boots, and I think buffalo shoes too. I did as I had been instructed, and it helped.

My Theodor[6] came home sick from Addison. He had it in the throat. He brought a letter from the director: They had wanted to keep him there, but he had insisted on going home. The doctor had said it was not diphtheria. I fetched our Dr. R. right away, and he also said it was not yet diphtheria at that point. The next day he came back: "Yes, it is diphtheria." Now the house was quarantined. My Otto, the youngest, soon got it.[7] His sister Maria[8]—we called her Mamie—nursed him with all diligence, but she gets it too. Mama contracted erysipelas [*die Rose*][9] and I now had four invalids. Every morning there would be a call outside. Out there would be someone with bread, the next day with soup, the next with a roast, the next with cake, the next with a roasted turkey, etc.

One time there was knocking at the door. There stands the dear Lydia P. with a small parcel under her arm. "Child, what do you want?"

"I want to stay with you, sir, and help you out."

"Dear child, you simply cannot do that. I simply cannot do that."

"I am not at all afraid of getting infected."

"Child, it isn't going to work."

"Then please let me get the house straightened up and see Mamie, then I will be off again."

---

4. Since Strieter later says he was in Wisconsin at the time, this was either the regular synod convention held on October 14ff, 1863, or the special convention held on October 19ff, 1864.

5. Kipskin is leather prepared from the hide of small or young cattle, intermediate in grade between calfskin and cowhide. Strieter spelled it keepskin.

6. See Appendix II, no. 12.

7. See Appendix II, no. 14. Since Otto passed away on Jan. 18, 1891, the events described here took place in the days and weeks leading up to that date.

8. See Appendix II, no. 10.

9. Carl adds "in the face."

That I permitted.

Soon Mother Sch. came and stayed with me. The doctor thought I had handled everything exactly right.[10]

Mamie grew so sick that for three days I couldn't even get a knife between her teeth, and we thought that her time could be up any moment. Theodor got better.[11] Otto did too, but he had such terrible nosebleeding at first that we had absolutely no clue what to do. The doctor thought it was not good since it could easily lead to cardiac arrest. And so it did. He was lying in another room. All of a sudden he started in: "I want to go by my mama." I tried to calm him down, but he kept at it. I took him in and laid him by her, but could tell that the end was at hand. Mama can too and begins to pray with him. He prays along, but then he stops and has passed away.

Now we tried to make sure Mamie didn't notice it from over there, but she noticed it anyway, and the deathly ill child jumps up and comes over, throws herself on the corpse and cries, "O my Otto, my Otto."[12] From that moment on she improved.

My congregation took care of the funeral, so that it didn't cost me even a cent.

A little boy also died on us in Peru[13] and the dear congregation also took care of that funeral themselves. The child was buried in the city cemetery because the congregation did not have their own. Later the congregation bought themselves a plot for a church cemetery. Then they exhumed our child and put him in their cemetery.

My dear Director Lindemann in Addison was a great comfort to me. We often took turns visiting each other. I especially enjoyed his examinations and commencement addresses for the graduates. I would always go with my teachers to listen to them.[14] Oh, how the address would flow from his lips there, how skilled he was at praising the ministry [*Amt*] the young men were entering, encouraging them to faithfulness, showing them God's comfort, and extolling his blessing. How the news of his sudden death struck me like a thunderbolt.[15] At the funeral I was able to keep myself together fairly

---

10. Strieter seems to be telling the story in such a way to highlight Lydia's youthful naiveté. It appears that this young woman was a friend of Mamie's and thus probably around her age, nineteen (see n. 12 below), and with his wife sick, Strieter at age sixty-one truly could not accept her offer without creating an awkward and uncomfortable situation for himself and his neighbors. The "Mother Sch." who eventually came and stayed with him was doubtless an older woman of repute whose stay was much less likely to raise any eyebrows.

11. However, as Strieter will note, Theodor would die of pneumonia less than six years later.

12. Otto was twelve years, four months, and twenty-five days old. Mamie was a little over nineteen years and two months old.

13. See Appendix II, no. 8. This son, also named Otto, passed away on Nov. 20, 1869, at age two years, five months, and twenty days.

14. A roughly ten-mile trip from his home in Proviso

15. The opening page of vol. 35, no. 3 (Feb. 1, 1879) of *Der Lutheraner* contained the announcement of Director J. C. W. Lindemann's death. It reported that he had gently and blessedly fallen asleep after one p.m. on January 15 after a short but difficult battle during which he ardently called on God for help and joyfully confessed Christ his Redeemer.

well, but on the way I was suddenly overcome by such intense grief that I just had to let out all my weeping and sobbing. But still took comfort in the fact that the dear brother was now released from his many crosses. He was a great cross-bearer.

Fig. 43. C. F. W. Walther, engraving printed in his *Amerikanisch-Lutherische Evangelien Postille* (11th ed.). Walther was pastor of (Old) Trinity Lutheran Church in St. Louis (1841–1887), founder of *Der Lutheraner* (1844), president of the Lutheran Church-Missouri Synod (1847–1850, 1864–1878), president of Concordia Seminary-St. Louis (1850–1887), and the most influential figure in the history of American Lutheranism.

The dear Dr. Walther was also very comforting to me. How glad I was at the synod conventions where I got to hear him speak. The words flowed from his lips into my heart like balm. What instruction, what comfort I derived from his presentation on the Bible as God's word, on God's providence, on predestination, and others. One time I was lamenting my weakness to him and he said to me, "Our dear Lord God also uses filling stones."[16] How very comforting that was to me up to the end of my ministry [*Amtes*]. His lingering illness was painful for me, but I comforted myself with the thought that our dear God would graciously reward him for it in full.[17]

---

16. *Füllsteine* was also a heading regularly employed in *Der Lutheraner* (which Walther had edited for many years) for miscellaneous stories or tidbits used to fill up space in the paper.

17. See Appendix X, nos. 1 & 2.

Wagner and I accompanied each other to his funeral.[18] We went in a sleeping car and even got an upper berth. In the morning a little lady crawled out of the bed beneath me. As I put on my coat, I say, "If this coat is mine, it certainly doesn't feel like it at all," and I noticed that she smiled. My Wagner went in search of a place to smoke, and I am sitting alone with the lady. I start in: "Are you German, ma'am?"

"My mother tongue is French, but I can speak French, German, and English equally well."

"Are you a Jewess?"

"Yes."

"Where is your home?"

"In Texas. I come from Saginaw. I wanted to stay there a while, but I grew restless and had to be off again. If I am at home, I get restless; if I am away, it's the same thing. I know well that it is pure nonsense, but I still cannot help it."

"What you are missing, ma'am, is peace of the heart. Believe in Jesus Christ, your Savior, then you will have peace."

"Why is it though, that you Christians hate and persecute us Jews so much?"

"I[19] do not hate you at all, ma'am. You have to admit though, that there are different kinds of people among the Christians, since it's the same way among the Jews."

"I cannot understand how God can condemn me, even if I don't have your faith. I am not aware of anything bad I have done or am doing."

"Do you have a husband, ma'am?"

"Yes."

"If you come home and you heard that he had done wrong by you according to the Sixth Commandment, what would you do?"

"I would get a divorce immediately."

"You see, ma'am, God is one who has planted that sense of justice in you, but he has it too. He gave his Son in the flesh to be your Savior, and in doing so he contracted a covenant of grace and requires nothing but that you accept this redeemer.[20] If you won't, then God's zeal is kindled and you must face his wrath."

"There are many Christian churches in my city, English ones. What good is it for me to go there and hear about temperance and the like? What good does that do me?"

"Let me give you some advice, ma'am. Buy yourself a New Testament—French, German, or English doesn't matter. Look up the Gospel of John and read especially Chapters 13, 14, 15, 16, and 17, but read a little at a time. Read it without any

---

18. See Appendix X, no. 3.

19. Leutner replaced this with "We".

20. Many Lutherans nowadays do not like the word *accept*, because it has been hijacked by evangelicals and given the human-centered meaning of "to make a conscious decision of your own free volition to admit [someone or something] into your heart." But in itself, the idea of faith being an accepting of Christ in response to the free invitation of the gospel, enabled entirely by the Holy Spirit—who, as the Formula of Concord puts it, makes the unwilling willing and then dwells in the willing—is entirely biblical and Lutheran.

preconceived notions, read it slowly, read it with serious reflection, and you will find peace. But now we are in St. Louis and I have to get off."

"Oh, that's too bad. I should very much have liked for you to keep traveling farther. But now, sir, one question before you depart: You are a clergyman, aren't you?"

"Yes."

"I thought so." She squeezed my hand so affectionately when I left.[21]

In Peru I also experienced this astonishing thing: The number of members, as already noted, continued to dwindle. What did the remaining ones do? Whenever another person died or left, this person took this much more upon himself, that person this much, until they had covered the shortage, so that I still received my salary. They kept on doing this again and again. And you could say that all of them were poor. How many had no home of their own and also still had to pay rent out of their daily earnings. How badly I felt for them, and yet how much this willingness to make sacrifices also comforted me.

In Proviso we were one time at B.'s house for a visit. As we were getting into the two-wheeled cart, B. said, "You're going to need a new buggy pretty soon, sir." It stuck in my head, since my twenty-five years were coming up. Sunday arrives and I think, "You need to stop this before it starts, just like so many times before." When the service ended, I stayed standing at the altar and say that they surely knew as well as I did that my twenty-five years were nearly concluded. But they had better not make any fuss over it. They should give the money to another fund that needed it. I didn't need anything; I was supplied with everything. They had often followed my direction at other times; they should also follow it now. I was asking them sincerely.

Pretty soon I had the Supper, go home afterwards, and lie down after dinner to rest a little, not suspecting anything whatsoever. There is a knock at the door, and in come two administrators with white gloves on. I am startled and ask what they wanted. They wanted to take me to church for the celebration. I say, "It is still too soon."

"Please come."

I have to come along, and Mrs. Pastor does too. Outside stood a carriage that we have to get into. We were scarcely on our way, the bell begins to ring. I was worried: No one better get into that pulpit for me who is going to give me some extravagant gush-mush [*eine Lobhudelei*], or I am running out. Into the church; everything was crowded full. We have to sit up in front. The organ begins. I notice there's someone different playing; it was Prof. Käppel from Addison. Who should appear before the altar and then get into the pulpit? My Lindemann, the second, from Addison. I cheered up then; he was sensible. And he did deliver a glorious sermon in which he gave God the glory.

---

21. In the manuscript, this sentence was crossed out in pencil, then in red ink. In its place, the book simply reads: "We part."

After church we went around the corner, there stood my horse in front of the sacristy with a new harness on its back and hitched to a new top buggy. M. gives a speech, and now we're supposed to get in the new buggy and drive home. I express my thanks, and we get in.

Here comes Karl's boy. Mama says, "Fatty! Now where did you come from?"

Fig. 44. The parsonage in Proviso, Ill., photo printed in *Lebenslauf des Johannes Strieter* (1905)

"All of us are here." Right he was. When we open the door, the house is full of children and grandchildren. A horse harness, a buggy, a couch, and 112 pieces of fine utensils for the wife were the gifts. By now I was happy about it though, namely the show of love.

In the latter half of my time there, the congregation was small. We came down to sixty. Here's how: We had to exclude a number of them, i.e. resolve that they had excluded themselves, since they were evading the final step of admonition. A portion of them, renters, moved west, and many we transferred to other congregations in the area. By the end we were completely surrounded by congregations. To the east was Lyons, at six miles;[22] to the northeast Harlem, at five miles;[23] to the north Mellrose;[24]

---

22. See p. 150, n. 18.

23. This appears to have been St. John Lutheran, Forest Park. However, according to their website, the original church was located "at the corner of Marengo and Franklin Streets," which would have put it seven miles away, not five (http://www.stjohnforestpark.org/history; accessed July 12, 2017).

24. Strieter's spelling of Melrose Park. Today this is St. Paul Lutheran on Lake Street, about six miles from Immanuel.

to the northwest Elmhurst at five miles;[25] to the west York Center at five miles;[26] to the southwest Hinsdale at five miles;[27] to the south La Grange at four miles.[28] We transferred members to all, especially to Hinsdale.

By the end of my time, my congregation was in an excellent condition. As far as I can recall, no big cases of sin came up any more. Church and congregational meetings were well attended. No one left during the Catechism instruction, or before the end when we held the Supper. Earlier the baptisms were conducted after the service had ended; without my prompting, conducting them during the service was introduced. Congregational meetings were held on a regular basis every quarter. Special meetings when necessary. Little things were taken care of right after the service. If there was something that concerned all of them, I kept all of them present. In Communion, Proviso was among the top in the entire synod, according to the annual statistical report. In giving, my dear brothers and sisters in the Lord became very generous. There was Supper every month and a collection every time. On the chief feast days a collection was taken for the synod treasury as a standing rule. We never ignored any solicitation letter that I can recall. How many poor students we helped from the Poor Fund, which was the Sunday penny collection. My own young'uns were supported too. One time I asked my treasurer how much we gave that year for the kingdom of God.[29] "A little more than 300 dollars."

The salaries were paid on a regular basis each month. They gave me 600 dollars per year, the teacher 550 by the end. We had free housing and each had some land. The honorariums were very good by the end. I seldom received less than two dollars for a baptism. For confirmation there was many a five-dollar gold piece by the end. For instructing a sick child at home, the mothers would give me five five-dollar gold pieces. My people were very kind to me and bore very patiently with my weakness. We sent a delegate to all the conventions. After it was over, the synodical report would be gone through—Catechism instruction after the sermon on one Sunday, information from the convention on the next.

I visited my sick members diligently. Several frail old mothers were bedridden for a long time. Visiting them was often very refreshing for me. I had one sick brother, when I myself was in bad shape, who often begged me to take it easy and not come so often. One time I had to go there on foot. I had to go through a grove; in the middle of it I was suddenly seized with an unusual weakness. My limbs were quivering

25. Today this is Immanuel Lutheran, Elmhurst. The current location is closer to six miles from where Strieter lived.

26. Today this is Trinity Lutheran, Lombard. The current location is closer to six miles from where Strieter lived.

27. See p. 151, nn. 23 & 24.

28. See p. 151, nn. 22 & 26.

29. Carl translates: "how much we gave for outside purposes." It does appear that here Strieter means the kingdom of God at large, not counting the ministry of his own congregation.

and I broke out in a sweat and I couldn't go one step farther. I sighed to God that he please not leave me lying in the woods. It got a little better and I dragged myself all the way there. When I came to the sick man: "My dear pastor, you look terrible! And how is it I hear that you came on foot, sir? I ask you, why do you do that? Why do you not take it easy?"

When it was time for me to go, he sent for his son from the field. He had to hitch up and drive me home.

I had one man who was pretty rough at first; he was especially very brash with his judgment. He came to church regularly and grew more and more attentive, and he changed a lot. He was elected as an administrator and was very faithful. He grew more and more quiet. He got sick and I visited him. By the end I said, "All my fathers and brothers are leaving me. That's hard enough and now you want to go too, sir," and I was seized with such a feeling of grief that I couldn't keep myself from crying any longer.

He said, "Please cheer up, my dear pastor. God has not left you yet, sir, and he's not going to leave you either. Just let me go home; you too will follow soon enough."

One man became blind and it persisted ten to twelve years until he died. He was a very lively person and staying put and being quiet were nearly impossible for him. How he grew more and more quiet. How calmly he sat in his corner. At first he still came regularly to church and to meetings. Other things started going wrong too and he couldn't come anymore. Not long before his end, he was lying on his bed and said he wanted to sing me some of his songs. He sang, but you could tell things wouldn't be right again, couldn't even get the melody straight, but he sang to the end. He soon fell silent, folded his hands, and closed his eyes. That was the last, for he soon fell asleep peacefully.

A little old mother was suffering from cancer. By the end I was visiting her every day and had to commune her every week.

One brother suddenly got sick and advanced toward his end quickly. He told me, "My dear God never let go of me. He went after me again and again and always pulled me back to himself. Now I will go to him."

One brother suddenly got sick. He sent for me and desired the Supper. When he had communed, he placed his hands together: "So, now I am ready."

One dear old father's eyesight was fading on his deathbed. When I sat down next to his bed one time, he grabbed my face and felt my beard. "Yeah, that's him. Go ahead and talk, sir."

I often read from Luther to my sick members, especially from the Lord's farewell address. I would pick out a passage, dissect it, reflect on it, and even if I didn't write something down every time, I would collect my thoughts and knew then exactly what I wanted to say.

The small conferences were refreshing for me too. When I came to Peru, I proposed to Jox in Logansport that we should start small conferences. He agreed to it. We got together with our teachers on a regular basis every month throughout the year, one time at my place and then at his place. Schlinckmann also joined. Heinz from Crown Point, who still belonged to Ohio at the time, often came too. I was assigned to provide an essay on Dietrich's Catechism every time. I worked through all of Dietrich that way.

When I came to Proviso, I started another. Grosse from Harlem, Bohlen, Gotsch, Trautmann, and Uffenbeck all came. The teachers were also there. At first we met at my place every month and it was called Proviso Conference. Later it moved around. I worked through Dietrich there too. I would richly supply my essay with citations from Luther. Later this conference expanded and the work was divided up.

Fig. 45. Johannes and Elizabeth Strieter, unknown year, photo.
Image courtesy of Nelson Wesenberg.

I especially include my marriage with these experiences. God gave me an exceptionally wonderful wife and has preserved her for me up to the present hour. She is sixty-six, and even though she has given birth to fourteen children, in mind and body she is still as healthy as a girl of eight. She was very well liked in all my congregations. Often I had to hear, "You should really visit us sometime, sir; you haven't been here in so long." When I would say, "What? Wasn't I just there however many days ago?" they would say, "Yeah, but you didn't bring Mrs. Pastor along." Schwan would frequently say, "She simply does not age." One woman told me in Wisconsin, "When you come next time, please bring your wife along. I must see her again."

Fourteen children were born to us, of whom nine are still living, four sons and five daughters. One baby boy died on us at a quarter-year old in Newburgh and is buried there. One little boy died on us at three years old in Peru and is buried in the church cemetery. A baby girl was stillborn on us in Proviso, but not really too early. The midwife said, "It's a mystery to me why the child is dead." My Otto, the youngest, died at twelve years old in Proviso and is buried there. My Theodor died at twenty-two years old and had already been teacher in Antigo, Wis[consin], for two years. He was very well liked there and God was greatly blessing his work. He died from pneumonia, but was buried in Proviso. Pastor Grimm even came along and Mr. Dir[ector] Krauss gave the funeral address. My wife had three children on her birthday, August 24—Karl, Lizzie, and Otto.

Fig. 46. *Pastor Strieter's Familienbild*, c. 1892, photo printed in *Lebenslauf des Johannes Strieter* (1905). *Standing (L to R)*: Hermina Volberding, Karl, Ernst, Theodor, Wilhelm, Friedrich, Emma Querl. *Sitting (L to R)*: Elisabeth Sohn, Elizabeth née Ernst, Mathilde, Johannes, Maria.

My oldest, Friedrich, is a professor at the seminary in Seward, Nebraska. He has a large family and his second wife already, Rector Schick's daughter, and one of his sons is already a teacher in Des Peres, Missouri.

The second, Willie, is a carpenter.

The third, Ernst, is teacher in Frankenmuth, Michigan, and also has a large family.

The fourth, Karl, is teacher in La Porte, Indiana, and also has a strong family.

My oldest daughter, Emma, has Pastor Querl in Toledo, Ohio. They only have three children, but from them we already have a great-granddaughter, Erna. We have a cute little picture with the sixty-four-year-old great-grandmother and the four-year-old great-granddaughter next to her.

The second daughter, Hermine, is married to Th[eodor] Volberding and resides in Reinbeck, Iowa; she has three sons and three daughters.

The third,[30] Lizzie (Elizabeth), is married to Teacher A[ndreas] Sohn in Mayville, Wisconsin, and has six little daughters.

The fourth, Mamie (Maria), is married to Teacher H[einrich] List in Frankenlust and has two little sons and two little daughters.

My youngest, Tillie, is in Reinbeck, Iowa.

While in Proviso, I was asked to preach several times in Aurora, several times in Yorkville, several times in Squaw Grove, several times in Wisconsin—one time for the mission festival in the same place where years ago the Methodists had held their camp meeting, which I reported on earlier,[31] and one time for the twenty-fifth anniversary. One time I even preached again in Peru, Indiana.

My Newburghers had me for the dedication of their second church building. Schwan was supposed to preach in the morning, Niemann in English in the afternoon, and I in the evening. Schwan got hoarse though, so I had to go in the morning.[32] Another time they called on me for the dedication of their new school and twenty-fifth anniversary of their much loved teacher, Aug[ust] Schefft.[33]

The visits from the children and grandchildren and other relatives and friends were also glorious occasions. When July was approaching, we would say, "Here they come." Friedrich was frequently there, Ernst frequently with wife and children, or by himself too, Willie, Karl, Theodor, Emma with her little children, her husband too. The good Pastor Querl was completely down and out one time, but Grandmama nursed him back to his feet again. A[ndreas] Sohn was also completely down and out one time, but he too recovered at Grandmama's. Hermine was there with her little kids, Lizzie with her little daughters, Hanna, Karl's wife, with her children, Mamie with her husband and her Edwin. Often the house was full. Mama would raise chickens in the spring, then there would be young roosters who then had to give up their lives. Then the little ones would call out, "Grandmama, a drumstick [*ein Schickebein*]!" Lizzie's girls would sing so sweetly under the green trees. Tillie would sit down at the melodion and the singing would begin. We would often go for a drive; about twelve or more would get in and take their seats and we'd go do some fishing.

---

30. Strieter got off in his count here; he had "fourth" here and "fifth" for Mamie.
31. See pp. 122–24.
32. See Appendix IV, no. 11.
33. Aug. 25, 1895, according to St. John's Anniversary Committee, *History of St. John's Evangelical Lutheran Church, Garfield Heights, Ohio* (1929), 69.

Fig. 47. Johannes Strieter relaxing under the green trees, unknown year, photo. Image courtesy of Nelson Wesenberg.

Whenever the exhibition was in Chicago, the house was full. People came from all sides. My brother-in-law Reichle would arrive with a tin pail full of oysters. I needed a lot of money, but Treasurer M. would hand it over and keep on handing it over and told me I had better come get him when I needed any. By the time the hullabaloo was over, quite a few times I was fifty dollars ahead on my salary.

I also cannot pass over notable instances of God sparing our lives, if I am to honor him. In Aurora I had, as mentioned earlier, a small corner on the second floor at the southwest corner of the house for my study. The stairs going up made a right turn at the top; at the top was a window on the left to the south, straight ahead led through the door into the study and to the west was a window, the only one, and my desk stood next to it. If I wanted some air, then I had to open the window on the west side, the door, and the window in the hall.

One day I was sitting at the desk, it was very hot, and I hear thunder in the distance. The storm was approaching from the west and it was getting very dark and the thunder was getting louder and louder. I think, "You need to go down to your family," but I leave everything open. Mama goes up the stairs, without me noticing it, to close the windows. There is a terrible boom. The kids scream and run into my arms and I reassure them.

Then I hear a weak voice from above: "Papa, come get me."

I hurry up the stairs; there stands Mama in my little study leaning against the wall, and she says, "The lightning hit me. I cannot walk; I cannot straighten my knee."

I help her downstairs and hold her. Then she said, "As I was entering through your door to close the window, fire shoots in through the window, as if a tin pan full of burning coals were being tossed in. The fire fell to the floor and slid past me, through the door and out the other window. As it was going past me, my leg jerks up, so that my heel was stuck against my upper thigh." As she was telling the story, she said, "Now I can straighten my leg again. Now my calf is tingling . . . now my heel . . . now my toes . . . now it's gone."

How our dear God protected me. If I had stayed sitting, the lightning would have hit me in the left ear. And dear Mama was so miraculously preserved. That lightning ripped the gutter down and struck the elder bush in the neighbor's yard.

In Peru there was fine sledding one time, and I borrowed the neighbor's sled and plan on driving Mama around in the sled a little. We drive up the street toward the main street and veer left onto it. Across the street is a small elevation on which the people can walk. When my sled jumps over it, the pin that holds the singletree flies out, the shafts fall down, and my horse pulls me out of the sled, but I do not let go. The sled shoots to the left (the horse had been running fast) right into a dray that was standing in front of a smithy—it belonged to my administrator Gysin—and Mama flies out and hits the pointy axle of the dray and there she lies. Gysin sees it and runs to Mama right away and carries her into the shop. Another man runs after my horse, who was trying his best to get away, and grabbed it by the bridle. Gysin fixes the sled right away and we head home and immediately send for our Dr. R. Mama is moaning and having trouble breathing. The doctor comes right away and says we shouldn't be afraid; it had hit her in the best possible spot on the entire body, beneath the ribs. The pain abated and the black spot also went away again. If Mama had crashed into the axle with her head, it would have certainly smashed her brains in. So there too our dear God did a swell job keeping Mama safe.

South of Peru, up six miles or so, was a village, whose name I have forgotten, where two railroads intersected.[34] I wanted to ride home with the one to Peru.[35] On one corner stood the station and in front of it a platform, three feet high or so off the ground, which formed a sharp corner at the intersection. I ask the agent about

---

34. Bunker Hill

35. Today the Nickel Plate Trail follows the stretch of railroad from Bunker Hill to Peru. The route of the other railroad is clear from a satellite image of Bunker Hill. The intersection of the two railroads was located between what is today West Broadway, North Elm, and Main Street. In 1901, the station was located on the northeast corner of the intersection.

the train. He says the passenger train is coming later, but a freight train was coming soon that I could ride on. The train came and slowed down somewhat, but the caboose is still back there. I am thinking the train will go forward and then hold still so that I can board [*einsteigen*]. But it didn't do that. I am about to climb on [*aufsteigen*] quick, but at that moment feel something touching me on either side. I quickly step back and my train goes past, a handbreadth or so away from the platform. The agent is standing above, claps his hands together, and says in English, "O my, a little more and you would've been cut in two."[36]

One time I was about to drive over the tracks with the sled in La Grange. The boys were hanging on to it, suddenly jumped off, but said nothing.[37] On the left stands a shed where the workers kept their handcar. As I come up to the tracks, a train comes out from behind the shed. I crack the horse a good one and get across, but my sled flew to the side.[38] I was that close to getting run over, if God had not protected me.

I also include this with my pleasant experiences: In 1902 and 1903 I saw Mrs. Pastor Sievers again, but she was no longer the blossoming figure she had been in 1850, but an old widow and completely hunched-over. I visited her often and she me. She would tell stories and I would tell stories. I also read to her from Luther, comforted her and her daughters Agnes and Renata, for they were distressed on account of their pastor, who had caused a lot of grief. He soon resigned his position though and Pastor P[eter] Andres came. He came as a widower and Agnes became his wife.

Fig. 48. Karoline (*or* Carolina) Sievers. Image courtesy of St. Paul Lutheran-Frankenlust, Bay City, Mich.

---

36. Trying to picture exactly what happened here is difficult, but Strieter seems to be saying that he averted (or rather, an angel kept him from) a collision with the sharp corner of the platform.

37. These appear to have been local boys simply catching a free ride (Carl translates, "some boys"), or perhaps catechumens.

38. In other words, as Carl translates, the back of his sled "got a bump" from the front of the train.

Fig. 49: Rev. Peter P. Andres, pastor of St. Paul Lutheran-Frankenlust, Bay City, Mich., from 1903–1915. Image courtesy of St. Paul-Frankenlust.

In the winter of 1904, after Christmas, I grew so very deaf that I almost couldn't understand a single word at all anymore, and I was too hesitant to visit my dear old Grandmother S[ievers] and refrained from seeing her for some time. Then she came to me and laid a piece of paper on my desk which read: "Dear friend! How very sorry I am that you do not come at all anymore, and that we cannot converse at all anymore. Could we not try it with sign language once? There was a deaf-mute painter in my father's house and I could interact well with him in sign language."

I replied, "Dear little mother, I am simply much too old to learn sign language at this point. But I have written down ten short sermons, and I can read one or the other of them to you from time to time." She was very happy with that.

I read two to her in her house and promised when I left that I would read the third. Then toward evening the pastor's little daughter came running and looked so scared, turned right around again and my daughter Mamie followed her. I was sitting upstairs and thought, "The dear grandmother is sick and about to die." My wife went over there too. I felt miserable and lay down. In the morning my wife wrote for me on a piece of paper: "Yesterday evening around ten o'clock I closed the grandmother's eyes; she died of a stroke."

"God be praised," was my first thought. "Now she is home." At her coffin I was permitted to say a few words in the church. She was a half-year older than I.[39]

In the spring of 1902 we arrived at my son-in-law's, Teacher Heinrich List, in Frankenlust. We soon visited our son Ernst and our other relatives; my wife has a sister

---

39. This sentence was struck through in both pencil and red ink and omitted from the book.

living there, Mrs. H[einrich] Reichle, and H.'s parents live there.[40] From there we headed to my brother in Sebewaing, who died soon afterward,[41] to my old sister Katie, who is still living in the middle of her eightieth year, but is unfortunately blind. I preached there frequently, also in Unionville,[42] where we also have relatives. We were also in Pigeon[43] and visited a few former members from Proviso, who were very happy to see us. We went to see our nephew in Deerfield, Pastor Müller, and I preached there too; also to Tillie Burger in Adrian,[44] daughter of my youngest sister, and to other relatives there, and I also preached several times for Pastor Fackler. I preached for Pastor Querl in Toledo for their mission festival.

We traveled to see Mother Müller in Bridgewater, my brother-in-law Karl Müller's second wife, and her two sons. There I took a horse and buggy and drove Mama around, showed her where my siblings had lived and the old homestead. We drank water from the well that my father had dug and walked around on the land. Drove her over to Lake Pleasant and showed her the spot where I had nearly drowned earlier. Six lakes are there on a stretch of seven to eight miles, which she saw. We were also at the cemetery in Freedom where my parents are sleeping. Visited also a female cousin and some other people. Were also at the churchyard in Bridgewater, at the graves of my dear brother-in-law Karl Müller and his first wife, my sister Rosina.[45] Visited relatives in Saline, where I preached for Pastor Lederer a few times. We were in Scio and I preached at the place where I was confirmed, except there's a new church there. Looked up the log house where my father moved into in 1837; visited several people whom I knew and then moved into the winter quarters in Frankenlust. That winter I preached frequently in Salzburg, a few times in dear Sievers's pulpit, frequently in Amelith, also one time in Monitor, in Saginaw, and at Pastor Jüngel's.[46]

In 1903 it was back to traveling in the summer, but this time to [Teacher Andreas] Sohn in Wisconsin. There I preached frequently in the lower church where our children lived, also in the upper church, Hochheim.[47] Also preached frequently

---

40. It is unclear from the manuscript whether he means Teacher List's parents or H. Reichle's parents. Leutner added an "L." after the "H."; perhaps he knew Strieter was referring back to Teacher List.

41. According to the "Find A Grave" website, Jacob died on Sept. 13, 1902.

42. Five and a half miles south of Sebewaing

43. Fourteen and a half miles northeast of Sebewaing

44. About thirteen and a half miles west of Deerfield

45. Leutner misread Müller as *Mutter*, and thus inserted *seiner*, so that the phrase in the print edition read: "the graves of my dear brother-in-law Karl, his mother, and his first wife, my sister Rosina."

46. This was a son of the Heinrich Jüngel mentioned multiple times earlier; this son served in Munger, Michigan.

47. You can read about the history of Immanuel, Mayville, here: http://immanuelmayville.com/history.php (accessed Nov. 17, 2017). Only the cemetery of the upper church in Hochheim remains today, on the south side of Hochheim Road; the brick church burned down in 1941, was rebuilt, then burned down again in 1956. The congregation then amalgamated with the lower church along the Rock River (present address N8092 County Road AY, Mayville). A "separate school with a teacherage was built" at the lower church in 1885. "This is the present limestone structure which stands

for Pastor Wilhelm in the village of Mayville.[48] Also gave a mission talk at Pastor Rathjen's. Then we headed to our old home in Proviso, Illinois. There we visited our dear old friends and I preached several times in the old pulpit. Preached also in La Grange, in Grossdale, and in Hinsdale. Then it was back to the winter quarters in Frankenlust. That winter I did not preach.[49]

Fig. 50. St. John Ev. Luth. Church in Newburgh, Ohio (second church building in Garfield Heights), photo printed in *Lebenslauf des Johannes Strieter* (1905)

In the summer of 1904 we received an invitation from the congregation in Newburgh, Ohio, for their golden anniversary, with which we complied. The festival was on the first Sunday in July. In the morning Pastor Wambsgans preached, one of their former pastors. After him I gave a brief address. In the afternoon, L[ouis] Hölter from Chicago preached, a son of the congregation, and after him Kolbe, a former pastor of the congregation, gave an address. In the evening Pastor Wischmeyer preached in English. Pastor Rathert had resigned his position, their most recent pastor. On

south of the church."

48. St. John's Lutheran, Mayville

49. Here Leutner includes a portion from an addendum: "Included with my pleasant experiences I still have to mention this too: When I was over in Wisconsin visiting my children in 1903, there came in the mail, among other things, a golden watch for my birthday."

Monday there was a children's festival in the grove, where I said a few words to the dear children. I preached to the congregation during their vacancy, at their request, and gave my sixth sermon on the Twelfth Sunday after Trinity, August 21.[50] At the desire of the congregation, I am supposed to give a mission sermon in the grove on the Thirteenth Sunday after Trinity, August 28,[51] and hold a service with Communion on the Fourteenth Sunday after Trinity, September 4.[52]

With that, my life story up to the present is now at an end, and so I must conclude, since the future is closed to me.

When I now look back over my long life, two things stand out to my soul—for one, my great weakness, many deficiencies, failings, and sins which, however, are all forgiven in the merit of Jesus. Second, my God's great love and the many, many kindnesses which he has shown me out of his grace. I speak from the heart: "Praise the Lord, my soul, and what is in me, praise his holy name; praise the Lord, my soul, and forget not the good he has done for you [Ps. 103:1,2]"

Written in the home of my dear sister-in-law, the second sister of my wife, widow Sophie Franz, in the valley,[53] six miles south of Newburgh. Finished today, August 26, 1904.

To God alone the glory!

Johannes Strieter

Addenda

1.

Included with my pleasant experiences I still have to mention this too: When I was over in Wisconsin visiting my children in 1903, there came in the mail, among other things, a golden watch for my birthday. And the other day two dear girls from Proviso, former members, came for a visit unexpectedly, Ardina Meine and Martha Meyer. How delighted we were. They also brought along some nice presents. May God reward it all.[54]

---

50. These sermons are preserved in the book *Lebensbrot: Predigten gehalten der Ev. Luth. St. Johannes-Gemeinde, zu South Newburgh, O., während der Vakanz von Juli bis Oktober, 1904, von ihrem ersten Seelsorger, Johannes Strieter, Pastor Emeritus* (Cleveland: Geo. Gotsch, 1906). The "sixth sermon" he refers to here was on 2 Corinthians 12:9a under the theme, "Be satisfied with grace."

51. He did so on Mark 16:15 under the theme, "The mission of Christians, a divine privilege and a divine duty."

52. His confessional sermon was on Matthew 26:26–28 under the theme, "The Holy Supper, the New Testament."

53. Leutner wrote "at Tinker's Creek" above "in the valley."

54. See n. 49 above. Strieter later expanded on the latter part of this paragraph in the next addendum. Thus Leutner crossed out these last four sentences and did not include them in the book.

PLEASANT EXPERIENCES

2.

Fig. 51. August J. C. Schefft, teacher of St. John's Lutheran School, Garfield Heights, Ohio, from 1870–1911

On August 7,[55] I was lying in bed not feeling well, when two dear girls from Proviso, Illinois, arrived quite unexpectedly, Ardina Meine and Martha Meyer, bearing beautiful gifts for me and my wife. On Sunday, Trinity 13, our dear God granted me strength to give a mission sermon in the grove by the church in Newburgh, which the dear girls attended.[56] They then went to Niagara Falls. On the way back they visited us again and again brought along beautiful presents[57] for me and my wife, along with seven dollars cash in brand new banknotes. On Trinity 14, I gave the confessional address in St. John Church[58] and Pastor [Otto] Kolbe gave the sermon. On September 9, my birthday, when I concluded seventy-five years, the dear Mr. Teacher of the congregation in Newburgh, A[ugust] Schefft, who has still never occupied any other position, arrived in the evening at the house of my dear brother-in-law, Adam Reiber, husband of my dear Sarah, the fourth sister of my wife. He came with his administrators.[59] He handed me the following congratulatory letter:

> To our highly esteemed Mr. Pastor, J. Strieter:
>
> In a congregational meeting, held on September 4, 1904, it was gladly and unanimously resolved by the St. John Congregation of this place to pass along

---

55. Leutner added the year, 1904.
56. See n. 51 above.
57. Leutner added that they were birthday presents.
58. See n. 52 above.
59. Leutner adds that there were two of them.

their most sincere congratulations and prayers for God's blessing to their old, truly deserving pastor, Pastor J. Strieter, on the occasion of his seventy-fifth birthday on September 9, 1904. In passing this resolution, we remember the devoted work that you did in our midst fifty years ago in your youth, at the founding of this congregation. But we especially remember now the glorious, instructive sermons that you, sir, have gladly and willingly preached to us during our vacancy in your advanced senectitude.

Thus we wish you also in the future the protection and blessing of our faithful God, and that he would richly repay you all the love and faithfulness you have shown us, and we hope that he would continue to preserve you in our midst for a long time.

At the behest of St. John Congregation,

A. J. C. Schefft,

Secretary

Newburgh, Ohio, Sept. 9, 1904

Twenty-five dollars in cash was presented to me with this letter.

The dear girls took their leave on September 3. It was hard to see them go. Ardina, since I can't hear, handed me these lines:

> Now we must say goodbye. God grant that you continue to be preserved in the best health for a really long time, so that you can still visit us again sometime in Proviso. Please do not forget to write very often and to write a lot, so that the homesickness doesn't get so bad again. May our dear God grant that we get to see each other yet again in this world. But if not, it will most certainly happen in heaven.

On Trinity 15 I preached again to the dear Newburghers.[60] In the evening seventy of them came to celebrate my birthday. After dear Sarah had fed them all, there was conversation for awhile. Then three candles were hung up on the porch, Mama and I were surrounded, and we sang hymn no. 2, "Abide, O Dearest Jesus." Then the following was read:

> To our dear brother-in-law, grandpapa, uncle, and great-uncle on his seventy-fifth birthday:
>
> Our most deeply heartfelt congratulations and wishes for God's blessing. As we wish you God's rich grace and continued blessing, we present you with a cash gift that was gathered by all of us today.
>
> You may also say something about it to your dear, faithful Lisbeth.
>
> On behalf of all your relatives,

---

60. He preached on 2 Corinthians 9:12b under the theme, "The power of the Lord is mighty in the weak."

Yours,

Fritz Franz

After that we sang hymn no. 341.[61] The gift was seventeen dollars. Some gave some more privately. Fifty-seven dollars in total. May God be pleased to reward all of it richly.

---

61. "Praise to the Lord, the Almighty"

Appendix I

Strieter Ancestry

This is not meant to be an exhaustive ancestral study. I simply wish to satisfy interested readers' curiosity about Strieter's grandparents and great-grandparents, as well as give any interested Strieter descendants a starting point for studying their ancestry.

The earliest mention of the name Strieter in connection with Affalterbach, the market town in which Johannes was born, dates to 1473. The Marbach Jurisdiction's stock book (*das Lagerbuch des Amts Marbach*) for that year includes, among other names, Hans Strietter (*sic*), Clemens Strieter, and Martin Struter (probably Strieter) as inhabitants of the town.[1] A Martin Strieter was the town's magistrate in 1634, when the population numbered 321.[2] And a Jerg Strieter is mentioned as burgomaster (*Burmeister*) on a panel inscription from 1730, presumably made on the occasion of a town hall renovation.[3]

Strieter Ancestors

Johannes' father was *Johann Jacob Strieter*, first a shepherd, then a farmer.

Born: July 17, 1789, in Affalterbach

Married: Jan. 23, 1814, in Affalterbach, to Maria Catharina Wiesenauer

Died: July 27, 1848, age fifty-nine,[4] in town of Freedom, Washtenaw Co., Mich., U.S.A.

---

1. Paul Sauer, *Affalterbach von 972–1997: Weg und Schicksal einer Gemeinde in 1025 Jahren* (Affalterbach from 972–1997: The Development and Fortunes of a Community through 1025 Years), new edition (Stuttgart: Chr. Scheufele, 1997), 26.
2. Sauer, 106. The population had numbered 540 just twelve years earlier.
3. Gerhard Gall, e-mail message to translator with photograph, Sept. 15, 2015.
4. Cp. Chapter 1, p. 13, where Johannes gives his father's dying age as sixty.

APPENDIX I: STRIETER ANCESTRY

Johann Jacob's father (Johannes' grandfather) was *Johannes Strieter*, a Lutheran by profession and shoemaker by trade.

Born: Sept. 11, 1742, in Affalterbach

Married: Sept. 29, 1767, in Affalterbach, to Dorothea Jung

Died: May 4, 1796, age fifty-three, in Affalterbach

Johann Jacob's mother (Johannes' grandmother) was *Dorothea (Jung) Strieter*.

Born: Oct. 28, 1748, in Affalterbach

Died: Oct. 1, 1834, age eighty-five, in Affalterbach

Children:

Johann Strieter, farmer

Born: March 29, 1777, in Affalterbach

Married: Jan. 28, 1801, in Affalterbach, to Eva Catharina Lang; then on Nov. 11, 1834, in Affalterbach, to Christina Catharina Rosin (d. Aug. 5, 1851)

Died: Feb. 20, 1855, age seventy-seven, in Affalterbach

Rosina Catharina (Strieter) Büchele

Born: April 20, 1782, in Affalterbach

Married: May 17, 1803, in Affalterbach, to Jacob Friedrich Büchele, small town shepherd (d. Sept. 27, 1850)

Died: May 13, 1844, age sixty-two, in Affalterbach

Note: Rosina Catharina and her husband served as Johannes Strieter's baptismal witnesses; he was their nephew.

Johann Jacob Strieter (see above)

Johannes' father (the autobiographer's great-grandfather) was *Martin Strieter*, a Lutheran by profession and butcher, keeper of the Lamb Inn,[5] church custodian, and magistrate by trade.

Born: Jan. 31, 1701, in Bittenfeld

Married: Nov. 18, 1721, in Affalterbach, to Barbara Rössle (d. June 7, 1733); then on Feb. 15, 1735, in Affalterbach, to Rosina Catharina Wolf

Died: Dec. 30, 1753, age fifty-two, in Affalterbach

5. See p. 2.

Note: Seven of Martin's children from his first marriage died in infancy; four lived to adulthood—Sara (Faber), Christiana (Läpple), Catharina (Schweizer), and Johann Daniel. Six children from his second marriage also died in infancy.

Johannes' mother (the autobiographer's great-grandmother) was *Rosina Catharina (Wolf) Strieter*.

> Born: March 16, 1711, in Nellmersbach
>
> Died: Dec. 29, 1753, age forty-two, in Affalterbach[6]
>
> Children:
>
> Margaretha Christina (Strieter) Sanzenbacher
>
> Born: Jan. 19, 1736, in Affalterbach
>
> Married: Nov. 27, 1759, in Affalterbach, to Josef Sanzenbacher, freeman and farmer (d. Feb. 26, 1785)
>
> Died: Feb. 8, 1801, age sixty-five, in Affalterbach
>
> Rosina (Strieter) Jung
>
> Born: Sept. 20, 1739, in Affalterbach
>
> Married: Jan. 29, 1760, in Affalterbach, to Johann Georg Jung, farmer and vine dresser (d. June 11, 1781)
>
> Died: Dec. 9, 1799, age sixty, in Affalterbach
>
> Anna Barbara (Strieter) Stroh
>
> Born: May 6, 1741, in Affalterbach
>
> Married: June 25, 1765, in Affalterbach, to Johannes Stroh (d. ?)
>
> Died: ?

Johannes Strieter (the autobiographer's great-grandfather; see above)

Note: The autobiographer's Great-Great- and Great-Great-Great-Grandfather Strieter were both named Georg Strieter.

Wiesenauer Ancestors

Johannes' mother was *Maria Catharina (Wiesenauer) Strieter*.

> Born: Nov. 28, 1791, in Bürg by Winnenden

---

6. Note that her husband died the following day.

Married: Jan. 23, 1814, in Affalterbach, to Johann Jacob Strieter (d. July 27, 1848)

Died: Oct. 4, 1847, age fifty-five,[7] in town of Freedom, Washtenaw Co., Mich., U.S.A.

Maria Catharina's father (Johannes' grandfather) was *Johann Martin Wiesenauer*, a Lutheran by profession and linen-weaver by trade.

Born: May 19, 1762, in Bürg by Winnenden

Married: Jan. 25, 1785, in Bürg by Winnenden, to Anna Maria Juditha Seybold (d. before 1786); then on Feb. 3, 1786, in Hertmannsweiler to Maria Agnes Layer

Died: Feb. 14, 1832, age sixty-nine, in Affalterbach

Maria Catharina's mother (Johannes' grandmother) was *Maria Agnes (Layer) Wiesenauer*.

Born: May 2, 1760, in Breuningsweiler

Died: ? in Affalterbach

Children:

Georg Jacob Wiesenauer, weaver

Born: May 9, 1789, in Bürg by Winnenden

Married: Jan. 23, 1814, in Affalterbach, to Margaretha Anders (d. Jan. 15, 1815)

Died: Jan. 28, 1848, age fifty-eight, in Affalterbach

Maria Catharina (Wiesenauer) Strieter (see above)

Maria Dorothea (Wiesenauer) Höllwarth

Born: June 1, 1796, in Bürg by Winnenden

Married: April 25, 1819, in Affalterbach, to Johannes Höllwarth, freeman and vine dresser (d. Nov. 24, 1857)

Died: Jan. 9, 1868, age seventy-one, in Affalterbach

Johann Friedrich Wiesenauer

Born: Feb. 15, 1798, in Affalterbach

---

7. Cp. Chapter 1, p. 13, where Johannes gives his mother's dying age as fifty-six.

APPENDIX I: STRIETER ANCESTRY

Married: ?

Died: ?

Anna Barbara (Wiesenauer) Gall

Born: Jan. 8, 1800, in Affalterbach

Married: Feb. 17, 1833, in Affalterbach, to Johannes Gall, freeman and mason (d. ?)

Died: ?

Jacob Friedrich Wiesenauer

Born: June 18, 1802, in Affalterbach

Died: Jan. 6, 1803, age six months, in Affalterbach

Johann Martin Wiesenauer's father (the autobiographer's great-grandfather) was *Johann Georg Wiesenaur*, a Lutheran by profession and freeman and vine dresser by trade.

Born: March 5, 1721, in Ödernhardt

Married: Nov. 17, 1751, in Winnenden, to Anna Barbara Gerstenlauer

Died: Oct. 17, 1798, age seventy-seven, in Bürg by Winnenden

Johann Martin Wiesenauer's mother (the autobiographer's great-grandmother) was *Anna Barbara (Gerstenlauer) Wiesenauer*.

Born: Feb. 24, 1724, in Bürg by Winnenden

Died: Dec. 24, 1796, age seventy-two, in Bürg by Winnenden

Children:

Anna Maria (Wiesenauer) Schlitter

Born: Sept. 13, 1751, in Bürg by Winnenden

Married: Jan. 18, 1774, in Bürg by Winnenden, to Christian Schlitter, shoemaker (d. ?)

Died: ?

Elisabetha Magdalena Wiesenauer

Born: April 29, 1754, in Bürg by Winnenden

Died: Aug. 12, 1754, age three months, in Bürg by Winnenden

Elisabetha Magdalena Wiesenauer

Born: Nov. 30, 1755 in Bürg by Winnenden

Married: ?

Died: ?

Georg Jacob Wiesenauer

Born: April 24, 1759, in Bürg by Winnenden

Married: ?

Died: ?

Johann Martin Wiesenauer (see above)

Jakob Friedrich Wiesenauer, freeman, weaver

Born: Aug. 19, 1768, in Bürg by Winnenden

Married: Feb. 7, 1798, Bürg by Winnenden, to Friederike Müller (d. May 21, 1824)

Died: May 7, 1836, age sixty-seven, in Bürg by Winnenden

Note: The autobiographer's Great-Great- and Great-Great-Great-Grandfather Wiesenauer were both named Hans Jerg. His great-great-great-great-grandfather Michael Wiesenauer was born in 1618 and died on Dec. 12, 1692, in Welzheim.

Appendix II

Strieter Children

The following were the children of Johannes and Elizabeth (Ernst) Strieter. Most of this information was obtained from the *Familien-Register* in the Strieter family Bible, but in some cases church records and the "Find A Grave" website were also consulted. *Italic* typeface indicates the name by which the person was called, if known.

Fig. 52. Family of Friedrich Strieter (Johannes's oldest son), c. 1910, photo. Image courtesy of Frederick J. Strieter. *Standing (L to R)*: Edgar, Gertrude, F. Winfried, Immanuel C., Ann (Albrecht) Strieter (Immanuel's wife), Theophilus W., Fred L., Martin E. (photo inserted), Marie, George Bernecker, Lucy, Ottomar, Ida (Galmiefski) Strieter (Winfried's wife), Lillie (Strieter) Bernecker. *Middle row (adults, L to R)*: Prof. Friedrich Strieter, Elizabeth (Ernst) Strieter, Johannes Strieter, Marie (Schick) Strieter (Friedrich's wife). *Front row (children, L to R)*: Bert, Winfried, Elmer, Ruth, Lucy Bernecker.

1. Johann *Friedrich* August

   Born: Dec. 26, 1854, in the town of Independence, Cuyahoga Co., Ohio

   Baptized: Dec. 26, 1854; sponsored by Friedrich Auch, Maria Dorothea Auch, and Anna Kunigunda Ernst

   Married (first): Dec. 27, 1877, to Louise "Lucy" Zumhof (1860–1885)

Married (second): May 21, 1886, to *Maria* Emilie Louise Schick (1858–1933)

Died: Dec. 15, 1927, age seventy-two, in Davenport, Iowa

2. *Emma* Eleonora Strieter

Born: Aug. 20, 1856, in the town of Independence, Cuyahoga Co., Ohio

Baptized: Aug. 24, 1856; sponsored by Emma Schwan, Friedrich Toensing, Eleonora Toensing

Married: July 16, 1874, to Hermann Wilhelm Querl (1845–1921)

Died: April 2, 1933, age seventy-six, in Los Angeles, California

3. Ernst *Emanuel* Strieter

Born: March 24, 1858, in the town of Independence, Cuyahoga Co., Ohio

Baptized: March 27, 1858; sponsored by Ernst Boehning, Ernst [illegible], and Maria Hoelter

Died: June 25, 1858, in the town of Independence

4. Maria Clara *Hermina*

Born: June 11, 1859, in the town of Independence, Cuyahoga Co., Ohio

Baptized: June 13, 1859; sponsored by Hermann Kuehn, Maria Hoelter, and Clara Boehning

Married: Nov. 17, 1881, to Theodor Heinrich Volberding (1859–1915)

Died: April 17, 1910, age fifty, in Livingston, Montana

5. Jacob *Wilhelm* "Willie" Michael Strieter

Born: May 20, 1861, in the town of Crystal Lake, Marquette Co., Wisconsin

Baptized: May 26, 1861; sponsored by Johann Jacob Hoffmann, Wilhelmine Gudrean, and Michael Schmidt

Died: March 15, 1935, age seventy-three, in Cook Co., Illinois

6. *Ernst* Julius Heinrich

Born: Sept. 20, 1863, in the town of Crystal Lake, Marquette Co., Wisconsin

Baptized: Sept. 22,[1] 1863; sponsored by Heinrich Lossner,[2] Julius Breitenfeld, and Johanne Rosinalde Erneste[3] Hoffmann

---

1. The family Bible has Sept. 27, but Johannes' church records have Sept. 22.
2. See p. 85, n. 30.
3. The family Bible has "J. R. Ernestine Hoffmann."

Married: July 25, 1886, to *Mathilde* "Tillie" Emma Prescott (1869–1930)

Died: Feb. 8, 1949, age eighty-five, in Chicago, Illinois

7. *Karl*[4] Heinrich Gotthold

Born: Aug. 24, 1865, in Aurora, Illinois

Baptized: Aug. 27, 1865; sponsored by Ernst Heinrich Dress, Johann Heinrich Rang, and Auguste Fickenscher

Married: July 19, 1888, to Johanna Sophie Dorothea Haben (1871–1944)

Died: Aug. 21, 1952, age eighty-six, in Elgin, Illinois

8. *Otto* Paul Christian

Born: May 31, 1867, in Aurora, Illinois

Baptized: May 31, 1867; sponsored by Johann Christoph Wilhelm Lindemann, Michael Grometer, Anna Margaretha Grometer, and Maria Muschler

Died: Nov. 20, 1869, in Peru, Indiana

9. Anna Katharina *Elisabeth* "Lizzie"

Born: Aug. 24, 1869, in Aurora, Illinois

Baptized: Aug. 29, 1869; sponsored by Anna Dress, Katharina Barth, and Jacob Barth

Married: July 18, 1889, to Johannes *Andreas* Sohn (1865[5]–1951)

Died: Aug. 5, 1955, age eighty-five, in Chicago, Illinois

10. *Maria* "Mamie" Dorothea Henriette

Born: Nov. 12, 1871, in Peru, Indiana

Baptized: Nov. 12, 1871; sponsored by Maria Conradt, Dorothea Schmidt, and Heinrich Kors

Married: July 15, 1894, to Johann Georg *Heinrich* "Henry" List (1871–1946)

Died: Jan. 2, 1948, age seventy-six, in Frankenmuth, Michigan

11. Unnamed daughter

Stillborn: Nov. 7, 1873, in the town of Proviso, Cook Co., Illinois

Buried: Nov. 7, 1873

---

4. This is spelled Carl in the Strieter Bible, but since Johannes spells it Karl throughout his autobiography, I have retained that spelling here.

5. This is the birth year on the "Find A Grave" website. It appears to be 1864 in the Strieter Bible.

APPENDIX II: STRIETER CHILDREN

12. Martin Albert *Theodor*

    Born: Oct. 17, 1874, in the town of Proviso, Cook Co., Illinois

    Baptized: Oct. 18, 1874; sponsored by Georg *Theodor* Gotsch, Katharina (Kiefer) Gotsch, and August Heidorn

    Died: Dec. 29, 1896, age twenty-two, in Antigo, Wisconsin

13. *Mathilde* "Tillie" Sophie Wilhelmine

    Born: Jan. 11, 1877, in the town of Proviso, Cook Co., Illinois

    Baptized: Jan. 21, 1877; sponsored by Mathilde Elisabeth Lindemann, Sophie Heidorn, and Johann Christoph Wilhelm Lindemann

    Married: June 21, 1899, to Adam Elmer Sibert (1873–1904); divorced in 1902[6]

    Died: Jan. 26, 1959, age eighty-two, in Chicago, Illinois

14. *Otto* Hermann Louis

    Born: Aug. 24, 1878, in the town of Proviso, Cook Co., Illinois

    Baptized: Aug. 25, 1878; sponsored by Friedrich Heinrich Christian Louis Wesemann, Louis Theodor Ahrens, Katharine Dorothea Wesemann

    Died: Jan. 18, 1891, age twelve, in the town of Proviso, Cook Co., Illinois

---

6. One of the additional pages of German notes on the Strieter children that I received from the family, as best as I can make out, reads, "A. E. Sibert soon [after his marriage] died an inglorious [*ruhmlos*] death and Tillie reassumed her family name." "An inglorious death" probably refers to a death caused by or during an immoral action or activity. Although Johannes refers to her as Tillie, her gravestone bears the name Mattie. Her divorce and the "inglorious" death of her ex-husband explain why Johannes only mentioned her briefly when talking about his children (see p. 169).

Appendix III
Indian Missions in Huron and Saginaw Counties, Michigan

1. August 8, 1846[1]

The Michigan Synod and Its Mission to the Heathen

In southern Michigan there are several German settlements, founded for the most part by immigrants who were originally Lutheran. They were initially served with Word and sacrament by the Rev. Pastor [Friedrich] Schmidt [sic] in Ann Arbor, who later trained some young men for the ministry [Dienst] of the Church and formed a synod with them, which they called a "mission synod." Its primary focus was directed at mission work among the Indians of Michigan. Its name was A German Lutheran Synod of Michigan. By being called to the Lutheran congregation of Monroe, which had previously been served, among others, by Mr. Pastor Schmidt in Ann Arbor, [Wilhelm] Hattstädt, a pupil of the Lutheran Pastor Löhe from Franconia in Bavaria, became a member of this synod. In this synod he found commitment to all the symbolical books of our Lutheran church of the pure confession, and even though there was also some ignorance about Lutheranism, he found seemingly good intentions. This caused him to bring this synod and the activity they had begun among the heathens of Michigan to the attention of his Lutheran friends in the old homeland. The result was that a correspondence was struck up from Franconia. In response to the definite declaration that the mission work would only be conducted from the position of the Lutheran Church and that all missionaries would be pledged to all the symbols of our church, the Franconian Lutherans pledged themselves to joint participation in the venture, to the extent that the Lutheran ministerial candidates Trautmann and Lochner were sent to minister to [zum Dienst an] the German Lutheran congregations

---

1. *Der Lutheraner* 2, no. 25 (Aug. 8, 1846) 98–100. Each of these articles is titled by the date given in the article itself or, if no such date is given, by the date of the issue of *Der Lutheraner* in which it appeared. *Der Lutheraner* (The Lutheran) was the first official newspaper of the Missouri Synod. In addition to devotional and instructive articles for the members of the synod, it also contained updates on work being carried out in the synod, reports on official acts and meetings within the synod, and announcements regarding upcoming conferences, conventions, books for sale, etc. Many, if not all, of the original issues are viewable on the internet.

under the oversight of this synod that were lacking pastoral care. And for the purpose of mission work to the heathen, a small German Lutheran mission congregation set out from Franconia in order to station herself with her called pastor, A[ugust] Crämer, on the Cass River in Saginaw County in the state of Michigan, and to conduct mission work among the heathens in conjunction with the missionaries of the Siboying [Sebewaing] station, who had been sent there from Ann Arbor. The Franconian Lutherans also sent large sums of money for the support of this mission. Meanwhile, a graduate of the Basel Mission Institute, the Rev. Mr. [J. Simon] Dumser, arrived to help at the Siboying station. He had been ordained in the old homeland, but had not been pledged to the symbols of our church. In fact, he later declared that an *unqualified* commitment to our symbolical books was a violation of conscience for him. It also came to light that several mixed congregations[2] had previously been blatantly served *as such*[3] with Word and sacrament. Pastors Hattstädt, Crämer, Trautmann, and Lochner immediately submitted a joint protest against these abuses, insisting on the excommunication of the un-Lutheran Missionary Dumser and on a public purification of the synod on account of the accusation of having serviced mixed congregations *as such*. But at the synod's convention in June of this year, the first motion to excommunicate the un-Lutheran Missionary Dumser failed right away, even though he stubbornly persisted in his refusal to be pledged without qualification to the symbols of our church. Pastors Hattstädt, Crämer, Trautmann, and Lochner therefore felt compelled in their conscience not only to leave the Michigan Synod and to submit a protest on account of the synod's failure to purify itself, but also to put the reasons for their withdrawal in writing and to deliver them personally to the synod president, exactly as they are printed at the end of this article. The brothers who have withdrawn will immediately be joining the pure Lutheran synod that is being organized in Fort Wayne, Ind., and the mission on the Cass River will be run all the more conscientiously from the position of the Lutheran Church. In fact, the church constitution of the German Lutheran Mission Congregation on the Cass River, which has been solemnly signed by pastor and congregation, already sets down the following conditions with respect to purity of doctrine:

> Chapter 1
>
> §1. We confess ourselves to all the confessional writings of the Lutheran Church—the Augsburg Confession, its apology, both catechisms of Luther, the Smalcald Articles, and the Formula of Concord—or in short to the Lutheran Book of Concord of 1580, as it was first published in Dresden. Precisely in so doing, we confess ourselves to the Lutheran Church itself. We and our children, our church and school, our pastors and schoolteachers belong to it without qualification.

2. That is, consisting of both Lutheran and Reformed members

3. That is, without any attempt to make a confessional or doctrinal clarification or give confessional instruction.

§2. Our preachers and schoolteachers swear themselves to the complete contents of the Lutheran Book of Concord of 1580, not merely *quatenus* (*insofar as* it agrees with the word of God) but *quia* (*because* it agrees with the word of God), not merely for the sake of conformity and obedience, but out of their own deepest conviction. This stipulation is to be included in the oath of ordination.

Chapter 2

§22. If the man elected (the newly elected pastor in a case of vacancy) is an already ordained parson, he will be presented to the congregation by the synod president or his representative, and office and authority will be entrusted to him. Whatever the case, the man elected also then publicly and solemnly attests to his loyalty to the Book of Concord.

In this pure denominational consciousness, the mission on the Cass River all the more courageously asks all brothers of the Lutheran faith in North America for their active participation and support,[4] seeing as it has already zealously begun the work of proclaiming God's word among the heathens with faith and prayer. A mission house has been built; seventy acres of land have been purchased for the mission; a translator has been hired. The Indian tribes on the Cass, Swan, Pine, Cacallin [Kawkawlin], and Belle Rivers have been visited several times. Eleven heathen children are already being instructed and cared for; other are expected in greater numbers every day. A heathen boy of sixteen years has expressed desire for holy baptism after six weeks of religious instruction. The lack of a witness versed in the language and a pressing business trip by Crämer are the only things postponing its performance.

May the Lord bless this work of his and cause it not just to redound to the establishing of the glory of his holy name through the proclamation of his pure word and the administration of his unadulterated sacraments among the heathens of Michigan, but also to rebound upon Lutheran congregations and their denominational consciousness with animating and invigorating effect.

Declaration of Withdrawal

Reverend Mr. President!

We, the undersigned pastors, hereby announce to An Honorable Synod of Michigan our formal withdrawal from the same on the basis of the following reasons:

1. We came over here from our fatherland to serve the Lutheran church and mission and to serve *it alone*, and we offered our services to, and membership in, the synod mentioned above under the specifically stipulated condition that it was a *pure Lutheran* synod, and that consequently all its pastors and

---

4. Freewill contributions should be addressed to the current treasurer: Rev. W. Hattstaedt, Monroe, Michigan. Reception in good order will be noted in *Der Lutheraner* [footnote original].

missionaries pledged to all the symbolical books of the Lutheran Church *without qualification*, and did so not *insofar as*, but *because* they agree with Holy Scripture. In the Instruction they presented, the undersigned also not only gave notice that they were not able to serve any mixed congregations (which are organized *as such*), but also furnished testimony against all such service.

2. It has nevertheless presently come to light that one of the missionaries to the heathen sent out by the Michigan Synod had not been pledged to the symbolical books of our church in any way, and in fact later declared repeatedly that he refused to be pledged *without qualification* to our symbolical books. Likewise it has actually been proven that up to the present mixed congregations have blatantly been served in this synod *as such*.

3. The undersigned therefore felt compelled in their conscience to propose the excommunication of the un-Lutheran missionary, Mr. Dumser, at a conference that had been arranged. But when we made this motion, we were referred to the sessions of this year's synod convention. In a formal petition to the then-president of the synod, we also unanimously moved for purification on account of the non-denominational [*unkirchlichen*] service of mixed congregations as such that had previously taken place, and indeed for public purification on the part of the synod as a whole.

4. At this year's synod convention beginning on June 24, we formally renewed our original motion on account of the un-Lutheran missionary, Mr. Dumser, in public session. But even before our motion was called, the Missions Committee of the Michigan Synod cast their vote by re-confirming Mr. Dumser in his position and sending him off to his post, even though he repeatedly and publicly declared that he refused to be pledged to all the symbols of our church *without qualification*. Thereupon we undersigned pastors formally declared our withdrawal from the Michigan Synod. Today we put this announcement in writing and, having signed our names, deliver it personally to the synod. With it, we add a solemn protest against the neglect of the other point, namely the public purification on account of non-denominational service of mixed congregations *as such*.

As we depart, we are deeply disturbed by the un-Lutheran position that the synod maintains in spite of all the pure testimonies we have furnished. We ask the Lord of the Church that he would soon bring the Michigan Synod to a conviction of how dangerous such a position is, especially amid the denominational conditions that prevail in this country, and of how necessary it is for the health of our precious church of the pure confession that there be resoluteness and firmness in *doctrine* and *practice* of the same, so that Lutheran synods can thrive.

Ann Arbor, Washtenaw Co., Michigan
June 15, 1846,

the Commemoration of the Presentation of the Augsburg Confession

W. Hattstädt, pastor in Monroe, Mich.
A. Crämer, pastor of the Lutheran mission congregation of Frankenmuth, Sag. Co., Mich.
Fr. Lochner, pastor in Toledo, Ohio
J. Trautmann, pastor in Danbury, Ohio

2. February 23, 1847[5]

Frankenmut [sic], on the Cass River, Michigan

The third day of Christmas was for our small mission congregation a day of special grace and joy, for on that day in our new little forest church the firstfruits of our mission work, a heathen boy of eighteen years and his two younger sisters, were baptized after they had renounced the devil and his works[6] and had confessed their faith. The boy received the name Abraham, the older girl the name Magdalena, and the younger girl the name Anna. They had been home with their sick mother for a considerable time throughout the entire summer and had to endure many rigorous tests there, since they were surrounded by the English Methodist missionaries who did not hesitate to employ every measure to stir up the Indians' prejudice against us using the coarsest lies. But after their mother died, they came back to us and were all the more attentive during religious instruction, even though we had very limited teaching aids at our disposal. But the Lord, who reserves the glory for himself alone, blessed what little we had and caused it to bear fruit. The hardest part for us was convincing the boy of his sinfulness, since he was a sober, honest, and industrious youth. What Paul says to the Romans in Chapter 5 was clearly evident in him: "Where there is no law, there one gives no thought to sin." But when he heard about the fall into sin from Scripture and how all people since then are already impure and under God's wrath through their sinful birth, the Spirit of God soon had him convinced that a bad tree could not bear good fruit, and that everything he had done and refrained from doing up till then was nothing but sin, and he became desirous of salvation. He now asked what he would get from baptism, and when he was told that it worked forgiveness of sins, life, and salvation, he expressed his desire to be baptized on repeated occasions. His sisters too, although more quiet and reserved, declared with tears that they wanted to be baptized. The act was actually supposed to take place on the first day of Christmas, whose meaning was explained to them, but the baptismal witnesses who were invited could not come on account of the thaw, to the boy's great chagrin. He himself then suggested closer neighbors who were versed in the language. When we headed out for the church to perform the baptism, the boy expressed his great joy

---

5. *Der Lutheraner* 3, no. 13 (Feb. 23, 1847) 73.
6. German: *nach geschehener Abrenunciation*.

that he was now going to be washed clean of his sins. Fourteen days after the baptism, the one girl suddenly died from paralysis of the lungs as a result of whooping cough. How happy the grieving brother was when he heard that she was now with the Lord Christ in his eternal glory, since he had received her in her baptism.

Church and cemetery are thus already consecrated for their purpose, and although, as already mentioned, we are boxed in by the fanatical Methodists, we still already have influence with two large tribes. In fact, from the one tribe the chief's own son is now attending our school, a candid, talented boy. Lutheran Christians, you who are reading this and rejoicing, pray to the Lord with us for the advancement of his work and open up your hearts and hands for actual support. Here the Church is giving birth to children from foreign tongues, not by means of human compulsion, the way the sects try to make Christians, but through the only means of grace, Word and sacrament. Now may the Lord graciously grant that many more such children be born, that the number might soon be filled up and he might come and lead us home to his eternal kingdom of joy and glory. Amen.

A[ugust] C[rämer]

3. September 20, 1847[7]

Mission News

Frankenmut [sic], Saginaw Co., Mich.

Since mission work to the heathens is the Church's business, and in this country mission work among the Indians should lie quite especially close to our hearts, I cannot refrain from once again releasing a brief report on our mission work among the Chippewas in northern Michigan.

---

7. *Der Lutheraner* 4, no. 2 (Sept. 20, 1847) 14–15.

Fig. 53. Crucifix with skull and serpent at its foot in the possession of St. Lorenz Lutheran, Frankenmuth, Mich., 2020, photo. The original crucifix spoken of in this article allegedly had its serpent pulled off at some point. This replica from Germany was given to the congregation in the twentieth century.

After several fruitless attempts, we succeeded in getting another translator at the end of May of this year and hurried into the woods to visit the tribes on the Pine and Swan Rivers and especially to inspect the damage that the foe had caused in the meantime. We were deeply disturbed to see how furiously he had rooted around in our grainfield with his Methodists, but we also rejoiced to observe that the Lord, our mighty God, had set a boundary for them. They had pestered Chiefs Pemasike and Sauaban for a long time to no avail, in spite of being repeatedly and earnestly refused. Especially the former told them that he did not want them and that he already had in me a missionary for himself and his tribe who possessed his trust. They then began sneaking around into houses here and there, especially on the Pine River, and managed to take captive a few little old women and young, inexperienced people. These then separated themselves, set up their tents on a neighboring hill, and since then have been filling the woods with their terrible howling every day. They tried to do the same among Sauaban's people, but with even less success, though there too they managed to bring a few to their side after plenty of coaxing and compelling. In the process, they once again made use of abominable lies and slanders in order to undermine the

APPENDIX III: INDIAN MISSIONS IN HURON AND SAGINAW COUNTIES, MICHIGAN

trust the Indians had in us, wherever possible. Among other things, they told Sauaban's people that we didn't know how to talk about anything but a serpent; we were not even Christians, but worshiped a serpent. They supported this with the following story. The previous summer a Methodist Indian boy from Cacallin [Kawkawlin] attended our school for a short time. The iron crucifix that was meant for our altar but was still in my house at the time attracted his attention. He curiously examined the skull and the serpent at the foot of the cross and asked what all of that meant. So we gave him a good answer and told him how the crucifix represented the Lord Jesus Christ, who had died on the stem of the holy cross for our sins, and we explained to him those symbols of death and sin (the latter by telling him exactly what Genesis 3 says), which lay at the foot of the cross to symbolize how they had been defeated by the One who conquered sin, death, hell, and the devil. We thought we had done the ignorant boy a service, and now we hear and are astonished at how they had turned this scriptural instruction into such a shameful lie. Because we worship the One who has crushed the serpent's head and put our *entire* confidence in him alone—not in our own holiness, our own preparation, spasms of repentance, zeal for prayer (or rather howling), etc., like the Methodists do—we therefore must be serpent worshipers. It is in fact an equally horrible counterpart to their former lie, that we were calling upon the holy virgin Mary, namely because we cry to the One who is Mary's son according to the flesh. But how is it going to help you, you holy Methodists, to try to spread your name by such unholy, shameful means? Even the heathens will discover your deceptions and detest you. Too bad that they will be defaming the name of the Lord at the same time. For although you like to call yourselves Methodists and put more stock in your methods and devices than in God's eternal word, you still also want to be treated as Christians, yes, as the only genuine ones, just as your missionary was bold enough also to try to make the heathens believe there was nothing to be had with the rest of us and that he alone was the the man with whom God spoke! But you cannot put a stop to the work of the Lord. God be praised: You intended it to cause evil, but God intended it to bring about good [cf. Gen. 50:20]. The Indians only received us with that much more trust. Not long after our visit, Chief Pemasike paid us a ten-day visit in return and, in addition to the two boys who were already in our school during the winter, he brought along another three children, including another one of his own sons, a younger one. We also have three boys and two girls from Sauaban's tribe now. The students number seventeen in total, not including the three children of our translator, although they are of half-Indian blood on their father's side.[8] There is the expectation of new growth every day, especially also from Point au Gres, to which we intend to travel as soon as possible. So too, an old Indian, who lives with his large family on our mission property, has formally transferred two of his own small children and two of his small grandchildren to the mission for eventual education and cultivation, whom we baptized immediately with his full approval—even though he

8. In other words, their father, the translator, was half-Indian.

himself, as has been the case thus far with all older Indians, refuses baptism because he one day wants to be in the same life where his fathers are. He also wanted to have two of his grown children and a mature granddaughter baptized by us, who have been attending our schools since last winter and are making good progress. But look what came to light when we questioned the children? These three children, a girl of about sixteen years, another of fifteen, and a boy of ten years, went with an older Methodist brother to a camp meeting in Lapeer last summer. There, after plenty of howling and raving, inquiries were made all around as to which of the Indians present were not yet baptized. All who said they hadn't been, according to the children (who also belonged to that number), were then put into a group and were baptized one after the other—seemingly as mere people, who first could have been and should have been instructed—without even caring whether they wanted to be baptized or not. None of the three children knew his or her baptized name anymore. None of them even knew just the wording of the holy Ten Commandments, the Creed, the Lord's Prayer, all of which we would have had to teach them first. But of course, why would the Methodists care about that, when they can simply trumpet to the world that they have yet again fabricated this and that many dozens of new Methodists. We can only sigh, "O Lord, look down from heaven, behold!"[9] This is not how "genuine" Christians should go around with God's holy means of grace. This is not how the true Church should behave with her children—taking them into her lap without a thought, only to leave them without teaching and instruction for years, or in the best case scenario, taking the one who can scream the loudest from those she has newly converted and appointing him to be their preacher. One of their preachers openly confessed to us that he knew nothing at all about God's word; he simply preached to them how they should conduct themselves according to his own insight.

Nevertheless, we must also thank God from the bottom of our hearts that he has continued to leave an open door among the poor Indians in our neighborhood for his pure Word and his unadulterated sacrament. He has also sent a faithful assistant to our difficult field of labor in the person of Mr. Eduard Baierlein, a graduate of the Dresden Mission Society, who is already conducting an Indian service for the Indian children every Sunday with the help of the translator.

May the Good Shepherd and faithful Savior Jesus Christ continue to bless the work of our hands and open the hearts and hands of many of our brothers in the faith to contribute with their prayers and their gifts, so that many more of them are gathered to the throng of the thousands upon thousands, of whom those who have completed their course are already singing, "Holy, holy, holy," around the throne of the Lamb. Amen.

A[ugust] C[rämer]

9. Quoting the first line of one of Martin Luther's hymns, paraphrasing Psalm 12.

4. August 1848[10]

Frankenmuth, Cass River, Mich.
August 1848

Since, dear readers of *Der Lutheraner*, you have always so diligently remembered our mission with your gifts of love, I cannot refrain from reporting to you now and then on its status and how it is prospering under God's blessing. In doing so, I trust that my simple recounting of that which the Lord is working here with his Word and grace will bring you heartfelt joy, since Christian people can certainly not help but rejoice with their Savior at the spread of God's kingdom among the heathens. And then I also intend to draw you more and more into our blessed enterprise of love by persuading you to join us in faithful prayer and to offer your kind assistance. May the Lord, the merciful God, grant his blessing, so that the following lines also meet this twofold goal.

What I am most eager to tell you about is our small, promising boarding school [*Pflanzschule*] and about the Indian children who have been entrusted to our school and instruction, nineteen of whom we have now baptized already. When I recently returned from the convention after a month-long absence, they ran to meet me with such eager haste and such joyful cries, that I had to clasp them against my heart with fresh and renewed affection—aside from the fact that the Lord Jesus cherished the children that were brought to him and expressly stated, "Let the little children come to me and do not restrain them, for the kingdom of heaven belongs to such as these" [Matt. 19:14].

Truly, if anyone has ever had the opportunity to observe small savages like these in their native forests—how they crawl around the tents of their elders covered in filth, how they fill the air with a piercing alarm and flee into the thicket like shy deer at the sight of a white man—and were then to find twenty of them here, who are neatly washed and combed, their nakedness sufficiently covered, appearing for breakfast in the morning with happy, healthy faces and, in spite of their youthful eagerness to eat, not sitting at the table before the morning blessing and table prayer have been spoken; if anyone were to then see and hear them hurrying off with their reading and writing slates first to our German school, then learning to spell, read, write, and count in German, and later coming to religion and English classes, where they recite Luther's Small Catechism in their mother tongue and spell two- and three-syllable English words with decent fluency; if anyone were to see them sitting at their simple dinner table at noon positively beaming with joy, and were to observe them in their afternoon free time, as the boys go hunting for birds with bow and arrow or hurry off into the woods to look for berries, or while the girls are occupied with sewing and knitting, and are now and then easily solicited for work in the garden and in the field as if it were but a game; if anyone were to be there in the evening to hear their candid "Good night," as they shake hands with everyone before going to bed, even with strangers who should

---

10. *Der Lutheraner* 5, no. 1 (Sept. 12, 1848) 3–4.

happen to be present; if anyone were to experience and see a Sunday here, as most of them first attend our German services of their own volition and pray the Lord's Prayer and the Creed very devoutly with us, and then as all of them together attend their own services in the Indian language, singing songs together, praying loudly and decorously in unison, and attentively listening to the readings from Genesis and from the Gospels; if anyone were to see all of this with benevolent eyes, he would certainly have to join us in sincerely rejoicing over it and he would thank God for counting us worthy to be instruments of his mercy to these poor children. But precisely for that reason, every honest Christian soul must certainly also be filled with indignation at the spite of Satan, who has already attempted several times to use false reports from the mouths of Methodist Indians to rob us of the trust of these children. Thus we were recently deprived of a girl, who was already on her way to us, by the shameful slander that we had a cudgel as thick as an arm in our schoolroom which we used to beat children to death (!). Then too, for all that gives us cause for rejoicing, there are also plenty of things that depress us and recommend themselves to your intercession. I will just mention this one thing that greatly distresses us—that the children are so often called home by their parents, who don't understand how things work. Yes, they usually promise to send them back after ten to fourteen days, but then they not uncommonly keep them at home for two to three months, so that when they finally return, we often have to start all over again with them.

We are also gaining more and more access to the older Indians, in spite of the malice of our enemies. The best and most gratifying proof of this in recent time is that the chief on the Pine River himself expressed the desire that we build a schoolhouse in his village and come over there to instruct them on location—not just the children of his tribe, but also the elders themselves. In spite of our sparse means, we made sure he didn't have to ask us twice. A house has already been erected there and Missionary Baierlein has left to go there with the translator. The first Sunday he organized an assembly there in order to preach the message of the cross to them, his audience numbered seventy people. Let us diligently pray that the Lord would grant power to his words and open many of their ears and hearts, so that they are converted from darkness to light and from the power of Satan to God, to receive forgiveness of sins and the inheritance together with us who are sanctified through faith in Christ [cf. Acts 26:18].

Another chief, whose son is already attending our school, has asked to purchase a piece of land from us, which he intends to pay off with the money that they still have to receive from the United States every year. We have also complied with this request, and they have already begun to clear an area for regular cultivation. The Indians on our mission property have likewise been induced by the beautiful fruits of their diligence, which the Lord bestowed upon them this year, to prepare another area of land for themselves for the coming year. At the same time, the Methodists are also certainly not taking a break from causing their same old mischief. Not only do they continue to plow in foreign fields with tremendous shamelessness, but on top of that they also keep on making use of the same old lies, for example, that the Indians will be removed if they don't become Methodists, that they won't get any more money, and more of the same. In doing so, they frequently accomplish nothing more than quickly fabricating them into Methodists using all sorts of persuasion, only to shamefully neglect them, either by giving them no instruction whatsoever in God's word or by appointing preachers right from their own midst who themselves know nothing at all about God's word. For example, we recently had a boy run away from our school who was never able to commit the Lord's Prayer to memory while he was with us. The Methodists not only converted him just like that, but also immediately made him a preacher of the Word, even though he cannot read it, much less teach it, and has only heard them howling about it on a few occasions. But he definitely possesses a good throat and is a capable screamer, and so he has the necessary characteristics of a Methodist preacher.

This is exactly why we need to set up our opposition with prayer and to earnestly implore that the Lord would own our good cause as his own, since it is his own, and that he would put a stop to such misconduct. So then, join us in diligent prayer, and help however else you can, especially since so little help can be expected from Germany now. We recently read that the Barmen Mission Institute has already had to close down due to lack of participation. The same sad fate has supposedly fallen to the one in Basel. That wouldn't bode well for our poor Lutheran mission either, but we do hear that the Central Association [*Centralverein*] of Nuremberg is becoming more and more inclined to lend stronger support to Lutheran missions with its Lutheran money.

May the Lord, the merciful God, prosper the work of our hands and open many people's hearts, so that more and more we become a people who are diligent in good works, and also that through us his name may be spread further and further, and the kingdom of darkness, as far as it affects us, may be destroyed.

A[ugust] C[rämer]

5. March 6, 1849[11]

Mission News from Frankenmuth

We have once again shared some news with our friends from our small mission here in northern Michigan in this volume of *Der Lutheraner*—in the very first issue, in fact.[12] Now the merciful God has graciously given us the opportunity to report some gratifying news about it yet again, for which we wish to thank him above all, from the bottom of our hearts. The readers might still recall that the talk in our last update was about an Indian school that we had just erected in Chief Pemasikeh's village on the Pine River.

11. *Der Lutheraner* 5, no. 14 (March 6, 1849) 109–110.
12. See the preceding article in this appendix.

With the help of God, this young nursery has already produced some seedlings of salvation. When we were up there recently to baptize a baby girl belonging to Mr. Missionary Baierlein, who works there, the chief not only acknowledged with visible emotion that we had come from such distant lands to teach them and to instruct and nurture their children, but also, in light of his advanced age and his frail health, transferred his five small children (three of which attend the school, while the other two are still minors) and two infant grandchildren to the mission, himself expressing the desire that they be baptized. Now since there were three catechumens besides these, three promising boys, who also desired baptism, we had ten heathen children to baptize at the same time. In fact, the chief's two adult children, a married son and a daughter, also wanted to be baptized without further ado, but were not yet properly instructed in the Catechism. They now promised to undertake this necessary instruction more regularly. The chief, however, who is already fairly well acquainted with the saving truth, has already declared on a few occasions, and did so again on this occasion, that he would let himself be baptized next spring. Even though we made the danger of postponing it most emphatically clear to him, he could not be persuaded that the devil was fooling him with such appointed times and simply wanted him to miss the opportune time, which was now [cf. 2 Cor. 6:2]. Once he had declared that he would not let himself be baptized until next spring, without being able or willing to cite even a single reason for it, he remained in that sudden indifference that so often seizes the Indians and seems to border on complete stupor, standing by his decision as if it were the unalterable decree of a Great Mogul. May God be pleased to graciously have mercy on him, to free him from these chains of darkness that still hold him captive, and to transplant him into his dear kingdom, which he has also brought to these children of death and has caused to take root among them through his Word and sacrament. And as he has made us competent to plant, so may he also be pleased to make us competent to water, and be pleased not to deny us his gracious success [cf. 1 Cor. 3:6,7]!

He has also once again enlarged the Indian school in Frankenmuth, by four children, and has added two more promising boys to his dear Church through holy baptism here—back in September of last year, in fact. He has also given our more mature students no small joy in the fact that they have now advanced far enough in reading and spelling that they are beginning to read God's dear word in their mother tongue. Considering that their words are often enormous, this is certainly no small task at times.

Now while our wonderful God is providing rich blessings like these on the one side, on the other he is testing our faith and your love by withdrawing the support for our mission from Germany that had flowed in so abundantly until now. The most recent intelligence definitely makes it clear that, for the time being, we can expect nothing more from Germany. There might not be any money in the treasuries, and the promises they might make us today they often might not be able to keep tomorrow, even with the best of intentions. So then, it all comes down to you Lutherans in this country doing a bit more diligence than before. This work that has been begun and that God has blessed far beyond our asking and understanding [cf. Eph. 3:20] we are also asking you, for your part, to support with your gifts of love as much as you are able. And now, because I have been asked by several parties at some point to give advice for mission presentations [*Missionsstunden*][13] and to provide material about our mission for them by means of regular communications, permit me therefore to express my thoughts on this freely and openly.

In these last, troubled days people are compelled to carry out the holy business of mission work through mission presentations [*sogenannte Missionsstunden*], if not entirely through special societies in the end, and these presentations are then mostly just aimed at arousing a whimpering feeling of pity (often by means of a dreadful depiction of the heathens' physical needs more so than their spiritual needs) and at extorting donations in this way. (I know this choice of words won't please everyone.) This isn't true religion, but rather a pitiful disgrace. The exultant throng of the redeemed in the first, blessed centuries of Christianity, and afterwards around the grace-filled time of the Reformation, did not require any such thing. They were so inwardly filled up with the kingdom of God, they so actively carried its weal and woe on their souls, that they probably would have treated such artificial means of inducing people to zealous service of the church and to a generous demonstration of love with utter contempt. Now then, let the good old days become young among us again. Let us use the eternally young, powerful Word of truth to paint so vividly for the souls of our hearers their profound need caused by their sins, so that they are thoroughly terrified by it. But let us also then portray Christ crucified so beautifully before their eyes, so that their hearts also rejoice and they praise his holy name, and then, as his redeemed people, also grow diligent in good works. Then, with a firm grasp on their own sinful need, they will easily be able to appreciate at once that of the blind heathens. Moreover, whenever collections are gathered for heathen mission work, the people will then contribute their willingness too, which alone makes the gift pleasing in God's sight [2 Cor. 8:12; 9:7]. That way, he will bless the gift not merely on the receiving end, but also and primarily on the giving end.

But if there really do need to be mission presentations, then I would think that people could perhaps read the holy book of Acts, the true and proper book of the Church and her mission. In this book, the Holy Spirit teaches us how the Church was planted, namely through the gospel of God's grace, through the message about faith, the message which gives the Spirit. And then they can show how the kingdom of all grace has also come to us through Word and sacrament, entirely apart from any merit or worthiness on our part, and how we have from God not just the vocation, but also the holy duty of love to continue to relay the message of the cross to those who still sit outside in darkness and the shadow of death [cf. Luke 1:79]. In so doing, they can then certainly also relate how and where our mighty God powerfully proves

---

13. Mission presentations (*Missionsstunden*, lit. "mission hours") and mission festivals (*Missionsfeste*) were just coming into vogue.

himself in the souls of the heathens through his Word still today, in the simple way that Acts teaches, without any of the sweet fancy talk one finds in most mission reports. But if there is a congregation where the members have not yet learned to think like the Church, then it would be better to wait for that mindset to develop and not turn mission work into a commercial enterprise. Otherwise, in the end, the members will think that they're just swell people for giving this or that amount to mission work, instead of thanking God, as they ought, for giving even to them the ability and privilege of contributing to the spread of his kingdom.

Now may the Lord, who directs our hearts like watercourses [Prov. 21:1], give us all true faith, fervent love, and much fruit.

A[ugust] C[rämer]

6. September 18, 1849[14]

Concerning the Cause of Mission Work

Report of the Committee that Was Appointed by the German Evangelical Lutheran Synod of Missouri, Ohio, and Other States to Confer with the Mission Society in Ann Arbor, Mich., about the Transfer of the Siboying [Sebewaing] Mission Station

Honorable Synod!

By the gracious assistance of our faithful God, we are already in a position to be able to give the following gratifying report on the execution of the task that was assigned to us, "to negotiate with the Mission Committee in Ann Arbor, Mich., on behalf of the synod, concerning the transfer of the Siboying [Sebewaing] Mission Station that they offered us."

When we had made it as far as Monroe on our return trip from the synod convention in Fort Wayne, we were not only met there with an urgent invitation from Mr. Pastor Schmidt [sic] in Ann Arbor to visit him on the matter in question, but we also encountered Mr. Missionary Auch, who deeply regretted that he had been so delayed by unfavorable winds, that he was no longer able to come to our convention in Fort Wayne in a sufficiently timely manner. He also greatly wished that we would seize the favorable opportunity and go with him to Ann Arbor immediately which, after mature deliberation, we had to acknowledge as the most suitable course of action. Now since Brother Gräbner was not present, who had been appointed to the committee along with the present author and Pastor Sievers, we filled the empty position with Brother Hattstädt and headed out for Ann Arbor on Thursday, June 21. The official negotiations between us and the Mission Committee there took place on Sunday, the

---

14. *Der Lutheraner* 6, no. 2 (Sept. 18, 1849) 11–12.

twenty-fourth; their committee was put together from Mr. Pastor Schmidt and six of his congregational administrators. Since they unanimously declared themselves in favor of transferring the Siboying Station to our synod, providing it could be done in an orderly way, and since at the same time Mr. Missionary Auch declared on behalf of his colleague, Mr. Missionary Mayer [Maier], that they would both be happy to join our synod, we therefore presented the conditions under which the synod had declared herself prepared to accept the transfer—namely, that the mission had to be conducted under the direction and oversight of our Mission Commission, and accordingly on the basis of the saving doctrine represented in all of its purity in our symbols contained in the Book of Concord of 1580, which are based on the entire word of God as the sole rule and standard for faith and life; and that the missionaries would be required not only to pledge themselves without qualification to these collective symbols of our precious Lutheran Church, but also to subject themselves to a colloquy prior to their formal admission to our synod. Since their Mission Committee originally simply had in mind that, through joint operation, the mission work in this area's field of labor might flourish and grow even more, they referred us to their former missionaries Auch and Mayer with our conditions; these conditions were no hindrance to surrendering the Siboying Mission Station to our synod on their part. At this point, Missionary Auch publicly and solemnly declared to the committee that he and his colleague had come to the conviction that the Lutheran Church alone confessed the saving faith in all its purity, while the other church denominations adhered to spiritually pernicious errors contrary to the clear Scriptures—errors that made it impossible to exist in religious and brotherly fellowship with them, as long as they continued to adhere to such errors. They had come to this conviction not through any sort of human persuasion, but through faithful study of our symbolical books. He therefore plainly declared on behalf of himself and his colleague that he was in complete agreement with our stated conditions, which were in complete harmony with our synodical constitution, which they had already examined. The negotiation that now followed over the movable and immovable property that the Ann Arbor Mission Society possesses in Siboying was soon concluded to this effect: The use and enjoyment of that property was to be surrendered to us for the time being, until the society figured out what else they might wish to do with it. In fact, the prospect was held out that it might entirely fall to our synod one day, and that Mr. Pastor Schmidt's congregations would not stop remembering the Siboying Mission Station with their gifts of love, which they would send in to our treasurer. According to later reports, however, this latter prospect might still prove false for the immediate future, since a large portion of the congregations there are supposedly not too happy with the transfer of the Siboying Mission Station to our synod on the part of the Ann Arbor Mission Committee, which has now taken place conclusively, formally, and without qualification.

The colloquy with Missionaries Auch and Mayer was conducted later by Brother Sievers, at a conference in Siboying. The subject of discussion was the doctrine of justification, and the outcome was that we no longer have any doubts as to the orthodox convictions of these brothers. Their mission assistant, Sinke, also submitted himself to the same colloquy with the same result. He intends to continue his faithful and honest service to the mission there with his school-teaching and his skilled needle.[15] All three formally declared their admission to our synod, as well as their joyful approval of our synod constitution, which were included in the conditions of their conducting of the mission that were presented to them.

When we used the opportunity to take a tour of the Siboying mission field, we found many things to be happy about. The school, which is attended by eight promising boys and a few small children of the translator, is in good condition, and we are very happy to report that two of the boys will likely be qualified for advanced theological studies [zum Studiren]. It was especially uplifting for all of us to visit a small tribe numbering perhaps thirty souls, encamped eight miles from the mission house. They have immigrated from Canada, where they fell prey to the Methodists. Soon after the Methodists had enrolled their names in the long register of their newly converted souls and had set them a very shocking example at wild camp meetings, they completely neglected and forgot about them. The Siboying missionaries found them in the most miserable condition spiritually and physically. But through God's help they soon succeeded in winning their trust, and the gospel they preached was accepted by these hungering souls with great joy. The entire village organized itself into a small congregation which, through their diligence and by readily following the wholesome counsel that the missionaries gave them, is now flourishing outwardly too, and is in possession of some marvelous corn and potato fields. Our visit was a source of genuine joy for them. When we told them that they should let the merciful love of their Savior move them to be a light to their brothers according to the flesh who are either still heathens or are being misled by the Methodists, the reply rang out loudly from every throat: "Ah!" ("Yes!")[16] The requisite materials for the building of a small little church have already been procured, but they need at least a competent architect for it, who could then be hired from our treasury. And in order to secure the future of this very promising post, the purchase of forty acres of land, which would only cost fifty dollars, is absolutely necessary. Perhaps six acres would be reserved for church and school, and the church would be built on it immediately. The rest would gradually be paid off by the Indians and would become their property.

The missionaries also still have an open door on the far side of the lake, at Point au Gres, although so far none of the Indians there have yet been caught in the net of the gospel [cf. Matt. 13:47].

A second tribe of neglected Methodist Indians, only six miles from Siboying, has already asked if the missionaries could also conduct services among them, since their

---

15. See p. 13.
16. Cf. https://ojibwe.lib.umn.edu/main-entry/eya-pc-disc (accessed May 28, 2020).

preacher (?), a man from their own midst who cannot even read Scripture, much less interpret it for them, is not going to obtain any real respect among them at all.

Finally, the dear cross is also not lacking in Siboying. They not only have just as many freebooting Methodists to put up with as we have already had occasion to complain about, but they also have their beloved trouble with the chief of the Siboying tribe himself, who is growing more and more hardened and is ruining nearly all the influence that the missionaries have had on his large tribe, who for the most part are actually kindly disposed towards them, but don't even dare to send their children to the school because they are afraid of the chief. May the Lord, the faithful God, see fit to grant his saving Word access also among these blinded and bound people, so that it may carry the strong away as plunder!

To him, the Father of all mercy, be praise, honor, glory, and thanks, for once again so graciously espousing our cause, significantly expanding our field of labor, increasing the number of those serving him with the pure Word and sacrament, and visibly consolidating our sphere of activity in the midst of threatening dangers. May he now also be pleased to stir up the hearts of many members of our synod and generously open up their hands, since it is certainly clear how much the needs of our mission have been increased through this gratifying expansion, and since it seems that the gifts flowing in from outside, especially from our old fatherland, will increasingly fail to materialize.

And really, even if someone were to show his thanks to God in this way, how small that gift would still be, in comparison to the great, fatherly grace and blessings which the Lord allows us to enjoy in ever richer measure. To him alone be the glory.

Also on behalf of Brothers Sievers and Gräbner,
August Crämer,
Lutheran pastor in Frankenmuth

7. November 27, 1849[17]

Rejoinder

In issue 12 of the *Missionsbote* (vol. 2), the official paper of the Michigan Synod and her Mission Society, one can find a letter by P[astor] Schmidt [sic] in Ann Arbor, from which we excerpt the following:

> For about half a year now, we have noticed a tendency and disposition expressed in the letters of our missionaries Auch and Maier, indicating that they would no longer be able to remain in our Mission Society according to their conscience and inner conviction, if we did not collectively join the Old Lutheran Church or the Lutheran Synod of Missouri in doctrine, confession,

---

17. *Der Lutheraner* 6, no. 7 (Nov. 27, 1849) 54–55.

and practice. The readers of the *Missionsbote* are aware how, when we founded the Indian mission in Saginaw Co. in the state of Michigan, the brothers from Bavaria set their hand to the holy task with us . . . but how in 1846 a separation occurred on account of certain differences in opinions of an unessential nature, especially regarding worship.

Further along it reads:

We already articulated ourselves in issue 9 of the previous volume of the *Missionsbote* with respect to the doctrine and confession of the Lutheran Church, and we testify here once again that, by God's grace and the power of the Holy Spirit, we have continually held purely to the word of the Holy Scriptures, as the Lutheran Church teaches, and have never been ashamed of the confession of our church. But to affiliate ourselves with the Missouri Synod unconditionally, as our missionaries and several brothers in that synod desire, and thereby also to embrace the practices and ceremonies of the Old Lutheran Church, which are unfamiliar to most of us and must be regarded as matters of secondary importance anyway—that we can and will never do. Accordingly, there was nothing left for us to do but surrender our brothers Auch and Maier, along with the Sibiwaing [sic] Mission Station, where the Lord had clearly blessed his work up till then, to the Missouri Synod—a transfer that took place in an orderly way.

To this an anonymous author adds, among other things, the following remark:

We respect the convictions of every single person, and so too those of Missionaries Auch and Maier. It's just that the Holy Spirit has yet to convince us that the ceremonies of the Old Lutheran Church are appropriate for our own time and especially for Lutheran Christianity in North America. We do acknowledge that we have shortcomings, also with respect to worship, but we confidently believe that we have to focus primarily on the main shortcoming, the true Christian life, and once this has been reawakened, the Spirit of God will have no problem creating the proper form of worship for future Christianity, a form that corresponds to the inner life of the Church, and this form will certainly not correspond to any of the currently existing ones. We therefore deem it foolish to foist any predetermined form upon a Christian congregation that has been gathered from heathendom, for the Spirit creates his own form, and the only true worship form is one that corresponds to the Spirit as he wields his influence in the congregation. And that form will also vary according to the different circumstances prevailing in each country.

* * *

Everything said here can only lead the one who reads it to conclude that we left the Michigan Synod and her Mission Society on account of a certain obsession with ceremonies, because they wouldn't accommodate themselves to our desire to embrace Old

Lutheran ceremonies. After all, it is clearly articulated here that the Michigan Synod and her Mission Society continually held purely to the word of the Holy Scriptures, as the Lutheran Church teaches, and has never been ashamed of the Lutheran Church's confession. We accordingly could not have had any other reason for separating from them than the one just cited.

Now, apart from the fact that, in the opening, Mr. Pastor Schmid probably should have tripled the time he gave in order to match the facts, so we in turn, in order to match the facts, cannot help but confess here publicly: We *never*, either directly or indirectly, stipulated *any such condition*, that we could only remain with the Michigan Synod's Mission Society in good conscience if it joined *the Old Lutheran Church* or the *Lutheran Synod of Missouri* in doctrine, confession, and practice. We do not know of any Old Lutheran Church, nor do we recognize either an Old or a New Lutheran Church, but *only one Lutheran Church, as she appears before everyone in her symbols, in doctrine, confession, and practice*. But if people desire to label the Missouri Synod (with which we also gladly number ourselves) "Old Lutheran"—a synod that faithfully clings to the confessions of her fathers, not just *insofar as*, but *because they perfectly agree with God's holy word*, and defends them against all attacks not through syllogisms but from God's word—then let them go ahead and do what they can't help but do, but let them first prove to that synod that she has fallen away from the symbols of the Lutheran Church before they justly attach that name to her. For our part, we make no secret of the fact that we repeatedly asked our society to please bid farewell to the false union of our days (to which we too were still genuinely devoted just a few years ago, but were liberated from it by God's grace), to their confessional laxity and anti-Lutheran practice, and to return to the confession, doctrine, and practice of the Lutheran Church, in accord with her symbols. We also freely confess that it certainly does go against our conscience when a Lutheran (?) synod and society pledges their missionaries to the collective symbols of our church at their ordination, without requiring them to *study* those symbols, and that this procedure was compatible with our conscience only as along as we remained unfamiliar with those symbols. We *must* also confess that it would no longer harmonize with our conscience that we had signed a constitution in which each member of the synod pledged to adhere to the Augsburg Confession as a confession of faith, doctrinal norm, and norm of practice, as well as to handle the instruction of the youth, especially the confirmands, in the most faithful manner, when in fact the Augsburg Confession was effectively rejected in Article 14, and the latter was carried out in such a way that children who might barely be able to read were confirmed and admitted to the Holy Supper with a week's worth of confirmation instruction. Yes, it even happened, while one of us was staying in Ann Arbor, that children were confirmed with anywhere from two to eight days' worth of instruction, and the man who had been tasked with instructing them, as Mr. Pastor Schmid even said after he returned, for the most part taught them purely rationalistic tenets, e.g., that the Lord Jesus had become a martyr for his teaching, and so on.

It is also against our conscience and conviction that Catholics, Methodists, and Reformed were admitted to the Holy Supper *as such* at the aforementioned place, without first renouncing their error. We also sincerely confess that it militates against our conscience when a Lutheran synod admits new members, later making them the editor of her official paper,[18] who reject Article 10 of the Augsburg Confession and believe in (and also teach?) only a spiritual partaking of the Holy Supper, which happened in Woodville, Ohio, at a mission festival. We publicly testify here that we do not and never did desire of our synod and society that they embrace any sort of Old Lutheran ceremonies, only the confessional ceremonies of *the Lutheran Church*, and that they remedy the already cited abuses for God's sake and for the sake of our conscience. Why then does that entire letter seek to put all the blame for the separation on us like that? We have no choice but to rebuke our former society with the Eighth Commandment in all seriousness:

> You shall not give false testimony against your neighbor.

With that, we leave it to every truth-loving reader to decide for himself whether or not the Bavarian brothers' separation from the Michigan Synod in 1846 was caused by "opinions of an unessential nature."

Finally, to the anonymous gentleman who thinks that it is "foolish" to *foist* a predetermined form upon a congregation gathered from heathendom, because *the Spirit* creates his own form, etc., we would like to say in brief: As of yet, we have never found it necessary to foist any part of the "predetermined form" upon our heathen congregation, which has become a Christian one by God's grace. They have rather been very happy with it, as well as with Luther's Catechism, and especially with the pure Word and sacrament that is proclaimed and administered to them. We furthermore reject the clever idea that this respected gentleman possesses and recommends, because by God's grace we have recognized and become acquainted with some of the forms created by the spirit he is talking about (if we are not mistaken)—among the many sects who boast about this spirit. We have especially recognized those forms among the Methodists who work here among the Indians. They create a form for themselves, as we have witnessed with our own eyes, that we wish to have nothing to do with. For we believe that, if "the Spirit" causes feet to hang out over the pulpit in front of the assembled congregation, if "the Spirit" furthermore causes the stove to be upset during the sermon, the candles to be blown out during their nocturnal meetings, people to be baptized two or three times, etc., etc.—then that is indeed a spirit, but *not the Spirit who wields his influence in the Holy Scriptures.*

---

18. Based on all the clues shared in this article and the next one (no. 8), it appears that the "anonymous author," the "respected gentleman" (mentioned later in this article and again in the next), the current (at the time) editor of the *Missionsbote*, and the "learned" subject of the next article are all the same person—an apparently young or recent convert, or at least a young/recent addition to the Michigan Synod.

In conclusion, we ask the clever gentleman for the time being, until he has persuaded us from the Holy Scriptures and the symbols of our church that our predetermined form is unbiblical, to excuse us for our foolishness. But if he cannot do this—and we permit ourselves to doubt that he can from the outset—then we rebuke him with the words of the apostle in 1 Timothy 3:6 and ask him to be honest enough to set aside the Lutheran name.

Missionaries
J[ohann] J[acob] F[riedrich] Auch
F[riedrich] Maier

8. May 2, 1850[19]

A Few Remarks in Response to the "Rejoinder" of the *Missionsbote,* Regarding Missionaries Auch and Maier

Sibiwaing [sic], May 2, 1850

The threat that was issued against us from Ann Arbor seems to have finally been fulfilled, namely that "someone far more learned than us would come, who would put us in our place." He has appeared in the person of the publisher of the *Missionsbote.* He puts us in our place in the third volume, no. 3, telling us that we are "people who are fast asleep in unscrupulousness, hypocrites, dishonest, slanderers," etc. Now these expressions certainly sound strange enough coming from the mouth of the man who bitterly complains in the same article that the religious newspapers of the Lutheran Church are run in such a "vulgar way," and that they defend the truth with "insults and abuse" at the expense of "Christian cultivation and love," and he reassures his readers that he will not respond to our accusations in the same temperament (which should really read: in such a vulgar way). Meanwhile, it is supposedly a fairly common flaw in those who are "learned" that they demand propriety from others, but do not show it to others. And this man must definitely be learned, if he may dare to charge our church with errors, when no learned person has yet succeeded, and cannot succeed, in providing proof of those errors from Holy Scripture.

Now as for the reproach that, at the time of the mission festival in question (cf. *Der Lutheraner* 7, no. 6),[20] we must have been fast asleep in unscrupulousness, since we did not stand up against the respected gentleman at the time and ask him, "How can you let yourself be pledged to the Augsburg Confession, when you reject that one article in it?"—we kindly ask the gentleman to think back to that mission festival once more, if his memory is not deliberately too short. There he will certainly find that we were unable to say anything about it to him, since Missionary Auch

---

19. *Der Lutheraner* 6, no. 21 (June 11, 1850) 166-67.
20. See the preceding article.

was confined to his bed due to illness and was not present at that session where the conversation in question, about the Holy Supper, took place. Nor was Missionary Maier in any better position to say anything about it, since he departed already before the synodical session. He will nevertheless also recall that there was still no lack of consciences disturbed by it, since the local pastor had quite an intense argument with him, called his view on the Holy Supper a rationalistic one, and spoke against his admittance to the synod's organization.

But even supposing that it happened as the publisher erroneously thinks, in that case he would only succeed in proving that we had now definitely awoken from that "sleep," which is certainly much better than continuing in a good "Evangelical" sleep.

With respect to the "false" conclusions that we have supposedly drawn from his words, we refer the readers to the convictions this "honest, conscientious thinker" has reached "by virtue of the Holy Spirit," and shares with us in his paper, confusing in some parts but straightforward in others. First he says: "It is true that I believe that we receive the *glorified* body and the *glorified* blood in bread and wine and not anything *physical* in the Holy Supper." And he thinks that one must arrive at the latter error if he "takes such a strict position on the Formula of Concord, which decrees that with, in, and under the bread we receive the body and blood of Christ." "For," he adds, "something in, with, and under the bread and wine can only be thought of physically and Capernaitically, and that is not taught by the Scriptures, but is verging on Roman Catholic doctrine." According to the sublime thoughts of this learned champion, which ultimately dissolve into a fog of nonsense, glorification must in fact be the kind of process whereby a body ceases to be a body, and yet still remains a body. Now if Mr. Publisher does not believe that we receive the body of the Lord in the Holy Supper—since a body without anything physical to it is certainly not a body any more—how then can he maintain that he accepts Article 10 of the Augsburg Confession, which plainly and succinctly teaches that "Christ's true body and blood are *truly* present under the form of the bread and wine in the Supper and are distributed and received there"? And how can we possibly have drawn false conclusions from his words in this regard?

In the meantime, his own loquaciousness clearly enough betrays the hideout in which he thinks, given the situation, he has cleverly concealed himself. He himself says that "the Lutherans and German Reformed were agreed about the essential thing in the doctrine of the Holy Supper" (by "Lutherans" he naturally only means the kind to which he belongs). Now in order for this assertion to be true, it must be drawn from the Heidelberg Catechism, one of the confessional writings of the Reformed. There we read Question 47: "Then is Christ not with us to the end of the world, as he has promised us?" and these words in reply: "Christ is true man and God. *According to his human nature is not on earth now*, but according to his divinity . . . he never withdraws from us." Now if our Lord Christ is locked up in heaven according to his glorified humanity, how can he give his glorified body and his glorified blood to us, when we are still on earth? But the answer to Question 76 knows how to address that. It teaches that to eat the crucified body of Christ means to accept Christ's entire suffering and dying with a believing heart and thereby to receive forgiveness of sins and eternal life, and at the same time to become ever more and more united with Christ's blessed body through the Holy Spirit, who dwells both in Christ and in us, so that we, even though he is in heaven, etc. Here everyone can easily see that, according to this teaching, only bread and wine, or a symbol of the *absent* body and blood, are enjoyed in the Holy Supper, and it is up to faith to raise itself to heaven, in order to be able to enjoy Christ there through the working of the Holy Spirit. Now if Mr. Publisher agrees with this doctrine, then our conclusions are certainly not false, but vindicated as true by the man himself. And if he calls us Lutherans Capernaites for clinging simply to the word of the Lord, "This *is* my body," without trying to ferret the word "like" out of there, then he can wait and see what kind of end he meets for attaching an insult like that to the Lord, since the Lord is the one who said it, and we believe *him*.

Finally, as for our "dishonesty," we will gladly put up with it if Mr. Publisher prefers to apply that label to our withdrawal from the Union.[21] But if he is referring to some other dishonesty or disloyalty, then let him or whoever else is able prove it, before giving false testimony so unscrupulously. We were compelled to give those explanations in *Der Lutheraner* by the dishonesty of our opponents, who did not report this affair in a way matching the facts, but instead, in order to appear innocent themselves, shoved the blame on us like "Adam and Eve."[22] If the gentlemen who are always accusing us Lutherans of hatred and slander for conducting ourselves honestly with people, using the Word and in accord with the Word, would take a little bit better look around at home with an upright heart, they would find both of those traits still today where the blessed Johann Gerhard found them back in his day. Before he died, he said to his son, "And definitely be on your guard against the syncretists"—those who mix different faiths together—"for they are faithful neither to God nor to mankind." In connection with these words, we would like to pose just one more question to Mr. Publisher: If you, sir, have already been striving to become a good "Evangelical" Christian for a long time, why then did you seek to conceal this intention of yours under the name "Lutheran"? If you, sir, are the honest man that you claim to be in your rejoinder, why didn't you furnish any proof of honesty in that regard?

In love,
J[ohann] J[acob] F[riedrich] Auch,
F[riedrich] Maier

---

21. In reference to the Prussian Union, not the United States.

22. I am unsure what the quotation marks represent; perhaps they are meant to refer more to the account (as a heading) than to the individuals as such, though either reference would fit. Adam shoved the blame on Eve; Eve shoved the blame on the serpent.

9. September 6, 1850[23]

Lutheran Mission Update 2[24]

Frankenmut [sic], Bridgeport P. O.
Saginaw Co., Michigan
Sept. 6, 1850

It was on the morning of June 27 of the current year when we set sail with a brisk wind from the mouth of the small Sibiwaing [Sebewaing] River into the turbulent Lake Huron. We were headed over to the Indian village of Shebahyongk [sic], eight miles away, a place that no doubt, dear reader, occupies a pleasant place in your memory from previous reports. Our small little ship was teeming with a motley crew on this occasion. It was not only carrying all the members of our private conference here, consisting of four pastors and three missionaries, which had just met in Sibiwaing; two newcomers from Germany and a German migrant also found themselves on board. Then there were the two wives of Missionaries Auch and Maier, together with the entire mission family, i.e. the festively adorned boys of the Sibiwaing Indian school. Even some German farmers, who are settled around Sibiwaing, had turned up in their best Sunday coats, and the old Indian doctor from Frankenmut [sic], whom you will likewise still remember, rounded out the bunch. If you had seen us flying there over the waves like that, our faces beaming with joy, you would have immediately detected from the sight that that day was a happy one for us. And why should we not have been happy and joyful? After all, with the help of God the small Indian chapel at Shebahyongk had finally been finished.[25] And that day it was to be consecrated and at the same time Mr. Missionary Maier, in the presence of his young congregation from the heathens, was to be installed in it as their called preacher. Yet how our joy was first heightened when, after a short voyage, we drew near the small cove where the Shebahyongk empties and we saw the immaculate log chapel gleaming out from between the green trees, bearing a massive cross on the eastern peak of its roof, a silent yet eloquent symbol of peace emitting beaming rays over the dark forests that had been covered with the thick darkness of paganism for so long! We

---

23. *Der Lutheraner* 7, no. 3 (Oct. 1, 1850) 23–24.

24. So named because it was immediately preceded by "Lutheran Mission Update 1"—a report from the Bethany Station in what is today St. Louis, Michigan.

25. This article confirms what Strieter says in his autobiography and makes it clear that the Shebahyonk mission house was dedicated on June 27, 1850. Unfortunately, the Historic Site marker outside the Luckhard Museum in Sebewaing and Charles F. Luckhard's *Faith in the Forest* give the incorrect year of 1849. The error might trace back to Crämer's abbreviation for "of the current year" in this article, *l. J.*, which Luckhard may have mistaken for *letzten Jahres*, when it actually stands for *laufenden Jahres*. (The abbreviation for "of last year" is *v. J.—vorigen Jahres*.) Furthermore, from Strieter's description of the house as a "long log house, made of squared fir trunks," from Crämer's description of it as a "small Indian chapel" and a "log chapel" here, and from his description of its location here, the Luckhard Museum cannot be the mission house described here, as it purports to be, but must have been built later.

really would have liked it if the river's mouth had been a little less shallow, so that we could have just quickly hurried over there and viewed everything up close. Finally, after a lot of difficult pushing with the oars, we reached our destination and now we made for the church at full speed, in order to inspect it from the inside. New joy took us by surprise when we saw the walls beautifully decorated with green sprigs and wreaths made of leaves and flowers by Indian hands, like the kind they had noticed here [in Frankenmut] on Pentecost. A neatly covered altar and a stately lectern, which took the place of a pulpit, also presented a very cheerful appearance. But another, more beautiful decoration was now soon to fill the bright space, when the small host of Christians who had been gathered from the heathens arrived in festive attire, and men and women, boys and girls took their respective seats with happy yet reverent faces. The service was held, as necessity dictated, in both the German and Indian languages. Pastor Gräbner, who was responsible for the installation, preached first on 2 Corinthians 5:17–21 in German. In keeping with the text, he talked about the ministry that preaches reconciliation. He set forth its divine institution and its comfort and necessity in vivid speech. Then followed the installation rite, which was followed by the Holy Supper. Finally, Missionary Auch, who has gathered this small congregation, addressed them in the Indian language by means of an interpreter. He set forth for them in a simple way the significance of what was happening before their eyes, and he exhorted them very earnestly and emphatically to the sacred duties incumbent upon them as a Christian congregation with respect to their teacher and spiritual shepherd. Joy, emotion, and gratitude could be very clearly and refreshingly detected on many of the red faces. In the afternoon the entire crowd assembled once again, this time to hear a church dedication sermon, which Mr. Missionary Baierlein gave them in their language through the interpreter. During the service Lutheran hymns in the Indian tongue were taken up with robust voices, so that the walls reverberated with the sweet sound. After the service concluded, the Indians expressed their wish that the author of this report, as their old friend, would also give an address to them. This then took place, and this festive occasion was used, in the first place, to really portray for them the blessed fellowship of the saints, and in the second place, to remind them of the high calling they now had, as a firstfruits congregation and as those favored by our kind God with the pure gospel and the unadulterated sacraments, also to be a true light among the nearby heathens [and] among those of their tribe whom the Methodist fanatic has taken control of in such deplorable fashion. It was stirring to hear the reply of the committed chief, spoken in loud and solemn tone, in which he not only expressed a heartfelt joy to be standing in religious fellowship with us white Christians who had come from afar and with our brothers still in the old fatherland, but he also spoke quite a few insightful and fitting words concerning the task they had received from the Lord of the Church. Little wonder that on our joyful return voyage we gave vent to our grateful hearts in word and song and praised the Father of our Lord Jesus Christ, who has done such great things for us unworthy people for the sake of his dear Son. But another joy was in store for us the next morning, right when we were getting ready to begin our journey home from Sibiwaing—a burdensome journey that had, however, been richly sweetened for us. Namely, the Sibiwaing chief now showed up too, who, it seems to us, had intentionally gone out of his way to talk with us. As you might imagine, we seized the opportunity yet again to impress really vividly upon his soul the great faithlessness he had displayed up till then, the miserable condition of his heart, the terrible danger that was threatening to drive him to hell as an old, unconverted sinner, just like the old Pemasikeh, and on the other hand the ready help that had already been offered to him often. Now the Lord provided our words with some sort of opening into the rock-hard heart of this gray-haired sorcerer and scoundrel. He was visibly concerned and promised that things would now finally be different with him and his poor band that had been enslaved by him. And we hear that so far he has kept his word at least to this extent, that since then he has been living in good friendship with the missionaries there, is regularly sending his children to the school, and no longer prevents one father from his band from turning up for the catechumen instruction. May he become a firstborn of all the others, who have thus far had such direct access to the Word and have spurned it for so long out of fear of the chief. I was also able to perceive another good aftereffect of this beautiful festival. The old Indian doctor has become quite contemplative since then; he comes to the services diligently and listens attentively. Recently he earnestly declared that he wants to be baptized, as soon as he has grasped and retained what is necessary, which is definitely going very slowly with him. We asked him if there was any way he could find some more time to show up during the week for extra instruction, seeing as he had already begun anyway. But he excused himself, citing the approaching corn harvest. He did promise to pay that much better attention on Sunday and hoped to be prepared for baptism in several weeks. May God grant that these are not just avenues for escaping again that the devil, whom he has served for so long, made available to him in order to keep him fully in his servitude.

Also in Point au Gres things have finally taken a turn for the better in an entirely gratifying way. During Missionary Maier's last visit, the small band declared that they would let themselves be instructed and baptized whenever they receive a missionary of their own. Now certainly for the moment we are lacking everything we need for something like that. For one thing, we don't have a missionary. For although Mr. Strieter, a brother-in-law of Auch, has presented himself for mission work and is with me right now to prepare for Fort Wayne, it will still be years before he has received his necessary training. But then we are also lacking the money required to found a station there. For, with the long distance and isolated location of the spot, such a station would not be inexpensive. And what's more, such a station would not at present hold much promise for the future anyway, since apart from the hitherto inaccessible Sable Indians, there are no others in the vicinity. So we find ourselves in a pretty bad dilemma here. At any rate, since that band is on friendly terms with the one in Shebahyongk, we are cherishing the optimistic hope that they will be persuaded to move, either there or at least into the vicinity, where we would then certainly be compelled to purchase land for their sake. But how nice would it be if in this way the congregation there was strengthened, our operations were concentrated, and thus further work could be carried out from a fixed station. Now the Lord knows what we need and will direct things differently if that is his holy pleasure. Now join us in diligently praying to him, and also open up your hands, so that we are put in a position where we can satisfy the many demands made of our poor Mission Fund. You have certainly heard so many gratifying things in this report. Let it move you to praise and thank God, and then demonstrate your gratitude however you can, including with your willing actions. But in order that the cause the Lord is advancing here through us weak instruments might become more and more dear to you, and that you might become more and more at home with us here in the far north, I plan in the near future, as the Lord affords me grace and strength, to furnish you with an overview presentation of all the mission work here, from its initial beginnings up to the recent, joyous occurrences, in short installments.

To the Lord alone be glory!

August Crämer

10. November 28, 1850[26]

Mission Update

Sibiwaing [sic]
Nov. 28, 1850

Most Reverend Mr. President!

A difficult task has been assigned to me by the Lord, that of informing you and our entire synod of the terrible misfortune that befell our mission on the fifteenth of this month. Mr. Missionary Maier and another man by the name of Haushahn, a resident here, found their grave in the Saginaw Bay on the just-mentioned day. They set out from Sibiwaing on the twelfth with the purpose of bringing winter provisions back home, and set sail from Lower Saginaw[27] for the return trip on the fifteenth with a favorable, though very strong wind, and when it grew stronger and stronger, and there was also such a thick fog on the sea that they could only see a short distance ahead, they came right into the worst spot of breakers on the entire east side of the Saginaw Bay, and here they were shipwrecked, perhaps a half mile from shore and six miles from Sibiwaing. Just as I was returning to Sibiwaing from Shiboyank

---

26. "Missionsnachricht" in *Der Lutheraner* 7, no. 8 (Dec. 10, 1850) 63–64.
27. That is, Bay City

[Shebahyonk],[28] Mr. Missionary Maier's place of residence, where I had held divine service in his absence, I found a man at my door with a note from a merchant who had been so kind as to bring the boat's cargo into his custody. This note contained the terrible news. Mrs. Missionary Maier[29] was actually staying with us during her husband's absence and was now notified of her husband's misfortune at the same time we were. I will not describe the heart-rending scene that followed. May the Lord from whose hand this distress came also comfort us according to his great mercy. To him be praise, thanks, and honor for such mercy!

The next day I rode out to the spot and found things as they had been reported to me, the mast on the boat broken off, the boat itself overturned, and the cargo scattered over a half-mile stretch of the shore. Although I rode back and forth along the shore nearly eight miles, the only thing I could find was Mr. Maier's cap drifting along the shore. How terrible I felt! The day after that I went back to the spot of the accident with our German settlers here, who proved very devoted and sympathetic to the cause and flipped the boat back up in the water. But after we had once again searched all around in the water for the bodies for a long time and to no avail, we returned home to Sibiwaing with the badly damaged load of flour.

I then discontinued any further searching until last Monday, the twenty-fifth. On that day, I once again went out to the spot in the company of our interpreter, Mr. Maier's brother, who had made his way here at the news of his brother's death, and with another man. Two miles above the site of the accident, I and Mr. Maier's brother climbed ashore and, while the other men continued in an Indian boat, we went searching along the shore. On the way I found a coat belonging to Mr. Maier, in addition to other small articles from the boat. Finally we came to the place where we had found the most flour and as I turned my gaze forward, I saw Brother Maier on his face in front of me, his coat over his head, the waves beating against him, lying on the shore in water perhaps four inches deep. Calling out to his brother, I hurried over. Ugh, what a sorry sight! We turned him over, his hands were washed snow-white, his face was puce, his skull bashed in. Maier's brother was wailing dreadfully. I did my best to comfort him with God's word, but the pain my own heart was in to see my brother-in-law in that condition right there in front of me—there are no words to describe it. We also found the other man just sixty paces away from Mr. Maier. We returned home. On the next day we buried them and thereby sowed the first seeds of grain on the mission property here in Sibiwaing that are looking forward to a blessed resurrection [cf. John 12:24,25].

---

28. See p. 207; also p. 13, n. 29.
29. The sister of the author of this article

Fig. 54. The final resting place of Missionary J. F. Maier in Immanuel Lutheran Cemetery, Sebewaing, Mich., 2020, photo.

Mr. Missionary Maier *was faithful in his calling.* I can vouch for this on his behalf in good conscience. He *lived* to his Lord in faith, and so we also have the assurance from God's unchangeable word that he has also died to the Lord [cf. Rom. 14:7–9]. He lived to the age of twenty-seven years, one month, and eleven days.

His death has left a gaping hole in our mission. Who is going to fill it?

Our Indian congregation is very sorrowful. When I comforted them with God's word, the chief told me, "Yes, we now have a spiritual shepherd *under us*, who is proclaiming God's word to us; I sincerely rejoice with my people in that fact. I was intending to see myself soon put into a position where I would be able to teach God's word *myself*, but what are our prospects now? Night and darkness now surround us again, when I think of going to school. Yet I do believe what you told us from God's word, that 'for those who love God, all things must serve for the best'" [Rom. 8:28].[30]

---

30. The author seems to be quoting the chief of the Chippewas at Shebahyonk. See n. 36 on p. 16, and pp. 215–17.

"..."

I have now taken over Shiboyank again, trusting in God's assistance. I have promised to hold service there every Sunday and, when the weather permits, once during the week too. I have also started up Indian school again. Here in Sibiwaing I am responsible for the Indians and perhaps eight German families. Consequently, there is not a single hour in which I do not see myself surrounded with work on all sides. Oh, how unfit I feel for such a serious calling! There are many times I almost do not know how to keep my faith from dwindling. If God's word were not my comfort, I would surely perish. I therefore ask the entire synod and especially you, dear Mr. President, to remember me in your petitions to the Lord as your lowly fellow brother. May the Lord show mercy and provide another shepherd for the abandoned sheep in Shiboyank in the near future! These sheep have begged me to please earnestly stress to the synod how dire their situation is, along with the request that they be sent another spiritual shepherd in the near future. God grant it, etc., etc.

J[ohann] J[acob] F[riedrich] Auch

Appendix IV

Announcements Pertaining to Strieter's Ministry

1. Johannes Strieter's Ordination[1]

Most Reverend Mr. President!

I am hereby supplying the report I owe you, that Mr. J. Strieter, formerly a pupil at the Fort Wayne seminary, after he had received an orderly call from the German evangelical Lutheran congregation in and around Elyria, Loraine [sic] County, Ohio, was, at the behest of the vice president, ordained by me and at the same time solemnly bound to all the confessional writings of our church on April 6 in the presence of his congregation and with Mr. Pastor Steinbach assisting.

Our brother's field of labor is small by outward appearances; may the Lord be pleased to compensate for that by making it that much more fruitful through his blessing!

H[einrich] C[hristian] Schwan
Cleveland, May 6, 1853

2. Installation in the Town of Independence, Cuyahoga County, Ohio[2]

After a number of members of the Cleveland congregation formed their own parish with our consent, St. John's Congregation in Independence, and issued an orderly call to Mr. Pastor J. Strieter, who had been in Elyria and Vermillion [sic], he was committed by me to his new office, at the behest of the Most Reverend President of the Middle District of our synod, Mr. Dr. and Prof. Sihler, on the Eighteenth Sunday after Trinity [Oct. 15], with Mr. Pastors Kühn and Steinbach assisting, and the newly erected church was dedicated at the same time.

Now may our dear fellow believers include also this congregation in their prayers.

---

1. "Kirchliche Nachrichten" in *Der Lutheraner* 9, no. 21 (June 7, 1853) 142.
2. "Kirchliche Nachricht" in *Der Lutheraner* 11, no. 7 (Nov. 21, 1854) 56.

H. C. Schwan
Address:
    Revd. J. Strieter,
    Newburgh P. O., Cuyahoga Co., O[hio]

3. Pastor Strieter Preaches for a Church Dedication in Holmes County, Ohio[3]

This past Seventeenth Sunday after Trinity [Sept. 26, 1858] was a day of celebration for St. John's Evangelical Lutheran Congregation in Holmes County, Ohio, for they had the great joy of consecrating their newly erected frame church. In the morning Pastor Lindemann preached on Galatians 2:16 and presented on that basis: What the true adornment of an evangelical Lutheran church is, namely 1. the pure message about justification, and 2. the listeners who make this message their own in true faith. In the afternoon Pastor Strieter preached on Luke 19:1–10 and showed from that text: 1. how Christ has moved into this church, and 2. how we should serve as his hosts.

W[ilhelm] Engelbert, Past[or]

4. Installation in the Town of Crystal Lake, Marquette County, Wisconsin[4]

After the honorable J. Strieter, up till now the pastor in Newburgh, Ohio, was called as pastor in an orderly way by the four evangelical Lutheran congregations in the town of Christal [sic] Lake, Newton, Shields, and Mechan [sic], Marquette County, Wisconsin, and he had accepted the call in agreement with his former congregation, he was installed into his new office by the undersigned on the Second Sunday after Epiphany [Jan. 15] at the behest of the Rev. Mr. President of the Northern District.

    May the faithful God, who has assigned a large field of labor to this servant of his in that area, now also graciously grant that his activity there would result in the salvation of many souls!

    Mr. Pastor J. Strieter's current address is:
    Stonehill [sic] P. O., Marquette Co., Wisc.

P[eter] H[einrich] Dicke

---

    3. "Kirchweihen" in *Der Lutheraner* 15, no. 13 (Feb. 8, 1859) 103.
    4. "Kirchliche Nachrichten" in *Der Lutheraner* 16, no. 14 (Feb. 21, 1860) 110.

5. Pastor Strieter Ordains J. J. Hoffmann[5]

Mr. J[ohann] Jacob Hoffmann, candidate for the holy preaching ministry [*des heil. Predigtamtes*], was recently sent to me from Fort Wayne as an assistant and, after receiving a call, he was ordained by me and solemnly bound to all the symbols of our church on Invocavit Sunday [Lent 1], the seventeenth of M.,[6] at the behest of the Mr. President of the Northern District.

J. Strieter
Address:
    Rev. J. Jacob Hoffmann,
    Stone Hill, Marquette Co., Wisc.

6. Pastor Strieter Installs J. J. Hoffmann in Rural Wausau[7]

Today, namely on the Thirteenth Sunday after Trinity [Aug. 25], Mr. Pastor J. Jacob Hoffmann, my former assistant preacher, after first being issued a call, was installed by me in his congregation near Wausau at the behest of the most honorable presidium of the Northern District. May the Lord make him a blessing to many.
    The address of the dear brother is:
    Rev. J. JACOB HOFFMANN,
    Box 38, Wausau, Wisc.

J. Strieter

7. Urgent Request on Pastor Strieter's Behalf[8]

Of the five pastors in Wisconsin from our synodical organization who were selected by lot for military service in the most recent draft, one has been declared fit for duty and has thus been forced to buy a replacement at a high price. This is Mr. Pastor *J. Strieter*. Now since Mr. Pastor Schwankovsky has been absolved of military service due to physical inadequacy and therefore no longer requires the payoff amount pledged for him by pastors, teachers, and delegates during the synod convention, the undersigned thought he could safely assume with Mr. Pastor Strieter that the respective underwriters would transfer their contribution to the latter, and so the

---

    5. "Kirchliche Nachrichten" in *Der Lutheraner* 17, no. 16 (March 19, 1861) 127.
    6. The "M." was either a mistake by Strieter or a misprint by the editor. Invocavit Sunday fell on February 17 in 1861, not March 17.
    7. "Kirchliche Nachrichten" in *Der Lutheraner* 18, no. 3 (Sept. 17, 1861) 23.
    8. "Dringende Bitte" in *Der Lutheraner* 21, no. 8 (Dec. 15, 1864) 62.

amount of $740.00 was raised by congregation members here in a short time.[9] In the certain hope that this request is not being made in vain, the undersigned accordingly requests that the pastors, teachers, and delegates in question *would send their contribution this way immediately upon receipt of this information.* It will also be noted that from the congregation of Mr. Pastor Strieter only limited assistance can be expected, perhaps even none at all. Therefore, should others who have not made any pledge also feel compelled to make a contribution, it will be accepted with that much greater thanks, and any potential surplus will be reserved for assistance of the same nature in the future and conscientiously used at the proper time.

F[riedrich] Lochner
Milwaukee, Nov. 20, 1864

8. Installation in Aurora, Illinois[10]

Mr. Pastor J. Strieter, who had followed a call from the congregations in Aurora and Yorkville, Ill[inois], was installed in Aurora by the undersigned on Oculi Sunday [Lent 3, March 19] at the behest of the presidium of the Synod of Missouri, Ohio, and Other States, Western District.

God grant that he may produce much fruit.

J. P. Beyer, Pastor

9. Installation in Peru, Indiana[11]

After my parish had grown into six congregations under our dear God's gracious assistance and I could no longer provide the service the people needed, even with an assistant preacher, we branched off three congregations into their own parish—the congregations in Peru, Rochester, and North Grove, which together number some eighty-five families. The faithful God, in his great love, has also given us a proven minister of his Church for this new parish, namely Mr. Pastor J. Strieter, hitherto active in Aurora, Illinois. I then performed his installation here in Peru yesterday, the Twenty-First Sunday after Trinity, at the behest of our Rev. Mr. President Schwan.

May the Lord bless the shepherd and the flock for his name's sake. Amen.

9. Note that there is a $15 discrepancy between the amount reported here and in Strieter's autobiography (see p. 117). This is perhaps due to Strieter's faulty memory or to a gratuity added to the loan amount as a token of gratitude to Mr. Pritzlaff. It also remains unanswered whether the reference to "congregation members here" is an attempt to conceal Mr. Pritzlaff's identity, or is an indication that Pastor Lochner's congregation (Trinity Lutheran, Milwaukee) paid back Mr. Pritzlaff and assumed the debt as a whole.
10. "Kirchliche Nachrichten" in *Der Lutheraner* 21, no. 15 (April 1, 1865) 118.
11. "Kirchliche Nachrichten" in *Der Lutheraner* 26, no. 7 (Dec. 1, 1869) 55.

J[ohannes] H[einrich] Jox
Peru, Oct. 18, 1869
Address: Rev. J. Strieter, Peru, Ind.

10. Installation in Proviso, Illinois[12]

This past Oculi Sunday [Lent 3, March 16] Mr. Pastor *J. Strieter*, who had accepted a call from the evangelical Lutheran congregation in Proviso, Cook County, Illinois, with the consent of his previous congregation in Peru, Indiana, was installed by me in his new church, with Mr. Pastor Th. Gotsch assisting, at the behest of Mr. President Pastor Franke. Mr. Pastor Gotsch preached on the basis of 2 Timothy 2:3–6.

May the Lord now be pleased, in his grace, to continue to acknowledge dear Pastor Strieter and his work as his own in this new field of labor!

C[hristian] A[ugust] T[homas] Selle

11. Pastor Strieter Preaches for a Church Dedication in Cuyahoga County, Ohio[13]

On the Fourth Sunday after Trinity [July 6] the new, beautiful church of the St. John Congregation in *Independence*, Ohio, was dedicated. Mr. Pastor Strieter delivered the main sermon; Mr. Pastor Niemann preached in the English language in the afternoon.

O. Kolbe

12. Pastor Strieter Reports on a Church Dedication in Du Page County, Illinois[14]

On the Twentieth Sunday after Trinity the first German evangelical Lutheran church in Hinsdale, Du Page Co., Ill., was dedicated (a fifty by thirty-two wood building with steeple). Pastor H. Sieving delivered the dedication sermon, and in the afternoon a short address was given by the undersigned.

Joh. Strieter

---

12. "Kirchliche Nachrichten" in *Der Lutheraner* 29, no. 13 (April 1, 1873) 102.
13. "Kircheinweihungen" in *Der Lutheraner* 35, no. 15 (Aug. 1, 1879) 118.
14. "Kircheinweihungen" in *Der Lutheraner* 44, no. 25 (Dec. 4, 1888) 199.

13. Pastor Strieter Installs J. F. C. Molthan in Hinsdale, Illinois[15]

On June 1, Trinity Sunday, I installed Mr. *Pastor J. F. C. Molthan* in Hinsdale, Du Page Co., Ill., at the behest of Mr. President Wunder.

Joh. Strieter.
Address: Rev. J. F. C. Molthan, Hinsdale, Du Page Co., Ill.

14. Pastor Strieter Ordains Alex Ullrich in La Grange, Illinois[16]

On the Fifth Sunday after Trinity [July 2], Candidate *Alex.*[17] *Ulrich* [sic] was ordained and installed by Joh. Strieter in St. John Evangelical Lutheran Congregation in La Grange, Ill., at the behest of the Rev. Mr. President Succop. Address: Rev. Alex. Ulrich, La Grange, Cook Co., Ill.

15. Pastor Strieter Installs Christoph Drögemüller as His Replacement[18]

At the behest of the Rev. President Succop, Pastor *Christoph Drögemüller* was installed by Joh. Strieter in Immanuel Congregation in Proviso, Ill., on Rogate Sunday [Easter 6, May 4], assisted by Pastors Ullrich and Gübert.

---

15. "Amtseinführungen" in *Der Lutheraner* 46, no. 13 (June 17, 1890) 106.
16. "Ordinationen und Einführungen" in *Der Lutheraner* 49, no. 15 (July 18, 1893) 118.
17. This may be short for Alexander, but even in one of his obituaries and on his gravestone his name is simply given as Alex.
18. "Einführungen" in *Der Lutheraner* 58, no. 10 (May 13, 1902) 155.

Appendix V

Sketch of the Parents of the Ernst Girls by Henry F. Rahe

The following sketch by a nephew of Johannes Strieter, already in English, was shared with me by Susan Hawkins, a great-great-granddaughter of Johannes Strieter, via email on Sept. 5, 2015. I have made some minor editing adjustments, including the numbering of the paragraphs, and reformatted it to fit these pages.

1. I know very little in detail of the history of the lives of my grandparents, Caspar Ernst and Anna Kunigunde Wittich Ernst. For some reason the name of Wittich was changed to Wittig. All the descendants of this family go by the name of Wittig. On my mother's confirmation certificate in 1859 the name was spelled Wittig.

2. I will tell you first what I know of Grandfather Ernst. He was born about 1808 in Hessen-Kassel, Hessen, Germany. He was left an orphan when seven years old and was raised by a sister and brother-in-law. How and with whom he came to this country in 1830 I do not know.

3. He was a cabinet maker and ship carpenter by trade, and that probably accounts for his locating at Vermilion, Ohio. At that time the town was quite a harbor and ship-building center on Lake Erie. There were three brothers in America but I do not know their given names. One lived in Philadelphia, Pennsylvania. He was well-to-do, and I have heard from my mother and aunts how, on the occasion of a visit of this brother and his wife to Vermilion, Grandmother Ernst put on the best dishes and tablecloths. (And Grandmother Ernst had some very fine hand-worked linens.)

4. The Ernsts must have had some means when they came here. The other brother, who lived in or near Vermilion, had a large farm, sent his four or five children to college and was prosperous. It was his son Louis, your mother's cousin, who wished to give her an education and send her to college at his expense. That family went in for education. This Louis was a teacher and professor all his life. He and a younger sister went to California in the early seventies. Another cousin, Casper Ernst, was killed in the war of the Rebellion.

5. Another of the boys, Washington Ernst, was also a well-educated man. For a time he lived in Saginaw and Frankenmuth, Michigan, where he taught school for a

while and then did other work. When I was in Frankenmuth at the age of five years, he was in the grocery and meat business with Uncle Reichle's brother Fred. He eventually married a Frankenmuth girl, Sabina Ruff, and moved to a farm in Kansas where he lived for many years until his death.

6. Another cousin, Elizabeth (Betsy), married Isaac Smith. In the spring of 1864 they emigrated to the west with a company of friends and acquaintances from around Vermilion. They went to the promised, and at that time much advertised, land of Kansas and Nebraska. Aunt Sarah Ernst accompanied her cousin Betsy. They traveled with oxen, cattle, horses, covered wagons—a regular caravan. When they got to the Mississippi, the first section, which had made very good time in traveling, had to wait for the second section to come up before crossing the river. While waiting there, Aunt Sarah ran into Adam Reiber. Neither knew that the other was traveling with the caravan. They had known each other since childhood and were sweethearts. But Grandmother Ernst did not favor their keeping company and objected to it. To forget some of their troubles each decided, though unknown to the other, to join their friends and go west. They were married in Illinois on December 23, 1866. (Grandmother Ernst objected to all of her daughters' selection of husbands unless the choice fell either on a minister or teacher.) But I am getting way off from the story of the Ernst family. Cousin Betsy Smith settled in Garfield, Nebraska, where she lived until her death some ten years ago. Her children and descendants still live there.

7. Grandfather Ernst was a six foot tall, broad shouldered, good-looking man. He had black hair and was dark-skinned. He was easygoing and good-natured, but his weakness was drink. Knowing Grandmother Ernst as I did, although I was rather young to form an opinion, the trouble was that Grandmother would not stand for his weakness and she got a divorce sometime in 1848 or 1849. As stated before, the Ernst brothers must have brought some means with them from the old country. Grandfather Ernst bought about an acre of land in the center of Vermilion and built a fair-sized frame house on it. This property and some money he gave to his wife at the time of the divorce.

8. The Vermilion Telephone Exchange, a small brick building, now stands on the northeast corner of the property. The old house is still standing and is still occupied. This property Grandmother Ernst sold very cheaply to her brother, Conrad Wittig, when she and the whole family moved to Newburgh, Ohio, in 1854 to live with the preacher, John Strieter, who had married her eldest daughter Elizabeth.

9. All of the Ernsts whose photographs I have seen were good-looking people, and your mother and her five sisters did not get their good looks from the Wittig side of the family but from the Ernsts. Uncle Leutner always said, "Those Ernst girls were regular belles, no matter what they wore, if it was only a calico dress." (And a calico dress was about the only kind worn during the Civil War and even after the war.)

10. Grandfather Ernst died in 1850 at the early age of forty-two, of typhoid fever, which was a deadly disease in those days. He was buried in a Vermilion cemetery along Lake Erie. The cemetery has since been washed into the lake.

Grandmother Wittig Ernst

11. Anna Kunigunde Wittich was born March 16, 1811, in Bebra, Kreis Rotenburg, Hessen, Germany. Her parents were well-to-do and she received a good education for those times. She had a command of a fine High German and later in America acquired a good English. She was a very fine seamstress and a past master in fine knitting and crocheting. None of her daughters ever reached the perfection of their mother in these accomplishments. She had the misfortune to lose her mother by death. Her father married again and our grandmother did not get along very well with her stepmother. Some of her cousins, the Gleins, the Kropfs, and some friends decided to come to the United States. She thought it would be fine to accompany them here and if she would not like America, she could return to Germany. They left Germany in March 1836. At least that is the date on Grandmother Ernst's passport, the original of which is in my possession. It gives a very good description of Grandmother and also politely asks all officials and authorities coming in contact with her on her journey to courteously extend to her any needed protection and assistance. The passport, of course, is in the German language and I herewith submit a translated copy. The schoolteachers of the family have OKed the translation, so you may rest assured that it is correct.

> Passport No. 103. Good for One Year.
> Electorate of Hesse, Province of Lower Hesse.
>
> | | |
> |---|---|
> | Age | 25 years |
> | Height | 5 ft. 1 inch |
> | Hair | brown |
> | Forehead | arched |
> | Eyebrows | brown |
> | Eyes | blue |
> | Nose | pointed |
> | Mouth | medium |
> | Teeth | good |
> | Chin | full |
> | Face | long |
> | Complexion | healthy |
> | Stature | slim |
> | Special description | xxx |

APPENDIX V: SKETCH OF THE PARENTS OF THE ERNST GIRLS BY HENRY F. RAHE

Signature

A. Kunigunde Wittich

All civil and military authorities are requested to allow the bearer, Anna Kunigunde Wittich, single, born at and resident of Bebra, this district, free and unhindered travel to North America and return if she so desires, and to courteously extend to her any needed protection and assistance.

This Pass, valid for one year, was issued at the behest of the local administration. Attested by the municipal administration [*Orts-vorstandes*] in Rotenburg on March 24, 1836.

One Thousand Eight Hundred Thirty and Six.

The District Commissioner [*Der Landrath*]

Remelie

12. The company of travelers was on the ocean eleven weeks. It was a voyage of calms and storms as related to me by my grandmother. They made the entire trip here by water. From New York they went up the Hudson to Albany, thence by Erie Canal to Buffalo, and by lake boat to Cleveland. Just how Grandmother got to Vermilion I do not know. My supposition is that some of her countrymen were interested in boat building and she accompanied them to the busy little boat-building center of Vermilion. One of the men, Philip Minch, became a big lake boat builder and vessel owner. Years ago, some of you older members may remember, in one of the worst storms in lake history, the Philip Minch, at that time the largest boat on the lakes, broke in two and sank with everything and everyone on board.

13. At Vermilion, Ohio, is where the married life of happiness and trouble for Casper Ernst and Kunigunde Wittich commenced, was lived, and ended. They were married in 1837 by a justice of the peace. I always supposed that all of the children were born in Vermilion, but in the book, Strieter's *Lebenslauf* [his autobiography], your father gives Brownhelm, a place six or seven miles from Vermilion, as the birthplace of your mother, Elizabeth.[1] The other girls were born in Vermilion.

14. The life in Vermilion was the usual life of a small town. Vermilion, on account of the shipbuilding, always had quite a few transients and life was somewhat livelier than in the ordinary town of that date. While they lived there, the Lake Shore Railroad was put through the town. It was a big event. Your mother, Elizabeth, had a number of friends and acquaintances among the men working on the railroad. The engineer on the work train would always blow the whistle every time he passed their house, which was right along the railroad right-of-way, and Elizabeth was always there to give them the high sign. The arrival and departure of boats, the building and the launching of

---

1. See p. 58.

new boats, rivalry among the fishing boats, and other aquatic events kept the life of the inhabitants quite busy.

15. As stated before, Grandmother Ernst would or could not put up with the weakness of her husband and divorced him in 1848 or 1849. So with this act he passed out of the life of Grandmother Ernst and family. In 1853 the preacher, John Strieter, comes into the life of the Ernst family. He was a missionary trying to round up Lutheran people into the congregations. He failed to form a congregation in Vermilion, but he found a wife there, Elizabeth Ernst. They were married January 17, 1854. In October 1854, after selling her property, Grandmother Ernst and family moved to Newburgh, Ohio, with Rev. John Strieter, who had received a call to the St. John's Lutheran Congregation there.

16. When they got to Newburgh, Rev. Strieter could not support the widow Ernst and her five daughters, and besides, the parsonage was too small. Aunt Martha worked out and they farmed out Sophie, Anna, and Sarah (all under eleven years of age) to other pastors. They had a hard life of it. Aunt Sophie, who resembled her mother in stature, temperament, and will power, more than any of the other girls, would not put up with this farming out proposition and they had to take her home and keep her there until after her confirmation. She then went to work for Rev. H. C. Schwan. It no doubt was a hard thing for Grandmother Ernst to send her girls of eight, nine, and ten years old to other people, even if they were ministers. It was her own doing and Uncle Strieter was to blame for much of it. All relatives, both from the Ernst and Wittig sides, opposed her determination to go with the Strieters and promised her all the help she would need to raise her family. This act estranged her from all her relatives, especially her brother. She never corresponded with any of them or visited them. She was the one who was estranged and not the relatives. In later years and especially in her last illness (Uncle Leutner, in whose home she died, told me this), conscience pangs bothered her on account of her conduct toward her relatives, especially her brother and her separation from her husband. I once spoke to Uncle Strieter about this moving of the family from Vermilion and he admitted that it would have probably kept the family together had they remained in Vermilion and would have been "better according to human reason, but what was to be, was to be."

17. They lived in Newburgh until the call came to Rev. Strieter to be missionary in the state of Wisconsin. He accepted the call and in November 1859 he and his family went to Wisconsin. Grandmother Ernst and the other girls moved to Cleveland. Martha was already working in Cleveland and after their confirmation Sophie, Anna, and Sarah also found their work in Cleveland. Grandmother and Aunt Mary kept house together. This continued during the Civil War.

18. In 1867 Grandmother became very ill at our house. She eventually recovered but was never really well again. After Aunt Mary married Uncle Fred Leutner, Grandmother made her home with them except in the summer months, when she would visit with us or with Aunt Sophie Franz. In the winter seasons she kept close to the

APPENDIX V: SKETCH OF THE PARENTS OF THE ERNST GIRLS BY HENRY F. RAHE

house. She had a bronchial trouble. In the late winter of 1874 she became much worse and after several weeks in bed, died March 23, 1875. The funeral was March 25, 1875. The body was first placed in a vault in the Erie Street Cemetery. On April 4, 1875, she was buried on our church cemetery—St. John's Lutheran in Garfield Heights, Ohio. Here she rests with three of her daughters, Sophie, Anna, and Sarah, and their husbands, and fifteen grand- and great-grandchildren.

19. Grandmother had a large circle of friends among our church people and had many acquaintances among teachers and ministers of our synod.

20. The six daughters of this marriage were:

1. Elizabeth (Mrs. John Strieter), b. August 24, 1838; d. December 6, 1924

2. Martha (Mrs. Henry Reichle), b. February 14, 1843; d. August 21, 1924

3. Sophie (Mrs. Fred Franz), b. June 26, 1844; d. May 7, 1925

4. Anna (Mrs. Henry H. Rahe), b. October 16, 1845; d. June 30, 1925

5. Sarah (Mrs. Adam Reiber), b. December 17, 1846; d. October 7, 1925

6. Mary (Mrs. Frederick Leutner), b. March 3, 1848; d. September 18, 1894

21. I have written and addressed this story of the life of Casper Ernst and Anna K. Wittig Ernst, of whom we are all descendants, to my cousin Carl Strieter, who is, as I am, of the third generation. They were our grandfather and grandmother.

Henry F. Rahe
Son of Anna Ernst and Henry H. Rahe
Cleveland, Ohio
July 12, 1942

Appendix VI

Beginnings of Organized Lutheranism in Marquette County, Wisconsin

The following letters are contained in The Wisconsin Evangelical Lutheran Synod Presidential Papers: Early Presidents Collection, located in the Wisconsin Evangelical Lutheran Synod Archives in Waukesha, Wisconsin. Their numbering here corresponds to their numbers in that collection. The interested reader can also refer to the WELS Historical Institute Journal *37, no. 2 (Fall 2019) 1–58.*

No. 77: Johann Schultz to Synod President Johannes Muehlhaeuser (Jan. 8, 1855)

January 8, 1855
Princeton, Marquette Co., Wis., N[orth] A[merica]

Reverend Mr. Preacher!

    The Germans who established themselves here two years ago have been lacking in spiritual care from clergymen. For this reason many are inclining toward the Albright people, which is causing a splintering in doctrine and confession to surface. As Prussians we belonged to the United Church, and since last Pentecost we have been induced by Mr. Preacher Stephan of Mayville, Dodge Co., to cross over to the pure doctrine of the Augsburg Confession, and this doctrine has already born blessed fruits among us in this short time. The distance from here to Mayville is some sixty miles, and Mr. Stephan cannot have a satisfactory impact on our four settlements, which amount to more than a hundred families, thereby giving the Albright people free rein in the area. Several committed Germans examined the basic tenets of the Albright people and found in their practice an extreme mysticism which, when coupled with a sensitive nervous system, degenerates into fanaticism and even visions. I was therefore called upon by the four congregations to initiate reading services among them, which are also now taking place at five stations. On my own I have already been giving independent discourses for a year now, so that I have succeeded through God's assistance in enjoying the approval of the congregations among which I preach on rotation. This winter the instruction of the confirmands was entrusted to me; their confirmation will take place at the hands of Mr. Stephan on Feb. 5 of this year, at which we are likewise planning to celebrate the Lord's Supper. But since we are able to receive clerical encouragement only on rare occasion, due to the distance and even the cost, since there's simply no way on earth Mr. Stephan can visit us all the time without detriment to his congregations, the four congregations, to which the fifth is in the process of joining, are agreed on it to elect me as their preacher. Most of my fellow members are already familiar with me from back in Germany, and an affectionate attachment has linked us together. We are kindred spirits.

I therefore take the liberty of asking you, Reverend Sir, to be so very kind as to relay to me the date at which I may appear there for an examination?

The following sketch might serve to inform you of my past and present circumstances: I was a teacher for thirty years in the province of Posen, belonging to Prussia, and received my training in a teachers' seminary in Bromberg.[1] I am still able to prove my qualification for the teaching profession with testimonials, if required. Born in the year 1800, I definitely find myself already at an advanced age, yet still in possession of sufficient energy to defend what is true and good and of a gentle spirit to have a richly blessed impact on my fellow brothers. Self-interest is certainly not leading me to take this step, since I am self-sufficient, possess forty acres here, and my children are so far grown that the youngest of them, a son and a daughter,[2] are being confirmed by Mr. Stephan. In Germany I occupied a very difficult position, since for the most part I had to work with 200 children and instruct in German and Polish. My supervising clergyman only held divine service in my congregation six times a year, which is why I was obliged to conduct the reading service in the intervening Sundays. Any independent discourse, however, was strictly prohibited there, and the teacher was not allowed to venture into the realm of theology, under threat of punishment, which is why—I will freely confess it—an intimidation comes over me when I think of my impending examination. Also, owing to a cause unknown to me, my singing voice is no longer as melodious as it once was. As a teacher I could make up for it with the help of an instrument, but I cannot make use of that as a preacher.

It would be up to you to determine whether I should present you my certificate of election via mail or when I arrive.

I obtained your address through one of my friends. If you should find it necessary that I would have to be examined in Buffalo by the estimable synod there, then on account of the cost I would certainly have to abandon my plan, seeing as I do not possess the means for such a trip. This does not mean, however, that I would stop doing everything in my power to contribute to the building of our church, and seeking to bring about in it that the kingdom of God would draw closer to us.

In anticipation of a favorable answer, I sign myself most respectfully,

1. Polish: Bydgoszcz.
2. Carl Friedrich and Ernestine Charlotte, respectively.

Your Reverence's
faithfully devoted servant,
Farmer Johann Schultz

No. 80: Johann Schultz to Synod President Johannes Muehlhaeuser (Jan. 24, 1855)

January 24, 1855
Princeton

Reverend Mr. Preacher!

At the present time of year a trip to see you would be attended by unpleasant conditions, and so I am hoping, if God grants life and health, to visit you first thing in the month of March. Your dear letter fills me with hope and confidence, and I believe to have found in your estimable person a guide whose suggestions I will faithfully utilize.

In reference to my former relation to the church, I believe I will have to share with you the following additional information. Since 1817 the two sister churches, the Lutheran and Reformed, were united in Prussia; this union is supposed to have been effected primarily by then Bishop Eilert.[3] We called ourselves Evangelical Christians. Later, however, the Lutheran Church re-emerged as a separate church, especially through the efforts of Scheibel in Breslau.[4] It was suppressed at first, but ever since the current king ascended the throne it has regained its former legitimacy.[5] All the local emigrants, a good portion of which are still my pupils, belong to the Evangelical Church. Fourteen days after my arrival in America (1852), a traveling preacher from the Evangelical Association,[6] Eslinger,[7] turned up here. His operations did differ

---

3. Rulemann Friedrich Eylert

4. Johann Gottfried Scheibel (1783–1843), of Breslau in Silesia, continued to use the old Wittenberg liturgical agenda and sacramental rites of the Lutheran Church after the new Union agenda had been adopted. He was forced into exile to the Kingdom of Saxony in 1832.

5. Friedrich Wilhelm IV ascended the throne of Prussia in 1840. The organization of free or independent Lutheran churches was permitted beginning in 1841.

6. That is, the Albright Brethren.

7. According to *The History of Columbia County, Wisconsin* (Chicago: Western Historical Company, 1880), the advent of the Albright Brethren "into Columbia County dates back some thirty years ago, when a class was organized in the town of Lewiston. A similar organization was effected soon after in Portage, Samuel Schleifer being the prime mover. The Rev. George Eslinger (then the only minister of the Albrecht persuasion in the extensive circuit in which were included the present circuits of Portage, Westfield, Brandon, Winnebago, Fox River, Berlin, Marquette and Oshkosh, at present comprising an aggregate membership of fifteen hundred souls), presided every second Sunday. It was his custom to fill a small provision pouch with hard crackers and other imperishable food, and set out from Portage on foot, making his tour and reaching Oshkosh in seven days" (p. 629).

considerably from those of our German clergymen, but we believed we had to soothe ourselves with the thought: "We live in America now." As we subsequently became acquainted with other clergymen of that sort and their religious teachings—and their method of holiness, repudiation of confirmation, indifference toward holy baptism, and so forth struck us as being incompatible with the Bible besides—a separation between them and us was brought about. But where to get a preacher now? I wrote to Mr. Preacher Geyer of Lebanon County [sic], but it wasn't until eight weeks later that this gentleman gave us the disappointing directive to apply to his colleague, Mr. Stephan, in this regard. Meanwhile, I probably need not mention at this point that the Albright people around here were not idle. Like the Italian and Spanish Jesuits, they sought to cause divisions, and they definitely succeeded with many individuals who were weak in faith. During this turmoil, I was sent as a representative of the local evangelical congregations to a one-time preacher and headmaster named Nohl, who lives twenty-six miles distant from here. He, however, declined our invitation to hold the Holy Supper for us, due to the inconvenience. Finally a letter also turned up from Preacher Stephan. He did agree to help us, but his agreement was accompanied by so many accusations of Calvinism that we weren't really sure about him either. The United Church in Prussia had never accepted the doctrine of election,[8] or the partaking of the Holy Supper only as a mere memorial meal, but this was expressly presumed in his letter. Nevertheless, we came to a mutual understanding, and this past Pentecost festival we had the good fortune of receiving the Holy Supper at his distribution. On Feb. 4 he will once again hold Lord's Supper at four stations; in addition he will likewise appoint a day for the confirmation of the children. Up till now the Sunday reading service has been conducted at six places by the farmers Teske, Gruhlke, Stelter, Kopplin, Ernst Schultz (my son), and by myself. I have been the superintendent of these congregations in the sense that I have visited them on rotation, preached among them, and exhorted them to unity. The congregations are seven, nine, ten, and sixteen miles distant from me, yet in the summer months I have made the trip there and back on foot in one day, and that included preaching for them. Along the way I would memorize my sermon, in addition taking turns imploring God for his grace and for his blessing on behalf of myself and the listeners, and my work has been successful every time. My domestic circumstances are just passable, and full of trials besides. I have still not as yet been able to acquire my own team, and an otherwise robust twenty-five-year-old son[9] has suffered from epilepsy since early childhood and makes my days bleak. On Nov. 8 of last year the youngest of my children[10] died on me, a promising boy of ten years.

    8. Schultz appears to be unfamiliar with this doctrine as a whole. He is probably referring to double predestination. Confessional Lutherans do believe in predestination or election, but only an election to salvation, not to damnation.

    9. Carl August

    10. Friedrich Rudolph

APPENDIX VI: BEGINNINGS OF LUTHERANISM IN MARQUETTE COUNTY, WISCONSIN

Fig. 55. Ernst Adolph Schultz, the son of Johann Schultz, unknown year, photo.
Image courtesy of John Dolan.

I do not feel that I am called to distribute the holy sacraments, though I have performed emergency baptism on some sickly children at the request of the parents. There are currently several children here in need of baptism, whom Mr. Preacher Stephan will baptize.

The formalizing of marriages has been effected by the town justice in question, due to the lack of a clergyman. Afterwards we have then added to the ceremony with our songs and prayers.

I was also responsible for the burial of the dead in Germany at my congregation there. Burials are also done here with singing and the reading of a fitting funeral address.

Finally, I will permit myself to append to my present letter the additional note that, a few years before my departure from Germany, I lost my entire library in a disastrous fire at night, including a few valuable works on church history. Wouldn't it be possible for me to obtain a work of that sort through you, Reverend Sir, sent through the mail? I would deliver it back to you with thanks upon my arrival.

My relation to Mr. Preacher Stephan you may see for yourself from the enclosed letter I am taking the liberty of sending along to you.[11]

I pray God for your good health, and sign myself with deep respect,

---

11. See the next letter, no. 73.

Your Reverence's
most faithfully devoted servant,
Farmer Johann Schultz

No. 73: Rev. Martin Stephan to Johann Schultz (Dec. 18, 1854)

Esteemed friend and brother in Christ,

Your dear letter dated the first of this month made me very happy, for I can see from it that nothing unwelcome has happened; rather, most welcome advances are being made. I have given some thought to the best arrangement for my coming there, and I think this would be best: Since my ministerial duties make it impossible for me to come out there immediately after Christmas at the turn of the year, I am hereby scheduling the next available date, *Friday, January 26*, as the day of my departure; I would thus be arriving at Mr. Teske's on Saturday toward evening. On that Sunday, I was planning to make my appearance in the early morning at the closest preaching station with my guide and so forth, and would like it, if it could be arranged, if that same day I could also preach and so forth at the station closest to that one right away, but if not, on the next day, Monday. During the week I would give the confirmands their final preparations for their confirmation and partaking of the Lord's Supper; those solemnities would take place the following Sunday, February 4. With that the first three preaching stations would be taken care of; I could take care of the fourth either in the course of the same week I just mentioned or on Monday, Feb. 5.[12]

Fig. 56. Rev. Martin Stephan, Jr. (1823–1884), unknown year, photo.

12. Here Schultz was referred to a note in the left margin: "Since, however, Friday, Feb. 2, is the Feast of the Purification of Mary, it would be very fitting if a sermon, etc., were given on that day at one of the four stations."

However, this entire plan can also be postponed to an even later date, and I therefore ask you to report to me in a timely manner if a postponement should be desired on your part or on the part of our other friends. The time of year is definitely not particularly conducive. But I will happily and heartily assume such minor physical inconveniences, if it means I am able to contribute something to the spread of Christ's kingdom—considering how much he himself assumed, and he was the innocent lamb of God!

I will see to the four catechisms you asked for, and I hope to obtain them from Philadelphia by then; I first have to order them from there. I am very glad that this splendid little book is finding admirers among you. God grant that through a truly active Christianity the Holy Spirit be given room to work in those families, so that he may build himself a Zion there out of living stones, founded on the cornerstone, Jesus Christ. That is my wish and prayer. Only through a *living* Christianity can the sectarians be opposed there; for a *dead* one they are certainly more than a match, morally speaking, even if they do err in a number of points.

I would also add that, for the location where the confirmation will take place, if at all possible a public schoolhouse should be chosen, since the church is also entitled to the most decorous order and solemnity possible, also as far as the space is concerned. No one will certainly think anything of the miles it takes to go, for example, from Mr. Teske's residence to the nearest schoolhouse. At Mr. Welke's the *space* lent a lot to the service in terms of solemnity. Enough on that.

If there are children to be baptized and they cannot be brought to the assembly on account of the cold weather, then I ask you to give timely consideration to how I can save the most time in traveling to the residence of the parents. The expenses that I will have for the horse this time will certainly be more significant than the other time, but since four little congregations are sharing them, it won't be too burdensome for any of them.

If there are any more reminders you need to give me in advance, there's still of course plenty of time to do so. Please give my greetings to Mr. *Gruhlke*, though I cannot recall who he is. The Lord and Chief Shepherd of his flock, Jesus Christ, who has entrusted the pasturing of his lambs, fill you both with his Spirit, so that you become tools in his hand through which he himself prepares those young hearts for eternal life, so that they are born again from the imperishable seed of the living word of God, the word that endures eternally! Likewise please give my friendliest greetings to our other friends *Teske*, *Welke*, and *Holz*. *Fischer's* religious defection saddens me deeply. I commit all of you to God's faithful and fatherly hand and to the protection of his holy angels.

Hoping for a speedy, healthy, and joyful reunion,
your friend and brother in Christ,
M. Stephan

Mayville, December 18
1854

No. 85: Johann Schultz to Synod President Johannes Muehlhaeuser (May 19, 1855)

May 19, 1855
Princeton, Marquette Co.

Most Reverend Mr. President!

Please do not accuse me of any indecency for not having sent you your book as of yet.

With help from my son-in-law,[13] I have built myself a residence this winter, since I was living in a makeshift cabin for such a long time. I thus had to put this time to good use, since my son-in-law is compelled by his circumstances to go looking for work elsewhere throughout the summer months. Once we have finished planting, however, I will pay you a visit and bring the book along. It's in a safe place with me. I will defer telling you how the local churches are doing until then.

May God preserve you and your dear ones in the best of health. This is the sincere wish of:

Your faithfully devoted servant,
Farmer Johann Schultz

No. 116: Johann Schultz to Synod President Johannes Muehlhaeuser (May 14, 1856)

May 14, 1856
Princeton, Marquette Co., Wis.

Most Reverend Mr. President!

The undersigned most obediently takes the liberty of acquainting you with the state of local church affairs and of asking you for your kind advice on behalf of several evangelical congregations in this area.

From an earlier letter to you on my part, Mr. President, you will still recall that we had chosen Mr. Preacher Stephan, in Mayville, Dodge Co., as our guest preacher until the establishment of our own parish system. Recently,[14] however, Mr. Stephan

---

13. Possibly August Hasse

14. Various details from these letters and Immanuel Lutheran-Mayville's records make it clear that Schultz is referring here to a trip Rev. Stephan made in December of 1855. Even though Schultz is

did not wish to administer the Holy Supper to us on account of the fact that, on his way here, an inebriated fellow member from our church alliance denied that we will one day rise bodily from the dead, in a conversation they had started up. As further reason for refusing us the Supper Mr. Stephan cited the incorrect understanding of the Augsburg Confession on our part. Since then a strained relationship has set in between Mr. Stephan and us, and it is unlikely to be resolved at this point. But the fault lies with Mr. Stephan. If he had kept in mind all the many different elements that have combined to form the church community in this area, that we previously belonged to the United Church and that the matter could accordingly only gain acceptance with slow and careful steps, and if he had lastly kept in mind that the rejection of more than 150 communicants, many of whom lived more than twenty-five miles away from here, could do nothing but cause bad blood—if, I say, he had kept this in mind, he would have dealt with us more sensibly. Because of this incident, the members of the congregation here are now firmly determined to remain with the United Church, and to stick with a guest preacher until they are in a condition to establish their own parish system, which is not too far off. Ever since I have had the honor of making your acquaintance by letter, I have continually advised that we should put the matter completely into your hands, and I am now getting their approval.

Would it not be possible, Mr. President, for you to honor us with a visit yourself, to administer the Holy Supper to us, and to introduce the further steps required for us to join your organization? You could take the railroad to Watertown and ride with the mail coach from there. You would get to know us personally, and we would comply unconditionally with your kind advice. You would be rewarded for your trouble. If, however, your position will not permit this trip, then we earnestly beg you, sir, to be so kind as to provide us with the name of a preacher to whom we can turn. Might not your brother-in-law, Mr. Conrad, be a suitable option?

If you do visit us, we would inform you of your accommodations and the places where the Supper is held later on.

Looking forward to your kind reply at your earliest convenience,

Farmer Johann Schultz

No. 144: Marquette County Administrators to Rev. Gottlieb Reim[15] (March 3, 1857)

March 3, 1857
Princeton, Marquette Co.

---

writing this five months after the fact, "recently [*in jüngster Zeit*]" is a relative term, and could encompass a much longer period of time in those days, when the pace of life wasn't as rushed as it is now.

15. Gottlieb Reim (1828–1882) was a Wisconsin Synod pastor in Ashford at the time.

Most Reverend, Most Esteemed Mr. Preacher!

When you were last here, you expressed the wish that a compilation of the evangelical Lutheran Christians in this area be drawn up, so that you could obtain an accurate standard for establishing a church association.

This wish of yours should have been satisfied sooner, but thus far absolutely no results could be confirmed on account of the overly high snow and the overly great distance between the individual members. Today, March 1, the delegates elected by the individual congregations are now meeting. They produced a list of their members, and it resulted in the following tally:

1. The Princeton congregation numbers	40 heads of household,
2. The Montello	54
3. The Mecan	50
	= 144 heads of household

The congregations are large enough to warrant the necessity of a clergyman. You, Mr. Preacher, are already somewhat acquainted with the congregations here; we can, however, give you the assurance that at least ten more heads of household on the other side of Montello are joining, so that a number of 154 can very readily be assumed.

Now this would be our request to you, sir: to be so kind as to present our circumstances to the president of your synod and to do what you can to get a spiritual shepherd sent to us.

The raising of a salary, we believe, will then be able to be accomplished once the assurance of a preacher is made known to us.

Please be so kind as to forward to the president the enclosed letter addressed to His Reverence, accompanied by your recommendation.

The religion book sent to Schultz he has received in good order, but we still wish that the instruction might be given by our future preacher.

August Schwancke, Sigemad [sic] Luetke
Ferdinad [sic] Bahr, Wilhelm Krenz
Wilhelm Stelter, Martin Tagatz

No. 145: Two Letters to Synod President Johannes Muehlhaeuser, Enclosed with No. 144

March 3, 1857
Princeton, Marquette Co., Wis.

Most Reverend, Most Esteemed Mr. President!

We are so bold as to entrust you with the pressing need of a spiritual shepherd for the following congregations:

The Princeton congregation consists of	40,
the Montello	54, and
the Mecan	50 heads of household.

Mr. Preacher Reim, at Ashford, who has already held service here twice, is also certainly convinced by now of the urgent need for a preacher, and all the more so considering that the Albright people are doing their utmost to make the people waver in their faith and are endeavoring to steal the sheep away from the rightful Shepherd.

In an enclosed letter we have entreated Mr. Pastor Reim to present our situation to you, and we live in the conviction that Mr. Reim will place the matter on your heart as a pressing need.

We would then raise the salary for our future preacher immediately, and if it is required, send it to you.

A kind reply is most humbly requested by:

The administrators,
August Schwancke, Siegemud [sic] Luetke
Ferdinand Bahr, Wilhelm Krenz
Wilhelm Stelter, Martin Tagatz

[Written on the back side:]
Most esteemed Mr. President!

I cannot do otherwise than comply with the wish of these people; chalk it up to mere modesty that they did not write you in a more urgent tone than they did. Their need is great; their eager willingness to hear God's word no less great. One cannot but wish that this field of labor be occupied as soon as possible. Since I have already spelled out their necessity in detail several times, it seems superfluous to do so repetitively here, and will therefore content myself with this recommendation.

With most respectful greetings,
Pastor G. Reim
Ashford, April 15, 1857

No. 146: Johann Schultz to Synod President Johannes Muehlhaeuser (March 11, 1857)

March 11, 1857
Princeton, Marquette Co., Wis.

Most Reverend Mr. President!

Through my neighbor Luetke, who is traveling to Milwaukee on business, I am taking the liberty of sharing with you a short digest of the progress of the church alliance in this area.

In accordance with the wishes of Mr. Pastor Reim of Ashford, administrators were elected for the 3 evangelical congregations in this area—Princeton, Montello, and Mecan. These men were to assemble their heads of household and announce their affiliation with us by getting their signatures in their own hand.

Due to the high snow and the widely scattered residences of the members, their recording could not take place until the final days of February, and on March 1 the administrators got together and reported the number of their heads of household at 144.

Even if Mr. Pastor Reim, in keeping with our request, has already sent you word of this occurrence, or will do so later, surely you will not hold it against me, Mr. President, if I myself share with you what has happened here and make my own appeal to you, placing on your heart the urgent need for a spiritual shepherd for the evangelical Lutheran congregations in this area. The raising of the pastor's salary would take place according to your stipulation and be sent to you,[16] and in this connection let me remark that everything possible will be done on our part to make the pastor's stay among us a pleasant one.

The instruction of the confirmands here will probably be conducted by me, in accordance with Mr. Pastor Reim's desires, but due to the bad weather nothing at all has been able to be done thus far.

Unfortunately, in sharing this news, I also cannot keep it hidden from you that the Albright people in this area are making every conceivable effort to stir up divisions among us in order to turn church members away from us, and they have again recently succeeded in doing so with some people. Degradation of others, particularly of German clergymen; forcing people to the bench of repentance; limitless soliciting; insipid, unbiblical drivel, instead of the pure word of God; popular melodies, e.g. "God Save the King";[17] exaggerated figurative concepts in song lyrics; and perfect sanctification—these are the most outstanding abnormalities of the Albright people, by which they incur, if not the sheer contempt, then at least the sorrow and pity of every true Christian.

Surely no one would acknowledge it as a God-pleasing action if I caused separations between spouses or children, or enticed members of other religious parties to come over to my church service like a highwayman. And yet these are the

---

16. Probably not the salary itself, but the documentation of who would give how much and the total amount.

17. German: "Heil dir im Siegerkranz [Hail to Thee in the Victor's Crown]"—the royal anthem of the Kingdom of Prussia at the time, with the same tune as "God Save the King," also used for "My Country, 'Tis of Thee." Schultz first wrote "popular songs," then crossed it out and wrote "popular melodies," since the Albright Brethren undoubtedly did not actually sing the royal anthem itself, but other religious songs set to that tune.

prominent characteristics of the Albright people. Their confessional writings and their publications do not even articulate a tenth of the silliness that their clergymen and members put on display in various forms. It cannot be denied that the position of a clergyman would probably be a difficult one, at least at first. I nevertheless live in the hope that with correct handling and otherwise faithful spiritual care, many Albright people will rejoin our church.

We have only seen a preacher among us five times in the course of six years, while two, even as many as seven, Albright preachers work on some forty people for days, yes, weeks at a time. Thus it is no wonder if now and then they draw someone to their side and make heads spin with that kind of activity.

My neighbor Luetke will be staying in Milwaukee for several days, and I flatter myself with the prospect of receiving an answer from Your Reverence through him.

With exceptionally deep respect, I remain

Your Reverence's
most faithfully devoted servant,
Farmer Johann Schultz

No. 149: Rev. Martin Stephan to Synod President Johannes Muehlhaeuser (April 2, 1857)

Oshkosh, Wis., April 2 [?], 1857

Reverend Sir,

Having returned from a trip to a congregation by Princeton, I feel compelled to write you a few lines with respect to this congregation.

From the beginning she has been served by preachers of the Missouri Synod. Most recently by me. A portion of the same gave me occasion to practice the church discipline commanded in God's word (Matt. 7:6 and ch. 18) on account of their manifest worldly mindset and unbelief. On that account, in their resentment toward me they turned to you, and there they acquired a preacher of their mindset. Up to this point I have no objections. But now another portion of the congregation did not resent the church discipline practiced by me, as the other portion did, even though it was something new to them at the moment. This portion called me to serve them from time to time, which I also would have done, had I not accepted a call to Michigan shortly before that. But now I am back in Wisconsin, as you can see from my date, and I now intend to serve that congregation.[18] No one can challenge my valid claim

---

18. Martin Stephan, Jr. (1823–1884), son of the infamous Martin Stephan, Sr. (see Walter O. Forster, *Zion on the Mississippi* [St. Louis: Concordia, 1953]), was ordained and installed as the pastor of Immanuel Lutheran in the town of Theresa near Mayville, Wis., by Pastor Ludwig Geyer of Immanuel Lutheran, Lebanon, on May 1, 1853. From there he made his first trips to rural Princeton

on this congregation without committing an injustice. That congregation also would have really appreciated my service to them, if they were not expecting a preacher from your camp because of a promise made to them. Now if it should be the case that this congregation has been or will be alienated from me and my synod, by any party whatsoever, it will in any such case be a sin.

Now this is my well-intentioned desire, that you, Reverend Sir, would seriously take to heart the circumstances detailed above in sending a preacher to Princeton, leave my portion of the congregation entirely out of your consideration, neither deny nor obscure the obvious difference between your doctrine and the doctrine of my synod in order to capture the people, and in general not covet or snatch what belongs to your neighbor. Cf. the Ninth and Tenth Commandments with Luther's explanation; also the passages 1 Pet. 4:15; 2 Cor. 10:13–16; Rom. 15:20,21; and Gal. 2:9. I would have to term it a glaring injustice if your emissary would permit himself any kind of encroachment on the rules fixed by God in the passages just cited. It is your job, though, to guard and govern. Please do let me be cheated out of the legitimate fruits of the bitter pains that I took on my frequent horseback rides to that congregation in all sorts of weather. If your emissary confines himself to the portion that I have conceded, he will find first of all those who share his spirit and plenty of people to boot. But only by dishonorably forcing and enticing away could he take the portion faithful to me and united with me in spirit and fasten it to the other portion.

Finally, I attest to my good, Christian, loving intention in these lines, in conformity with the truth, for I love sincerity and hate insincerity, especially that despicable piracy sailing under Lutheran colors. But perhaps, in view of the forthcoming general Lutheran conference, all those calling themselves Lutheran will at last be imbued with one Lutheran, brotherly spirit, and people will learn to be ashamed of calling themselves Lutheran when, in fact, they are not. You, sir, will certainly share this wish with:

Yours truly,
Martin Stephan, Pastor

In between the preceding and the following letters, Konrad Diehlmann was installed as the pastor of the congregations mentioned in the preceding letters. In 1856 Diehlmann had been serving as a pastor in Rainham on the Niagara Peninsula in Canada, west of Buffalo, New York. But the president of the Missouri Synod himself, C. F. W. Walther,

---

and Montello in 1854 and 1855 (see nos. 80 & 73 above). In 1856 he accepted a call from a Lutheran congregation in Kalamazoo, Mich., and was installed there on Oct. 23. However, the congregation disbanded shortly thereafter, and by December Stephan was staying with Dr. Wilhelm Sihler on the seminary campus in Ft. Wayne, Ind. He received a new call to serve "two Lutheran congregations in and near Oshkosh" in the early part of 1857 and was installed as their pastor on March 1. As you can see from the date, he wrote this letter shortly thereafter. He served in Oshkosh until he accepted a call to be an assistant preacher in Ft. Wayne and was installed there on June 27, 1858. For more on Stephan Jr., see *WELS Historical Institute Journal* 37, no. 2 (Fall 2019) 31–47.

made a winter trip from St. Louis to visit him and to convince him to move to St. Louis and take over as the editor of the St. Louiser Volksblatt, *a German newspaper, an offer he accepted that same year. (He was already editing the* Illustrirte Abendschule, *a family-oriented periodical, and continued in that capacity in St. Louis.) According to the Wisconsin Synod historian J. P. Koehler, Diehlmann became "more moderate in his confessional stand" while in St. Louis. He became acquainted with Pastor Wilhelm Streissguth of the Wisconsin Synod, who persuaded him to come to Wisconsin and to join the Wisconsin Synod (The History of the Wisconsin Synod [1970], 52). When Diehlmann came to Wisconsin, he took over the above-mentioned congregations and officially joined the Wisconsin Synod at their 1857 convention in Oak Creek from June 7–10. He also attended the synod convention in Milwaukee the following year, but was absent without excuse from the 1859 convention in Racine. (The letter he submitted to excuse himself was judged by the Excuse Committee to be an improper "intermingling and exchanging [of] synodical with personal matters.") At the 1860 convention in Fond du Lac, President Muehlhaeuser reported that "soon after last year's convention Pastor Diehlmann requested his release from the synod," and was granted his request. The following letter helps to answer some, though not all, of the questions as to what happened.*

No. 386: Rev. Gottlieb Reim to Synod President Johannes Muehlhaeuser (Nov. 27, 1859)

Helenville, Nov. 27, 1859

Dear Brother Muehlhaeuser!

With warmhearted greetings I am finally taking the time to comply with your wishes and to report that which is most newsworthy, if anything by us really qualifies as such. After I had received Pastor Diehlmann's letter, I set out from here on Nov. 14[19] to go to Princeton. Since Bading happened to be in Watertown, and I had a lot to discuss with him about Watertown, I spent the midday in Watertown. Here and in Lebanon the Missouri preacher Strassen [sic][20] had spread rumors that our synod had joined a non-Lutheran synod (the General Synod?) and that, furthermore, I had supposedly been with Strassen in Princeton and on that occasion Diehlmann had confessed in the presence of me, Strassen, and a congregational administrator that he had committed adultery. These rumors had provoked great agitation, especially in Lebanon. Bading strongly urged me to go with him to Lebanon, preach, and clear the synod's name. I did so, and exposed the unfounded nature of these slanders in the presence of many from Geyer's congregation.[21]

19. A Monday

20. Carl Strasen had been installed earlier that year (Pentecost 6, July 31) as the pastor of St. John Evangelical Lutheran Church in Watertown by Pastor Ludwig Geyer of Immanuel in Lebanon.

21. Geyer's congregation was Immanuel (see previous n.). According to Immanuel's online history

The next morning[22] at four o'clock we then drove to Horicon together, and from there I took the railroad to Cambria. I arrived at Diehlmann's in the evening.[23] He gave me a truly friendly welcome and informed me candidly of the situation in Princeton. We discussed for a long time what should be done, and after lengthy consideration finally came to the conclusion that a personal visit would do more harm than good under the present circumstances. The reasons why are summed up as follows:

1. Pastor Strassen was in Princeton and has a following there. If I gain one too, which would certainly be possible, perhaps likely, that would break up the settlement and turn it into an endless battlefield. If we wanted to hold our ground, we would need to have a man who would be more than a match for the Missourians. But there is no such man currently available to us. To gather a following and hold out hope for later occupation is therefore dangerous, since that would already be issuing a challenge to the Missourians.

2. It is fairly certain that the Missourians will fizzle out sooner if we seemingly surrender the field to them. Then they will make a genuinely Missourian appearance right from the start and alienate themselves from the people. But if we get ourselves involved, that would induce them to be more moderate and to make sacrifices that we are unable to make.

3. Diehlmann's complete ruin would be an almost inevitable result. The conflict would already be there. The Missourians would turn Diehlmann's case into a bone of contention in a downright malicious way. In the end there would be nothing left for us but to keep silent and leave the matter sitting there on our shoulders. And the fact is that there is something to the accusation, even if the slander as presented is a lie. That's precisely why Diehlmann won't take a stand against it, and we cannot either. Any intervention in the Princeton affairs on our part could get Diehlmann worked up so much that he would be pushed to his limits. If the matter stays where it is, then we are protected against every attack. No complaint from Princeton came before the synod; consequently, we could not be aware of the matter. The blame would chiefly fall back on the people in Princeton themselves, since, instead of taking the proper, Christian course of action, they are running from one synod to the next.

(https://www.ilcol.org/4.html; accessed July 5, 2018), a controversy arose "in 1856 when the teacher Philipp Wetzel and other members objected to private confession that Rev. Geyer insisted on. One hundred members broke away and formed St. Matthew's congregation and built their own church on the south end of Old Lebanon. It disbanded in 1926." It is doubtless this St. Matthew's Congregation to which Bading and Reim went. See also A. Wagner, "Erklärung," in *Der Lutheraner* 15, no. 25 (July 26, 1859) 199.

22. Tuesday, Nov. 15

23. From this and other sources (church histories and census information), Diehlmann appears to have been living with the Anson Root or Martin Bender family on the western border of the town of Randolph in Columbia County—along the eastern side of what is today Inglehart Road, west or northwest of Friesland in the town of Randolph, Columbia Co., Wis.

In view of these circumstances, especially the last reason, I couldn't follow through with going to Princeton, even though I was charged with doing so. Instead we decided to maintain a written correspondence with persons who are influential and averse to the Missourian influence. That way, when the right moment had come, we could take back the entire field that much more easily.

Whether I have hit upon the right choice and have acted in accordance with the president's wishes, I do not know. At any rate I tried, and did so according to my best judgment. It was no small thing for me to have to come to such a conclusion about a field so close to my heart. Diehlmann's current congregation could perhaps be some compensation for us; it would then be an outpost for Princeton at the same time. It would be good if Diehlmann were called upon by the synod to prepare the congregation for joining. It would also be very good if Diehlmann could be visited by a preacher now and then. He is hurting badly. If I didn't have to spend a night somewhere on the way, I would visit him frequently; he is very much in need of it.

On Saturday evening[24] I returned to Watertown, where I then preached at noon on Sunday. In the evening the serving of the congregation was discussed in a meeting. So much for the report on my trip.

On Saturday evening[25] Candidate Strube arrived here. I am very sorry that no instructions were sent along with him in keeping with the discussion at the conference. I definitely made it a requirement there, and it is also extremely necessary. It would eliminate many false preconceptions. Occasionally it might prevent discrepancies. If the young people are not advised right away as to the proper relationship between them and their congregation, they will want to be waited on like barons. And when that doesn't happen, how galled they are! How they have been wronged! And what good are they now. I have already experienced this several times. That's why I brought the matter up at the conference, and I was sure that by taking this measure people would seek to protect me from such experiences. . . . It wouldn't be surprising if a man's desire for this vanished before he even got started. . . .

Here in the congregation[26] things are going quite smoothly. The construction of the church is proceeding somewhat slowly. But we will be able to celebrate Christmas in it. I am especially happy that the old bickerers are unlearning their bickering. Bulwinkel's influence is diminishing considerably. I have hopes that the congregation here will become a good congregation in time. Certainly there is still much to be done to reach that point. It is no small task to get so shattered a congregation back on the right track.

In our small family things are also going really well, praise God. Admittedly my wife is still never quite healthy, but things are going quite smoothly. Adolph is quite healthy, plump, and thriving, exceptionally well-behaved too.

24. Nov. 19
25. Nov. 26
26. In Helenville

In closing, sir, my truly warmhearted regards to you and your dear wife and children.

Most respectfully,
G. Reim, Pastor

No. 387: Johann Schultz to Synod President Johannes Muehlhaeuser (Dec. 1, 1859)

December 1, 1859
Princeton, Marquette Co.

Most Reverend Mr. President!

You will have hopefully received my letter dated Nov. 1 of this year. I have read Mr. Pastor Reim's letter. It treats the same subjects that yours does. Incidentally, it is true that the administrators in this area have applied to Mr. Stephan for a preacher, which I am not in a condition to prevent.[27] It pains me to have to share this news with you. Having said that, an important event has recently transpired here, which I herewith most humbly report to you:

An evangelical Lutheran congregation (Shields congregation)[28] was desirous of joining our church alliance when Mr. Pastor Diehlmann was here, but for reasons unknown to me pastor Diehlmann turned them down. The congregation consists of some thirty heads of household. Since they didn't want to be without services, they entered into an agreement with a farmer named Gruhlke, who was a teacher in Prussia, whereby he would lead services and perform religious functions for them, except for the distribution of the Holy Supper.

The congregation has increased greatly in number in a short time, and especially since Diehlmann's dismissal, and now even the Princeton congregation has joined together with it. The latter congregation intends to build a church in Princeton, along with a parsonage. Gruhlke is already holding a service there every three weeks, and doing so with active participation.

On the First Sunday in Advent,[29] I also attended the service there. In accordance with the wishes of the administrators, I had already previously put down their declarations in writing, which Mr. Gruhlke read to the assembled congregation after the conclusion of the service. They all gave their approval.

---

27. Cf. p. 65. Stephan was Dr. Sihler's assistant preacher in Ft. Wayne at this time.

28. Original: Siels. Judging from the ensuing letters from August Gruhlke, who is soon to be mentioned, this is a misspelling for Shields, a township in Marquette County bordered by the towns of Crystal Lake (north), Harris (west), Mecan (east), and Montello (south).

29. Nov. 27

As for Gruhlke's personality, he is a man in his thirties,[30] was a teacher with me in the province of Posen under a superintendency, and was prepared for his office at the seminary. He is in no way lacking in oratory talent, but this is surpassed by his bright mind, his unsparing devotion, and his selflessness.

Wouldn't it be possible, Mr. President, for this man to receive the pastorate there through your gracious consent? I am convinced that you will not be conferring the office on an undeserving man. Whatever measures Gruhlke has to take in this regard I ask you to transmit to me, since I am also addressing the present letter to you at their behest.

When I was there, the congregation voiced their wish that I ask you if you would kindly be present to handle the founding and formation of their church fellowship in person. I advised against it, however, since it can be anticipated that the duties of your office will not permit it.

I very sincerely ask you, sir, for a speedy reply, and I would be profoundly happy if you might be gracious enough to comply with the wishes of these two congregations, as well as my own wishes!

With the greatest respect
for Your Reverence,
Farmer Johann Schultz

No. 395: August Gruhlke to Synod President Johannes Muehlhaeuser (Dec. 29, 1859)

December 29, 1859
Shields[31] near Montello, Marquette Co., Wis.

Most Reverend Mr. President!

Please permit me, the undersigned, whose name you have become acquainted with in Mr. Johann Schultz's letters, the liberty of conveying the following letter.

In 1834 I was appointed the provisional evangelical teacher in Prussia, in the Bromberg Region,[32] Chodziesen District,[33] in a substantial village named Radwonke,[34]

---

30. Gruhlke was actually forty-two at the time. See n. 35.

31. Original: Schilds. See also n. 28.

32. The administrative region of Bromberg, so named for its capital city, was the northern of two such regions of the Grand Duchy of Posen (later simply the Province of Posen) in the Kingdom of Prussia.

33. Chodziesen was one of nine districts or counties of the Bromberg Region. Its name was changed to Kolmar in Posen in 1877.

34. Arnold Lehmann read Kadewonke in his transcription, but there was no such village in the Chodziesen District (the village with the closest spelling was Kamionke, but its statistics do not fit Gruhlke's description). Radwonke (today Radwanki) was about six miles southeast of the city

at the age of a little over seventeen.³⁵ The only reason for my leaving the seminary so early (for I was just three to four years in) was that the administration desired that the director of the seminary propose three pupils from the institution who possessed the necessary skills for three simultaneous positions in which instruction had to be given in German and Polish. This lot fell upon me, since I was the only one who appeared to possess the necessary skills for this. From the three positions proposed I chose the one mentioned above and, after I took the required examination in Bromberg two years after my appointment, I received my provisional and, not too long afterwards, also my final certification. My activity in that position (it was at the same time a very difficult task to instruct at least 140 children of both confessions³⁶ in two different languages) lasted seventeen years, up until the time I tendered my resignation and emigrated to the United States,³⁷ where I settled as a farmer on the present site. During this time I have led some of the accustomed church services for my nearest neighbors, who mostly consisted of my former schoolchildren, though I have done nothing more than I was obligated or permitted to do in keeping with my former official duties. For the most part, however, I lived only for myself and my family and fulfilled my political duties (for I have held one or a few town positions every year), which I also have to fulfill now as town treasurer amid the most trying circumstances. I dare say that I possess the public confidence in a high degree, although this did not make the slightest impression on my mind until about three to four years ago.³⁸ That was when some neighbors came to me one day and complained how the Methodists were putting such hard and terrible pressure on them to convert to their fanatical heathen abomination. And you, Reverend Sir, must already be aware of what cunning and impudence these ignorant people who call themselves preachers exhibit, and of every method concealed beneath the cloak of religion that they consider permissible—yes, even a duty—in order to achieve their goal. And it was this alone that had compelled those men to come to me, and they came out with the declaration that, if I would not support their cause, then they would probably end up being persuaded by them after all, since they had no one to defend our holy religion. I myself was terrified by the danger; since I could see no other way for the time

---

of Chodziesen (today Chodzież). In 1847 it had a population of 480 souls (of both confessions, as Gruhlke says later) in fifty-nine houses (*Topographisch-statistisches Handbuch des Preussischen Staats* [Magdeburg: Verlag von Emil Baensch], 198).

35. According to his gravestone and obituary (available at https://www.findagrave.com/memorial/69306874/august-ludwig-gruhlke), August Gruhlke was born on July 16, 1817, which would put his appointment in the year 1834.

36. Namely, Evangelical/Protestant and Roman Catholic

37. According to his obituary (see n. 35), he emigrated in 1852 (Schultz also gives that year in his letter dated Jan. 24, 1855); that year fits with Gruhlke's information here if we assume an emigration in the first half of the year.

38. That is, between Dec. 1855 and Dec. 1856. The events Gruhlke goes on to describe seem to have happened after Rev. Stephan's disciplinary action in Dec. 1855 (referred to in nos. 116 & 149 above).

being, I said that I would see how far I could get under the guidance of the almighty God. And I can tell you frankly, Mr. President, that I have done more than I believed myself capable of. My spirit, roused to the occasion, found nourishment enough as one congregation after the other came to get strengthened in faith and to find comfort and refuge. I thank my Lord most sincerely that by his grace I have succeeded in strengthening the weak, bringing the unbelieving back to understanding, and bringing many a stray back into the protective fold. However, my dear Mr. President, my inner urge will not be satisfied; it seeks the rights of the church. I am culpable, since I came forward as an unordained preacher, although I have stayed away from the distribution of the Holy Supper, and will continue to stay away as long as I do not have the right and the duty to distribute it. This is what I am seeking to obtain from you, and my soul would not have strength enough to endure a refusal. My heart is too full to sum up everything it might well say in order to be strengthened. Next to God, you are the only one I can depend on for this strengthening, Mr. President. Although Paul's words in 1 Tim. 5:22 are apropos, that the minister of Christ should not be in a rush when he does not have sufficient knowledge of the man who is aspiring to the teaching office, I nevertheless implore Your Wisdom to see if you can afford me ways and means of attaining to my goal. To begin with, I am asking for your kind and speedy reply, and whether I might take the liberty of imposing upon you in person in Milwaukee. Although my means are limited enough, I am nevertheless prepared to make every sacrifice to procure rest for my soul. I admit that I possess no theological expertise, and do not even possess so much as one work for studying church history. But so great is my confidence in you (after the love of God), in which my friend Schultz strengthened me even more, that Your Kindness will find the means to curb this deficiency too. In closing I commend myself and my family to you,

Obedient to Your Reverence,
August Gruhlke

No. 408: August Gruhlke to Synod President Johannes Muehlhaeuser (Feb. 3, 1860)

Shields[39] near Montello, February 3, 1860

Most Reverend Mr. President!

You will most kindly excuse me if I am bothering you with another letter. In the closing days of the month of December of last year, I took the liberty of appealing to you, Mr. President, for obtainment of the preaching office. I sought to lay my motives before your keen insight, and at the same time urgently asked for a speedy decision

---

39. Original: Schilds. See also n. 28.

(favorable to me). Unfortunately I have had to continue managing without. I must surely presume that, as president of a synod and at the same time a clergyman, you, Reverend Sir, are overwhelmed with very extensive tasks, or the letter I sent to you might have gotten lost in the mail. Whatever the case, I most earnestly repeat my request for you to disclose ways and means to me as soon as possible, whereby I might provide my pressing urge with nourishment. At the same time, however, I do not hesitate to tell you that everyone's eyes are intently watching with the keenest interest to see how this will turn out, both my friends and my adversaries. After all, it is I who, all on my own, have not just maintained, but enlarged our church's three congregations, consisting of more than seventy families, for three to four years, and I have fortified them to such an extent that only your refusal of my request is in a condition to shake and dismantle this fortification. And if, Mr. President, you were compelled by the exercise of your faithful duty to be unable to admit me to the preaching office, then I must give up these congregations, and in that case they will be lost for your synod forever. Why? That is easily answered. There is already a preacher named Strieter[40] living a few miles from here. He was sent there from Ohio by the Missouri Synod shortly before Christmas upon the application of certain administrators. Before he came here this man was not yet a real preacher, just a tolerated one, and he received his ordination scarcely two weeks ago through a pastor from Watertown.[41] In spite of that, this man also seems to be working with very little approval, and consequently with not much blessing either, as is evident from how many people have become dissatisfied in such a short time and from the many persons, numbering in the forties, who went over to the Methodists two weeks ago when they dedicated their church two miles from that Missouri preacher.[42] From this, then, your keen insight will also realize the fate to which these congregations are exposed with this kind of rift. The Methodists would seize upon a portion of them—the majority, I fear—since every single member wants to be a big shot proselytizer, and the weaker, now vulnerable portion would fall to that Old Lutheran preacher. But since this preacher does not seem to have the right touch either, even though he claims to have worked in Ohio for five years already,[43] your keen wisdom will conclude what miserable confusion would inevitably set in here in short

40. Original: Stritter. The reference is to the subject of this book.

41. As Strieter's autobiography and other sources testify, Gruhlke is mistaken as to the facts of Strieter's case. Strieter had, in fact, been a "real" preacher, graduating from Fort Wayne after his examination in July 1852 and receiving his ordination in Elyria, Ohio, from Rev. Heinrich Christian Schwan on April 6, 1853. He was subsequently called to St. John Lutheran Church in what is today Garfield Heights, Ohio, in October 1854, before accepting the call to Wisconsin in November 1859. Strieter was then installed (not ordained) into his new office on Sunday, January 15 (Epiphany 2), 1860, by Rev. Peter Heinrich Dicke of Mayville (not Watertown).

42. See p. 70, n. 9. This likely refers to the church built on what is today the site of Emmanuel Evangelical Crystal Lake Cemetery on the east side of State Highway 22, one and a quarter miles from the site of Strieter's house.

43. See n. 41; Strieter had already worked in Ohio for seven years, five of them in what is today Garfield Heights.

order. If you will weigh all of this, Mr. President, and be disposed to my humble yet urgent application, then I ask you to send me a church history book if possible, and in any case I look forward to a speedy and kind reply.

Obedient to Your Reverence,
August Gruhlke

No. 413: August Gruhlke to Synod President Johannes Muehlhaeuser (Feb. 19, 1860)

February 19, 1860
Montello, Marquette Co., Wis.

Most Reverend Mr. President!

Your very precious letter came into my possession on the eleventh of this month. Even though I was looking forward to a reply with the greatest longing and, I permit myself to say, also with trepidation for a decision as to how my lot would fall, I nevertheless acknowledge with the most profound gratitude that, according to the content of your kind letter, I am to some degree pushed along in a hope to reach my goal, even if it is still far down the road. I would have replied most obediently right away with the next mail delivery, only I could not. My listeners, whom I regarded as my children, had to share in my joy with me, because my work is so very closely attached to your soul. You will accordingly, Mr. President, most kindly pardon my immodesty.

As for the position at which you have arrived, Reverend Sir, I accord it childlike respect and agree with it completely. Nothing would delight both me and my members more than if you yourself, Mr. President, appeared in our midst and at the same time distributed the Holy Supper here. Only this will probably not be feasible due to your likely advanced age and due to the widespread duties of your office. Nevertheless, I ask you earnestly, if you send a preacher, to communicate to him at the same time, by my request, which I am expressing on behalf of my congregations, that he should distribute the Holy Supper here. This would have to be done at two stations at least and, in addition, would especially give the preacher the best opportunity to get better acquainted with the church situation and the needs of the congregations than he would otherwise. You, Mr. President, or that preacher of our synod would certainly be so kind as to prearrange the particulars for this. Those who intend to commune at the celebration of the Supper, I, with your gracious permission, would prepare for doing so with the assistance of our Lord. You are also quite correct, as a true servant of the Lord, when you do not doubt that I would gladly bow out if I felt that the Lord had not called me. Only I believe that I addressed that in my first letter, and also say it now, that my soul will only find rest when it has completed its[44] work in the name of the Author and Finisher of our faith [cf. Heb. 12:2], as often as there is work to be done, and my soul would not be strong enough to be able to endure a refusal peacefully. True, my knowledge is fragmentary and my prophesying is fragmentary [cf. 1 Cor. 13:9]; I do not possess any resource for my training (apart from the Hirschberg Bible, which is accompanied with explanatory notes)[45] and would be able to accomplish a lot more if I possessed the most necessary works for getting acquainted with different viewpoints. That is also why I have all the more reason to praise the grace of God; it, not I, is responsible for the work being done. For the Methodists your kind letter has become a veritable terror (I read the content of the letter after the sermon to the congregation here) since they would have easily won the victory if I had gone down in defeat. Now, however, they not only see a barrier, but their ramparts can also be easily threatened. As I bid you a fond farewell, please permit me the liberty of adding the request that I might be kindly informed of your opinion in the near future, if possible.

Reverentially obedient to Your Reverence,
A[ugust] Gruhlke

No. 433: August Gruhlke to Synod President Johannes Muehlhaeuser (April 7, 1860)

Montello, April 7, 1860

Most Reverend Mr. President!

On April 6[46] I learned, after conclusion of the service, that there was a letter for me at the post office, but that the postmaster would not surrender it to me without an order. I therefore went to Montello myself that day to retrieve the letter, since I presumed that it had to be a message from you, Reverend Friend, for which I and my congregation members had been waiting with longing. Unfortunately I was disappointed; the letter addressed to me had disappeared from the post office, even though the postmaster, a friend of mine, told me that a letter for me from Milwaukee really had arrived, and some people had also been there trying to retrieve it, but he had

44. Usually when Gruhlke capitalizes *Ihr*, he is referring to Muehlhaeuser (polite form of "your"); this would then be translated, "when it has performed your work [namely, the public ministry of the gospel]." However, since he also capitalizes *Ihr* later when referring to the Methodists, along with other capitalization quirks throughout his letters, it seems that his capitalization practice is somewhat random. The smoother, simpler translation above is therefore to be preferred.

45. The Hirschberg Bible (*Hirschberger Bibel*) was a reprint of Luther's German translation of the Bible along with brief and pointed annotations and parallel references by Ehrenfried Liebich, pastor at Lomnitz and Erdmannsdorf, Silesia (today Łomnica and Mysłakowice, Poland), assisted by Johann Friedrich Burg of Breslau, Silesia (today Wrocław, Poland). It was printed at Hirschberg, Silesia (today Jelenia Góra, Poland), 1756–1763.

46. Good Friday

refused it to them, and now he absolutely could not recall where the letter must have gone to. He himself was very concerned and asked me to write you back immediately as a precaution (although he was also hoping to re-obtain the letter, which perhaps had gotten to a wrong address), and to ask for the kind contents of the just-indicated letter. This is accordingly my fond request, and one that likely requires haste. I will conclude then with the Christian wish that you, Reverend Sir, might enjoy a happy and holy Easter celebration, and that you think of me with affection.

With veneration for Your Reverence,
A[ugust] Gruhlke

No. 434: August Gruhlke to Synod President Johannes Muehlhaeuser (April 8, 1860)

Princeton, April 8
Twelve o'clock noon, 1860

Most Reverend Mr. President!
A happy Easter.

With true, glowing love I pick up the quill, even on this First Holy Easter Day, to write back to the man whom I truly love and revere as a father, even without having seen him. Briefly, the occasion for writing such an unpardonable letter on this day is as follows:

I presume that you, Reverend Mr. President, already received my letter addressed to you from Saturday, the seventh of this month, which informs you of the loss of the letter you sent to me. When I came home in the evening, a man showed up in my residence at eight o'clock, a Methodist, and handed me your precious letter with these words:

One of their preachers had retrieved the letter from the post office several days ago, because he believed the address belonged to one of his people. He, the preacher, had then delivered the letter to him, the one now bearing it, and he had left it lie for three days already. He still would not have brought it to me even today, if he had not heard about all the inquiries being made about the letter. So, Reverend Friend, I nevertheless found myself deeply delighted to possess the letter, yet in a situation not all that delightful. You had written your letter on March 17, I received it on April 7, and the preacher is supposed to arrive here on April 13, this Friday. However, on Sunday, the First Holy Easter Day, when I had to preach in Princeton, I was given the assurance that the reply to your kind letter would still work with their schedule. I accordingly declare most humbly that I agree with your arrangement completely, and add that a team of horses will be waiting in Ripon, on schedule, for the arrival of the preacher on the thirteenth of this month, and that the first service will thus be held on

Saturday the fourteenth, seven miles from Princeton, where I live. The next service in Princeton on Sunday the fifteenth. At both stations the distribution of the Holy Supper is not only desired, but urgently requested. But I myself will add one more request, that I *greatly, greatly* desire, if it would be possible, that you yourself would come. A whole lot is hanging in balance for our synod with this visit. A Methodist contingent will also not be lacking. Everybody is extremely anxious; everything else I can tell you in person. I submit to you like a child in every respect. As I and my friends bid you a fond farewell, Reverend Mr. President, I remain most reverentially:

Your true f[riend],
A[ugust] Gruhlke[47]

There is no further correspondence from Johann Schultz or August Gruhlke in this collection. We can deduce from the proceedings of the 1860 Wisconsin Synod convention in Fond du Lac (May 31—June 7) that the preacher who arrived in Ripon on April 13 to visit the congregations that met in Princeton and at the Gruhlke farm was Wilhelm Streissguth of Milwaukee. According to his obituary available online (see n. 35), Gruhlke moved to Waseca County in Minnesota in 1862. Pastor J. J. Kern, associated with but not a member of the Wisconsin Synod, eventually took over in Princeton. See Appendix IX.

47. Alternative translation: Yours truly, F[armer] A[ugust] Gruhlke

Appendix VII

Early Relationship between the Missouri and Wisconsin Synods

The following two articles were submitted to Der Lutheraner, *the Missouri Synod's main periodical. They illustrate the relationship between the Missouri and Wisconsin Synods at the time Johannes Strieter arrived in Wisconsin. The second one also contains an allusion to letter no. 149 in Appendix VI.*

The Wisconsin Synod Is, According to the Testimony of Her Own President, "New Lutheran"[1]

Sent in by Past[or] J[ohannes] H[einrich] Jox[2]

New Lutheran! What sort of new sect and party is this? What does it believe, teach, and confess? Where does it originate? In this enlightened and celebrated nineteenth century has there also appeared a new and second Luther?

These are perhaps the questions that this or that reader will ask in curiosity. Now in order that we may get our proper bearings here right from the start, we simply cannot forget that we are in a free country, where everyone can call himself whatever he likes and whatever his heart desires, regardless of whether or not he and the object in question are defined by the name he gives himself and that object. That is certainly not the case in Germany, where one usually calls everything by its proper name. New Lutherans like the Wisconsin ones also exist over there, but there they are called "United."[3]

What? Does that mean that the New Lutheran Wisconsin Synod is completely *United*, and their label "New Lutheran" means *confused, mixed-up, lax* and *lukewarm*?

---

1. *Der Lutheraner* 16, no. 10 (Dec. 27, 1859) 78.

2. J. H. Jox was the pastor of Immanuel Lutheran in Kirchhayn (closed in 1974, but the last church building and the cemetery still exist on W. Mill Road in the town of Jackson, Washington Co., Wis.) from 1858–1865.

3. That is, the result of the Prussion Union of 1817, which combined the Lutheran and Reformed and compromised confessional Lutheran doctrine.

Absolutely! That the Wisconsin Synod is not Lutheran, but United, she herself clearly proves, and these proofs are so powerful and striking that they cause all her claims about being Lutheran to collapse into nothingness.

But if the Wisconsin Synod still confesses herself to the symbols of the Evangelical Lutheran Church like we do, how can she be thus accused of unionism? The Wisconsin Synod certainly does confess herself to the confessions of the Lutheran Church, but in exactly the same way as all the sects and fanatics confess themselves to the Bible, i.e, she uses these symbols only as a signboard. Her doings and dealings do not follow them at all, but are contrary and opposed to them. Consequently, her confession to the Symbols is merely a confession of the lips, and therefore no confession at all. If the Wisconsin Synod actually confessed herself to the Confessions, it would be a matter of the heart for her. Indeed, if this were the case I should think that she would also have to know that the Symbols forbid a Lutheran from all church- and altar-fellowship with Reformed, United, and all other heterodox people. This, I say, she would know, and would also believe, teach, confess, and act accordingly. But how very different the reality is with her! It isn't just that she formally serves United congregations and admits them to her synodical organization,[4] but she also stands in religious union with completely United mission institutes in Germany, gets her preachers from them, etc. In addition, she has also quite recently (for she is even progressing in her New Lutheranism) opened the way for an alliance with the well-known *unionistic-rationalistic* preacher seminary in Springfield, Ill., in order to have her preachers trained there.[5]

Now is this Christian? Biblical? Lutheran? Never! For God's word and the confessions of our church curse and condemn all false teachings and forbid us from all religious fellowship with the heterodox. Thus speaks St. Paul in 2 Cor. 6:14–18: "Do not tug at the foreign yoke together with unbelievers. For what partnership does righteousness have with unrighteousness? What fellowship does light have with darkness? What agreement does Christ have with Belial? What portion does the believer have with the unbeliever? What likeness does the temple of God have to idols? But you are the temple of the living God, just as God says, 'I will dwell among them and walk among them, and I will be their God, and they shall be my people. Therefore go out from them, and separate yourselves, says the Lord, and touch no impure thing. Then I will accept you and be your father, and you shall be my sons and daughters, says the

---

4. Should the Wisconsin Synod demand proof of this, we stand ready to provide it at any time.—footnote original

5. Committee No. 9 of the Wisconsin Synod's 1859 convention (June 18–24) had indeed discussed the possibility of a working relationship with Illinois State University, operated by the Illinois and Northern Illinois Synods. But the committee of five men charged with pursuing it were "to ascertain under what conditions such access [to the university] would be granted" and to "seek further to ascertain officially the confessional stand of both synods." To accuse the Wisconsin Synod of affiliating with these synods without waiting to see how the committee's work played out was not exactly fair. In fact, at the Wisconsin Synod's 1860 convention, further negotiations were broken off and the committee was disbanded. However, the reason cited is a bit confusing and requires clarification—"because of the prevailing confessional movement in both synods and the named university."

Lord Almighty.'" And again in Romans 16:17: "But I admonish you, dear brothers, to watch out for those who cause division and scandal alongside the teaching that you have learned, and withdraw from them." And to these biblical passages, to which plenty of others could naturally be added, the Confessions say Yea and Amen.

Oh, that the Wisconsin Synod would just reflect on this, abandon their lazy and groundless position by God's grace, not just carry God's word and the confession of the church on her lips, but also take it to heart and demonstrate it in her actions and life, so that God would truly be honored by her and the church would not be torn down, but built up.

Church News from Northern Wisconsin[6]

Sent in by Fr[iedrich] Ruhland, Past[or][7]

On the Second Sunday after Trinity,[8] the newly constructed, cheerful little church of St. John's Ev. Luth. Congregation in New London, Waupaca Co., Wis., which has been served from the Oshkosh base as an ancillary congregation since Pentecost 1859, was most solemnly dedicated to the worship of the triune God. In the morning the undersigned spoke the dedication prayer and delivered the dedication sermon on Genesis 28:16–19. In the evening Mr. Candidate Chr. Kraenzlein preached on the Gospel of the day.[9] Recalling the note added by the editorial staff to a church dedication report in vol. 15, no. 26, p. 205 of *Der Lutheraner*,[10] I take the liberty of adding the following brief remarks on the origins of this small congregation:

Already in the years 1857 and 1858, the former pastor in Oshkosh, Mr. Pastor Martin Stephan, had also visited New London with the saving message of the gospel on several occasions. During the lengthy vacancy of the pastorate in Oshkosh that followed him, Mr. Pastors Lochner, Ahner, Steinbach, Wagner, and Brose most faithfully occupied themselves with the now preacher-less congregations. Nevertheless, this vacancy struck a neighboring preacher of the "New Lutheran" Synod of Wisconsin[11] as the right time to take possession of the Oshkosh parish, along with all

---

6. *Der Lutheraner* 17, no. 3 (Sept. 18, 1860) 20–22.

7. See pp. 115–16.

8. June 17, 1860

9. Luke 14:16–24, the invitation to the great banquet.

10. The report, by G. K. Schuster, was on the dedication of a new frame church in Bremen, Marshall Co., Ind. (today St. Paul's Lutheran Church), and included some remarks on the origins of the congregation. The accompanying editorial footnote read: "Reports on the origin and development of congregations in this country are in most cases more useful than even the most vivid descriptions of church dedication ceremonies; such descriptions are, as a rule, all the more boring, the more detailed they are."

11. The reference is to Gottlieb Fachtmann, the first man called to be a part-time traveling preacher (*Reiseprediger*) for the Wisconsin Synod shortly after her 1858 convention (held from May 30—June

the ancillary congregations belonging to her, through an audacious *coup de main*, to pass on what had been thus won to the "New Lutheran" partnership of Wisconsin, and then, crowned with fresh laurels by the chief of the house, to relax comfortably in Oshkosh. This gentleman was on the move at once, "to act out of genuine love and compassion by tending to the needs of the poor souls that had first been fettered by Missouri in Old Lutheran chains and had then been completely neglected by her." As far as Oshkosh itself, his fervent wishes now remained unfulfilled and his diplomatic skills had no effect; he initially had more luck, however, in the ancillary congregation in Winchester and also in [New] London. Many at the time were still too greatly lacking in the necessary knowledge, in confessional loyalty and spirit-testing talent [cf. 1 John 4:1], to be able to resist the persistent coaxing of such an eager suitor. It was bad enough that this man knew how to take his time working on the people and how to influence them in his favor using all sorts of pretenses, so that they actually let him preach and administer the sacraments several times (and administer them in an extremely flippant manner), but without calling him in an orderly way [cf. Augsburg Confession, Article 14]. Later, however, after these two small congregations were informed that the Oshkosh preaching position would soon be filled again, as they were expecting, they also declared that they really wanted to go back to their former and rightful relationship and be served from the Oshkosh base by a Lutheran preacher of the Missouri Synod. But by now that salesman was most keenly intent upon thwarting this plan. With the purpose of throwing sand in my eyes over the existing relationship that those two congregations had with me and the Oshkosh pastorate, and of hindering me from making contact with them right from the start, this gentleman paid me a visit just a few days after my arrival in Oshkosh and disclosed to me without any shame that he was planning to travel to Winchester and [New] London, respectively, that same day yet, in order to distribute the Holy Supper in the former congregation and in [New] London, on the other hand, to help the Lutherans there set up an orderly congregational entity *at their express wishes*; I therefore didn't need to trouble myself with them anymore, etc. Now I had been sufficiently briefed, by both Mr. Pastor Stephan and members of the Oshkosh congregation, on the constituent parts and conditions of my field of labor, as well as on the preferred practices of the Wisconsin Synod. I therefore, with God's help, did not let myself be dazzled and bamboozled by this preacher's loving and considerate expectations. I rather admitted to him my doubts as to the truth of his assertion and asked him kindly, yet insistently, to please desist from any further (and also from the present) illegitimate and sinful encroachments on my

---

3). Fachtmann's base of operations was a dual parish in the town of Polk and Richfield, Wis., but as a result of his work he accepted a call to Fond du Lac early in 1859. He was a talented and zealous gospel preacher but, in addition to the confessional weaknesses detailed in this article, he seems not to have cared too much about trespassing on the fields of other Lutheran preachers or synods. Fachtmann's activity is covered primarily in two sources: John Philipp Koehler, *The History of the Wisconsin Synod*, ed. Leigh D. Jordahl (The Protes'tant Conference, 1970), 54–56; and Arnold Lehmann, "Wisconsin Synod *Reisepredigt* Program" in *WELS Historical Institute Journal* 6, no. 1 (Spring 1988) 23–27.

ministry and field of labor, since I would otherwise be compelled to testify against him publicly. But Mr. New Lutheran Preacher persisted in his assertion and his intentions, criticized our Missouri Synod, laughed me to scorn, and walked off sneering, "The rank and file in London will rally around me, you'll see." To which I retorted, "I will gladly let you have the multitude, but the congregation is going to remain with Christ."

Naturally I considered it my duty to oppose these announced freebooting plans on location immediately, to learn the facts of the matter for myself, and if necessary to faithfully warn all honest Lutherans in the two small congregations, who had probably not yet been informed of my arrival in Oshkosh, against the Wisconsin preacher as a false teacher. For he had documented himself as such in my presence through the following statements:

> 1. With respect to the acceptance of our symbols [i.e. the Lutheran Confessions], the question of *because* or *insofar as* they agree with God's word was *rationalistic fancy talk*, with which he (the Wisconsin preacher) would not occupy himself at all.

> 2. *Whatever might still be true in our time was not true anywhere beyond that.* It might very well be found in God's word, *but no one had it, wielded it, or taught it perfectly—not he and not I (the undersigned). It was therefore foolish and incongruous with love to keep on insisting on pure doctrine, since no preacher could be entirely certain if he was wielding it.* (Note, dear reader—this is New Lutheran doctrine!)

Our dear, faithful God, who had now given me the desire to carry out my plan also gave me success. Since I could no longer use the steamboat without traveling together with the "New Lutheran," a member of the congregation in Oshkosh drove me that same day on the country road to [New] London, thirty-two miles away, where I arrived the next morning, twenty-four hours earlier than the Wisconsin man, who was still wandering around in Winchester for the time being. I called the members together, most of whom were occupied with woodcutting in the bush, shared with them the primary reason for my visit, at which they were astonished in no small measure, and then learned from them that they had served the Wisconsin pastor not a *letter of invitation*, but one *of refusal*, and so his assertion to me was nothing but a *big fat lie*.

After that I preached for the first time in [New] London in the afternoon. Another service was scheduled for the following morning, and just as I was getting ready to head over to the Presbyterian church with the people for the service,[12] the Wisconsin man showed up, not a little taken aback at my presence in [New] London, not ashamed to face me now as a manifest liar, but rather still brazen enough, in spite of my request, to go into the church with us making derisive remarks, in order to jeopardize the devotion and attention of many hearers just by being there. Nevertheless,

---

12. No doubt they had an agreement with the owners to hold their Lutheran services there for the time being.

he did eventually prefer to take to his heels soon afterwards, in consequence of his failed enterprise, after the last anchor he had thrown out in desperation—accusing me of being a belly priest [cf. Rom. 16:18]—also wouldn't catch any ground. Now the small New London congregation called me to be their preacher and spiritual shepherd in an orderly way and since that time has been visited by me every five to six weeks on average. However, the Lord had still more salutary trials in mind for her. The same thing happened here as did in the parable of the fishing net [Matt. 13:47–50]. The gospel had also caught quite a few who soon afterwards were manifested as rotten fish by the bad odor they started to give off. After half a year had passed, more than half of the members fell away, since they could not continue as members while living in the manifest works of the flesh without being punished (which is what they wanted). They ganged up, forced the small congregation that had melted down to fifteen voting members out of the schoolhouse, which was the only building left in which she could hold services, and did everything possible by which they could expect to ruin her. But the Lord did not take the eyes of his mercy off of this very weak congregation. Purified by tribulation [cf. 1 Pet. 1:6,7], she proceeded, with one accord and an optimistic spirit, amid the scornful laughter of her foes, to build a church. And our gracious Lord God has allowed her to succeed in this.[13] May his name be praised for all his undeserved kindness. May he also then strengthen and preserve for himself a little band here, who will serve him in honest faith and true love, and may he guard it from all evil. So now the congregation does belong to Christ. And to whom does the rank and file belong? Notice, the "New Lutheran" did get one thing right. No, the multitude did not rally around his estimable person, but they did rally around the person of his worthy colleague and business successor,[14] who had recently been requisitioned to [New] London after setting up business in a neighboring congregation, which had likewise been gathered by Mr. Pastor Stephan and had been regularly served by him for a considerable time. But what's the use? The New Lutheran synod definitely has good hopes for new growth and acquisitions with it. Still, I would have gladly kept these old stories to myself and not published them, if my congregations and I did not have to keep on suffering at the hands of the terrible New Lutheran practice of the Wisconsin Synod again and again, and if

---

13. German: *Und der gnädige Herrgott hat es ihr doch gelingen lassen.* Ruhland seems to be alluding to the fourth line of the third German stanza of Luther's hymn "A Mighty Fortress": "*es soll uns doch gelingen.*"

14. Friedrich Waldt had been assigned to Menasha and Neenah prior to the 1859 Wisconsin Synod convention (held from June 18–24) and was then accepted into the synod's membership during that convention. In the autumn of 1861 "a number of Lutheran families in Oshkosh organized an Ev. Luth. congregation, and requested a pastor from [the Wisconsin] synod. The group called Pastor Waldt of Menasha at the beginning of the year [1862]. He moved there and . . . also serv[ed] his former congregation as a sister congregation" (1862 Proceedings). After the 1865 convention, he accepted a call to St. Paul's in the town of Eldorado, Wisconsin. After the 1867 convention, he accepted a call back to Neenah. In late 1870 he accepted a call to First Ev. Luth. Church in Racine, where he served until 1887.

the last vestiges of hope that it might be corrected had not faded away. That business successor, as a well-practiced huckster, has not only stolen his way to [New] London, but also, in derision of all my urgent protests and admonitions, into the Winchester congregation; has established an opposition congregation;[15] has strengthened the malice of carnal people who had withdrawn from us; has confused the consciences of weak persons and those lacking in knowledge through false representations of our synod, my doctrine, and my life; and in short, has brought untold sorrow upon our congregation. Even Oshkosh has not been spared by this man. A man who had been banned from the congregation here, a man steeped in manifest vices and detested even by respectable worldlings, this Wisconsin man allows to participate in the Sacrament without any hesitation. And when questioned by me regarding this sacrilegious action and asked for justification, he replies to me in an insulting letter saying that I understood nothing of such matters, had no basis for questioning him and asking for justification, was a Jesuit, and therefore he also would not give me an answer for such a question, etc. Many other vitriolic and defamatory charges against the Missouri Synod and my miserable person I do not wish to repeat. Certainly what has been cited will suffice to give all true Lutherans yet another indication of what one should actually make of the article "New Lutheranism," which has recently been issued by the alleged "Lutheran Synod of Wisconsin" for inclusion with the other "New Articles of Doctrine and Faith" being fabricated in this America. We have now seen some more samples of it, namely shameful practices.

And what kind of *doctrine* should one infer from such practices? No doubt a rotten one, which has to be all the more rotten, the less they talk of doctrine at all in the Wisconsin Synod. (I once asked the aforementioned business successor why the previous year's Wisconsin Synod convention report did not make any mention of confession and doctrine. Answer: "We spoke *privately* about doctrine.") Yes, thus far the Wisconsin Synod has had the Lutheran doctrinal confession hanging like a signboard above the door, but the already cited assertions of one of her most celebrated preachers testify as to what she thinks of it and how she confesses herself to it. Each of her pastors thinks what he wants, does what he wants, believes and teaches what he wants with regard to the church's confessions—today Lutheran to the Lutherans, tomorrow Reformed to the Reformed, the next day unionistic to the United. But ministering in the last way seems to all of them to be the most practical for their business, and they now give themselves the name "New Lutheran" only so that they do not betray themselves completely and so that they can please everyone. They still go by "Lutheran" in order to blind the eyes of Lutherans lacking in knowledge wherever possible, but "New

---

15. Rev. Waldt actually ended up organizing two such opposition congregations very close to the original Winchester congregation (also known as Immanuel, Rat River)—St. Peter's Lutheran Church on what is today County Road MM, one mile east of the Rat River congregation, and the other in Zittau, one and a half miles north of the Rat River congregation. The Zittau congregation even adopted the same name, Immanuel, causing even more confusion and the eventual establishment of yet another Lutheran church three miles north of the Zittau congregation, Zion Lutheran Church.

Lutheran" in order to pay their respects to all unbelievers, sects, and enemies of the Lutheran Church. But while the Wisconsin Synod may be able to deceive humans in this way, she will certainly never be able to deceive God and his word, by which she has already been judged as "neither hot nor cold" (Rev. 3:15,16). Whoever calls himself New Lutheran does not wish to be called just Lutheran anymore, and whoever does not want that also does not want to *be* completely and exclusively Lutheran anymore, but is instead practicing a spiritual prostitution with this or that ancient or recent false doctrine or sect. New Lutherans are therefore no longer true children of their mother, the orthodox Lutheran Church, but apostates and bastards. And the New Lutheran or Wisconsin Lutheran confession? It is basically just a cake baked from imported unionistic clay and rationalistic dishwater, which is then covered with as much frosting as possible so that everyone will bite into it blithely and eagerly. Well then, whoever doesn't want anything better, let him eat his fill of this cake and take care lest he eats up the eternal death of body and soul along with it. Honest Lutherans have no desire to taste it; it disgusts them. They rather have a sincere desire to have their souls fed with the unadulterated Bread of Life, which is what the Lord Jesus offers them richly in the pure Word and Sacrament of the Evangelical Lutheran Church. May then this faithful Savior enlighten all pious Christians more and more through the power of the estimable Holy Spirit as to the inestimable worth of this heavenly food, the only food that saves, so that they learn to hold it above all else in high and precious esteem through daily and diligent use and, in so doing, acquire such a taste for this bread that they immediately recognize the "New Lutheran cake" and avoid it as poison, even when it too is foisted upon them under the name "bread of life."

Earlier I made mention of a Mr. Candidate Kraenzlein, who may very well be known only to a few members of our synod, since he has joined her and begun to serve the kingdom of God in her fellowship only recently. Mr. Candidate Kraenzlein is from the Kingdom of Bavaria and was initially sent by Mr. Parson Löhe[16] to the former schoolteacher seminary in Saginaw, Mich. Up until a year ago he belonged to the Iowa Synod and was preparing himself at the preacher seminary in Wartburg, Iowa, for the holy preaching ministry [*das heilige Predigtamt*]. After passing his examination, he functioned as an assistant preacher for Mr. Pastor Deindoerfer in Madison, Wis., though without being ordained. His very frail physical constitution forced him to give up preaching, however, whereupon he traveled to Milwaukee with the intention of devoting himself to a different vocation. Here it also pleased our very faithful and gracious God to convince Mr. Kraenzlein of the unscriptural nature of certain teachings adopted by the Iowa Synod—those of the Church, of ministerial and church authority, and of the Last Things—and to cause him to find the only correct teaching on these points in our synod. In the meantime it seemed like his physical condition had improved, and along with that the propensity within him to proclaim the truth of the gospel awakened anew, and now that he fully understood that truth, he desired to

---

16. See p. 21, n. 1.

do so in union with us. When I asked him to extend me a helping hand with the rather difficult ministry to my five small congregations by preaching the Word to them, he came to Oshkosh very willingly (after I had already gotten acquainted with him beforehand through Mr. Pastor Lochner) and has preached in [New] London, as the dear reader now knows. But already after two weeks, as a result of several sermons and the inevitable physical strain accompanying them, his old chest pain flared up more intensely than before, and as depressing as it had to be for him, he still recognized the counsel and will of God and came to the conviction that any further preaching would wear him down completely. Instead he declared his willingness to serve the Church from now on, with God's help, as a schoolteacher [*im Schulamte*], and since at exactly the same time the teacher's position [*Schulamt*] here was vacated by Mr. Teacher Hoppe's acceptance of another call and Mr. Kraenzlein declared he was ready to assume it, especially since he found the healthy climate here to have a very therapeutic effect on him, my congregation here therefore called Mr. Kraenzlein in an orderly way to be their schoolteacher, after obtaining a recommendation from the Most Reverend Presidium of the Northern District and after being convinced of his orthodoxy and teaching ability. I then inducted him into his office on the Twelfth Sunday after Trinity, solemnly binding him to the symbols of our church at the same time. May the Lord Christ grant our dear brother the necessary physical powers and spiritual gifts, so that he may faithfully carry out his new office with rich blessing. Amen.

Oshkosh, September 1860
Fr[iedrich] Ruhland, Past[or]

Appendix VIII

Johann Jacob Hoffmann

It is difficult to surmise exactly how the lyrics for the "sad song about Hoffmann"[1] would go, in large part because the Concordia Historical Institute does not have any collection for Carl Strasen, and H. C. Schwan destroyed most of his correspondence before he died. What we do know is as follows:

Johann Jacob Hoffmann (usually referred to by his middle name) was born on June 12, 1840, in Kuehndorf, Prussia, to Johann Valentin and Maria Christiane (Hohmann) Hoffmann. He was one of seventeen children. He immigrated with his family to the United States around 1845 when he was around five or six years old. They lived for a while in Buffalo, New York, where his father worked as a tailor. Eventually the Hoffmanns moved to Michigan, where Jacob's father farmed until his death.[2]

Jacob began his studies for the public ministry of the gospel in Buffalo, then continued and finished them at the seminary in Fort Wayne. He was sent to serve as an assistant to Pastor Strieter in Marquette County, Wis., early in 1861, where he was ordained on February 17. On March 11, the Lutherans in the town of Berlin northwest of Wausau called him to be their pastor and he accepted. As Strieter notes, this was somewhat rash on his part, but Strieter installed him on August 25. From his base in the town of Berlin, Marathon Co., Hoffmann served at least twenty preaching stations, traveling even as far as rural Neillsville.

---

1. See p. 102.
2. "Pastor's Son Marries Neighbor Girl" in *Berlin's Memories in 1976*, edited by the Berlin Bicentennial Committee (Town of Berlin, Marathon Co., Wis., 1976), 11. This article also contains some of the information that follows.

APPENDIX VIII: JOHANN JACOB HOFFMANN

Fig. 57. Street Scene, Naugart, Wisconsin, 1909, postcard. Today this is the intersection of Berlin Lane (the visible road) and Naugart Drive. The white house in the middle of the picture was serving as the Naugart Post Office at the time. The frame schoolhouse pictured on the right (later replaced by a brick schoolhouse), just north of present-day St. Paul Lutheran Church, is standing where an original log schoolhouse stood. This was where J. J. Hoffmann was called to be the first full-time pastor of the Evangelical Lutherans in the town of Berlin, Marathon Co., on March 11, 1861. This congregation was the mother congregation of all the Lutheran churches eventually founded and built in the area. Johannes Strieter would have also driven through this intersection, and seen it basically as pictured, when he came to preach for the church anniversary celebration in 1910 (see Appendix XI).

Fig. 58. Rev. Eduard Moldehnke, traveling preacher (*Reiseprediger*) of the Wisconsin Synod from 1861–1863 and president of Wisconsin Lutheran Seminary from 1863–1866

In a December 2, 1861 report to Johannes Bading, president of the Wisconsin Synod,[3] traveling missionary Eduard Moldehnke wrote of a chance meeting with Hoffmann in Wausau on September 23, during a mission trip to the area. Moldehnke reported:

> On September 23, I traveled thirty-five miles by stagecoach to Wausau, a village surrounded by a ring of black stumps. It has a charming location on the Wisconsin River and is basically the last village in that direction. I arranged to stay at the home of Mr. Paff. In the evening I preached to about thirty people. Earlier I had just so happened to meet a Missouri man, Hoffmann. He would like to live there, but the people are rejecting him. He has a congregation in the bush about ten miles from Wausau, but he hurries by horse to about thirty stations and fails to accomplish anything substantial by splintering his efforts this way, meager as they already are. He was very rude to me, even though he is only about twenty-one years old. Naturally I repudiated his attacks, though too mildly, I fear. . . . With his domineering manner Hoffmann has caused scandal everywhere he's preached. Even some in his own congregation would gladly be free of him. So he preached in Wausau in a private home and when Mr. Paff asked him how he managed to preach there without permission, he said that he was a preacher and had the right to preach anywhere, and so on.

On January 20, 1862, Jacob was united in marriage with Johanne Rosinalde Erneste von Anschuetz (in records, Jacob referred to her as Rosine or Rosa for short) by Rev. Friedrich Lochner in Milwaukee. Rosine was eighteen. God blessed their marriage with eleven children:

1. Ernst August Wilhelm, b. Oct. 7, 1862
2. Johann Valentin Ernst, b. March 31, 1864
3. Johann Jacob Ernst, b. Dec. 10, 1865
4. Ernst Georg Heinrich Martin, b. Dec. 10, 1865
5. Clara Renata Coeleste, b. Jan. 13, 1868
6. Theophilus Oscar Ernst, b. July 2, 1869
7. Adolph August Ernst, b. Aug. 28, 1871
8. Otto Wilhelm Ernst, b. Jan. 15, 1874
9. Eduard Oscar Arthur, b. Dec. 31, 1875
10. Wilhelm Philipp Ernst, b. Aug. 18, 1878
11. Harry Hubert, b. Nov. 1, 1882

---

3. No. 567 in the Early Presidents Collection (see introductory par. in Appendix VI).

APPENDIX VIII: JOHANN JACOB HOFFMANN

The first nine Hoffmann children had six, six, eight, six, eight, five, seven, five, and nine sponsors, respectively, including six different pastors and a schoolteacher. Rosa was a capable and intelligent mother, teaching her children in the evenings.

In August 1864 he made a mission trip to the Upper Peninsula of Michigan. After he returned he sent a report to Prof. August Crämer in Fort Wayne, Ind., who in turn submitted it to *Der Lutheraner*. Since the article provides insight into Hoffmann's character, not to mention the Missouri Synod's character at the time, I provide it here in its entirety:[4]

* * * * *

For a long time already it has been a real desire of the members of our dear Wisconsin Conference that the region along Lake Superior belonging to the state of Michigan might be visited for once, since so many of their former congregation members have moved there and they had received repeated requests from them to be visited. This summer they now called upon our Pastor J. J. Hoffmann to undertake a trip there. He was found agreeable to the task, set out on foot on August 8 of this year, thankfully covered the distant, wearisome, and perilous journey under God's protection, and provided me the following report about his arrival at the place of his destination and what he accomplished there, which I simply must share with the dear readers of *Der Lutheraner*:

> Finally I came to Rockland on Monday at midday. The Rockland, Minnesota, and National Mines are in that city.
>
> Already shortly before my departure I had heard that there was a German preacher in Minnesota (now called Rockland); he was also purported to be Lutheran. If everything had not been arranged already, this news might have induced me to postpone the trip for a bit and to gather more information first. As matters stood though, by this point I had to make the trip. In addition, I did know that he was not from our synod and that his service was therefore of no use to our former congregation members anyway. I now inquired after this preacher with my innkeeper first, who was a well-cultured man, an old soldier, and had served in Italy and in France. Now he was lying on his deathbed though. He had had a stroke at the top of the stairs in his house, fallen down, and from then on had completely lost all feeling from his chest on down. Even though no one was supposed to disturb him, the condition he was in nevertheless required that much more that I speak with him. I soon found that he too was one of the poor people who had fallen away from their faith on account of the baseness and the shameful greed of a large part of the so-called spiritual leaders in Germany. By one such clergyman he had been defrauded of his father's entire estate of some 30,000 thalers. To the question of whether

---

4. *Der Lutheraner* 21, no. 4 (Oct. 15, 1864) 28–30.

he then considered what was written in God's word to be true, he only kept on saying that he had formed his own ideas on that. He was nevertheless tolerating it when I was preaching law and gospel over and over again between our conversation, and although he never said anything in response, one tear was chasing the next.

He also informed me about the pastor and had someone bring me to him. The pastor was an alumnus of the mission institute in Basel. It was therefore no surprise to me when I learned he was not a Lutheran. Nevertheless, he agreed with me when I said that calling it the Basel Mission Institute was actually an absurdity since, for instance, when it sends out its graduates with Reformed leanings and those with Lutheran and United leanings, it has to and does say to all of them alike: "It is true that you all have differing convictions, but each of you should just make the most of the conviction he has. It is all from the Holy Spirit, and so each of you should just act and teach according to his conviction." The institute also has absolutely no confession whatsoever that could be considered Lutheran—not once is Luther's Small Catechism promoted there, nor is the Augsburg Confession. It has fallen squarely in the middle of the current of the spirit of the times and wishes precisely to train people who are only going to preach "Christ," as if that could happen without preaching his doctrine pure and whole. And from this kind of institute the Michigan and Wisconsin Synods get their preachers and still want to be called Lutheran synods, even though their pastors who come from the institute are not at all acquainted with the symbolical books of the Lutheran Church, and thus not their doctrine either. I used these facts to show him how the Michigan Synod, to which he belonged, could not be truly Lutheran. This too he granted, and seemed in general to have a desire to become truly Lutheran. I told him I would not preach in Rockland and asked if he knew anyone there who had formerly been in our fellowship. He said no. When I later returned to Rockland again, I simply could not understand how it had escaped his notice that many Missourians were there, apart from concluding what I subsequently found out. Tuesday morning I traveled twelve miles by stagecoach to Ontonagon, a sizable city along Lake Superior to which the pastor in Rockland laid no claims. I was looking for a Lutheran there and happened to meet him as soon as I got off the stagecoach. He ran an inn and poured me some beer there. He was in other respects a very noble man, but right away he said, "You won't have anything to do here; the people will probably not come. I don't go to any church myself, though my wife and a few other women like to go." Another man said, "A pricher? Gimme a break! The parson! I need the parson like I need a . . ." A third man said, "The folks here are too smart; they're nobody's fool. There won't be anyone who comes" ("and I won't either," he might as well have added). Another woman said: "There are not many Lutherans here"—even though there are eighteen families—"and many of them go to the English church. I go there too, since I can understand English as well I do German," and with that she murdered some English so badly that it might have moved someone to pity me just for having to be there to hear it.

On the other hand I also met many honest souls; they also greatly bemoaned the lack of love for God's word. But most of all they lamented the fact that the people had become even more indifferent through ignorant preachers, and they accordingly wished very much that a competent man would gather them. So too at many places along the lake I met several people who had moved there from our congregations. They were very happy beyond measure at the assurance that our synod would provide them with a preacher at their request, and they asked me to please see to that. So I now collected addresses of people in the following places: Buchanan,[5] Burlington,[6] and Portland[7] in Minnesota; Superior City, La Pointe, Bayfield, and Bay City,[8] along with Ashland in Wisconsin; and Marquette and Munising in Michigan. I also met a number of people from Portage Lake[9] that reported to me that close to a hundred families (and probably even more) were living in the neighborhood who were without a preacher, and they too expressed the desire that I would see to it that a competent man come there. I told these people that Pastor St. in Rockland had applied to his synod on their behalf, but they declared that they knew nothing about that and wanted to have nothing to do with it, since they could not continue to rely on that synod.

On Wednesday evening, then, I held church, to which the Presbyterians came, since it was the exact time their weekly service was held and since their preacher is in the war. I spoke to them, at their wish, on Psalm 32. To the Germans I spoke on the summary of all gospel passages, John 3:16–18. After church I met another Missourian with whom I spoke quite a while longer and who also came back in the morning because he couldn't get enough. I also succeeded in posting a few copies of *Der Lutheraner* and *Lehre und Wehre* as missionaries and certainly these will produce abundant fruit under God's blessing. I also put a copy of the *Abendschule* to work, and this too is certainly more conducive to making the reader into a healthy Christian than many so-called Lutheran papers. The *Herold* also happened to fall into my hands and I found the article on the slave-drivers in the Missouri Synod. You can imagine what effect it had on former members of our congregations. If they had previously considered the *Herold* to be a good, Christian paper, now their eyes were opened regarding this pet child of the Michigan Synod after I explained to them the whole story of the history of this writeup. About eight o'clock in the morning I rode back to Rockland again, since I unfortunately did not

---

5. Today the closest community to this location is Knife River. There is a Buchanan Historical Marker three and a half miles southwest of Knife River along Highway 61.

6. Now named Two Harbors

7. Now part of Duluth

8. Formerly northeast of Ashland along the coast of Chequamegon Bay

9. The Houghton and Hancock area

have time to accept the various invitations because the steamboats here have such unpredictable travel schedules. When I arrived there at midday, my innkeeper's health had gotten worse and worse. I asked him if he would permit me as a preacher to speak a few words with him. To all such inquiries he would only say that his head could not take it. When I asked him if he at least wished that I would pray for him, that God would make him healthy or be gracious to him in any case, he answered in the affirmative: "I thank you kindly for that, sir." Friday morning I found him completely withered away. I stood for while at his bed by myself and shooed the flies away. Then he cried out suddenly in great agitation, perhaps ten times one after the other, "Pastor! Pastor!" The word "pastor" I understood quite clearly; I'm guessing that the second word, which I could not make out as clearly, was the name of the pastor through whom he had lost his father's estate. I bent over him and asked him loudly if I should pray with him, to which he clearly mumbled, "Yes," as he bowed his head. I knelt down and grabbed hold of his already cold hands and prayed. This was his last word. I thought that he would at least make it until evening yet, and since his wife came in and cried out anxiously, "Ah, leave my husband alone, sir! Leave my husband in peace!" I left to go and have a look at the mines. I rode down 1,200 feet with my escort in a box. Then we got out and went zigzagging around in the mine, and after we had come back to 1,200 feet from 1,500 feet underground, we sat down and consumed our midday meal. Afterward I rode up alone—in two minutes I was back on the surface of the earth, and now I heard that the innkeeper had died. I also found a few Missourians now, but they belonged to the congregation, and I was asked to please preach to them on Sunday, and since it was okay with their pastor, who seemed to have honest intentions on the whole, that's what I did. After church many Missourians remained standing at the church doors, and when I asked them if any of them were from our congregations, I received multiple "I am" and "Me too" answers. In the evening the people now held a meeting, and there I found out something I never would have guessed. The congregation was founded by Missourians, who banded together as "Zion's Evangelical Lutheran Congregation," and the church property had also been procured through their efforts. The former preacher was also from the Michigan Synod. After he moved away the board of administrators had applied to our synod for a preacher through Mr. Pastor Stecher.[10] Meanwhile the Michigan Synod had sent the present Pastor St. to the congregation without their desire or knowledge. So the congregation had taken him in *pro tempore*, as it were, until one of our own would come, which had not yet happened by that point. Since they were looking for advice, I was compelled to tell them that, since the congregation was supposed to be an evangelical Lutheran one and had been founded as such, they should also make every effort to see to it that Lutheran doctrine and practice held sway in the congregation. But if that could not be accomplished,

---

10. Rev. Anton Daniel Stecher of Trinity Lutheran, Sheboygan

then they could not remain in affiliation with that congregation or that synod. The pastor was present at this meeting and also seemed to see the necessity of adhering firmly and exactly to Lutheran doctrine and practice, or of dropping the name "Lutheran" if that was not the case. The Lord grant that this congregation become more and more that which it was founded to be.

So then, this trip accomplished this much at any rate: We now know those whom we have to keep track of, and I can now fully inform the brother who will serve as missionary there exactly what the situation is with the people and the area. God only grant that these poor people who are looking for help might also soon be able to be helped. To that end we must then persistently ask the Lord of the harvest to fill up the hearts of our students, and of many others who will join their number in their future, with real love for Christ and their fellow redeemed, so that they devote themselves to the grueling task [*Dienst*] of mission work with commitment and dedication. We must also pray that he would open the hands of our congregation members so that such energetic pupils, but especially the poor ones, are able to be trained, and that he would also bless the work of our precious Pastor Brunn to that end, so that we are able to answer the cry for help of our dear, scattered fellow brothers and are thus also able to help fill the heavenly storehouses of our Savior.

I do not wish to burden you further, sir, with the details of my return trip. Let me just say that I departed on Monday morning at nine o'clock and made it back to Jenny,[11] the boundary of my parish, on Saturday morning at 9:30, August 27. I was so tired though that I could hardly walk the length of my living room any more. From here to Minnesota [i.e. Rockland] it is a good 200 miles, even though it might not amount to that much according to the measurement indicated on a map. By now, God be praised, I have recovered again to some extent; at first, though, I was nearly lame for two weeks. But now I ask you, worthy Mr. Professor, to work with me at getting the synod to send a competent man to that area. Material for congregations is available in abundance and little by little more and more people could be assembled, and then the desire of those Christians would be fulfilled, and those who were not seeking God would learn to seek him again and how to find him.

May then the Lord of the great harvest be pleased to help in this regard too, according to his grace, for the sake of his name. Amen.

Yours,
J. Jacob Hoffmann

* * * * *

Hoffmann accepted a call to St. John's in Portage in February 1867. There he took pride not only in preaching but also in teaching, writing in the back of the church

---

11. That is, Merrill, Wisconsin, which used to be called Jenny Bull Falls, or Jenny for short.

record book, "My attention was directed at the school above all." When he began teaching in June of 1867, there were twenty-two children. By 1868 the congregation had erected a new schoolhouse and there were seventy-five children. At the dedication of the school in December, Pastor Hoffmann read a document he had composed in which he boasted of his accomplishments. In his concluding remarks he said:

> I sincerely and earnestly ask that every father please send his children punctually and consistently each day when school is being held. I beg that every father please buy his children the necessary chalk tablets and books. I furthermore ask that every father please punctually pay the trivial amount for exercise books, ink, and quill pen, which I supply the children myself, just as I do the German books. That way they will come by them fairly and will always be provided with what they need.
>
> One more note in closing: I will do my best to continue to hold school in the future as much as possible. I will also continue to do my best to do it as well as possible. I will do my best to teach every child what is necessary and beneficial at the proper time. But I ask you trust me enough to assume that I must know what is most necessary and what a child needs to learn first. Nevertheless, everyone may make his wishes known to me, and if they are acceptable, I will take them into consideration.

This excerpt is part of a nine-page feature that he wrote about himself in the back of St. John's record book, after having devoted just over one page to all five of his predecessors combined.

St. John's one hundred and fiftieth anniversary booklet says that 1870 was a stormy time in the history of the congregation, supposedly owing to "great opposition to strict biblical practices." It also reports that Pastor Hoffmann resigned "'for the sake of peace' and with broken health" sometime around the middle of July 1872. He appears to have moved to East Tawas, Michigan, near Tawas City. (His parents were living in that vicinity.)

APPENDIX VIII: JOHANN JACOB HOFFMANN

Fig. 59. Rev. J. J. Hoffmann. Image courtesy of St. John Lutheran, Plymouth, Wis. See also Fig. 36.

Hoffmann then accepted a call to St. Paul's in Sheboygan Falls and St. John in Plymouth, Wisconsin, at the end of 1872 and was installed in January of 1873. His firstborn son Wilhelm died on June 4, 1873, at 3:30 p.m. from fever and smallpox. He was ten years old. In recording his son's death in the records, Hoffmann called him "a gem of a Lutheran and a gem of a Missourian." It was probably not long before or after this that his second son Ernst, at age nine, fell down the cellar and broke his leg below his hip, which crippled him for life. What effect these tragedies had on Hoffmann's psyche is not known.

In June of 1878, the one hundred and fiftieth anniversary book for St. John, Plymouth, reports that Hoffmann went on a missionary tour through the Lake Superior region for several weeks. "Adverse reports occasion the resignation of Pastor Hoffmann from the Sheboygan Falls-Plymouth parish in November." In the record book for St. Paul, Sheboygan Falls, Hoffmann made his final entry in the Confirmation section as follows:

> On [Saturday] the twenty-third of November, 1878, the following children were confirmed by me in the Lutheran church in Sheboygan Falls, Wisconsin, and admitted to the Holy Supper, by special, fervent request on the part of the children:
>
> 1. Johann Jacob Ernst Hoffmann, born December 10, 1865 [twelve years old]
>
> 2. Ernst Georg Heinrich Martin Hoffmann, born December 10, 1865 [twelve years old]
>
> 3. Clara Renata Coeleste Hoffmann, born January 13, 1868 [ten years old]
>
> The two twins had already finished confirmation instruction in 1875, and again in 1877, and had thoroughly learned all of Dietrich's [edition of Luther's]

Catechism at that time. The girl had also taken part in all of the confirmation instruction in 1877 and had learned well the chief questions and all the passages in Dietrich's Catechism.

All three of them were, as far as knowledge is concerned, some of the best of the confirmands, and just because of their young age had to stay back from the Holy Supper, which all three of them have already desired most passionately. Therefore I was no longer able to refuse them given the situation.

God bless them in time and eternity. Amen. J. Jacob Hoffmann, Pastor.

A note was later added in the margin by Hoffmann's successor:

> J. J. Hoffmann was already deposed [from his office as pastor] at the time and consummated the action [of confirmation] without witnesses. J. M. Hieber

The following "Announcement and Warning" appeared in the July 15, 1879 edition of *Der Lutheraner*:

> The Northwestern District of the Synod of Missouri, Ohio, and Other States hereby announces that J. J. Hoffmann, formerly pastor at Sheboygan Falls and Plymouth, Wisconsin, is no longer to be regarded as one of your own. He has been officially dismissed from his position because he has occasioned much scandal and offense by his conduct, in spite of all our admonition.
>
> Representing the above-named synodical district,
>
> C. Strasen, President

Later reports from the *The Lutheran Witness* place him in New Orleans spreading slanders against the Missouri Synod and her leadership and ministering to a French Lutheran mission congregation. In 1882 he accepted a call back to Wisconsin, to serve some of the same members he had previously served. This occasioned a lasting split among the Lutherans in the area and the founding of Grace Lutheran Church in the town (now village) of Maine, northwest of Wausau—a Wisconsin Synod congregation. Hoffmann served in the area until 1885. From 1890–1895 he served in Sheboygan and was unaffiliated with any synod. He appears to have returned to New Orleans in 1895, but he drops off the radar after 1897. By the time eight Lutheran congregations northwest of Wausau celebrated a joint fiftieth anniversary in 1910, the *Wausau Daily Record-Herald* reported that Hoffmann was deceased.[12] However, his seventh son's obituary reported that, after founding and conducting "a non-sectarian mission" in New Orleans, J. J. died and was buried there in 1919.

---

12. See Appendix XI.

Fig. 60. Taegesville, Marathon Co., Wis. (oriented eastward), 1911, photo. The road pictured is the present-day County Road A. This photo captures well the split occasioned when Immanuel Lutheran Church (prominent church in the foreground, today occupied by a gravel parking lot for Schmidt's Ballroom) called Rev. J. J. Hoffmann back to the area in 1882. Due to doctrinal and personality concerns, thirteen families objected and founded their own congregation that year, Grace Lutheran. In 1884, they constructed their own church just a quarter-mile east (steeple visible further uphill in the background). Immanuel relocated her church building about four miles SW in 1923 and the congregation dissolved in 1969. The members of Grace worship in essentially the same church to this day. (I suspect, but am unable to confirm, that it is the oldest Lutheran church building in Marathon County still in use.) The local name for the area, Taegesville, dates to 1891, when the Maine Post Office was renamed the Taegesville Post Office after Postmaster Wilhelm Taege. Although the post office closed in 1901, the intersection continued to be referred to as Taegesville locally, and the name is still used occasionally today.

All of these pieces are part of the "sad song about Hoffmann" that Strasen and Schwan could sing once upon a time. There does not appear to have been one super-scandal that ruined Hoffmann's ministry. Rather, his life and ministry seem to have been characterized by a steady buildup of headstrong activity. He thought of himself more highly than he ought to have (cf. Rom. 12:3), craving attention, recognition, and praise, and wanting always to do things his own way, without concern for what his brothers in the ministry thought or what his members thought, whom he probably perceived as being ignorant and uninformed by comparison. He also seems to have been lacking in tact. His knowledge, intelligence, skill, and energy are undeniable, but so are his arrogance, self-centeredness, and foolhardiness.

Appendix IX

J. J. Kern Letters

The following letters are contained in The Wisconsin Evangelical Lutheran Synod Presidential Papers: Early Presidents Collection, located in the Wisconsin Evangelical Lutheran Synod Archives in Waukesha, Wisconsin. Their numbering here corresponds to their numbers in that collection. Johann Jakob (or John Jacob) Kern was born in or near the hamlet of Stöckenburg (today part of Vellberg) in the Kingdom of Württemberg on June 21, 1835. After his mother's passing, he immigrated to the United States in the fall of 1859, landing in New York on Oct. 14. After a brief stint in eastern Iowa, where he married Henrietta Marburg on June 21, 1860, he moved to Springfield, Illinois, where he taught at Illinois State University, which was jointly operated by the Illinois and Northern Illinois Synods. According to his obituary, "the sons of [Abraham] Lincoln attended his classes" there. His correspondence with the Wisconsin Synod also begins during his time there. This correspondence is included here primarily because of the role Kern ended up playing in Princeton, Wisconsin, as Strieter's opponent toward the end of Strieter's ministry in Marquette County. Kern details this opposition extensively—an opposition which helped to effect a lasting division in the Lutheran churches of Marquette and Green Lake Counties. The reasons Kern reached out to the Wisconsin Synod are not entirely clear, though as his correspondence and the facts of his life make abundantly clear, his innate wanderlust or itchy feet certainly contributed.

No. 678: J. J. Kern to Synod President Johannes Bading

Springfield, Ill.
March 23, 1863

Rev. J. Bading
Watertown, Jefferson Co., Wis.

Reverend Mr. President!
Beloved brother in the Lord!

In response to my asking if a fitting position for me might not be open in the Wisconsin Synod, Mr. Pastor Muehlhaeuser shared with me last week that the preacher position in Fond du Lac[, Wisconsin,] needed filling and it would be nice if I accepted it, if my health would permit it. Now since my health has already greatly improved during the few weeks' vacancy and my ill health consisted entirely in exhaustion, I see no reason why I should not venture to accept that position, trusting in the One who gives power to the weary and strength to the incapable [cf. Isa. 40:29]. Accordingly, I have replied to Mr. Pastor Muehlhaeuser that I am ready to assume that position and, if no obstacle stands in the way, to depart from here already on April 6. But I did still desire a more definite answer and actual call beforehand, to have as a firm basis for setting out. It would also be nice for me to have more exact information about whether a parsonage is available or not, how far the two ancillary congregations are from the city, whether I need a horse (and cart) and whether I would therefore be better off taking my horse and cart along (which certainly would not be cheap) or selling them at a loss, whether the congregation will reimburse my traveling expenses or at least a portion of them. I would furthermore appreciate receiving information about your arrangement with regard to installation. Could I not be installed right away on the first Sunday I am there, which would be Quasimodogeniti Sunday,[1] and give my inaugural sermon either that same day or the next Sunday? I must insist on the favor of information about these and similar things.

Enclosed is my release from the Northern Illinois Synod. My certificate of ordination I will hand over when we meet together in person. Looking forward to this in advance and awaiting a speedy reply,

Your lowly brother,
J. J. Kern

No. 735: J. J. Kern to Rev. Gottlieb Reim[2]

Fond du Lac, Wis.
Sept. 17, 1863

Rev. G. Reim
Helenville,[3] Wis.

Dear Brother!

---

1. I.e., the Second Sunday of Easter. It received this Latin name from the old Introit appointed for that Sunday, from 1 Peter 2:2, "Like newborn babies..."
2. Pastor Reim was serving as the president *pro tem*, since President Bading was on a trip to Germany to collect funds for the construction of a seminary.
3. Original: Helensville

Let the following serve as an answer to your correspondence from the eleventh of this month:

1. It is true that on Pentecost in the Fond du Lac congregation—after the preparation sermon in which I spelled out the essence of the Holy Supper, just as I have always done—I invited even those who were non-members of the congregation or those in attendance who were perhaps members of other fellowships, who after listening to the sermon felt a longing for the Holy Supper, to announce with me personally. Hereupon some non-members came forward, including a Reformed man; although he associates with our congregation, he still was not able as yet to resolve upon the switch. Since the discussion came out to my satisfaction, I admitted them. Their names are noted in the record book.

2. It is true that I introduced prayer- and Bible-hour, and in two of these made the attempt to invite a different member of the congregation, whom I considered to be qualified, to say a prayer at each. Since, however, I could not help but notice myself that my members are not yet far enough along for that, I discontinued the practice on my own. Would to God that our congregations were in a better condition in general.

3. It is true that, about a year ago, I spoke to Pastor Off[4] for ten minutes at the station on his journey through Springfield. Basically, as I believe I am able to recall, the subject of the conversation was, among other things, why I had not joined their association, even though I had been directed to it from Basel? Answer: My Lutheran confession. I cannot recollect stating what you cited, that I was looking for an opportunity to join the Association, and the assumption that I said anything of the sort is absurd, since the most fitting opportunity possible presented itself when the Evangelical congregation in Nashville, Washington Co., Ill., issued me a call. And when I answered them in the negative and remarked that I had decided to go to Wisconsin in order to join the German and more Lutheran (than the Northern Illinois Synod) Wisconsin Synod, they sent another call after me to Fond du Lac with the implication that, if I were not to find any fitting position in Wisconsin, their congregation was still open to me with their very attractive offers, and that if I did not want to join the Association, I could also remain a member of a Lutheran synod. Did I do the right thing by not following this call? Yet I could conceivably have said yes; it could, in fact, still happen that I join the Association one day, although I could scarcely have made an assertion of that kind. Since then I have never come into contact with Pastor Off again; I do not know his address and have also never written to him. But it seems to have been the

---

4. In 1862 this Pastor Off served a congregation today known as First Congregational United Church of Christ, Lake Mills, Wis. He was a member of the German Evangelical Church Association of the West (*Der Deutsche Evangelische Kirchenverein des Westens*) which considered itself related to the Evangelical Church established by the Prussian Union.

purpose of the Hon. Wisconsin Synod to push me into taking such a step, but she will find herself deceived if she thinks that I am a swaying reed.

For some time now I have been receiving letters from brothers in your synod from time to time, some in a benevolent style, breathing love and respect, several in a contemptuous tone, some with biting accusations.[5] Then I also now see from Boehner's own conduct that he and the majority of the synod harbor bitter hatred and animosity towards me, even though I had forgiven and forgotten everything, and was defending and protecting Boehner especially since the convention or, where defending him was not possible, turning the conversation to something else by saying, "That is all forgiven and forgotten; that's in the past." Then all sorts of conversations in general are being resurrected since the church dedication in Eldorado.[6] I also hear that I was accused of having given out the reason for Boehner's dismissal from Basel, whereas I have never said anything to his disadvantage, apart from the one time, in a state of great agitation over Boehner's choices,[7] in the presence of three persons who were members of my congregation. I am amazed at how Boehner can talk badly about me like that, even though we were on good terms in the Mission House.[8] He should re-

---

5. In this and what follows, Kern appears to be alluding to the momentous 1863 synod convention (held at Grace Lutheran Church in downtown Milwaukee from May 29—June 3) and what had transpired since then. The proceedings at that convention say that Kern was one of those "present in order to be accepted into synod membership." Also present as a voting member was Pastor C. F. Boehner, who had arrived from Basel in August 1859, was elected to take over the congregation in Fond du Lac, examined by the Northwest Conference on Sept. 30, and ordained on Oct. 2; he had officially been accepted as a pastor of the synod at the 1860 convention. After laboring in Fond du Lac for three years, the 1863 proceedings report that Boehner had "received a call from the Ev. Luth. Congregation in Beaver Dam" towards the end of 1862 and had accepted it and moved to his new congregation at the beginning of Jan. 1863. The same proceedings furthermore report that Pastor Kern had come to Wisconsin "in Easter week" of 1863 and "preached on the festival days in Fond du Lac whereupon the congregation there called him as their preacher and minister." Pastors G. Reim, C. Koester, J. Conrad, C. Gausewitz, and H. Quehl were appointed to Committee #2 of the 1863 convention to deal with the "acceptance of pastors applying for membership in the synod." In the afternoon session of May 29 they gave their report and eleven men were accepted into the synod, including F. Hilpert, a candidate who had arrived in Watertown in Dec. 1862 from Chrischona near Basel; Kern was not mentioned. Not until the afternoon session of June 1 was Kern "presented to the synod and it was resolved that committee No. 2 would report on his request for membership in the synod." In the afternoon session of June 3, "committee No. 2 brought up its report concerning the acceptance of Pastor Kern. Resolved that the report be shelved." Later that same session, "Pastor Boehner . . . informed the synod that the Ev. Lutheran Congregation in Eldorado, Fond du Lac Co., urgently desires Pastor Hilpert to be its preacher. In regard to this request it was resolved that the secretary of the synod [Christian Philipp Koehler of Manitowoc] inform said congregation that Pastor Hilpert would be willing to accept a call from them as soon as such could take place." See *WELS Historical Institute Journal* 16, no. 2 (Oct. 1998), and 17, no. 1 (April 1999).

6. St. Paul Evangelical Lutheran Church, of which only the cemetery remains today, along County Road I northwest of Fond du Lac, was built and dedicated in 1863 on land purchased that year from John and Wilhelmine Buntrock.

7. Alternate translation: "the choosing of Boehner"

8. I.e., in Basel

ally be ashamed to slander me like that—he was dismissed; I was sent out honorably. I am very sorry for this venting, which has escaped me in my vexation, but please keep in mind that I have been provoked. I now demand that an investigation committee come up here and investigate the entire matter on location and that from now on everyone's yapper gets stuffed. If I am not granted this privilege, I will know how to vindicate myself on my own, but then the Honorable Synod also need not expect me to let myself be admitted to her membership. For now I am still a member of the Northern Illinois Synod.

Your brother in Christ,
J. J. Kern

P.S. I am resolved to give the congregations here back to the synod any time it is requested. I will also never attempt to entice them away from the synod. But if the congregation should separate on their own, that would only be the fault of the synod herself.

No. 745: J. J. Kern to Rev. Gottlieb Reim[9]

Fond du Lac, Wis.
[Nov.][10] 25, 1863

Rev. G. Reim
Helenville,[11] Wis.

Reverend President!
Beloved brother in Christ!

Last week I received a letter from the "Free German Congregation" in New Holstein, Calumet Co., Wis., in which they express the wish that, since they were willing, if it was possible, to join our synod (the Free Lutheran Synod of Wisconsin),[12] I would acquaint them with the synod's constitution and, if at all possible, give them a talk, for which they were agreed on five dollars and offered to bring me there and back. A few days later an administrator, Mr. Oesan, came to me himself to talk with me some more in person. He told me that they had combined their sixty (heads of household) to form a free congregation, mostly well-to-do farmers, some of them wealthy and educated, consisting almost entirely of Holsteiners (a number of our members here are

---

9. See n. 2.
10. A guess based on the content; Kern does not give any indication of the month.
11. Original: Helensville
12. Kern qualifies "our synod," since he is still technically a member of the Northern Illinois Synod; he does not quite get the name right either.

also from Holstein), and they desire a Lutheran preacher from the Wisconsin Synod, whom they promise to give a salary of at least $300 or even $400, that they were also willing to build a church at once out of their own means and, if they get a suitable man, another forty members easily will join. For the present they are asking the preacher to hold school a few days a week, but would soon like to employ a separate teacher, etc. Mr. Oesan struck me as a really intelligent man, but it seems to me that a good portion of these people are simply rationalists, and it calls for a man, to start with, who can deal with the people where they are at. Up to the present these people are carrying on without preaching or God's word. Their children are not confirmed and probably not baptized either, but it seems to be their earnest intention to get a preacher now. Every member pledged to contribute at least five dollars annually to the preacher's salary for three years, for the time being. A Reformed preacher was there, only the vast majority didn't want to become Reformed or to accept their Reformed congregational constitution. And yet they also do not want "to become Old Lutheran." Oesan asked me whether or not I was Old Lutheran; I said yes, I certainly was Old Lutheran. He seemed to be satisfied with the constitution that I showed him, after lengthy discussion. I then promised him, if the president approved, I would pay them a visit on the Fourth Sunday in Advent and consider the matter. Now this is what I consider to be my informed opinion: We should take up this congregation, this large field, and send a man there who is equal to this position, an educated, clever, and sociable man, who unites true piety and confessional loyalty with these characteristics. Not just any preacher is fit for these people. From the church in Calumet it is roughly another fifteen miles, roughly twelve miles from Stockbridge on the other hand. In this way we would have and obtain an entire network of congregations in this area. I could definitely use some help, and could use it very soon. If I had an assistant teacher, who could lend assistance with preaching after a while, I would procure myself another horse and cart and go searching for some more preaching stations and also keep better track of the people here. If you can do anything in this matter, I would be greatly obliged. A young person like this could receive instruction from me early in the morning and I would have him provided with a thorough preparation for the seminary; in exchange for his help I would give him board, in addition to instruction, and cover all his other needs like clothes, books, etc. The school requires most of my energy and I can find no time for home visits, and without those a tremendous number of benefits are lost. We would thus have the following stations to be called upon and served here:

1. Fond du Lac
2. Forest
3. New Holstein
4. Calumet
5. Stockbridge

6. Greenbush

7. A place five miles from here[13] in the bush, where the Methodists have been working (or doing business) for a year

8. Another field, twelve miles from Forest, that the Methodists have picked up.

The names of the last two stations aren't coming to me. These could be divided like so:

1. The brother stationed in New Holstein could also take over Stockbridge at first.

2. The brother stationed in Calumet or Forest could take over both of these stations and Greenbush and the next station.

3. I would take Fond du Lac and the surrounding area, for which I could still use a helper.

No one would lack food or clothing. I am asking for serious consideration of this request. I am now resolved upon dedicating all of my energy to the Wisconsin Synod and wish to forget and forgive everything in the past, just as I ask for the same in return for the sake of the Master. Please write me a reply soon and impart some instruction to me with regard to New Holstein, so that I can give them an answer. It would certainly be good if you yourself could travel there and inspect the situation. If I receive no direction, I will go there, Deo volente, on the Fourth Sunday in Advent. I bid you and your dear ones a fond farewell as:

Your brother in Christ,
J. J. Kern

P.S. You or another brother aren't by chance aware of a reliable yet inexpensive buggy (and riding horse), are you? I really need to get one, since the residents of Forest only pick me up, if someone just so happens to be here, but never bring me back. For that I have to run.

No. 786: J. J. Kern to Rev. Gottlieb Reim[14]

Fond du Lac, Wis.
Dec. 20,[15] 1863

Rev. G. Reim

---

13. It is unclear whether "here" refers to Greenbush or his home base in Fond du Lac.
14. See n. 2.
15. The Fourth Sunday in Advent that year

Helenville,[16] Jefferson Co, Wis.

Reverend Mr. President!
Dear brother in Christ!

Having just now returned from [New] Holstein, let me share with you the result of my visit.[17] A congregation has now organized itself there with seventy heads of household as members, which can quite easily grow as high as a hundred; by comparison, there are 200 Protestant, mostly Holsteiner families in the town of Holstein. The entire congregation is in favor of joining the Wisconsin Synod; not even one voice was opposed. All were satisfied with the constitution of the synod. The articles of the congregation only pertain to the external organization of the congregation, and the name "Free Church Congregation" presents no obstacle either, since they still did not know which church body to join and therefore chose this name for the time being. It can be changed to "Evangelical Lutheran" at any time, though I did not push for that, since not all the members were in attendance and the congregation as such would be best organized as a congregation by the president of the synod. The congregation has a permanent foundation, insofar as the members make commitments for at least three years at a time and consequently cannot break up right away at every opportunity that the startup of a congregation can easily afford. I could find absolutely nothing in the constitution that was at variance with the synodical constitution. The people are mostly intelligent and I confess that, if I had a suitable successor for Fond du Lac and if the work begun here would not suffer, I would take on the Holsteiner congregation right away; they even asked me about that. To be sure, amusements are very commonplace there, only I find that to be the case here too and cannot control it either. What the congregation would need, however, is the kind of man who can accommodate himself to the people and who knows how to approach them from the proper angle. He cannot be blunt in his views; he must be sociable and yet reserved, and be a capable teacher. For now, though, it is only required of him that, in addition to the English instruction in the district school, he provides a few hours of German instruction and a few hours of religious instruction every week, and some private instruction in the evening besides, until eventually a separate teacher can be appointed. Since I overwork myself here, I would wholeheartedly prefer a position like this and the Holsteiners expressed their wishes to that effect, only I did not get their hopes up. If, however, a man for Fond du Lac should be found, I would gladly take on Holstein, if my congregation here were able to be satisfied with it. Now please appoint a day in the near future on which you plan to go to Holstein. This important place cannot be neglected.

Forest must furthermore have its own preacher too, since I cannot keep serving it along with my other stations longer than this year (up to April '64) on account of the hardships and because Fond du Lac wants and needs to have a preacher all to

---

16. Original: Helensville
17. See Kern's previous letter (no. 745).

itself. A man in Forest could use that location as a base for preaching in the Missouri congregation that I want to visit at New Year, since she is without a preacher, and for preaching in Greenbush. He would take his position for at least $200 and should preferably receive mission assistance his first year.

In Calumet the Albright people are preaching, but it should be occupied with a self-sacrificing brother.

The Free German School here has lost its preacher and has now received a man who does not hold out much promise and who is unpopular. If we had the right man now, our school could soon outstrip that one. Please make your trip over here and inform me of it in a timely manner, since I would have many things to talk with you about in person and I want to notify the Holsteiners of your visit. Other than that, I bid you and your dear family members a fond farewell as:

Your brother in Christ,
J. J. Kern

No. 836: J. J. Kern to Rev. Gottlieb Reim[18]

Fond du Lac, Wis.
March 1, 1864

Rev. G. Reim
Helenville,[19] Wis.

Dear brother in Christ!
Reverend Mr. President!

I have to report to you that my city congregation has resisted my wishes and put me on notice. This is how it happened. A short time ago I stipulated that, if I was expected to hold yet another year of school, the congregation had to install a parsonage above the new schoolhouse. The board of administrators would not agree to that, but desired that I preach in Fond du Lac alone and then content myself with $350.00, whereas up till now I had been receiving $140 and $280 from both stations for a total of $420.00. I declared that in either case I would not and could not make do with less than I had thus far, and that I was not holding any more school unless the parsonage was completed above the schoolhouse. Then the administrators told me there were some members who were wishing that I move along and who wanted to retract their financial subscription if I was going to stay here. Up till then I did not know or believe that I had such opponents. They added that I had picked up some new ones in the congregational meeting a few weeks back, when I had sharply opposed those who were

18. See n. 2.
19. Original: Helensville

pushing for changes to the congregation's constitution. I said that they should and could do as seemed best to them, but that I was not backing down from my demand one bit. This demand was not unreasonable, since the congregation has literally doubled in size since I have been here and I lose too much precious time in covering the long distance between my house and the school, especially in winter when I have to be there quite some time before school starts in order to fire up the stove, and a cold midday never agrees well with my stomach. A congregational meeting was quickly called, for which only a few more than half showed up. After lengthy, heated quarreling, it was proposed and supported to take the fight to a vote whether or not I should stay, and I . . . lost. I simply did not imagine that something like this could happen, but am happy to be free from holding school. I had just been in Forest on that Sunday.

I am now undecided as to what I want and ought to do. On the Sunday after Easter I am giving my farewell sermon.[20] Then I intend to continue serving Forest by itself and to stay here still and to give some private instruction until another open door shows itself to me. For I must confess that I am also afraid to go to *[New] Holstein*, since I believe that it is going to be a difficult post initially and I might not have the proper patience for this post. If you desire it, however, and give me the order to propose myself also to the Holsteiners, then I will take the risk. I cannot go to *Calumet*, since I made the repugnant and now excommunicated people my bitter enemies by thwarting their plans and re-establishing a Lutheran congregation, with the Lord's help, on a better foundation than had hitherto existed. I could not easily win these people back. So then I will stay here for the time being. If, however, in the course of the year you find[21] one or two suitable country congregations among whom order already prevails and where I do not need to hold any school, except for a few months and for four days a week tops, and where I could perhaps still practice medicine, I will accept such a position. Meanwhile I will devote myself to the study of Holy Scripture and to medicine on the side.[22] I must confess, I am very discouraged. I would like best to give up the preaching ministry entirely and take up anything else at all. No! Begone, you thoughts! It isn't that I am resentful toward my congregation here on account of their ingratitude. No, I am in fact asking you to fill the position as soon as feasible, for Fond du Lac is an important place for our Lutheran church and is going to keep on growing. Certainly there is still many a battle to be fought out there, and perhaps all too soon a crisis will take place as a result of which either a Reformed or United congregation will be organized in addition to the Lutheran one. The tinder is there; one could see it in the second-to-last congregational meeting when the motion was made to alter the congregation's constitution, and it is made further susceptible by Reformed papers recently introduced from Sheboygan, which

---

20. April 3 that year
21. This verb is a guess; in the midst of all his subordinate clauses Kern neglected to insert one.
22. Alternate translation: "and [to the study] of medicine on the side."

are now being read among the families who are fundamentally Reformed. Write me[23] soon and impart some brotherly advice to me.

Your lowly brother in Christ,
J. J. Kern

No. 837: J. J. Kern to Rev. Gottlieb Reim[24]

Fond du Lac, Wis.
March ,[25] '64

Rev. G. Reim
Jefferson Co., Wis.

Dear Brother Reim!

    I read your valued letter after my return from a short excursion to Watertown, Milwaukee, and New Berlin. The previous week I had received a short letter from Brother Moldehnke, in which he invited me for a visit and proposed two stations, namely Kilbourne Road (the congregation of the departed Brother Koester)[26] and New Berlin, as two suitable posts for me. I figured a short trip couldn't hurt me any, commended myself to God and the snorting steam horse,[27] and spent the night from Thursday to Friday at Brother Moldehnke's, then went to Milwaukee, spoke with Pastor Muehlhaeuser, to whom the congregation here had already written. He thought I ought not abandon Fond du Lac entirely until the posts here were filled. He said there were no prospects in Caledonia[28] and a trip there was unnecessary for me, since the people desire Brother

---

    23. In the original, Kern wrote, "Schrieben ~~Sie~~ mir bald," which, whether intended or not, has the same effect as writing, "~~Please w~~Write me soon."

    24. See n. 2.

    25. The blank is original. Based on a) the fact that Kern penned this letter to Reim between a letter to him dated March 1 and another one dated March 28, b) the fact that Kern received a reply to his March 1 letter before writing this one and received a reply to this one before writing his March 28 letter, and c) the contents of this letter, Kern probably penned this letter during the week of March 13, most likely on or around the fifteenth.

    26. Kilbourne Road is now named 27th Street. From the church website: "1852: Pastor Conrad Koester accepts the call to serve St. John's, now consisting of only 16 families. But with an influx of immigrants from various areas in Germany wanting to settle in the region, the congregation begins to flourish again. Like [Johannes] Weinmann, Koester works tirelessly as a missionary to multiple congregations in the area, including Caledonia (now Trinity), Tess Corners (now St. Paul's, Muskego), and Root Creek (now St. John's on Forest Home Avenue). He is also remembered for introducing the use of Martin Luther's Small Catechism in his confirmation instruction. He served St. John's until his death in 1864" (http://www.stjohnsoakwood.org/history#/st-johns-history; accessed June 6, 2020).

    27. The German version of "iron horse," i.e. locomotive.

    28. Caledonia seems to refer here to St. John's on Kilbourne Road and its sister congregations mentioned in n. 26.

Goldammer. He proposed that I still go to New Berlin at my earliest convenience. I went there that same evening and overnighted in Waukesha[29] with a Christian innkeeper named Nohl, who made a good impression on me. He told me Pastor Huber[30] had preached in Waukesha every two weeks the last year he was there, though that had not been sufficient at all. The Albright people there have had their own church for fifteen years, and it was so jam-packed every Sunday that it had been resolved (I think that's what he said) to build a new, larger church. But the Lutherans were also firmly determined to do something now, and if the preacher held school for at least six months out of the year, a man could live well off of Waukesha. I spoke with Rev. Alexander from the Presbyterian church, a nice man. He gave me permission to preach in their church on Sunday afternoon. On Sunday morning I preached in New Berlin. The congregation elected me as their pastor. But I did not accept the call yet, since the people wanted the United catechism to be retained, and because they, the seventy members, had only raised $160 for Brother Huber in the last few years which, to me, indicates some sort of greed. A list is going to be passed around now and then sent to me. The house also leaves much to be desired. In Waukesha, even though it was not adequately advertised, a respectable assembly came[31] together. These people want me to come to them. They plan to hold a meeting on Easter Monday. The Congregationalist church is now available for purchase at favorable terms and they don't want to let this opportunity slip away without taking advantage of it. They believe that they would have at least thirty members to start with, perhaps sixty (families). Rev. Alexander, the principal of the college there, wants me to take over the station there and at the same time to teach mathematics at the college, in return for which he will let me have use of a hall in which I could give German instruction in the afternoons. This might be an advantageous offer. What to do? Waukesha and Berlin, a mere four miles from each other, can easily be combined. Brother Moldehnke is advising me to take over this station. The touchy issue is the catechism. I would have to insist on ignoring the United catechism right from the start.

As for things here, it is certainly an awkward thing to dismiss the pastor without being able to cite any reason at all. I myself still do not know the reason to this day. The board of administrators and some members set the whole thing up and caught the congregation off guard. All sorts of stories are making the rounds now, such as that I demanded a parsonage, $400 salary, and also what the school brings in besides, which is simply not true. Since then, I have already been asked by various parties if I wouldn't change my mind and stay, if the vote would turn out completely different today. I

---

29. Original: Waukeshah. Kern spells it three different ways in this letter—this way, the correct way, and Waukeschah.

30. Daniel Huber had been based in New Berlin from 1860–1863.

31. Here in the original letter appear three struckthrough lines which read: "To/For the married couple Herrmann Heinrich Hartmann and his wedded wife Anna Elisabeth Wilhelmine, née Reichmann." Clearly unrelated to this letter, they appear to be an excerpt from an official entry of some sort, such as in a church record book or elsewhere. Perhaps Kern had used the sheet of paper to practice writing the entry before entering the information in the proper place.

admittedly have no great desire to do so, and on the other hand I am also not happy to be going, since I am now encountering all sorts of demonstrations of love and attachment. What should I do? Would it not be good if you, sir, were to come this way for a visit? I leave the matter in the Lord's hands. The week after Easter is conference in Oshkosh. Write me back soon and give me your kind advice. With warmhearted greetings to your dear family I am:

Your lowly brother in Christ,
J. J. Kern

No. 851: J. J. Kern to Rev. Gottlieb Reim[32]

Fond du Lac, Wis.
March 28, '64

Rev. G. Reim
Helenville,[33] Jefferson Co., Wis.

Dear brother in Christ!

    I received your valued letter. I am extremely unhappy about changing places yet again and this affair is helping to make me feel most miserable. The reproach you mentioned that Fond du Lac is making against me is an empty excuse. And I did not always use an outline, and when I did, it was only because too much work was generally demanded of me and I was meticulous about developing my sermons properly. This has ultimately helped me, though, to free myself completely from an outline now. But the main reason is this, that I didn't preach what their ears are itching for. Or why then did I always have a full church? Is not the Sunday School thriving? Have I not brought c. thirty issues of our various (Lutheran) church papers into the congregation, which previously had read not more than a single one, as well as fifty-two *Jugendfreunde*[34]? When I used an outline, was it not well developed every time? I can put most of them in front of me still today. However, I will never need to do this again.

    I am still hoping to go to New Berlin, although I have quite a few misgivings. Administrator Kern, to whom Pastor Muehlhaeuser directed me, belongs to the United party. Perhaps he would try to influence me from the get-go in favor of his position; briefly, he knew nothing about the fact that the Lutheran catechism would

---

    32. See n. 2.

    33. Original: Helensville

    34. This seems to refer to *Der neue Deutsche Jugendfreund* (The New German Childhood Friend, for Nurturing and Cultivating the Youth), edited by Franz Hoffmann. It was first published in Wriezen in 1846; from 1849 it was published in Stuttgart, and beginning in 1864 it was published under the title *Franz Hoffmann's Neuer Deutscher Jugendfreund*. Kern appears to have distributed this reader in connection with his schoolteaching, as it was not a religious publication.

have to be introduced. I shared with him the synodical resolution that pertains to it; he acted completely ignorant. Since I was not present at the congregational meeting in which I was elected, Admin. Kern shared the result with me afterwards, adding that the congregation wanted everything to stay as it had been with respect to the catechism and such. I explained to him, however, that there could be no talk of that, that I could not accept the United catechism. For another member had told me in town the day before that if the United component would not conform, then they would separate and form their own congregation.[35] I wrote to Brother Huber the other day and questioned him about the situation. It is furthermore very strange to me that the people were not prepared either to cover my modest traveling expenses or even to set a firm amount as my salary. Pastor Huber received just $160 the last few years. The parsonage is in very bad shape.[36] In Waukesha they want church services just as much as in New Berlin and need them just as much, but also at least six months of school, and in New Berlin at least three months. So there would be plenty of work once again. A sermon every Sunday at two places, and at three in the summer. The other thing I didn't like was that the New Berliners were telling me how much money Pastor Huber had made, and yet he had such a small salary. From everything, I got the clear impression that the people are very stingy; the fact that seventy members raised $160 is nothing too commendable. The difficulty will be founding and serving Waukesha properly, without New Berlin becoming dissatisfied.

I am finding that, in order to perform marriages, it is necessary to have one's "credentials of ordination" as well as one's membership in a synod on record, and that a fine of $500 is in place for neglecting to do so. Now since I simply cannot consider myself a member of the Northern Illinois Synod any more and am also not a member of Wisconsin, which I would nevertheless like to join, I am asking for official information as to whether I am considered a member of the synod and will be taken up in the next session, and if so, I ask you to instruct the secretary of the synod to issue me a certificate concerning it, so that I am an official member of the synod and also to be able to perform weddings in the future without being liable to penalty.

I also ask on behalf of the *Forest* congregation, against whom I am have no complaints, that their post be filled quickly. Likewise on behalf of the *Calumet* congregation, twenty families strong, for a preacher. Both places can also be combined with each other at first. Or another option: Both stations each receive their own preacher and *Stockbridge* is combined with *Calumet* and Pastor Hilpert goes to *Forest*, which is able and would be willing to purchase a suitable little frame house, a type of shanty with adequate space and an acre of garden land very nicely cultivated, for a reasonable price as a parsonage. Pastor Hilpert is willing.

With that, receive the warmhearted greetings of:

---

35. According to the New Berlin Historical Society's website, this split did in fact take place a few years later.

36. Alternate translation: "The parsonage is very plain."

Your brother in Christ,
J. J. Kern

No. 855: J. J. Kern to Rev. Gottlieb Reim[37]

Fond du Lac
Apr. 6, '64

Rev. G. Reim
Helenville, Wis.

Dear brother in Christ!

In response to my firm declaration that I would have nothing to do with the United catechism, the New Berliners sent me the enclosed letter. I have no idea what I should do now. Perhaps it would have been better to say nothing about the matter and then simply to ignore the United catechism. Please advise me in this matter.

The people in Waukesha, whom many from the country wish to join, thus want a man all to themselves, one who will teach school at the same time, and they have probably engaged a man by the name of Fleischer, on whom they were very keen when I was there.

In case you propose other places for me, I would prefer to get country congregations, even several, and good Lutheran ones. For I find that the discord in the congregations does not stem from the Lutherans, but from un-Lutheran elements.

Requesting your affectionately fraternal advice, I am in Christ Jesus:

Your lowly brother,
J. J. Kern

No. 864: Rev. Philipp Koehler[38] to Rev. Gottlieb Reim[39]

Manitowoc, Wis.
April 14, 1864

---

37. See n. 2.

38. The secretary of the Wisconsin Synod at the time. Koehler was one of the pastors of the Northwestern Conference (so-called because it was northwest of the synod's headquarters in Milwaukee), who exerted a decidedly confessional Lutheran influence on the fledgling Wisconsin Synod. These men continue to be honored today in the name of the synod's official publishing house, Northwestern Publishing House.

39. See n. 2. This letter reveals an attempt on Rev. Reim's part to fulfill Rev. Kern's request in no. 851.

Dear Brother Reim!

I received your dear letter yesterday evening; permit me to give you your answers by return mail.

I just finished the invitations to the pastors you mentioned; they will go out in the mail today. As for the reminder about the collection for the synod, I consider that to be superfluous. Reference is made in the invitation to §49 and §56, and that collection is mentioned in the latter; I think that is a sufficient reminder.

I would very gladly be in Watertown on May 3, but if I want to be there on the appointed date, then I have to set out from here already on Saturday[40] and cannot then be in my congregation that Sunday or Ascension Day.[41] I entreat you to take this into consideration and accordingly not to take it the wrong way if I do not come for the cited reason. I would come regardless, if it were absolutely necessary, but as I see from the charter, it is just fine if only a majority of the trustees are present. So I will not come, unless you write me once more beforehand that it is unavoidably necessary to come.

I have no desire to take over Koester's congregations;[42] I will stay in Manitowoc for now. If I should still wish to get away from here, I could go to Newton, since that congregation has given me a call.

Now at last, concerning the certificate of accreditation for Past[or] Kern, I cannot bring myself to issue it. I am sorry that I cannot comply with your wishes once again, but I cannot help it. Why do you in turn put such demands on me? To be sure, I have issued such a certificate for others, but that still does not mean that I also have to issue one to Pastor Kern. Pastor Kern was refused by the synod last year and will hardly be admitted this year. You know that as well as I do; thus it is simply not the same with him. You cannot give Pastor Kern any official information that he is viewed as a member of the synod or that he will be taken up during the next convention, so how should the secretary[43] be able to certify that Past[or] Kern is a regular member of our synod? I will not do so therefore.

Bartelt's and Kern's letters enclosed. We are—thank God—pretty much all well again. Warmhearted greetings from us to you and your dear family.

Your brother in Christ,
Phil[ipp] Koehler

---

40. April 30

41. May 1 and 5, respectively

42. The 1864 convention proceedings report that C. Koester, listed in the 1863 proceedings at Caledonia Center, had passed away after "suffering terribly" on a "difficult and painful sickbed."

43. Koehler himself

No. 866: J. J. Kern to Rev. Gottlieb Reim[44]

Fond du Lac, Wis.
Apr. 19, '64

Rev. G. Reim
Helenville, Jefferson Co., Wis.

Dear brother in Christ!

I received your valued item dated the ninth of this month, though certainly too late to have a detailed discussion with Brother Giese about his field of labor. I have, however, already written to him on that score.[45] Judging from what he said about it and from what you wrote me, I would be inclined to take it over, especially since I would not have to hold any school, on which point I wish to follow Brother Giese, except for religious instruction and what is connected to it, for no one can serve two masters and satisfy both. For this reason I would hereafter like to be and become exclusively a preacher and leave everything else aside. I have written a letter of declination to New Berlin.

I have sold my house without coming out at a loss, but if I still have no post for much longer, I will have to look around for a rental place soon.

Brother Giese has not given the congregation here much hope that he will accept the position, since he is hoping to be called to the seminary.[46] The people are docile right now, and the board of administrators has asked me on behalf of the congregation to keep on preaching for as long as I am here. I complied with this wish and last Sunday I once again preached in front of a large assembly. Pastor Koehler has addressed an invitation to the convention to me, and I will make an appearance at the same.

Both of my children[47] have the measles.

With the most cordial greetings to your dear family I am:

Your lowly brother in Christ,
J. J. Kern

Addendum. The Calumet folks were again at my place while I was absent and are asking me to intercede with the synod on their behalf and to ask that a preacher just for them might please be sent to them very soon. But if there is no other option, they are okay with getting a preacher to share with Forest, which I think is best for now,

---

44. See n. 2.

45. The reference is to E. Frederick Giese, whose field of labor at this time was in the town of Herman, Wisconsin. See the 1864 convention proceedings in the *WELS Historical Institute Journal* 17, no. 2 (Oct. 1999) 8.

46. See *Jars of Clay: A History of Wisconsin Lutheran Seminary (1863–2013)*, 32–34.

47. Georg Friedrich (b. Aug. 19, 1861) and Johann Martin Herman (b. Jan. 19, 1863).

since Fond du Lac no longer wants to or can team up with Forest anymore, and Forest definitely cannot be neglected. The current members of the Calumet congregation and especially the administrators are dear, order-loving people, and I ask that this request be given serious consideration, if at all doable.

I am concerned about Holstein, except that I am not the right man, not imposing enough, and especially for that reason the position might be too difficult for me. It would perhaps be good to send them a German teacher for the time being, if we don't have any more people as preachers.

No. 899: Rev. Gottlieb Thiele to Synod President Gottlieb Reim

Ripon, Wis.
June 9, 1864

My Esteemed [*Herr*] President,

In my opinion, I am excused from executing your commission to turn my attention once again to the Princeton congregation, due to the fact that her circumstances have turned out exactly as I foresaw. As I learned upon returning here, Pastor Kern had traveled to Princeton via Ripon on Thursday.[48] Today he showed up all at once from P[rinceton], arriving at my house, and he told me that he was waiting for his family to arrive here from Fond du Lac so that he could bring them to Princeton, his new home. He told me that, after he had preached in P[rinceton] on Sunday,[49] he informed the people that he did not belong to the Wisconsin Synod, to which they had replied to him that he could just remain with them all the same whether he belonged to a synod or even to none; it didn't matter to them either way. So he is now in P[rinceton], and will remain there.

I for my part think the synod has wronged Kern badly by being so difficult with his acceptance into membership. Pastor Kern has the intention of rejoining the Illinois Synod, to which he belonged earlier.

I think the synod will have nothing to object to in my continuing to be on good, neighborly terms with Kern. He is certainly no Methodist, no Baptist either, but truly a "good Lutheran"!

Most respectfully,
G[ottlieb] Thiele

---

48. June 2
49. June 5

No. 906: J. J. Kern to Synod President Gottlieb Reim

Princeton
June 17, 1864

Rev. G. Reim
Helenville, Jefferson Co., Wis.

Dear Brother Reim!

I received your letter yesterday. In it you write that I went to Princeton contrary to agreement. Now a firm agreement was never made and besides, here in America one may often avail himself of the English saying, "Help yourself." My acceptance into the synod was forced and unconstitutional. With repeated voting I still might have ended up being rejected after the continuing agitations.[50] Various older brothers therefore advised me to withdraw. I borrowed a hundred dollars, left my family behind and went to Princeton,[51] where my effects had already arrived (and I was planning to forward them onward). I told the people that I had not been accepted into the synod for such-and-such reasons, as well as they were known to me, relayed the whole story to them and shared with them my decision to go to a different place, where the congregation was viewed as belonging to the Wisconsin Synod and the synod had been applied to for the sending of a preacher.[52] The leading members came together that same day and asked me to remain at least until Sunday. They were hoping that I would remain here. On Sunday after the sermon the congregation declared unanimously that it was their wish that I stay, whether I belonged to the Wisconsin Synod or to any other synod or to none at all. At this I decided to remain and that is what I will now do, sir, come what may. But I do not therefore have in mind to alienate the congregation from the synod—far from it. That is why I have even presented the church constitution of the Wisconsin Synod to the congregation, and it was adopted, except the article on the

---

50. Even though the previous letter (no. 899) from Pastor Gottlieb Thiele (newly accepted into the Wisconsin Synod himself) also talks about difficulties attending Kern's acceptance into the synod's membership, there is no record in the official minutes (as translated and printed in the *WELS Historical Institute Journal* 17, no. 2, and 18, no. 1) detailing how his request for admittance into the synod was handled. The minutes list Kern in the roll call as one of those who "placed themselves at the disposal of the synod and were accepted as advisory members," and they list the committee (Committee 2) appointed to deal with the "acceptance of new pastors." But when presenting Committee 2's report, Kern's name appears neither there nor anywhere else in the remainder of the minutes. Thus the nature of this "forced and unconstitutional" acceptance into the synod remains a mystery.

51. As Gottlieb Thiele's letter (no. 899) makes clear, Kern didn't abandon his family but sent for them later.

52. Perhaps the curious *mit* Kern went back and inserted at the beginning of this clause indicates that the traits he was looking for in his new location were also more or less true of the Princeton congregation (in this case, less true, since Kern goes on to show that the Princeton congregation did not really consider herself a member of the Wisconsin Synod). If so, that could be an indication that he was subtly baiting the congregation to consider him as a viable option for their new pastor.

preacher says that he must belong to a recognized Lutheran synod. The congregation itself will not join any synod as long as I am serving them (unless I were a member of the Wis. Synod). I have even spoken in favor of the synod and defended her, when some of the most respected people were grumbling and saying the Wisconsin Synod had not cared for them thus far, they could not expect anything from her, they would just as well join some other synod. I came to the Wis. Synod's defense and said that I agree with her in matters of faith and hope that they never join any other synod. For me though, it is a necessity, for if I remain any longer without synodical affiliation, no other synod will admit me into her association anymore either. I now have to choose between the Illinois and the Missouri Synod, and I believe that even the latter would not refuse me. If, however, the Wisconsin Synod should still wish to accept me into her midst, I remain ever ready to enter into her association. But I am not going to do any groveling. If she admits me, that will be just fine and I will work for her faithfully and diligently; if she does not admit me, that will also be just fine and I will never seek to do her harm. The love that individual brothers have exhibited toward me has gladdened me, even as I also thank you for your part. If I had the definite assurance that I will be accepted into the association of the Wisconsin Synod, I would see to it that it was still put into the statutes, before the incorporation of the congregation, that the preacher and congregation have to join the Wisconsin Synod. But until then, for the sake of my own security, I will not push for it.

With warmhearted greetings to you and your dear family, I am:

Your brother in Christ,
J. J. Kern

Postscript: Be so kind as to inform me at once as to whether I can be accepted into the synod a year from now or, if not, whether I might still serve the congregation for the longer term even if the § [section] on the preacher were amended to read that the preacher, along with the congregation, has to join the Wisconsin Synod. For I love good order and wish that the Lutheran congregations in Wisconsin would belong to the Wisconsin Synod. But I want to have assurance and will not let myself be intimidated by threats. If I am still hoping to be accepted into the synod, I do so not for my own sake, but for the sake of the congregation, so that future controversies may be prevented.

No. 907: J. J. Kern to Synod President Gottlieb Reim

Princeton, Greenlake [sic] Co.
June 17, 1864

Rev. G. Reim
Helenville, Jefferson Co., Wis.

Most esteemed Mr. President!

I hereby notify you, sir, that, after the congregation in Princeton elected me in an orderly way to be their preacher and spiritual shepherd, they refused to let me move on; that accordingly, instead of moving to another state and joining a different Lutheran body, I have resolved to remain here and therefore hereby retract my withdrawal from the synod.

Yours most respectfully,
J. J. Kern, Lutheran preacher

There are two mysterious factors at work here: 1) the relationship between this letter and Kern's previous letter (no. 906), which bears the same date, and 2) the nature of Kern's membership (or quasi-membership, or non-membership) in the Wisconsin Synod at this point. Regarding no. 1, it almost seems as though Kern had already penned this notification early the same day, but when he received President Reim's letter, he then penned his other letter dated June 17 and mailed the two together. The other possibility is that Kern thought that a separate letter was needed regarding the retraction of his withdrawal from the synod, for the sake of good order. Regarding no. 2, there is a lot of conflicting information in his two June 17 letters and in Gottlieb Thiele's June 9 letter (no. 899). Thiele was brand new to the synod, having just been accepted into the synod's membership during the convention at the end of May. He mentions the synod "being so difficult with [Kern's] acceptance into membership." Originally, Thiele had gegen (against) in this clause (which would alter the English translation somewhat), but then crossed it out and put bei (with), which seems to imply that Kern was in fact accepted, but that it wasn't pretty. Then Kern himself says in his other June 17 letter that he was accepted, but that it was "forced and unconstitutional." He then mentions being advised to withdraw, of which we have no record. (Did all of this take place at the convention, and that is why Secretary Hoenecke never included action on Kern's membership in the minutes?) From then on, Kern writes as someone not belonging to the synod, even asking Reim in the postscript of no. 906 to inform him at once whether he might be taken into the synod's membership at the next convention, but also making clear that he will not be intimidated into taking that step. But then here (no. 907) he gives President Reim official notice of the retraction of his withdrawal from the synod (perhaps to grease the skids for his future acceptance?). It is all quite confusing, to say the least.

No. 1013: J. J. Kern to Synod President Gottlieb Reim

Princeton, Greenlake [*sic*] Co., Wisconsin
Dec. 1, 1864

Rev. G. Reim
Hellenville [sic], Jefferson Co., Wis.

Dear Brother Reim!

I am finally getting around to replying to your valued letter today, since my time has also been pretty well occupied. Let me start by attesting to my heartfelt sympathy for the illness of your dear wife. If Christians in general cannot exist without the cross, that much less can a preacher of the gospel do without it; he must be drawn into the fellowship of the cross even more deeply than others, so that all his doings and testifying acquire more and more a heavenly character and flavor. Yet the Lord does not burden his children with more than they can bear, and he also certainly knows when he should turn our suffering away.

As for me and my congregation, everything is proceeding steadily. The services in the schoolhouse are plentifully attended. Our[53] choral society is blossoming with success and may soon occupy a level equal to any society I know of. I introduced liturgical singing right away.[54] The Word also seems to be dividing.[55] In the beginning everybody came; now the most godless seem to want to stay away entirely, not through my fault—I didn't try to drive anybody away. They just cannot bear it when harlotry and boozing are called by their proper names. For in this respect Princeton surpasses everything that I have seen so far. Six of our members here are innkeepers, and besides that there are still four other saloons here. Sundays are desecrated with boozing and dancing, though much has changed. Apart from that I am very happy to be here; the people show me a lot of love and put their confidence on display in all sorts of ways. Even if the salary is only coming in sparingly, the people bring various gifts and I am therefore also better off than in Fond du Lac. I have absolutely no desire to change places any more. Sixteen miles from here in Indianland I have taken over a congregation of twenty-two members, and am holding service every six weeks in the schoolhouse one mile away from P[astor] Strieter.[56] The people from Strieter's congregation are also favorable toward me, by and large. I was already called upon for three funerals from his congregation, and even if it won't work now, the time is going to come when all these congregations will fall to me, D[eo] v[olente].

Things are going sadly where Diehlmann is preaching. He does not want to resign and his people don't want to just chase him away, and if he remains for several

---

53. It appears that Kern originally wrote "My" here.

54. The following two sentences are written in the left margin of the first page: "I have begun confirmation instruction with fourteen confirmands and fourteen auditors. Our Sunday School numbers about eighty children and six teachers."

55. Perhaps a reference to Hebrews 4:12 or Luke 12:51

56. See the schoolhouse on Michael Schmidt's property in Fig. 28, located at the northwest corner of what is today the intersection of Dover Ave. and 14th Ave. Though the schoolhouse was just a bit more than one section of the township removed from Strieter's parsonage, the distance was about two miles, not one.

more years, only a few families will still remain for the Lutheran Church; the Albright people are settling in[57] shamefully. How should I conduct myself in this situation? Would it be excusable for me to step up against Diehlmann publicly? The people send their children to me for school and I generally have their complete confidence, but I would not consider it appropriate to incite them against the man who has been their preacher up till now.

On the Reformation festival I gathered a collection for the seminary and sent it to P[astor] Moldehnke. I will also do what I can for the seminary in other respects for the sake of the cause, which is great and precious to me. My congregation is poor, however, since our richest people do the least, out of natural indifference, greed, and worldly mindedness.

I would gladly attend the conferences if they were not so far out of the way, which costs me too much money in these expensive times. Nor can I get away in the foreseeable future on account of other domestic circumstances. P[astor] Strieter was drafted, but for $725 he satisfied a replacement and thus remains back here. He is very hostile to me. Other than that, nothing of significance.

Your brother in Christ,
J. J. Kern

No. 803: J. J. Kern to Synod President Gottlieb Reim

Princeton, Greenlake [sic] Co., Wis.
Jan. 5, 1865[58]

Rev. G. Reim
Hellenville [sic], Wis.

Reverend Mr. President!

About ten weeks ago twenty members—i.e. *the total membership* of the evangelical Lutheran congregation in Crystal lake [sic], Marquette Co., called the Schmidt congregation, which had been served by Pastor Strieter up to that point—turned to me with the request to serve them, since they had been abandoned by P[astor] Strieter. I came to the people and inquired about the reasons for the separation from P[astor] Strieter in front of the assembled congregation. These were stated to me as follows: The Schmidt congregation is the first and original congregation (Pastor Strieter lives within it)[59] and always had service every two weeks, and a church was supposed to be

---

57. German: *hausen*. Alternate translation: "going door to door."

58. Kern made a classic New Year mistake and wrote 1864, which is also what accounts for the numbering of this letter.

59. This is an example where we see the semantic blend between "congregation" and "community."

built in their area. But now a church had been built in Newton. Alternating services are now to be held there and in the schoolhouse by Mr. Dagatz [*sic*][60] every two weeks, at one place in the morning and at the other place in the afternoon, and the Schmidt congregation has c. three to four and five miles to each place.[61] In their own schoolhouse, on the other hand, no more services are to be held on Sundays; they are instead supposed to divide themselves between those congregations. They said Strieter simply told them he was not coming anymore. Those are the pure facts of the case, as I also heard them elsewhere. At this, they proceeded to call me, and were all the more delighted to do so since they had been eager to be rid of Strieter for a long time. I formally took over the congregation when I was there again on Advent 4, and in three weeks they plan to adopt the church constitution of the Wisconsin Synod as I introduced it in Princeton[62] and to join the Wisconsin Synod. But then, seven weeks ago, I received an obscene letter from Strieter. I answered him with composure. Then he answers me back and asks me for the address of my synod's headquarters [*meines Präsidiums*], which I have no problem sharing with him. He calls me an invader, wolf, scamp, etc., and that I cannot put up with. The call came without my having anything to do with it; indeed, I only accepted it once I was convinced that Strieter had abandoned the congregation. He was willing to preach to them during the week as often as they desired, that is true. But the people were not agreeable to that. In his second letter he now says that he would also have preached to them every six weeks, like I am, but that he promised them that or expressed himself to that effect earlier is a lie. Now if a complaint against me should arrive, I will be able to defend myself.[63]

Since Christmas I have also been serving the congregation hitherto served by Diehlmann. When four more families went over to the Methodists, I preached in the schoolhouse there unsolicited and the people all declared themselves against Diehlmann, saying that he was derelict in his duty, and they called me as their spiritual shepherd. Their children had already been coming to me for instruction for a long time anyway. Even this United congregation will adopt the Lutheran church constitution of the Wisconsin Synod.

I also preached in Dartford on Second Christmas Day in front of twenty-three persons. In time a congregation can also be gathered there.

Even so, this remark is misleading; all other indications are that if Strieter lived within any congregation/community, it was the one that met at the Tagatz schoolhouse, mentioned later.

60. "Dagatz" should be "Tagatz."

61. These appear to be the distances to the Newton church and the Tagatz schoolhouse, respectively, but he is using the maximum distance certain members of the Schmidt congregation had to drive to each place. The distance from the Schmidt schoolhouse to either meeting place was less.

62. See no. 906.

63. The correspondence between Strieter and Kern, referred to here, can be read in its entirety in no. 1057, soon to follow.

It will not be long before Pastor Strieter abandons his congregation, as he can no longer live off his meager salary. At that point, if God wills, I will also get one or the other congregation.

My wife was delivered of a healthy daughter on Dec. 27.[64]

How should I conduct myself with respect to Strieter? Wishing God's rich blessings for the new year, I am:

Yours, J. J. Kern

[Postscript:] Could you please send me some altar chants to choose from? I have introduced altar chanting in Princeton.

No. 1051: J. J. Kern to Synod President Gottlieb Reim

Princeton, Greenlake [sic] Co., Wisconsin
Jan. 16, 1865

Rev. G. Reim
Hellenville [sic], Wis.

Dear Brother Reim!
Reverend Mr. President,

On Jan. 29, that is, the Fourth Sunday after Epiphany, I am preaching in Crystallake [sic].[65] Since Strieter now intends to leave in order to restore unity,[66] everyone[67] wishes that either my congregation join with them or else that they unite with us. Because of this, now has come exactly the right moment for our synod to reconquer the entire Indianland; if it doesn't work now, it may not happen ever again. For that reason, I am inviting you, Mr. President, to arrive here the Friday before the above-mentioned Sunday and to ~~go~~ ride[68] with me to that congregation on Saturday. I have also already made firm arrangements accordingly,[69] or in the event you yourself cannot come, then please send another experienced brother, but this much is certain

---

64. Anna Dorothea, whom J. J. baptized on Jan. 25.

65. That is, Kern was scheduled to preach at the Schmidt schoolhouse that Sunday. He was scheduled to preach there every six weeks.

66. See p. 129.

67. He appears to mean everyone in the Schmidt congregation, which he was serving, and the two neighboring congregations that Strieter was still serving, which were meeting at the Newton church and the Tagatz schoolhouse, respectively.

68. The German *gehen* can also mean "walk"; Kern changed it to *fahren* to avoid any confusion.

69. For more on these arrangements, see the letter from Kern to Mr. Schmidt that Strieter shares in his protest, no. 1057, pp. 318–19.

[*aber gewiß*].⁷⁰ If you do this, sir, then I can promise you this entire area for the synod. Please answer me right away as to what you intend to do. There is no time to lose; that same Sunday a candidate⁷¹ from Missouri is preaching in the congregations. About 400 congregation members are at stake; an entire future is at stake.

In the congregation I just took over two weeks ago that had been served by Diehlmann things are looking dismal. Almost everything is corroded by Methodism, so that only a few faithful souls are left for the Lutheran Church. Every night these fanatics have their assemblies in the homes of our wavering members one after the next, lasting into the early morning, and therefore in two weeks I plan to preach against Methodism in that settlement every evening, as Luther did against the iconoclasts.⁷² I should be very glad if a capable brother could assist me with this. The existence of this congregation is at stake, which has the current potential to number fifty to sixty families, though it has just eight (to twelve) members who are still faithful and reliable. So if you could spend two more evenings with me in that settlement after Advent 4,⁷³ it would certainly be of great benefit. If you are unable to come, please send another capable brother. But please do not leave me stuck in a tight spot. The negative results would affect the synod and the church at large. As I eagerly await a prompt reply, I remain:

Your lowly
J. J. Kern

No. 1058: Rev. Adolf Hoenecke⁷⁴ to Synod President Gottlieb Reim

Farmington
February 2, 1865

Dear Brother Reim,

---

70. This could also possibly be translated, "but of course" in the sense of "at the very least." But the above rendering seems more natural, in spite of the disjointedness it creates (which is already on display in this sentence anyway).

71. This usually refers to a seminary graduate, or soon-to-be graduate, who has not yet been ordained.

72. The reference is to Luther's so-called Invocavit sermons—a series of eight sermons he preached on consecutive days beginning on March 9, 1522, after returning to Wittenberg from the Wartburg, in order to restore order after the iconoclasm Andreas Karlstadt had incited.

73. This was a mistake; it should read "Epiphany 4," as per the first sentence of the letter.

74. The secretary of the Wisconsin Synod at the time, nearly thirty years old.

APPENDIX IX: J. J. KERN LETTERS

On Tuesday[75] I returned from my wolf hunt, i.e. the wolf is all mine.[76] I think I did so at the right time, even if it was too soon for Brother Kern; I did not want to stay and mess around with the Methodists for him on Monday evening though. Had my reasons too. If I tackle the Methodists and accomplish something, afterwards Kern is all the more exposed to them and to his congregation if he is not a match for the Methodists. But in addition, the seminarians also need to have their instruction; was therefore not advisable to sacrifice another day to Kern when synodical interests were not strictly involved. I will also remark here right away that Kern gave five dollars for the seminary out of his own pocket. Am also more and more firmly convinced that he is a decent guy and that we are lacking any reason to refuse him yet again.

Now to the report on what I accomplished in the Indian land. Let me start by illustrating my report with a map.

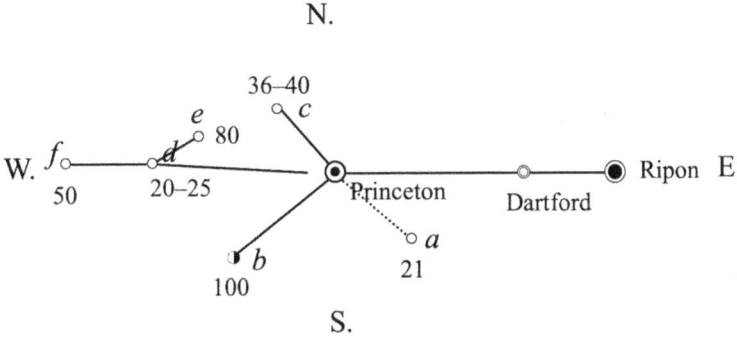

From Princeton, where I arrived on Friday evening,[77] I rode with Kern on Saturday to Congregation b,[78] which numbers a hundred members. The point was naturally, as much as possible, to get some clarity on the disposition of the people. But it did not work to get the church from the administrator for Sunday morning (in the afternoon Strieter was going to preach), in order to get a chance to negotiate with the congregation. As for why I attempted to get the church in the first place, I had decided to do so in view of the fact that 1) Strieter had declared he wanted to leave and the congregation had unanimously made the counter-declaration that they were releasing him; 2) accordingly Strieter's position at the time was a provisional one; and 3) the congregation had not joined the Missouri Synod.

---

75. Jan. 31

76. German: *d.h. der Wolf ist ganz auf meiner Seite*. This expression seems to borrow from the saying, "*Das Vergnügen* [or *Die Ehre*] *ist ganz auf meiner Seite*"—"The pleasure [or The honor] is all mine" (in response to someone saying, for example, "It's a pleasure [or an honor] to meet you"). In this case, Hoenecke is saying that his trip was successful; the wolf, whom he will shortly identify, has been incapacitated and has lost every advantage.

77. Jan. 27

78. In Strieter's Feb. 3 complaint to Reim (see no. 1061), he identifies this congregation's administrator as Buchholz, thus identifying the congregation as what is today Emmanuel Lutheran, Big Mecan, to the east of Montello.

Now since it did not work to address the congregation *in pleno* [as a whole], I had as many as possible invited to a schoolhouse, in order to negotiate with them after delivering a sermon. I think I spoke carefully enough in my negotiations. I namely told the people that I had not come to force my way in on them *à tout prix* [at all costs]. I had heard, though, that they had released their current pastor. Now since they were certainly not obligated, as an unaffiliated congregation, to take another preacher from the Missouri Synod, there was perhaps an opportunity for the Wisconsin Synod to right a wrong that had been committed against their will. We had sent them a preacher earlier;[79] he had proven unfaithful; now we would supply them a faithful one, if we were given the opportunity.

The men in attendance, c. seventeen, declared themselves to a man in favor of the Wisconsin Synod and also remarked in addition that they were annoyed with Strieter, not on account of his admonitions but on account of his crudity. He called them dogs, asses, swine, etc.

At this point there was nothing further we could do with this congregation for the present, other than to give them the suggestion, in a careful way, that they, if by chance the matter were to come up in the entire congregation on Sunday, they[80] should not simply let a preacher of the Missouri Synod be foisted upon them by Strieter and a few administrators.

On the ensuing Sunday[81] I rode with Kern a distance of some seventeen miles to Congregation *d*. This congregation was abandoned by Strieter, or rather forced into separating by his authoritarian, Missourian-papistic conduct.[82] He had simply decreed that the services in this congregation would be discontinued and the people should come to the services of the other congregations. They would not put up with this and accordingly sent an orderly call to Kern, who took them into his service.

It was in this congregation that I now preached. There were also a number of members from Congregations *e* and *f* present. After the sermon I expressed myself in a similar way as I had to Congregation *b*. An old teacher who opposed me I reduced to complete silence.[83] He said the congregations had already called a pastor. I asked, "Who? The administrators, or the congregation after a meeting was held?" "No, the administrators." "Okay," I said, "then it is not true what you say, sir, that the congregation has called the new preacher." After that the good man was completely compliant.

The way the song ended was that the people from Congregations *e* and *f* declared they wanted to have me as their pastor. Even three men from Congregation

79. I.e., Konrad Diehlmann

80. This redundancy is also in Hoenecke's original.

81. Jan. 29

82. This paragraph shows that this is the same congregation, the so-called Schmidt congregation, discussed in Kern's Jan. 5 letter to Reim and in Strieter's protest and Feb. 3 complaint to Reim—nos. 803, 1061, and 1057, respectively.

83. Perhaps Wilhelm Fierke, who was forty-seven at the time.

e did this, all three of which have the name Tagatz and carry the greatest respect in that congregation. I was supposed to come with them immediately; they wanted to present me to the congregation and elect me. Kern indicated to them that I could not come, but we would send them a capable man. They were satisfied and said if someone from the Wisconsin Synod came and was a capable preacher, they would rather elect him than one from the Missouri Synod, since then the congregation that had gone to Kern would also rejoin them.

So at this point the circumstances in these congregations are very favorable.

From the other congregation (*b*), another report came to me Monday morning, that there too the greater part want to go to the Wisconsin Synod and, if Strieter stays or appoints a Missourian as his successor, they will secede from the congregation, since Strieter has declared all those who wanted to go to the Wisconsin Synod to be condemned.

So there too we have the best odds going for us. For even those who are perhaps inclined toward Missouri will not let it come to a separation. For they can never keep a preacher only as a partial congregation, and even if this congregation were not divided up, they would give in as soon as Congregations *e* and *f* declare themselves for us, and that, as I already said, is beyond question. The reason why even those sympathetic to Missouri do not want to have it come to a separation is that the congregations are quite dreadfully poor. They can only support a preacher sufficiently if they all stay together.

Now it is up to you to act. A man must be sent there to give an election sermon[84] as quickly as possible. If we send a capable man, we win everything; if we don't send one, we win nothing. For my mission field will have hardly expected that my goal was to induce the people to declare themselves for our synod as a whole and to make them eager, then to wait quietly until we can send them a man when we get the chance. I believe Baikmann would be energetic enough for the field of labor; the only concern would be whether he too would not expose himself with respect to his teaching. For there are a number of people there who know very well what Lutheran teaching is.

In conclusion, I should just remark that, first of all, there is no prospect of all these congregations joining the synod with firm commitment. Strieter didn't secure that either. But we are still able to do everything necessary to gain a firm footing there. Remember, it is almost an entire county that we are gaining.

I will now settle a few more unrelated business matters right away. First, the report that Gensike, Lauer, Ewert, Hass, Sauer, and Thiele have received their mission money. I had previously written to Opitz in keeping with the conference resolution and his letter does not give any occasion for sending him money. He himself declines it.

Second, it will soon be time, I think, to convoke another conference. Perhaps for the end of February or beginning of March. I just wanted to remind you in this

---

84. That is, a trial sermon which would (hopefully) prompt the people to elect him as their pastor.

connection that Br[other] Mayerhoff has asked me that the conference take place by him this time.

I would gladly send you the ordination certificate for Klein right away, but I do not have time to draw it up right this moment.

A warmhearted greeting then. Do something with respect to the Indian land. One more thing. There will naturally be a coarse article in *Der Lutheraner*; I think people will ignore it completely.

Greet your wife and sister.

Your brother in Christ,
Adolph Hoenecke

No. 1059: J. J. Kern to Synod President Gottlieb Reim

Princeton, Greenlake [sic] Co., Wis.
Feb. 2, 1865

Rev. G. Reim
Helenville, Jefferson Co., Wis.

Dear Brother Reim!
Reverend Mr. President!

Br[other] Hoeneke [sic] will have reported to you everything as he found it here. Pastor Strieter is completely ticked off at me and was even going around in my congregation this week and reading the enclosed protest to them,[85] and trying, if possible, to incite the people against me. Everywhere in this protest, however, Strieter does not tell the truth. It is not true that the Schmidt congregation was offered the fourth Sunday; at this point they would certainly be ready to take anything. It is not true that I am sneaking into houses hither and thither; I simply went to Administrator Buchholz in the Mecan congregation and entreated him, since Strieter was going away and two other preachers are supposed to preach, that a preacher of our synod also be permitted a hearing, since the majority of the congregations were in favor of the Wisconsin Synod anyway. I did not offer myself and took [*ging*] the usual path. It is not true that I am emitting my poison against Strieter on all sides; I rather acknowledged the merits of Strieter everywhere when I had the opportunity and it does not occur to me to drive him away, but since he himself is leaving and he and the congregations have mutually given themselves up, we the Wisconsin Synod have just as much right as the Missourians to send them a preacher for election. But Strieter wants to foist one on the people, even if it should cause the congregations to split. In the Mecan congregation

---

85. See next letter.

the majority have now seceded and are loudly demanding a preacher from us or wish to merge with Princeton; the Tagatz and Newton congregations are unanimously for us. Under these circumstances it is necessary to send them a preacher at once, then we will have won. If we do not, Strieter might still succeed in smuggling a preacher in for them and then it will be too late for us. The people would like Br[other] Hoeneke best; he was to everyone's liking and in order to win a congregation for good, it would certainly be good if he would follow that call. There is no danger of the synod losing Farmington anymore. Besides, this area is larger and more important.

The congregation among whom the Methodists have gained ground has adopted the church constitution of the Wisconsin Synod and twenty heads of household have signed and wish to be taken up into the affiliation of the Wisconsin Synod. Br[other] Hoeneke promised to preach there on Monday, but did not keep his word so that he could be with Br[other] Thiele for a day. When I arrived, besides our people all the Methodists were also there; they were all waiting for something new. I had the text from Isaiah 45[:22]: "Turn to me and you will be saved, all you ends of the world," and the four parts: Who is speaking; to whom; what he promises; on what condition. During the first three parts, which pleased the Meth[odists], the Amen calls, the God-grant-its and so forth, and other cries eventually grew so great, that I had every fear that my preaching would be completely interrupted, as well as the people's meditation; accordingly told the people to refrain from such noise, since that didn't come from the Spirit but from the flesh. But now they started laughing, talking softly, I thought they might start kicking each other with their feet and so forth. In the fourth part I came to the Luth[eran] way of salvation and repudiated the Method[ist] method, spoke of baptism and the Supper and their significance as sacraments, yet in a gentle way, inviting more so than repelling. After the blessing, the Methodists then surrounded me and directed a question at me; instead of referring them to the sermon they had just heard, I started to answer them, only before I had said a few words, the uproar of the Methodists, the women and men, was already so great that I could not understand myself anymore. A few called me a liar, etc., and it took great effort for us to reach the doors. When our administrator called for silence, he was shouted down; they also had a right to speak here, etc. In short, it was a comedy and there was a real threat of a large-scale brawl. But our people conducted themselves quite peacefully and the wrath of those people unconverted to the truth and their fanaticism could be very clearly seen there. These people are so angry at me that they could kill me, and I now understand Br[other] Hoeneke, who wanted to avoid such an encounter with them and told me ahead of time they would surround me like a swarm of bees.

Please inform me, sir, whether anyone will come for the congregations in the Indianland, and who it is. I will then gladly relinquish the congregation in Crystallake [sic], which is way out of the way for me, in favor of a congregation in my vicinity which has likewise been served by Strieter till now. But please send someone as soon as possible, if possible Br[other] Hoeneke, and all will be right.

Excuse my haste and the fact that I am sending a sheet smudged with ink; my little boy knocked the ink over and I had neither time nor inclination to copy it again. With warmhearted greetings to your dear family and wishes for improvement of health for you yourself, I remain:

United with you in Christ,
J. J. Kern

P.S. Two delegates from the Mecan congregation were just here and shared with me that on February 12 Strieter is preaching there again and then it will be decided whether the entire congregation is going to turn to the Wisconsin Synod or if a separation will take place. Whether our party as the majority would keep the church or as the minority be forced to hold services in the schoolhouse, they were commissioned in the event of a separation to call me as their spiritual shepherd. But the people would prefer it if the congregation stayed united and then, as a congregation more than a hundred families strong, got a preacher of their own, who also understood English though, so that he could also run the district school. In that case two preachers should be sent here, one for this congregation and one for the congregations where Strieter lives, namely Newton with c. forty to fifty families I'm guessing, Schmidt's with twenty-one families, Tagatz's with eighty families, the one in Neshkoroh [sic] with fourteen families and from Harrisville with c. twelve to fifteen families, and one congregation with forty families would still fall to me. Strieter is trying everything, however, to retain at least one portion and portions of his congregations for his synod. I therefore ask that you not spare any effort. The congregations will gladly triple the salary. The reason Strieter received little from those many people was because he was unpopular.

As I heard from my confirmands today, the Methodists have uttered actual threats on my life, and I was warned by a few of our members to watch myself with a few Methodists. Big promises were also made to some of our faithful members if they went to the Methodists. Other flatteries are being attempted with others.

J. J. Kern

No. 1057: J. J. Kern's Copy of Strieter's Public Protest

Copy[86]

---

86. This protest is the one referred to in no. 1061, but this copy was made by J. J. Kern and enclosed with the previous letter (no. 1059), as that letter itself makes clear, together with his editing (see nn. 90 & 99) and handwriting here. The original protest appears to have been composed between Thursday and Saturday, Jan. 26–28, 1865.

I. N. J.[87]

Protestation and public testimony,
as I intend to answer for it before God's holy countenance,
and which every truth-loving heart will corroborate for me.

First: I protest against it when I am reproached *with having abandoned the congregation at Schmidt's*. It is true that Sundays, on which they had had services for five years, were taken away from them. But who was responsible for that? Did Strieter do that or the congregation at Donning's? Whoever says that Strieter did it is grossly lying against the truth. No, that congregation did it, as is publicly known. And why did they do it? Because it is, in fact, completely unnecessary that three devotions be held within such a short distance as that between Tagatz Schoolhouse and Donning's church (eight miles), as I myself frequently attested. At two stations, namely in the schoolhouse and there in the church, is enough, and all the people can either come this way or go over there, and in so doing can have God's word every two weeks instead of every four weeks. Nevertheless, at the time I protested in all earnest against the demands of the congregation at Donning's, as is also publicly known, and I wanted to see the old arrangement continue until we had also built a church here,[88] and it was actually for the sake of love that I wanted it, so that we wouldn't snub these people, since they didn't want to go along with those folks'[89] idea. But when those folks followed through with their plans, we held a meeting in the schoolhouse at Tagatz's, at which the majority from the Schmidt congregation were present. There they were given the option of going to the church at Donning's, which those folks also invited them to do, as Schwanke's letter openly testifies; they were given the second option of coming this way to us in the schoolhouse; they were given the third option that the congregation at Tagatz's would relinquish a Sunday to them every four weeks (but not until after the Schmidt congregation had already called and elected Pastor Kern and had already been served by him for some time)[90]; they were given the fourth option that I would preach to them during the week as often as they desired. Is this not the honest truth? Or where is there a person so depraved as to deny this? And who can now maintain, in the face of this truth, that Strieter has abandoned them? The congregation at Schmidt's listened as these offers were made, but did not definitively agree to anything. They did not say what they were thinking, but at the end they took their leave of us on friendly terms, so that we were all of the opinion that they would come to us in the schoolhouse from now on. Only Mr. Peter Meyer said one more thing to me as he was leaving: "It

---

87. Abbrev. for *In nomine Jesu*: "In the name of Jesus."

88. Namely, at or near Tagatz's, to replace the schoolhouse as a worship facility.

89. "Those folks" in this paragraph always refers to the congregation at Donning's in the town of Newton.

90. This parenthetical remark was added by J. J. Kern.

will become church as usual in time, but the fact that those folks are now going to get their way is a thorn in my heart." Dear Meyer, are those not your words? Yet look what happened! Without saying a word to us, without renouncing me, behind our backs, they turned to Princeton and fetched the pastor there. Isn't it obvious from this that I did not abandon them, but they me, and not for any reason on my part—for I boldly challenge friend and foe in all of Injunland to show me where I have gone wrong either in teaching or in practice—but out of spite toward that congregation at Donning's, as Meyer's words clearly testify? I now wrote to these brothers, i.e. to the congregation at Schmidt's, and asked them in a brotherly and sincere manner to please recognize their wrong and to come back, but they would not listen. I will repeat this request once more here: Please consider, O you poor people, what you are doing! You are not actually despising and rejecting Strieter, which is of no consequence whatsoever. No, by your actions you are despising God your Lord himself, for it is the preaching ministry that he has established among you through my person that you are despising and rejecting, without reason, out of spite and stubbornness. Please, please consider what you are doing! God says of his preaching ministry, "Whoever despises it is despising me" [cf. Luke 10:16], and God will not be mocked [Gal. 6:7]; he will certainly take action and avenge it in due course. This shall be my final word to you. If you will not listen, then I commit you to God's justice. He knows that I have sincerely loved you all and still do; he knows that I have conducted myself among you faithfully; he knows that I have preached his word to you faithfully; he knows that I have sought nothing but your salvation; he also knows that I have not abandoned you but that you have abandoned me and deserted me behind my back. Before his throne everything will be revealed, and that is where I summon you, if you will not listen here.

Second: *I protest against Mr. Pastor Kern's conduct.* Hear this, Mr. Pastor Kern; hear this, his president, or any of his brothers who will listen; hear this, each and every truth-loving heart. This Mr. Pastor Kern came to the Schmidt folks at their request and preached to them, distributed the Supper to them, and accepted them as his congregation, without any sort of consultation with me. I protested against this in a letter dated Nov. 7, 1864, which read as follows:

> Esteemed Mr. Pastor! Since you preached in my parish without my knowledge yesterday, the Twenty-Fourth Sunday after Trinity, my duty compels me to address the following lines to you: According to Acts 20:28, where the H. Spirit, through the mouth of St. Paul, exhorts the bishops or parish supervisors [*Pfarrherrn*] not just at Ephesus, but up until the Last Day, with the following words: "So attend to yourselves and to the entire flock, among which the H. Spirit has appointed you," and so on—it is clear, or at least it should be even to a child, that the bond between a pastor and his congregation is no mere human one, but a divine one. When therefore a congregation, or a portion of one, or even just a single member, wishes to separate from their[91] rightful

---

91. The pronoun used here and for the following "them," which could be either masculine or

APPENDIX IX: J. J. KERN LETTERS

pastor (and thus the one appointed for them by God) and to join themselves to one strange and unfamiliar to them, then it is the stranger's duty, according to *Scripture, conscience,* and *natural law,* to inquire of the pastor loci[92] as to what is going on, so as to learn whether he has the right and duty to enter into the desired union or not. This you did not do, sir. Instead, without my knowledge, you invaded my congregation by preaching to those people, who are members of my congregation; who have never pointed out, nor are able to point out, the slightest wrong either in my teaching or in my practice; who never emitted even a single word to me about wanting to separate from me and to turn to Princeton; to whom, after devotions in the schoolhouse at Schmidt's were discontinued, the congregation to which they had previously belonged offered the free use of their church; to whom the congregation in which I live offered the free use of their schoolhouse, i.e. that they could go to church by us; to whom I offered to preach to them during the week as often as they desired. In 1 Peter 4:15 you are forbidden from meddling in another man's ministry, which is what you have done. In the Seventh, Ninth, and Tenth Commandments you are forbidden from breaking into your neighbor's house, and his congregation even more so, since that is and must be much more precious to him than all earthly possessions, for it is his flock that has been entrusted to him by God. Now if you still have any sort of conscience in your body, then please put away this wickedness from your hands, yes, if you are a man who simply lays claim to a manly character, then do what is right and just. But if you have committed this sin knowingly and intentionally, then please know that you are an unprincipled, feckless person, a vagabond[93] and fanatic [*Schwärmer*], yes, not even a real man, but a scamp. J. Strieter

To this letter, in which I thus pointed out to Mr. Pastor Kern that it had been his duty according to Scripture, conscience, and natural law (the last of which even a respectable heathen still observes) first to inquire of me as to what was going on before he took over my congregation; that it had therefore been a godless action on his part; that, if he had done it out of ignorance, he should put away this wickedness from his hands; but if he had done it out of spite, that he was a scamp—I received the following reply from him, dated Dec. 21, 1864:

Esteemed Mr. Pastor Strieter! I received your letter from the seventh of last month and would have replied to you at once, had I not preferred to speak with

---

neuter, reflects the fact that Strieter especially has in mind "a portion of [a congregation]." The German word for *portion* can be either masculine or neuter, but *congregation* is feminine. In some places Strieter refers to all of his preaching stations together as his congregation (as he is doing here), but in others, he refers to each preaching station as a congregation (as he does later in this letter).

92. I.e., the local pastor, or the pastor of that place.

93. German: *Läufer*, lit. "runner." It seems here to denote someone who runs around from place to place, finding work (or income) wherever and however he can. It was even occasionally used of pirates.

you about the matter in person. In general, I had been wanting to make your acquaintance for some time already, which is also why I have extended you the invitation several times now, through some of your members, to visit me when you are driving past my house in Princeton. As for the Schmidt congregation, they turned to me for a guest sermon without my involvement or foreknowledge, after they had been abandoned and forsaken by you. Before I preached there and before I later took over the congregation, I asked for the exact reasons for the separation from their previous pastor, as I did not wish to promote disorder or to meddle in another man's ministry, and I also stand on the same confessional foundation as the Hon. Missouri Synod, namely on the collective confession of the Evangelical Lutheran Church. Not until I had made sure that you yourself had abandoned the congregation did I yield to the desire of those people and take the congregation into my service. And I had every right and duty to do so, and a number of different preachers of the Hon. Missouri Synod have preceded me in doing likewise. But I regret that I now have to see and hear you resorting to vulgarities and seeking everywhere to call my name and character into question, even as your letter itself exudes hostility. That is also why I then did not wish to visit you, sir. Instead I will inform you by this means that I have taken the above-named congregation into my service and from now on consider it to be my own. A tough log requires . . . This proverb occurred to me, only I was too ashamed to be a tough wedge.[94] J. J. Kern.

(What fine and holy shame! But wrongfully taking over my congregation for me—you weren't too ashamed to do that. This is exactly what the fanatics, the Methodists, do. When confronted with the truth, they refuse to give it one syllable's worth of its due, but start complaining right away about the rudeness they have to endure, and then they want to be holy, innocent martyrs after the fact. How can a person not think of the fable of the wolf and the sheep here? The wolf stood upstream and accused the lamb of muddying the water for him.[95] So Mr. Kern commits the most horrible injustice against me and yet passionately complains when I tell him so.) To this letter I replied with one dated Dec. 28, '64, which read as follows:

Mr. Kern! So you are going to continue to serve the congregation at Schmidt's. Propping yourself up with this supposed fact: I abandoned them. Did I not write to you, sir, that after church at Schmidt's discontinued, the congregation at Donning's offered them the free use of their church (where they were going

---

94. The full German proverb is: *Auf einen groben Klotz gehört ein grober Keil*, "A tough log requires a tough wedge." To paraphrase: Rudeness must be met with rudeness. In other words, Kern had thoughts about replying to Strieter's insults in kind, but thought better of it and chose the high road.

95. To summarize the fable: The wolf wants to eat the lamb, but since the lamb looks helpless and innocent, he tries to find a good reason for doing so. He first accuses her of muddying the water. When the lamb points out that he is upstream, he accuses her of spreading lies about him the previous year. When the lamb says she wasn't born until the present year, the wolf accuses her brother, and eventually says, "It was someone in your family anyway," and carries her off. The moral of the story is that the unjust will always find an excuse for their injustice and will not listen to the reasoning of the just.

not all that long ago), until we had built one;[96] that the congregation at Tagatz's offered them their schoolhouse; that I offered them that I could preach to them during the week? Where is the abandoning here? This is a change in service arrangement, nothing more. They still had God's word and sacrament; yes, if they would have gone along with the last arrangement, they would have had it more than before. It is a shameful lie to say that they were abandoned. No, they were the ones who abandoned us out of spite toward those folks,[97] without saying a word, and then turned to you. So who told you that they were abandoned? They did. But you should have listened to me, the other party, to learn if it was so. How can you be certain, if you have not heard the other party, and if the other party is in fact loudly protesting against it? I ask you, sir: What would you think of the sort of ruler who, after Fritz had complained to him that Hans had tried to kill him, tied Hans up to a tree without further ado, without questioning Hans? You don't even have to tell me! The person who tramples on every rule of justice has either no understanding or is a profoundly feckless person. But you, sir, have acted just like that kind of ruler, for as soon as you heard their complaint, you declare them in the right and condemn me for having abandoned them, without even listening to me to learn if it was so. I stand by my position; I have not spoken rudely and crudely, but *truthfully*. When you say, "Your letter exudes hostility," you should know that I cherish no hostility toward your person and it is impossible for me to do so, since personal hostility always presupposes personal acquaintance. But now if I still have never met you, how can I have hostility toward such a person? But I am genuinely hostile to your feckless action. When you say that you "stand on the same confession," I ask you: Are your actions found in Article 14 of the Augustana[98]? Do you call it an *orderly* call when that congregation says to you, "Come," and you come, without first consulting me, their rightful pastor, whom they had never renounced or who had never renounced them, but on the contrary had made them every possible offer? From my brothers in my synod, I do not know a single case where one of them has intruded on the ministry of another like you have in mine. I am thus obligated by love to regard it as a lie until you prove it. When you reproach me for not having visited you, you should know that I have been here for five years and you for one-half. Reason would therefore dictate that the onus was on you to visit me, not the other way around. Please be so kind as to apprise me of your president, along with his post office. J. Strieter

96. By "we," Strieter seems to mean the portion of his parish that met at Tagatz's schoolhouse, though it is unclear whether Kern would have understood that.

97. As in the first part of his protest, Strieter is referring to the portion of his parish that met at the church at Donning's, but again, it is unclear whether Kern would have recognized the antecedent.

98. Another name for the Augsburg Confession, from its Latin name, *Confessio Augustana*. Article 14 reads: "Regarding the supervision of the church, we teach that no one should publicly teach or preach or administer the sacraments in the church without a call issued in a regular and orderly way."

To this letter I received the following reply, dated Jan. 17, 1865:

> Mr. Strieter! I would have very gladly gathered information from you about this dubious matter before serving them, except that I am aware of cases where such inquiries were made of pastors of the Missouri Synod in similar affairs, in the friendliest way, and these Missouri Synod gentlemen replied in such a coarse and vulgar way—like bullies and ragamuffins might typically reply, but not a civilized person, let alone an honest Lutheran pastor. Your own letter is a strong testimony that you are accustomed to behaving in the same way, and certainly no one is to be blamed if he prefers to avoid such obscene letters for his own part. I also make absolutely no claim on being recognized by you as an orthodox Lutheran, and am far from viewing you as a model orthodox Lutheran. And it would not be difficult to prove that your synodical brothers have intruded on the ministry of other pastors, only I will also avoid doing this, since there is every reason to fear that a person could be treated to vulgarities—something I am not fond of. You can rest assured, sir, that I constantly make it my business to study the precious Augustana diligently and to order my practice according to it. J. J. Kern.
>
> P.S. I should also note that I do not expect any more replies from you. J. J. Kern.

So I cannot reply anymore to this letter, since Mr. Kern has forbidden it. I therefore have to do it here. He would have very gladly obtained information from me, but he was aware of cases, etc. My, my! How nicely the gentleman knows how to get himself out of a predicament. Will that also vindicate you before God—that you had to commit wrong and robbery because you were avoiding vulgarities? And how did you know about me, before I had even written, that I would treat you like a bully? Yeah, yeah, that's what a guy has to say. That's what all fanatics, vagabonds, prowlers, robbers, and wolves do, which is what my Mr. Kern now perfectly shows himself to be. Or am I going too far again? Am I using vulgarities again with this fine, esteemed gentleman, who is so genuinely Lutheran and so diligently studies the Augustana, especially Article 14, on the legitimate call? Well then, I will prove that my accusation is true. Here follows another letter, from Mr. Kern's quill, which a congregation member brought over to me. It reads thus:

> My dear Mr. Schmidt! On Jan. 29 I will preach by you as arranged and will bring along another brother of our synod with me. I ask you therefore to pick us up already on Saturday and also to make arrangements with the people accordingly and, if it would be possible, also at one more place, e.g. in the Tagatz schoolhouse or in Newton, since it is maybe possible and also best for all the congregations to assemble there to elect a preacher of our synod as successor to Pastor Strieter who, as I heard, is going to be leaving the congregations. Now, I am placing all confidence in you, sir, to arrange everything wisely as

may prove best for the church. May the Lord be pleased to direct everything for the best. With warmhearted greetings to you and your dear family, I remain: United with you in the Lord, J. J. Kern, Pastor

Is is still not clear that Mr. Kern is a prowler, a wretched person, and a wolf?! He does not content himself with taking a portion of my congregation to himself without my knowledge and consent, but he also wishes to unite my entire parish under his scepter, and in order that he may better succeed in doing so, he plans to bring another man with him. So I am not asking Christians anymore; I ask heathens, Turks, and Jews, yes, oxen and cows: Is it right, is it Lutheran, is it Christian, is it manly to try to use his administrator to get a meeting organized behind my back in my congregation, which I have legitimately through an orderly call, in my schoolhouse, in my church? Is this not going about things the way Methodists and Satan do, trying to oust me so secretly? Is it not the stuff of robbers, bullies, and ragamuffins, is it not the stuff of thieves and swindlers to steal my congregations away from me like this—congregations at which I have faithfully labored for five years under much trouble and difficulty, under sighs and prayers to God—and in this way to reap where I have sown? And my administrators told me this past Tuesday that Mr. Kern has done the same not just here, but everywhere, i.e. in my other congregations too; has already offered and smuggled himself in everywhere; already demanded over yonder at Buchholz's that they should open the church for him so he could preach there (that's not true; he merely asked the administrator to let a Wisconsin preacher preach too, before it came time to choose, since, as people were telling me[99] everywhere, the majority of the congregation members would like to have a preacher of the Wisconsin Synod and the congregation did not actually belong to the Missouri Synod). If Mr. Kern does bring one of his brothers along, then I hereby appeal to that man's conscience—seeing as Mr. Kern has thus revealed himself to be an infamous person—and call upon him to judge in this matter. I will listen and see if he also sanctions and approves of this. Whoever he is, let him hold on to these simple facts: Kern is taking over my congregation without saying one little word to me; he is sneaking around in my congregation, as his letter and many witnesses prove, is soliciting and cajoling and trying in this way to make the flock averse to its rightful shepherd. How is this not shameful, robber-like, and wolfish? Is this not a sin against the Seventh, Eighth, and Ninth Commandments, against Peter's saying that no one should meddle in another man's ministry [1 Pet. 4:15]? All of you, you who have even a little regard for God's word, a little fear of God, judge. If you sanction this along with Kern and his party, then know that you are wolves, thieves, robbers, and swindlers along with him and will have the devil's blessing for your reward. But if you do not sanction it, then open up your muzzle with me to rebuke such godless and robber-like conduct.

---

99. The switch to the first person pronoun here, together with the content of the remark as a whole, betrays that this parenthetical remark was added by Kern.

To close, I will insert here a short excerpt from Luther:

> The secret preachers [*Winkelprediger*] go sneaking around in houses without a call and emitting their poison, before the parish supervisor is aware of it. These are the thieves and murderers of whom Christ speaks in John 10:8, who intrude on church domains belonging to others, who meddle in another man's ministry that has not been committed to them, but forbidden to them.[100] Each and every parish supervisor has his appointed church domain or parish, which St. Peter in his first epistle also therefore calls a *kleros* (5:3), i.e. a portion, so that every single one has his portion of people entrusted to him, as St. Paul also writes to Titus. Within that portion, no other person or stranger should presume to teach that man's parishioners without his knowledge and consent, either secretly or publicly, and no one should listen to him either, on pain of body and soul, but should report him and notify his parish supervisor, etc., etc.[101]

J. Strieter

No. 1061: Johannes Strieter to Wisconsin Synod President Gottlieb Reim

Chrystal [*sic*] Lake
Feb. 3, 1865

Esteemed Mr. President!

I am herewith bringing the following grievance to your attention:

Mr. Pastor Kern from Princeton broke into my parish already in the fall in a robber-like manner.

One portion of one of my congregations got angry at the other over a completely minor change to the service arrangement and—out of spite toward them and probably toward me too, though they do not say the latter, since they have no basis in fact for doing so—turned to Mr. Pastor J. J. Kern, asking him to preach to them.

Now this gentleman did not consult with me, their rightful pastor, a single syllable; instead he began serving those people immediately. I protested against this in writing, but this Mr. Kern just complains about my rudeness and refuses to discuss the matter.

I composed a lengthy protestation and public testimony, in which the whole story is treated in detail; you are welcome to it.

---

100. Cf. Erlangen Ausgabe 39:253; Weimarer Ausgabe 31/1:210.

101. Cf. EA 39:254; WA 31/1:211. Strieter appears to have taken this quote from a secondary source; it is very similar to the wording found on the cover page of *Der Lutheraner* 2, no. 18 (May 2, 1846). However, he does cite the EA in his Feb. 3, 1865 letter to Gottlieb Reim (see next letter).

In the meantime I receive a call letter from Illinois and no sooner did Mr. Kern hear this than he went and got himself an accomplice, Hennicke,[102] and the two gentlemen went to my larger congregation, completely behind my back, and demanded of the administrator (Buchholz) that he open the church for them so that they could address the people—and without further ado messengers were sent around to invite the people to the church on Saturday, Jan. 28. When he refused them this, they, Hennicke,[103] preached in the schoolhouse and offered the people that they would get them a capable man from their synod, etc. They went on Sunday, Jan. 29, to that renegade bunch[104] and also spurred those people on—and there were plenty there from my congregations—to take a preacher of their synod.

All of this is happening in a congregation that has been mine as long as I have been here—and I have not even accepted that call yet—without anyone having invited or requested them.

Do you approve of this, sir? Can you reconcile this with 1 Peter 4:15; with Article 14 of the Augustana;[105] with Luther's testimony against the sneaking preachers in the Erlangen Edition, volume 31, page 214, and volume 39, page 253, etc.?

Please, sir, take action in this matter that is in keeping with the duty of your office.

Whether Hennicke is the correct name of that gentleman, I do not know for sure. He is supposedly a pastor in or near Watertown and the secretary of your synod.[106]

Signing myself most respectfully,
J. Strieter, Pastor
Address: Harrisville, Marquette Co., Wis.

No. 1076: J. J. Kern to Synod President Gottlieb Reim

Princeton
Feb. 20, 1865

Rev. G. Reim
Helenville, Jefferson Co., Wis.

Dear Brother Reim!

---

102. See n. 106.

103. Both men were present, but "Hennicke" (see n. 106) preached the sermon.

104. I.e., the Schmidt congregation

105. Another name for the Augsburg Confession, from its Latin name, *Confessio Augustana*. Article 14 reads: "Regarding the supervision of the church, we teach that no one should publicly teach or preach or administer the sacraments in the church without a call issued in a regular and orderly way."

106. Nos. 1058 and 1059 confirm that it was in fact Adolf Hoenecke, the secretary of the synod, who accompanied Kern. Hoenecke was serving in Farmington at the time, roughly ten miles south of Watertown. (Hoenecke was subsequently called to Watertown itself in 1866.)

Pastor Zernecke is now pastor in the Indianland and will move up with his family this week yet and will have his residence just one to two miles from Pastor Strieter, who now intends to stay back, or rather to stay a while longer for the present, since it seems it was only a lie that he had a call from another congregation! Now he will get his passport, however, since staying will no longer be an option for him. Pastor Zernecke now has two congregations for the time being, with c. a hundred families combined, and there is not the slightest doubt that the remaining congregations won't fall to him one and all, and it now makes me sincerely happy that I was enabled to bring this affair that had been commenced to such a speedy conclusion through the arrival of Pastor Zernecke.

Now I just wish that *Berlin-Dartford* is soon occupied by a man who can put a stop to the Methodists, even if he would have to have support from us,[107] for the Methodists just recently made inroads into Br[other] Thiele's area[108] and snatched a number of families away from him, and Br[other] Thiele, being inexperienced in these matters thus far, is not a match for these people in my opinion. I certainly hope that now they will not make any more advances in my area. The congregation by Sommer[109] among the Methodists now encompasses twenty-one families, and I believe these people are now reliable. They have signed the church constitution of the Wisconsin Synod and wish to be taken up into the affiliation of the synod. Though poor and mostly tenants [*Rentleute*],[110] while the landowners have gone to the Methodists, who now constitute approximately forty to fifty families, they still want to build a church this year if they get a better harvest, since the Methodists are now trying to oust us from the schoolhouse that we have been using thus far. The congregation has the name "St. Stephen's Ev. Luth. Congregation in the town of Dayton and Princeton, Greenlake [*sic*] Co., Wisconsin."

I should very much wish that a conference were formed here under the name "Fox River Conference," since it is too far for us to attach ourselves to the Central Conference. At the same time, I hope that many more fields of labor can be discovered and filled within this area.

With warmhearted greetings to your dear family, sir, I remain:

Your brother in Christ,
J. J. Kern

---

107. I.e., financial support from the synod

108. G. Thiele is listed as being stationed in Ripon in the 1865 synod convention proceedings.

109. The same congregation that he previously described as belonging to Pastor Diehlmann.

110. In its original, proper sense, *Rentleute* or, more commonly, *Rentner* were people who lived off of *Renten*—regular, especially annual, revenues or earnings—and were not salaried by others. Today *Rente* usually denotes a pension, and so *Rentner* are pensioners or senior citizens. Kern, however, seems to be using the term in opposition to *Gutsbesitzer* or landowners.

No. 1091: J. J. Kern to Synod President Gottlieb Reim

Princeton, Greenlake [sic] Co., Wis.
March 2, 1865

Rev. G. Reim
Hellenville [sic], Wis.

Dear Brother in Christ!

I received your letter dated Feb. 24 yesterday. Pastor [August] Zernecke has been in his congregation in Crystallake [sic], which I relinquished to him, since last Friday, thus for almost a week, together with his son. His wife and daughter are still with us though. The former had a strong attack of dysentery, probably as a result of catching cold. As I understand it, however, Pastor Zernecke has still not taken a single step toward obtaining the other congregations; until that has happened, the work is only half done. In the Mecan congregation there are sixty-eight members who have declared themselves in favor of Zernecke, thus the vast majority. It was Br[other] Zernecke's wish that I conduct his installation there next Sunday, except I thought better of it. I have no commission from you as the president, and with the bad postal communication it would probably be too late to get a reply if I submitted a request. In addition, it is better if someone else does the installing, seeing as I am still not actually a member of the synod anyway and the people could also say that the matter was proceeding from me, since the Strieter party simply hates me now. In addition, the administrators still have the keys to the church and are Strieter's strongest adherents, and the Strieter or Missourian party is refusing to surrender the church, even though no church constitution, much less a formal joining of the Missouri Synod, has ever been made, so the congregation has the freedom to elect whomever she wants, and now the disgruntled minority still want to claim the property of the ~~church~~ congregation. I hear the deed is made out to the administrators, but they are still in place only in the name of the congregation. The day before yesterday two people from there were at my place and asked me for advice. I gave it as best I could and am convinced that they are within their rights and if the minority leaves [*abtritt*],[111] they should simply elect themselves new administrators and on Sunday, after the Missourians have read their sermon, they should stay and Pastor Zernecke should preach and they should assert their rights, then the Missourians might sue. But that is why I believe it would be good if you yourself came here to conduct an investigation and also the installation. We admittedly cannot charge Strieter of anything either in teaching or in conduct that would have significance (though there have been plenty of lies), but the question is whether I and Br[other] Hoenecke are wolves and Br[other] Zernecke is the devil, as

---

111. It seems like a *nicht* ("not") is missing here, so that the clause would read: "and if the minority does not give in."

Strieter preaches, whether we have committed any injustice at all, whether we have been sneaking around, if we are accepting an orderly call without having a hand in getting it, from a congregation to whom their old preacher has given notice and abandoned and from whom he has been released by any standard of justice, and which has also never let itself be persuaded to join the Missouri Synod, has in fact specifically declared that it never wants a Missourian again. We are fully within our rights and this judgment would have to be awarded to us in any investigation. Go right ahead and offer Strieter an investigation. Besides, Strieter will leave his position here in just a few days and move to his new position; but then a candidate from St. Louis is supposed to come here, and for the time being individual Missouri preachers are going to fill the position. It won't come to that, however. I hope Br[other] Zernecke will succeed in winning everyone yet, since those who are firmly committed to Strieter and have their own opinion are only very few and the scales will fall from the eyes of those people too. Strieter was asked one day by one of his members, who was at his place along with four or five others of his adherents: "So what is the actual difference between the Missouri and Wisconsin Synods?" Str[ieter] said, "Sure, let me tell you. We distribute Christ's body and blood in the Supper, but the Wisconsin men distribute mere bread and wine, like the Methodists and all the sects." That was something new to the previously zealous adherent of Strieter; he said, "Yeah, then they certainly have no rights." But in order to make sure about it, the man comes to me the next day and asks me very concisely how we distribute the Holy Supper. At first I didn't understand him, but once I noticed that it had to do with the doctrine, I told him the answer and as proof I showed it to him black and white in the agenda. Then the man, quite astonished, related the occurrence with Strieter to me and said, "So Strieter is a liar and slanderer," and since then he's been standing behind us most zealously.

A man from Mecan just told me that Strieter and the administrators were in Montello last Monday and had the deed for the congregational property changed and reworded. If that's true, what can we do?

It is therefore my opinion that it would be good if you would set up an investigation right away and install Pastor Zernecke afterwards. In addition, you would then also get better acquainted with the circumstances here, which I cannot describe that well for you in writing.[112]

Greeting you warmheartedly, together with your dear family, I remain:

Your brother in Christ,
J. J. Kern

[The postal stamp on the back side of third page of this letter shows that it was mailed from Princeton on March 3.]

---

112. This is the gist of these sentences, which I cannot translate precisely due to a missing section in the original.

No. 1094: J. J. Kern to Synod President Gottlieb Reim

Princeton, Greenlake [sic] Co., Wisconsin
March 4, 1865

Rev. G. Reim
Helenville, Wis.

Dear Brother Reim!

I received your valued letter yesterday. At the same time a professor at the homeopathic institution in Chicago, Dr. Small, dean of faculty, wrote to me and I hope to follow his advice, since it seems to me to be the best. This is what he writes (in English):

> If you wish to add the profession of physician to that of the ministry I would advise you to attend the regular course from Oct 10th to March, which will qualify you very much for such duties. On attending two fall courses you can become a regular candidate for the Doctorate and then you will have something substantially beneficial in the way of aiding you in gaining a support for your family, while you serve the Lord in preaching the Gospel.

Accordingly I now plan on taking the regular course this coming winter, if God wills, and by the time I finish, it should also be clear whether or not I can attend the institution again the following year in order to earn the doctorate. The money should not be a problem for me, although I know that it will cost me a significant amount. If God grants me a fairly long life, it will yield its interest. In any case, I am more inclined toward this than toward the preaching ministry [*Predigtamt*], which I intend to give up for the present. Therefore I also entreat the Honorable Synod to send me a successor by October or sooner, since I will no longer be serving the congregations anymore. Both have shown willingness to be admitted into the synod and if a capable man comes here, he can also win a third congregation, served by Strieter thus far. We are currently in the process of purchasing the Congregationalist church here, except there are only twenty-five to thirty members we can count on safely. The others have moved away or enlisted or give nothing for God's word. But they want to put $500 towards it, if they can get it for that much. I will tender my notice to the board of administrators already on July 1. If, however, a fitting man should be found sooner, before October, you may send him here at any time.

I will probably come to the convention though, since I desire that the congregations be admitted into the synod, even though no one from the congregation can or wants to attend, and even though I myself also do not want to be admitted this time and therefore wish that no one brings it up. However, I have nothing against the synod in the least and would petition for membership if I were staying here longer. It's just that, as much as it pains me to take this step, I have to take it. More than anything else, I have to care for my family and be mindful of my health, and my health has been suffering for some time. Every little agitation, every little circumstance, e.g. in the school, brings on a tightening of my chest [*Brustbeklemmung*], fainting-like spells, often shaking, etc. On the other side, I am more in the mood for quiet studying than usual. The reason for this is precisely because all kinds of upsetting things occur daily and I try to keep my displeasure to myself. A person has to just keep quiet in response to way too many things. E.g., up till now I had a wretched church administrator, who often stayed sitting in the saloon instead of going to church; fortunately the congregation elected a different man at the last meeting. Another man, not an administrator, the rich Thiel, a horrible person, always does all the talking, e.g. at congregational meetings. I'm now holding school and give it all imaginable effort three days a week and yet many parents do not send their children, or send them to the English school. I only have c. twenty-five children at present, while I occasionally had fifty or sixty last fall and winter (from various congregations). Some people are moving on from here without paying their overdue salary. No one concerns himself with school and church affairs; I had to rent the school venue myself last fall and get it furnished out of my own pocket. And when I started up school again in a different venue last week and wanted to check on the desks and benches, more than half were missing, etc., etc. But those are trifles. On the whole there is still a small, good core here, though one has to have all patience with them. On the whole the people do a lot and make every effort, but I just cannot make do with my family with this small congregation, and since I now also have the internal liberty to take the above-mentioned step, I do not want to defer any longer. Whether I am making the best decision, only time will tell. I have no inclination to remain in the preaching ministry [*Predigtamte*] any longer. On the other hand, there is a good chance I can take on another congregation later, yet I do not want to be dependent on her. I do not believe that I am now acting of my own accord. If a respectable brother has some better advice for me in my situation, I will gladly take it, and will gladly take some chastisement and humbling too. I will always continue to have our church very much at heart.

Pastor Zernecke is indeed deep in debt, though I am very sorry to have let out any comment about it,[113] since I consider him a thoroughly honest man and think highly of him. He has also already paid off seventeen dollars to me, has likewise paid ten dollars toward a wagon that cost eighty, and the Mecan congregation has put down $155 for his horse (without harness), so that the total is no longer so great. In Chicago where he pawned his golden timepiece, he has now also paid twenty-one dollars. What he owes me is for stove, furniture, groceries, etc., all of which were the most expensive yet, especially here in this den of deceit. Then he supposedly owes

---

113. It is unclear whether Kern is referring to the words he just wrote (which appear to have been in response to something Reim wrote in his letter) or to something that Reim perhaps reported to have heard from Kern secondhand (e.g. from Thiele or Moldehnke, both of whom appear to have had some contact with Kern).

Br[other] Moldehnke fifty dollars, as Br[other] Thiele told me, and likewise P[astor] Bading.[114] Furthermore, what might his trunks cost from New York to St. Paul and then here? But unfortunately he has no news about where they are right now. They are in dire straits. They just won't admit it. Their girl told my wife they are sleeping on straw and using their clothes as covers. For this reason Br[other] Hoenecke should not install him in Crystallake [sic] but in Mecan, so that he doesn't have to visit them, which would otherwise put them in great embarrassment. Br[other] Hoenecke should just stay with me.

Other than that, if you could give me some good advice in my case, I would be sincerely grateful to you. In particulars I am still not entirely decided either as to what I should do, where to leave my family, etc. In the meantime receive warmhearted greetings from:

Your lowly brother in Christ,
J. J. Kern

No. 1098: J. J. Kern to Synod President Gottlieb Reim

Princeton, Greenlake [sic] Co., Wis.
March 8, 1865

Rev. G. Reim
Hellenville [sic], Wis.

Dear Brother in Christ!

When I brought Mrs. Pastor Zernecke, who until then had been staying with us together with her daughter, to the town of Newton, where they are now residing, I learned more exactly from various persons how matters stand. Today Pastor Strieter is retreating from there, after he has first done his utmost to make the schism in the congregations last. For the present, matters still stand as they did when P[astor] Zernecke was here the first time. He is currently serving the Schmidt congregation (hitherto served by me) and the congregation at the Mecan, where there are still c. thirteen opponents who are refusing to surrender the church. Both congregations are asking for an investigation, as you can see from the enclosed letter.[115] Since the one from the town of Mecan, which is similarly worded, did not reach me because there are no administrators there and therefore it is simply being signed by individual members and might therefore take awhile, I am sending off the one for the time being. At the

---

114. It is unclear if Zernecke likewise owes Pastor Bading fifty dollars, or if Pastor Bading likewise told Kern that Zernecke owes Moldehnke fifty dollars.

115. The enclosed letter, the request from the Schmidt congregation for an investigation, was apparently forwarded to Strieter (see no. 1108), and thus has been lost.

town of Newton the views are split, but I believe that the entire congregation there will join company with Pastor Zernecke. In the Dagatz [sic] congregation, on the other hand, twenty-eight members are firmly resolved not to let Pastor Zernecke into their schoolhouse and to be served by the Missouri Synod. Yet I believe here too it would just require some clearing up and refuting of the preconceptions and slanders and a chance for the people to hear Pastor Zernecke preach in order to win the people. The congregation closest to Princeton, which had been kindly disposed towards us up till now, has been all riled up ever since Strieter's hostilities, and Mr. Theske [sic] in particular, in whose house you have already held devotions[116] and who until seven weeks ago was almost a regular attendee of the services here, though also a venerator of Strieter. Ever since Strieter gave his notice, he has most vigorously taken his side and is seeking to stir up the people not to join company with Princeton nor with P[astor] Zernecke, since Strieter is in the right; he is saying we are wolves, thieves, and devils. Yet I hope the congregation will nevertheless turn to me. Only I cannot visit the people, so that no one may rightly be able to call me a prowler. I therefore think it would be good for you to come and spend some time here at the various congregations, investigating, mediating, and advising, so that everything can soon get back on the right track. I would not have expected this opposition from some people. But the slander is too great. Already people are insisting that Zernecke is a Methodist, that he caused various mischief in Germany, that he was forced to go to America, in short, that he is an unscrupulous man, since he is a thief who steals the sheep, even worse than the little padre [*Pfäffchen*] in Princeton, etc.

With warmhearted greetings to your dear family, I am:

Your brother in Christ,
J. J. Kern

[Written beneath Kern's signature in a different hand:]
Dear Br[other] Mold[ehnke],

I received these letters from Br[other] Kern. I am sending them to you to get your insight. Once you have finished using them, send them back to me.

With regards,
Your brother G. Reim

No. 1108: Johannes Strieter to Wisconsin Synod President Gottlieb Reim

Aurora, Kane Co., Ill.
22/3/65

---

116. See Appendix VI, nos. 144 & 145.

Esteemed Mr. President!

Your letter, sir, has been forwarded to me from Wis[consin]. I can scarcely travel back to Injunland for an investigation now, since I have just arrived here; for that the investigation would have had to be initiated earlier, while I was still there. If the congregation that was still faithful to me is ready for such an investigation, then my place can be taken by my protest, of which you possess a copy, provided that the copy is complete. Even if I were there, I could not tell you anything different than what is said there. It only ought to be noted for you here that my accusation and the letter from Schmidt that was shared with me are not contradictory like you thought. Schmidt makes a false accusation, which you will find neither in my accusation nor in my protest. He accuses me of stating that Kern had "snuck into" *their* congregation and had "alienated" them, and I never made that claim. I had four main congregations in Injunland. It was from the one in the town of Newton that those at Schmidt's, Meyer's, Bartz's separated themselves. My complaint against Schmidt's congregation was *that they separated from me without sufficient grounds*, as you will find in my protest; and the accusation against Kern in regard to this congregation was *that he accepted the congregation without first inquiring with me as to what was the matter;* but in regard to the congregation by Buchholz, in the town of Mecan, that he "snuck his way in" and "alienated" them,[117] as you will likewise find in my protest.

Yours,
J. Strieter

No. 1110: J. J. Kern to Synod President Gottlieb Reim

Princeton, Greenlake Co., Wis.
March 27, 1865

Rev. G. Reim
Helenville, Wis.

Dear Brother in Christ!

I am finally sending you the enclosed petition from the Mecan congregation.[118] I couldn't send it until now, because after I had sent off the one from the Crystallake congregation, a short letter from Brother Hoenecke arrived, which prompted me to wait for a reply from Pastor Zernecke first—a reply which has yet to come. Instead Pastor Zernecke writes me a different letter that makes it clear that he has not even

---

117. Strieter double-underlined this last clause.
118. See the next letter, no. 1095.

received that letter yet, even though I sent it off immediately.[119] The letter does say that some more people have joined. But there still remains a considerable opposing faction, who intend to call a candidate from Missouri, but I hope that doesn't happen.

In my opinion, arrangements should be made for the congregation in Berlin, which was served by Strieter every six weeks, to be served by us and not to be occupied by other Missourians again. Berlin is a very important place—even more important than Ripon in my opinion—and a preacher just for them should be stationed there right away if possible. I have no horse and have no way of getting any news about the circumstances there, otherwise I would have already gone there myself. Yet I can't stop thinking about it and if I were charged with doing so, I would go there immediately in order to gather information.

On Palm Sunday I have twenty-four children from four different congregations to confirm. My family is well and I hope the same is true for you and your dear family.

With warmhearted greetings,
Your lowly
J. J. Kern

No. 1095: Mecan Representatives to Synod President Gottlieb Reim[120]

We the undersigned most very humbly petition Your Reverence, since we have learned that Pastor Strieter has submitted accusations and charges against Pastors Kern and Hoenecke with the Wisconsin Synod for having stolen into the congregations and estranged them from Pastor Strieter, that you would submit this case to an investigation, since we wish that rest and peace would soon set in once again in the scattered congregations, and we should like it best, sir, if you yourself would assume the investigation and install our pastor while you are here.

Mecan, March 6, 1865.
Johan Bartz
Johnn [sic] Judas
Jakob Beutler
Friedrich Menge
Michael Banick
Gottlieb Tonn
Ludwig Job

---

119. That is, immediately after receiving Hoenecke's letter, Kern sent Zernecke a letter in which he asked him to respond to certain information and/or inquiries.

120. This was enclosed with the preceding letter, no. 1110. The note itself, minus the signatures, is written in Rev. August Zernecke's handwriting.

Eduard Lehmann
Jo: Schmudlach
John Otto
August Lück.

No. 1121: J. J. Kern to Synod President Gottlieb Reim

Princeton, Greenlake Co., Wis.
April 19, 1865

Rev. G. Reim
Helenville, Wis.

Dear Brother Reim!

Since my salary here is so modest that I can[121] barely manage to get by only by being very frugal, I have made up my mind, after mature deliberation and prayer and after discussion with Brother Thiele and my wife and their approval, to go to Chicago for two months until July 1 and to study homeopathy in the Hahnemann Homeopathic College[122] there. I am therefore asking for a vicar to take my place during that time. He can be a student and does not have to be ordained. He merely has to preach and to teach school a few days during the week, perhaps also attend to the funerals. I will pay the traveling expenses and give him free board and lodging, and I will send the institution some money to compensate for the loss. My congregation, to whom I won't actually be presenting this until next Sunday, should not have any objections to it. In a number of ways I can tell that my congregation loves me. It's just that she is too small and too weak overall, and the richest people do very little proportionately. Everything is in the best order and running smoothly. Except in the country congregation the Methodists are making themselves felt more than ever before. They once again held a large assembly for a week and, to my extreme sorrow (it made me very depressed for a few days), they succeeded in getting two families, who had received the Holy Supper from me on Good Friday and had even given me assurances that they would never become Methodists, and on Easter, when I did not preach there, they went to the bench of repentance and crossed over.[123] That little group is getting small, though some firmly-grounded souls do remain. I have not grudged any toil or sweat and have asked for nothing for my work, apart from what they might offer me out of free will, and these people have done nothing, and nothing was demanded from them either.

Please fulfill my wish, sir; both little congregations will join the synod. In the course of this year very many people have moved away from Princeton, which makes

---

121. This word is missing in the original.
122. The Hahnemann Medical College had opened in 1860.
123. Good Friday fell on April 14 (the day Abraham Lincoln was shot) and Easter on April 16.

the congregation smaller, but the church attendance is better than ever. (I put up security for Pastor Zernecke for c. $100.00. He already has debts of nearly $500.00, by my calculation. I fear for him.)

I will already depart next week, God willing, since the course has already begun. If I am not granted a vicar, I would actually also not be too opposed to being sent a successor, but the congregation will not be happy with that. And yet I must take this step or some other one, if I do not want to lose all my money in a few years. This is the step I therefore choose to take.

Am asking for an immediate reply. I am also writing to Prof. Mohldenke [sic]. We are all well, except I look a bit worn out. On my way to Chicago I will visit you, God willing.

Your lowly brother in Christ,
J. J. Kern

No. 1124: J. J. Kern to Synod President Gottlieb Reim

Princeton, Wis.
April 22, 1865

Rev. G. Reim
Helenville, Wis.

Dear Brother in Christ!

I would like to add the following to my last letter, which you will have received by now. Since my wife has, for a long time actually, been longing to get out of Wisconsin, and I too have no great inclination to remain here for reasons already known to you; since furthermore the Methodists make my life bitter and my poor health has actually been having a noticeable effect on me for some time now—an effect that has already astonished others too; I would therefore really appreciate it if I were completely released from my duties for a time and could get a capable successor who would continue and complete what I have built up with much toil. I wish to withdraw from the preaching ministry [Predigtamt] entirely for the time being and, with a temporary leave of absence from my family, to recover in Illinois in the company of my friends and in the next few months to receive further training in homeopathy in Chicago. I would be sad to leave this place, for I know it will upset my congregation here, since she loves me. But I have to think of my health and family first and foremost. If I were to die today, they would be in the direst of straits. And there are no provisions in the Wisconsin Synod for such cases. At present I am still able to leave [gehen],[124]

---

124. Alternate translation: "still able to get along."

since in the last few days I received another $150 from the money I have on deposit in Fond du Lac. If I do not leave, that will be used up too. About eight families from the congregation moved away from here recently, including G. Lueck among others, because the land in this area is much too poor, as this past dry summer and the resulting total crop failure made all too clear. Nevertheless, $280 in preacher's salary came in for me. $240 was pledged, but $320 was promised. In addition, I received forty dollars income for occasional services and c. forty dollars in school money and various gifts amounting to c. twenty dollars. I still haven't received anything from the country congregation. She will do what she can, but the people are poor. I didn't ask for anything for baptisms, funerals, school, confirmation—I was too good in that regard, receiving only $17.00 from twenty-four confirmands, so that when I subtract the expenses (certificates, gifted catechisms and unpaid-for hymnals, wood, etc.), I am left with scarcely $12.00. Yet the people generally did what they were able to and we could get by fine in a pinch. Also, some people who gave twelve dollars this year promised to do even more next year. A young man will therefore be able to get by fine, especially if he can also get the Strieter congregation closest to Princeton, which to a man has yet to join either me or Zernecke because Strieter prejudiced them against me too deeply, though many come to our services here, which are well attended overall. I am accordingly asking you for an immediate reply and for your kind opinion on the information shared above. If no successor can come, then I ask for a substitute (for two months), who can also be a student.

With warmhearted greetings to you and your dear family, I am:

Your brother in Christ,
J. J. Kern

No. 1134: J. J. Kern to Synod President Gottlieb Reim

Princeton, Greenlake Co., Wis.
May 14, 1865

Rev. G. Reim
Helenville, Wis.

Dear Brother Reim!

I know that Brother Hoenecke was just here a week ago and I had replied to your valued letter just a few days before that.[125] But I already have some more news to share.

Last Tuesday, Pastor Strassen [*sic*] from Watertown came this way to inspect the Indianland for himself, and the result of his efforts is not a happy one for us. More

---

125. This letter does not appear to be preserved in the archives.

people who ally with the Missourians are congregating there every day. The number of families already exceeds a hundred, and after Pentecost[126] a candidate from St. Louis is coming to distribute the Holy Supper there and to stay there. The congregation four to five miles from Princeton[127] is against me and Zernecke; she consists of thirty families. But she would join Princeton if another preacher were here instead of me. Otherwise she will join the Missourians and then they will gain another firm foothold. It also turns out that about five families, the more well-to-do families of our congregation, reside in that direction. One of them was an administrator, but the congregation replaced him with another man on account of bad conduct. These five families got riled up by this person and (they expressed themselves to this effect) are apparently going to join there. That will leave me with just two small congregations. Now since I was planning to leave this fall, I don't know what else to do except to beg you, sir, to send a man before Pentecost who can take over the two congregations here. Then that aforementioned congregation will also join right away and the schism will be averted. If not, a preacher will no longer be able to maintain himself here. A man like Hoenecke—who, I might say in passing, would be the perfect man for the job; he is the one they all want—would have no problem keeping the Missourians out of the field. I kept on hoping that I could win over these people by Princeton. But now I see that I am not going to. I have already foreseen this for quite some time, but I didn't really want to own up to that fact. Now it is right in front of my eyes. Swift, energetic action can still make everything right. I am now just waiting on your reply, so that I can immediately tender my notice. I will not stay any longer. My wife cannot see why I am taking this step, but this is what is necessary for the field to stay intact for the synod. All of this can still be stopped. If I don't take this step, the Missourians might once again retake the entire field.

I admittedly still do not know what to do and am looking at an obscure future. I have lost almost all courage and joy for the preaching ministry [Predigtamt], although preaching is easier for me than ever before. I am not happy to be leaving. In spite of the difficulties, the congregation has become dearer to me than any I've had and the people love me on the whole. But I view this as a necessity. At present I feel completely well again, but news like what I received today from the Indianland, as well as the Missourians, always keep beating me right to the ground. I await your news and ask for discretion. Not everything that I write to you as a brother belongs in the public forum.

Your brother in Christ,
J. J. Kern

---

126. Pentecost fell on June 4 in 1865.
127. This is the congregation that Strieter says was meeting at Peter Warnke's.

No. 1136: Princeton Administrators to Synod President Gottlieb Reim

Princeton
May 18, 1865

Your Reverence, we take the liberty of directing the following request to you:

We must give our preacher and spiritual shepherd Kern the testimonial that he has faithfully and conscientiously fulfiled[128] the duties of his office and has also concerned himself with the up-and-coming youth with all love and care. It was all the more painful for us when Preacher Kern informed us in the last few days that he was no longer willing and able to discharge the preaching position here, and as much as this news surprised and troubled us, we still cannot label his decision as anything but one that does every honor to his character, since we can do nothing but consent to the reasons that are prompting him to leave.

Your Reverence is no doubt aware that, after the departure of the previous preacher Striter [sic], west of Princeton in Marqette [sic] Co., the congregation split into two parties, the one and indeed the majority joined Preacher Zernicke [sic], while the rest insist on calling a preacher from the Missouri Synod. Preacher Strassen from Watertown Preached for them last week and urged them to faithfully cling to Luther's doctrine and the Missouri Synod and gave them reason to expect that they will receive a preacher from the Missouri Synod in June. A congregation four miles away from here have [sic] declared that if a capable, energetic man and a good speaker were entrusted with the preaching position here, they would likewise join Princeton, if this congregation joined, the calling of a preacher from the Missouri Synod would be made much more difficult or perhaps be prevented entirely, and that is what we desire with all our hearts, since we are not in agreement with the Missouri Synod. We acknowledge with all thanks the sacrifice that Preacher Kern is willing to make for the cause and therefore hope all the more that Your Reverence will, as soon as possible [sic], appoint us a preacher for the preaching position here and the congregation that wants to join and will send him this way to deliver a sermon, this is what we desire, a man that has already held a position in the Wisconsin Synod for some time and possesses the gifts needed to win over the hearts of the people. The congregation that wants to join Princeton has declared that they will not join the Missouri Synod as soon as they just receive the promise from Your Reverence that the kind of preacher they desire will soon be coming. However, in order to prevent the calling of a preacher of the Missouri Synod, it would be better if a preacher from the Wisconsin Synod were sent this way as soon as posible.

---

128. There are various misspellings, grammatical mistakes, and run-on sentences in the German original, some of which I have attempted to reflect in the English translation.

If it would be posible for Your Reverence, we beg you to come here yourself and Personally see how the circumstances are situated with your own eyes, in which case we can talk about a lot more.

Moreover, Pastor Kern has declared that, if there is the prospect of another preacher of the Wisconsin Synod coming here to serve us soon, he will stay here and discharge his office until he does.

We ask that Your Reverence would make this a matter of true urgency and either come here yourself or that you would give us a speedy answer.

With deep respect,
The administrators of St. John's Lutheran Congregation in Princeton:
G. Jahnke
C. Lemke
S. Lütke

The address is:
G. Jahnke
Princeton, Green Lake Co.
Wis.

No. 1177: J. J. Kern to Synod President Wilhelm Streissguth[129]

Princeton, Greenlake Co., Wis.
July 3, 1865

Rev. Streissguth
Milwaukee, Wis.

Reverend Brother in Christ!

I wrote to Mr. Pastor Reim, your brother-in-law, from Iowa and excused myself with regard to my absence from the convention. But as I have since learned that Brother Reim is no longer president, I'm guessing that my letter didn't even come before the convention, which is too bad. As I already shared with the president two months ago, it was advisable for me to leave my position, if it gets filled again right away. I went on a restorative trip with the secondary purpose of simultaneously looking around for a fitting place where I could remain. To that end I made a stop in

---

129. A few days before the opening of the Wisconsin Synod's annual convention on June 22, President Reim suddenly and unexpectedly resigned. Thus the presidency devolved upon the vice president, Wilhelm Streissguth (1827–1915), associate pastor at Grace Lutheran, downtown Milwaukee. Rumors circulated that President Reim had committed adultery. However, such does not appear to have been the case. See Lynn E. Wiedmann, "The Helenville Problem," https://essays.wls.wels.net.

Beaverdam [sic], but since Reim was not home, instead of going to Watertown I went to La Crosse via the train that had just arrived. Once there, I was unsure whether to go to Minnesota or down the Missisippi [sic]. I chose the latter and came to Navou [Nauvoo], Ill., where the Lutheran congregation is vacant, since the congregation dismissed her previous preacher, Eisenbach, from his office on account of adultery. Two preachers had already preached before me and in the afternoon another one preached after me. I was elected by a large majority (some of the people knew me from earlier when I was serving in Iowa) and the few who were in favor of Zaiser, when they saw that they couldn't do anything, gave their consent and only required that I bring along good testimonials from the synod. The congregation wants to have nothing more to do with the Illinois Synod, since the committee defended the preacher half and half and did a poor job. The congregation is a good one and has a good chance of tripling in size in a short time. But since for years I have no longer belonged to a synod and was not admitted this time by Wisconsin at her convention at my request, I also will not be able to take over the congregation and will consequently resign from the preaching ministry [*Predigtamt*] for good, in the event that the Honorable Wisconsin Synod should refuse me admittance and therefore also a release or testimonial. In that case, I will start a high school in Franklin Center, Lee Co., Iowa, for the well-to-do Germans there, who live there in great numbers. I attended the sessions of the Iowa Synod convention (English-German) as a guest. This synod has cleansed herself of her impure elements and has positioned herself on a firm Lutheran base. The German Conference of the synod, consisting of seven preachers, desires permission to send its pupils to Watertown and to co-support the institution there, and when I left, they asked me to greet the Wisconsin Synod and to inquire about this possibility. On account of some mild health issues that developed, I was prevented from making it to the convention in Watertown in time and therefore wrote an excuse to President Reim. My position here, which I am leaving a week from today, must now be filled right away, if it is going to be filled at all. The Methodists have been causing mischief during my short absence. They are currently holding a camp meeting with twelve preachers. Perhaps Berlin can be combined with here into a single parish. If a preacher cannot come soon, I would rather the people take a Missourian than become Methodists. I therefore ask that my three congregations be staffed as soon as possible. At the same time I ask that the enclosed dollar be accepted for synodical purposes as a contribution from my own pocket. My overdue twenty dollars as my contribution for the founding of the seminary, which I will continually support to the best of my ability, I will send in when it is more convenient for me. And now I ask to be apprised by return mail of the status of my admittance into the synod. If a letter can no longer reach me here, then please address it to Franklin Center, Lee Co., Iowa. If I were at least granted an honorable release so that I could join the Iowa Synod, I would be grateful to the Wis. Syn. I believe I have earned that much from the synod anyway. At least I am not aware of having done any wrong that would prevent me from being admitted. If I am prevented, that will mean the same for me as being removed from the preaching ministry [*Predigtamt*], since currently I can no longer be admitted into any proper synod without being able to prove that I was formally affiliated with Wisconsin.

As I greet your dear family warmheartedly, sir, I am:

Your lowly brother in Christ,
J. J. Kern

The Methodist preacher here will start holding service every Sunday right after my departure; I was just told and given definite assurances of this.

No. 1180: J. J. Kern to Synod President Wilhelm Streissguth

Princeton
July 10, 1865

Rev. W. Streissguth
Milwaukee, Wis.

Dear Brother Streissguth!

I am leaving here tomorrow. I am parted from here with a heavy heart. It wasn't until I gave my farewell sermon that I really learned how much I loved the congregation and the congregation loved me, and if the step had not already been taken, I probably would not leave. Unfortunately the country congregation who belonged to Strieter and who promised that they would unite with Princeton if I moved away—which then was also the main reason I took this step—has already joined the Missourian party, which is receiving a preacher a week from now. The Methodist preacher here has cast his net around my entire area and within it and even though he still does not have a single soul within a two-mile radius. Ever since the murmur started that I would be leaving, he has settled in Princeton; during my four-week absence he preached in all the various schoolhouses within the narrower and wider radius of Princeton, rotating every day. Last Sunday[130] he preached here for the first time and now plans on preaching here every Sunday. He has already visited every single member of my congregation and with some of them, he is basically breaking into their homes. Now they are cheering and rejoicing, as if they already had my entire congregation in their possession. And my congregation is frightened and discouraged and they are worried that they won't ever get another preacher. Yesterday the entire congregation was crying. They presented me—all on their own and without my asking—the best testimonial that I could desire or wish for. Also, another forty

---

130. July 2

dollars was voluntarily collected and presented to me; a mere $240 had been pledged and $320 promised, so it all ended up coming in.[131]

The congregation is currently very weak, but they do what they can. And I beg you, sir, to remember this hard-pressed congregation and to send her a faithful shepherd and teacher as quickly as possible. If there is no one here, I cannot guarantee that the Methodists won't cause some irreparable damage. The congregation is weak, but she is worth it. But if help does not come in a timely manner, then it might be too late and the field might be forever lost for the Wisconsin Synod. It would pain me greatly if the two little congregations that I gathered and preserved with a lot of sweat were scattered by the wolf and brought to ruin. Perhaps the congregation in Berlin served by Brother Thiele, though eighteen miles away, could be combined with Princeton for the time being.

While I was writing this, your letter came into my hands. I am very satisfied with the content of the testimonial and thank you for it.

If you wish to communicate with the congregation, please contact the administrators: C. Lemke, Sigismund Luethe, or G. Jahnke.

With warmhearted greetings to you, sir, and your dear family,

Your lowly brother in Christ,
J. J. Kern
In haste

No. 1221: J. J. Kern to Synod President Wilhelm Streissguth

Franklin Center, Lee Co., Iowa
Sept. 17, 1865

Rev. W. Streissguth
Milwaukee, Wis.

Dear Brother in Christ!

Please pardon my delay in replying to your valued letter. The sickness and death of my mother-in-law, the construction of a schoolhouse and boarding house, the founding of my school and the many things associated with it would not permit me to come when you called.[132] I did not accept the call from the congregation in Navou [Nauvoo]. She has called Brother Kiesel in Davenport in the meantime, and his

---

131. Kern had told Reim in his April 22, 1865 letter (no. 1124) that $280 had already come in—forty dollars more than what was pledged. That's why he refers to "another forty dollars" in this sentence and why he can say that the full $320 has come in.

132. Kern is speaking metaphorically; "coming at your call" is the same thing as "replying to your letter" here.

successor there will be Brother Ritter. The German brothers of the Iowa Synod would like it if Ritter joined their synod, since the congregation belongs to it and the German element would be strengthened if he joined. As for me, I have begun a high school here, and have good prospects for the future. In doing so, I have ventured into a realm that is not foreign to the preaching ministry [*Predigtamt*], since indeed the Lord also says to Peter, "Tend my lambs" [John 21:15].

I am very sorry that Princeton had to be without a shepherd for so long. If it has still not been filled, I ask again that it be filled quickly. I left it with good intentions, in hopes that, if the position were quickly filled again, a Missouri congregation would join with Princeton and that would make it impossible for the Missourians to establish themselves. As for the German Conference of the Iowa Synod, it is not actually formed yet, but will hold its first meeting in the near future and organize itself then. In any case, the head person is Pastor F. W. Strobel in Fort Madison, secretary of the synod, who has also already supported the seminary in Watertown with sixteen dollars.

With warmhearted greetings to you, sir, and your dear family, I am:

Your brother in Christ,
J. J. Kern

No. 1514: J. J. Kern to Synod President Wilhelm Streissguth

Bath, Mason Co., Ill.
March 25, 1867

Rev. W[ilhel]m Streissguth
Milwaukee, Wis.

Reverend Brother, cherished in Christ!

Your valued letter did not find me in Franklin anymore, since I accepted a call not long ago from a vacant congregation consisting of c. sixty families of Hanoverians and Wuerttembergers. They live in the country, are all well off and rich, have a church, parsonage, and schoolhouse and, lastly, were previously served by a Missourian. Yes, Franklin was not a good place for me to stay either. Everybody there is a member of the club and, since I wouldn't join too, I was a thorn in the side of Parson Braschler, the United preacher there. He also tried to put all sorts of obstructions in the way of my school, and although my school was thriving nonetheless, it just wasn't sitting right with me,[133] and it was pushing me back into the preaching ministry [*ins Predigtamt*] and, paying attention to the signs [*Winke*] the Lord was giving, I then accepted

---

133. German: *so war mirs doch dabei nicht wohl zu Muthe.* Alternative: "I just wasn't feeling good about it."

this call upon the advice of brothers—a call that adequately secures my livelihood. Pastor Bredow of Dubuque installed me into my office, at my request and at the behest of the German Iowa Synod. You can see from this that, even if I am not yet a member, I am on friendly terms with the German Iowa Synod. I still belong to the English Iowa Synod, though I am not happy with it at all. Through my efforts the German Conference has been established. At the next conference on May 1 in Davenport, it is supposed to be discussed and decided what steps we wish to take. I and Pastor Strobel were initially in favor of joining with Wisconsin, but since we were acquainted with the German Iowa brothers and have developed a real trust in them, and since we also are not keen on having two like-minded synods in one area, we are in favor of joining with Iowa. Whether everyone will go along with it, I do not know.

Now as for Pastor A. Pfister, who belongs to our conference, we would really like it if he would find a small place somewhere outside our synodical circle, so that we would be free of him. For he is no adornment to a Lutheran synod. The good brother certainly means really well: He is extraordinarily diligent, runs another ten miles from Farmington on Sundays in order to preach to a little group of four to five families, does a good job visiting the people, teaches school, and the children learn fairly well. It's just that he is very poorly gifted and has a limited education. In the pulpit he uses the Zurich dialect, doesn't write out his sermon (which we've often advised him to do, but he is unable to do it), and then he screams his head off, moving and gesturing this way and that, until at last he is bathed in sweat and is unable to utter another word. The prayer that follows the sermon seems that it will never come to an end and has no structure at all. He is not at a loss for words and turns of phrase, but the ones he uses—when you hear him the first time, you're instinctively tempted to laugh, especially since he makes all kinds of strange grimaces. And then there's the high opinion he has of himself, etc. He is an alumnus of St. Chrischona and came over with Brother Hilpert, isn't any taller than him either. But Hilpert has a great humility, whereas with Brother Pfister, in spite of all his efforts to appear humble, he can't ever succeed. He has obtained an excellent wife, a former pupil of mine. I am really sorry to have to draw such a picture for you, sir, and I do not wish the good brother any ill. God knows that, but I still wanted to and had to draw you an accurate picture. He was ordained by the Michigan Synod. The fact that he is a Lutheran seems to have happened completely by accident, but now that he is, he does want to be a good Lutheran. In the surrounding area, he is known as the Methodist because of his yelling and praying. But if he gets assigned a suitable field of labor, he might be and and prove a useful laborer in the Lord's vineyard. If that happens, it would be good if he were placed under the oversight of an older, capable brother. I hope that he is still willing to take a lot more advice. If my people in Farmington—whom, by the way, I first visited eight years ago and organized into a congregation—were not such a small congregation and not such truly fine, contented people, there's no way Pfister would have lasted these three to four years there. Incidentally, for the past one and a half years he also has been quite actively trying to get a different place of service, but he hasn't really been able to succeed. On the one hand, I harbor the desire to get rid of this brother, and for that reason I would very much like to recommend him to you. The fact that I am not doing so should lead you to recognize my integrity, by which I seek to validate the trust placed in me. The brothers of the German Conference are: Strobel, Kiesel, Schumacher, Brecht, Lutz, Pfister, and I. Ritter, as far as I know, still belongs to your honorable synod.

The reason I did not answer you at the time was because I was very overwhelmed with business and at the same time could not report anything significant or certain. Later the matter was forgotten.

You will not take it as an act of hostility that I am in favor of the Iowans. After all, since we now belong to the same general church body,[134] it is more fitting for us to belong to the synod in whose area we are living and to whose meetings we can easily come. I will therefore continue to disseminate the *Gemeinde-Blatt* and to leave it up to the people which paper they wish to read—the *Kirchenblatt*, which is too deep for ordinary people, or the *Gemeinde-Blatt*.

I would also have a request of you, sir. Since I no longer know the letter box[135] of Brumder, your brother-in-law, I would like to request of you that you give him the enclosed dollar and request that he send me wafers [*Hostien*] in exchange.

As I pass along the most warmhearted greetings to you and your dear family, along with Mr. Brumder, I am:

Your brother devotedly connected to you in Christ Jesus,
J. J. Kern

Kern's correspondence with the Wisconsin Synod's leadership ended here, but his adventures did not. The year 1873 found him in the Hebron, Nebraska area. In December 1874, he helped organize Trinity Lutheran Church in nearby Friedensau—a community which he also helped found. The church joined the Missouri Synod early the following year. Kern apparently had to give up his ministerial duties due, in part, to conflicts resulting from his community business dealings with parishioners. Kern's hopes for a large return on his Friedensau investments were dashed when the Rock Island Railroad was installed through Deshler along Spring Creek in 1887, instead of through Friedensau along the Little Blue River. In 1889 he moved to Portland, Oregon, where he eventually founded the Nachrichten, *a German newspaper. Five years later he turned it over to his son Albert and founded the Farmers' Mutual Insurance Company. After his first wife passed away in 1911, he married Julia Panek, a widow thirteen years his junior,*

---

134. At the time, there was serious talk about both the Wisconsin and Iowa Synods joining the General Council. See E. C. Fredrich, *The Wisconsin Synod Lutherans* (Milwaukee: Northwestern, 1992), 40ff.

135. That is, PO Box.

on Feb. 16, 1913, at age seventy-seven. Less than three months later, he passed away from heart failure after breakfast on Saturday, May 3. He was buried in the Rose City Cemetery. His will stipulated that each of his children was to be left one dollar, "as they have already either got more than their share and have mistreated me, or because they are well off and will not mind the trifling share that would fall to them." Most of his estate, which included a piano, writing desk, books, and twenty acres of alfalfa land in Pecos County, Texas, was, ironically, left to Concordia College in Portland, a Missouri Synod institution. His daughter Meta DuMond successfully filed suit for the return of the piano later that same year, claiming that "the piano was given to her when she was a little girl in payment for services in aiding her mother in keeping a boarding house." The money of Kern's estate was left to his wife.

Appendix X

Death and Burial of C. F. W. Walther

Walther's Fiftieth Anniversary in the Ministry[1]

This issue of *Der Lutheraner* is festively decorated,[2] and rightly so, since the man who founded this newspaper in 1844, who ran it by himself for years, who, even after its editorship was placed into the hands of the St. Louis seminary faculty, has labored most faithfully on its behalf and carried its welfare on his heart up to the present, namely Mr. Doctor C. F. W. Walther, celebrated his fiftieth anniversary in the ministry on January 16.

Now if it is already a great and gracious gift of God when a servant of the Church has labored for fifty years in one or more congregations, then we should extol it as an especially great and gracious gift when such a man has completed fifty years in the ministry [*Amtsjahre*] who has served not just as a pastor, but whose service has extended into far reaches. And this is the case with our beloved celebrant. Passing over his abundantly fruitful activity as a pastor, he has functioned as editor of *Der Lutheraner*, as author of many significant doctrinal and polemical writings, as long-standing president of our synod, as professor and president of our St. Louis institution, as tireless speaker and consultant at synod conventions, as correspondent and adviser not just here in America, but also all the way into the farthest reaches of our church, to Europe, Asia, Africa, and Australia. Not just friends, but even opponents are compelled to acknowledge this abundantly fruitful activity. Thousands owe a debt of thanks to him, right after God. Our paper therefore has fittingly put on festive adornment in honor of this joyous occasion for its founder.

The Celebration of the Fiftieth Anniversary in the Ministry of the Most Reverend Mr. Dr. C. F. W. Walther on January 16, 1887

This celebration, which for many months now had occupied the hearts of the St. Louis congregations and of most of the congregations in the synod, now lies behind us.

---

1. *Der Lutheraner* 43, no. 3 (Feb. 1, 1887) 17,18b.
2. There was a large picture of the aged Walther on the front page of this issue.

During this time, ardent prayers have ascended to the throne of divine grace, asking that our faithful Savior would please permit our faithful teacher to enjoy this great and rare day of honor in good health and with all his former mental vigor, and that he would permit us to celebrate a truly joyful day of jubilee. But it has pleased the Lord, in his unsearchable wisdom, not to answer our prayers in the way our hearts implored; otherwise we would be able to report today on a larger public celebration. If all of our human wishes and plans had been achievable, this day would certainly have been a day of jubilee for the entire synod, led by the St. Louis congregations, and the presidents and delegations from all our synodical schools and pastoral conferences would have made an appearance. For, God be praised, everyone in our synod was saying the same thing, that we had to honor the celebrant as the spiritual father of the synod, whom God has so richly endowed with such extraordinary gifts, because it is chiefly due to him that our synod has spread out so rapidly, that she has enjoyed such unity in faith and confession with corresponding practice, and that each one of her congregations enjoys such glorious freedom and independence, limited only by the clear word of God. And since this is true only by God's free grace, this day was accordingly also supposed to be prepared as a day of rejoicing and of pure thanks and praise for God's superabundant grace, which he has so undeservedly shown us through the celebrant.

These were our human thoughts. But God had other things in mind. The illness of our dear doctor, which had already cropped up in September of last year, grew all the more rampant as he strenuously carried on with his work in his old self-denying way, without permitting himself a moment's rest, until he finally exhausted himself completely and broke down. The illness had now grown so strong that all the skill of the doctors seemed wasted and we even despaired of his life. But God answered the prayers of his children that were certainly being sent up to him from all over the synod on behalf of this precious life. The illness slowly abated, but a completely extraordinary infirmity remained, which still left us in a constant state of concern for his life. Naturally, this extremely critical condition soon threw all plans for a larger celebration up in the air and, when asked about it, the doctors unanimously declared that, while they did have confident expectations for the dear invalid's eventual recovery, an exciting, outdoor celebration was also out of the question for the time being. However, they were optimistic that a quieter, short congratulation ceremony in his room with not too many visitors, as the expression of sincere love and grateful veneration, would be much more likely to have a beneficial effect on him.[3]

---

3. The remainder of the article, not provided here, continues in three more columns on the next two pages. At the end it is signed with the initials O. H.—possibly Pastor Otto Hanser, who later spoke at Walther's graveside.

Announcement of Walther's Death[4]

✠ Dr. C. F. W. Walther ✠

So the sad occurrence has now come to pass. Although it was not unexpected, all our hearts are still filled with the deepest grief. Our dearly beloved and highly respected father and teacher, Dr. C. F. W. Walther, has passed away.

What this dear, departed man has meant to our synod, yes, to the Church both near and far, and what we therefore have now lost by losing him, we need not highlight here. What we have him to thank for, right after God, we highlighted in *Der Lutheraner* when we had occasion to report on his fiftieth anniversary in the ministry, and the synodical address and synodical sermon printed in this issue show how we rightly mourn, yet not without hope.

We will therefore limit ourselves here to a brief recounting of our blessed Walther's final days on earth and of his blessed departure.

The aforementioned issue already reported on the illness he had contracted. Since that time, with every passing week, the hope that this faithful, tireless laborer would be restored to his work in the Lord's vineyard increasingly dwindled. His strength continued to wane. Indeed, at first the departed was entertaining the hope that he would still recover at some point; indeed, the man who was accustomed *only* to work on behalf of God's kingdom was thinking that he would be able, even if only in a limited way, to take up his usual work once again. But later he gave up these thoughts and looked forward to his release from bondage and eagerly anticipated his redemption.

He often confessed that he experienced great joy when he called to mind all of the many great blessings which God had shown him during his long life. Right up to the end, he often praised it as a special grace of God that God had protected him from severe spiritual afflictions in this final illness, which he had not been spared in past illnesses. He also comforted himself with God's gracious election, and was comforted by others with it. One time he mentioned that many people probably considered him a truly stubborn man who would not be dissuaded from his opinions, but he was certain that this "obstinacy," with which he had held firmly to the truth he had come to know, was a *donum Dei* (gift of God). Regarding special wishes and concerns for the future, he expressed several times that he had nothing in particular on his heart—just one matter that Mr. Pastor Stöckhardt took care of at his wish. Only in general terms did he frequently declare: Oh, if our synod will simply persevere in what she has! God has shown her such extravagant grace. And if she will only preserve a devout ministerium and not let any unworthy persons into the ministry [*ins Amt*]!

In his final weeks he often slept and was unconscious. Visitors could speak with him very little. During this time, when writers, upon taking their leave, would say to him, "The Lord will not leave you or forsake you; he will stand by you with his power,"

---

4. *Der Lutheraner* 43, no. 10 (May 15, 1887) 77–78.

the wearied man would turn his head a little and say, "Especially in the final hour!" Often the sigh would rise from his heart: "God, have mercy!" Often he would pray: "Jesus, your blood and righteousness My beauty are, my glorious dress," etc. When Mr. Pastor O[tto] Hanser took leave of him and asked him if he was looking forward to the glory of heaven, he answered, "Yes."

Concerning his final days, Mr. Pastor Stöckhardt reports as follows:

> At 5:30 this evening (May 7), our Dr. Walther was finally set free from his prolonged suffering and transferred to the company of those who have overcome. His final days were a truly peaceful conclusion to a difficult confinement in bed. While he was almost continually without consciousness a week ago, since Wednesday one could once again speak with him intelligibly and he understood everything that was said to him. At the start of the convention, his son reminded him that the convention was now beginning, but that he would soon be called to another assembly, that of the patriarchs, prophets, and apostles. To that he replied, "That will be glorious!" Indeed he still did much sighing: "God, have mercy! O God, do not forsake me!" But right up to the end he also affirmed the deathbed comfort that people shared with him from God's word with "Yes," or by nodding, or with a handshake. When an old church member visited him the day before yesterday and began to speak Psalm 23, he recited the entire psalm. Yesterday evening we prepared ourselves for the end. At his request I prayed one more time with him and his relatives and then read the verse from the evening hymn: "Should this night be my final night In this dark vale of tears, Let me behold your Son in light With your elected heirs," etc. When I was finished, he said, "May God grant it!" I then posed him this question: Was he now also ready to die confidently in the same grace of the Lord Jesus Christ to which he had testified throughout his life? He answered it with a loud and clear "Yes." Toward midnight he seemed to have terrible pains one more time, and then he said, "That is enough!" After that, he seems to have experienced no more agony. The whole day today he was, as they say, at the point of death, but he did remain conscious right up to the end, and he made it clearly known that he had no problem understanding what his son, Prof. Schaller, and I said to him. One hour before his death, I was called straight to another dying man and, when I came back, I found him departed. In short, it was a truly peaceful, quiet, uplifting conclusion to a prolonged and often gloomy period of suffering.

We bow down beneath the hand of God. It is sorrowful for *us*. It is wonderful for *him*. He has entered into his Master's happiness. We can only imagine the joys with which the soul of this devout and faithful servant was received! O how glorious, how great his reward will be!

APPENDIX X: DEATH AND BURIAL OF C. F. W. WALTHER

The Burial of the Blessed Dr. Walther[5]

On May 7, during the synod convention, on its fourth day of sessions, Dr. Walther fell asleep. So that the convention would not be interrupted and so that a truly large number of the synod's members could take part in the burial, the burial was postponed at the desire of the convention.

On Friday, May 13, in the afternoon, the embalmed body was brought into the seminary building and placed on the bier in the main hall [*großen Halle*] there, near the lecture rooms. When it was time to depart from the house of mourning, Mr. Pastor Stöckhardt gave an address and said a prayer. The coffin, carried by eight students, was followed by the grieving survivors—the two sons of the deceased, Mr. Pastor Ferdinand Walther and Mr. Constantin Walther, Mr. Pastor St[ephanus] Keyl and his wife and daughter,[6] and Mr. Pastor H[einrich] Niemann, whose wife, the youngest daughter of Dr. Walther,[7] was unfortunately prevented from attending by illness. The rest of the students followed after them.

The seminary building was draped in black both inside and out. Even the professors' residences, as well as those of the church members who live here, were hung with black. The students took turns keeping guard.

On Saturday evening, at the desire of Americans, an English funeral service was held in the main hall [*Aula*] of the seminary. Mr. Pastor Birkner from St. Louis was the speaker.

On Sunday afternoon the body was brought to Trinity Church. Great was the number of those who made an appearance for this solemn occasion. The main hall [*große Aula*] could not hold them all. Mr. Pastor Stöckhardt gave the address for this, printed in this issue. A great multitude followed the corpse on foot, in spite of the threatening weather. Trinity Church was decked in mourning crape both inside and out. Many, many additional people came into the church on that day and on Monday and Tuesday morning, in order to have one last look at the countenance of the cherished deceased man.

At midday on Tuesday the body was brought to its final resting place. Around eleven o'clock the students, professors and pastors, from both here and elsewhere, teachers, congregational administrators, and others assembled in the schoolhouse on Barry Street, in order to proceed from there to Trinity Church in solemn procession. Around twelve o'clock the funeral service began, in which Mr. President Schwan preached on Psalm 90 and Mr. Professor Crämer spoke at the altar on 2 Kings 2:12. The pallbearers on this solemn occasion were the professors of the seminary and the

---

5. *Der Lutheraner* 43, no. 11 (June 1, 1887) 86–87. This is the original title (except translated in English).

6. Stephanus Keyl (1838–1905), the oldest son of Pastor Ernst Gerhard Wilhelm Keyl, was taken into the custody of C. F. W. Walther, his uncle, in 1847 when his father accepted a call to Milwaukee. He ended up marrying Walther's daughter Magdalena (b. Nov. 22, 1842), his first cousin, in 1862.

7. Julie (b. July 27, 1849)

pastors of the city. From all parts of our country pastors of our synod had hastened this way to pay their last respects to the beloved deceased. Even other synods were represented: the Hon. Minnesota Synod by her president, Mr. Pastor Albrecht; the Hon. Wisconsin Synod by Professors Notz and Gräbner from her seminary in Milwaukee; and the Hon. Norwegian Synod by her president at large[8] and Mr. Professor Larsen from Decorah. Certainly there has been no funeral for a theologian in America in which that many theologians have taken part. Certainly the city of St. Louis has scarcely seen a larger funeral.

At the grave Mr. Pastor O[tto] Hanser gave the graveside address on Daniel 12:2,3. Mr. Professor Larsen (of the Norwegian Synod) could not refrain from giving a short speech, in order to testify for how much also the Norwegian Synod has the cherished departed to thank. We impart his heartfelt words here:

> Included among the great host of mourners who have assembled on this sad occasion are a small number of pastors from the Norwegian Synod, including the president at large of this synod. On behalf of so many of our brothers, we would very much like to express the heartfelt gratitude that we feel toward God and his servant, the cherished Dr. Walther, now of blessed memory, for every good thing God has poured out through him, on us as well. And so we cannot pass up the opportunity also to convey our thanks to the entire synod, so strongly represented here, who had him as her leader. The Missouri Synod has demonstrated such great and sacrificial love to us for nigh unto thirty years now. Since the year 1858, surely without interruption, we have had students in her theological seminaries. Approximately half of our pastors have studied at these seminaries, and most of them have had the benefit of Walther's instruction. Who can measure the blessings they have reaped from this, and the blessings reaped through them by their congregations and our people? But also others of us, including some older persons in our synod, who did not receive formal instruction here as enrolled students—did we not sit at Walther's feet too? Certainly we did, and far from being ashamed of it, we rather count it as an honor and, more than that, as a great blessing which we have been allotted thereby. Our people have also been blessed by Walther and the Missouri Synod in that quite a few writings from here have been translated into our language and have been distributed among our fellow countrymen. We mention especially Walther's *Evangelien-Postille* [Gospel Sermons] and the glorious little book, *Die rechte Gestalt einer vom Staate unabhängigen evangelisch-lutherischen Ortsgemeinde* [The Proper Form of an Evangelical Lutheran Local Congregation Independent of the State].
>
> Walther and the synod who had him as her leader gave us such strong guidance and encouragement in faithfulness, both in preserving the divine truth and in striving for true holiness. Let it be our earnest wish and prayer

---

8. Herman Amberg Preus (1825–1894), president of the Norwegian Synod from 1862.

today that this faithfulness might long survive the dear departed both in our synod and in his own! May it be so for Jesus' sake! Amen.

It should go without saying that the students sang their funeral songs at the grave of their beloved teacher, just as they had for the preceding solemnities. Mr. Pastor Sieck spoke the collect and blessing, and Mr. Pastor Wangerin, after he and the assembly had finished singing the antiphonal burial song, "Now Lay We Calmly in the Grave,"[9] spoke the Lord's Prayer. The grave into which the coffin was lowered is lined with masonry. A heavy stone slab covers the coffin.

---

9. A hymn by Michael Weisse (c. 1480–1534), no. 476 in the *Evangelical Lutheran Hymnary*.

Appendix XI

Jubilee Report

Aged Church Organizer Celebrates Jubilee[1]

The Rev. Johannes Streiter [sic], 90 [sic] Years Old, Knew Wausau as
"Big Bull"—2,000 Evangelical Lutherans at Berlin Hold Greatest
Religious Gathering in History of County

The joint celebration held by eight Evangelical Lutheran congregations at Henry Krueger's grove in the town of Berlin, yesterday, was undoubtedly the greatest event in the church history of the county and possibly of the entire state. Attended by over 2,000 people, the event also proved the greatest gathering of old settlers and their descendants from city, village and country, ever held in the county.

The presence of Rev. Johannes Strieter, the missionary pastor, of Bay City, Mich., who paid his respects to "Big Bull" as Wausau was known in the olden days, and who organized the first congregation in Marathon county, added immensely to the success of the great jubilee. Few, even of the earlier settlers[,] remembered this pioneer missionary pastor, who fondly recalled "Big Bull" and all his experiences in this vicinity when the sturdy woodsmen inhabited the surrounding country.

The Rev. Strieter favored the press with an acount [sic] of his first experiences in this portion of the state. He has partly lost the faculty of hearing, but is in full possession of all his other faculties and as a reconteur [sic] of past reminiscences has but few rivals.

Relates History.

Full of vigor and possessed of bright intellect, he told with vivid interest how he was first attracted to Northern Wisconsin. "I was pastor on the Indian reservation which in that day lay between Montello, Plainfield and Princeton, when I met a young man from "Big Bull" who informed me that the people in this vicinity were very anxious to be served by a pastor. I took my horse and buggy and drove to "Big Bull" but

---

1. The article transcribed here was the first headline on the first page of the *Wausau Daily Record-Herald* 3, no. 833 (Aug. 15, 1910).

before I reached this hamlet, my buggy was all in pieces. The road was full of holes and my horse became lame. With the help of some of the earlier pioneers whom I met enroute and who had heavier teams and wagons, I safely reached "Big Bull." But here there was no one.

"It was impossible for me to preach the gospel at a place where scarcely anybody lived. I remember a man who had a store near the river, I believe his name was Kickbusch, where I stayed over night. The next morning I went to the town of Berlin, where a large number of people gathered in various homes and listened to my preaching.[2]

Fig. 61. August and Mathilda Kickbusch, unknown year, photo.

---

2. There was probably some error in transmission from German to English, and Strieter may have grown fuzzier in some of the details, but this does appear to supplement what he shares in his autobiography (see p. 94). His buggy probably was starting to fall apart already before he headed out from Wausau to the town of Berlin, and he did almost certainly stay with a man named Kickbusch on Oct. 2, 1860—August Kickbusch, to be exact, who had arrived from Milwaukee earlier in 1860 and had opened a store in a little shanty on Clarke's Island. Clarke's Island today is primarily occupied by Big Bull Falls Park beneath the Stewart Avenue Bridge. Kickbusch eventually became Wausau's first mayor.

First Congregation.

"On Ascension Day, 1859, I organized the first congregation at this place.[3] My following trips were made with much difficulty as I met with snow and the roads were impassable. With the help of oxen, the earlier pioneers were enabled to make their way through the vast banks of snow. It was with their assistance, that I was enabled to reach Big Bull successfully."

The old gentleman, who is about ninety [sic] years old, remembered the names of his different horses as clearly as though the events had happened yesterday. His jocose laughter added a happy vein to his rehearsal of his past experiences. Sincere and sympathetic, his narration was animated by a lofty spirit. He was modest and when told that the press wished to be informed of his early experiences in "Big Bull," he laughed heartily and said that he was a poor old man and therefore was of no interest to newspaper readers.

"Big Bull" Only.

He told of the efforts made by the Rev. Theodore Hartwig, pastor of the Berlin congregations, to secure his presence during this jubilee. The Rev. Hartwig had written him a letter in which he asked him if he was the Rev. Strieter who had organized the Berlin, Hamburg and Maine congregations in this county. Rev. Strieter replied to this letter that he remembered "Big Bull" thoroughly and had known this section only by this name.

When asked by the Rev. Hartwig for his presence at this function, he replied that his presence could not be worth the expense but the Rev. Hartwig persisted that he be present and to bring with him his wife. That these efforts of Rev. Hartwig were fully appreciated, was easily to be seen from the interest that centered about this pioneer pastor, who organized not only congregations in this vicinity, but as well in Eau Claire, Chippewa Falls, etc.

He visited this section about once a year and in 1862 [sic], estalished [sic] the Rev. J. J. Hoffman [sic] as his assistant to take charge of the local congregations. The Rev. Hoffman was the first regular pastor of the congregations in Marathon county and is now deceased.

Only Charter Member.

Another personage around whom much interest centered was Edward Nass. Mr. Nass is the only living charter member of the first Berlin congregation. While unsteady from

---

3. He was still living in Ohio on Ascension 1859. He also did not officially organize any congregation in the Wausau area, though he did help prepare them for organization.

age, his sturdiness was apparent and he conversed freely. He is sixty-eight years of age and was about eighteen years of age when he signed the charter.

In spite of the claims of present day missionaries and of young men's clubs that the young men of the past did not show an interest in church work, the interest of the youths in the organization of the first congregation in Marathon county, was greatly manifested and has resulted in a flourishing growth of the church in the western part of the county.

Strieter's Sermon.

The program of the day was opened with a sermon by Rev. J. Strieter, who spoke so distinctly and so interestingly, that the entire assemblage listened attentively to his good words and found recollections of the old Pomeranians who first cleared the farms of Marathon county. Following the opening address of Rev. Strieter, the Rev. [Philip Samuel] Estel delivered a sermon, which although not as clear as that of the senior reverend, was filled with elevated thoughts and fond reminiscences. This concluded the morning service and a bountiful spread awaited the onslaught of the visitors who joined heartily in the open air banquet.

Afternoon Addresses.

After the dinner hour, which was given to the meeting of friends and acquaintances as well as the association of the older settlers, the afternoon program was commenced. Rev. William Bergholz, who served the congregation from 1881 to 1889[,] was the first to address the assemblage in the afternoon. Rev. J. Glaiser [sic], who was pastor of the Berlin congregation from 1889 to 1900 [sic] gave the second address of the afternoon. Rev. H[erman] Brandt, who was pastor at Naugardt [sic] from 1900 to 1904, gave the closing sermon of the afternoon service. All three sermons were appropriate to this great festival and were full of thanksgiving and praise to God for having given His children this joyful opportunity for comparing the great transition from the pioneer days of Marathon county to the present advanced stage of development.

APPENDIX XI: JUBILEE REPORT

Congregations Present.

Fig. 62. View of Naugart, Wis., 1912, postcard. This is essentially the view Pastor Strieter would have had as he headed back home from the anniversary celebration in Henry Krueger's grove. We can only imagine what he was thinking as he saw the beautiful church building, farmhouses, barns, and cultivated farmland, and recalled his trips to the area when it was bush-land just beginning to be cleared.

The congregations represented in this joint celebration and who jointly celebrated their fiftieth anniversary were as follows: The St. Paul and Trinity congregations in the town of Berlin, the Trinity, St. Paul, St. John and Salem congregations in the town of Hamburg and the Grace, and Zion's congregations in the town of Maine and the St. John congregation in the town of Scott, all of the Evangelical Lutheran faith.

In addition to the sermons the choirs of the St. Paul church of Berlin and Salems' [sic] church of Wausau as well as the cornet band of the St. John's Evangelical Lutheran church of Merrill, furnished music. Refreshments were sold at stands and many brought lunch baskets. The great event closed at about 5 o'clock.

Appendix XII

Johannes Strieter's Obituary

Death Notice[1]

On August 24 of this year Pastor *Johannes Strieter* completed his course, at the age of close to ninety-one years. Born in Affalterbach, Wuerttemberg, at the time when rationalism held sway, his Bible-believing parents sowed the seed of the pure gospel in the heart of their young boy. In the Franconian settlement in Michigan, the sapling of faith was first tended especially by our later Professor A[ugust] Craemer, and then its growth furthered at the preaching seminary in Fort Wayne. And to spend himself in the service of his Savior—for that our Strieter was always ready. He soon had to step into the work against his wish. Our synod was small in number in the early years of our orthodox fathers. Confidence had to be won first, and the orthodox church had to be built up from the rough, and all this for the most part amid almost unbelievable hardships. It was into such work that our pioneer, too, set foot. God had equipped him for precisely that purpose. At his very first mission settings his faith was put to some hard tests. He seemed to labor in vain, to harvest almost nothing but hostility. Despite a salary of only sixty dollars per year he nevertheless entered into matrimony on the advice of brothers in the ministry; he would not have been able to find greater compensation anyway. Our synod did not yet have mission funds at that time like the ones that exist among us now. Afterwards God let him remain a few years and find refreshment in a newly founded congregation in which God's word bore fruit, namely in Independence, Ohio. Then he sent him to a far-flung mission field in Wisconsin. Strieter relates in his autobiography: "Here I preached never fewer than four, and never more than nine, times a week and I always traveled by horse, about 6,000 miles per year, mostly on so-called Indian trails." Amid what adversities! In hunger, at the risk of his life. Unfortunately in a necessarily brief report only allusions can be made. Today one can find over forty congregations on this mission field, some of them rich with members. After six years of this pioneer work Father Strieter's health was ruined, even if his faith and courage were most certainly not. God now led him into another work. From 1865 to 1869 he served the congregation in Aurora,

---

1. *Der Lutheraner* 76, no. 21 (Oct. 19, 1920) 347.

Illinois, then the congregation in Peru, Indiana, until 1873, and lastly, he was active in ministry in Proviso, Illinois, until 1902. But his mission zeal never ebbed.

In 1902, to the regret of his final congregation, he finally had to resign his office on account of deafness. For eighteen straight years this congregation took four collections every year which she contributed to him for his livelihood. May God reward her for her kindness out of his grace! He found a retirement home in the home of his daughter and her husband, Teacher H. List, in Frankenlust, Michigan, and God let his faithful spouse remain at his side to take care of him. He is survived by eight of his fourteen children, of whom one is a professor in Seward and two are in the teaching ministry, and by over sixty grandchildren and forty-two great-grandchildren. In his retirement, writes Pastor Nuechterlein, he diligently read his Bible and Luther, later just the Bible still, and at the end only the Psalter.

Fig. 63. Johannes Strieter reading, with his wife Elizabeth standing nearby, unknown year, photo. Image courtesy of Nelson Wesenberg.

At the funeral in Frankenlust Pastor Budach delivered an address in the home, and Pastor Nuechterlein delivered the sermon in the church on Luke 2:29–32 [the Song of Simeon]. In Proviso, where the corpse now rests, the undersigned preached in the church on 2 Timothy 4:6–8[2] and Pastors Dannenfeldt and Roehrs delivered addresses at the casket, and the latter officiated at the grave. Henceforth there is "set aside for [him] the crown of righteousness," for the sake of his Savior.

L[ouis] Hoelter

Fig. 64. The final resting place of Johannes and Elizabeth Strieter in Immanuel Lutheran Cemetery, Hillside, Ill., 2013, photo.

---

2. "For I am already being offered up, and the time of my departure is at hand. I have fought a good fight, I have completed my course, I have kept faith. Henceforth there is set aside for me the crown of righteousness, which the Lord, the righteous judge, will give me on that day, but not to me alone, but also to all who love his appearing."

About the Translator

Nathaniel Biebert is the oldest of eight children, seven boys and one girl, born to Rev. Timothy and Linda Biebert of Wisconsin. He was born and baptized in California and attended Lutheran grade schools in Wisconsin. He graduated from Luther Preparatory School (2001), Martin Luther College (BA with a minor in confessional languages, 2005), and Wisconsin Lutheran Seminary (MDiv, 2009) after serving a vicarship (pastoral apprenticeship) in New Hampshire (2007–2008). Upon his seminary graduation, he received a one-year assignment to be a dormitory supervisor and instructor at a Lutheran high school in Nebraska, where he was ordained into the pastoral ministry. In 2010, he was reassigned as the pastor of two rural parishes northwest of Wausau, Wisconsin—parishes which, as he soon found out, owed their existence to Pastor Strieter's mission work in the 1860s. There Nathaniel also taught religion part-time at a nearby Lutheran high school. In 2017, he accepted a call to serve a Lutheran parish in South Austin, Texas.

In 2012, God united him in marriage with Katherine née Sternberg. Among other things, they enjoy bicycling, traveling, camping, reading, watching good movies, and attending classical music concerts together. Nathaniel also enjoys hiking, fly fishing, fly tying (still a novice), and historical research, including translating German and Latin works.

Nathaniel is the author of *Luther at the Manger* (Milwaukee: Northwestern, 2017)—a translation of a 1531 sermon series—and the translator and editor of *Heaven Is My Fatherland: The Life and Work of Michael Praetorius* (Eugene, OR: Resource Publications, 2020). He has authored articles and translations for the *Wisconsin Lutheran Quarterly* and *Forward in Christ*. He is a 2018 recipient of the Concordia Historical Institute's Award of Commendation for his serial in the *WELS Historical Institute Journal*, "Johannes Strieter: Raconteur of Past Reminiscences."

Subject Index

(For names of churches, see Place Index. "c" refers to a caption. *Italicized* page numbers refer to an illustration.)

Abendschule. See *Illustrirte Abendschule*
absolution, 11, 124
accident, 46–48, 89–90, 171
administrator, 50, 64, 74, 75, 78, 80–81, 84, 89, 129, 130, 131, 134, 141, 145–46, 156, 163, 166, 171, 177, 206, 242–44, 245, 248, 251, 255, 275, 285, 289, 292, 293, 297, 298, 307, 308, 310, 311, 319, 321, 323, 324, 325, 326, 327, 334, 335–36, 339, 348
Albright Brethren, 65, 119, 126, 127, 234, 236–37, 244, 245–46, 289, 292, 303. *See also* Methodists/Methodism
anniversary (church/congregation), xvii, xviii, 94n53, 104n76, 105n80, 169, 175, 270, 277, 278, 279, 351–55
anniversary (marriage), xxv–xxvi
anniversary (ministry), 163–64, 169, 344–45, 346
announcing for Communion. *See* Lord's Supper (announcing)
apology. *See* confession (of wrongdoing)

baptism, xii, xix, xxiii, 1, 7, 35n36, 70n6, 82, 85n30, 87, 94n53, 96nn60f, 104n76, 105n77, 109, 110–11, 113, 120, 124, 125, 126–28, 148, 153, 156, 165, 182, 193, 195–96, 198–99, 200, 203, 211, 217, 237, 238, 240, 286, 305n64, 311, 333
Baptists, 298
bass viol, 6, 84
bear, 19–20, 97–98
beer, 29, 106, 111–12, 137, 150, 273
bells, 4, *28*, 29, *31*, 151n24, 163
bench of repentance, 124, 245, 331
blasphemy, 120, 135–36, 141
blindness (physical), 166, 174
blindness (spiritual), 204, 208, 266
Book of Concord. *See* Confessions, Lutheran

brewery, 86n33, 106, 107
bribery, 84–85
Buffalo Synod, 88n39, 96n62, 235
buggy, xii, xviii, 19, 47, 49, 54, 55, 56n51, 75, 80, 85, 89, 92–95, 101, 102, 104, 113, 115, 116, 121, 124, 133, 138, 163, 164, 174, 282, 286, 287, 351–52

call (divine), xvii, xx, 12n25, 21, 32n23, 36, 37n41, 42, 51, 62, 65, 74, 75n14, 101, 102n71, 104n76, 129, 130, 131, 132, 138, 141, 143, 144, 151, 157, 191, 192, 215, 222, 223, 224, 225, 226, 232, 234, 238, 246, 247n18, 255n41, 256, 262n11, 263n11, 265, 268, 269, 270, 276, 278, 279, 280c, 282, 283, 284n5, 291n26, 292, 296, 297, 304, 308, 311, 312, 313, 317, 318, 319, 320, 321, 322, 324, 330, 339, 340–41, 348n6
canal, xii, 8, 39, 42, 45, 155, 231
catechism/catechesis, 11, 30, 41, 42, 43, 61n65, 84, 96, 132, 134, 135, 137, 142, 145, 165, 167, 192, 200, 203, 211, 213, 217, 240, 273, 279–80, 291n26, 292, 293–94, 295, 333
chanting (liturgical), 24, 302, 305
Chippewa (Native American people). *See* Ojibwe
church bells. *See* bells
church council(man). *See* administrator
church discipline. *See* discipline (church)
church service. *See* service (divine)
Civil War, xii, 87c, 94n54, 109–110, 132, 228, 229, 232, 274
clarinet, 150
clearing land, 9, 10c, 51n32, 53n37, 88, 201, 354, 355c
coffee, 91, 105, 111

361

SUBJECT INDEX

cold weather, 20, 33, 69, 89–92, 96, 97, 98, 99, 140, 152, 159, 240, 290
colic, 106, 136
comfort, 6, 48, 70, 81–82, 83, 110, 160, 161, 163, 166, 172, 216, 219, 220, 221, 254, 346, 347
Communion, 4n5, 24n13, 96, 102, 165, 166, 176, 256. *See also* Holy Supper *and* Lord's Supper
conferences, xxiii, 23, 24, 26–27, 65, 67, 113, 115–16, 129, 152, 156, 166–67, 191n1, 194, 206, 215, 247, 250, 272, 284n5, 293, 295n38, 303, 309–310, 322, 337, 340, 341, 342, 345
confession (of wrongdoing), 50, 60, 64, 79, 80, 134, 138, 248
confessional subscription, 12n23, 23, 191, 192–94, 206, 210, 212, 222, 224, 261, 268
confession and absolution, 11, 103. *See also* private confession
Confessions, Lutheran, xiin2, 12n23, 23, 27, 28, 61n65, 66n18, 76n17, 102n71, 191, 192, 193, 194, 195, 206, 210, 211, 212, 213, 222, 224, 234, 242, 261, 262, 263, 264, 268, 273, 316, 317, 321
confirmation, xxiii, 11, 25, 55, 76, 85, 111n96, 121, 123, 134, 135, 146, 155, 156, 165, 174, 210, 228, 232, 235, 237, 239, 240, 245, 278–79, 286, 291n26, 302n54, 312, 333
counseling, 53–54, 80–82, 129, 143, 147, 162–63, 241, 291, 293, 295, 326, 327
Creed (Apostles'), 199, 201
crying, xxiii, 6, 10, 11, 27, 31, 48, 52, 64, 70, 84, 109, 117, 160, 161, 166, 219, 273, 338

dancing, 3, 6, 16–17, 83, 144, 146, 147n14, 148, 149–50, 302
deafness, xxiv, xxv, 113, 151–52, 173, 178, 357
debate, 27, 119, 121–22, 124, 125–28, 213
Der Lutheraner, 161c, 161n16, 191–227, 260–68, 272–76, 279, 310, 344–50, 356–58
Deutsche Evangelische Kirchenverein des Westens, 283n4
devil, 60, 80, 102, 116n122, 120, 122, 138, 140–41, 144, 149, 150, 156, 157, 195, 197, 198, 203, 217, 323. *See also* Satan
devotion (family), 61, 64, 158
Dietrich's Catechism, 135, 167, 278–79
diphtheria, 159
discipline (church), 74, 80–81, 83, 132, 137, 141, 145, 149, 150, 164, 192, 194, 242–43, 246, 290
discipline (corporal), 5–6, 10, 52, 153, 154

divine service. *See* service (divine)
doctor (medical), 20, 33–34, 44, 48, 140, 141–42, 151–52, 159, 160, 171, 325
drunkenness, 6, 17, 51, 79, 83n26, 112, 137, 146, 150, 242
duck-duck-goose, xii, 116n120
dumb ague, 15, 17, 18

elder. *See* administrator
election (doctrine), 161, 237, 346
erysipelas, 159
excommunication. *See* discipline (church)

fanaticism, 65, 108, 119–28, 196, 216, 234, 253, 261, 306, 311, 315, 316, 318
ferry, 106, 107, 109
fever, 15, 17, 18, 24n12, 140, 230, 278
fire, 4, 15, 17, 52, 53, 88, 89, 92c, 171, 174n47, 238, 290
fireworks, 2
fishing, 18, 25–26, 89, 93, 169, 232
food, 7, 17, 18, 36, 37, 40, 45, 54–55, 59, 65, 91, 111–12, 125, 126, 159, 169, 236n7
forgiveness, xii, xv, 61n64, 64, 79, 80, 81–82, 105, 111n96, 176, 195, 201, 214, 284, 287
funeral, 42, 50, 77, 84, 92, 133, 142, 153, 154, 156, 160, 162, 168, 219, 233, 238, 302, 331, 332, 348–50, 358

games, xii, 115–16, 146, 200
Gemeinde-Blatt, 342
generosity, xiv, xvii–xx, 39, 64, 101n70, 108–9, 118, 138, 152, 160, 164, 165, 208, 357
German Evangelical Church Association of the West, 283n4
gifts, xiv, xvii, xxv, 3, 85, 101n70, 164, 177–79, 200, 302, 333
greed, 13, 84, 112, 272, 292, 303

heaves, 94, 106
Heidelberg Catechism, 213
Herold, 274
history, xi–xii, xvii, xix, xx, xxiv, 21n5, 35n36, 62n3, 78n23, 85n33, 96, 118n128, 124n145, 130n3, 151nn24&26, 161c, 174n47, 215n25, 228, 231, 236n7, 238, 248n21, 254, 256, 274, 277, 351
Holy Supper, xii, 11, 24, 29, 42, 51, 53, 76, 78–81, 83, 87, 89, 96, 110, 121–22, 123, 124, 134–35, 137, 141, 142, 145, 149, 152, 154, 156, 163, 165, 166, 176n52, 210, 211, 213–14, 216, 235, 237, 239, 242, 251, 254, 256, 259, 263, 278, 279, 283, 311, 314,

324, 331, 334. *See also* Communion *and* Lord's Supper
horse, xxiv, 6, 15, 20, 25, 32, 33, 34, 42, 45–46, 47, 48–49, 58, 71, 89, 91, 92–97, 98–100, 101, 102, 103, 104, 105, 106, 107, 109, 110, 111, 113, 115, 116, 117, 122, 131, 138, 142, 146, 150, 164, 171, 172, 174, 229, 240, 258, 271, 282, 286, 287, 326, 330, 351–52, 353, 356
horseback riding, xii, 15, 20, 30, 32, 33, 34, 42, 48–49, 95, 96, 99, 104, 106, 107, 109–111, 142, 247

incantation, 135–36
Illinois Synod, 261n5, 281, 298, 337
Illustrirte Abendschule, 248, 274
Indianland, 6, 69, 70, 88, 94, 103, 109, 119, 124, 125, 128, 302, 305, 307, 310, 311, 314, 322, 329, 333, 334
Iowa Synod, 44n1, 88, 267, 337, 340, 341, 342

Kirchenblatt, 342

lawsuit, 30, 80, 131, 150, 153, 154, 323
lightning, 171
lodge membership, xxiv, 137, 141, 153–57
Lord's Prayer, xxiv, 61, 82, 199, 201, 202, 350
Lord's Supper (announcing), 11, 53, 78–80, 149, 283
Lord's Supper (doctrine), 42, 51n34, 78–79, 121–22, 123, 134–35, 213–14, 324
Lord's Supper (frequency), 29, 141, 145, 165
Lutheran Confessions. *See* Confessions, Lutheran
Luther's works, 61n65, 66, 67, 83, 95, 97, 101, 124, 147n14, 166, 167, 172, 192, 199n9, 200, 211, 247, 265n13, 273, 291n26, 306n72, 320, 321, 357

maid. *See* service (domestic)
measles, 287
medicine, 20, 44n5, 52, 106, 290
medicine man, 35n36, 215, 217
melodion, 56, 169
Menominee (Native American people), 69n3, 71c
Methodists/Methodism, 99n66, 108, 119–28, 155, 169, 195, 196, 197–98, 199, 201–2, 207–8, 211, 216, 253, 255, 257, 258, 259, 287, 298, 304, 307, 311, 312, 316, 319, 322, 324, 328, 331, 332, 337, 338, 339, 341. *See also* Albright Brethren
Michigan Synod (First), 12, 24n13, 191–94, 208, 209–210, 211
Michigan Synod (Second), 24n13, 273, 274, 275, 341

Missionary Synod of the West. *See* Michigan Synod (First)
mission festival, 13n27, 169, 174, 204n13, 211, 212
mission presentations, 175, 204–5
Missionsbote, 208–9, 211n18, 212–14
Missouri Synod, xii, xxiv, 12nn23&25, 21, 24, 25n13, 31, 37n41, 39n46, 44n1, 45n7, 77n18, 97n62, 102, 105n79, 108n89, 113n105, 115c, 130n4, 137n16, 151n21, 161c, 191n1, 205, 206, 207, 208, 209, 210, 222, 224, 225, 233, 246, 247, 248, 249, 250, 255, 260–68, 271, 272, 273, 274, 275, 278, 279, 289, 300, 306, 307, 308, 309, 310, 316, 317, 318, 319, 323, 324, 328, 330, 334, 335, 337, 338, 340, 342, 343, 344, 345, 346, 349, 350, 356
musician, 6, 83, 84, 149, 150, 159, 163, 169, 355

Native Americans. *See individual people groups*
New Lutheran, 210, 260–61, 262, 263, 264, 265, 266–67
Northern Illinois Synod, 261n5, 281, 282, 283, 285, 294
Norwegian Synod, 102, 349–50

Oddfellows, 141, 153, 154, 155
Ohio Synod, 21n2, 24n13, 39n46, 88n39
Ojibwe (Native American people), xxiv, 12, 13, 15–17, 23, 24nn12f, 25, 31, 32, 33, 35, 44, 69n3, 191–221
Old Lutheran, 24n13, 208, 209, 210, 211, 255, 264, 286

parsonage, xx, 8, 28, 29, 34, 35, 49n25, 62, 70–71, 72, 74, 75c, 86n35, 87c, 91c, 140, 143, 164, 232, 251, 282, 289, 292, 294, 302n56, 340
Pennsylvania Dutch, 45, 68, 125, 135, 139, 142
periodical, 88, 248, 260. *See also individual periodicals*
perspective, xii, 7, 24n13, 67, 83n26, 112–13, 176, 257
physician. *See* doctor (medical)
piano, 159, 343
Pietism, 8n15, 66n18, 76n16, 83n26, 147n14
Plumpsack, 116
pneumonia, 160n11, 168
prayer, xv, xviii, xxiv, 4, 6, 8, 11, 17, 25, 26, 29, 54, 61, 62, 64, 81, 82n24, 83, 96, 99, 101n71, 103, 110, 112, 121, 125, 126n150, 128, 148, 151n26, 160, 178, 193, 194, 196, 198, 199, 200, 201, 202, 218, 221, 222, 238, 240, 262, 275, 276, 283, 319, 331, 341, 345, 347, 348, 349, 350

SUBJECT INDEX

predestination. *See* election (doctrine)
presents. *See* gifts
private confession, 29, 78, 249n21
protection (divine), xi, xii, xx, 2, 20, 46, 170–72, 178, 240, 272, 346
providence, xxiii, xxiv, 19, 25–26, 38, 55–56, 99, 108, 159, 161, 356
Prussian Union, 22n10, 44, 51n34, 65, 67, 97n62, 157, 214, 234, 236, 237, 242, 260, 261, 266, 273, 283n4, 290, 292, 293, 294, 295, 304, 340

railroad, xii, 37, 39n47, 45, 58, 59, 69, 88, 95, 102, 103, 113, 117, 118, 130, 133, 139, 171–72, 231, 242, 249, 291, 337, 342
reconciliation, 60, 61, 64, 79, 80, 81–82, 134, 216
riverboat, xii, 7, 111, 112–13
Roman Catholics/Catholicism, 10, 11, 12, 24, 38, 41n54, 60, 61, 94, 137n14, 211, 213, 252n36

sacraments, 3n3, 23n12, 24n13, 119n134, 126, 191, 192, 193, 196, 199, 203, 204, 208, 211, 216, 236n4, 238, 263, 266, 267, 311, 317, 321n105. *See also* baptism, Communion, Holy Supper, *and* Lord's Supper
sailboat, 17–19, 215–16, 218
Satan, 24, 52, 201, 319. *See also* devil
school, xii, 5–6, 9, 10, 13, 15, 24n12, 25, 28, 30, 50, 51, 52, 54, 55, 59–60, 64, 66, 69, 76, 85, 125, 131–33, 139, 141, 143, 145, 146, 151, 153, 154, 155, 158, 169, 174n47, 177c, 192, 196, 198, 199, 200, 201, 202, 203, 207, 208, 215, 217, 220, 221, 228, 277, 286, 288, 289, 290, 292, 293n34, 294, 295, 297, 303, 312, 326, 331, 333, 337, 339, 340, 341
schoolhouse, 9, 10, 28, 30, 50, 51, 52, 55, 59, 61, 63, 71, 72, 73, 74, 75, 76, 89, 99, 101n71, 102n71, 104, 105, 107, 108, 119, 124, 125, 131, 132, 133, 134, 135, 139n3, 143, 151, 201, 240, 265, 270, 277, 289, 302, 304, 305nn65&67, 308, 312, 313, 315, 317, 318, 319, 321, 322, 328, 339, 340, 348, 355
Schwärmerei, 119n134. *See also* fanaticism
sermon preparation, 66–67, 83–84, 293, 341
service (divine), 8n15, 9, 29, 36, 49, 50n30, 52–53, 56, 60, 65, 80, 94, 97, 103, 107, 109, 112, 117, 119, 129, 131, 132, 134, 138, 151n24, 156, 158, 163, 165, 176, 199, 216, 219, 221, 235, 237, 240, 244, 245, 251, 257, 258–59, 264, 274, 302, 303, 317, 320, 338, 348, 354
service (domestic), 28, 32, 52, 81, 84–85, 94, 100, 134
shenanigans, 15, 114–16
ship, 6, 7–8, 15, 18, 25, 36n37, 38, 39n47, 56, 215, 228
singing, 3, 11, 19, 28, 29, 31, 40, 42, 49, 64, 76–77, 107, 108, 109, 125, 132, 133, 155, 158, 166, 169, 178, 179, 199, 201, 216, 235, 238, 245, 302, 350
sled, 15, 71, 85, 89, 96–97, 98–99, 131, 171, 172
sleeping during sermons, 53–54
snow, 52, 89, 96, 97, 98–100, 243, 245, 353
spells, 135–36, 147
spiritual growth/maturity, 53–54, 85, 134, 135, 165, 166, 217, 220–21
stagecoach, xii, 50, 88, 103, 104, 105, 271, 273
steamboat, 8, 45, 111, 112, 264, 275
stool of repentance. *See* bench of repentance
storytelling, v, xi, xii, xv, xvii, xix, 134, 158, 159, 172, 265, 292, 351
Strieter, Elizabeth née Ernst (1838–1924)
    appearance of, 59, 83, 167, 229. *See also* pictures of *below*
    birth of, 58, 168, 231, 233
    death of, 233
    grave of, *358*
    health of, 140, 159, 167
    intelligence of, 59–60
    marriage of, xxiv, 58–59, 167
    nursing the sick, 140, 143, 169
    pictures of, *xxv, 58, 167, 168, 187, 358*
    struck by lightning, 171
    youth of, 55, 59–60, 231
Strieter, Johannes
    baptism of, 1
    beard of, *v, xxv, 58, 96, 113, 114, 115, 118, 166, 167, 168, 170, 187, 357*
    birthday celebration of, 175n49, 176, 177–79
    birth of, 1, 356
    burial of, 358
    confirmation of, 11, 25, 27n18
    death of, 356
    debating. *See* debate
    decision of, to enter the ministry, 13, 25–26
    elementary education of, 5–6, 9–11
    emigration of. *See* immigration of
    grave of, *358*
    handwriting of, *57*
    health of, 13, 15, 17, 18, 52, 54–56, 92, 106, 113, 128, 141–42, 165–66
    horses of, 71, 91, 93, 94–95, 101, 131, 353
    immigration of, 6–9

letters by, 123, 314–15, 316–17, 320–21, 328–29
marriage of, xxiv, 58–59, 167
ordination of, 54, 222
pay of, 108–9, 165. *See also* salary of *below*
pictures of, *v, xxv, 58, 114, 167, 168, 170, 187, 357*
pre-seminary education of, 27–28, 36
public protest of, 310, 312–20, 329
rebuking, 53, 61, 79, 80, 83, 136, 137, 145, 148, 150, 155
reported on by others, xxiii–xxiv, 124n143, 217, 229, 232, 255, 302, 303–4, 305, 307, 308, 309, 310–11, 312, 322, 323–24, 325, 327–28, 330, 333, 338, 351–54, 356–58
residences of, 2, 8–9, 15, 19, 27–28, 39, 51, 52, 53, 54, 60, 62, 70–71, 72, 130–31, 140, 143, 152, *164*
salary of, 51, 64, 109, 165
seminary education of, 39–45
traveling problems and suspense of, 32, 92–95, 96, 98–99, 102–3, 104, 105, 106, 142, 172, 351–52
vomiting, 15, 113
weakness of, 64, 161, 165
Sunday School, 293, 302n54
symbols. *See* Confessions, Lutheran

Ten Commandments, 41–42, 50, 148–49, 162, 199, 211, 247, 315, 319
threats, 81, 128, 300, 312
tragedy, 15, 40, 55, 82, 92, 160, 168–69, 218–21, 278
train. *See* railroad
translating, xiv–xv, xix, 25, 30, 35, 193, 197, 198, 199, 201, 207, 230, 349
typhoid, 13, 230

United Church. *See* Prussian Union

wagon, 6, 45, 46–47, 48–49, 69, 70, 94, 105, 106, 121, 122, 128, 326
walking, xii, 6, 11, 15, 27, 30, 31, 35, 36, 37, 43, 50, 54, 55, 61, 66, 88, 99, 103, 104, 150, 165–66, 174, 236n7, 237, 272, 276, 348
Wausau Daily Record-Herald, v, 279, 351–55
wedding, 3, 58–59, 83, 84, 104n76, 147n14, 231, 238, 271, 294
widow, 21, 39, 41c, 48, 50, 55, 58n54, 61, 64, 109, 111, 135, 153, 155, 172, 176, 232, 342
Wisconsin Synod, 71n9, 75, 107, 108nn89f, 124n143, 130n4, 242n15, 248, 259, 260–68, 270, 271, 273, 279, 281–342, 349
witnessing (personal), 82, 112, 119–20, 162–63, 217
worship. *See* service (divine)

Name Index

(For names of churches, see Place Index. For names of synods/church bodies and Native American peoples, see Subject Index. For the names of Johannes Strieter's ancestors not listed here, see Appendix I. Birth and death years, if known, are given in parentheses for Strieter's contemporaries. "c" refers to a caption. *Italicized* page numbers refer to an illustration.)

Abel (Cain's brother), 3
Abraham (Ojibwe convert), 195–96
Adam (first man), 3, 134, 214
Ahner, Friedrich August (1835–1907), 262
Ahrens, Louis Theodor (1838–1891), 190
Albrecht, Christian Johann (1847–1924), 349
Alexander, William, 292
Allen, Lillie, 11
Ämilie Juliane, countess of Schwarzburg-Rudolstadt, 31n22
Amman,[1] Karl Gottlieb (1812–1877), 31
Andres, Agnes née Sievers (1859–1922), 172
Andres, Peter (1859–1915), xxv, 172, *173*
Anklam, August (1812–1883), 86n35
Anklam, Dorothea Sophie née Lau (1811–1890), 74, 85, 86
Anna (Ojibwe convert), 195
Anton, Paul, 83n26
Arndt, Johann, 3
Arnold, Daniel (1814–1899), 45n11, 48n22
Arnold, Georg (1821–1903), 45n11, 48n22
Arnold, Heinrich (1825–1904), 45n11, 48n22
Arnold, Jacob (1787–1865), 45, 46, 47, 48–49, 68
Arnold, Jacob (1823–1888), 45n11, 48, 49
Arnold, Johann (1817–1894), 45n11, 48n22
Arnold, Jonas (1825–1906), 45n11, 48n22
Arnold, Ludwig (1829–1910), 45n11, 48nn22f
Auch, Dorothea née Strieter (1818–1886; Johannes's sister), 2, 6, 7, 9, 11, 12, 13n27, 15, 27, 32, 33, 187, 215
Auch, J. Christian (1791–1868), 8

Auch, Johann Jacob Friedrich (1817–1905), 12, 13, *14*, 15, *17*, 18, 19, 23, 24, 25, 26, 27, 32, 33, 34, 35, 36, 39n47, 187, 205, 206, 208–214, 215, 216, 217, 218–21
Avery, Jared Newell (1825–1880), 94n54
Avery, William (1817–1892), 94n54

Bach, Christian (1823–1884), 13
Bach, Christiana née Strieter (1822–1893; Johannes's sister), 2, 6, 7, 9, 11, 13, 19, 37
Bach, Elizabeth. *See* Liken, Elizabeth
Bading, Johannes (1824–1913), 108n90, 124n143, 248, 249n21, 271, 281–82, 327
Bahr, Ferdinand, 75, 243, 244
Baierlein, Eduard (1819–1901), 25, 26, 44, 199, 201, 203, 216
Banick, Michael, 330
Bartelt, H., 296
Barthel, Martin C. (1838–1899), 77
Barth, Katharina (1835–1893), 189
Barth, Jacob (1833–1892), 189
Bartz, Johan, 330
Barz, Daniel, 74
Beilke, Auguste née Neumann (1831–1916), 124n145, 128
Beilke, Heinrich (1833–1884), 101n71, 124, 125, 128
Beilke, Johann Heinrich Carl (1860–1938), 125
Bemassikeh (Ojibwe chief). *See* Pemasike
Bender, Martin (1810–1876), 249n23
Bergholz, William (1848–1935), 354

---

1. Strieter spelled it Ammann.

367

NAME INDEX

Bernecker, George (1883–1972), 187
Bernecker, Lillie née Strieter (1883–1969), 187
Bernecker, Lucy (1907–1982), 187
Bernthal, Friedrich[2] (1825–1862), 35
Bernthal, Georg Martin (1787–1857), 35
Besel, Friedrich (1815–1901), 44, 45, 46–47, 48, 49–50, 68
Betzner, J., 139
Beutler, Jakob, 330
Bewie, William Henry (1843–1935), 131–32
Beyer, Johann Nicholas (1825–1870), 118
Beyer, Johann Paul (1832–1905), 129, 225
Bicker, Heinrich (1826–1899), 64
Birkner, Heinrich (1857–1932), 348
Blank (Albright Brethren preacher), 123–24
Boehner, Carl F., 284–85
Boeling, Friedrich (1827–1900), 115n112
Bohlen, Wessel (1853–1926), 150, 156, 167
Böhning, Clara née Titgemeier (1840–1920), 188
Böhning, Ernst H. (1833–1916), 64, 188
Böhning, Hermann Heinrich (1798–1871), 64, 65
Böhning, John (1838–1883), 64
Böhning, Maria Eleonora née Stoffer-Blase (1799–1874), 65
Böhning, Mary D. (1842–1925), 64
Böhning, Wilhelm (1835–1861), 64
Bollhagen, Laurentius David, 76, 77
Borges, Clara née Meyer (b. 1813), 65
Borges, Ernst (1813–1868), 65
Borges, Mary C. (1841–1915), 64
Bornemann, Mrs. (widow), 39
Borsack, Wilhelm (1823–1885), 99, 120, 122
Böse (family), 51, 60
Brandt, Herman J. (1859–1934), 354
Brandt,[3] Nils Olsen (1824–1921), 103, 104
Braschler (Evangelical pastor in Franklin Center, Iowa), 340
Brauer, Karl (1831–1907), xxiv, 152
Brecht (Iowa Synod pastor), 342
Bredow (Iowa Synod pastor), 341
Breitenfeld, Julius (1840–1895), 74, 82n25, 89n45, 188
Brenz, Johannes, 3
Brose (pastor in Woodland, Wis.), 262
Brumder, Mr. (resident of Milwaukee), 342
Brunn, Friedrich August (1819–1895), 276
Buchholz, Michael (1819–1907), 71, 75, 76, 77, 78, 80, 92, 94, 103, 122, 130, 307, 310, 319, 321, 329

Budach, Paul R. (1860–1937), 358
Bul(l)winkel, Mr., 250
Buntrock, John, 284
Buntrock, Wilhelmine, 284
Burg, Johann Friedrich, 257n45
Burger, Johann Georg (1816–1847), 21
Burger, Mathilda née Killinger (1851–1947), 174
Busse, Charlotte née Jacobson, 82
Busse, Gottlieb, 82
Busse, Julie (b. 1851), 82

Cain (first murderer), 3
Catenhusen, Anna Elisabeth (b. 1863), 109n93
Chemnitz, Martin, 66n17
Clarke, John C. (1831–1906), 85n33, 352n2
Clöter, Ernst Ottomar (1825–1897), 22, 26, 114, 115
Conrad, Jacob (1828–1890), 242, 284n5
Conradt, Maria née Smith (1831–1916), 189
Crämer, August (1812–1891), xii, xxiv, 16n36, 21, 22n10, 23, 24n12, 26, 27, 28, 29, 30, 31, 32n23, 35, 36, 39, 40, 42, 44, 50, 100, 102, 115, 192, 193, 195, 196, 199, 202, 205, 208, 215n25, 216, 218, 272, 276, 348, 356
Crämer, Dorothea (1817–1884), 36
Crämer, Eva, 10
Crämer, Heinrich (1840–1881; August's adopted son), 35–36
Cramer, Jerry, 10
Cronenwett, Georg (1814–1888), 12nn23&26
Crull, August, 31n22

Daenzer, Mr. (teacher), 145
Dannenfeldt, Heinrich (1859–1945), 358
Dartt, E. J., 69n3
David (psalmist and king of Israel), xxi
Deindoerfer, Johannes (1828–1907), 267
Dicke, Peter Heinrich (1822–1911), 75, 76, 116, 223, 255n41
Diehlmann, Konrad (1820–at least 1880), 70, 74, 75, 119, 247–50, 251, 302, 303, 304, 306, 308, 322n109
Dietrich, Veit, 67n20
Donning, August, 71, 74, 77, 313, 314, 316, 317n97
Donning, Gottlieb, 74
Douglas, Stephen A. (1813–1861), 117
Dress, Anna, 189
Dress, Ernst, 85, 131, 189

2. Strieter mistakenly guessed that the second Bernthal son was a tailor (p. 35). Friedrich was actually the third, Johann (1820–1905) and Leonhard (1821–1911) being the first and second.

3. Strieter spelled it Brand.

NAME INDEX

Drögemüller, Christoph (1867–1911), 152, 227
DuMond, Meta née Kern (1878–1951), 343
Dumser, J. Simon (1817–1857), 13n27, 192, 194

Engelbert, Wilhelm (1823–1878), 68, 223
Ernst, Adam (1815–1895), 21
Ernst, Anna Kunigunde née Wittig (1811–1875), 55, 56, 58, 59, 62, 64, 69, 187, 228, 229, 230–33
Ernst, Caspar/Casper (c. 1808–1850; Elizabeth Strieter's father), 228–30, 231, 232
Ernst, Caspar/Casper (Elizabeth Strieter's cousin), 59, 228
Ernst, H., 59
Ernst, Louis, 59n57, 228
Ernst, Sabina née Ruff, 229
Ernst, Washington, 228–29
Eslinger, George, 236
Estel, Philip Samuel (1843–1920), 354
Eve (first woman), 3, 134, 214
Ewert, Michael (1812–1888), 309
Eylert, Rulemann Friedrich, 236

Fachtmann, Gottlieb (1813–1877), 262–65
Fackler, Johannes P. (1846–1913), 174
Fenske, Andrew, 74
Fickenscher, Auguste, 189
Fierke, Caroline née Buth/Butt (1821–1860), 92
Fierke, Gustav (1848–1860), 92
Fierke, Wilhelm (1817–1894), 74, 78n21, 84, 92c, 308n83
Fischer, Mr. (resident of Berlin, Wis.), 117
Fischer, Samuel, 74, 240
Fleischmann, Philipp (1815–1878), 40
Francke, August Hermann, 83n26
Franz, Frederick (1844–1887), 179,[4] 233
Franz, Sophie née Ernst (1844–1925), 55, 56, 62, 64, 69, 176, 229, 231, 232, 233
Fresenius, Johann Philipp, 66, 67
Friedrich Wilhelm IV, king of Prussia, 236
Friedrich, Wilhelm Julius (1837–1900), 105n80
Fürbringer, Ottomar (1810–1892), xxiv, 105, 115, 129

Gausewitz, Carl F. W. (1828–1910), 284n5
Gensike, Traugott (1827–1905), 309
Gerhard, Johann, 3n2, 51n34, 66n17, 214

Gerhard, Mr. (brewer in Chippewa Falls), 106, 107
Gerhardt, Paul, 4n4
Gernand, Lucy née Strieter (1891–1967), 187
Geyer, Ludwig (1812–1892), 237, 246n18, 248, 249n21
Giese, E. Frederick, 297
Gishaemanido (Ojibwe spirit), 15
Glaeser, Johannes G. (1865–1933), 354
Glenz, Gottlieb, 75
Goldammer, C. F. (1821–1896), 292–93
Gosenheimer (family), 19
Gotsch, George (1871–1955), 176n50
Gotsch, Katharina née Kiefer (1833–1899), 190
Gotsch, Theodor (1825–1908), 167, 190, 226
Götz/Goez, Carl Gottlieb (1782–at least 1837), 4, 5, 6
Götz/Goez, Christiane Friederike née Römer (1794–1882), 5
Grabau, Johannes Andreas August (1804–1879), 97
Gräbner, August L. (1849–1904), 349
Gräbner, Johann Heinrich Philip (1819–1898), 21, 26, 30, 205, 208, 216
Graverad, Jacob, 16n36, 25, 33
Griebel, (Wilhelm Georg? [1803–1885]), 39
Grimm, A. F. W. (1864–1922), 168
Grometer, Anna Margaretha, 189
Grometer, Michael, 189
Grosse, Traugott Johannes (1844–1919), 152, 167
Gruhlke, August (1817–1895), 74, 75, 78n21, 237, 240, 251–59
Gübert, H. C., 152, 227
Guderjahn, Wilhelmine née Krueger (1817–1909), 188
Gudrean, Wilhelmine. See Guderjahn, Wilhelmine
Gysin,[5] Mr. (resident of Peru, Ind.), 171

Haag, Daniel (1825–1872), 53, 54
Habermann, Johann, 126n150
Hanser, Otto (1832–1910), 345n3, 347, 349
Hardekopf, Friedrich (b. 1828), 131, 132
Hartmann, Anna Elisabeth Wilhelmine née Reichmann, 292n31
Hartmann, Herrmann Heinrich, 292n31
Hartwig, Theodore (1859–1921), 353

---

4. The signature on this page could not have been made by Fred Franz, since it was written in 1904 and Fred passed away in 1887. His wife Sophie, who had doubtless become accustomed to signing things in her husband's name while he was still alive, appears to have continued the practice in his memory even after he died. Or there may be some other explanation that is not yet apparent to me (e.g. another Fritz Franz of whom I am unaware).

5. Strieter spelled it Gysen.

Haserot(h), Mr., 50
Hass, Friedrich Wilhelm (1818–1890), 309
Hasse, August (1826–1905), 241n13
Hattstädt, Wilhelm (1811–1884), xxiv, 21, 23, 37n42, 191, 192, 193n4, 195, 205
Haushahn, Johann Georg (d. 1850), 218
Heckel, Gertrude née Strieter (1896–1983), *187*
Heidorn, August (1823–1884), 190
Heidorn, Sophie (1835–1896), 190
Heinz (pastor in Ind.), 167
Hensler, Erna M. née Furstenberg (1899–1996; Johannes's great-granddaughter), 168
Herter, Mr. (teacher), 145
Hieber, Johann M. (1850–1901), 279
Hiller, Philipp Friedrich, 11
Hilpert, F., 284n5, 294, 341
Hoenecke, Adolf (1835–1908), 301, 306–310, 311, 321, 323, 327, 329, 330, 333, 334
Hofacker, Ludwig, 8
Hoffmann, Adolph August Ernst (b. 1871), 271, 272
Hoffmann, Clara Renata Coeleste (b. 1868), 271, 272, 278–79
Hoffmann, Eduard Oscar Arthur (b. 1875), 271, 272
Hoffmann, Ernst August Wilhelm (1862–1873), 271, 272, 278
Hoffmann, Ernst Georg Heinrich Martin (b. 1865), 271, 272, 278–79
Hoffmann, Franz, 293n34
Hoffmann, Harry Hubert (b. 1882), 271
Hoffmann, Johann Jacob (1840–1919), 86n35, 97n63, *100*, 101, 102, 124n143, 125n148, 188, 224, 269–77, *278*, 279–80, 353
Hoffmann, Johann Jacob Ernst (1865–1905), 271, 272, 278–79
Hoffmann, Johanne Rosinalde Erneste née von Anschuetz (1843–1923[6]), 188, 271, 272
Hoffmann, Johann Valentin (c. 1814–1888), 269, 277
Hoffmann, Johann Valentin Ernst (1864–1899), 271, 272, 278
Hoffmann, Maria Christiane née Hohmann (c. 1816–1880), 269, 277
Hoffmann, Otto Wilhelm Ernst (1874–1930), 271, 272
Hoffmann, Theophilus Oscar Ernst (b. 1869), 271, 272
Hoffmann, Wilhelm Philipp Ernst (b. 1878), 271
Ho(hen)berger, Mr., 19

Hölter, Louis (1848–1922), xiv, xv, xxiv, 175, 358
Hölter, Maria née Böhning (1828–1902), 188
Hol(t)z, Andrew (1817–1903), 74, 240
Holz, Ferdinand, 74
Huber, Daniel, 292, 294
Hubinger, Anna (1823–1889), 29c
Hubinger, Johann Georg (1823–1909), 29, 30
Hubinger, Johann Matthias (1820–1903), 29, 30
Hügli, Johannes Adam (1831–1904), 118
Huntington, William P., 71

Jahnke, G., 336, 339
Jahns, Michael, 121, 123
Job, Ludwig, 300
Johansen, G. (ship captain), 7, 8
John (apostle), 78, 136, 157
Jox, Johannes Heinrich (1831–1893), xxiv, 115, 116, 138, 141, 166, 226, 260–62
Judas, John, 330
Jüngel, Heinrich (1829–1911), 54, 65, 66, 67
Jüngel, Theodore H. (1871–1960), 174

Kaeppel, Albert. *See* Käppel, G. C. Albert
Kaeppel, Mr. (teacher), 145
Kahler, Marie née Strieter (1899–1983), *187*
Kalb, J. Paul (1828–1858), 40
Kalbfleisch (family), 6
Käppel, G. C. Albert (1861–1934), 163
Keith, Mr. (merchant in Manchester), 19
Kern, Albert E. (1875–1949), 342
Kern, Anna Dorothea. *See* Struve, Anna Dorothea
Kern, Georg Friedrich (1861–1934), 297
Kern, Henrietta née Marburg (1843–1911), 281, 305, 327, 331, 332, 334, 342
Kern, Johann Jakob (1835–1913), 129, 259, 281–343
Kern, Johann Martin Herman (b. 1863), 297–98
Kern, Julia formerly Panek (b. 1848), 342–43
Kern, Meta. *See* DuMond, Meta
Kern, Mr. (resident of New Berlin, Wis.), 293–94
Keyl, Julia Wilhelmina (1884–1951), 348
Keyl, Magdalena née Walther (1842–1936), 348
Keyl, Stephanus (1838–1905), 348
Kickbusch, August (1828–1901), 94, 128, *352*
Kickbusch, Mathilda née Schochow (1833–1891), 352
Kiesel (Iowa Synod pastor), 339, 342
Kiesow, Friedrich, 71, 73, 74
Killinger, Johann (1810–1860), 13

---

6. This death year is given in her son Otto Wilhelm Ernst's obituary. She is allegedly buried in Merrill, Wis.

Killinger, Margaretha née Strieter (1826–1857; Johannes's sister), 2, 4, 6, 7, 9, 11, 13, 21, 37
Kittel, Herman, 108n90
Klempe, Gottlieb, 73
Koch, August (d. 1867), 33, 34
Koch, Friedrich Carl Ludwig[7] (1799–1852), 26, 27, 34
Koehler, Johann Philipp (1859–1951), 248, 263n11
Koehler, Philipp (1828–1895), 284n5, 295–96, 297
Koester, Conrad (d. 1864), 284n5, 291, 296
Kohnke, August (1827–1898), 74
Kohnke, Johanne Henriette née Krenz (1833–1910), 74, 85, 86c, 96
Kohnke, Ludwig, 74
Kolbe, Otto (1834–1914), 175, 177, 226
Kollmann, Anna. *See* Neusüs, Anna
Kollmann, Friedrich, 131
Kollmann, Wilhelm (1833–1913), 131, 132–33
Kopplin, August, 74
Kopplin, Johann, 73, 237
Kors, Heinrich (1833–1911), 139, 140, 141, 189
Kraenzlein, Christ., 262, 267–68
Krauss, Eugen Adolf Wilhelm (1851–1924), 151n24, 168
Krenz, Friedrich (1830–1905), 86, 87c, 101n71
Krenz, Johann Daniel, 86n35
Krenz, Wilhelm (1824–1869), 75, 243, 244
Krenz, Wilhelmine née Gennrich (1841–1906), 86, 87c
Krieger, Catharine Henrietta née Schaible (1843–1922), 51n32
Kronenwett, Georg. *See* Cronenwett
Krueger, Ernestine Charlotte née Schultz (1841–1907), 235
Krueger, Henry (1857–1913), 351
Krueger, Ludwig, 74
Krumsieg, Theodor Gustav Adolph (1836–1900), 104n76
Kufahl, Anna née Schunkeler (1805–1890), 158
Kufahl, Carl (1809–1890), 94, 113?, 158
Kufahl, Carl (1832–1877), 158
Kufahl, Daniel (1846–1901), 158
Kufahl, Emilie née Nass (1837–1911), 158
Kuhn, Christian Lorenz (b. 1863), 109n93
Kühn, Hermann (1818–1898), 22, 26, 27, 28, 31, 62, 65, 83, 188, 222
Kundinger, E., 27, 28

Lange, Joachim, 83n26
Larsen, Peter Laurentius (1833–1915), 349
Lederer, Carl August (1847–1926), 174
Lehmann, Eduard, 331
Lemke, C., 336, 339
Leontine (ship), 7
Leutheusser, Mr. (teacher), 145
Leutner, Friedrich (1848–1916), xiii, xxvi, 10n21, 19n41, 20n43, 25n15, 33n27, 34nn29f, 35n33, 36n38, 40n49, 43n58, 45n13, 48nn19–21, 51n33, 54n42, 55nn46&48, 59n56, 60n62, 66n16, 70nn4&8, 85nn30f, 89n42, 94n54, 111n98, 113n104, 115n113, 117nn125f, 118nn127&129, 119n131, 123n139, 125nn141f, 126n151, 127n152, 128nn154–56, 129nn157&159, 133n8, 136n11, 139n2, 141n6, 145nn6&9, 146nn10&12, 150nn16f, 153n30, 154n32, 155n35, 157n37, 158n1, 162n19, 174nn40&45, 175n49, 176nn53f, 177nn55ff, 229, 232, 233
Leutner, Mary née Ernst (1848–1894), 55, 56, 62, 64, 69, 229, 231, 232, 233
Leyser, Polycarp, 66n17
Liebich, Ehrenfried, 257n45
Liken,[8] Elizabeth née Bach (1863–1946), 3
Limb, Margaretha Maria née Schaible (1837–1921), 51n32, 54
Lindemann, Friedrich (1851–1907), 163
Lindemann, Johann Christoph Wilhelm (1827–1879), xii, xxiv, 65, 66, 67, 68, 131, 146, *147*, 160, 189, 190, 223
Lindemann, Mathilde Elisabeth, 190
Link, Georg (1829–1908), 116, 128
List, Edwin O. (1896–1978), xiv, 169
List, Heinrich (1871–1946), xxv, 152, *153*, 169, 173, 174n40, 189, 357
List, Maria née Strieter (1871–1948), 143, 159, 160, 167, *168*, 169, 173
Lochner, Friedrich (1822–1902), 22, 23, 28c, 35n36, 118, 191, 192, 195, 225, 262, 268, 271
Loescher, Valentin Ernst, 83n26
Löhe, Johann Konrad Wilhelm (1808–1872), 12, 21, 22, 23 (caption & n12), 31, 37n41, 39n46, 191, 267
Lossner, Heinrich (1841–1896), 85, 188
Louise (ship), 7, 8
Lücke, Martin (1859–1926), 41c, 115c
Luckhard, Charles F., xix, 16, 215n25

---

7. Strieter called him Bergrat Koch (p. 26). Bergrat, "counselor of mines," was his title, denoting an expert in mining and related manufacturing operations.

8. Strieter spelled it Leiken.

Luckhard(t), Friedrich (1813–1888), 13
Luckhard(t), Katharina née Strieter (1820–1907; Johannes's sister), 2, 6, 7, 9, 11, 13, 37, 174
Ludke, Emil, 75
Lueck, August, 331
Lueck, G., 333
Luecker, Louis, 151n26
Luethe, Sigismund (same as next?), 339
Luetke, Si(e)gesmund, 75, 243, 244, 245, 246, 336
Luther, Martin, 3n3, 61n65, 66, 67, 83, 95, 97, 101, 123, 124, 147, 166, 167, 172, 192, 260, 306, 320, 357
Lutz (Iowa Synod pastor), 342

Machimanido (Ojibwe spirit), 15
Machmeyer/Machmeier, Johann Ludwig Heinrich (1863–1954), 110n94
Mack, Mr. (teacher), 145
Mackwitz, W., 41c
Magdalena (Ojibwe convert), 195, 196
Maier, Dorothea née Auch (1828–1908), 25, 27, 215, 219
Maier, Friedrich (1823–1850), 13, 15, 23, 24, 25, 27, 206, 208–214, 215, 217, 218–220, *220*
Maier, Mr. (Friedrich's brother), 219
Marchetti, Louis (1846–1931), 85n33
Mary (mother of Jesus), 10, 141, 198, 239n12
Math, Cathariena (*sic*), 7n14
Math, Leontine, 7n14
Mayerhoff, E., 310
Meganigischik (Ojibwe chief), 16n36, 216, 220
Meine, Ardina (1874–1961), 176, 177, 178
Meine, Martha née Meyer (1873–1947), 176, 177, 178
Memmel, Mr., 50
Menge, Friedrich, 330
Metzger, Georg Wilhelm Emmanuel (1800–1855), 12
Meurer, Moritz, 28n20
Meyer, Peter (1825–1901), 313–14
Miessler, Ernst Gustav Hermann (1826–1916), 44
Minch, Philip, 231
Moldehnke, Eduard (1836–1904), 107, 108, 124n143, 125n148, *270*, 271, 291, 292, 303, 326n113, 327, 332
Moll, Andreas, 27
Molthan, John F. C. (1865–1952), 151, 227
Muehlhaeuser, Johannes (1804–1868), 234–39, 241–42, 243–47, 248–59, 260, 282, 291, 293

Müller, August J. (1862–1938), 174
Müller, Christian (1858–1925), 174
Müller, Jacob Friedrich (1844–1927), 9, 174
Müller, Karl (1807–1880), 8, 9, 13, 20, 174
Müller, Magdalena née Klager (1823–1910), 174
Müller, Rosina née Strieter (1816–1855; Johannes's sister), 2, 6, 7, 9, 11, 20, 37, 174
Muschler, Maria née Schnerzingor (1832–1915), 189

Nage-jikamik (Ojibwe chief), 16, 17, 33, 208, 217
Nass, Edward (1842–1917), 353–54
Neumann, David (c. 1791–1875), 128
Neumann, Louisa née Schwan (1796–1889), 128
Neusüs, Anna née Kollmann (1856–1932), 133
Nicholas I, Tsar of Russia (1796–1855), 6
Niemann, Heinrich (1848–1910), 169, 226, 348
Niemann, Julie née Walther (1848–1898), 348
Nocktschikome (Ojbiwe chief). *See* Nage-jikamik
Nohl, Christoph (1823–1884), 292
Norden, Herman Heinrich (1844–1919), 135
Notz, Eugen A. (1847–1903), 349
Nuechterlein, J. George (1874–1963), 357, 358

Oesan, Mr. (resident of New Holstein, Wis.), 285–86
Off (Evangelical pastor in Lake Mills, Wis.), 283
Oglajo (Ojibwe medicine man), 35, 36, 198–99, 215, 217
Oldshim. *See* Oglajo
Opitz, A. (pastor in Slinger, Wis.), 309
Orff,[9] (Gottlieb? [1822–1888]; resident of Ft. Wayne, Ind.), 159
Ottmann, Friedrich (1829–1900), 40, 42
Otto, John, 331

P., Lydia (born c. 1871), 159
Paff, Jacob (1824–1895), 271
Paul (apostle), xxiv, 135, 156, 195, 261, 314, 320
Peisch, Amalie née Würtenberger (1846–1869), 110–11
Peisch, Johann, 111n97
Pelton, Gust, 59
Pemasike(h) (Ojibwe chief), 197, 198, 201, 202, 203, 217
Peter (apostle), 136, 319, 320, 340
Pfister, A., 341–42
Phillips, Ruth née Strieter (1906–1986), *187*
Pinkepank, Johann Heinrich August (1826–1856), 27
Poach, Andreas, 67n20

---

9. Strieter spelled it Orf.

NAME INDEX

Polsdorfer, F., 145, 151n26
Preus, Herman Amberg (1825–1894), 349
Pritzlaff, John (1820–1900), xii, 118, 225n9

Quehl, H., 284n5
Querl, Emma née Strieter (1856–1933), 69, 99, 117, 143, 167, *168*, 169, 171
Querl, Hermann W. (1845–1921), 168, 169, 174, 188

Rahe, Anna née Ernst (1845–1925), 55, 56, 62, 64, 69, 228, 229, 231, 232, 233
Rahe, Henry F. (1866–1951), xxvi, 228, 233
Rahe, Henry H. (1842–1918), 233
Rang, Johann Heinrich (1839–1918), 189
Rathert, Friedrich C. (1869–1950), 175
Rathjen, Henry J. (1872–1928), 175
Rauschert, Jakob (1828–1882), 39, 41
Reiber, Adam (1845–1931), 177, 229, 233
Reiber, Sarah née Ernst (1846–1925), 55, 56, 62, 64, 69, 177, 229, 231, 232, 233
Reichle, Fred, 229
Reichle, Henry C. (1845–1908), 170, 174n40, 229, 233
Reichle, Martha née Ernst (1843–1924), 55, 56, 62, 64, 69, 173–74, 229, 231, 232, 233
Reim, Adolph (1860–1932), 250
Reim, Anna née Brumder (1827–1911), 250, 302, 310
Reim, Gottlieb (1828–1882), 75, 242–43, 244, 245, 248–51, 282–312, 320–36, 337, 339n131
Reinke, Augustus (1841–1899), 138
Richter (pastor), 12n26
Ritter, J., 340, 342
Röbbelen, Karl August Wilhelm (1817–1866), 12n25
Röder, Edmund (1827–1902), 44
Roehrs, Henry (1862–1928), 358
Root, Anson (d. 1861), 249n23
Rörer, Georg, 67n20
Rörke, Mr., 71
Röske, Carl Friedrich, Jr. (b. 1841), 85
Röske, Carl Friedrich, Sr., 85n32
Röske, Louise née Goethe, 85n32
Röske, Mr., 76
Röske, Wilhelm Ferdinand (b. 1844), 85, 89, 90, 117
Rudelbach, Andreas Gottlob (1792–1862), 88
Rudisill, Mr., 43
Ruhland, Friedrich (1836–1879), xxiv, 115, 116, 262–68

Salos, Mr., 59, 60

Sargent, George B., 71
Satan, 24, 52, 201, 319
Sauaban (Ojibwe chief), 197, 198
Sauer, J. J. E. (1827–1889), 309
Schaefer (Methodist preacher), 125–28
Schaible, Carl Heinrich (1851–1927), 51n32
Schaible, Caroline (1848–1910), 51n32
Schaible, Catharine Barbara née Ramsayer (1817–1873), 51n32, 54, 55, 60
Schaible, Catherine Henrietta. *See* Krieger, Catherine Henrietta
Schaible, Jacob (1807–1874), 51, 54, 55, 56, 60, 61
Schaible, Jacob E. (1845–1921), 51n32, 60–61
Schaible, Johann Friedrich (d. 1875), 51n32
Schaible, Margaretha Maria. *See* Limb, Margaretha Maria
Schaller, Johann Gottlieb Michael (1819–1887), 37, 38, 45, 347
Schaller, John (1859–1920), 37n41
Schefft, August (1851–1912), 169, *177*, 178
Scheibel, Johann Gottfried, 236
Schipinsky, Anna Friederike (b. 1860), 111n97
Schipinsky, August, 111n97
Schipinsky, Barbara née Ander, 111n97
Schipinsky, Emilie Clara (b. 1854), 111n97
Schipinsky, Louise Wilhelmine (b. 1855), 111n97
Schipinsky, Pauline Wilhelmine (b. 1852), 111n97
Schleifer, Samuel, 236n7
Schlinckmann (pastor in Ind.), 167
Schmid, Friedrich (1807–1883), xix, 8, 9, 11, 12, 13, 23, 24, 25n13, 37, 191, 205, 206, 208, 210
Schmidt, August, 101n71
Schmidt, Dorothea, 189
Schmidt/Smith, Michael (1819–1874), 71, 74, 101, 129, 188, 302n56, 303, 304, 305nn65ff, 308n82, 310, 312, 313, 314, 315, 316, 318, 321n104, 327, 329
Schmudlach, Johann, 331
Schreiner, Heinrich (1863–1943), 110n94
Schult, J. P. v., 76n16
Schultz, Carl August (b. 1830), 237
Schultz, Carl Friedrich (1839–1907), 235
Schultz, Ernestine Charlotte. *See* Krueger, Ernestine Charlotte
Schultz, Ernst (1820–1912), 75, 78n21, 237, *238*
Schultz, Friedrich Rudolph (1844–1854), 237
Schultz, Johann (1800–1874), xix, 75, 78n21, 119n133, 234–42, 243, 244–46, 251–52, 253n37, 254, 259
Schumacher (Iowa Synod pastor), 342
Schuster, Georg Konrad (1819–1869), 262n10

NAME INDEX

Schwan, Emma (1828–1915), 188
Schwan, Heinrich Christian (1819–1905), xxiv, 45, 50, 54, 62, 65, 66, 102, 167, 169, 222, 223, 225, 232, 255n41, 269, 280, 348
Schwan, Paul (1851–1937), 45
Schwanke, August, 75, 243, 244
Schwankovsky, Johann C. (1824–1915), 224
See, Mr., 139
Selle, Christian August Thomas (1819–1898), 226
Sherman, William Tecumseh (1820–1891), 87c
Sibert, Adam Elmer (1873–1904), 190
Sieck, Henry (1850–1916), 350
Sieling, Louis, 151
Sievers, Agnes. *See* Andres, Agnes
Sievers, Carolina. *See* Sievers, Karoline
Sievers, Ferdinand (1816–1893), xxiv, 21, 22, 23c, 26, 34, 174, 205, 206, 208
Sievers, Johanne[10] (1855–1926), 172
Sievers, Karoline née Koch (1829–1904), 34, *172*, 173
Sieving, Hermann (1843–1901), 226
Sihler, Christian (1848–1919), 39
Sihler, Wilhelm (1801–1885), xxiv, 39, 40, 41, 42, 44, 65, 69, 101n70, *115*, 116, 119, 143, 222, 247n18, 251n27
Sinke, Georg, 13, 207
Small, Alvan E. (d. 1886), 325
Smith, Elizabeth née Ernst, 229
Smith, Isaac, 229
Socrates Scholasticus, 78n23
Sohn, Andreas (1865–1951), 169, 174, 189
Sohn, Elisabeth née Strieter (1869–1955), 143, 167, *168*, 169
Sohn, Flora (1897–1957), 169
Sohn, Ruth Henriette (1900–1988), 169
Sommer, F. (resident of Green Lake Co., Wis.), 322
Sommer, Wilhelm (1826–1878), 26, 40
Sozomen, 78n23
Springer, Gertrude (1848–1875), 142
Springer, Jacob (1801–1876), 139, 142
Stecher, Anton Daniel (1820–1893), 42, 115, 275
Steinbach, Ferdinand (1826–1883), 39, 50, 51, 54, 55, 56, 58, 62, 66, 115, 222, 262
Stelter, Gottfried (1820–1894), 74
Stelter, Marie née Buge (1823–1922), *77*
Stelter, Wilhelm (1817–1907), 65, 69, 70, 74, 76, *77*, 78, 104n76, 119, 121, 237, 243, 244
Stephan, Martin, Jr. (1823–1884), 74, 234, 235, 237, 238, *239*, 240, 241–42, 246–47, 251, 253n38, 262, 263, 265

Stöckhardt, Georg (1842–1913), 346, 347, 348
Strasen, Carl (1827–1909), 102, 115, 116, 128, 159, 248, 249, 269, 279, 280, 333, 335
Streissguth, Wilhelm (1827–1915), 108n90, 248, 259, 336–42
Strieter, Adolph A. (1891–1987), 164
Strieter, Ann née Albrecht (1887–1974), *187*
Strieter, Barbara (Johannes's sister), 2n1
Strieter, Bert (1909–1991), *187*
Strieter, Carl. *See* Strieter, Karl
Strieter, Christiana (Johannes's sister). *See* Bach, Christiana
Strieter, Christiana née Trinkler (1823–1899; Johannes's sister-in-law), 13, 37
Strieter, Dorothea (Johannes's sister). *See* Auch, Dorothea
Strieter, Edgar H. (1901–1984), *187*
Strieter, Edwin J. (1898–1989), xiv
Strieter, Elisabeth (Johannes's daughter). *See* Sohn, Elisabeth
Strieter, Elizabeth née Ernst. *See* Subject Index
Strieter, Elmer (1909–1995), *187*
Strieter, Emanuel (1858–1858), 167
Strieter, Emma. *See* Querl, Emma
Strieter, Emma née Prescott. *See* Strieter, Mathilde Emma
Strieter, Ernst (1863–1949), 143, 167, *168*, 169, 171, 173
Strieter, F. Winfried (1881–1967), *187*
Strieter, Fred L. (1894–1952), *187*
Strieter, Friedrich (1854–1927), 69, 91, 99, 117, 167, *168*, 169, *187*
Strieter, Hermina (Johannes's daughter). *See* Volberding, Hermina
Strieter, Ida née Galmiefski (1876–1940), *187*
Strieter, Immanuel C. (1878–1941), *187*
Strieter, Jacob (1789–1848; Johannes's father), xix, 1–9, 11, 13, 14c, 19, 55, 174, 181, 182
Strieter, Jacob Friedrich (1824–1902; Johannes's brother), 2, 4, 6, 9, 11, 13, 20, 36, 37, 55, 174
Strieter, Johanna née Haben (1871–1944), 169, 189
Strieter, Johannes. *See* Subject Index
Strieter, Karl (1865–1952), xiv, 49n24, 136n11, 143, 145nn7f, 146n11, 151n26, 152n27, 157, 158, 159n9, 164, 165n29, 167, *168*, 169, 171, 172nn37f, 189, 233
Strieter, Katharina (Johannes's sister). *See* Luckhardt, Katharina
Strieter, Louise née Zumhof (1860–1885), *187*

---

10. This appears to be the daughter Strieter calls Renata, which was perhaps a middle name.

Strieter, Margaretha (Johannes's sister). *See* Killinger, Margaretha
Strieter, Maria (Johannes's daughter). *See* List, Maria
Strieter, Maria Katharina née Wiesenauer (1791–1847; Johannes's mother), xix, 2, 3, 5, 6, 7, 9, 11, 13, 14c, 20, 174, 183, 184
Strieter, Marie née Schick (1858–1933), 168, *187*, 188
Strieter, Martin E. (1887–1979), *187*
Strieter, Mathilde (1877–1959), 167, *168*, 169
Strieter, Mathilde Emma née Prescott (1869–1930), 169, 189
Strieter, Otto (1867–1869), 140, 160, 167–68
Strieter, Otto (1878–1891), 159, 160, 167, 168, 190
Strieter, Ottomar (1892–1977), *187*
Strieter, Rosina (Johannes's sister). *See* Müller, Rosina
Strieter, Theodor (1874–1896), 159, 160, 167, *168*, 169, 190
Strieter, Theophilus W. (1889–1965), *187*
Strieter, unnamed stillborn daughter (1873), 167, 168
Strieter, Wilhelm (1861–1935), 99, 117, 143, 167, *168*, 169, 171
Strieter, Winfried (1905–1991), *187*
Strobel, F. W., 340, 341, 342
Strube, Ernst (1829–1918), 250
Struve, Anna Dorothea née Kern (1864–1902), 305
Stubbe, Carl, 74
Stubbe, Florendine Caroline (b. 1860), 104n76
Succop, Heinrich H. (1845–1919), 157, 227

Taege, Wilhelm (1851–1901), 280c
Tagatz, Anna Justine née Mesall/Missal (1810–1874), 70
Tagatz, August (1831–1885), 74
Tagatz, Christoph (1836–1916), 70, 71, 74, 80, 100, 304, 305n67, 308–309, 311, 312, 313, 317n96, 318, 328
Tagatz, Louise née Schätzke (1838–1903), 70
Tagatz, Martin (1802–1867), 70, 95, 243, 244
Teske, Gottlieb, 75
Teske, John, 74, 75, 237, 239, 240, 328
Teske, John Ludwig, 75
Theisen, Maria Elizabeth née Theiss (1810–1884), 50, 52, 60
Theisen, Peter (1805–1889), 50, 51, 52, 54, 55n49, 60
Theisen, Sarah M. (b. 1852), 60
Theiss, Agnes Barbara née Schaible, 51n32, 54n44, 60

Theiss, Barbara née Hoffman (1824–1901), 51n31, 59
Theiss, Friedrich Gottfried, 50n31, 51n31, 60
Theiss, Heinrich (1819–1894), 51n31, 55n49, 56, 59
Theiss, Jacob, 51n31
Theiss, Philipp (1816–1905), 50, 51n31, 55, 56, 59
Thiel, Mr. (resident of Princeton, Wis.), 326
Thiele, Christian (1834–1916), 144, 148, 149, 150
Thiele, Gottlieb, 298, 299nn50f, 301, 309, 311, 322, 326n113, 327, 331, 339
Thiele, Margareth née Bernhart (1854–1935), 144, 148
Tonn, Gottlieb, 330
Tönsing, Eleonora née Böhning (1830–1905), 188
Tönsing, Friedrich (1825–1886), 64, 65, 66, 188
Trautmann, (C. August? [1848–1903]), 167?
Trautmann, Jakob (1815–1900), 167?, 191, 192, 195
Trinkler, Christiana (1823–1899; Johannes's sister-in-law) 13, 37

Uffenbeck, William (1841–1942), 167
Ullrich, Alex (1872–1946), 151, 152, 157, 227

Vockerodt, Gottfried, 83n26
Voigt, Mr. (teacher), 145
Volberding, Hermina née Strieter (1859–1910), 69, 99, 117, 143, 167, *168*, 169, 171
Volberding, Theodor H. (1859–1915), 168, 188

Wagner, Anton (1830–1914), xxiv, 162, 249n21, 262
Waldt, Friedrich (1822–1908), 265–66
Walther, C. F. W. (1811–1887), xii, xxiv, 37n41, 66, 77n17, 112, *161*, 162, 247–48, 344–50
Walther, Constantin (1847–1905), 347, 348
Walther, Ferdinand (1847–1933), 348
Wambsgans(s), Philipp (1857–1933), 175
Wangerin, Gustav (1844–1925), 350
Warnke, Johann Friedrich, 74
Warnke, Orlan, xi, xiv
Warnke, Peter, 71, 74, 76, 79, 122, 334n127
Weisse, Michael, 350n9
Welke, Johann Gottlieb (1810–1900), 71, 75, 119, 240
Werfelmann, Heinrich (1827–1905), 39, 41
Wesemann, Friedrich Heinrich Christian Louis (1848–1919), 190
Wesemann, Katharine Dorothea née Menthe (1849–1936), 190

NAME INDEX

Wetter(r)oth, Wilhelm Heinrich (b. 1860), 109n93
Wetzel, Philipp, 249n21
Wiegrefe, Mr. (teacher), 145
Wiesenauer, Johann Martin (1762–1832; Johannes's grandfather), 3, 184, 185, 186
Wiesenauer, Maria Katharina. See Strieter, Maria Katharina
Wilhelm, Philipp (1869–1933), 175
Wines, Elizabeth née Tilley, 41c
Wines, Marshall S., 41c
Wischmeyer, E. Henry (1853–1926), 175
Wittig, Conrad (1818–1868), 229
Wolf, Johann Georg (1819–1862), 41
Wolter, August (d. 1849), 42c
Woltersdorf, Ernst Gottlieb, 4n5
Wunder, Heinrich (1830–1913), xxiv, 129, 227
Wünsch, Karl/Carl (1837–1888), 132
Wüst, Amalie Caroline (b. 1857), 110–11
Wüst, Anna Louise (b. 1856), 110–11
Wüst, Carl Friedrich W., 110–11
Wüst, Johann, 111n97
Wüst, Maria née Damas, 110–11
Wyneken, Friedrich (1810–1876), xii, xxiv, 21n1, 39n46, *115*, 116

Zehnder, Herman, xiv, 16nn33&36, 35n36
Zeising, August Wilhelm (b. 1863), 109n93
Zernecke, August, 130n4, 322, 323, 324, 326, 327, 328, 329, 330nn119f, 332, 333, 334, 335
Zorn, C. M. (1846–1928), xxvi

Place Index

(European territories and locales are listed first, then those in Canada, then those in the United States. Locations in the United States are grouped by state, then county. When deemed helpful, entries are further subdivided into "Communities and Townships" and "Churches and Institutions." "c" refers to a caption. *Italicized* page numbers refer to an illustration.)

European (Mostly German) Territories and Locales

Affalterbach, xix, 1, 2, 4n7, 5, 6, 7, 181, 182, 183, 184, 185, 356
Barmen, 202
Basel, 8, 24n13, 44, 192, 202, 273, 283, 284
Bavaria, Kingdom of, 21n1, 22c, 23n12, 27c, 51, 130, 137, 191, 209, 211, 267
Bebra, 230, 231
Berlin, 97n62
Bittenfeld, 182
Bremen, 6, 7
Bremerhaven, 7
Breslau (now Wrocław, Poland), 236, 257n45
Breuningsweiler, 184
Bromberg (now Bydgoszcz, Poland), 235, 252n32, 253
Bürg (by Winnenden), 183, 184, 185, 186
Chodziesen (now Chodzież, Poland), 253n34
Darmstadt, 66n18
Erdmannsdorf (now Mysłakowice, Poland), 257n45
Erfurt, 97n62
Franconia, xxiv, 21, 22, 24, 27, 29, 31, 39n48, 40n50, 191, 192, 356
Frankfurt am Main, 66n18
Giessen, 66n18
Hanover, 39n48, 64, 65n15, 130
Hertmannsweiler, 184
Hesse (unspecified), 9, 19, 51, 60, 61, 130
Hesse, Electorate of, 230
Hesse-Darmstadt, Landgraviate of, 54n39
Hesse-Kassel, Landgraviate of, 228
Hirschberg (now Jelenia Góra, Poland), 257n45
Kuehndorf, 269
Lomnitz (now Łomnica, Poland), 257n45
Lusatia (Prussian), 44n3
Lusatia (Saxon), 40n51
Marbach, 2, 5
Martinskirche-Affalterbach, *1*, *3*, *5*
Nagold, 8n17
Nassau, 68n21
Nellmersbach, 183
Neuendettelsau, 21n1, 22c
Nieder-Wiesen, 66n18
Nuremberg, 202
Ödernhardt, 185
Pomerania, 74, 76n15, 86, 87c, 88n36, 123n139, 125, 354
Posen, 70, 235, 252
Prussia, Kingdom of, xvii, 44nn2f, 49, 50, 51n34, 97n62, 214n21, 234, 235, 236, 237, 245n17, 251, 252, 269, 283n4
Radwonke (now Radwanki, Poland), 252–53
Rotenburg an der Fulda, 231
Saxe-Weimar, Duchy of, 39n45
Saxony, Kingdom of, 236n4
Silesia, 236n4, 257n45
Stöckenburg, 281
Stuttgart, 293n34
Vellberg, 281
Walddorf, 8n17
Welzheim, 186

Winnenden, 2, 6, 183, 185
Wolfsölden, 4
Wriezen, 293n34
Württemberg, Kingdom of, 1, 8, 9, 11, 12n25, 24n13, 51, 130, 281, 356

Canada

Niagara Falls, 177
Rainham (near Fisherville, Ontario), 247

United States

CALIFORNIA

Los Angeles, 188

ILLINOIS

Cook County

COMMUNITIES AND TOWNSHIPS

Chicago, xxiv, 24, 44, 129, 143, 150, 170, 175, 189, 190, 325, 326, 331, 332
Grossdale (now Brookfield), 151, 157, 175
Harlem (now Forest Park), 164, 167
Hillside, xix
La Grange, 151, 152, 156–57, 158, 165, 172, 175, 227
Lyons, 150, 164
Melrose Park, 164
Proviso, xi, xviii, 143–46, 148–50, 153–54, 156, 159–60, 163–64, 167, 168, 169–70, 175, 176, 177, 189, 190, 226, 227, 357, *358*

CHURCHES AND INSTITUTIONS

Concordia University Chicago, 146n13
Hahnemann Medical College, 325, 331, 332
Immanuel Lutheran-Hillside, xix, 143, *144*, 145–50, 151nn23ff, 152, 153–54, 156, 160, 163–66, 226, 227, 357, 358
St. John Lutheran-Forest Park, 164n23
St. John's Lutheran-La Grange, 151nn22&26, 156–57, 227
St. Paul Lutheran-Melrose Part, 164n24
Zion Lutheran-Lyons, 150n18
Zion Lutheran-Summit, 150n20

DeKalb County

Hinckley, 130n2, 135
Pierceville, 130, 131, 132, 133–35
Squaw Grove, 130, 131, 132, 133–35, 169

DuPage County

COMMUNITIES AND TOWNSHIPS

Addison, 85, 131, 146, 147n13, 152, 159, 160, 163
Downer's Grove, 151
Elmhurst, 165
Hinsdale, 151, 152, 154, 165, 175, 226, 227
York Center (now Lombard), 165

CHURCHES AND INSTITUTIONS

Immanuel Lutheran-Elmhurst, 165n25
Lutheran Teacher Seminary-Addison, 146, 147n13, 151n24, 160
Trinity Lutheran-Lombard, 165n26
Zion Lutheran-Hinsdale, 151, 226, 227

Hancock County

Nauvoo, 337, 339

Kane County

COMMUNITIES AND TOWNSHIPS

Aurora, xi, 129, 130–31, 132, 135–37, 138, 140, 151, 169, 170–71, 189, 225, 328, 356
Elgin, 189

CHURCHES AND INSTITUTIONS

Iglesía Luterana San Pablo-Aurora, 130n1
St. Paul Lutheran-Aurora, 130, 131, 135–38, 225, 321, 356

Kendall County

COMMUNITIES AND TOWNSHIPS

Kendall, 131n5
Long Grove, 130
Plano, 130, 131
Yorkville, 129, 130, 131, 132, 138, 169, 225

CHURCHES AND INSTITUTIONS

Brown's schoolhouse, 131
Immanuel Lutheran-Yorkville, 131–33, 138, 225

Madison County

Collinsville, 7

PLACE INDEX

Mason County

COMMUNITIES AND TOWNSHIPS

Bath, 340

CHURCHES AND INSTITUTIONS

St. John's Lutheran-Bath, 340–41

Sangamon County

COMMUNITIES AND TOWNSHIPS

Springfield, 22n10, 115c, 261, 281, 283

CHURCHES AND INSTITUTIONS

Concordia Theological Seminary, 22n10, 115c
Illinois State University, 261, 281

Washington County

COMMUNITIES AND TOWNSHIPS

Nashville, 283

CHURCHES AND INSTITUTIONS

St. Paul UCC-Nashville, 283

INDIANA

Allen County

COMMUNITIES AND TOWNSHIPS

Cedar Creek, 43n57
Fort Wayne, 21n4, 27, 36, 38, 39–42, 44, 45, 65n15, 68n21, 75n14, 85n30, 101nn70f, 137, 159, 205, 217, 222, 224, 247n18, 255n41, 269, 272, 356
Nothstein, 42–43

CHURCHES AND INSTITUTIONS

Lutheran Theological Seminary-Fort Wayne, 21n4, 27, 28, 36, 39–40, *41*, 42, 43n57, 44–45, 65n15, 68n21, 75n14, 101n71, 222, 247n18, 255n41, 269, 356
St. Paul's Lutheran-Ft. Wayne, 42, 101n70

Cass County

Logansport, 166, 167

Fulton County

Rochester, 139, 225
Whippoorwill, 139

Huntington County

Huntington, 31, 42

Lake County

Crown Point, 167

LaPorte County

La Porte, 168

Marshall County

COMMUNITIES AND TOWNSHIPS

Bremen, 262n10

CHURCHES AND INSTITUTIONS

St. Paul's Lutheran-Bremen, 262n10

Miami County

COMMUNITIES AND TOWNSHIPS

Bunker Hill, 139n4, 171–72
Harrison, 139, 142
Moorefield, 139, 142. *See also* North Grove
North Grove, 139n3, 225. *See also* Moorefield
Peru, xix, 138, 139–42, 160, 163, 166, 167, 169, 171, 189, 225–26, 357
Pipe Creek, 139n4

CHURCHES AND INSTITUTIONS

St. John's Lutheran-Peru, xix, 138, 139, *140*, 141, 142, 143, 160, 163, 167, 357

IOWA

Clayton County

Wartburg College, 267

Grundy County

Reinbeck, 168, 169

Lee County

Fort Madison, 340
Franklin (Center), 281, 337, 339–40

Scott County

Davenport, 188, 339, 341

Van Buren County

Farmington, 281, 341

Winneshiek County

Decorah, 349

LOUISIANA

New Orleans, 279

MARYLAND

Baltimore, 37n41, 65

MICHIGAN

Alger County

Munising, 274

Arenac County

Au Gres, 198, 207, 217

Bay County

COMMUNITIES AND TOWNSHIPS

Amelith, 174
Bay City, xix, 15, 22n7, 34c, 76c, 153c, 172c, 173c, 351. *See also* Lower Saginaw *under* Saginaw County
Frankenlust, xxv, 22, 23, 26c, 34, 75n14, 152, 169, 172–73, 174, 175, 357, 358
Hampton, 23
Monitor, 174
Munger, 174
Salzburg, 174

CHURCHES AND INSTITUTIONS

St. Paul Lutheran-Frankenlust, xix, xxv, 22n7, 26c, 34, 76c, 153c, 172, 173c, 358

Gratiot County

COMMUNITIES AND TOWNSHIPS

St. Louis (formerly an Ojibwe settlement), 23, 25n14, 193, 197, 201, 202–203, 215n24

CHURCHES AND INSTITUTIONS

Bethany Lutheran Mission, 23, 25, 44n5, 201, 202–203, 215n24

Houghton County

Hancock, 274n9
Houghton, 274n9
Portage Lake, 274

Huron County

COMMUNITIES AND TOWNSHIPS

Pigeon, 174
Sebewaing, xix, 3, 13, 14c, 16n36, 19, 24, 25, 26–27, 32–34, 35n34, 39n47, 40, 174, 192, 205–214, 215, 217, 218–19, 220, 221
Shebahyon(g)k, 13, 15, 16n36, 17, 24, 25, 33, 207, 215–16, 218–19, 220–21
Shebeyang. *See* Shebahyonk
Shiboyank. *See* Shebahyonk
Sibiwaing. *See* Sebewaing
Siboying. *See* Sebewaing
Weale, 13n29

CHURCHES AND INSTITUTIONS

Luckhard Museum, xix, 14c, 35n34, 215n25

Iosco County

East Tawas, 277
Tawas, 269, 277
Tawas City, 277

Jackson County

Jackson, 37

Kalamazoo County

Kalamazoo, 247n18

PLACE INDEX

Lenawee County

Adrian, 21, 174
Deerfield, 9, 174

Marquette County

Marquette, 274

Monroe County

Monroe, 21, 45, 114–15, 191, 193n4, 195, 205

Ontonagon County

COMMUNITIES AND TOWNSHIPS

Minnesota. *See* Rockland
Ontonagon, 273–74
Rockland, 272–73, 274–76

CHURCHES AND INSTITUTIONS

Zion's Lutheran-Rockland, 275–76

Saginaw County

COMMUNITIES AND TOWNSHIPS

Bridgeport, 23
Frankenmuth, xviii, xix, 21, 22, 23, 24n12, 25n14, 27, 28, 29, 30, 31, 32, 33, 35–36, 39n47, 168, 173–74, 189, 192, 193, 195–205, 208, 215–18, 228, 229, 356
Frankentrost, 21, 23, 30, 32, 35, 65, 75n14
Lower Saginaw (now called Bay City), 15, 18, 22, 34, 218
Saginaw, xix, 15, 18, 22, 23, 26, 27, 30, 35, 162, 174, 228, 267

CHURCHES AND INSTITUTIONS

Holy Cross Lutheran-Saginaw, 22n8
Immanuel Lutheran-Frankentrost, xix, 21n6, 30
St. Lorenz Lutheran-Frankenmuth, xviii, xix, 21n5, 28, 29, 30, 35, 192–93, 195–205, 215–18

Tuscola County

Frankenhilf (now Richville), 22, 23, 27, 31
Richville, 22n9
Tuscola, 23, 30
Unionville, 174

Washtenaw County

COMMUNITIES AND TOWNSHIPS

Ann Arbor, xix, xx, 8, 9, 12, 15, 23, 36, 37, 191, 194, 205–206, 208, 212
Bridgewater, 9, 13, 37, 174
Freedom, 9, 10, 13, 19–20, 36–37, 39n47, 174, 181, 184
Manchester, 9, 19
Saline, 174
Scio, 8, 9, 11, 20, 33, 174

CHURCHES AND INSTITUTIONS

Bethel Evangelical-Freedom, 9, 14c
Bethel United Church of Christ-Freedom, 9n20, 14
Salem Lutheran-Scio, xix, 8, 11
University of Michigan, 12

Wayne County

Detroit, 8, 22, 36, 37–38, 39n47, 45

MINNESOTA

Lake County

Burlington, 274
Knife River, 274n5
Two Harbors, 274n6

Ramsey County

Saint Paul, 327

Saint Louis County

Buchanan, 274
Duluth, 274n7
Portland, 274

Wabasha County

Reads Landing, 111–12

MISSOURI

St. Louis

xiii, 28c, 32, 37n41, 76, 77n18, 95, 112, 113, 114, 137, 157, 161c, 163, 248, 324, 334, 344, 345, 348, 349

CHURCHES AND INSTITUTIONS

Concordia Seminary, 161c, 344, 348
(Old) Trinity Lutheran, 161c, 348

St. Louis County

Des Peres, 168

MONTANA

Park County

Livingston, 188

NEBRASKA

Seward County

Seward, 168, 357

Thayer County

COMMUNITIES AND TOWNSHIPS

Deshler, 342
Friedensau, 342
Hebron, 342

CHURCHES AND INSTITUTIONS

Trinity Lutheran-Friedensau, 342

NEW YORK

Albany County

Albany, 97n62, 231

Erie County

Buffalo, 8, 97n62, 231, 235, 247, 269

New York City

8, 231, 281, 327

Niagara County

COMMUNITIES AND TOWNSHIPS

Wolcottsville, 116n115

CHURCHES AND INSTITUTIONS

St. Michael's Lutheran-Wolcottsville, 116n115

OHIO

Coshocton County

Coshocton, 44, 49, 50n28
Jackson, 50
Roscoe Village, 49, 50

Cuyahoga County

COMMUNITIES AND TOWNSHIPS

Cleveland, xxvi, 45, 50, 51n31, 65, 66, 69, 222, 231, 232, 233
Euclid, 62, 65, 83
Garfield Heights, v, xix, xxvc, 63c, 67c, 169n33, 175c, 177c, 255nn41&43. *See also* Independence *and* Newburgh
Independence, 62, 63, 64–65, 66, 67, 187, 188, 222, 226, 356. *See also* Newburgh
Newburgh, 61, 62, 119, 167, 169, 175–76, 177–79, 223, 229, 232. *See also* Independence
Ohio City (now West Cleveland), 65

CHURCHES AND INSTITUTIONS

St. John Lutheran-Garfield Heights, v, xix, xxvc, 58c, 62, 63, 64–65, 66, 67, 169, 175, 176, 177–79, 222, 226, 232, 233, 255n41
St. Paul's Lutheran-Cleveland, 45n8
Zion Lutheran-Cleveland, xxvi, 45n7, 62

Erie County

Sandusky, 45
Vermilion, 54, 55, 56, 58, 59–60, 61, 222, 228, 229, 230, 231–32

Franklin County

Columbus, 65

Holmes County

COMMUNITIES AND TOWNSHIPS

Mount Hope, 44n1, 68c
Salt Creek, 44, 49, 50, 68

CHURCHES AND INSTITUTIONS

St. John's Lutheran-Mt. Hope, 49, *68*, 223

Lorain County

COMMUNITIES AND TOWNSHIPS

Amherst, 65
Brownhelm, 58, 231
Elyria, 50–55, 56, 58, 59, 60–61, 222, 255n41, 356
Oberlin, 59

CHURCHES AND INSTITUTIONS

Oberlin College, 59
St. John Lutheran-Elyria, 51–55, 60–61, 222

Lucas County

Toledo, 22n10, 38, 45, 168, 174, 195

Medina County

COMMUNITIES AND TOWNSHIPS

Liverpool, 12, 50, 54, 55, 56, 58, 62, 66
Medina, 50
Valley City, 12n25

CHURCHES AND INSTITUTIONS

Emmanuel United Church of Christ-Valley City, 12n25
St. Paul Lutheran-Valley City, 12n25, 50n29, 54n39
Zion Lutheran-Valley City, 12n25

Ottawa County

Danbury, 195

Sandusky County

Woodville, 211

Stark County

Massillon, 45

Summit County

Akron, 45n9

Wayne County

Eagle Tavern-Mount Eaton, 48
Mount Eaton, 48
West Lebanon, 46, *47*

OREGON

Multnomah County

COMMUNITIES AND TOWNSHIPS

Portland, 342–43

CHURCHES AND INSTITUTIONS

Concordia College, 343
Farmers' Mutual Insurance Company, 342

PENNSYLVANIA

Philadelphia County

Philadelphia, 37n41, 228

WISCONSIN

Ashland County

Ashland, 274
Bay City, 274
La Pointe, 274

Bayfield County

Bayfield, 274

Buffalo County

Mondovi, 110n94

Calumet County

COMMUNITIES AND TOWNSHIPS

New Holstein, 285–86, 287, 288, 289, 290, 298
Stockbridge, 286, 287, 294

CHURCHES AND INSTITUTIONS

St. John's UCC-New Holstein, 285–86

Chippewa County

Chippewa Falls, *87*, 106–107, 353
Goetz, 107

PLACE INDEX

Clark County

Neillsville, 269

Columbia County

COMMUNITIES AND TOWNSHIPS

Cambria, 249
Friesland, 249n23
Lewiston, 236n7
Pardeeville, 88, 103, 113
Portage, xix, 88, 237n7, 276
Randolph, 71n9, 249

CHURCHES AND INSTITUTIONS

St. John's Lutheran-Portage, xix, 276–77

Dane County

Madison, 267

Dodge County

COMMUNITIES AND TOWNSHIPS

Beaver Dam, 284, 337
Herman, 297n45
Horicon, 249
Lebanon, 115, 237, 246n18, 248, 249n21
Mayville, xix, 75, 116, 169, 174–75, 176, 234, 239–41, 246n18, 255n41
Theresa, 246n18
Woodland, 115

CHURCHES AND INSTITUTIONS

First Lutheran-Beaver Dam, 284n5
Immanuel Lutheran-Lebanon, 116n121, 246n18, 248nn20f
Immanuel Lutheran-Mayville, xix, 75n14, 174, 234, 241n14, 246n18
St. John's Lutheran-Mayville, 175
St. Matthew's Lutheran-Lebanon, 249n21

Douglas County

Superior, 274

Dunn County

Menomonie, 107, 108n90, 109

Eau Claire County

COMMUNITIES AND TOWNSHIPS

Brunswick, 110–11
Eau Claire, 88, 103, 104n76, 109, 110, 111, 353
Fall Creek, 74, 77, 88, 103–104, 105, 107, 111

CHURCHES AND INSTITUTIONS

St. John Lutheran-Fall Creek, 77, 88n40, 104n76, 105n80, 353

Fond du Lac County

COMMUNITIES AND TOWNSHIPS

Ashford, 242n15, 244, 245
Brandon, 236n7
Calumet, 286, 287, 289, 290, 294, 297, 298
Eldorado, 265n14, 284
Fairwater, 71, 76, 103
Fond du Lac, 87, 248, 259, 263n11, 282–95, 297–98, 302, 310, 333
Forest, 286, 287, 288–89, 290, 294, 297–98
Ripon, 69, 75, 87, 95, 102, 258, 259, 298, 322n108, 330

CHURCHES AND INSTITUTIONS

St. Paul Lutheran-Eldorado, 265n14, 284n6
St. Peter's Lutheran-Fond du Lac, 282–95, 297–98, 310
Zion Lutheran-Fairwater, 71n11

Green Lake County

COMMUNITIES AND TOWNSHIPS

Berlin, 71, 76, 87, 93, 98, 99, 102, 111, 117, 118, 236n7, 322, 330, 337, 339
Dartford, 304, 322
Dayton, 73, 322
Green Lake. *See* Dartford
Hamilton, 73
Marquette, 73, 236n7
Princeton, xix, 69, 70, 73, 74, 79, 103, 124n143, 129, 234, 236, 237, 239, 241, 242, 243, 244, 245, 246, 247, 248, 249, 250, 251, 258, 259, 281, 298–306, 307, 310–12, 314, 315, 316, 320, 321–28, 329–30, 331–39, 340, 351
Seneca, 73
St. Marie, 73

Churches and Institutions

St. John's Lutheran-Berlin, 71n11
St. John's Lutheran-Princeton, xix, 74 (#20), 251, 259, 298–306, 310–12, 321–28, 329–30, 331–39, 340
St. Paul's Lutheran-Fairburn, 71n11
St. Stephen's Lutheran-Dayton, 73, 302–303, 304, 306, 307, 311, 322, 325, 331

Jackson County

Black River Falls, 87, 105

Jefferson County

Communities and Townships

Farmington, 306, 321n106
Helenville, 248–51, 282, 285, 288, 289, 291, 293, 295, 297, 299, 300, 302, 303, 305, 310, 321, 323, 325, 327, 329, 331, 332, 333
Lake Mills, 283n4
Watertown, 102n73, 108n90, 115, 248, 250, 255, 281, 291, 296, 333, 335, 337, 340

Churches and Institutions

First Congregational UCC-Lake Mills, 283n4
St. John Lutheran-Watertown, 248n20
St. Peter's Lutheran-Helenville, 250
Wisconsin Lutheran Seminary-Watertown (original location), 270, 282n2, 297, 303, 337, 340. See also under Milwaukee County

La Crosse County

La Crosse, 87, 108n90, 112, 113, 337

Langlade County

Antigo, 168, 190

Lincoln County

Communities and Townships

Jenny Bull Falls/Rapids. See Merrill
Merrill, 87, 276
Scott, 355

Churches and Institutions

St. John's Lutheran-Merrill, 355
St. John's Lutheran-Scott, 355

Manitowoc County

Communities and Townships

Manitowoc, 284, 295
Newton, 296

Churches and Institutions

First German Lutheran-Manitowoc, 296

Marathon County

Communities and Townships

Athens, 100c
Berlin, xvii, 86, 87c, 101, 102n71, 124–28, 269, 270, 276, 280, 351–54, 355
Big Bull. See Wausau
Edgar, xix
Hamburg, 353, 355
Little Bull Falls. See Mosinee
Little Chicago, 87n36, 88n36
Maine, xvii, 94n53, 158, 279, 280, 353, 355
Marathon, 87n36
Mosinee, 86n33, 87
Naugart, xin1, 270, 354, 355
Stettin, 101n71
Taegesville, 280
Wausau, v, xvii, xviii, 74, 85, 86, 87, 94, 96, 100, 101, 108, 113, 123n139, 124, 125n148, 128, 158, 224, 269, 271, 279, 351, 352, 353, 354, 358

Churches and Institutions

Faith Lutheran-Maine, 87n36
Grace Lutheran-Maine, xvii, 87n36, 280, 353, 355
Immanuel Lutheran-Maine (then Stettin), 88n36, 94n53, 280
Salem Lutheran-Hamburg, 355
Salem Lutheran-Wausau, 355
St. John Lutheran-Wien, xix
St. John's Lutheran-Hamburg, 87n36, 353, 355
St. John's Lutheran-Scott, 87n36
St. Paul Lutheran-Hamburg, 355
St. Paul Lutheran-Naugart, xi, xvii, 86n35, 87 (caption & n36), 88n36, 100c, 101n71, 102, 128n153, 224, 269, 270c, 271, 353, 355

St. Peter Lutheran-Little Chicago, 87n36
Trinity Lutheran-Berlin, 87n36, 355
Zion Lutheran-Maine, 87n36, 355

Marquette County

COMMUNITIES AND TOWNSHIPS

Budsin, xx, 77c, 99n66
Crystal Lake,[1] 65, 69, 70, 72, 85, 89, 90, 91, 95, 99–100, 101n71, 103, 113, 119–24, 128, 129, 159, 169, 188, 223, 224, 237, 251n28, 255, 269, 303, 305, 311, 320, 323, 327, 329, 356
Germania, 71n12
Harris, 72, 85n32, 251n28
Harrisville, 72, 89, 312, 321
Mecan, 73, 223, 234–42, 243, 244, 245–46, 251–52, 310, 312, 323, 324, 326, 327, 329, 330
Montello, xix, 69n3, 72, 87, 103, 104, 243, 244, 245, 251n28, 252, 256, 257, 324, 351
Neshkoro, 70n9, 71, 73, 119, 312
Newton, xx, 72, 92, 101n71, 223, 237, 304, 327, 328, 329
Oxford, 69n3
Packwaukee, 72
Shields, 72, 101n71, 223, 237, 240, 251, 252–59
Westfield, xix, 71, 236n7

CHURCHES AND INSTITUTIONS

Borsack school, 99
Emmanuel Evangelical-Crystal Lake, 255
Emmanuel Lutheran-Big Mecan,[2] 71, 72, 73, 75, 76, 77, 79, 80, 92, 103, 119, 122, 130n4, 307, 308, 309, 310–11, 312, 319, 321, 323, 326, 327, 329, 330–31, 335
Immanuel Lutheran-Westfield, 71n11
St. John Lutheran-Budsin,[3] xx, 71, 72, 76, 77c, 80, 89, 99n66, 100, 119, 304, 305, 306, 307, 308–309, 311, 312, 313, 315, 317, 318, 321, 328, 329
St. John's Lutheran-Harrisville, 312
Stone Hill Post Office, 69, 72, 99–100, 223, 224

St. Paul Lutheran-Crystal Lake,[4] 71, 72, 74, 101, 129, 302, 303–304, 305, 307, 308, 310, 311, 312, 313–19, 320, 321, 323–24, 327
St. Paul Lutheran-Newton,[5] xx, 71, 72, 74, 77, 129, 304, 305, 306, 307, 308, 309, 311, 312, 313, 314, 315, 316, 317n97, 318, 320, 321, 328, 329
St. Peter's Lutheran-Germania,[6] 71, 73, 74, 75 (#24), 76, 79, 122, 307, 312, 325, 328, 329, 333, 334, 335, 338, 340
Trinity Lutheran-Little Mecan, 71n11, 130n4, 335
Zion Lutheran-Neshkoro, 71n11, 312

Milwaukee County

COMMUNITIES AND TOWNSHIPS

Milwaukee, 22n10, 69, 116n115, 117–18, 129, 225, 245, 246, 248, 257, 259, 267, 271, 284n5, 291, 336, 338, 340, 348n6, 349, 352n2
Oak Creek, 248, 291
Root Creek, 291n26

CHURCHES AND INSTITUTIONS

Grace Lutheran-Milwaukee, 284n5, 336n129
St. John's Lutheran-Milwaukee (Forest Home Ave), 291n26, 296
St. John's Lutheran-Oakwood, 291, 296
Trinity Lutheran-Milwaukee, 225n9
Wisconsin Lutheran Seminary-Wauwatosa, 349

Monroe County

Tomah, 88, 103

Ozaukee County

Freistadt, 115, 116n115

Pepin County

Albany, 110
Durand, 109

---

1. Includes references to Strieter's home and neighbors in Wisconsin
2. Includes references to the Welke schoolhouse and to Buchholz's
3. Includes references to the Tagatz schoolhouse
4. Includes references to the Schmidt schoolhouse
5. Includes references to Kiesow's and Donning's
6. Includes references to Warnke's

Portage County

COMMUNITIES AND TOWNSHIPS

DuBay, 85n33
Stevens Point, *87*, 94–95, 96, 98

CHURCHES AND INSTITUTIONS

St. Paul Lutheran-Stevens Point, 87n36

Racine County

COMMUNITIES AND TOWNSHIPS

Caledonia, 291
Racine, 129n158, 248, 265n14

CHURCHES AND INSTITUTIONS

First Lutheran-Racine, 265n14
Trinity Lutheran-Caledonia, 291n26, 296

Sheboygan County

COMMUNITIES AND TOWNSHIPS

Greenbush, 287, 289
Plymouth, xix, 278, 279
Sheboygan, 279, 290
Sheboygan Falls, xix, 278, 279

CHURCHES AND INSTITUTIONS

St. John Lutheran-Plymouth, xix, 278–79
St. Paul's Lutheran-Sheboygan Falls, xix, 278–79

Washington County

COMMUNITIES AND TOWNSHIPS

Jackson, 260n2
Kirchhayn, 115n107, 116, 260n2
Polk, 263n11
Richfield, 263n11

CHURCHES AND INSTITUTIONS

Immanuel Lutheran-Kirchhayn, 115n107, 260n2

Waukesha County

COMMUNITIES AND TOWNSHIPS

New Berlin, 291, 292, 293–94, 295, 297
Tess Corners, 291n26
Waukesha, 281, 292, 294, 295

CHURCHES AND INSTITUTIONS

Carroll College, 292
First Presbyterian-Waukesha, 292
First United Methodist-Waukesha, 292
St. Paul's Lutheran-Muskego, 291n26, 296

Waupaca County

COMMUNITIES AND TOWNSHIPS

New London, 262, 263, 264–66, 268

CHURCHES AND INSTITUTIONS

St. John's Lutheran-New London, 262–66, 268
Zion Lutheran-Fremont, 266n15

Waushara County

Plainfield, 95, 96n59, 98n65, 351
Wautoma, 71, 98, 99, 103

Winnebago County

COMMUNITIES AND TOWNSHIPS

Menasha, 265n14
Neenah, 265n14
Oshkosh, xix, *87*, 116n115, 236n7, 246–47, 262, 263, 264, 266, 268, 293
Winchester, 263, 264, 266
Winnebago, 236n7
Wolf River,[7] 118

CHURCHES AND INSTITUTIONS

Immanuel Lutheran-Rat River, 266n15
Immanuel Lutheran-Zittau, 266n15
St. Peter's Lutheran-Rat River, 266n15
Trinity Lutheran-Oshkosh, xix, 262–64, 266, 268

---

7. The area referenced formerly belonged to the town of Winchester.

Scripture Index

Genesis

2:17	122
2:21–22	134
3	195
3:1–5	140–41
3:4–5	122
3:11–13	214
3:15	198
24:31	88
28:16–19	262
50:20	198

Exodus

20:2–17	149, 199
20:3	148
20:7	148
20:8	148
20:12	149
20:14	50, 162
20:15	41, 42, 315, 319
20:16	211, 319
20:17	247, 315, 319

Deuteronomy

5:6–21	149, 199
5:7	148
5:11	148
5:12	148
5:16	149
5:18	50, 162
5:19	41, 42, 315, 319
5:20	211, 319
5:21	247, 315, 319
6:5	148
6:16	40
31:6	107, 346

1 Samuel

7:12	31
16:7	120

2 Kings

2:12	348

Job

9:8	6

Psalms

12	199n9
23	347
32	274
33:15	xxiii
51:5	195
51:12	83
71:18	347
90	348
91:11,12	46
103:1,2	xxi, 176
115:1	176, 208, 218

Proverbs

13:24	153
19:17	118
21:1	205
31:10	xx

Ecclesiastes

1:5	4

Isaiah

6:3	199
8:20	123
40:29	282
45:22	311

Jeremiah

17:5	156

Daniel

12:2,3	349

Matthew

1:18	141
4:1–11	80, 141
4:7	40
4:10	156
5:28	83n26
6:1–4	138
6:9–13	199, 201, 202, 350
6:11	xxiv
6:12	61, 81
6:14,15	61, 79
6:24	297
7:2	120
7:6	78, 246
7:17,18	195
8:23–27	8
9:38	276
11:7	284
13	44, 45
13:47–50	265
13:47	207
13:52	xxiv
16:24	302
18:15–17	164, 246
19:14	200
22:37,38	148
25:14–30	xxiii
25:21	347
26:26	51n34, 214
26:26–28	176n52, 213
26:26–29	121, 135
27:46–50	31
28:19	110–11
28:20	213

Mark

4:35–41	8
8:34	302
10:14	200
12:30	148
14:22	51n34, 214
14:22–25	121, 135, 213
15:34–37	31
16:15	176n51
16:16	111n96

Luke

1:35	141
1:79	204
2:22–24	239n12
2:29–32	358
4:1–13	141
4:12	40
6:38	118
6:43	195
7:24	284
8:22–25	8
9:23	302
10:2	276
10:16	314
10:27	148
10:29	36
11:2–4	199, 201, 202, 350
11:3	xxiv
11:4	61, 81
12:51	302n55
14:16–24	262n9
16:13	297
18:16	200
19:1–10	223
22:19	51n34, 214
22:19–20	121, 135, 213
23:44–46	31
24:27	82

John

2:1–11	147
3:3	112
3:5	127
3:6	195
3:16–18	274
3:16	119
3:30	xv
5:28,29	68
6:35	267
10:1–18	54
10:8	320
12:24,25	219
13–17	162

14-17	166	9:12	178n60
21:15	340	10:13-16	247
		12:9	176n50
		13:10	262

Acts

2:38	111n96, 195
8:20	80
20:28	314
20:32	152
22:16	111n96, 195, 196
26:18	201

Galatians

2:9	247
2:16	223
3:1	204
3:26-27	111n96
5:19-23	83n26
6:7	314

Romans

2:16	314
4:11	127
5:13	195
6:23	84
8:28	220
12:2	149
12:3	280
13:1	149
13:14	83n26
14:7-9	220
15:20,21	247
16:17	192, 262
16:18	84, 265

Ephesians

2:3	195
3:20	204
5:4	83n26

Colossians

2:11-12	111n96
3:17	149

1 Thessalonians

4:13	346

1 Corinthians

3:6,7	203
3:6-9	xxiv
4:1	78
6:1-6	105
6:10	79
9:14	108, 109
10:13	302
10:21	149
11:23-24	51n34
11:23-25	121, 123, 135
11:27-32	78n23
13:9	257
15:42-44	68
15:51,52	68

2 Thessalonians

3:6-12	106

1 Timothy

3:6	212
5:22	254

2 Timothy

2:3-6	226
4:6-8	358

Titus

1:5	320
3:1	149
3:4-7	111n96, 195

2 Corinthians

5:17-21	216
6:2	203
6:10	xxiv
6:14-18	261
6:14	156
8:12	204
9:7	204

Hebrews

4:12	302n55
6:13-20	82

Hebrews (continued)

11:6	195
12:1	120
12:2	257

James

5:16	78

1 Peter

1:6,7	265
1:23,25	240
2:2	282n1
2:4–6	240
3:7	112
3:20–21	111n96, 195
4:15	247, 315, 319, 321
5:3	320
5:4	240

1 John

1:9	78n22
4:1	263

2 John

9	157

Revelation

3:15,16	267
4:8	199
13:8	1
21:27	1

www.ingramcontent.com/pod-product-compliance
Lightning Source LLC
Chambersburg PA
CBHW080406300426
44113CB00015B/2409